FINDING
FLORIDA

Also by T. D. Allman

Unmanifest Destiny

Miami: City of the Future

Rogue State

As Coauthor and in Anthologies

Cambodia: The Widening War in Indochina

Reporting Vietnam: American Journalism 1969–1975

Conservatism as Heresy: In Defence of Monarchy

Provence: An Inspired Anthology

The Florida Reader: Visions of Paradise

Spain: True Stories. The King Who Saved His Country

Why Bosnia?

Miami, the American Crossroad: A Centennial Journey, 1896–1996

Busted: Stone Cowboys, Narco-Lords and Washington's War on Drugs

Killed: Great Journalism Too Hot to Print

These United States: Original Essays by Leading American Writers

Marguerite Yourcenar and the USA: From Prophecy to Protest

FINDING
FLORIDA

THE TRUE HISTORY
OF THE
SUNSHINE STATE

T. D. ALLMAN

Atlantic Monthly Press
New York

Published simultaneously in Canada
Printed in the United States of America

FIRST EDITION

ISBN-13: 978-0-8021-2076-2

Atlantic Monthly Press
an imprint of Grove/Atlantic, Inc.
841 Broadway
New York, NY 10003

Distributed by Publishers Group West

www.groveatlantic.com

13 14 15   10 9 8 7 6 5 4 3 2 1

For
CHENGZHONG
与你同行 旅程别样风景

Quid terras alio calientes sole mutamus?

Patria quis exul se quoque fugit?

Why do we flee to lands warmed by a foreign sun?
What fugitive from his own land can flee from himself?

—Horace (65–8 BC),
quoted by Michel de Montaigne (1533–1592)

CONTENTS

PROLOGUE
NATURES AND NAMES

The sky opened up over Jacksonville. Wet vengeance descended: the rain that drowns civilizations and floats arks. The French, the first Europeans here, not the Spanish, would have said it was raining ropes along the waterfront esplanade, but right there beside the St. Johns River was a pavilion with bins and bins of books for sale in it. While the rain cannonballed I searched the bins. Maybe I'd find some revealing book about Florida. In a way I did.

The book was *The Pleasure of Finding Things Out*, by the famous physicist Richard Feynman, a man with the kind of mind it takes to understand a place like Florida, where conventional concepts of how history works and why people do things break down. Professor Feynman, who lived from 1918 to 1988, won a Nobel Prize in Physics and was one of the creators of the atomic bomb. He also investigated the 1986 *Challenger* space shuttle disaster. Unlike everyone else, he got to the bottom—or almost to the bottom—of why all those astronauts were killed.

In Feynman's book I found an observation that unlocks the door to understanding Florida, along with lots of other things. In it he describes how his father was different from other boys' fathers when it came to satisfying his son's curiosity. His friends' fathers, Feynman relates, taught their sons the names of birds when they went on nature walks. Feynman's father taught him not to confuse names with knowledge. Once, he recalled, a playmate asked him the name of a bird they saw. When Feynman said he didn't know, the other kid laughed at him. "'Your father doesn't tell you anything,'" the kid said. "But it was the opposite: my father had taught me," Feynman remembered:

"Looking at a bird he says, 'Do you know what that bird is? It's a brown throated thrush; but in Portuguese it's a . . . in Italian it's a. . . . ,' 'in Chinese it's a . . . , etcetera. 'Now,' he says, 'you know . . . what the name of that bird is [but] you'll know absolutely nothing whatever about the bird. You only know [what] humans in different places . . . call the bird.'" The understanding his father imparted to him set Richard Feynman on the road to amazing discoveries. "He knew the difference between knowing the name of something, and knowing something," he remembered all those years later.

One of the things Florida teaches you is that calling it a river doesn't make it a river. Florida's St. Johns "River" is actually a series of accidentally interconnecting water systems. The portion of the St. Johns at Jacksonville is part of an ancient intra-coastal lagoon. Hydraulically speaking, it is more like an ocean inlet than a river. Knowing a "river" isn't a river doesn't change the surface of things. You still need a bridge to cross the St. Johns. Ships can still dock in it and (pollution permitting) fish can still swim it. But when you probe deeper, you find that the misunderstanding about the nature of that particular body of water is part of a much grander misunderstanding about the physical reality of Florida and its possibilities which has warped events and misguided people for hundreds of years. My favorite example is the search for gold. Florida is the only state which has no metals, yet that did not stop the Spanish from wreaking havoc on the place searching for gold there. By insisting on searching for gold where no gold existed, they set in motion a centuries-long series of irrational events, as explosive as a nuclear chain reaction.

Infesting everything in Florida is a fateful ambiguity of water and land. Until people started turning it into real estate, Florida was less Promised Land than anteroom of the sea, a watery place where land loses its meaning. In Florida tens of millions of people today build their houses and drive their cars across a crust of sea-shaped muck and rubble over which and beneath which flow enormous quantities of water, or they live on dredged-up soggy soil that until very recently was under water and, if nature had its way, would soon resubside.

Not so terribly long ago—about one hundred thousand years ago—ocean levels were about twenty-five feet higher than they are today. All of south Florida from Sarasota around to Palm Beach and then up the Atlantic coast to Jacksonville was under water. The future sites of Fort Lauderdale, Miami, Key West, and Fort Myers were deep under water and far out to sea from the shoreline Florida had back then. It's a thought to ponder as you read the headlines about climate change. Seas would not have to rise three hundred feet, or even fifty feet. A mere twenty feet would suffice to plunge beneath the sea the homes, highways, and cities where the great majority of all Floridians dwell today. If, instead of rising, ocean levels fell by two or three hundred feet, Florida would nearly double in land area. Florida could be everything; it could be nothing. That macrogeological equivocalness plays itself out in every Florida backyard. Fell that pine barren; build a theme park; construct your gated community. Then watch as the sinkholes swallow up your Florida fantasy, an alligator devours your fox terrier, and the palmetto bugs—Floridaese for giant flying cockroaches—infest your life.

Florida is the Play-Doh State. Take the goo; mold it to your dream. Then watch the dream ooze back into goo. People are constantly ruining Florida; Florida is constantly ruining them back. For at least five hundred years that has been Florida's defining theme—whoever the protagonists are, whatever their dream is, whatever flag they wave.

Attempting to explain Florida's distinctive shape and geography, Thomas Jefferson theorized it had been "formed by deposition of the sands by the Gulf Stream in its circular course round the Mexican Gulf," but he was wrong. Florida retains its distinctive north-south shape because beneath its shifting sand it is one of the earth's most stable geographic formations. To understand, think of Florida as a gigantic alligator, with its tail (the Florida Panhandle) curled behind it, its snout (south Florida) pointing toward Cuba. When sea levels are low, Florida looks bigger but it hasn't gotten bigger; it's just that, since water covers less of it, we can perceive its full extent more clearly. When sea levels are high, Florida seems smaller because all that's left above the waterline is the alligator's snout, his eyes, and the ridge running along his back.

Florida's stability is patly due to its location. Glaciation has never reworked Florida as it has so many other parts of the United States; it is located south of the southernmost advance of the glaciers. No volcanoes or earthquakes shake and reshape Florida. It is north of the seismic zones of the Caribbean and Latin America, but Florida's own underlying geological structure is the essential reason why it is so stable. Instead of "dirt" or rocks sticking up out of the dirt, Florida is composed principally of tough, inert, though porous limestone which is honeycombed with interconnecting underground cavities and passages. Even more than a recumbent alligator Florida geologically speaking resembles a gigantic, fossilized sponge. Water, instead of eroding it or moving it, percolates through it.

Every year stupendous amounts of water flow out of the highlands of the southeastern United States, but no great river flows out of the southern Appalachians the way the Ohio and the Tennessee Rivers do farther north. Instead vast quantities of water gurgle over, under, and through that Florida sponge. The Okefenokee Swamp at the north is the place where "dry land" first dissolves into a soggy morass. Florida ends, some four hundred miles to the south, where its watery muck gets so watery it's called Florida Bay. What distinguishes Florida from the sea is not the presence of "land" but the absence of salt water. Where there is fresh (or even brackish) water, mangrove trees root in the muck; earth stabilizes around the mangrove roots. The ensuing "island" in due course attracts other life-forms, including a vacationing fisherman, who builds a fishing camp and then, uprooting the mangrove trees, subdivides it into lots. Water pressure, created by the influx of fresh water, as well as accumulated rainwater in Florida's subterranean aquifers, until recently sufficed to keep the salt water out and keep the Florida system alive. So omnipresent and multiform was the water that you could get in a canoe on the Georgia border and, except for some portages, paddle the length of Florida. You would traverse maybe seven hundred miles of waterways called by different names—"lakes," "rivers," "swamps." Whatever you called them, the pressure of Florida's immense quantities of fresh water kept you afloat.

Its underlying structure explains why Florida is so different from that other great Sunbelt magnet state, California. Florida has no gold so there was never a Florida gold rush. In addition to having no metals, Florida lacks alluvial soil, so agricultural production is largely limited to crops which like limestone, such as citrus, tomatoes, and strawberries. This near-complete absence of what normally are considered "natural resources" raises a question which Florida's conquerors ranging from those Spaniards seeking gold to the real estate speculators of today almost never have asked themselves. How to make the place pay? How to create wealth there instead of destroying it? To consider that question seriously would deter any rational investor. The result, tautologically, is that Florida's history has been dominated precisely by those kinds of people who do not rationally consider the consequences of what they do. For five hundred years successive wave of conquerors, ignoring the reality of Florida, have tried to re-create, in Florida's alien clime, a more perfect—sometimes outright hallucinatory—version of the society they left behind. A new Castile, where every Spaniard is a gentleman on horseback, his saddlebags bulging with gold doubloons! A new Ohio, where every house is located in a crime-free suburb, only with a swimming pool, and it never snows!

To understand Florida's geology is to understand many things that initially seem perverse. Why is its capital, Tallahassee, so capriciously isolated from the rest of the state? The reason is that the area around Tallahassee is the only significant part of the state that is not part of the underlying Florida limestone monolith. This made it the only part of Florida well suited to cultivating cotton, which in turn explains why American southerners were so intent on seizing Florida from Spain and establishing slavery there. As a slave state Florida endured a mere fifteen years, yet as late as 1920 more than half its population still lived within fifty miles of the Georgia border. Nearly half those people were black because black slaves grew the cotton. Florida's Confederate legacy endures to this day because the soil around Tallahassee isn't limestone.

In a Florida of extremely limited physical possibilities, small variations can have big consequences, as an even slighter geological anomaly, at the opposite end of Florida, demonstrates. In Coral Gables, in metropolitan Miami-Dade County, what Floridians grandiloquently describe as the "Atlantic Coastal Ridge" rises to its summit—a full twenty feet above sea level. This limestone "ridge" runs along the east coast of Florida all the way from Jacksonville to Miami. In many places it is less than ten feet high, but in a geographic realm as low-lying as Florida, this slight elevation is important. It divides the Everglades from the Atlantic, and farther up the peninsula it is the reason why the St. Johns River cannot flow directly into the sea but instead must flow north. It also prevents the giant expanse of Lake Okeechobee from being invaded by the sea. The limestone ridge is so hard that people sometimes have to blast holes in their backyards, and then fill them with imported dirt, if they want shrubs to grow around their houses. It seemed useless for anything until, toward the end of the nineteenth century, rich people Up North started noticing that you could run a railroad the length of Florida down that ridge, all the way to Palm Beach and Miami.

At the end of World War II, Florida was a buggy, second-tier Cracker state with some local peculiarities (Miami Beach; the Cubans in Tampa then, not Miami). Today it is the pivot of America. Time and again America has watched—touched, amused, appalled, annoyed, but never able to look away—as hurricanes have lashed the state, rockets carrying human beings into space have exploded, and the seas surrounding Florida have yielded up sunken treasure, drowned Haitians, and gobs of sticky oil. Attracting even more attention are Florida's perpetual human dramas. What will happen to little Elián? To Terri Schiavo and her comatose state? To Trayvon Martin's killer? The nation stares at its TV screens as these telenovellas confront the basic dilemmas of our lives—until another "breaking news" banner bursts on-screen and another melodrama begins.

Because the media treat Florida as a series of disconnected breaking news events, they miss what Henry James, who wrote illuminatingly about Florida, called the pattern in the carpet. Look for those underlying patterns: you'll discover that what makes Florida important is not its quirkiness, its seeming otherness, or its unpredictability. It's that Florida provides a true mirror of what America is becoming—what it already is, in fact.

The most important revelation Florida forces on us, if we are willing to adjust our perspectives, is how irrelevant our narratives are. What we consider the aberrations, the disasters, the exceptions —they are the real narrative. We are the aberrations, the ones who imagine that the hurricanes, the epidemics, the killer frosts, and the human catastrophes constantly sweeping over Florida are not the natural state of affairs. To get an idea of what I mean, imagine a Floridian of the early twenty-first century standing on the balcony of his oceanfront condo. He looks out toward the watery horizon. He sees a tropical storm coming that wasn't mentioned in the weather report, or he sees a flotilla of boat people heading straight toward his marina. And what does he think? He thinks the hurricane has no right to be there. He thinks those boat people should go back where they belong. It does not occur to him, as he calls the security desk, that he is the one who is out of place—that it is his logic which does not apply here.

Leave the fancy dress ball that supposedly constitutes its "history," and you find that Florida is full of fascinating real-life human dramas no one could invent. The people introduced in the following paragraphs have three things in common. All of them were major protagonists who helped make Florida what it is today. Second, because what they did and who they were did not conform to the constantly evolving future stereotypes of what Florida is supposed to have been, they were trivialized, marginalized, or excised from the conventional Florida narrative. The third thing they have in common is that the effort to turn them into nonpersons was for the most part successful, yet you can't understand Florida—and much about America, too—unless you understand what they made of Florida, and what Florida made of them.

Who's ever heard of Dr. Frederick Weedon, or Henry R. Schoolcraft, or Adam Jacoby Slemmer? Slemmer was Florida's original Civil War hero, but don't look for his name on any monument. Schoolcraft, though you've never heard of him, misshaped history so successfully that you probably still believe his fictions are true. Dr. Weedon pioneered the grotesqueries now commonplace on *Dexter* and *CSI: Miami*, yet you never see his name when the credits roll. John Titcomb Sprague, Florida's greatest historian, was expunged from history, too. James Dean (the Florida jurist, not the movie icon) was a rebel with a cause, but no movies are made about him. Alligator and Jumper were warrior-statesmen widely admired at the time, not rock musicians or TV wrestlers, yet you won't find them mentioned in any index either.

Florida's forgotten lovers could populate season after season of successful TV series—except that Antonio González and Annie Maloney, like Dewey McLaughlin and Connie Hoffman, weren't the right demographic to be remembered. Senator Charles W. Jones's passion for Clothilde Palms, like Ida Alice Shourds Flagler's for the tsar of Russia, was so unbounded that today they'd get a reality show. Instead they were shut away in asylums. When Zephaniah Kingsley, Florida's extraordinarily insightful social theorist, wasn't preaching it, he was putting into practice his theory that interracial sex was redemptive. His love affair with the stupendously resourceful Madgigine Jai makes *Aida* seem suburban, yet you'll never find her held up as a role model for Florida's girls and women. Then there is Ossian Hart: Ossian Hart! Never was there a more valiant Floridian, a nobler American. His name should be spelled Heart, yet this greatest of Florida's homegrown heroes has been expunged entirely from Florida's memory of itself.

Billy Powell is probably the greatest Floridian whose name you don't know. He was just a little boy when his mother took him to Florida, which first transformed him into the famous "Indian chief" Osceola and ultimately into one of its most grizzly souvenirs. You also need to understand how Florida reconfigured his nemesis, José—a.k.a. "Joe"—Hernández.

Names and reality in Florida are so utterly uncontingent it is also possible for two different names in the history books to apply to the same person. That's the case with David Levy and David Yulee: two entries, one scoundrel. It's also true of Harold Schwartz Jr. and H. Gary Morse, who, in addition to being one and the same person, are probably the most important unknown Floridian of recent times. To understand Florida you also need to appreciate that this is a place where the nonhuman protagonists, famous ones like Jose Gaspar and Mickey Mouse, but also unknowns like *Schizoporella floridana*, often have more impact than the plutocrats and politicians.

Because it possesses so few useful resources, the notion that it must be "sold" infests every warp and weave of Florida. The false advertising isn't limited to swampland; a horror of the truth infests most supposed Florida scholarship. The fakery also populates Florida's road maps. North Miami Beach is nowhere near Miami Beach, or any beach. Up in the Panhandle, I once passed a place selling "New Used Tires." The motels, diners, trailer parks, and other such establishments located at least one mile inland with Seaview, Gulf View, and Ocean Vista in their names could fill a phone book. Even so it's worth mentioning Ocean Pond, near which Florida's only significant Civil War battle was fought. It is sixty-five miles from the ocean: Floridians were mislabeling things before tourism replaced slavery as the dominating activity. It freezes in Frostproof.

As Feynman's father would have pointed out, those names tell us "absolutely nothing." Then he would say, "Let's look at the bird." When you do look at Florida, you discover that everything is interconnected. Michelangelo was painting the ceiling of the Sistine Chapel at the exact moment voyagers from Europe were tracing their first symbols in the Florida sand, trying to get the original inhabitants to show them where the gold mines were. Michelangelo, up there on his scaffold, the immense void of the Sistine ceiling pressing down on him, realized he had to abandon his fixed perspective if the great enterprise he set for himself was not to end in ruin. "He used no consistent rule of perspective, nor is there any fixed point of view," his biographer Giorgio Vasari wrote. To find the real Florida you too must tear up the picture postcards! Get rid of the plumed conquistadors and Confederate cavaliers! Dispense also with the notion that it never gets cold in Florida.

Once you do rid yourself of the illusion that learning the names of things teaches you the nature of things, you discover something interesting. Florida is so powerful in its peculiar passive-aggressive way that it provides its own perspectives—and, as events never cease to demonstrate, woe unto those who imagine they can shape the great viscosity of Florida into what they have decided it should be.

FINDING
FLORIDA

PART ONE

INVASIVE SPECIES

Ships at a distance have every man's wish on board.

—Zora Neale Hurston, *Their Eyes Were Watching God*

1

BELIEVE IT OR NOT

You don't need a GPS to search out the meaning of Florida, though it helps. To get started, tap in the following address: 11 Magnolia Avenue, St. Augustine. You'll know you're drawing close to the wellspring of Florida's identity when you reach the intersection of Ponce de Leon Boulevard and Matanzas Avenue. Those names mark a traffic intersection. They also describe an intersection of myth and reality. Generations of Americans have grown up believing Ponce de León discovered Florida while searching for eternal youth, but what does "Matanzas" mean? As they drive along Matanzas Boulevard, or power-boat along the Matanzas River, few understand that this mellifluous-sounding Spanish name means "slaughter" or "massacre." Thus, in English, St. Augustine's marina-fringed harbor, Matanzas Bay, could be rendered "Slaughter Bay."

You'll know you've almost reached your destination when you find yourself peering up at an ancient-looking arch. Across the top you'll see displayed, in Ye Olde English–type lettering, an inscription. It reads: FOUNTAIN OF YOUTH. The lettering is meant to evoke long-vanished times of chivalry and derring-do, but one detail marks it as indubitably Floridian: the sign is made of neon tubing. In the gathering subtropical twilight, the FOUNTAIN OF YOUTH sign glows and sputters like the VACANCY sign on a state highway motel. According to press releases provided by the Fountain of Youth Archaeological Park, which is what this venerable tourist attraction currently calls itself, this is the very spot where "Ponce de León landed in St. Augustine in 1513 searching for a Fountain of Youth." The local ruler "welcomed the Spanish as guests," the official Fountain of Youth

History of St. Augustine relates. "The Spanish were impressed with the beauty and strength of the natives," it adds; "they asked the Timucua to tell them the source of their physical vigor. The natives pointed to the spring."

Juan Ponce de León never visited and never could have visited St. Augustine: St. Augustine was not founded until forty-one years after his death, in 1565. Ponce did not discover Florida. Many Europeans had been to Florida before he got there; many more knew of its existence. The first European to sight Florida may not have been Spanish at all, but Portuguese or Italian. According to long-standing belief, the Italian Giovanni Caboto (better remembered as John Cabot), who discovered Newfoundland in 1497, was the first European to lay eyes on Florida after he failed to discover a Northwest Passage to China. Finding "that there was no appearance of passage, he tacked about, and ran [south] as far as Florida. . . . Here, his provisions failing, he resolved to return to England," according to a history of the United States published in 1830.

The first repeat visitors to Florida were Spaniards. They came hunting for people to kidnap and enslave in the new Spanish dominions of the Caribbean. In one early foray from Santo Domingo, five hundred people were lured onto Spanish ships with gifts of ribbon and jewelry. Two-thirds of those abducted died before the ships returned to port. Every one of the surviving captives also died soon after being enslaved. Ponce himself came upon proof of earlier European landings when he encountered a native inhabitant who already spoke Spanish, but the greatest proof of earlier contact is the hostility he met wherever he landed. People learned quickly that these vessels with ghost-white sails carried horror and death in their holds. "In all his attempts to explore the country, he met with resolute and implacable hostility on the part of the natives," observed one chronicler. "He was disappointed also in his hopes of finding gold."

Documentary evidence of prior European exploration can be found in early maps. The Juan de la Cosa Map, published in 1500, depicts Florida in a rudimentary fashion a full thirteen years before its supposed discovery. The 1507 Waldseemüller Map, today housed in the Library of Congress, shows a southward-projecting peninsula so clearly that anyone familiar with a modern road map would recognize it immediately as Florida. The most famous of them, known as the Peter Martyr Map, was circulated in Europe in 1511, two years before Ponce made his "discovery."

If anyone whose name we know deserves specific credit for having reached Florida first, it could be the Portuguese navigator Gasper Côrte-Real. He first sailed to America via the North Atlantic route in 1500, then made two more voyages in 1501 and 1502. The third time his luck ran out; he disappeared along with his ship. A second ship did return safely to Portugal, providing a scenario in which at least three ships from three successive voyages return with new knowledge of the Atlantic coast of North America. Decades before the official "discoveries," sailors ranging from cod fishermen to pirates ventured into North American waters deliberately, or because their ships were blown off course, then mapped the coasts as they sailed along them. Back in Europe a mapmaker fitting together the resulting bits of geographical data as though they were pieces of a jigsaw puzzle would have perceived Florida growing from the southeast corner of North America like a physical appendage.

Today hardly anyone in Florida is aware Gaspar Côrte-Real, existed but nearly two thousand miles northeast of St. Augustine, in St. Johns, Newfoundland, a statue of the Portuguese navigator stands in front of the House of Assembly, one of the oldest parliaments in the New World. The statue is a reminder that, right from the beginning of the European era, Florida's destiny was shaped by forces converging on it from both north and south. Why were there no further Portuguese efforts to colonize North America? Portugal was barred by solemn treaty from colonizing what today are the United States and Canada. Only two years after Columbus reached the New World, the Spanish and Portuguese had split the world up between themselves. Their agreement, called the Treaty of Tordesillas, followed at least one papal bull or decree that delineated which parts of the world Portugal and Spain could colonize.

At that time Portugal and Spain were the only European powers capable, in today's parlance, of projecting naval power globally. The aim was to prevent conflict between the two Catholic superpowers.

This the pope did with the simplicity of cutting the Gordian knot—
splitting the world north to south with an imaginary line of longitude
running the length of the Atlantic Ocean. Everything east of the
pope's line (that is, the whole of Africa and Asia) was made Portugal's
preserve. Everything to the west was allotted to Spain. At first this
partition suited the Portuguese fine. By excluding Spain from Africa
and Asia, it gave them a monopoly of the East Indies trade. The
explorations in America changed the balance of the bargain by giving Spain a monopoly on the New World's newly discovered riches.
Portugal wanted a piece of the new action, so the new treaty was
negotiated. It shifted the global dividing line farther west—from 100
to 370 leagues beyond the Azores. Even with this adjustment, these
early maps show, the whole of North America lay beyond the pope's
dividing line—therefore beyond Portugal's right to colonize it.

Even before Florida was discovered, its destiny was a by-product
of great power politics. It was also an early example of the impact
of the law of unintended consequences. Because of the 370-leagues
provision, Newfoundland and Virginia would never become Portuguese dominions, but Brazil did protrude sufficiently far to the
east to be eligible for Portuguese colonization. By getting the papal
line shifted, Portugal hit the imperial jackpot in South, though not
North, America. Another unintended consequence: in the Far East,
as a result of the papal line being moved, the Philippines came under
Spanish rule for four hundred years.

Like Gaspar Côrte-Real, Juan Ponce de León was one of only
a few thousand European sailors and soldiers who, in the late 1400s
and early 1500s, changed the world suddenly and forever with
their exploits. He first enters history in early 1492. That January
Ponce, at the time a page boy, is said to have witnessed the triumph of Their Catholic Majesties, Isabel and Ferdinand, over the
Muslim caliph of Granada. One year later, Ponce de León sailed
with Columbus on the Great Navigator's second voyage across the
Atlantic. Unknown and penniless, he was just one of the men, boys,
and beasts crowded onto the fetid ships of Columbus' flotilla, but
once in the New World Ponce transformed himself from a face in
the crowd of conquest into a leader renowned for his ruthlessness.

Fourteen years later, in 1507, Ponce de León reached the peak of his personal fortunes as the king of Spain issued him patents royal to explore—and, he hoped, to exploit for his own profit—Puerto Rico. In 1508 Ponce established the island's first European settlement, then set about enslaving its inhabitants and working them to death. Ponce expected he would be rewarded for his efforts with the right to rule the island as his own domain. Instead Columbus' son Diego was made governor. As a consolation prize, Ponce was given the right to colonize Florida.

By March 1513, when Ponce and his private flotilla of three ships sailed north to claim the new land, there was no need to "discover" Florida. Ponce's expedition was meant to address a quite different question: how to secure, settle, and finance the administration of this new land that had fallen within Spain's ambit? Conferring an official name on such a place was an important ritual, akin to baptizing a new land, but why "Florida"? It was not because of any profusion of flowers. Look into any Florida backyard; even today you'll see a somber palette of greens. Leafiness, not floweriness, is the hallmark of Florida's vegetation. What flowers you see are mostly imports. The significance of the name was religious. It was a custom among the conquistadors to name places according to the dates of the liturgical calendar. Columbus discovered the island of Trinidad on the feast of the Trinity, hence that island's name. Pascua Florida was a poetic name for Palm Sunday. By the time Ponce went ashore in early April 1513, Palm Sunday, which fell on March 20 that year, already had passed, but when it came to names his choices were often fanciful, and sometimes macabre. He called the Florida Keys "The Martyrs" because, poking out of the sea one after another, they reminded him of the decapitated heads of Christians who had died for their faith.

Ponce's own log of the voyage establishes that the place where he first landed on the Atlantic shore of Florida was probably south of Cape Canaveral, which was more than one hundred miles south of the future site of St. Augustine. The Gulf Stream provided one reason Ponce did not sail farther north. The Spaniards were astounded, at one point, to see two of their ships, even though their sails were full of wind, moving backward in relation to the land. Avoiding the Gulf

Stream—whose northeastward-coursing current could have carried him away into the vastness of the Atlantic Ocean—Ponce sailed south, hugging a shoreline that, centuries later, would be adorned with motels, bingo halls, and boulevards bearing his name. Encounters with the native Timucua, Tequesta, and Calusa peoples were few, but from the beginning unhappy. These people treated Ponce and his men as dangerous intruders who nonetheless brought with them tools the Indians coveted. The first recorded instance of a white man shooting a gun at Indians in Florida (indeed in the whole of the future United States) occurred when a group of tribesmen tried to steal the Spaniards' longboat. Ponce himself, taking aim, fired the first shot in a war of white men's conquest that would not end in Florida until 1858.

After a two months' sail, Ponce rounded Cape Florida and headed up the Gulf coast. There for the first time he established more than glancing relations with the local people. Within a week of first contact, bitter fighting erupted. Following an attack by Indians in war canoes, Ponce made the intelligent decision to cut and run without establishing any settlement of any kind anywhere in Florida. Nothing better rebuts the Fountain of Youth claptrap than the false triumph Ponce de León orchestrated for himself when he returned to Spain following his failed expedition. What the king wanted was gold, and gold the king was given—5,000 gold pesos. This treasure did not come, and could not have come, from Florida. The gold came from Ponce's holdings in Puerto Rico. His private wealth had financed the expedition; now his personal fortune alchemized failure into success, at least in the eyes of the court. What if Ponce de León actually had returned to Spain with vials containing a liquid he assured everyone contained the elixir of immortality? Would he simply have been considered mad? Or—darker possibility—would this have been seen as evidence of witchcraft, and Ponce de León passed into the hands of the Inquisition?

His expedition had taught Ponce de León what many others would refuse to learn: Florida was no place to get rich quick. To the contrary, it was a sinkhole of wealth. Ponce might never have sailed there a second time had not another man's greater good fortune once again prodded him to act. In 1519 Hernan Cortés astonished the world with his conquest of Mexico and its gold. Suddenly all the old myths gained new force. El Dorado did exist! A less proud man, a less vigorous man might have stayed in Spain, but here we get to the fatal truth behind the future myth: Ponce de León was not the quixotic old gent the Fountain of Youth billboards later made him out to be.

Ponce de León was probably thirty-eight or thirty-nine in 1513. He was forty-six or forty-seven or so when he embarked on his second Florida expedition, about the same age as Columbus when he first crossed the Atlantic, some seven years younger than Pizarro was when he began his conquest of the Incan Empire. On his first voyage to Florida, the chronicles note, he traveled with his mistress as well as his favorite horse. The idea that local Indians informed the Spaniards of the Fountain of Youth's supposed existence also is fiction; "no Indian had ever heard of it." Like smallpox and the orange blossom, belief in the fountain was an import; "it came to the New World in the mental baggage of the conquistadors," as Samuel Eliot Morison felicitously puts it. As another historian explained nearly seventy years ago, the Fountain of Youth "is a legend that crossed the Ocean with Columbus' companions, together with the myths of the Earthly Paradise, of the Amazons, of St. Thomas' wonder-working tomb, of the Ten Tribes of Israel, of Gog and Magog, and of the monsters of which Columbus inquired after his landing." "It is possible that Ponce may never have heard of this legend," the historian David O. True concluded following a close study of the Spanish historical records. "It seems ridiculous," he added, "that a robust adventurer and explorer would have been influenced in the least by such a fable, even if he had heard it." The logs Ponce kept of his voyages describe his Florida landings as searches for fresh water, not magic fountains.

Since sailing to America with Columbus twenty-eight years earlier, Ponce de León had killed, bullied, and bribed his way into the back tier of that small group of figures who were the makers of Spain's New World empire. Now, in 1521, envy and pride impelled him into his second Florida disaster. Ponce's 1521 expedition—financed, again, at his own expense—was meant to make him into the equal of Cortés, but he was not Cortés and Florida's hostile tribesmen were not the temporizing Aztecs. Ponce reached the Gulf coast of Florida with two hundred men and some women, along with fifty horses, all crowded into two ships. Once again he went nowhere near St. Augustine. Instead he made the mistake of landing on the Gulf coast at the same place where, eight years earlier, he had been attacked.

The logistics do not seem particularly arduous, but to get an idea of the difficulties, someday at a Florida marina try to get one horse on and off a cabin cruiser. Now try it with fifty horses while Calusa warriors shoot arrows made of sharpened fish bone at you that have the projectile velocity of major league baseballs and the penetrating power of Swiss Army knives. Ponce de León's thigh wound might not have been fatal, but infection flourished in the subtropical damp and dirt, and the Spaniards were as indifferent to sepsis as they were alert to heresy. The wounded Florida land speculator was medevacuated to Cuba. There he suffered a slow death of gangrene and fever. Ponce de León expired in the all-penetrating damp of the Caribbean summer in July 1521.

It turns out that the person most responsible for spreading the myth of Ponce and the Fountain of Youth was none other than Washington Irving, the inventor also of "Rip Van Winkle" and "The Legend of Sleepy Hollow." Though today Washington Irving is remembered for his fiction, in his own time he was infamous for the liberties he took with the facts—in this case those found in the Spanish archives. No contemporary account mentions any quest for eternal youth by Ponce, or any other of the conquistadors, but in 1535, some fourteen years after Ponce died, the Spanish archivist Gonzalo Fernández de Oviedo, without mentioning any fountain, remarked in passing that Ponce was searching for a remedy for "*el enflaquecimiento del sexo.*" More than half a century after Ponce's death, in 1575, a second unsubstantiated reference to Ponce appeared in a compendium of fact and fantasy dealing with an entirely different person. This one did mention a fountain.

A third volume published in 1610, nearly one hundred years after Ponce supposedly "discovered" Florida, conflated this largely fictional and unrelated adventure with the history of Ponce de León's actual career, while mixing in other irrelevant and fantastical details.

That was it—three baseless, passing references to Ponce de León over a period of nearly three hundred years, until Washington Irving turned up in Spain in the 1820s. There the brilliant young American storyteller began what he promised would be an accurate translation of Oviedo's immense opus, which filled dozens of volumes, but Washington Irving was far too inventive to be anyone's interpreter. Finding his undertaking tedious as well as gargantuan, Irving turned his "translation" into a far briefer work, dealing only with Pizarro, Cortés, and Ponce de León. Then, when he got back to America, he published what he had written under his own name, not Oviedo's. Irving, one of America's first best-selling authors, understood the importance of comic relief. Taking Ponce's supposed *"enflaquecimiento"* as his starting point, he spun out a tale that is still as entertaining and deceiving as it was when he wrote it.

Thanks to Irving's narrative skills the false Ponce became a star performer in a fiesta of illusion that persists to this day. As the five hundredth anniversary of its "discovery" by Ponce de León approached, millionaires donated money, academics composed screeds, and politicians lauded Florida's made-up history while people all over the state were caught up in the street parades, the beauty pageants, and, occasionally, the attempts to convene serious intellectual colloquia in commemoration of Florida's definitive fake event. A great historical continuity was on display, though not the one they imagined they were celebrating. For the latest of countless times people in Florida cavorted, ignorant of the events that had led them to perch on this soggy former annex of the sea—uncaring, too, as to what this disregard for the past might bode for their future.

2

THE JOHNNY APPLESEED
OF PIGS

Fighting at an altitude of twelve thousand feet, the Spaniards conquered Cuzco, the Incan capital in Peru. The high peaks of the Andes
did not keep them from colonizing the pampas of Argentina, nor
did the jungles of Panama stop them from expanding their power to
the Pacific Ocean, yet Florida stuck in the Spanish craw. In Florida
conquistadors who had won pitched battles in the oxygen-starved
mountains of South America went mad and wandered madly, before dying of fever. Such was the fate of Hernando de Soto. Ponce
was Florida's first failed land speculator. De Soto was the first of
the protean superrich who, having triumphed everywhere else, ruin
themselves in Florida

De Soto seemed ideally qualified to succeed where others failed.
Before arriving in Florida he had saved Pizarro's empire in Peru for
him, then returned to Spain with a fortune in melted-down gold
and silver that made him one of Europe's richest men. Deciding
Florida would be his new Peru, and his alone, de Soto landed on
the west coast of Florida in 1539, a stranger to failure. Then, in the
course of three years of futile wandering, he destroyed his fortune,
his expedition, his reputation, and himself. Even more than Ponce's,
his subsequent transmogrification from marauding killer into gallant
protagonist epitomizes the persistent denial of the tragic element in
accounts of Florida's past.

De Soto arrived with nine ships and more than six hundred
men; more than eighty years later the *Mayflower* would sail with

101 souls aboard. He came questing after the two great illusions Florida embodied: gold and a shortcut to China. In May 1542, having exhausted his men, his supplies, and his physical and mental capacities, de Soto died on the banks of a river which may or may not have been the Mississippi. Here is how one of his less feverish biographers describes the pathetic figure he had become: "A moody, irritable, discontented man. He no longer pretended to strike out on any grand undertaking, but, stung with secret disappointment, went recklessly wandering from place to place, apparently without order or object, as if careless of time and life, and only anxious to finish his existence." All authentic accounts make it clear the expedition was a disaster, so where do we get the schoolbook version of the intrepid explorer discovering the Mississippi River? One of the most influential and untrustworthy books on Florida ever published is *The Conquest of Florida Under Hernando De Soto*. It is so abusive of the truth that it might have been written by Washington Irving. It almost was. Its author was Washington Irving's nephew, Theodore Irving. At the urging of his best-selling uncle, he, too, took up the task of transforming Florida's chronicle of disaster, disease, and death into an adventure yarn.

De Soto never claimed he discovered the Mississippi. It was Theodore Irving, writing nearly three hundred years later, who conjured up this "fact" in the same matter-of-fact way that Jonathan Swift introduces us to the Lilliputians. "For seven days," he writes, "they traversed an uninhabited country full of forests and swamps. At length they came in sight of a . . . wide river." At this point, without supplying any evidence, he adds: "it was the same now called the Mississippi." The "great river" whose bottom feeders consumed de Soto's body may have been the Tennessee, or maybe only the Tuscaloosa River. It is indisputable that the body of Hernando de Soto, which otherwise might have found its final resting place in a golden sepulchre, was dumped into a big river.

The younger Irving's fantasy version was so popular that it spawned a hobby—finding the exact places where that now supposedly valiant explorer, Hernando de Soto, had pitched camp. Hundreds of years earlier the most trustworthy of de Soto's chroniclers, Gómez Suárez de Figueroa, explained why all such attempts were exercises in fantasy—also why de Soto "discovered" nothing and why his wanderings produced no useful knowledge. "They had no instruments with them by which they could compute distances. Their main object," he observed, was "silver and gold; consequently they gave themselves but little trouble to note down the route."

Almost everyone has heard of de Soto. We would understand Florida, the Americas, and ourselves better if his chronicler were as well known. Gómez Suárez de Figueroa, better known as Garcilaso de la Vega, was the son of an Incan princess and one of the Incan Empire's Spanish destroyers. One of the first mestizos in the cultural as well as genetic sense, he was at once a collaborator of the Spanish and a chronicler of their crimes, a victim of imperialism and also its pet. Gómez Suárez called himself "The Inca" in order to emphasize he was not a full-blooded Spaniard. Even so, he spent decades of his life in Spain attempting to claim legitimate inheritance from his father. While doing that, he sired an illegitimate son of his own. With "The Inca" are born the great themes of future Latin America—which today are also Florida's themes and, increasingly, those of the rest of the United States. These are—whether the realm is literature, vegetation, or politics—the triumph of the conqueror followed by the triumph of the conquered over the conqueror.

The Inca confessed he could make no sense of de Soto's route from the garbled accounts provided by the expedition's survivors, but some three hundred years later that did not stop Americans who knew no Spanish from announcing with certainty the precise locations where the famed explorer had pitched camp. The all-time champion of the de Soto hobbyists was Henry R. Schoolcraft, another of those forgotten inventors of Florida whose life—as opposed to the legends he invented—makes him a figure of genuine importance. Schoolcraft had noted that the names of certain Florida tribes mentioned in Irving's book sounded, to his ear, similar to the names of tribes he encountered as far north as Minnesota. From these supposed correlations, themselves based on unreliable Spanish and Portuguese renderings of the original names in a variety of Indian languages, he stitched together a squiggly line running first all over Florida, then wherever Schoolcraft's imagination took him.

If a tribe somewhere in Arkansas or Kentucky had a name that, to him, sounded like a name mentioned in some account written down hundreds of years earlier, that settled it. De Soto had been there. Phonetically Schoolcraft's approach was nonsense; anthropologically it was preposterous. Even had his research been more rigorous, Schoolcraft's findings would have remained specious for an even more fundamental reason. Most of the tribes that de Soto encountered (and whose descendants Schoolcraft now imagined he had identified) were extinct by then. Without realizing it, Schoolcraft remade the long-dead sixteenth-century Spaniard over into his own image and likeness. Nearly forty years earlier, Schoolcraft had falsely proclaimed himself the discoverer of the source of the Mississippi River. Now he proclaimed de Soto the discoverer of the same river on equally fallacious grounds. Schoolcraft also had something in common with The Inca. While working among the tribesmen of the upper Mississippi valley, he married a half-Indian woman. The Inca, a child of the Andes, would spend most of his adult life in Andalusia, writing books in Spanish. Schoolcraft, with his mixed-race family, would also live out his life on the far margins of the world into which he had been born.

If you are one of those millions who believe de Soto "discovered" the Mississippi, it is because the American educational system foisted on you a myth which, after Irving and Schoolcraft refined it, was propagated by generations of grade-school teachers and text book publishers. At taxpayers' expense a myriad of U.S. government agencies, including the Department of the Interior and the National Park Service, also purveyed as fact fictional versions of de Soto. In 1936, 385 years after de Soto's death by misadventure, Congress voted the money to fund the United States De Soto Expedition Commission. Through a kind of historical gerrymandering, Tampa Bay was declared to have been the site of de Soto's landing.

Two monuments erected in the Tampa area illustrate the scope of the fabrication. "On a sweltering day in May of 1539, Hernando de Soto and an army of over 600 soldiers splashed ashore in the Tampa

Bay area," kids are falsely taught when they visit the De Soto National Memorial, a federally funded facility located in an attractive waterfront area where Hernando de Soto is no more likely to have splashed ashore than, in faraway Yellowstone, Smokey the Bear is likely to have put out a forest fire. Staffers of the National Park Service give their young visitors the chance to "try on a piece of armor," just like what de Soto never wore. At the other monument, in downtown Tampa, de Soto is transmuted into the kind of gentleman Florida ladies in hoop skirts would be right proud to welcome to their garden parties. The De Soto Oak Plaque, as it is called, "marks the tree under which tradition says De Soto parlayed with the Indians," according to Floyd E. Boone's guide, *Florida Historical Markers & Sites*, but the oak is not native to this part of Florida. It could not possibly have been there when de Soto commenced his policy of kidnapping and enslaving whatever Indians he could find. Like those who invented it, the "tradition" of de Soto and the oak tree was a recent migrant into Florida. Looking at the De Soto Oak Plaque, you can almost see the tale of William Penn and the Treaty Elm taking off its plain Quaker garb, putting on a conquistador's plumes, and then, like so many Pennsylvanians later, moving down to Florida.

De Soto's greatest fame came as a by-product of the automobile age. Walter Chrysler called his first car the Plymouth. With its wholesome connotations of the first Thanksgiving, the Plymouth was marketed as America's modern means to pursue happiness, but what to name his other car, aimed at a more upscale market? Names of explorers were popular because Americans themselves now could explore their country from sea to shining sea. The competition already had appropriated Cadillac, but the name of another, by now acceptably noncontroversial explorer was still in the public domain. "De Soto had covered more North American territory than any other early explorer," notes Dave Duricy in his 2005 essay on the legendary gas-guzzler. The first DeSoto (spelled with a capital D, no space between the words) was the 1929 model, America's best-selling car the year of the great stock market crash. The DeSoto became America's car of the moment again in 1957, when its chrome-encrusted tail fins made it the automotive epitome of the Cold War consumer society.

For many years the best place to obtain a realistic view of de Soto and the fate that overtook him, counterintuitively enough, was in the grandiose Ponce de Leon Hotel in St. Augustine. There, filling much of one wall, hung a painting that within the boundaries of its immense frame contained more truth about Florida than many libraries do. The canvas, more than five feet high and nearly ten feet wide, was produced by the historical genre painter Thomas Moran in 1878. It was the age of Cinerama-like canvases portraying the scenic wonders of America and the intrepid explorers who discovered them. Moran, a businessman virtuoso of an artist, already had enjoyed success with a production typical of this genre, *Columbus Approaching San Salvador*. Hoping for another big sale, the artist now opted for "painting a subject featuring the Spanish conquistador Hernando de Soto."

Unlike many others who have defined Florida in paint or print, Moran took the trouble to visit Florida and to study its landscape. That led to his undoing because, instead of presenting the South Seas–Riviera version, he depicted Florida as it was. There are no pretty flowers in his painting, no swaying palm trees. Instead the figures in the painting find themselves lost in a somber kingdom of encroaching green darkness. The painting's pivotal figure is not the conquistador; it is a soldier holding a gun in the lower right-hand corner of the painting. He stares in the direction of some danger, which he neither can see nor understand, but which he knows lurks in the nearby forest darkness. On this immense canvas, fully 70 percent of the surface area is taken up by the gnarled trees, their roots and foliage, and the darkness they create. A stream in the background, instead of leading to some gold mine or sea route to Cathay, disappears into a swamp. A few Indians are also there; they have offered some animal hides to the Spaniards.

The scene depicted in the painting is a literal representation of an incident that Theodore Irving lifted from an earlier account known as the report of a "Portuguese gentleman" of de Soto's wanderings. It occurred "in a most wretched country"—that is, one without gold or silver. The local people are described, with some irritation, as a "peaceful race, nearly naked. They lived principally on herbs, root, and wild fowl." What especially dismays de Soto is the tribute the local chief offers: "two deer skins, which he seemed to think a considerable present." We also learn why, as shown in the painting, so few inhabitants come to greet the conquistador: "Most of the inhabitants of this miserable province fled to the woods on the Spaniards' approach, leaving few inhabitants in their villages, except the old, blind and infirm." The following passage explains why they fled: "Every morning, de Soto dispatched four or five parties of horse, in different directions, to scour the country; these cut down every Indian they encountered, and always returned at sunset, with the assurance that there was not one remaining within four leagues. In four or five hours afterwards, however, hordes of savages were again prepared to attack them."

For Moran, like de Soto, wealth was the objective. To satisfy putative purchasers, Moran put feathered headdresses and war paint on the Florida Indians, the equivalent of dressing up Knights of the Round Table in Viking helmets. In his effort to find a buyer, Moran took even greater liberties with his title. He hoped to sell the painting to the House of Representatives, but Congress already had paid for a triumphalist mural depicting the de Soto myth. Entitled *Discovery of the Mississippi by De Soto, 1602*, it dated de Soto's supposed discovery sixty years after his death. When it became clear Congress wouldn't buy a second de Soto–themed work, Moran switched the name of his painting. Instead of *De Soto in Florida*, he called it *Ponce de Leon in Florida*, even though his painting shows no ship, no seashore, no ceremonial naming of Florida—and no Fountain of Youth, though Moran easily could have slipped that last motif into his painting where the miasmic swamp was, and didn't. In spite of the name change, no government agency made an offer. No museum would take it either. This painting was too truthful. As often in Florida the truth was to be found in the mislabeling.

De Soto or Ponce de León? Moran's painting reflected the reality that, once ashore in Florida, names no longer mattered. All the conquistadors were interchangeable figures lost in the enveloping green. Finally, nearly twenty years after Moran finished it, one of the Ponce de Leon Hotel's interior decorators bought the painting because its name went with the new hotel. Then the painting disappeared, only to reappear episodically, just as de Soto himself had, in the most outlandish places. It would be displayed in an Oklahoma City used-furniture store before finding its way back to Florida; today it is on display in Jacksonville's Cummer Museum.

In the end all that remained of de Soto's immense wealth were "two slaves, three horse, and seven hundred swine." All were auctioned off to the survivors of the expedition and their camp followers. The winners agreed to pay for their purchases with Florida's nonexistent gold, "the money to be paid by the purchaser on the first discovery of any gold or silver mines." Hernando de Soto had become to pigs what Johnny Appleseed would be to apple orchards: "500,000 Feral Hogs Causing Problems in Florida," a story datelined Gainesville, Florida, announced in August 2005, more than 450 years after de Soto's swine began their Florida proliferation. "European pigs arrived in the country with some of the earliest settlers, and they either escaped or were released into the wild nearly 500 years ago," another report explained. "Since then they have migrated as far north as Canada, and into at least 35 states."

The conquest continues. In 2012, the National Feral Swine Mapping System showed that the beasts had colonized much of Oregon and almost the totality of California except for Los Angeles and a few other freeway-encordoned safety zones, "but they feel especially at home in Florida," one news report noted.

3

CHERT

Between 1513 and 1565 no fewer than eight expeditions were sent to Florida with the aim of establishing Spanish rule there. Florida stymied every one of them. In 1526 Lucas Vásquez de Ayllón arrived with a flotilla of six ships carrying more than six hundred people, including soldiers, settlers, their wives and children, doctors, and slaves from Africa. Here is an account of what happened to their settlement: "During the fall the colonists suffered from disease, lack of food and cold. Scouting parties were sent inland to locate native populations from which food could be obtained, but they were not successful. Many people died, including Ayllón. Some members of the colony moved to a nearby Indian village, but after several days their native hosts killed them. Raids took a toll on the Spaniards, and at one point some of the African slaves set fire to buildings. Defeated, the colonists abandoned the settlement in mid-November and set sail for home."

In 1528 Pánfilo de Narváez drowned in the course of his attempt to conquer Florida. Only four of the fifteen hundred men who started out with him survived. The most famous of the survivors, Álvar Núñez Cabeza de Vaca, found rescue only after he had walked from Florida clear across Texas. In 1548 Father Luis Cancer de Barbastro was clubbed to death on a Florida beach. Then, in 1559, Tristán de Luna y Arellano set out from Mexico. Pursuing the novel strategy of trying to conquer Florida from the north rather than the south, he and his expedition landed in the vicinity of present-day Pensacola just in time for a hurricane to destroy their provisions, supplies, and hopes. Tristán de Luna was successful by one measure: he was the first leader of a Spanish expedition to escape with his life.

The ruination the Spaniards inflicted on themselves was trivial in comparison to the horror they unleashed on Florida's original people. Smallpox, malaria, typhus, bubonic plague, pneumonic plague, measles, and yellow fever all arrived with the Europeans. As European diseases swept the Americas, the human population of all the islands from Cuba down to South America perished. So did the populations of Newfoundland and the Bahamas. In Florida, too, the insular quality of life had protected its people for millennia, but when the invasion finally came they were even less prepared to survive contagion than the continental populations were. As the native peoples died so did the conquistadors' dream of conquest. The two catastrophes engendered each other. The Spanish carried the diseases that killed them. By dying, the indigenous people denied the Spanish the labor essential to their system of empire.

A similar fate overtook Spain's spiritual empire. The cross following the sword, Franciscans and Jesuits eventually established more than one hundred Florida missions, the first of them in 1566, 203 years before the first of the famous California missions was founded. By 1705 every one of them had disappeared, along with the people whose souls they were meant to "save." These vanished unfortunates were as bad as us, as good as us, also as quick on the uptake as people are today. "Charity and kindness were here, 7,000 years ago," writes Robin C. Brown of *Florida's First People*. So were violence and cruelty, as archaeologists discovered in 1982 after a workman excavating a site for a real estate development at Windover Pond, eleven miles inland from Cape Canaveral, found human skulls in the muck and called the cops. It wasn't evidence from one of Florida's famous mass murders. These people had died thousands of years before Buddha, Socrates and Confucius were born. The misshapen spinal column of a youth, maybe fifteen years old, was the most revealing find; he had suffered from a birth defect called spina bifida. "The badly crippled youth could never have walked," Brown points out, "yet they cared for him." Archaeologists also found the remains of a murder victim; he had been trying to escape when his attackers speared him.

The initial peopling of Florida was a migrational rivulet eddying off a much broader peopling of the Americas. New findings keep pushing back the date of mankind's first apparition in the western hemisphere, but in terms of evolution it occurred so recently that no Neanderthals or *Homo erectus* ever roamed the western hemisphere; we are the only species of the genus *Homo* ever to reach the Americas. Like the Sunbelt migrants of today, these first people changed Florida irrevocably and forever by being there. Within fifteen hundred years all of Florida's large beasts, including supersized camels and giant five-hundred-pound beavers, were extinct. The horse also disappeared, though it would return with the Spanish. At the Museum of Natural History in Gainesville you can see the skeleton of a mammoth that lived in Florida some sixteen thousand years ago. Like the remains of the Windover people it was preserved in underwater muck. This magnificent creature was more than fifteen feet tall when it raised its mighty head, displayed its immense tusks, and bellowed. Until people got there, bigger had been better in Florida. The invention of the spear point changed that. Use of spears meant that small groups of emotionally bonded, task-driven, armed humans—the forerunners of the military platoon, and many other forms of teamwork—could battle, kill, then feed themselves, their mates and their offspring on the flesh of beasts that otherwise would have been invulnerable.

The inventions of the Paleolithic and Neolithic eras revolutionized the world's hierarchy of speciation, turning humans into the planet's dominant species, but how to have a Stone Age without stones? In addition to having no metals, Florida has no granite or quartz. You also won't find jasper or obsidian because those substances are the products of volcanic eruptions, and Florida has no igneous rocks of any kind, hence also no coal or diamonds or opals or any other "stones" in the usual sense of the word.

In Florida people mastered Stone Age technology though they had no stone. From the fossilized remains of dead sponges they manufactured daggerlike weapons efficient enough to render extinct whole species of megafauna. The most important toolmaking material they used is called chert. Chert in its finished form "is characterized by its extreme hardness, glass-like fracture, and the sharpness of the edges," notes one geologist. That made it ideal for the "manufacturing of axe heads, spear heads and arrow points," but chert doesn't occur in nature that way. Before it could be "napped" into tools and weapons, chert first had to be extracted from the thick layers of limestone encasing it, then broken down into manageable nuggets. Chunks of the material, weighing as much as seventy-five pounds, were then buried in sand, over which hot fires were made to burn for many hours. Once extracted from these Paleolithic furnaces, the nuggets were broken into smaller pieces. They in turn were laboriously transformed from a dusty gray substance, gritty to the touch, into a smooth, shiny substance with a palette of attractive hues, ranging from pastel pink to mahogany brown. These, depending on their structure and the inventiveness of the people working them, were fashioned into a variety of ornaments, tools and weapons.

This elaborate tempering process was a triumph of human inventiveness and organization, but chert was rare and hard to find so, even more remarkably, people in south Florida developed methods of transforming agatized coral into killing blades. Such implements prove that what is true of the age of nuclear weapons was also true more than fifteen thousand years ago. Man's intelligence, not the weapons he used, was what made him such an efficient killer. Bigger and heavier than the much more famous Clovis spear points, the chert spear points made in Florida worked so well they made themselves obsolete. As the big beasts these spear points killed disappeared the weapons, like the animals they were used to kill, became smaller and smaller. Right from the start people transformed Florida. As the evolution of their weapons technology reveals, Florida transformed them back—from big game hunters into baymen, fishermen, trappers, and scavengers.

Dinosaurs never roamed Florida; it was ocean bottom during most of the time they dominated the planet. There were no sheep, goats, or bovines, but when people arrived the alligator was waiting for them, as were the pelican and the manatee. In ancient Florida no one was ever stung by a bee but blackflies swarmed over everything.

Potatoes, tomatoes, chilies, and chocolate, though they originated in the Western Hemisphere, would reach Florida only when Europeans, having acquired them in Central and South America, brought them there. Corn, the nutritional mainstay among many of the Americas' indigenous peoples, only reached Florida thousands of years after it was cultivated elsewhere. The underlying limitations of the land help explain why, for so long, agriculture scarcely existed. The lack of food reserves to loot enraged the Spaniards nearly as much as the lack of gold mines did. They had stormed into the midst of a society that, in spite of its surface abundance, was far less productive and resilient than it seemed.

Dining on oysters, drinking teas made from local herbs, and wearing scanty but colorful clothing which they accessorized with jewelry of their own design, these early peoples, like Floridians today, were able to enjoy a standard of living their economic productivity did not seem to warrant. At Horr's Island in southwest Florida immense middens of discarded oyster shells arose, as gigantic as the Mount Trashmores Floridians have created from their castoffs in our own times. Thousands lived atop these man-made plateaux, which helped protect them from coastal storm surges, even though they lacked the support systems necessary for urban life, including agriculture and widespread trade routes. Early drawings show people who would fit right into the fashion parade you see, nowadays, in Miami's South Beach, with one difference. These ancient Floridians apparently felt no necessity to work out at the gym. In these early depictions both men and women are portly. The original Floridians seem not to have known hunger, let alone starvation, until the Europeans inflicted it on them, along with Christianity, slavery, and a multitude of diseases.

For at least a dozen millennia Florida's isolation had saved its people from the Black Death and other contagions. Now the common cold wiped out whole villages as rampant, unstoppable death arrived from the outside, and people there found themselves as unprepared for the onslaught, and as powerless to survive it, as the mastodon and the giant beaver had been. The first of Florida's modern human tragedies, their extinction was but one of many episodes in a biological melodrama of genetic advance and retreat that had been unfolding there since time immemorial, and continues to unfold all around us. All sorts of animals, plants, and microbes are constantly making bizarre apparitions in Florida because, in addition to the ambiguity of land and water, there is an ambiguity of air and temperature. Is it tropic or temperate, hot or cold, northern or southern? You may think you know the answer until the Jet Stream plunges south, bringing freezing winds and killer frosts with it. According to the National Weather Service, two of the ten most destructive natural disasters to strike Florida in the course of the twentieth century were fits of cold weather. Even in average years winter chills are a fact of life, yet people seem perennially unnerved when the cold front arrives. "I am greatly in need of a coat," Mrs. Clara Leonard, a Miami widow, wrote when chilly weather hit in December 1934. "If you have one which you have laid aside from last season, would appreciate it so much if you would send it to me. I will pay postage if you see fit to send it." Having composed her letter, Mrs. Leonard put a 3-cent stamp on the envelope and addressed it to Mrs. Eleanor Roosevelt, The White House, Washington, D.C.

The Denial of Frost is one of Florida's great recurring themes, but there are no hurricane deniers. Everyone has experienced it, if only vicariously: the howling winds, the storm surge slashing across the barrier islands; the hurricane turning life and property into its toys, then smashing them the way a petulant child does in the midst of a tantrum. Yet Florida's hurricanes, with one exception, have killed hundreds rather than thousands of people. This is because until recently Florida had so few people, and most of them did not live in the lowest-lying areas of peninsular Florida as they do today. The 1928 Lake Okeechobee hurricane led to the deaths, chiefly by drowning, of nearly three thousand people. They were killed when hurricane winds caused the waters of Okeechobee, which is three-quarters the size of the state of Rhode Island, to slosh violently over the dikes.

Zora Neale Hurston described Florida better than anyone else ever has, and maybe ever will. That goes for her description of people fleeing for their lives ahead of the Lake Okeechobee flood:

The monstropolous beast had left his bed. The two hundred
miles an hour wind had loosened his chains. He seized hold
of his dikes and ran forward until he met the quarters; uprooted them like grass and rushed on after his supposed-to-be
conquerors, rolling the dikes, rolling the houses, rolling the
people in the houses along with other timbers. The sea was
walking the earth with a heavy heel.
    "De lake is comin'!" Tea Cake gasped.
    "De lake!" in amazed horror from Motor Boat, "De lake!"
    "It's comin' behind us!" Janie shuddered.

"The mother of malice had trifled with men," Hurston wrote.
Actually it was the other way around. Had those man-made dikes
not existed, there would have been no fatal rush of water. Lake
Okeechobee would have spread gradually and benignly out over the
Everglades, providing a new injection of freshwater and vegetal nu-
trients rather than surging out in a homicidal rampage. The human
response, as always in Florida, was to distort the contours of the land
even more drastically. Today the dikes are so high you cannot see
Lake Okeechobee as you drive past it. Encasing Okeechobee was
only the start. The U.S. Army Corps of Engineers also constructed
what is known as the East Coast Protective Levee. Zigging and zag-
ging a hundred miles from Homestead, south of Miami, up through
Dade, Broward, and Palm Beach counties, the immense project
artificially separated the Everglades from its natural drainage out-
lets, transforming an immense swath of wetlands into momentarily
dry land. It amounted to a government-financed subsidy for urban
sprawl and real estate speculation in south Florida. It also constituted a disruption of Nature, which Nature sooner or later will find
a way to correct, the difference being that, this time, millions, not
thousands, of people will be endangered.
    Whether it's the behavior of air or water, animals or plants,
microbes or humans, explaining and propelling all that happens in
Florida is the melodrama of heat exchange. Just like in chemistry class,
heat expands on a global scale as air (wind) and water (oceans) try to
reach planetary equilibrium. The rotation and inclination of the earth

as it circles the sun make that impossible, but nature keeps trying so every year tropical storms carry immense quantities of warm air and moisture northward. Beneath the ocean's surface, immense volumes of warmer water are also flowing north. We call the northern-coursing warm waters that flow past Florida the Gulf Stream. The most powerful of the northward-moving air masses we call hurricanes. Different as they seem, the underlying symmetry of ocean currents and hurricanes is an elegant manifestation of how gases (such as heated tropical air) and liquids (such as heated ocean water) work out the same rules of nature in their own ways.

It is a case of shape and location, as well as geological formation, turning into destiny. Tectonics and geology have combined to create, in the form of Florida, a land formation which is both shaped like a bridge and acts like a bridge—and not just any bridge. Florida, because of its intermediate latitude, bridges two completely different climate zones, the temperate and the tropic. It also bridges what, over the past 500 years, have turned out to be two of the most historically volatile regions of modern times. One of these is tropical Latin America, which currently has one of the fastest-growing populations in the world. The other is temperate-climate North America. In less than 150 years it has been transformed from a vast, almost empty expanse, where bison roamed by the millions and passenger pigeons filled the skies, into home base of the greatest superpower the world has so far seen—the place where nuclear weapons, TV, iPods, and MIRVs, to say nothing of PCs and the Internet, were invented.

As migrants from the north move south, and migrants from the south move north, Florida's subtropical climate regime ensnares all sorts of creatures. To understand, think of insects and reptiles as well as people entering an environmental maze where things are not what they seem. Better yet, imagine a game of adaptational croquet played with pink flamingoes. More than fifty years ago, a flock of real pink flamingoes showed up at the Hialeah racetrack near Miami. For years to come the flamingoes, like characters in some avian tale by Damon Runyon, were faithful seasonal visitors to the track. Then, like a lot of people, the flamingoes stopped commuting, in their case to and from Cuba. They settled permanently in Florida. Other migrants which have made Florida their home include the cat, the mouse, the louse and the flea. The Cuban tree frog (actually it must have been a pair of them) invaded Florida in 1931, in a shipping crate. Its arrival violated U.S. Department of Agriculture regulations, but being an illegal alien has not stopped *Osteopilus septentrionalis*, to give its official name, from making it in America. "Celebrity Frog Makes Leap to 'Today' Show," the *Tampa Tribune* reported in 2005. In nearby Zephyrhills a pet tree frog named Prince Marchello had learned to pilot a toy scooter. In recognition of this accomplishment the amphibian had been booked to appear on national network TV.

Florida's biological melodrama of genetic advance and retreat goes mostly unnoticed until some video clip on YouTube, or scare story blaring from the tabloids in the supermarket checkout line, grabs people's attention: "Lizard Terrorizes Florida Neighborhood"— "Officials Hunt Pair of Hybrid Wolves"—"Florida on Guard Against Giant Snails"—"Python Population Out of Control." In October 2002, Florida's tendency to switch from postcard paradise into horror movie achieved epiphany when a north Florida woman named Dee Thompson entered her office in Fort Walton Beach and noticed it was infested by a multitude of small frogs. Outside, perhaps a million of the creatures, each about the size of a dime, had invaded the parking lot, the grounds and adjacent buildings. Over and over events in Florida had simultaneously satirized and symbolized America's dilemmas and foibles. Now, at Fort Walton Beach, Florida's own drama was mirrored in an event at once bizarrely implausible, yet propelled by an irrefutable Florida logic.

In addition to the where-else-but-Florida frogs themselves, there was that sense, so often felt in Florida, of glimpsing the zeitgeist in a fun house mirror. Partly this was because, years before it happened, Hollywood filmmakers not once, but twice, adumbrated the Fort Walton Beach frog infestation. The first movie to portray the event before it happened was a 1972 low-budget horror flick. Entitled *Frogs*, it not only depicted the infestation in advance, the movie was filmed only a few miles away from the actual site of the future, real-life frog invasion. Then in 1999, only three years before it happened, a more important film appeared. Like Florida, *Magnolia* was filled with sprawling, quirky, apparently unrelated events. This created a cinematic problem for its cult-status writer-director, Paul Thomas Anderson. How to end the movie? Anderson wisely decided to resolve his plot convolutions by having frogs fall from the sky. Now something analogous happened in Florida, though this being Florida the frogs did not fall from the sky. They oozed up out of the muck.

The real-life plague was infested with symbolism. For starters Fort Walton Beach, in name as well as event, recapitulates Florida's whole transformation from U.S. military outpost (Fort) to sybaritic American seashore (Beach). It therefore was fully appropriate that the frogs in question should choose that location to smite the notion that, in Florida, the American Dream, having crushed all resistance, had rolled on to total victory. The attack was even more precisely targeted than that. For Dee Thompson, the woman who found the frogs, was executive director of PAWS, the Panhandle Animal Welfare Society. Modern Florida had been founded on the notion that Nature could be trained to be cute, like a family pet. Now, by the hundreds of thousands, the slimy, gooey, unpleasant frogs were expectorating, defecating, and fornicating all over the carefully kept files on cute little missing dogs and oh-so-adoptable cats it was the mission of the Panhandle Animal Welfare Society to protect. They also were clogging the feed troughs and turning the litter boxes into green, throbbing messes of undifferentiated life.

Absurd though it seemed on the surface, the Fort Walton Beach infestation resonated with great themes going deep into Florida's unique geography and climate. Illuminatingly, however, Floridians reacted to the events at Fort Walton Beach the same way people in the rest of America habitually react to events in Florida. Weird! But what do you expect in a place like that? Then they returned to their usual life pursuits—momentarily diverted, but in no way enlightened.

Whether tropical storms are lashing northward from the tropics during the hurricane season, or a tidal wave of southward-swarming college students from Up North is breaking on its beaches during Spring Break, Florida's peculiar destiny is to get its history, along with its weather and practically everything else, both coming and going. In consequence most of what seems typically Floridian originated some place else, often brought by some military, political, economic, or cultural invader. Nothing seems more quintessentially Floridian than orange juice, unless it is the beautiful hibiscus blossom. Both originated in China, and then got to Florida via Europe. The music you hear in a Florida disco probably started out in the Caribbean, while the music you hear in a roadside bar is likely to have originated in the Appalachians. In Florida North constantly meets South. South constantly meets North, as the two jostle their way up and down Florida into each other's territory. Florida is not merely where South meets North and vice versa. It's where they collide, clash, combust and, more often than you'd suppose, caress and commingle.

One result of its intermediary position is that in Florida there is no such thing as stasis. Those bright clear mornings will be followed by afternoon thunderstorms. The same goes for human events. Nothing is permanent, though within this turbulence patterns occur and recur. We don't know what tree frogs expect to achieve by advancing into Florida. We do know what most people suppose when they conquer a country or make a down payment on a condo. They imagine that the particular version of reality they scratch into the mud or delineate on a map will be permanent, definitive, but Florida's North-South dynamic guarantees no such dreams of permanence ever come true.

The Spanish imagined they had conquered Florida for good in 1565 when, in the first mass killing of white by white men on the North American continent, they wiped out French colonization efforts there. The Americans thought they had settled Florida's future definitively when, following several rampages across Florida, they replaced the Spanish in 1821. For a long time the triumph of English-speaking North Americans seemed as irreversible as the earlier Spanish dominion had seemed. Events eventually proved that was an illusion too. By the end of the twentieth century a counter-influx of Spanish-speaking Latin Americans into Florida was remaking the state demographically, though that was not the end of it. By the time the twentieth-first century began, the northward-bound millions of Latin Americans were being counterbalanced by millions of southward-bound Baby Boomers advancing into Florida from the North on giant waves of retirement money. The ensuing social and cultural upheaval is to be expected, but one unexpected result of this commingling of humanity is the complementary roles the two groups have found for themselves in each other's lives. Florida, a state full of aging American retirees, also—with nobody planning it that way—has become a state full of immigrant health care workers. Meanwhile, every weekend, in singles bars from Tallahassee to Key Largo, dark dreamy eyes stare into bright blue eyes, and the two connect.

It would be wrong to say that, in Florida, every southward push is balanced by a reciprocal, northward shove; that's too simplistic. Florida, instead, operates as a kind of case study in chaos theory. Its consistencies emerge, like the Great Red Spot on the planet Jupiter, out of its swirling unpredictabilities. Water seeps southward through the limestone. Tropical storms carry immense quantities of water northward. Either way, Florida gets flooded. The midwestern retirees in their trailer parks and the Haitian boat people detained by the INS get to Florida by their different routes, for their different reasons. Both wind up living in cheap prefabs. Flight capital, whether it starts out in Caracas or Cleveland, tends to ensconce itself in gated communities. Exoskeleton or endoskeleton, after a few hundred years all that physically survives of both marine worm and man of destiny is a chalky white residue.

Florida had cockroaches of its own before such intruders as the giant Madagascaran hissing cockroach took up residence, but as a team of biologists points out in a study of Florida's insects: "The major pest species of cockroaches are all immigrants." Advancing from the opposite direction, the strangling killer kudzu vine entered Florida from Georgia around 1899 with the railroads. Also colonizing Florida is the Australian "pine." Though not a conifer, the first Australian pines were introduced into Florida because they reminded newcomers of real pines Up North. The problem is that the Australian pine proliferates like a gigantic, thirty-foot-tall weed when given the chance—and, it turned out, Florida's native trees and plants were unequipped to compete with this latest invader. Once valued for its "Mediterranean" look, the Australian pine is now one the principal threats to the Everglades.

Other invaders which have hit the jackpot include the brown citrus aphid, but in general only one out of ten invading species manages to survive once it reaches Florida. This is because for all species, including humans, Florida's most salient characteristic is its inhospitality. Except for that fringe at the top, Florida is too far south and soggy for cotton, let alone for tobacco, wheat, and the other cash crops that would make the rest of the United States the world's most abundant agricultural as well as industrial producer. Florida is also too far north for easy exploitation of the great tropical plantation crops. No bananas, no indigo, no pineapple or rubber plantations flourish in Florida because the place is neither temperate nor tropical. Instead ten months of sweat are followed by those spells each winter when the tourists shiver in their flimsy resort wear and Florida society women take their mink stoles out of storage.

None of these invading species compares remotely in importance with *Schizoporella floridana*, a.k.a. bryozoan. To understand, it's necessary to return to Florida's all-pervasive underlying fact of life, its limestone structure. Limestone does not naturally occur in and of itself; it is a by-product of chemical processes. Those chemical processes can be organic as well as inorganic. That is to say, living creatures can and do produce limestone, enormous quantities of it. When it comes to limestone-producing animals, coral is by far the most famous, but only a bit of Florida—the upper Keys, notably Key Largo—is of coral origin. The sea worm pitches in, too, creating a limestone crust around itself that eventually turns into some of the crunchy stuff that makes up Florida, but the bryozoan is the real hero of Florida's creation. The tiny animal has created vast areas of Florida, including most of the land underlying the Everglades. One reason bryozoan gets so much done is that it doesn't waste much time and energy on sex. The first member of each colony is created by sexual reproduction. This founding father-mother then clones endless reproductions of itself. Each creature, as part of its life cycle, excretes a self-defensive coating of calcium carbonate. In this way each individual, though less than a millimeter long, contributes to the eventual creation of immense land forms. Bryozoans come in more than five hundred species, but all of Florida's bryozoans belong to a one single species, *Schizoporella floridana*.

Different as they seem, *Homo sapiens* and *Schizoporella floridana* have two things in common so far as their impact on Florida is concerned. Their waste is their most enduring product. Also, both species are heedless of the consequences of their actions. Bryozoan didn't set out to create the state of Florida. It simply followed its impulses. The absence of reason is also one of the driving forces of Florida's human history. That accounts for the most ghastly aspect of the catastrophe which overtook the original people of Florida— its unavoidability. Human nature being what it is, it was inevitable that someday, somehow, human beings would find some way to end the separation of the two hemispheres, and once that happened? Florida shows that sometimes the catastrophes humans unleash on each other inadvertently can be more horrible than those inflicted as a deliberate result of their avarice, viciousness, cruelty, and pride. The behavior of Florida's conquerors was monstrous. The horror they unleashed transcended intent.

Before the arrival of the Europeans grown men in Florida were, on average, five feet nine inches tall, the same as well-fed Americans four hundred years later. Many Spaniards were not much more than five feet tall. In their dark northern climes, and on their filthy ships, they lived on denatured cereals infested with vermin, yet their sabers and daggers flashed sunlight into the eyes of people who had never before seen the glint of metal, or glass, or a mirror. Both sides were amazed by their physical differences, their differences of language, most of all by the differences in the objects they owned and made. Yet the most fateful difference—their different degrees of immunity to different diseases—was invisible to both of them.

We don't know what were the first words they said to each other. We do know that, very quickly, these people stole from each other and had sexual intercourse with each other. Right away they kidnapped and killed each other. While we know all those things happened, we will never know the name of the first Floridian to see the first European. We do know the name of the last Floridian. He was called Juan Alonso Cabale. Colonial records identify him as an

"Indian of the Timucuan nation." The same death certificate states that he lived to be fifty-five years old and had been born at a St. Augustine mission called Nuestra Señora de la Leche. His death date was November 14, 1767. Cabale did not die in Florida. His place of death was Guanabacao, Cuba. The circumstances of his death, like the extinction of his people, were a side effect of Europe's squabbles, wars, and truces. In 1763, a European peace treaty briefly took Florida away from Spain and put it under British control. By then Spanish Florida was so empty that, according to official statistics, only 3,096 people inhabited the colony. When the Spanish relinquished control, they simply put everyone there on boats, then sailed them off to Cuba. With Cabale's disappearance the final link in a chain of human existence going back to the last Ice Age disappeared.

The Florida into which those first Europeans heedlessly blundered is a lost world now. Nothing can revive it, but we owe it in simple decency to those who perished not to let perish the memory of what befell them. We also need to remember for our own sake. Florida shows how in every era people are killed, and cultures mutilated, and the earth ravaged because powerful men, from faraway, for vain and abstract reasons, on the basis of faulty information, and without sufficient attention to the consequences of following their impulses, authorize barbarities that benefit no one, including, in the end, themselves. As the subsequent history of Florida would demonstrate again and again, these early events taught lessons we ignore to our own great peril, yet traditionally Florida's "historians" have known nothing and cared less about what happened there before white men arrived.

The Spanish archives all along rebutted any notion that Florida was almost devoid of human population. They repeatedly describe a well-populated land—though with each successive intrusion the people become fewer. Archaeological research also refutes the notion that Florida's early peoples were artless as well as very few in number. In 1896, at a Marco Island site now covered by a housing development, archaeologists unearthed works of art as impressive as the tools found there were ingenious, yet historians went on purveying the notion that Florida before the Europeans arrived had been virtually devoid of human life, and even emptier of accomplishment. According to J. E. Dovell's two-volume history of Florida, first published in 1950, the population of Florida just before the first white male got there was "around 15,000," an impossibly low estimate. Things had not changed much by 1971, though that year Professor Charlton W. Tebeau, in his *History of Florida*, did almost double the original population with the click of a typewriter key, to "about 25,000."

Today the advocates of political correctness and multiculturalism increasingly hold sway; in consequence pre-European Florida has undergone a population explosion. "On the eve of Columbus's voyages," according to "a conservative calculation" provided by Dr. Henry F. Dobyns, "Florida's native inhabitants numbered approximately 925,000." The population levels of 1500 probably were not attained again until 1860 when the U.S. Census found just over 140,000 people, slave and free, living there. Possibly it was not until the great real estate boom of the 1920s, when the number of people in Florida reached the one million mark, that its population surpassed the level attained in 1500.

Whatever Florida's original population, all sources concur that by the time the United States took control in 1821 the number had fallen to zero. So far as most Americans were concerned it was as though they never existed. For them Florida's history began with the gallant Spanish conquistador, who in turn was followed by the valorous Confederate aristocrat and then by the multimillionaire visionary investor. That didn't keep visitors from literally tripping over evidence that Florida had a darker past than the tourist brochures admitted. In 1869 James Fenimore Cooper's niece, Constance Fenimore Woolson, visited St. Augustine. She, too, makes no mention of any Fountain of Youth, though she did have some practical advice. During romantic moonlit strolls, she cautioned, one should take care not to trip over the human bones. The future site of the yet-to-be-invented Fountain of Youth was a mass grave.

4

THE FORT,
NOT THE FOUNTAIN

Florida's true founder was a killer-courtier named Pedro Menéndez de Avilés. In the course of his tumultuous lifetime (1519–1574) Menéndez was painted by Titian, kissed the hands of Queen Mary Tudor of England, and was a prisoner of the Inquisition. Now, in Florida, in the month of September, in the year 1565, in the face of a howling hurricane, Menéndez executed the first mass slaughter by white men of white men in territory eventually to comprise part of the United States. At dawn on September 20 Menéndez started the killing. In only a few hours, he and his henchmen stabbed and bludgeoned to death more than 130 people at Fort Caroline, the French outpost on the St. Johns River near present-day Jacksonville. Nine days later he slaughtered another 110 or more Frenchmen, this time right near St. Augustine, on the shores of what thereafter was called Matanzas Inlet. In order to save gunpowder, Menéndez ordered his men to slit their victims' throats.

Menéndez founded St. Augustine. He was the one who finally secured Florida for Spain, but no bowling alleys or dry cleaning establishments are named after him. He has been airbrushed out of the American epic, making him the first of Florida's major protagonists to be excised from history because what he did violated future notions of what the past should have been. For generations it would be part of the national orthodoxy that the conquest of the New World marked deliverance from the crimes and corruptions of the Old World, but as Menéndez demonstrated, America's history would be morally indistinguishable from Europe's. From Florida to Quebec to Bunker Hill to Shiloh to Appomattox and then, as U.S. power expanded, to Vera Cruz and San Juan Hill, the history of the future United States, starting with Florida, would be a replication of Europe's blood feuds, a tale of dispossession, written in blood.

One of nineteen brothers and sisters, and a runaway at age fourteen, Menéndez learned seamanship and survival on the stormy Bay of Biscay between France and Spain. On those cold turbulent waters, violent and unforgiving as Menéndez himself turned out to be, he stalked French "pirates" in his sloop of war, slashed them to death with his cutlass, then sailed home to Spain, his corsair carrying rich booty. Menéndez made such a name for himself that he was barely thirty when the Hapsburg emperor Charles V commissioned him to rid the seas all the way to the Canary Islands of threats to Spanish shipping. This Menéndez did so efficiently that he next was put in charge of Spain's transatlantic traffic.

In theory these attacks on the ships of rival nations should have been unnecessary. Florida along with the whole of North America was supposed to be Spain's exclusive preserve, but the pope's bisection of the globe was workable only so long as obedient Catholics were the only ones at large in the watery world beyond Europe. It was a situation that couldn't last because the Age of Discovery coincided with revolutionary changes in Europe's religious landscape. In 1517 Martin Luther nailed his Ninety-Five Theses to the door of Wittenberg Cathedral. Simultaneously the growing power of France, England and the Netherlands created an increasingly nationalist challenge to Spanish supremacy. In Florida's case ideological fanaticism was added to great power hostility because France—like England, but unlike Spain—encouraged its religious dissidents to establish New World colonies. What the Pilgrims were to New England, France's Huguenots were to Florida, "heretics" as well as aggressors so far as Menéndez was concerned.

By excising France's Protestant settlers King Philip II aimed to simplify his family life as well as reimpose Spanish supremacy in Florida. Married twice as a prince, then twice again in the course of his forty-two-year reign, which lasted from 1556 to 1598, Philip had four wives and went bankrupt four times. His third and, at that time, his latest marriage, to a teenage French princess, Elisabeth of Valois, was ill-omened from the start. During prenuptial celebrations the child bride's father, King Henry II of France, was horribly wounded, then died an excruciating death when a sliver of wood from an adversary's lance pierced his eye and lodged in his brain in the course of a jousting match, leaving his crafty Florentine widow, Catherine de Medici, to run the show as Regent of France. As a result Philip found himself facing a strategic rival who was also his mother-in-law. It turned into a Cuban Missile Crisis in reverse, with the French base in Florida playing the role the Russian missiles did in Cuba four hundred years later. What's fascinating is how suddenly the sense of urgency overtook Philip and his advisers. By then kings and captains-general had been exchanging memoranda about what to do with Florida for more than fifty years. As King Philip himself correctly pointed out, "Florida's shoreline was too low and sandy, her countryside too poor in resources, and her harbors too barred and shallow to permit practicable settlement." The king banned further expeditions to the "accursed lands" of Florida. Then news reached Spain that her great rival, France, having established a colony in Florida, was about to resupply it. In an instant what previously had been an imperial liability was transformed into a strategic asset that must be denied the French, whatever the cost.

In his haste to smite the French Menéndez tore across the Atlantic, riding a fierce storm west toward the Antilles. Three of his ships vanished; hundreds drowned. To save his own life Menéndez ordered bronze cannons thrown overboard from his flagship, the *San Pelayo*. In his eagerness to kill Frenchmen he forsook efforts to save his own son's life. A year earlier Juan Menéndez had disappeared while on a voyage to the Americas; Menéndez initially intended to mount a search for him. Now his son's fate was forgotten. Frantic to reach Florida before the French supply fleet did, Menéndez bypassed Spanish Havana, where he could have repaired his storm-damaged ships while taking on new victuals and men. On the afternoon of September 4, 1565, this risky course of action produced its desired result. In a notable feat of dead reckoning, celestial navigation and intuitive empathy with his prospective victims, Menéndez sailed right into the broad estuary of the St. Johns River. There, near the future site of Jacksonville, was the French settlement, Fort Caroline. The French had every reason to be flabbergasted. So did Menéndez, for there, right in front of him, was a scene to wrench Don Pedro's ardent soul. Riding at anchor, protecting Fort Caroline from the Spanish flotilla, was the French supply fleet, commanded by the Protestant soldier and sailor Jean Ribault.

His whole strategy had rested on destroying the French settlement before reinforcements got there. Now—since the French could see him as clearly as he could see them—Menéndez had lost the element of surprise as well as the race to get to Fort Caroline first. Instead of attacking, expediency now dictated that he and his fleet withdraw. For one thing, Menéndez had not yet established his own Florida base of operations. His heavily laden, storm-battered ships were full of men, beasts, and provisions needing disembarkation after months at sea.

To Menéndez, such considerations were no more than cannons to be jettisoned in the storm. He had come here to attack the French. Attack them he resolved to do, there and then. He and his ships were advancing on the French as night fell and, once again, fate mocked him. The wind died, causing him to improvise yet another plan. He calculated—correctly, it turned out—that if, instead of trying to escape, he let his becalmed ships go on drifting, his Spanish fleet and Ribault's French fleet, in a series of uncontrollable encounters and collisions, would become entangled in the moonless darkness. That calamity, Menéndez had decided, was just what he wanted— because then, at first light, he and his Spaniards could spring from their ships, board the French ships, and kill the heretics! In the night, sound carried over the water as the Spaniards and French shouted imprecations at each other. Why wait for morning? the French taunted. So Menéndez ordered his boarding parties to attack then and there, producing still another calamity, for it was as though Menéndez had signaled the French, not his own men. In unison the French ships raised their sails and, taking advantage of the returning breeze, slipped out of reach, into the dark safety of the Atlantic Ocean.

Since arriving at Fort Caroline Ribault had repaired his ships and unloaded his cargo. Menéndez's ships—damaged in the Atlantic storm, still carrying their full cargoes—could not match the French for speed. This, Menéndez now decided once again, was just what he had wanted all along, for with the French ships gone he could attack Fort Caroline as originally planned. When dawn came, however, Menéndez saw that the French escape also had been a diversionary tactic. While drawing the Spanish away in the attempt to catch him, Ribault had left three of his ships to block the estuary when Menéndez returned. On shore, a French force was drawn up, bayonets bared, ready to repulse any Spaniards who got past the French ships. With enemies by land, enemies by sea, as well as no sanctuary and no lines of communication, who now was the hunter, and who the hunted? The nearest Spanish outpost, more than a week's sail away, was Havana—and in Havana, because of his insistence on secrecy, no one knew Menéndez was here. This was how all Spain's Florida expeditions had ended—ships, weapons, men vanishing into Florida as though it were quicksand.

His great need now being not to destroy the French but to save himself, Menéndez retired from Fort Caroline without attempting an assault. Keeping one eye cocked for the escaped French fleet, he worried his way down the coast past present-day Jacksonville Beach and Neptune Beach, seeking a suitable anchorage. After some fifty miles of searching he came upon the waterway today called St. Augustine Inlet. It was there, in the aftermath of his initial failure to destroy the French, that Menéndez opted to establish his own settlement. Though he now had a beachhead, Menéndez and his expedition remained in grave danger. One danger was that Ribault's nimble fleet would counterattack and defeat the Spanish flotilla in sea battle. Menéndez was so troubled by that possibility that, even before it could finish discharging its cargo, he ordered his cumbersome flagship, the *San Pelayo*, sent to Havana in order to get it out of harm's way. The flagship was his personal property; he would face financial as well as military ruin if the French seized it. In the event, the *San Pelayo* escaped just in time. At first light, Ribault's French ships appeared, prowling the coast. Menéndez and his troops scurried to get out of French cannon range, but instead of attacking, the French ships swept south.

Menéndez's enemies were now in hot pursuit of his flagship. On shore he and a thousand other Spaniards had no fortifications to protect their provisions, their weapons, and their lives, but at this moment, as it periodically does, the climate of Florida intervened to produce a reversal of fortune. As if written into the melodrama in order to change plot direction, a great storm howled onstage, and in this latest complication Menéndez perceived both the helping hand of God, and the outlines of another audacious new plan. The storm, Menéndez realized, made it impossible for Ribault's fleet to reverse course and sail north to protect Fort Caroline. The same storm, to be sure, also had made a seaborne attack by the Spanish impossible. In such weather an overland attack was also unthinkable—to anyone except Pedro Menéndez. The very irrationality of his latest scheme—to march overland through unknown territory in order to attack the French in the midst of a hurricane—was its most rational feature. If Menéndez could sneak up on Fort Caroline from behind, the French would have no inkling of the Spaniards' approach until the moment they were attacked.

Getting to Fort Caroline was a three-day ordeal of Menéndez goading soldiers who were tired, hungry, tormented by insects, and soaked to the skin on through muck and rain. Caught sleeping, weaponless, and naked in some cases, the French fled for their lives, the great majority of them without success. No Spaniard died. The toll of French stabbed or bludgeoned to death at close quarters was 132. Forty-five Frenchmen, swimming for their lives, managed to board two small ships and sail home all the way across the Atlantic Ocean. Among those few survivors was Jacques Ribault, son of the French commander, Jean Ribault.

This first of his massacres completed, Menéndez returned to St. Augustine where, in convenient batches, the storm delivered to him the rest of his victims. On September 29, Menéndez intercepted his first group of Frenchmen straggling northward along the beach. With their apparition, it was revealed how the other half of the drama had played out. While the *San Pelayo* had reached Havana safely, the storm had shipwrecked Ribault and his fleet. French survivors were now scattered along a stretch of Florida's Atlantic coast extending nearly one hundred miles from Matanzas Inlet past present-day Daytona Beach, to Cape Canaveral.

These castaways had been marching north for days, but south of St. Augustine they reached an impasse. The tidal channel was too wide and deep for the French to cross without a boat. As they pondered this dilemma, Menéndez and his troops appeared on the opposite side of the inlet. Two French officers were brought across to parley. The Spanish informed them of Fort Caroline's capture, but assured them that "their commander, who was a humane and merciful man, had sent [the French survivors] to France in a well-provisioned ship." The Frenchmen frankly informed the Spaniards of their desperate situation. It was a moment for chivalry—except the age of chivalry was dying. This incident was part of its death, an opening note in the overture to the great nation-state struggles for world power whose final strange flower would be the mass carnage of the twentieth century.

Menéndez, opting for deceit, "gave the promise under his seal that he would preserve the lives of Ribault and his men faithfully, without fraud, as an honorable gentleman." "A few prudent ones among them," unwilling to trust the Spaniards, turned back. The majority, including Ribault, accepted his offer of clemency. Once in Spanish hands, a survivor later related, they were "tied in groups of four, back to back." Ribault was stabbed to death. "Other Spanish soldiers were detailed to slay all the rest of the Frenchmen with clubs and axes, at the same time calling them Lutherans and enemies of God and the Virgin." Only four Frenchmen lived: the sailor who escaped to recount what happened, and three musicians, whose lives Menéndez ordered spared. Menéndez wasted no bullets or gunpowder on his victims. Sparing the musicians was also a practical matter. When he finally rounded up the last of the French stragglers—Menéndez sent the trumpeters out into the palmetto brush to summon them. He used the drummers to set the pace as he marched his prisoners up the beach.

Today you can drive down Route A1A to the exact spot, fourteen miles south of St. Augustine, where this happened. Fort Matanzas National Monument is located on the north side of the channel where, so long ago, Pedro Menéndez de Avilés lured his victims to their deaths. On the south side, the place where Ribault stood is occupied by a motel and restaurant. Ribault and Menéndez, as they face each other across that inlet, can be seen as historical marionettes, each personifying a different nation and system of beliefs, but visiting the actual spot allows you to understand it was also a human encounter. Each man, here in Florida, had aimed to build an empire and bequeath it to his son, but neither man would see his son again, though for different reasons. In this tiny war Menéndez was the "victor," but his son had been lost forever. Ribault had lost everything—except his son, who at that moment was safely on his way home across the Atlantic.

The Florida massacres created a scandal in Europe. King Philip evaded discussing the matter with the French ambassador for more than a month. When the opportunity arose the ambassador dressed down the king. "I have borne arms for forty years," Raimond de Fourquevaux, seigneur of Beccarie, informed the monarch, "and in that time the forces of the two crowns have often combatted each other, but never once has such an execrable deed occurred." The Spanish king could have retorted that France's internal Wars of Religion had led to the killings of many more heretics than his soldiers killed—or the Inquisition burned at the stake. Instead Philip blandly informed the ambassador that he, too, was "distressed that the matter had come, as it had, to the shedding of blood." Then the Spanish king added a telling comment. The intruding colonists, he observed, were heretics who obviously had gone to Florida without the approval of the French government. Therefore, he told the French ambassador, "exemplary punishment" had been justified in order to deter future trespassing. In this manner the king artfully turned the tables on the French. Did they wish to condone, or even claim responsibility for the supposed misdeeds of some criminal heretics?

The hasty choice of a site limited St. Augustine's possibilities from the start. The inlet there provides such poor protection from Atlantic storms that it would never be a major port. Instead Jacksonville would become Florida's first metropolis for the same reason the French chose it for their settlement nearly 450 years ago. The broad St. Johns still provides the best natural harbor on Florida's Atlantic coast.

Though St. Augustine owes its existence to Pedro Menéndez de Avilés, no statue, park, or monument there preserves his name. A hint of what he did does survive in the use of "Matanza" in the names of various restaurants, resorts, and real estate agencies. In Spanish "Matanza" is related to "matador," the killer in bullfighting. From Spanish it goes back through the Indo-European languages all the way to the Sanskrit verb "to kill." A trace of this old meaning survives to this day in English in "checkmate." Spain's checkmate of France's ambitions in Florida was the first great historical event to occur within territory presently comprising the United States of America. What's still impressive is how fast Menéndez made it happen. "If in the said coast or land there be settlers or corsairs of other nations whatsoever not subject to us, drive them out by what means you see fit," was how the king defined his mission. Menéndez sailed from Cadiz on June 27, 1565. By August 28, he had sighted Florida. He had hunted down the French by September 4. By October 11, date of the final massacre, French power in Florida had been crushed.

Menéndez killed for God and king, but this being Florida, illusion also propelled the mayhem. In this case the Holy Grail was the nonexistent Northwest Passage. Menéndez kept searching for this mythical body of water even though more than fifty years earlier, in 1511, Peter Martyr's map already showed that the American continents established a massive, north-south barrier to ambitions of reaching the East by sailing west. By 1540, the even more accurate maps of Sebastian Münster were available to every educated man in Europe, yet half a century after Balboa saw with his own eyes that the Panama Isthmus blocked passage between the two oceans, Spanish conquerors, including Pedro Menéndez, went on imagining they could find a way to sail east by sailing west.

"If the French or English should come to settle Florida," Menéndez warned the king, "it would be the greatest inconvenience, as much for the mines and territories of New Spain as for the navigation and trade of China and Molucca, if that arm of the sea goes to the South Sea, as is certain." "As is certain"—is there another phrase that has caused more mischief? This Florida expedition, most of all, showed how the world was changing. Menéndez was forty-five years younger than Ponce de León. In that interval, the Spanish Conquest of the Americas, which had begun as an extension of the Reconquista of Andalucía from the Muslims, had started to turn into a European great-power struggle for control of North and South America. The attempt to purge Florida of "Lutherans" was in spite of itself an opening paragraph in the secularization of world power politics. In the future fewer and fewer people would be killed because they were "Lutherans" or Catholics. More and more people, millions more in the age of nationalism, would be murdered because they were Spanish or French—or German, or Japanese, or Indonesian, or Rwandan, on into murderous infinity.

By establishing a Spanish colony in Florida Menéndez created an inviting target for French, English, and later American freebooters to attack. Vengeful Frenchmen raided St. Augustine within three years of the massacres. As early as 1586 it was plundered and burned by the English, so the Spanish spent the next few hundred years building and rebuilding a fortress to defend their worthless outpost. Menéndez himself quickly went broke. By 1602 royal inquiries were being held as to whether Florida would best be abandoned. The Spanish opted for inertia—and raising the walls of the fort a bit higher.

By far the most notable structure to have survived from Spanish colonial times in Florida, the Castillo de San Marcos never has gotten the kind of publicity the Fountain of Youth has. That helps explain why what goes on in Florida is so often so misunderstood. If you take Ponce and the Fountain myth as the beginning, events forever after seem nothing but a series of disconnected, rather silly events. Start with Menéndez de Avilés, what he did in Florida, and why he did it, and you begin to perceive an interconnected, comprehensible profile of events, stretching from the Protestant Reformation to the Cuban Missile Crisis and beyond. That pattern

consists of power politics, and the upheavals of peoples and products it reflects, along with the role in human affairs of force commingled with illusion, as wealth and power are both accumulated
and squandered.

It is the fort, so laboriously and futilely constructed, not the
Fountain, which tells the truth about Florida and makes what happened there understandable.

PART TWO

COVETING FLORIDA

The persistent desire of the United States
to possess the Floridas amounted almost
to a disease, corrupting the moral sense
of each succeeding administration.

—K. C. Babcock, 1906,
The Rise of American Nationality

5

THE WEST FLORIDA
LONE STAR BUTTERFLY EFFECT

At the beginning of the eighteenth century Florida's historical force field reversed itself the way the earth's magnetic poles periodically do. For the previous 200 years Florida's Caribbean exposure had been decisive; for the next 250 years events to the north would be determinant. Once again far-off events explain a seemingly unforeseeable transformation. The intellectual, spiritual, and commercial tumult of the Renaissance had projected Mediterranean greed and inventiveness all the way across the Atlantic Ocean. Now the consolidation of the northern European nation-states meant the end of the Iberian duopoly in the Americas.

The future marauded into Florida in 1702 as rampaging English colonial forces advanced down the coast, burning and looting. At St. Augustine they destroyed every house, foundry, shop, barracks, pier and stable, but the Castillo de San Marcos withstood the attack. For fifty days the Spaniards sat out the siege, gambling and playing stringed instruments. Another pastime, popular during hurricanes as well as sieges, seems to have been but little practiced. Only two children were baptized during the nine months that followed.

The Spanish held the fort and lost the country. That would be the story of how they clung on in Florida, off and on, for another one hundred years. The pretense that North America was Spain's alone had never been tenable. Banning the Portuguese made the power vacuum all the more inviting. Massacring the French had only opened the way for English expansion southward, nor was France deterred.

After losing their toehold in Florida, the French colonized Canada. Working south, French explorers seeking knowledge, not gold, were the ones who finally discovered the Mississippi—discovered its route, its resources, its possibilities. By 1698 the French were back in Florida, that far western part of it which today comprises the Florida Panhandle. That year they established an outpost at what today is Pensacola, followed in 1702 and 1720 by settlements at Mobile and Biloxi, finally founding New Orleans in 1723. Meanwhile more than 275,000 British migrants, not including slaves and Indians, had settled England's North American colonies, a population that would increase tenfold over the next one hundred years. While Spanish Florida's population had fallen to a few thousand, British North America was turning into a new colossus.

Like the 1565 attack on Fort Caroline, the 1702 destruction of St. Augustine had its origins in the complications of mammalian reproduction as played out in the life cycles of members of the Spanish royal family. The remarkable Philip II begat the unexceptional Philip III who begat the incompetent Philip IV. Philip IV in turn produced an heir, in the form of the future Carlos II, who was both physically and mentally incompetent to fulfill his dynastic responsibilities. His abnormally large tongue, which made his speech unintelligible and his dining habits unspeakable, Spaniards believed, had to be the work of the devil, hence his nickname "El Hechixado," the bewitched. Carlos II begat nobody. That dereliction of dynastic duty, amidst the tinderbox rivalries of Europe, and considering Spain's enfeebled but still far-flung place in the world, was tantamount to provoking a world war. Carlos II's heirless death, on the first of November, 1700, set off a struggle for the throne of Spain which the Bourbons ultimately won, but only after Spain had been devastated, and people all over the world killed and maimed because the last Spanish Hapsburg monarch had, apparently, an insufficient sperm count. St. Augustine's destruction by England's American colonists was one side effect of this royal dysfunction.

Diplomacy caught up with reality in 1763. That year, following yet another war among the Europeans, Florida finally was taken away from Spain and transferred to Britain. Europeans remember that conflict as the Seven Years' War. Americans still call it the French and Indian War, the difference in names reflecting the fact that the Americans were fighting for their own objectives, not Britain's. At first it seemed the colonists had gained everything they wanted. The French were obliged to give up Canada along with all their other possessions east of the Mississippi, including their toeholds in western Florida, but that was not the end of these territorial rearrangements. Having been forced to leave Florida, the Spanish were given those parts of French Louisiana lying west of the Mississippi River, along with the city and port of New Orleans. This Spanish presence in Louisiana, scarcely remarked in 1763, would become of great consequence forty years later when the newly independent United States sought to gain territory along the Gulf of Mexico.

The British were the first and last to impose some political coherence on Florida's geography. "Florida," like "Canada," had started out as a generalized term for a vast, undefined territory: early maps show "La Florida" extending from the Carolinas to Texas. By the time the British took charge, encroachment from the north had diminished Florida into a more limited though still far-flung territory. Eastern Florida included the entire Florida peninsula. Western Florida stretched along the northern coast of the Gulf of Mexico all the way to the Mississippi River. In addition to the Florida Panhandle of today, this western salient included the southern third of what now are Alabama and Mississippi, also that part of the future state of Louisiana where the state capital, Baton Rouge, is located. The British, recognizing the geographical absurdity of treating it as a single administrative unit, split Florida into two colonies. East Florida had its capital at St. Augustine. West Florida was administered from Pensacola. Then as later the Apalachicola River provided a natural boundary.

The British ruled Florida only from 1763 to 1784, but those twenty-one years, like Spain's two hundred, demonstrated Florida's capacity to lay low imperial presumption. In 1768 eight ships carrying more than twelve hundred colonists converged off the northeast coast of Florida. "This my Lord, I believe is the largest importation of white inhabitants that ever was brought into America at a time," the governor of East Florida, Colonel James Grant, wrote a titled friend. Most of these supposedly English colonists were actually Spanish, from the Mediterranean island of Minorca, at that time under British military occupation. The greatest Spanish colonization effort ever seen in Florida would unfold under the British flag at the instigation of a British real estate speculator, Dr. Andrew Turnbull. In addition to the Spaniards, Turnbull's indentured laborers included Greeks from the Ottoman Empire as well as some Italians and French. This exotic diversity flowed from the recurrent confusion in the Anglo-Saxon imagination between the swampy realities of Florida and the winy charms of the Mediterranean. Florida, the speculators in London recognized, was unsuited to the blue-eyed variety of colonization practiced farther north. On the other hand these southern Europeans, "accustomed to a hot climate and bred to the culture of the vine, olive, cotton, tobacco, etc., as also to the raising of silk," one promoter rhapsodized, would prove an ideal work force. That explained the Levantine name chosen for the colony: New Smyrna.

Within two years 627 of the 1,255 colonists were dead. When Turnbull discovered the survivors were planning to escape to the freedom of Spanish Cuba, he ordered exemplary executions. What ensued recalled the madness of de Soto as Turnbull turned New Smyrna into the Heart of Darkness, himself into the Kurtz of the future Sunshine State. Captain Bernard Romans, the deputy royal surveyor for the region, described what happened: "About fifteen hundred people, men, women, and children, were deluded away from their native country," he reported, "to this place, where, instead of plenty, they found want in the last degree; instead of promised fields, a dreary wilderness, instead of a grateful, fertile soil, a barren, arid sand." Starvation might have been avoided had Turnbull allowed them to fish, "but they were denied the liberty of fishing." Things got worse: "Again, behold a man obliged to whip his own wife for pilfering bread to relieve his helpless family; then think of a time when the small allowance was reduced to half." By the time the New Smyrna colony was abandoned in 1777, more Europeans had died as the result of Turnbull's scheme to grow wine grapes and breed silk worms there than had perished as a result of all Spain's efforts to save the Northwest Passage from the French.

The New Smyrna disaster, which continued the Florida tradition of such settlement schemes going horribly wrong, is significant for another reason. It is an early example of the "Blame the Victim" methodology that prevails in Florida historiography. The governing principle of this approach is that Nothing Unpleasant Ever Happens in Florida, at least nothing that can be blamed on English-speaking Protestant white men unless (later on) they are Yankees. When something does go wrong, the victims are to blame. In Florida's history books the New Smyrna victims are to blame, not the speculator who starved and killed them. Having "so many colonists of non-English language and religion more than offset any advantage that may have come from their knowledge of the growing of tropical products," complains one typical account.

In this, as in cases involving Indians and blacks, the worst troublemakers are the truth tellers. Captain Romans, author of one of the first important books on Florida to be written in English, *A Concise Natural History of East and West Florida*, was an unimpeachable source. Yet he, not Turnbull, is portrayed as the culprit, guilty of "animus toward colony management," according to a 1965 account called *Florida: From Indian Trail to Space Age*, one of those ever-upward-and-onward volumes that fill the shelves of Florida libraries. In her book on the New Smyrna colonists and their descendants, *Mullet on the Beach*, Patricia C. Griffin recounts the truth of what happened. "A diverse collection of individuals and families from traditional Mediterranean cultures," she writes, "full of hope, set out on a disorienting voyage to the New World, experienced a death-camp like existence on an indigo plantation, and . . . in desperation, they fled."

Following their escape, the survivors became known collectively as "Minorcans." Settling mostly in St. Augustine, they prospered as carpenters, clerks, teachers, surveyors, shipwrights, and dentists. So did their grandchildren and their grandchildren's grandchildren. The poet Stephen Vincent Benét was one of their descendants; so was the Hollywood singing cowgirl, Judy Canova. The Minorcans were the first Floridians in the modern sense. They still comprise a lively community and are the only people who can claim an unbroken Florida heritage going back further than the U.S. Declaration of Independence. Thanks to their endurance, Florida finally saw the establishment of a permanent European settlement.

While British efforts in Florida were descending into barbarism, Britain's hold on the whole of North America was crumbling. In 1763 the British were all-triumphant. By 1783 they had lost most of their American colonies. This immense realm went to pieces in just twenty years because the Americans no longer needed the British. Once the French were defeated, the Americans could continue the "Indian" part of the French and Indian War all by themselves. At least they could if the British did not stand in their way. And if they did? The Quebec Act, enacted by the Parliament in London in 1774, brought the Americans' sense of resentment to the boiling point. One of the first legal measures to explicitly guarantee "Civil Rights," it granted French-speaking Roman Catholics the same freedoms and protections colonists from Britain enjoyed. British attempts to stop them from seizing Indian lands west of the Appalachians enraged the Americans most of all.

When the colonies farther north rebelled, John Hancock and John Adams were burned in effigy in St. Augustine. "The Floridas," as they were jointly called, stayed loyal to the British; by the end of the War of Independence some ten thousand Loyalists had fled to the Floridas. Florida continued to defy stereotype as the governor of Spanish Louisiana, Bernardo de Gálvez, went on the attack against the British. In a series of successful advances the Spanish drove the British from Natchez and Biloxi in what now is Mississippi, but was then West Florida, as well as from Baton Rouge and Mobile. In a final victorious advance, Gálvez forced the British to surrender Pensacola. The Spanish "helped the United States gain its independence and that help came in the form of actual fighting, supplies, and money," writes Thomas E. Chávez in his study of *Spain and the Independence of the United States*. They also sought to enlist God's help. "We prayed fervently . . . for the success of the colonists under one George Washington, because we believe their cause is just and that the Great Redeemer is on their side," Father Junípero Serra, founder of the California missions, wrote in his diary. Although Washington and other leaders frankly acknowledged that "Spain was vital to the cause," Spain's Florida contribution to American independence, like many a future event there, would be excised from American history. Equally unnoticed, Gálvez lingers on in the name of Galveston; the Texas outpost was named in his honor.

For the British as for the Spanish and French, Florida had turned into a military and economic disaster. In 1783 Britain washed its hands of Florida; it gave both East Florida and West Florida back to Spain. Later there would be much muddying of the waters when it came to claims as to who owned what in the Floridas, but so far as law and treaty were concerned there never was any doubt. The 1783 Treaty of Paris, which recognized America's independence, defined the new nation's boundaries very clearly: Florida was entirely excluded, including those parts of it that today comprise the coastal areas of Mississippi and Alabama and, in Louisiana, the "Florida parishes" around Baton Rouge. U.S. exclusion from the Gulf of Mexico, many American nationalists claimed, threatened U.S. security as well as the prosperity of the newly settled lands west of the Appalachians, and therefore justified U.S. aggression against Spanish Florida. The legalities of the situation show that, too, to have been a myth. In 1795 Spain pledged by formal treaty to guarantee the United States port privileges at New Orleans and transshipment rights to the ocean beyond.

There matters stood until 1800, when yet another European upheaval produced an opportunity for another American land grab. That year Napoleon Bonaparte struck a secret deal with Spain for the return of the Louisiana territory to France. In the Third Treaty of Ildefonso the Bourbon king of Spain, Carlos IV, agreed that France would "be again placed in possession of the colony of Louisiana." In exchange, Napoleon promised to create a new Bourbon kingdom in Italy. Plus la change, the French said, the more things stayed the same. Only eleven years earlier, in 1789, the French had proclaimed the universal rights of man, supposedly ushering in a new era in which the caprices of kings and whims of tyrants no longer would dictate the course of human events. Now the First Consul of the French Republic treated with the Bourbon king of Spain in the same affable manner the decapitated Louis XVI would have. The king of Spain, for his part, manifested not the slightest scruple in treating most amicably with the French Republic, established though it was through the juridical murder of his cousin-king.

Ambition ruled Napoleon; vanity ruled the Bourbons. The Spanish king's Bourbon kinsman in Italy, the Duke of Parma, bore the title "royal highness" but had no kingdom to go with his title. The Treaty of Ildefonso set out to alleviate that distressing condition. Its express purpose was "the Aggrandizement of His Royal Highness the Infant Duke of Parma in Italy" into full-scale kingship. It was left to Napoleon to get the duke his kingdom, a service he was in an excellent position to provide: French revolutionary armies had recently invaded Italy. The Spanish king didn't care particularly what lands comprised the new kingdom. It could "consist of Tuscany," or if Napoleon preferred, "it may consist of the three Roman legations or of any other continental provinces of Italy which form a rounded state." It was naked cynicism on a global scale. Give me the Duomo in Florence, or the Leaning Tower of Pisa if you prefer. I'll give you the alligator-infested bayous and bison-thronged prairies of North America. In such a manner were the fates of the Sioux and the Tuscans conjoined, as a phantom empire in America was exchanged for a fool's-gold kingdom in Europe.

In 1565 the discovery that France not only had established a colony in Florida, but was preparing to reinforce it, sent Menéndez flying westward across the Atlantic. Now the prospect that France once again was going to establish itself in North America sent Jefferson's special envoy, James Monroe, speeding the other way across the Atlantic, to Europe. Florida, not Louisiana, was the focus of their attention. In order to secure an outlet to the Gulf of Mexico while avoiding a confrontation with France, President Jefferson had ordered the American representative in Paris, Robert Livingston, to explore the possibility of purchasing all or part of Spanish Florida, and perhaps the port of New Orleans as well. To that end, the president authorized Monroe to spend up to $10 million in order to "effectually secure our right & interest in the Mississippi, and in the country eastward of that."

The country eastward of that! Never before, never again would an American diplomatic démarche produce such an opposite, gargantuan and happy result. Jefferson was thinking of Florida, not Louisiana, but when Monroe got to Paris, he discovered that the whole Louisiana territory westward of the Mississippi was up for grabs. From his expedition into Egypt, in 1798, until his retreat from Moscow in 1812, Napoleon's grand enterprises traced the same trajectory, from magnificent conception to headlong retreat, and now it was happening again. Only three years earlier Napoleon had believed he could restore France's empire in the Americas when he enticed Spain to promise him Louisiana. By the time Jefferson sent Monroe to Paris, yellow fever and the world's first successful slave revolt had turned Saint Dominique—which the black insurgents called Haiti—into a French mass grave. With Haiti lost and Britannia once again ruling the waves, Napoleon understood, Louisiana would be as indefensible as Quebec had been in 1763. Since Louisiana was untenable, "to attempt obstinately to retain it would be folly," he informed his government. Therefore he would give up Louisiana even before France could take possession of it.

Napoleon's foreign minister, the famously imperturbable Talleyrand, was thunderstruck; Napoleon's brothers were appalled. When Joseph and Jerome Bonaparte tried to dissuade him, Napoleon, whom they had surprised in his bath, thrashed about so violently both brothers were drenched and a servant fainted, but Napoleon would not be moved. The only way to thwart the English, and so salvage something of his American disaster, he had decided, was to make the Americans an offer they could not refuse. "It is not only New Orleans that I cede; it is the whole colony, without reserve," he informed Talleyrand. "Have an interview this very day with Mr. Livingston." Having hoped to get New Orleans and perhaps some bits of Florida east of the Mississippi, the Americans found themselves offered the whole of Louisiana west of the Mississippi, all the way to the Rocky Mountains. The Spanish, the actual occupiers of Louisiana, were not consulted.

This magnificent opportunity in Paris created a dilemma in Washington. The U.S. Constitution did not authorize the president to acquire foreign territory in this manner. As Jefferson himself pointed out, "The general government has no powers but such as the constitution has given it; and it has not given it a power of holding foreign territory, & still less of incorporating it into the Union." Jefferson's solution was straightforward. If the Constitution did not confer such a power then it would have to be changed. "An amendment of the Constitution seems necessary for this," he argued. Jefferson went so far as to draft in his own hand a constitutional amendment for that purpose, but he never sent it to Congress and the states for ratification. Instead Jefferson, the most revered of the Founding Fathers, disregarded the Constitution's original intent.

Today many deride the notion that there is such a thing as a "living Constitution" and insist we adhere to "original intent." Jefferson, Madison and Monroe were directly involved in framing the Constitution: Madison is remembered as "the Father of the Constitution." Yet they never followed the path of what people today call "Originalism." As soon as it became expedient these Founding Fathers acted exactly in the manner that the "Originalists" of today would denounce as a betrayal of the Founding Fathers' original intent. In his eagerness to get Louisiana Jefferson had concluded what America's imperial presidents still do. When necessary or merely convenient, the powers of the presidency supersede the fundamental law of the land. As for treaties with foreign nations—whether European or Indian—the provisions of those agreements could be transformed at will on an ex post facto basis into whatever the president now wished them to be. Prior to acquiring Louisiana, President Jefferson insisted Florida was entirely separate from Louisiana. Once Louisiana was in U.S. hands, Jefferson reversed himself. He purported that parts of Spanish Florida did belong to the United States precisely because, he now suddenly alleged, they were part of Louisiana.

As Henry Adams later remarked, wittily, it was possible to make such a claim, though only by pretending "that Spain retroceded West Florida to France without knowing it, that France had sold it to the United States without suspecting it, that the United States

had bought it without paying for it, and that neither France nor
Spain, although the original contracting parties, were competent to
decide the meaning of their own contract." It was also possible to
claim that the Louisiana Purchase entitled the United States to no
land whatsoever. By selling Louisiana, Napoleon violated France's
treaty obligation to the Spanish "not to sell or alienate in any manner
the property and usufruct of this Province," rendering the trans-
action null and void in terms of international law. Others argued
Napoleon had no right to transfer Louisiana because the kingdom
he created for the Duke of Parma was only a ruse, part of a scheme
first to defraud Spain of Louisiana, then pass it off to the Americans
for his own profit. Napoleon's subsequent actions vindicated that
accusation. In 1807, only four years after establishing it, Napoleon
abolished the kingdom of Etruria as suddenly as he had created it,
and chased its supposed king into exile. The Spanish cried foul, but
in the end they did transfer Louisiana as promised—to the United
States, not France—while holding on to Baton Rouge and the rest
of West Florida. The Gulf coast east of the Mississippi, the Spanish
pointed out, never had been part of Louisiana, and who was better
qualified to know the extent Louisiana had "in the hands of Spain"
than the Spanish?

Up to the moment he handed the presidency over to James
Madison, Thomas Jefferson never doubted that the whole of Florida,
West and East, would fall to the United States as effortlessly as
Louisiana had. "We shall get the Floridas in good time," he wrote
to a Northerner. "The Floridas will fall to us peaceably," he assured
a Southerner. In the draft of the constitutional amendment he never
submitted for ratification, Jefferson specified that, in addition to
Louisiana, "Florida also, whenever it may be rightfully obtained,
shall become a part of the U.S." He added: "Its white inhabitants
shall thereupon be Citizens & shall stand, as to their rights & obligations, on the same footing with other citizens of the U.S." Less
than thirty years earlier, in the Declaration of Independence, he had
not felt it necessary to write that "all white men" were created equal,
but by 1803 the contradiction of building a country, economically,
on slave labor, while founding it philosophically on the proposition

that all men are equal, was no longer quite so uncontradictory as it had seemed in 1776. Calls already were being heard in England, and from some freethinkers in the United States, that slavery itself, not just the international slave trade, should be abolished.

America's slaveholders, for their part, were eager to add Florida to slavery's aggressively expanding empire, not realizing that ultimately they themselves would be among the victims of "an imperial expansion of the United States." Jefferson's expansionist policies, as Frederick Jackson Turner later observed, "laid the foundations for a readjustment of sectional power within the Union" that less than sixty years later would allow the slave-owning rebels of the South to be beaten into submission by a federal government that had grown vastly more powerful as a result of the acquisition of Louisiana.

Earlier Florida had held up a mirror to Spanish imperial illusion, then briefly reflected the maxim that the British Empire was won (and sometimes lost) in a fit of absent-mindedness. Now Florida held up a mirror to the often stunning gap between America's pretensions to moral superiority and how it behaves in the world. From the beginning eminent Americans put policy above principle and, when it suited them, let greed overrule the ethics they preached as universal in order to get what they wanted, in this case Florida. What drove these revered Americans to illegality was that the United States could find no way, as Jefferson put it, for Florida to be "rightfully obtained." The 1783 Treaty of Paris, the 1795 treaty with Spanish, and now the 1803 treaty with the French all made it clear that the United States had no rightful claim on any part of Florida, but so what?

Thanks to his willingness, as Jefferson himself put it, to "stretch the constitution until it cracked," the land area of the United States had nearly doubled. The United States also secured the outlet to the Gulf of Mexico it wanted. Who cared, now, about Spain's pathetic remnant of empire in Florida? Thomas Jefferson cared very much. So did James Madison and James Monroe, as well as Andrew Jackson and John Quincy Adams. For them Florida had become a kind of obsession. Covetousness of it darkened the happiest events, even so great a stroke of good fortune as the chance to acquire Louisiana. An immense prize had befallen America. "But the extent of that acquisition does not destroy the motive which existed before of acquiring the Floridas," Monroe wrote Madison in May 1803, only weeks after getting Louisiana, "nor essentially diminish it." Nor Essentially Diminish It: that phrase revealed all. On President Jefferson's successor James Madison, as on all those eminent gentlemen, Florida had the effect of an intoxicant or a narcotic. "The persistent desire of the United States to possess the Floridas," observed K. C. Babcock more than a century ago, in his 1906 chronicle of *The Rise of American Nationality*, "amounted almost to a disease, corrupting the moral sense of each succeeding administration."

With the Louisiana Purchase Jefferson had become the father of the imperial presidency. As a result of his Florida intrigues his successor, President Madison, became the godfather of U.S. covert operations. Though his intent was rape, Madison began his clandestine violation of Florida as though it were a seduction, by nibbling at its extremities—the territories that today comprise the "Florida parishes" of Louisiana. Spain retained sovereignty there, but the region had fallen increasingly under American influence because Spain, abandoning its traditional exclusionist policies, had started encouraging immigration from the United States. Jefferson recognized that the Spanish were inciting a stampede of Trojan horses into their domains. "I wish 10,000 of our inhabitants would accept the invitation," he wrote. "In the meantime we may complain of this seduction of our inhabitants just enough to make the Spanish believe it is a very wise policy for them."

Demographically and culturally the Florida parishes had become almost indistinguishable from Mississippi, just to the north, with one great exception. In Florida blacks, Indians and mixed race people could be free—as free as white folks in some ways, thanks to Spain's relative tolerance in racial matters, above all because of Spain's inability to control anybody, whoever they were. This lack of respect for the supremacy of the white race led many, though by no means all, of the area's white Americans to perceive themselves as new founding fathers, and the Spanish governor in western Florida, Vicente Folch, as the new King George III. Among the malcontents were the notorious and colorful Kemper brothers. Pirates, smugglers and political terrorists, the Kempers had tried, and failed, to grab control from the Spanish back in 1804. This time, with the support of the president of the United States, they would succeed.

Having decided to provoke a disguised military coup in West Florida, President Madison ordered secret agents and provocateurs into Spanish territory. As if by magic, grievances were suddenly proclaimed, the tyrannous yoke of the Spaniards denounced. As always in Florida, the link between words and meanings was tenuous, to the extend it existed at all. The Kempers and other disloyal elements called themselves "Patriots." Among their complaints was that the laws of Spanish Florida were not written in English. In the wee hours of September 23, 1810, a U.S.-instigated band chased the Spanish out of their run-down barricade at Baton Rouge. A Declaration of Independence was produced, a West Florida flag unfurled; a national anthem was sung: In this comic operetta real blood flowed. The "Patriots" killed two inoffensive Spaniards as they burst into the fort. They also killed fellow Americans. When William Cooper, a North Carolina–born loyalist, organized "a militia company to support the Spanish," he was murdered. "Like most of his neighbors, Cooper opposed the actions of the West Florida rebels," the parish history explains.

Thanks to Madison's subversion, Louisiana got Baton Rouge and such other towns as Slidell and Ponchatoula, but the Spanish clung on to the rest of West Florida, and all of East Florida as well. It would take the United States nearly twenty years to get Biloxi, Mobile, and the rest of Florida. As a result of this piecemeal aggression West Florida was chopped up like a sausage, into one big and three small pieces. The Florida parishes of Louisiana, plus the bits of Mississippi and Alabama sticking down to the Gulf, belong to those states as a result of Jefferson's long-forgotten and specious claim that they were part of the Louisiana Purchase. Even so, the eastern half of West Florida—from the Perdido River and Pensacola east to the Apalachicola—remained intact, under Spanish rule, eventually becoming the Florida Panhandle of today.

This splitting of West Florida produced what both chaos theorists and weathermen call a butterfly effect, by which seemingly insignificant, distant and unrelated events later produce enormous, far-away consequences. One unnoticed result was that the techniques of disguised aggression used in West Florida would serve the cause of American territorial expansion in other, more important places. First, Americans would arrive, buy or be granted land, and pledge loyalty to the country where they settled. Soon, however, the complaints about "tyranny" would arise, followed by the demand for "liberty." Then these subversives would rise up against the legitimate government and declare themselves free citizens of a free republic. In the final stage, the appeal to the United States for protection would lead to U.S. annexation. "It afforded at once an epitome and a prophecy of expansion in the Southwest," observed Professor Isaac Joslin Cox in his 1918 study of *The West Florida Controversy*. In Texas and California, also in Hawaii, the "Patriots" did the dirty work. Then, in Washington, the latest triumph of liberty would be proclaimed.

Though the West Florida "Patriots" were quickly discarded once they had served President Madison's purpose, the symbols of their subversion were assimilated rapidly into the permanent repertoire of America's nationalist self-rationalizations. West Florida's Betsy Ross is said to have been a woman named Melissa Johnson, the flag she stitched called the Bonnie Blue. Its most memorable feature was the single, large, five-pointed star which occupied the center of the blue field. It was the original version of the Lone Star flag that, twenty-six years later, similar "Patriots" would hoist in Texas. No one would remember President Madison's disguised aggression at Baton Rouge; everyone would remember the Alamo. If you look at the Lone Star in today's Texas state flag, you will see that the West Florida star still floats there on its original blue background.

President Madison's West Florida putsch produced its most spectacular unintended consequence in 2000, when his decision in 1810 to seize part, but not all, of western Florida became one of the causes of the constitutional crisis arising from the dispute over which presidential candidate, George W. Bush or Al Gore, had won in Florida. Had the state of Florida in the year 2000 still consisted of the entire territory it had under the Spanish—that is, had Florida extended all the way to the Mississippi River—George W. Bush would have carried Florida comfortably because the coastal areas of Alabama and Mississippi, along with the Baton Rouge area of Louisiana, voted heavily Republican. There also would have been no crisis had Florida by then consisted of two separate states, East Florida and West Florida. In that case, Al Gore would have won populous East Florida by a substantial margin and have won the Electoral College as well as the popular vote. Instead, thanks to Florida's curious borders, the peculiarities of the U.S. electoral system, and the geopolitical conniving of the Founding Fathers, the "world's greatest democracy" wound up with a president who had come in second when the people voted.

As for Madison's initial filching of Florida territory, Augustus Foster, the British minister in Washington at the time, accurately summed up matters. "This unjust aggression by the United States," he observed, was nothing more than "the ungenerous and unprovoked seizure of a foreign colony."

6

THE UNSEEN FOE

As a result of Jefferson's unauthorized expansion of presidential power, the United States had lassoed an elephant in the form of Louisiana. Now, under Madison, in the form of the Florida parishes, it had corralled a palmetto bug, but what about the rest of Florida? Napoleon had been capable of the grand gesture—putting on, then throwing off, Louisiana as though it were a magnificent cloak. The Spanish, in contrast, were clingers—capable of losing a mile and still not giving an inch. Earlier the Spanish had outfought the British in Florida; now they outfoxed the Americans there.

Madison had supposed a kind of domino theory would operate. The Spanish, he imagined, would take flight following their humiliation at Baton Rouge, whereupon the rest of West and all of East Florida would topple into Americans hands. Instead, the highest-ranking Spanish official in West Florida, Vicente Folch y Juan, turned American subversion to his own purposes. Following the seizure of Baton Rouge, Folch composed an extraordinary letter, addressed it directly to "the Executive power of the United States," then copied it to his superiors. "I have decided on delivering this province to the United States under an equitable capitulation, provided I do not receive succor from Havana or Vera Cruz during the present month," Folch announced to the astonishment of both the American government and his own. Harassed by American raiders, all but forgotten in Spain, Folch's audacious move briefly made him and his problems in West Florida the center of attention in Washington and, even more remarkably, in his own country.

President Madison swallowed Folch's bait hook, line and sinker. Calling Congress into secret session, Madison got $100,000 in order to finance, in the president's own words, "a subversion of the Spanish authorities within the Territory in question." Having used, then discarded, the Kemper brothers, President Madison now turned to a failed real estate speculator and disgraced ex-politician named George Mathews to implement the next stage in his Florida intrigue. You must send a man to do a man's job, it was said in Washington. And to run a fool's errand? President Madison's not-so-secret secret agent liked to be addressed as "General" George Mathews, even though instead of commanding troops he had spent most of the War of Independence as a British prisoner. Released, Mathews demanded that Georgia, in recompense, give him twenty thousand acres of free land. The legislature eventually did give him several thousand; thereafter Mathews remained possessed of a fascination with acquiring land without having to pay for it.

In January 1795, while serving as governor of Georgia, Mathews signed legislation authorizing the infamous Yazoo land grab, unleashing one of the most colorful scandals in American history. So all-consuming was the resulting outrage that, instead of merely being repealed, the offending law was publicly burned, while a crowd jeered, on the grounds of the state capitol. So it could be said that Heaven itself had reached down to incinerate the legislative abomination Matthews had signed into law, the fire was ignited using a magnifying lens to focus the rays of the sun on the hated text. When a constitutional convention abolished the entire state government from under him, Mathews decamped to the Mississippi Territory, where officials did not have to be elected, and finagled to have himself appointed governor there. That preferment was denied him when knowledge of his land speculations caused controversy in Washington.

In that unhappy situation destiny seemed to have marooned Mathews until January 1811, when President Madison summoned him to a secret one-on-one meeting, no witnesses present, no transcript ever made. Of all the self-servers and office seekers in Washington at that moment, Mathews was one of the very few who ever had been to West Florida, and apparently the only one actually to have met the now suddenly celebrated Señor Folch. The meeting ended with both men convinced the remainder of West Florida was ripe for the plucking. President Madison followed up his secret talk with Mathews with written orders to proceed to West Florida "with all possible expedition, concealing from general observation" the nature of his mission. Once there, he was to proceed "with the discretion which the delicacy and importance of the undertaking require." And if there was no Spanish capitulation? In that case he was authorized to manufacture "a suspicion of an existing design of any foreign Power" and, once that was done, call in the U.S. Army and Navy to "pre-occupy" the territory. In President Madison's vocabulary of dissimulation, "pre-occupy" meant launching a preemptive military seizure of Florida. The problem was that only aggression by some third power could justify such a strike, and no such threat existed. Napoleon, following his cession of Louisiana, had sworn off the Americas for good. Having given Florida away, the British did not want it back. More than that, thanks to Europe's ceaseless games of geopolitical musical chairs, Spain's great ally now was Great Britain, not France.

It bespeaks the quality of President Madison's judgment in matters concerning Florida that at the time he dispatched him on this singular mission Mathews was seventy-one years old, conspicuously corpulent, and eccentric of appearance as well as demeanor. His Irish brogue, apparently acquired from his immigrant parents, was so thick that Americans as well as Spaniards often found what he said incomprehensible. Eyewitnesses stress his fondness for wearing old-fashioned tricorn hats; it would appear Mathews more resembled Sancho Panza than Uncle Sam as he headed south on horseback. For decades those dealing with him had dismissed Mathews as a buffoon, but misadventure had left no dent in Mathews' self-esteem. According to one account, he "was known to acknowledge but two superiors: General George Washington, and the Lord Almighty. And as time passed, he questioned the high standing of Washington."

To put it another way, Mathews was a Florida natural. His pointless, fruitless marauding would be worthy of de Soto, but the Florida figure Mathews most resembled was Juan Ponce de León, both of them. Like the real-life Ponce, Mathews would see his dream of transforming Florida's empty acres into real estate turn into a nightmare that would cost him his life. Like the mythical Ponce, Mathews truly did go to Florida seeking rejuvenation. Having failed in Georgia and failed in Mississippi, in Florida George Mathews sought the glorious definitive conquest that, once and for all, would put the critics to shame and the naysayers to flight. With the arrival of George Mathews on the Florida scene, the language changes from Spanish to English; the story remains the same. His adventure casts into American frontier idiom Florida's perpetual role as the place where people come to reinvent themselves, regardless of the consequences, and God help them when they do.

Nearly a thousand miles south of the District of Columbia, away from its perennial ambitions and transient certainties, beyond even the borders of the United States, Madison's calculations and Mathews' dreams ended; the reality of Florida began. Upon reaching the border area, Mathews was greeted by shocking news. Capitulation no longer was on the table. In response to his threat to abandon West Florida, Folch had gotten "succor from Havana"—$50,000, along with orders to use the money to shore up West Florida's defenses. Unbeknownst to Mathews, Folch also had received precious aid from President Madison. Eager not to endanger the anticipated, peaceful transfer of West Florida to the United States, Madison ordered American forces in Mississippi to crack down on the "Patriots." Thanks to the protective vigilance of the U.S. Army, the borders of Spanish Florida were now secure. President Madison also had sent Folch a fawning, disastrously indiscreet reply. After informing the Spanish official that he would find it "advantageous" to betray his oath of loyalty to his own country, he announced that General George Mathews was on his way "to receive from you possession of the country in the name of the United States." Madison had blown Mathews' cover before he could get there. In his own hands, the Spanish official now had written proof that George Mathews was no loose cannon; he was the official, though no longer secret, agent of the president of the United States.

At Pensacola Folch received President Madison's envoy with courtesy, then informed him that he and his forces had been ordered to fight to the death any U.S. attempt to take possession of any part of Florida. Like a grand master with only a pawn left, Folch had gone on the offensive and pulled off a double coup. He had gotten military protection from the United States as well a cash infusion from his own government. Having been stuck in West Florida since 1787, Folch also got to go home. In response to his extraordinary accomplishments, he was court-martialed when he got there. Folch defended himself as resourcefully as he had West Florida, was exonerated, and lived to the age of seventy-five. There are not many figures over the centuries who, having wound up mired in Florida, manage to extricate themselves with honor and live to a ripe old age, but this forgotten Spanish official was one of them.

As a result of "staggering ineptitude on the part of almost everybody on the American side," as one scholar later put it, any chance of obtaining West Florida on the sly had been lost, but inside Mathews' agitated brain butterfly wings were flapping. Four hundred miles away from Pensacola lay St. Augustine, capital of Spanish East Florida. Hastening east on horseback Mathews, now seventy-two, initially intended to gallop down to St. Augustine and demand that the Spanish "surrender that province into the possession of the United States" then and there. He desisted only after Americans on both sides of the border warned him that the Spanish governor at St. Augustine was no Iberian gentleman like Folch, who would pour him rum and coffee while rejecting his demands. In St. Augustine the Spanish governor was a rough-and-ready Irishman like Mathews himself. Governor Enrique White, they warned, would throw him in the dungeon at the Castillo de San Marcos if he dared make such a demand.

Like the president who had sent him there, Mathews was eager to seize the entirety of Florida, both West and East, but in their haste to fabricate claims to land along the Gulf coast, Jefferson, Madison and Monroe had ensnared themselves in a trap of their own making. By insisting so strongly that Florida up to the Perdido River belonged to the United States, they had acknowledged that the rest of it—the whole of what today is the state of Florida—did not belong to the United States. Spain's sovereignty there was indisputable, but what if some "Patriots" in East Florida could be enticed into overthrowing Spanish rule, as they had in Baton Rouge? By then more than enough Americans had migrated into East Florida to overthrow the Spanish but, as George Mathews soon discovered, no one wanted to revolt. Economic freedom was the main reason the better sort of planter, along with the merchant class, as well as most of the yeoman salt-of-the-earth types, were content to remain under Spanish rule. Thanks to the international border separating Florida from the United States, smuggling slaves was as lucrative as smuggling booze would be during the Prohibition era—and drugs would be after that. All kinds of contraband flourished because the United States, in an attempt to avoid getting embroiled in Europe's latest wars, had banned trade with both Britain and France as well as their many allies. The trade embargo meant U.S. ports were stagnating but in Florida, conveniently close to the United States yet exempt from its laws, no cargo was forbidden.

Fornicators and miscegenists could come and go as they pleased too. Just north of the St. Marys River, on the Georgia side of the estuary, a man tempted fate if he consorted too openly with his Negro mistress. However rich he was, he lived knowing that, when he died, his white sons might sell his black sons down the river. In Florida a gentleman was free to cohabit openly with his black paramour, set their mixed-race sons up in business, and bequeath them land. On U.S. soil it was as much a crime for a black person to read a book as it was to carry a gun. In Florida blacks were able to arm and educate themselves. Florida's tradition of racial freedom was established as early as 1693, when Spain granted sanctuary to foreign slaves seeking refuge there. In 1738, near St. Augustine, self-emancipated black people established what Professor Kathleen Deagan, Curator of Historical Archaeology at the Florida Museum of Natural History, calls a "Fortress of Freedom." The "fort and town of Gracia Real de Santa Teresa de Mose," her archaeological excavations show, was "the first legally sanctioned free black community in what is now the United States." In 1740 when English colonists from Georgia invaded Florida, they were repulsed "in a pitched battle with the black, white and Indian Spanish forces."

Florida's freedoms were on display on Amelia Island, across the river from St. Marys, the Georgia outpost that George Mathews now made his base of operations. Life in the port town of Fernandina foreshadowed the diversity, license and energy synonymous with Florida today. In Fernandina the Irish saloon keeper was named Donohue; the German doctor's name was Karl Santage. Ezra Patch the carpenter, the blacksmith Mateo Gonsales, and Felicia the Fortune Teller all plied their trades. The "Indians" who strode into town, trading pelts and jerky for cloth and knives, were also newcomers. The original Florida Indians were long extinct, but as Yazoo-type land deals in Georgia and the Mississippi Territory made hundreds rich by dispossessing thousands, Indian tribesmen, escaped slaves and marginalized whites all found sanctuary in Florida.

In this place where no one had a certifiable past, men with plantation-perfect names like Lodowick Ashley and Farquahar Bethune played the role of aristocrat with as much aplomb and lack of birthright as any Hollywood star later did, but it was all an act. Cotton, indigo and tobacco do not grow in arid, barren sand. Estates with names like Ashley Plantation and Kingsley Plantation, which today lend their names to golf resorts and state parks, were contraband entrepôts. Like smuggling rum and cocaine later, smuggling slaves was a pervasive source of shame and profit, a traffic that touched almost everyone's life, whatever their claims to public uprightness and private morality.

Though dozens of influential men in Spanish Florida had black wives or mistresses, Zephaniah and Anna Kingsley, affluent residents of Amelia Island, were Florida's most prominent interracial couple. He was a migrant from Britain; she had started as a slave from Africa. Now he uncorked, and she passed the claret at their soirees. The source of all this vitality, tolerance and money was what today is called globalization. Just as Florida's position as a global and hemispheric nexus later made Miami the world center of the drug trade, and Orlando the world center of family-franchise vacations, geography, circumstance and human greed in the last years of Spanish rule made Fernandina one hell of a town. Rich whites, poor whites, blacks: the destinies of all these Americans by then already were intertwined in Florida. Together they already were starting to create a society that, no matter how rich it got, would always have poverty and, no matter how much it orated about equality, would always have the race stain in its soul. Beyond those three groups—rich whites, poor whites, blacks—were the "Indians," whose destiny it was to have no place at all. By the time Mathews arrived on the scene these four protagonist groups, in spite of their many differences, had one thing in common. All four were threatened by his scheme to impose the American system of race, class and dispossession on Florida. Florida's Indian, black and mixed-race people all "readily discerned that the maintenance of Spanish rule . . . in East Florida was essential to their well-being," as one academic later put it.

Mathews expected to be welcomed as Florida's liberator: he found himself to be a Paul Revere in reverse. By March 1812, more than one year had passed since his secret meeting with President Madison; Mathews was about to become impresario of the last great farce of his career. His inspiration for the East Florida Republic he was about to invent was the West Florida Republic. It took time, money and many unkeepable promises, but Mathews—still operating on the Georgia side of the border—finally did manage to round up nine individuals willing to sign their names to a Declaration of Independence. Since the declaration needed to be made on Floridian soil, Mathews and his protégés rowed across the St. Marys River, to the Florida side. There, on March 13, 1812, Mathews' nine Founding Fathers declared East Florida's supposed independence, then just as quickly pledged to relinquish "unto the United States of America all of the lands belonging unto the said Province." The proceedings creating this latest fake little nation would have been incomplete without the solemn hoisting of the official flag of the Republic of East Florida. The national symbol in this instance took the form of the silhouette of "a soldier in blue against a white background; the soldier, with his bayonet mounted, musket thrust forward," one historian later noted, appeared to be "charging the unseen foe." They then rowed back across the river to Georgia.

The question now was: what to do next? In the ensuing confrontation over the proper use of U.S. power Mathews prefigured the out-of-control CIA case officer. Lieutenant Jacint Laval, the commanding officer in St. Marys, Georgia, played the straight-arrow military man. To stop there, though, would be like describing Mathews as an ex-governor of Georgia, while not mentioning the Yazoo affair. In the aviary of eccentric protagonists the Florida border area by then had become, Lieutenant Jacint Laval's exotic plumage was second to none. A native of France, he had embraced the American cause out of revolutionary idealism. By the time his star crossed Mathews' Laval was simultaneously, and with no sense of self-contradiction, an honorable U.S. officer, a New World romantic, an avid gardener, an enthusiastic sexual adventurer, and an anti-Semite. If George Mathews is to be believed, Laval also borrowed money from the lower ranks and never repaid it.

Mathews wanted to use Laval's troops to invade Spanish Florida. Laval refused. He had received no such orders from his superiors. Even with such orders, letting Mathews use U.S. troops to invade the territory of a foreign country would amount to starting a war without Congress declaring it, and therefore be a violation of Laval's oath as an officer of the United States Army to protect and defend the U.S. Constitution. Laval was particularly outraged when Mathews demanded that he let him use his soldiers to invade Spanish Florida disguised as "Patriots." As Laval correctly pointed out, that would have turned U.S. Army troops into bandits. There was by then another reason why Laval refused to support Mathews' invasion plan. Mathews, having barged in on Laval, and occupied one of the two bedrooms in his riverside cottage for more than seven months, had turned into the house guest from hell. Day after day, and by night as well, Laval complained in a letter to the secretary of war, Mathews "almost tortured me to death to get me to cooperate" with what Laval called his "infamous scheme." "Is it possible that the government cannot be better furnished with officers," he demanded, than the kinds of "Jews, rogues, traitors, conspirators" he saw coming and going from his own house? The Jew in question was Ralph Isaacs, a Mississippi speculator whose courtesy title, conferred by the local militia, was "Colonel." In his early forays into Florida, Isaacs had operated as Mathews' advance man. Now they continued to act like a dysfunctional couple—Isaacs constantly warning Mathews of his folly while acting as his enabler. It was Isaacs who first established contact with Folch in West Florida—Isaacs, too, who composed East Florida's farcical declaration of independence, its signatories like Mathews being functionally illiterate.

In their dispute over the use of unauthorized violence Laval and Mathews personified a dialogue that for more than two hundred years has never stopped in the United States. Does being Americans gives us the right to violate the rules of civilized behavior, or does it confer on us an especial obligation to respect them? There was another continuity. History back then, as it is today, was being made by flawed human beings. It would be nice to portray Laval as grand and clean, like the statues of Jefferson and Lincoln in their great white memorials, but not even they were like that. It is equally tempting to treat Mathews humorously, but his actions were criminal as well as reckless. When Laval refused to provide troops for his invasion, Mathews incited mutiny. Laval stymied him by posting guards on his own troops, then stood guard himself the entire night.

With no U.S. troops to do the fighting, there was no way for Mathews to attack St. Augustine, let alone seize the entire "Province together with all the houses, arms and ordinances, military stores and fortifications with everything there unto appertaining," as East Florida's all-encompassing declaration of independence had invited him to do. But might he be able to seize the little port of Fernandina? A declaration of independence proclaimed by nine men carried little weight, but the Spanish defense forces were Lilliputian too. Nine, as it turned out, was also the number of soldiers comprising the tiny Spanish garrison there.

Deprived of artillery, Mathews unleashed a barrage of false promises. If only they threw down their arms, he promised, Fernandina's defenders would get the best of both worlds—U.S. freedom, plus handsome cash payments and the right to go on smuggling. Via various manifestos, Mathews promised an even more imaginative use for the secret funds Congress had appropriated. Once the United States took control, he added, it would (in clear violation of the Constitution) go on paying the stipends of Florida's state-supported Catholic priests. Meanwhile Mathews had been handing out guns and ammunition, as one early account puts it, to "all the wood choppers and boatmen in the neighborhood of St. Marys." In return for their support, these freelance invaders were promised happy looting, plus five hundred acres of Spanish land apiece.

As this undisciplined throng of "rag-a-muffins from the fag-end of Georgia," as one of Fernandina's defenders described them, ambled in the direction of Fernandina, the Spanish commander, Colonel Justo Lopez, convoked a committee of public safety. He then did what white Americans always feared most. He distributed arms and ammunition to slaves as well as free blacks. It reveals a great deal that not even that measure shook the loyalty of Amelia Island's white Americans to the Spanish.

This was no confrontation between Anglo-Saxon vigor and Latinate decadence. Though the Spanish flag still flew, the conflict already had become a dispute among Americans. The main men on Mathews' side were named McIntosh and Ashley. Lopez' chief assistants, on the Spanish side, were named Clarke and Atkinson. As at Bunker Hill earlier and Fort Sumter later, a battle between English-speaking white men over what kind of country America should be seemed in the offing, but no blood flowed because the utter irregularity of the situation gave Lopez, as it had given Folch earlier, a chance for maneuver which he adroitly seized. The essential question, the Spanish commander had the presence of mind to recognize, was whether or not the United States had authorized this aggression. When Lopez coolly asked the Americans to explain to him just who had ordered the attack, he encountered that classic symptom of a covert operation that has spun out of control—U.S. officials speaking with two opposing voices. "I have the greatest satisfaction in informing you that the United States are neither principals or auxiliaries, and that I am not authorized to make any attack upon East Florida,"

Lieutenant Laval informed the Spanish. "I have instructions from my government," Mathews informed Lopez, "to receive East Florida or any part of it from the local authorities, or to take it by force to prevent its occupation by a foreign power."

Sensing an opportunity, Lopez sent Clarke across in a rowboat to negotiate. The ensuing capitulation had something in it for everyone. In return for Mathews' calling off his attack, Lopez agreed to surrender Amelia Island to the "Patriots." They in turn agreed they would cede it to the United States within twenty-four hours. As Lopez knew, but apparently Mathews did not understand, this was a very significant diplomatic technicality. Since neither Spain nor the United States ever recognized the East Florida Republic, or anything it did, this later would allow both the Spanish and American governments to pretend that, juridically speaking, nothing had happened. Under those circumstances, Lopez could consider his surrender a temporary expedient, as in fact it turned out to be. Only the Georgia ragamuffins had reason for disappointment as the "Patriots" and the Spanish joined forces to preserve law and order. There would be no looting. No one would get the promised five hundred acres, either.

The next day, March 18, 1812, was the last truly glorious day of George Mathews' bizarre, long life as, on the Florida side of the border his East Florida flag, having been raised the night before, was lowered for the last time. On Mathews' orders the American Stars and Stripes was then unfurled. Nearly fourteen months after he and Madison had first hatched the plan, Mathews was finally getting some land in Florida handed over to him by an "existing local authority, amicable to surrender." Events on the Georgia side of the river that day were just as gratifying. After a long absence, Lieutenant Laval's immediate superior, Colonel Thomas Smith, had resumed command. The French-born lieutenant, delighted to scrape the mess Mathews had made from his boots, demanded and got a transfer. To George Mathews the road to glory now seemed wide open. Within days the "Patriots" were marching overland toward St. Augustine. Mathews proceeded by boat. As his little vessel was untethered so, simultaneously, were George Mathews' remaining links to reality. "On to Venezuela!" he declaimed.

Mathews' little force had tripled to about three hundred men by the time he got to St. Augustine. In violation of U.S. law and treaties, Laval's replacement, acting without orders, sent more than one hundred U.S. troops in full uniform to join the invasion. As they advanced, no one thought to ask: What if they won't surrender? It all had happened before—the headlong charge south, followed by the Spaniards' peevish refusal to give up the fort, the first time 110 years earlier, in 1702. Later, colonists from Georgia had twice attacked. On each occasion the fort held, even when the invaders burned St. Augustine. Now it was the turn of Mathews, the "Patriots," and U.S. Army troops to slap mosquitoes and bicker among themselves while, inside the Castillo, the defenders sat tight. On every previous occasion, after a few days or weeks, the attackers had been forced to withdraw. Now it was happening again, with one essential difference. On all those previous occasions, the country from which the invaders came had actually been at war with Spain.

Even if Mathews' marauders had the taste or training for actual combat, their force remained too small and poorly equipped to overrun the Castillo de San Marcos, where cannonballs bounced off the coquina limestone ramparts with no effect. While Mathews sat in his camp, churning out manifestos, supplies continued to reach the Spanish by sea, estuary, and land. It would have taken most of the U.S. Navy, one American military man judged, to blockade Matanzas Inlet successfully. Even that, he noted, would not have stopped hostile blacks, Spaniards, and Seminoles from picking off the invaders one by one. Mathews' followers had expected to be welcomed by dusky beauties offering them smiles and sweets. Instead the story soon circulated of a different kind of reception. It was said that some Americans, out for a swim, espied a party of lovely Minorcan ladies disporting themselves. Delighted, the Americans swam to the opposite bank. When they got there, Minorcan menfolk sprang into view and cut their throats. There comes a turning point in every failed siege when the besiegers' dream of victory is overtaken by the panic-stricken need to go home. As Mathews' forces started to dribble into nothingness, other stories of authentic provenance circulated. The Spanish had armed 150 black soldiers, as well as all the civilian blacks of St. Augustine, and more African troops were on the way from Havana. Pro-Spanish guerrillas had pounced on a detachment of Americans and killed fourteen of them. For Mathews' amateur conquistadors the Florida surrounding them had become the Florida surrounding de Soto in the painting in the Jacksonville museum.

Having been sent south to filch Florida on the sly, Mathews had created a military-political fiasco in which the United States faced the same two choices it would in some other controversial conflicts: either to admit defeat or escalate. A noted frontier fighter, Governor David Mitchell of Georgia, was sent down to see what could be done. Expected to call for a fresh influx of U.S. troops, Mitchell returned with the assessment that Mathews' force was primarily a danger to itself. As for chasing the Spanish out of St. Augustine, Governor Mitchell concluded that overrunning the Castillo de San Marcos would cost more money, and more lives, than it had cost the British to take Quebec during the French and Indian War. Thanks to America's freedom of the press, there was no need for official clearance to find out what a fool Mathews had made of the United States. "Disgraceful in the extreme," commented the *Charleston Courier* in an article criticizing the "farce of receiving the Province from a handful of insurgents" in such a manner.

In their démarches with Secretary of State Monroe and President Madison, Spain's representatives coolly asked the same question Lopez had in Fernandina—the same one Philip II implicitly had used, more than 250 years earlier, to turn aside French complaints about the Menéndez massacres. Had or had not the United States authorized the attacks on Florida? The brouhaha finally caused Secretary of State James Monroe to leaf through the reports Mathews had been sending to Washington. They demonstrated, as President Madison himself observed in a letter to Thomas Jefferson, that "Mathews has been playing a strange comedy," adding: "His extravagances place us in the most distressing dilemma."

The moment had come for an exercise in plausible deniability. "I am sorry to have to state," began the letter which Monroe sent to Mathews, "that the measures which you appear to have adopted for obtaining possession of Amelia Island, and other parts of East

Florida, are not authorized by the law of the United States, or the instructions founded on it, under which you have acted. You were authorized by law and instructions to take East Florida only on peaceful delivery by the governor or other existing local authority, or to forestall occupation by a foreign power." Monroe then modulated into an outright lie. "In any case," he continued, "a forceful wresting of the province from Spain was never contemplated, but only an occupation until a settlement could be reached by future amicable negotiation with Spain."

Mathews did not intend to be stopped now. Earlier, upon being denied the governorship of the Mississippi Territory, he had set out for Washington, intending to "chastise" President John Adams for his impertinence. The supposedly inflexible New Englander had turned away Mathews' wrath by appointing one of his sons to the interesting post of supervisor of public revenues in Georgia. Now Mathews headed north again; his aim, he wrote, was "ravange." Sputtering abuse to all who would listen, he vowed "to blow them all up in Washington." "Poor old Mathews," commiserated a fellow Georgian, "I am fearful will die of mortification and resentment." On August 30, 1812, while on his way north, George Mathews attained his seventy-third birthday; that same day he died. The same Governor Mitchell of Georgia who had recognized the folly of besieging St. Augustine did the best he could by way of eulogy. "Whatever political errors he may have fallen into, in the course of a long public life," he counseled, "let them rest in oblivion."

That advice was not followed. Instead of being forgotten, Mathews was turned into one of the first of American Florida's many fake heroes—a kind of proto-Confederate cavalier, the purehearted martyr to a noble, lost cause, "the victim of a covetous but vacillating administration which he had served faithfully." As late as 1954 Mathews was still being portrayed as a well-meaning victim. "His services in the Revolutionary War, his work in Congress, his contribution as governor of Georgia had almost been wiped from the memory of man by the Yazoo land frauds," wrote one admirer that year. "The secretary of war had denounced him, senators had shied away from him, and President Adams had failed him. During those long and lean political years he listened for opportunity's knock." Now, "in the evening of life," Mathews thought he heard that knock. Through the door he opened he perceived Florida. Then, in Mathews' real story, just as in Ponce's mythical one, his dream, as he acted it out in Florida, turned out to be nothing more than "the figment of imagination, the hallucination of old age."

"The repudiation of Mathews was but a paper maneuver," one chronicler later noted. President Madison still wanted Florida, all of it, but his little war there had produced an embarrassing disaster and 1812 was a presidential election year. Ready to do whatever it took to get a second term, the president now started a much bigger, far more disastrous war. When his local militia was summoned, Thomas Jefferson noted, all but 10 of the 241 men on the rolls crowded into town for the first muster, eager to attack America's neighbors. "The only inquiry," the ex-president informed Madison, "is whether they are to go to Canada or Florida?" The Florida historian Rembert Patrick compared the United States at this point to "a fledgling vulture [which] hovered outside the vortex of world conflict, hoping to snatch tempting morsels in North America from England and her weak and dependent ally, Spain." The vulture was about to lose a lot of its feathers.

Like Mathews' advance on St. Augustine, the U.S. attack on Canada began with a barrage of pronouncements about freedom, then quickly ran in reverse. Detroit was lost, along with parts of Maine and upstate New York. The war did get Madison his second term, but it was not until 1815 that the War of 1812 finally ended. By then Washington had been burned, Baltimore bombarded. The question now was whether Britain would give up the parts of the United States which it had taken, but it would be incorrect to state that there were no territorial gains. Having declared war on Britain, the United States had attacked the Spanish over in West Florida. Having failed to conquer Canada, it seized the two little bits of Alabama and Mississippi sticking down to the Gulf of Mexico. America's ostensible purpose had been to defend its rights as a neutral nation. Now, as a result of committing unprovoked (and ungrateful) aggression against a neutral nation that had helped them win their independence, Americans finally controlled the Gulf coastal strip which President Jefferson had first purported was America's in 1803. While giving back the part of East Florida that Mathews had seized with his right hand, President Madison had taken part of West Florida with his left. It was America's only territorial gain as a result of the war.

The U.S. seizure of Mobile at last produced the foreign threat the president had hoped to provoke. In response to the American action, the British took over the defense of nearby Pensacola. Had the tables been turned, Madison and Monroe would have announced that Pensacola had been "pre-occupied" in order to forestall further aggression. Instead the British move provided the excuse for yet another Florida invasion. In late 1814 U.S. troops advanced on Pensacola. It seemed the climactic battle in the British-American war was about to be fought on Spanish territory; then, suddenly, the British sailed away, having decided to attack New Orleans instead. U.S. forces, abandoning Spanish Pensacola as abruptly as they had seized it, got to Louisiana just in time. The British were expecting no more resistance there than they encountered when they burned Washington, but on January 8, 1815, U.S. forces killed and wounded a total of 2,055 British officers and men. Only 101 Americans fell. It was a veritable massacre, the most consequential slaughter of white men by white men in North America between the end of the War of Independence and the beginning of the Civil War.

7

AMERICANIZATON AT NEGRO FORT

"Mr. Madison's War," one critic predicted, had been "commenced in folly," was being "carried on with madness," and would "end in ruin." That was two-thirds right. The War of 1812 ended in Andrew Jackson. New Orleans was Jackson's Fort Caroline. His slaughter of the British there turned him into America's homegrown Pedro Menéndez de Avilés. All wars have unintended consequences; Andrew Jackson's unexpected rise to American supremacy was as consequential a result as one can get.

Jackson's enemies, appalled at the power his triumph brought him, pointed out it came only after the peace treaty had been signed. That was true but irrelevant. While Jackson's victory did not change the treaty, it transformed the military reality of North America. At Ghent the British pledged to withdraw from the U.S. territory they had taken, but only in exchange for a major concession on the American side. "Article IX of the Treaty of Ghent guaranteed that all lands taken from Indians during the War of 1812 would be returned to them." Jackson's victory turned that provision into a dead letter because in the aftermath of his slaughter at New Orleans no European power ever again would have the stomach to intervene militarily against the United States, no matter how many treaties it violated.

For that reason New Orleans also was the decisive victory in the generations-long war to dispossess America's original inhabitants so they could be replaced with landowners of European origin and, across the South, laborers on the land who were slaves from

Africa. Had this remorseless war of ethnic cleansing been fought in Europe, we might call it the Three Hundred Years War, for that is about how long it lasted. For the same reasons the War of 1812 more accurately could be called the "British and Indian War." After their defeat at New Orleans the British, like the French after their defeat in the French and Indian War, never again would intervene militarily in North America. This meant the Indians never again would have a European ally as they fought to salvage something for themselves in the face of American aggression. Jackson's victory also was a tipping point in the hemispheric and, eventually, the global balance of power. Less than fifty-five years earlier, the great strategic question had been whether Great Britain or France would dominate North America. Less than thirty-five after New Orleans, the United States would seize half of Mexico. The absence of a European counterbalance to U.S. power in North America would doom the Confederacy as well. Only thirty-five years after that, the United States would fight its first Asian land war, as the U.S. Army crushed the Philippines independence movement. Not until the Soviet Union backed Cuba in 1960 would an outside power directly challenge the United States in the western hemisphere.

Freed of all outside restraint following his New Orleans victory, Andrew Jackson set to work cleansing the southeast frontier of all Indians. Whichever side they had taken in the war it made no difference. All would be hounded along the Trail of Tears to oblivion. No word had existed for the kind of transformative violence Jackson unleashed until Noah Webster published *A Compendious Dictionary of the English Language*, which contained many new words of independent American origin. One of those new words was "hickory," defined as "noun: a tree, a species of walnut." To this day Americans call Jackson "Old Hickory" after the wood, sometimes also called pignut wood, used to whip horses and beat slaves. Another word which appeared for the first time was "Americanize." This Webster defined as "to render American." Following Jackson's victory, Spanish Florida was turned into a crucible of Americanization, with events there epitomizing two rampant impulses of American nationalism. One was the impulse to eradicate all alternatives to a society, as

Stephen Douglas later put it, dominated "by the white man, for the benefit of the white man, to be administered by white men, in such a manner as they determine." The other was the impulse "to render American" territories not belonging to the United States, that is commit aggression against America's neighbors. Here, as before and long into the future, Florida "afforded at once an epitome and a prophecy" as a two-pronged thrust of American expansion transformed the North American continent, then the western hemisphere, and ultimately the world.

You can get an idea of how American violence transformed Florida by visiting another fort which, like the one at St. Augustine, contains within its ruins long-ignored truths. This one is located in the Apalachicola National Forest in northwest Florida. You traverse Tate's Hell Forest. Then, just south of a wide spot in the road called Sumatra, a gravel track leads to a low bluff overlooking the Apalachicola River. In colonial days this marked the border between East and West Florida; this stretch of the river still divides the eastern and central standard time zones. Until July 1816, this place was the nucleus of an emerging community of free subsistence farmers. Here Indian, black and mixed-race people lived, worked, and tried to defend themselves and their families. Originally it was called Prospect Bluff. The Americans who, on General Andrew Jackson's orders, killed all the people there, called it "Negro Fort." Today its official name is the Fort Gadsden Historic Recreation Center. "Picnic tables, drinking water and vault toilets are available," the U.S. Department of Agriculture advises. Here, on July 27, 1816, U.S. forces perpetrated one of the worst massacres in American history. Hundreds of civilians were killed in the initial artillery attack. The survivors, including mothers with their children, were then murdered, their leaders tortured to death.

Understand what happened at Negro Fort, and myriad future events become intelligible. Banish it from mind and memory, and two hundred years of conflict and pain become disconnected, impossible to understand. You could say the massacre at Negro Fort was the signal event in the U.S. subjugation of Florida, except it sent no signal. To this day, almost no one is aware of what happened there.

"The explosion was awful, and the scene horrible beyond description," reported one eyewitness. "In an instant lifeless bodies were stretched upon the plain, buried in sand and rubbish, or suspended from the tops of the surrounding pines. Here lay an innocent babe, there a helpless mother; on the one side a sturdy warrior, on the other a bleeding squaw." The words "warrior" and "squaw" are of great significance in what supposedly was an expedition to chastise "runaway" black slaves; so is the identity of the witness. That testimony was provided by the U.S. Army officer who commanded the assault, Colonel Duncan L. Clinch. By Clinch's own account the great majority of those his forces killed were noncombatants; "more than 200 women and children" was his estimate.

The artillery attack on this civilian population followed the orders of General Andrew Jackson as relayed through Clinch's superior, General Edmund Pendleton Gaines. "I have little doubt of the fact, that this fort has been established by some villains for rapine and plunder," Jackson wrote, "and that it ought to be blown up, regardless of the land on which it stands; and if your mind shall have formed the same conclusion, destroy it and return the stolen Negroes and property to their rightful owners." Gaines entrusted the mission to Clinch. Military expediency could not justify the killings. The war with the British had ended one year and five months earlier. All across Georgia, Alabama, Mississippi and Louisiana, U.S. power was supreme. Even so, the existence of a free nonwhite community inside Spanish Florida constituted sufficient proof, so far as General Jackson was concerned, that the fortification at Prospect Bluff was manned by "villains" bent on "rapine and plunder." Accounts provided by white Americans involved in the attack inadvertently tell a different story—of people who were trying to lead peaceful lives when all was taken from them. "The force of the Negroes was daily increasing, and they felt themselves so strong and secure that they commenced several plantations on the fertile banks of the Apalachicola," wrote Commodore Daniel Patterson, head of U.S. naval operations in the region, in a report attempting to justify the attack. As white Americans saw it, blacks growing food for themselves on foreign soil was aggression against the United States.

U.S. Army and Navy units based as far apart as New Orleans and Georgia participated in the joint amphibious assault. By dawn on July 27, 1816, U.S. gunboats advancing upriver through Spanish territory from the Gulf of Mexico had linked up with Clinch's army detachment; it had advanced overland into Florida from the north. Though he commanded the operation, Clinch exempted himself from responsibility for the killings. One of the navy gunboats had fired a red-hot cannon ball into Negro Fort. That single shot, Clinch claimed, instantly killed 270 men, women and children; therefore it wasn't his fault. "The result appeared miraculous to the soldiers," a friendly account later noted, not without reason: "Neither vessel boasted of a furnace for heating balls." The cannon ball had other astonishing features. Surveying "the mangled corpses and torn arms and legs scattered hither and yon," the Americans found themselves "pleasantly surprised by the quantity of valuable stores that escaped destruction." The same explosion that killed 270 people left unscathed "163 barrels and nearly 500 kegs of gun powder," along with "500 carbines, almost 1,000 pairs of pistols, and 500 scabbard swords." In light of the accusations that the people at Negro Fort had been bent on "rapine and plunder," it was an interesting discovery that these weapons, abandoned by the British there when the war ended, were "still packed in the original shipping boxes."

The miraculous cannon ball also left the fort's two commanders unharmed. One of them was Indian, Clinch decided; no name for him is provided. The other, to American eyes, was "Negro," though he may have been of mixed blood, in fact a "Spaniard." In some accounts he is called "Garcon," the French word for "boy" or more generally, "servant"; in others he is called "Garcia." The customs of warfare dictated civilized treatment for captured enemy commanders but Colonel Clinch followed General Jackson's dictum, that the "laws of war did not apply to conflicts with savages." The two survivors who had led the defense of Negro Fort were tortured to death. In his report, Colonel Clinch explained why he was also not responsible for these gruesome murders. He had paid "friendly" Indians $50 per victim to do the killing. It was God's will, Colonel Clinch explained. "The war yells of the Indians, the cries and lamentations of the wounded," he later wrote, demonstrated "that the great Ruler of the Universe must have used us as his instruments in chastising the blood-thirsty and murderous wretches that defended the fort."

The Negro Fort Massacre involved a thoroughgoing failure of U.S. intelligence. The Americans' own accounts make it clear they had no idea who they were killing. According to Commodore Patterson, Prospect Bluff was controlled by the growing "force of the Negroes." Jackson himself had "little doubt of the fact" that the people there were "stolen Negroes," but when Clinch examined the bodies of the killed, he found most of them were Choctaw Indians. Colonel Clinch had another surprise in store. Such blacks as he did find at Negro Fort were "almost entirely Spanish-speaking Negroes from Pensacola." Having found no stolen slaves at Prospect Bluff, U.S. forces went on a kidnapping spree along the Apalachicola River. The only evidence that any of the people they seized actually were slaves, let alone "stolen" ones, came from the fact they looked "Negro." The captives were marched at gunpoint out of Florida, to a confinement camp on U.S. territory. There they were turned over to such friends and associates of their captors who wanted fresh slave labor, free of cost. "Georgia slaveholders," explains the National Parks Service in a recent account of these events, "justified their title to them by saying that their ancestors had owned the ancestors of the prisoners."

Clinch failed in his strategic mission, which had been to stop attacks on "U.S. citizens." As Clinch's own biographer later put it, "The destruction of the Negro Fort . . . did not frighten the hostile Seminoles." Instead, resistance to American intrusions grew stronger; failure nonetheless was spun into glorious victory. General Jackson commended Clinch and his troops for their "gallant conduct." Comparing Clinch's attack to American exploits during the recent war with the British, *Niles' Weekly Register* commented that the destruction of Negro Fort "yields in gallant daring and complete success to no incident that happened in the late contest." There was, however, the problem that this time the United States was not at war. In the absence of a legitimate state of war, Clinch's action therefore constituted what some had been so unchivalrous to describe as an "illegal action." The murdered people of Prospect Bluff left no records, but the accounts of those who encouraged, conducted and condoned the killings provide a clear view of what their real crime was. With the permission of the Spanish authorities, people of several races had set up farming communities "on the fertile banks of the Apalachicola." More than that, in a tradition going back to Fort Mose and the black defenders of St. Augustine, they had established "Negro militia and self-governing Negro communities in Florida." Their crime was being free. To use one of Jackson's favorite words, they were "chastised" for that crime with death.

A visit to the Fort Gadsden Historic Recreation Center reveals how small and fragile Negro Fort was. The encampment with its wooden palisades and earthen ditches had been hastily constructed under British supervision during the War of 1812. The main enclosure was not much larger than the basketball court at a modern high school. In 1816 the crowding together of some three hundred people in such a small place was an unusual event. Florida's two biggest settlements, St. Augustine and Pensacola, had only a few hundred people. These people had sought safety there because the combined advance of the U.S. Navy up the Apalachicola River and of the U.S. Army down the Apalachicola valley had caught them in a pincer of fear. A few years earlier, the British had wantonly exploited the hopes of Florida's nonwhite population by encouraging them to fight the "wicked People of the United States." Now the abandoned remnant of that failed effort—Negro Fort and its unopened boxes of weapons—raised the false hope of successful resistance. It was a fatal misapprehension. Clinch's army detachment numbered just over a hundred. With the support of the navy gunboats, he had sufficient firepower, and manpower, to slaughter hundreds of defenseless people crowded into one small enclosure. His attack force would have been powerless if the people at Negro Fort, instead of converging there, had dispersed, but trapped in a fight-or-flight situation, they had sought safety inside the fort at Prospect Bluff.

When it comes to Florida, Jackson often seems like a hurricane —roaring in, then out of the place like a caprice of nature. In reality Jackson's Florida terror campaign was a carefully calculated, premeditated endeavor. "From 1814 on," notes J. B. Bird of the University of Texas at Austin in his study of the Florida resistance, "Jackson sought pretexts for invading Florida." Portraying Florida as "a dangerous haven for fugitive slaves," Jackson "used this situation to build support for an attack." As always, Jackson promised to "chastise a lawless foe." That was how he habitually described the Indians he slaughtered. Now, in Florida, he avowed an even more emotive purpose. He was going to eliminate the "Negro brigands" who, he alleged, were "carrying on a cruel and unprovoked war against the citizens of the United States." Jackson's long-term purpose was to transform Florida—as he already had Alabama, Mississippi and his adopted home state, Tennessee—into a white supremacist slave state from which all "Indians" had been expunged, where all blacks were enslaved. Look at a map of Florida today; you will see what was evident to U.S. strategists in 1816. Negro Fort posed no threat to the United States. It did present a potential obstacle to further U.S. conquest. So did the Apalachicola valley's growing multiracial population. Jackson's order to "blow up" the fort, pointless as a defensive measure, did make military sense as a preemptive strike clearing the way for future aggression. It was Jackson, not his victims, who was plotting to launch "a cruel and unprovoked war."

In 1740 the free blacks at Fort Mose had helped thwart the attack on St. Augustine from Georgia. In 1812 black people once again joined Indians and Spaniards to thwart George Mathews' invasion. Now, in western Florida, a similar drama unfolded, though with the passage of the centuries the cast of characters changed. So did the meaning of the plot. This no longer was a struggle between Spain and Britain for control in Florida, as it had been as recently as 1783. Like the confrontation at Amelia Island, the bloodshed in the Apalachicola valley showed that the struggle for Florida had become a conflict among Americans. Jackson's own claims that the presence of "stolen Negroes" in Florida justified the U.S. attack implicitly conceded the real source of the conflict. It was the nature of American race relations, and the domestic crisis slavery already was creating inside the United States, that drove the violence that soon would engulf all of Florida, and eventually the whole United States.

Clinch's reference to the "Choctaws" at Negro Fort is also crucial to understanding why these early U.S. invasions, instead of crushing resistance, generated forty years of warfare in Florida. The "Choctaw warrior" whom Clinch had tortured to death was as American as Clinch himself, and not just in the sense the Choctaws and their ancestors had lived on what now was U.S. soil from time immemorial. One of the "Five Civilized Tribes," they were a literate people who had made the transition from the hunter-gathering stage of development to American-style agriculture, complete with log cabins, iron plows, and steepled churches. Many had English names and held registered deeds to the property Jackson and his men stole from them. The Choctaws understood that their own misfortunes were interconnected with the vaster turmoil of world events. Later, when the potato famine devastated Ireland, the Choctaws sent money to help the Irish because they knew, firsthand, what politically induced starvation was. The Choctaws did differ in one way from their neighbors. Because their skin was of a different color they would be hounded along the Trail of Tears to oblivion in the lands west of the Mississippi.

Generations before the Underground Railroad to Canada came into being, Florida provided refuge for a rainbow coalition of America's *Rebels and Runaways*, as Larry Eugene Rivers describes these diverse peoples in his aptly titled study of their early efforts to find freedom there. Out of the fusion of these various refugee peoples of American and African descent emerged what we have come to understand as the Seminole identity. One of Negro Fort's most important revelations is how, exactly, this fusion occurred. White repression had driven both Indians and blacks from the United States. Now both of them were attacked again. Dispossessed together, they tried to defend themselves together. "Garcon" and his Choctaw ally were killed, but following the massacre more and more Indians and blacks would make common cause in Florida, and their example encouraged more and more freedom-seekers to join them.

As the massacre at Negro Fort demonstrates, that early Florida posed one of the great questions of American nationalism. Would freedom truly prevail? Or would the future belong exclusively to white men like Jackson, Gaines, and Clinch? Today, from the distant prospect of the twenty-first century, a stupendous irony is on display in the food courts at every Florida shopping mall. Multiculturalism would triumph, though only generations after its precursors had been killed or enslaved. Americans today think of Andrew Jackson as the ancestor of their liberties. Their true antecedents, when it comes to how they live together and relate to each other, are the diverse peoples who on that horrible day in July 1816 found themselves trapped at Negro Fort.

None of this is evident at the massacre site, where cover-up masquerades as a "recreation center." The exhibits there show white people, along with some Indians, traversing the Florida wilderness as though on a nature hike. At Negro Fort not a single black face, figure, or artifact is shown. The murders of the women and children are nowhere mentioned. Every authentic account of the massacre, including Colonel Clinch's eyewitness description, makes it gruesomely clear that the two captured leaders were tortured to death. Some nineteenth-century accounts attempted to justify the killings by pointing out that, in earlier fighting, four U.S. sailors were killed. The modern display substitutes its own newly invented justification for the killings. In this recently concocted account the U.S. sailors are turned into innocent civilians, "Americans searching for water," leaving the reader to assume they died simply because they were white and thirsty. Such wanton savagery demanded that justice be done, so the "Indian chief and black commander were sentenced to death for the murder of the four Americans," it states. Not even those who killed them ever pretended there was a judicial process. Garcon was shot on the spot. The Choctaw was scalped, then stabbed to death.

The Negro Fort exhibits offer a paradigm of what might be called the Ongoing Florida Historical Method. It consists of suppressing, denying, or changing the facts whenever they controvert the celebratory version of events historians of the time, and their audience, prefer—and then suppressing, denying, or changing the facts yet again whenever a newer false version is needed. In this instance, through the straightforward expedient of lying, the victims of murder are turned, themselves, into "sentenced" murderers. Their killers become dispensers of justice. Negro Fort, site of the worst American massacre in Florida, provides the most complete example of how, over and over again, an illusion of American virtue is preserved by blaming the victims. Even Colonel Clinch gets marginalized in this process of turning the massacre site into an emotionally tax-free zone. Contrary to what you might expect, Clinch's name is not on the fort. It bears, instead, the name of Lieutenant James Gadsden, another Jackson protégé, because following the massacre Jackson ordered Gadsden to transform the site of the killings into a permanent base for the projection of U.S. power into Florida. He was so pleased with Gadsden's work that he ordered the new fort named after the subordinate who carried out his orders.

Far from being an act of self-defense, the bloody destruction of the multiracial communities of the Apalachicola valley was the latest step in Jackson's forward policy of Americanizing Florida. Clinch "cleared" the ground. Then Gadsden took charge of step two as he established the new fortification "regardless," to use Jackson's own word, of the fact that it was illegally located on foreign soil fifty miles beyond the borders of the United States. While falsely announcing that he had withdrawn U.S. troops from Florida, Jackson secretly ordered American forces to stay. They remained ensconced at the massacre site and at other clandestine posts even after President Monroe publicly ordered all U.S. troops to leave. The conflict between law and conquest that had erupted seven years earlier in the dispute between Lieutenant Laval and "General" Mathews had entered a new phase. This time two giants of American history, Monroe and Jackson, would be the protagonists.

This transformation of a peaceful civilian outpost into a projection of American military force prefigured Florida's history for generations to come. Though the exhibits on display at Negro Fort disguise that, the progression of the place-names at the massacre site tells the truth about what happened, both at the time and later. A geographical description ("Prospect Bluff") is turned into a place name carrying one of the most freighted, stress-filled words in American history. But then, thanks to a timely application of violence, history is made to turn out the way we are taught it should. The "Negro" in Negro Fort is excised, and replaced by the name of a vaguely remembered white man—"Gadsden." Finally the massacre site becomes, like Florida as a whole, a recreation center, the "Fort Gadsden Historic Recreation Center."

Clinch prepared the way. Then, in 1818, Jackson himself invaded Florida, gouging a mark so wide and deep it still shapes the state's political and psychological landscape. Whites, blacks, redskins: no one could accuse him of favoring one race over another when it came to slaughter. "My God would not have smiled on me, had I punished only the poor ignorant savages, and spared the white men who set them on," he remarked. Jackson's comment about killing white men referred to his murder of two British subjects, one a Scot, the other an Englishman, during his attack on Florida. Those killings attracted attention because the victims were white, but hundreds of others also were victims of the reign of terror Jackson inflicted, across an international border, upon the population of Spanish Florida.

Jackson found himself savaging Florida for the same reason George Mathews had wound up mired there six years earlier. President Monroe, like President Madison before him, wanted to obtain Florida on the cheap, without risking war even with enfeebled Spain, so once again an impetuous American invaded Florida. The ruse was the same, that the United States was not behind the mayhem. The objective was the same, to get Florida regardless of America's treaty obligations and the rights of its inhabitants. Jackson was as self-confident as Mathews had been. He would secure "the possession of the Floridas . . . in sixty days," he boasted.

Jackson's failure to grasp the reality of the Florida situation became clear as soon as he advanced on his first objective, the

little Spanish port of San Marcos de Apalache, today known as
St. Marks. Jackson claimed it was the headquarters of "a savage
foe, who, combined with a lawless band of Negro brigands, had
been for some time past carrying on a cruel and unprovoked war
against the citizens of the United States" but the only "brigand"
he found at St. Marks was a seventy-year-old British businessman
named Alexander Arbuthnot whom Jackson found having dinner
with a Spanish official. Jackson immediately had him imprisoned,
and later had him killed.

The Florida epicenter of the British-inspired, anti-American
conspiracy clearly wasn't at St. Marks, so Jackson next headed east
into the Florida wilderness, intending to find it there. Across the same
swamps and forests where, a quarter-millennium earlier, de Soto had
vainly sought gold, Jackson now raged. Jackson's "army made slow
progress," according to James Parton, whose laudatory biography
of Jackson was published in 1859, "wading through extensive sheets
of water; the horses starving for want of forage, and giving out daily
in large numbers" until, at last, Jackson and his troops seemed on
the verge of enacting a decisive massacre. The enemy headquarters,
supposedly friendly Indians assured them, was only six miles away.
"At sunset the lines were formed," writes Parton, "and the whole
army rushed forward." Where the great encampment was supposed
to be Jackson and his troops found nothing.

Jackson blamed his failure on one of his Florida victims. The
elderly Scotsman whose dinner Jackson had interrupted was alleged
to have written a letter to the Indians, warning them of his advance.
No authentic text of Arbuthnot's supposed letter was ever produced;
the text Jackson brandished was actually addressed to Arbuthnot's
son. Its purpose was not to warn the Seminoles that Jackson was
coming; that was obvious. It was to urge the Seminoles to avoid
bloodshed, and not resist "such a powerful force." The strangest
part of this story is the one that no American historian seems ever
to have challenged. Why would "savages" have needed a Scotsman
in St. Marks, 107 miles away, to write a letter in English informing
them that more than two thousand American troops were headed

their way? As his own staff reports make clear, Jackson's thunderous approach gave the Seminoles ample warning.

Jackson had aimed to provoke a decisive battle. Instead "the foe had vanished by a hundred paths, and were no more seen." It was a situation "to exasperate the mind of General Jackson" until one night a young Englishman named Robert Ambrister disrupted Andrew Jackson's sleep by arriving unannounced at his camp, seeking food and shelter. By then Jackson needed a scapegoat for his Florida failure, so he dragged his uninvited English guest back to St. Marks. When his own officers refused to condemn Ambrister to death, Jackson personally ordered him killed. After stealing his cargo, Jackson killed Arbuthnot by having the old man hanged from the yardarm of his own ship. It was a scene to dismay even Jackson's heartiest well-wishers. "Hapless Arbuthnot!" Jackson's biographer later exclaimed. Once again the victims were to blame—guilty, in the words of Jackson's comrade in arms, General Gaines, of being "self-styled Philanthropists who long infested our neighboring Indian villages, in the character of British agents—fomenting a spirit of discord (calculated to work to the destruction of the deluded savages), and endeavoring by pretended care and kindness to effect the destruction of these wretched savages."

The moral construct presented in that statement is worth examining because for generations to come it would be used to exculpate Americans from responsibility for their actions. As Gaines posits it, killers like Jackson and him are not responsible for "the destruction of the deluded savages." Those who offer them "care and kindness" are the guilty parties. It is their acts of "pretended" kindness, not American knives, guns, and bullets, that "effect the destruction of these wretched savages" by causing the Americans to kill so many more of them than would have been killed in the course of an unresisted American takeover. "The incident" observes J. B. Bird, "also betrayed a consistent turn of the American mind, with Jackson blaming foreigners for a conflict that had strong indigenous roots. It was, after all," he observes, "easier to blame the foreign agitators, and to execute them, than to admit that there was any justice to the cause of his enemies." Killing Arbuthnot and Ambrister was useful for another reason. Alive, they would have made powerful witnesses to the savagery and ineptness of Jackson's Florida expedition. Dead, they provided "proof" that a British conspiracy was afoot there.

Time was running out for Jackson; forty-four days had passed and all that he had to show for his exertions were two dead white men, a stolen cargo ship, and a trail of devastation. Jackson could plunge onward into the same "inaccessible retreats" that had swallowed up so many of Florida's other would-be conquerors, or he could choose survival. Jackson chose survival. Abandoning his pursuit of the "savage foe," he pounced on easier prey. Having assured the Spanish he had entered Florida in order to defeat "our common enemy," he now overthrew the Spanish government in Pensacola he claimed to have been protecting and installed a "provisional government" in its place. Jackson then marched home, whereupon even more bizarre events began to unfold. Jackson's first step was to proclaim his Florida failure a great victory. To prove it he made the bizarre claim that, as result of all that mayhem in West Florida, "East Florida, as he had promised, was now an American possession." Except for his abortive advance to the Suwannee River, Jackson had not actually ventured into East Florida. "The Seminole War," Jackson added, in his most bizarre comment of all, "may now be considered at a close." Forty years later, U.S. troops would still be fighting and killing Seminoles in Florida.

The eventual outcome of Jackson's 1818 assault was the introduction of monoculture slavery into Florida, followed by devastation in the Civil War, followed by generations of poverty and backwardness. The immediate result was "one of the most heated controversies in American history." Jackson, like Mathews before him, claimed to have received a letter confirming "that the president of the United States approved his proposal for the invasion of the Floridas." Monroe denied it, and "it was never possible to prove that President Monroe had authorized the 'Rhea Letter,'" as it was called. Never Possible to Prove: Madison's policy of plausible denial had been passed on to Monroe; he had used General Jackson the same way Madison had used "General" Mathews. Then, when this latest Florida ploy failed,

President Monroe disavowed Jackson just as President Madison had disowned Mathews earlier. The difference was that, unlike Mathews, Jackson would get his "ravange"—as president of the United States. Meanwhile Jackson, like Mathews before him, bellowed that the president of the United States was damned liar.

For nearly two hundred years the original Madison-Mathews dispute has been treated as inconsequential. In reality it, too, "afforded at once an epitome and a prophecy," in this case for one of the bitterest controversies of American history. The Jackson-Monroe dispute called into question the fundamental integrity of the president and the man who would be president. It raised profound questions about the abuse of American power not just in Spanish Florida, but in Washington. When we look at these two Florida controversies side by side, it is evident that the Madison-Mathews and Monroe-Jackson controversies are nearly identical. Monroe, like Madison before him, had authorized an unprovoked invasion of Florida in the false hope that killing and marauding down there would deliver Florida into U.S. hands without major military or political consequences. Then, when scandal, not capitulation, was the result, each president left the American whom he had sent on this sinister errand to take the heat. The difference was that Mathews was a spent force by the time Madison disavowed him, while Jackson, by the time Monroe disavowed him, was America's Hero on Horseback, its Man of Destiny.

Florida reveals both Jackson and Monroe to have been dishonorable, each in his own way. That double disgrace ever since has created a challenge for America's mythologizers. How to confect a version of events from which both Jackson and Monroe emerge blameless? The *Appleton's Annual Cyclopaedia and Register of Important Events of the Year 1877* summarized the cover story that is still the standard version. Since neither Monroe nor Jackson could be to blame, Monroe's Nixonesque disavowal is taken at face value: "The president was ill when Jackson's letter reached him, and does not seem to have given it due consideration. On referring to it a year later he could not remember that he had ever seen it, before." What about Jackson? He, too, emerges from this swamp of blood and lies with his boots as shiny as though he just got back from Sunday Bible class:

"There can be no doubt that, whatever the president's intention may have been . . . the general honestly considered himself authorized to take possession of Florida." Monroe, neither America's first nor last Teflon president, got away with it; he went on to be enshrined as the benign presiding genius of the Era of Good Feeling. And how could Congress punish Jackson, when he, too, was blameless? When the Military Committee of the U.S. House of Representatives issued a report documenting Jackson's many violations of U.S. law, the House rejected its findings by a vote of nearly two to one.

"All great world-historic facts and personages appear, so to speak, twice," Karl Marx wrote in a commentary on Hegel, "the first time as tragedy, the second time as farce." That may be true elsewhere, but as Jackson's rampage showed, events in Florida repeatedly unfold in the opposite direction, from farce to tragedy. Just as Menéndez and his massacres followed de Soto's farcical wanderings, the Mathews farce had been followed by full-fledged tragedy.

8

FLORIDA'S FAKE HISTORY

John Quincy Adams, acting as James Monroe's secretary of state, was the one who finally got Florida for the United States. He—like Jackson—would have laughed out loud at any claim that the United States "purchased" Florida. As everyone understood at the time, America finally grabbed away the whole of Florida by riding roughshod over the Spanish diplomatically as well as militarily.

Adams is often presented in gentlemanly contrast to the ruffian Jackson, but when it came to Florida he was as much a thug as Jackson was. When the Spanish ambassador asked for an inquiry into Jackson's outrages, Adams demanded an investigation into the behavior of Spanish officials. Had the Spanish been doing their job in Florida, he purported, there would have been no need for Jackson to ravage the place. Carrying this logic to its diplomatic extreme, he presented an ultimatum. Either the Spanish should make sure Florida no longer was a "post of annoyance," as he phrased it, or get out of Florida. Georgia, not Florida, was the real "post of annoyance." Had U.S. forces kept their side of the border orderly and peaceful, Florida would have been spared terror and devastation, but by then the Spanish faced a bigger threat than America's violent encroachments. From Mexico to Argentina independence forces were gaining strength.

While Spain fought to subdue its rebellious colonies, its officials feared, the United States might play the vulture once again, grabbing Texas and California and who knew what else. In America's covetousness of Florida, the Spanish perceived the chance to avert such a disaster. For three hundred years Florida had been a liability.

Could it now serve as a sacrificial pawn in a larger game? Spain had traded Florida away once before, in 1763, to get Cuba back from the British. Juan de Onis, the Spanish foreign minister, decided to give it a try. Following detailed negotiations, Spain agreed to relinquish all of Florida to the United States on the condition that the United States renounce all claims on Texas and the lands beyond, all the way to the Pacific Ocean, "forever."

In this case "forever" lasted twenty-six years. In 1845 Americans in Texas, modeling their revolt against Mexican rule on the West Florida Lone Star Republic, demanded to be annexed to the United States. President Polk, following President Jefferson's example, disregarded both America's treaty obligations and the U.S. Constitution. Falsely claiming that the United States itself had been attacked, Polk then went on to launch an unprovoked full-scale war of aggression. Mexico was compelled to cede to the United States all or parts of what today are the states of New Mexico, Arizona, Colorado, Utah, Nevada, Wyoming, and California. These conquests continued what had become a diplomatic-military tradition. Clever Europeans imagined they had dexterously bent these adolescent Americans to their purposes by getting them to sign some sinuously worded piece of paper. Then the Americans grabbed whatever they wanted anyway, according to "Originalist" notions that made—and still makes—America's acquisition of approximately one-quarter of its territory null and void.

In order to get the Spanish to relinquish Florida the United States additionally admitted its wrongdoing there, pledging to "cause satisfaction to be made for the injuries . . . suffered by the Spanish Officers, and individual Spanish inhabitants, by the late operations of the American Army in Florida." "Exonerating Spain from all demands in future, on account of the claims of their citizens to which the renunciations herein contained extend, and considering them entirely cancelled," it also undertook "to make satisfaction for the same, to an amount not exceeding five millions of dollars." In plain English, the United States pledged to pay its own citizens up to $5 million for any losses the Spanish government had inflicted on them, but what claim could Americans possibly have on Spain, when it was

Spain itself that had suffered losses at the hands of Americans? This, in essence, was a $5 million slush fund for all the "Patriots" who, in the course of subverting Spanish rule, claimed to have suffered loss or injury, and gone on to trump up claims against Spain. Had the treaty not declared these claims "entirely cancelled," various former marauders might have gone on pestering Spain in U.S. courts for decades to come. Spain, in turn, would have had grounds for delaying Florida's transfer to the United States.

That has not stopped generations of Americans from being taught that the United States purchased Florida fair and square. Anyone taking the trouble to read the actual treaty will find no mention whatsoever of any purchase. They will find that the treaty established America's western "boundary-line" as the Sabine River, which today is the border between the states of Louisiana and Texas. Though claims that American purchased it from Spain are fictional, the United States did pay dearly for Florida. In a speech he gave on the Fourth of July 1821, while still holding office as Monroe's secretary of state, Adams warned Americans of the costs, and dangers, of using violence to extend "freedom." "The fundamental maxims of her policy would insensibly change from liberty to force," he warned. What troubled him were the corrupting effects reliance on violence would have on the American people. America "might become the dictatress of the world," he conceded; "she would no longer be the ruler of her own spirit."

By the time the Spanish left Florida more than one-quarter of a millennium had passed since Pedro Menéndez de Avilés established St. Augustine. After all those centuries the total "Spanish" population of Florida was only about three thousand. Even they were mostly descendants of people who owed their presence to British, not Spanish, rule. The adaptable Minorcans had survived British mistreatment and Spanish neglect. Under the U.S. flag they would flourish. A few hundred other people of various exotic origins also stayed when the Spanish left, almost all of them clustered around St. Augustine and Pensacola and on Amelia Island. Virtually everyone else in Florida by 1821 was American—either born in the United States or of American origin. The killers and the killed, the enslaved and those who enslaved them, those who acquired millions of acres and those who lost everything: they were Americans one and all. The incoming whites, led and epitomized by Andrew Jackson, were American. The victims of U.S. rule were American too. What made these victims seem "un-American" was, simply, that most of them were not white.

It was a curiosity that Yellowstone, thanks to the Louisiana Purchase, was U.S. territory before Florida's beaches were. Annexation of Florida, now that it finally happened, was hailed as a triumph of symmetry as well as freedom. As Professor Isaac Cox put it, in his attempt to fit Florida into the frontier schema of conquest, "the southeast corner of the United States was filled out" now that "the Power of the Past," Spain, had been "constrained to hand its strategic but useless northern outpost over to the Power of the Future." That was Florida all right, "strategic but useless." Now Americans faced the same challenge that earlier befuddled the French, British, and Spanish. Whatever to do with the place?

Andrew Jackson gouged such a lasting mark there that it is hard to believe he visited Florida only three times. In 1814 he advanced on Pensacola, then marched his troops out of Florida in order to catch the British at New Orleans. He returned again in 1818; the memory of the ravages he instigated in the course of that foray still darkens the reputation of the United States in Spain and Britain. Finally, in 1821, he returned to serve as Florida's first American governor. That sojourn was also brief; within six months Jackson abandoned his post. He had anticipated that Florida would be an early proving ground for the "spoils system" he later used to fill federal posts when he became president, but in this matter, too, President Monroe pulled a fast one, appointing his own cronies to the most lucrative posts. "Had I anticipated this," Jackson complained, "I should not have accepted the Government." Contrary to his expectations, Florida also failed to provide enrichment in the private sector. "It is impossible under existing circumstances that any business can be profitable," he complained. Andrew Jackson finally had noticed what the Spanish and the British had learned earlier. Florida did not create capital; it consumed it.

The imposition of American white race supremacy in Florida, beginning with Jackson and protégés like Clinch and Gadsden, raises many disturbing questions about America's past and our understanding of it. One of them is at what point scholarship shades into complicity with the crimes of history. The problem is not merely that supposedly factual accounts endlessly perpetuate myths, such as the "purchase" of Florida. The deep contempt Florida's new American rulers felt for its people became a staple of what Americans were taught about their country's expansion. A collection of "runaway slaves, renegade whites and Indians, and foreign adventurers and pirates" is how one text book dating from 1971 defines the people who passed without their consent from Spanish to American control in 1821. Another modern historian goes so far as to describe Florida as populated principally by "criminally inclined persons" at the time of annexation.

Dehumanizing its "adventurers, fugitives, thieves, plunderers [and] robbers" helped justify the ensuing dispossession, murder, and enslavement of Florida's people, but by the time the United States annexed Florida, its pirates were mostly mythical. As for its "foreign adventurers," they apparently consisted exclusively of Arbuthnot and Ambrister. No "foreign adventurer" of any kind was ever again apprehended, let alone "punished," once Americans no longer needed that pretext to justify annexing Florida. The most revealing adjective in such passages is "runaway." Right across the twentieth century, in histories of the state of Florida, good slaves toil patiently; bad ones run away.

The myth of Floridian human defectiveness provided one justification for the inhumane policies the United States pursued there. The other great myth concerned national security. Virtually every book dealing with U.S. annexation describes the threat Florida's Indians and blacks supposedly posed to the security of the United States as though such a threat actually existed. Not one of those histories documents a specific instance of any such attack occurring after the War of 1812 ended. That is because the flow of terror was constantly in the opposite direction—from the United States into Florida. The more verbally dexterous of the accusers, notably Jackson himself, took care to denounce Florida's people for their attacks on "U.S. citizens," rather than on U.S. territory.

The truth was that these attacks occurred inside Florida, in response to violence inflicted on them by intruding Americans, yet in their eagerness to manufacture justifications for their aggression, Americans blamed unrelated mishaps on the U.S. side of the border on those they themselves were plotting to attack. In early 1816 fire broke out in the Georgia home of Benjamin Hawkins, the U.S. Indian Agent. It was claimed that the alleged arsonists had come all the way from Florida to do it. "The latter report proved false—the negligence of a servant was responsible for the burning of Colonel Hawkins' house," it was soon discovered, "—but this fact did not deter preparations against the Negro Fort." Here, too, Florida "afforded at once an epitome and a prophecy," in this case of the periodic use of disinformation to justify aggression.

Details of the 1816 massacre were available almost as soon as it happened; newspapers and magazines, relying on Clinch's account, provided the horrific details. Then, in 1837, Congress at long last got around to conducting an investigation. In a report entitled "A View of the Action of the Federal Government in Behalf of Slavery," Congressman William Jay of New York drew attention to the misuse of taxpayers' dollars that killing all those people had entailed. The massacre, he pointed out, had marked a turning point in the American acquisition of Florida—the moment when the inhabitants of Florida became the principal targets of U.S. violence, as opposed to their nominal rulers, the Spanish. Upon examining the evidence, Jay found that the killings had an even larger significance. The massacre, he concluded, inaugurated a new period of U.S. governmental activism in which the federal authority subsidized and promoted the expansion of slavery instead of merely tolerating it.

The Florida massacre got more attention when another congressman, Joshua Reed Giddings of Ohio, laid out in detail the U.S. government's use of violence in Florida. It was, he pointed out, the first time the armed forces of the United States had been used to run down, kidnap, and enslave people whose sole crime was that "they had sought their own liberty." The victims, Giddings observed, had been defamed as well as murdered. The posthumous "epithets of 'outlaws,' 'pirates,' and 'murderers,'" he pointed out, were part of an effort "to cast opprobrium upon the character of men who, if judged by their love of liberty or their patriotism, would now occupy a position not less honorable in the history of our country than is assigned to the patriots of 1776." The evidence of the times proves Giddings right, yet historians have repeated those libels as though they were the truth for generations.

With the passage of time, passions supposedly abate; the truth supposedly emerges from the rubble of accusations and self-justifications. In Florida the reverse constantly happens. The criticisms of the killings at Negro Fort, grudgingly acknowledged at first, have been airbrushed out of the picture entirely. Since the end of World War II, three general histories of Florida have been published, each presenting a less truthful version of events than was available in 1839 or 1816, or in the book that came before it. J. E. Dovell's two-volume, 995-page *Florida: Historic, Dramatic, Contemporary*, published in 1952, contains thousands of citations. Not even in passing does the author mention any of the criticisms the Negro Fort Massacre provoked. The unfounded allegations that the U.S. assault on Negro Fort was an act of national self-defense are presented as fact. "Negro banditti roamed the country committing crimes and causing such alarm," the author states, "that General Edmund P. Gaines, Jackson's subordinate in the area, offered fifty dollars for each captive Negro to friendly Indians if the fort were subdued." In this as in other accounts, not one specific example of such roving bands ever committing such crimes is ever mentioned, let alone authenticated.

The second of the three histories, Charlton W. Tebeau's *A History of Florida*, appeared in 1971. By then Florida was being physically reshaped by giant construction projects: highways, marinas, new residential developments. Tebeau presented the 1816 massacre as an internal improvements project. Killing the people at Negro Fort, he stated, "removed any immediate danger to users of the river." Such an approach abuses the past. It also stains the future by providing a false moral context for what people do today. For nearly forty years Professor Tebeau, a beloved figure in Florida academe, imparted his version of the past to thousands of students. Many went on to shape events during one of the most important phases of Florida's history. To a greater or lesser extent, their actions would be shaped by the idea that Americans are, and always have been, entitled to sweep away whatever stands in their way, whether it be "criminally inclined persons" or an ecosystem. They would carry with them an idea of the past that was factually false, but also morally false in its portrayal of American thought and feeling, for Professor Tebeau, like many others, not only writes as though it is acceptable to massacre people. He writes as though throughout their history all Americans have always agreed that massacre is a justifiable technique for achieving American goals. That is not true. Events like the Negro Fort Massacre tore at the American soul, with stupendous and tragic results, yet Tebeau's book, too, contains not so much as a hint that the Negro Fort Massacre had any negative implications for America's future.

The New History of Florida was published in 1996 under the editorship of Professor Michael Gannon of the University of Florida. A collective effort, it, too, recycles as fact the unfounded allegations that Seminoles and their black allies conducted raids into Alabama and Georgia. The Negro Fort Massacre, it goes on to relate, "did not end the problem, and in March 1818, General Jackson again invaded Spanish Florida." As late as 1996 blacks and Indians living peacefully together remains "the problem." In this book, as in the others, there is not so much as a hint that the use of the U.S. Army and Navy to expand slavery helped contribute to the national crisis that in the end ravaged Florida, almost destroyed the United States, and killed more Americans than the two world wars combined. That the U.S. attacks provoked a forty-year war in Florida is never acknowledged either, in any of these heavy volumes.

The same pattern of deception concerning Florida prevails in the many books on Andrew Jackson published each decade. *Meet Andrew Jackson* is typical of the primers put into the hands of American grade schoolers generation after generation. What lessons are the boys and girls of America to draw from having met Andrew Jackson? One lesson is that it was okay to kill the "two Englishmen" because he "believed that these two men had stiffed up the Seminoles against the United States." Children who read this book and the countless ones like it are taught, falsely and inevitably, that "Spain sold Florida to the United States." Having excused Jackson's murders in Florida, it goes on to present slavery as a benign institution. There would be nothing odd about that had this book been published by a regional press in 1850 or in 1950, but *Meet Andrew Jackson* was published in New York in 1967, at the height of the civil rights era.

Meet Andrew Jackson does let its young readers know that Jackson killed some people in Florida. That makes it a more reliable source of information than *The Age of Jackson* by the late Arthur M. Schlesinger Jr., who adopted a reverse-Schoolcraft approach to dealing with Jackson's outrages. In whatever empty corner he looked, Schoolcraft perceived a place where de Soto had pitched camp. Schlesinger surveys the bloodied terrain that Jackson pillaged and finds no trace of his hero's misdeeds anywhere. This allows him, in turn, to pretend that Jackson's emergence as America's dominant politician came out of the blue, as a surprise.

"Who was General Andrew Jackson, the new popular favorite?" Schlesinger asks. "In the War of 1812 he had shown great energy and resource in putting down some Indian uprisings, and in 1815, after the treaty of peace had been signed, he won at New Orleans the greatest American victory of the war." And after that? "For the decade past, his life had been mainly that of a Tennessee gentleman, living on a fine plantation near Nashville, entertaining his friends, racing his horse and heatedly talking politics," Schlesinger tells us.

Here the question of complicity in historical misrepresentation becomes inescapable. Following his 1815 victory at New Orleans, Jackson was deeply involved in military matters throughout 1816 and 1817, including the attacks he orchestrated in Florida. Jackson's 1818 Florida invasion was one of the major events of that period, not only militarily, but also politically because of the legal and constitutional controversies it aroused. As a result of his Florida exploits, Jackson was immediately embroiled in the political and diplomatic crises his killings of Arbuthnot and Ambrister provoked, and then embroiled for years after that in the national controversy over whether or not President Monroe had authorized his invasion. In 1821 Jackson had become the first American governor of Florida, a fact Schlesinger never mentions. Then, in 1824, he ran for president of the United States, an event he also does not mention. Although John Quincy Adams snatched the presidency away from him that first time, the disputed 1824 election remains one of the notable events of U.S. political history.

The period from 1815 and 1825 was crucial for Jackson and decisive for America. Concealing all that, Schlesinger purports that between 1815 and 1825 Jackson had spent his time relaxing. He portrays Jackson as a political innocent who, at the time he finally became president in 1829, had "experience neither in national nor in state politics." Jackson's experience in national and state politics went back to the 1790s, when he represented Tennessee in Washington, first in the House of Representatives, next in the Senate. How many other presidents have reached that high office having served as senator, representative, and governor, as well as a general in the army? Schlesinger does momentarily allude to his hero's Florida ravages, though only to discredit Jackson's adversaries. "His political opponents, building ardently upon incidents of his military past," the revered historian informs us, "managed almost to read into the records of history a legend of his rude violence and uncontrolled irascibility." A legend? Jackson's order to "blow up" Negro Fort is not mentioned, nor is his killing of Arbuthnot and Ambrister. A knowledgeable reader would assume that, at the least, Jackson's role in the Seminole War would be mentioned; that reader would be wrong. Not even the word "Florida" appears in Schlesinger's index.

Schlesinger's purpose, by his own account, was to demonstrate that the "heritage of Andrew Jackson, as President Roosevelt has said, is 'his unending contribution to the vitality of our democracy.'" Still quoting FDR, in a book published immediately after the U.S. victory in World War II, Schlesinger declares that "the enemies [Jackson] encountered" and "the victories he won are part and parcel" of the "victories of those who have lived in all the generations that have followed." Were killing Indians, enslaving blacks, violating treaties, and launching unprovoked military attacks during peacetime really "part and parcel" of the war to defeat Hitler and the Nazis? Were the "enemies" massacred at Negro Fort really the equivalent of the enemies Americans fought at Iwo Jima and on the beaches of Normandy? Schlesinger's Jackson fable won the Pulitzer Prize; it enjoyed the same vast popularity Washington Irving's tale about Ponce de León earlier had and, just like his Fountain of Youth fable, it propagated a false version of what happened in Florida, and what it meant for America, that came to be accepted, and repropagated, as fact.

Andrew Jackson's "Time Relaxing," 1815–1825

Date	Event
January 1815	Battle of New Orleans
May 1816	Jackson orders Negro Fort "blown up"
September 1816	Negro Fort Massacre
1816–1821	On his orders, U.S. troops secretly remain in Florida
March 1818	Jackson invades Florida
April 1818	Overriding military court, he orders Ambrister killed; Arbuthnot hanged
May 1818	Jackson attacks Pensacola, drives Spanish authorities from Florida
June 1818	He establishes illegal U.S. military rule at Pensacola
July 1818	Reentering U.S. politics, he falsely declares Florida victory
1818–1819	Jackson's Florida invasion bitterly polarizes U.S. politics
1821	Jackson first U.S. governor of Florida
1822	Jackson elected U.S. senator
1823	Continuing bitter controversy pits Jackson against Monroe
1824	Senator Jackson nominated for president
November 1824	Jackson wins most popular votes
December 1824	Jackson gets most electoral votes
February 1825	"Corrupt Bargain" in Congress denies Jackson presidency
October 1825	Jackson resigns Senate, resumes quest for presidency
1828	Jackson wins presidency on second try
1829	Inaugurated with "experience neither in national nor in state politics."

Unlike Schlesinger, Robert V. Remini, author of *Andrew Jackson and His Indian Wars*, published in 2001, does mention the killings at Negro Fort, though only to replace the old fictions with a new one. For 185 years every account specified that two leaders were killed, one of them black, the other Choctaw. In this newly invented version, the number of leaders killed suddenly becomes vague, but Remini, a longtime history professor at the University of Illinois and official historian of the United States House of Representatives, is not vague about their skin color. They were "black leaders," he states, stripping the events at Negro Fort of their multiracial significance. "So much for the 'negro menace,' " he adds.

It is a continuing process. In 2006 Sean Wilentz, a professor of history at Princeton University, produced another of the Jackson-Florida refictionalizations; "the nation's southern border," Wilentz declares, "[was] threatened by restive Creeks, Cherokees, Choctaws, and Chickasaws as well as the continuing Spanish possession of Florida." He adds: "Bands of Indians with settlements that straddled the Florida border . . . raided and harassed American settlements in south Georgia and escaped into Florida when Americans pursued them," recycling an accusation that, in this book as in all the others, is not supported by one single instance of any such event ever having happened. He then adds the long-discredited accusation that "the Spanish, goaded by British agents, were encouraging the attacks."

The Spanish, however, switch sides two sentences later. As in Remini's account, the victims also switch race: "250 fugitive slaves had taken over an old British fort," Wilentz writes, not mentioning the Indians there or considering the fact that many of those at Negro Fort were free men. He then adds a stunning new fiction: "With Spanish support, Americans destroyed the so-called Negro Fort and wiped out its inhabitants." With no sense of self-contradiction, he then transforms the Spanish back into enemies as he describes Jackson's unprovoked and gratuitous attack on "the Spanish command center at Pensacola." He concludes his account as Jackson concluded his Florida misadventure, by propagating the same ludicrous lie: "Jackson had promised, back in March, to complete his Florida campaign in sixty days. It took him slightly longer than that—but his triumph had come to include winning de facto military control over all of Florida." Though eyewitnesses portrayed Jackson as angry and frustrated following his failure at the Suwannee and his quixotic descent upon the hapless Spaniards at Pensacola, Wilentz nearly 190 years after the fact describes him as "flushed with victory," and why not? His rampage helped "pave the way to America's purchase of Florida."

The myth is that the United States "purchased" Florida. The reality, as one of Florida's first American jurists, Judge Isaac H. Bronson, put it, is that America's acquisition of Florida was "an episode in the general history of the nation, which, as an American citizen, I could wish might remain unwritten." The judge got his wish. It did go unwritten. Florida provided a cautionary tale of the destruction Americans are capable of unleashing on blameless peoples in the name of freedom, but it was a lesson that never would be learned because it would never be taught.

Way back in 1882 *The Critic*, a New York literary review, revealed why it was so "difficult to ascertain the truth about Florida from any published writings. For the most part," the magazine explained, "it has been concealed by one or all of three different methods: by intensely magnifying small facts, by withholding great facts and by actual misrepresentation." What had been true, by then, for nearly one hundred years would be equally true for the next hundred years and more, to the point that the broad outline of Florida history, as generally understood, is essentially fictional.

PART THREE

OSCEOLA'S HEAD

I would allow them to remain.

—General Thomas Sidney Jesup, 1838,
urging an end to ethnic cleansing in Florida

9

GOVERNOR DUVAL'S
CONSPIRACY

Head east from the Negro Fort toward Jacksonville and you pass towns, wide spots in the road, and former tracks through the forest whose names immortalize forgotten captains and corporals in the long war to "clear" Florida. Lloyd, Lamont, Greenville, Newbern, Day, Smith, Mann, Sanderson, Macclenney, Baldwin, Bryceville dot the way. Located in Duval County, Jacksonville was to the nineteenth century what Orlando is to the twenty-first century, the Florida metropolis where the possibilities and contradictions of a particular era converged. Everyone knows Jacksonville was named for Andrew Jackson, but who gave Duval County its name?

William Pope DuVal was Jackson's successor as Florida's governor. Like James Gadsden and Duncan Clinch, DuVal is one of the forgotten protagonists who made Florida what it is. Born into a poor farming family in Virginia, he made his mark as a politician in Kentucky. After serving as governor of Florida, he joined another former governor—Sam Houston of Tennessee—to seek more fame and fortune under the Texas Lone Star flag. DuVal's victories were celebrated as triumphs of American individualism but the federal government subsidized his every move, and remove. He is buried in a federal cemetery in Washington, D.C.

As hot-tempered in his youth as Andrew Jackson, and as devoted in later life as George Mathews to making a good story better with each retelling, Governor DuVal became famous for one particular anecdote. It concerned the time his father ordered his "good-for-nothing" son to get a log for the family fire. DuVal came back with the log twenty years later. In the meantime he had crossed the mountains to Kentucky, turned himself into a lawyer, and gotten himself elected to Congress. "Well," his father supposedly remarked when he finally reappeared with the log, "you were long enough getting it." In Florida, DuVal became what only later would be called a Carpetbagger—an outsider who, thanks to his connections with powerful outsiders, was awarded a post that made him powerful too. DuVal was appointed to one of the first U.S. judgeships there, but he owes his place in Florida's history to Jackson's impetuousness. When Jackson abruptly left Florida after than less than six months as governor, President Monroe had to find a replacement quickly.

DuVal's initial challenge was coping with the many problems Jackson claimed falsely to have solved, then coping with the host of new problems Jackson had created. DuVal himself then went on to pile tinder higher and higher on the smoldering conflict in Florida. As governor, DuVal presided over the period of nominal peace that separated Jackson's initial ravages (the First Seminole War) from the next violent phase of the U.S. subjugation, known as the Second Seminole War. In reality those "wars" were but different episodes of the same conflict, though while DuVal was governor intimidation and trickery—rather than simple violence—were used to deprive the Seminoles of their lands.

The gathering catastrophe might conceivably have been averted had the young United States of America been a nation that kept its word. Article V of the treaty with Spain stipulated that "the inhabitants of the territories which His Catholic Majesty cedes to the United States" were to be "admitted to the enjoyment of all the privileges, rights, and immunities of the citizens of the United States." At that time the single largest group of Florida's "inhabitants" consisted of those whom Congressman Joshua Giddings called *The Exiles of Florida*, a term which accurately described why these people had sought freedom there. No one could deny they were inhabitants of Florida, but the United States nonetheless resorted to a multitude of strategies which ensured that only white males would be allowed the "full enjoyment" of the rights guaranteed in the treaty.

This idea that the Indians must be expunged was not, as most people today assume, some age-old, deeply ingrained belief. It was a relatively new development in American thought and, like the proposition that all men are created equal, the notion that America's original inhabitants should be purged from the land was the brain child of Thomas Jefferson. Jefferson had long believed that the Indians should be treated as "our brethren of the same land." In January 1803 he officially proposed a policy of ethnic integration aimed at "bringing together their and our settlements" for the purpose of "preparing them ultimately to participate in the benefits of our governments." Following a period of cultural and economic assimilation, Jefferson predicted in a secret message to Congress, the Indians would "incorporate with us as citizens of the United States." That was before Napoleon offered his deal. By July 1803 Jefferson, abandoning his prior convictions, had decided to use "the acquisition of Louisiana [as] the means of tempting all our Indians on the east side of the Mississippi to remove to the West." The question, then as later, was what means of temptation would work. As Florida would show, Jeffersonian rhetoric would not turn the trick; Jacksonian violence would be necessary.

As territorial governor, DuVal was responsible for setting up the institutions that would prepare Florida for statehood, including a legislative council. Initially the council met alternately at St. Augustine and Pensacola, but delegates died trekking the wilderness of northern Florida, trying to get from one town to the other. Politicians drowned as well, trying to get to the annual meeting by sea. A new capital, equidistant from St. Augustine and Pensacola, seemed the logical solution, so DuVal named two commissioners to search for a site. It took the Pensacola commissioner, John Lee Williams, twenty-three days to reach St. Marks, a distance of about 215 miles. He and the St. Augustine commissioner, Dr. William H. Simmons, soon found a locale that delighted them, in part because it didn't look like "Florida" at all. "Every vegetable cultivated here is luxuriant, the cotton fields exceed by half any I have seen before; the sugar cane is better than the Mississippi ground affords," Simmons exulted. The area was so pleasing for two reasons. Geologically, the site was not part of the great limestone monolith atop which the rest of Florida sits. The other reason was that previous settlers from the United States had prepared the land and carefully nurtured what they planted there.

The most prominent of these entrepreneurs, a well-respected landowner originally from Georgia, was named Enemathla and of Creek origin. Upon their arrival at Tallahassee, Enemathla received his two visitors with every courtesy. Following a feast, young men entertained the visitors with a ball game. Only after having become the recipients of these kindnesses did Simmons and Williams inform Enemathla that he and all his people would have to give up this land, and all they had built and possessed there, and be transported to some other place; Americans would decide where later. Meantime, they informed their host, he and his people should prepare to abandon their vegetable gardens, their cotton fields, and their stands of sugar cane because these two visitors had decided this land should become the site of the white man's new city. Enemathla proposed a diplomatic solution. The land around them was almost unpeopled. Surely these two wise gentlemen, if they only searched a little more, could find an even better site for their settlement. Simmons and Williams went through the motions of complying. Then they informed him that, no, they had not found a place that better pleased them.

The full magnitude of American avarice was unveiled in September 1823, when the Seminoles were summoned en masse to a place south of St. Augustine called Moultrie Creek. As these people gathered to be informed of their fate, the moment was steeped in hope and tragedy. This was the greatest—and also the first and last—such general conclave that would be permitted to occur. Governor DuVal was the presiding officer, but James Gadsden stage-managed the affair. After rebuilding Negro Fort, Gadsden had been promoted first to colonel, then to adjutant general; even so, in 1822 Gadsden quit the U.S. Army. On Army orders he had searched Florida for the best places to establish more U.S. military installations. That had allowed him, at taxpayers' expense, to identify the choicest spots for real estate speculation. Resigning his commission, James Gadsden set out to cash in on the contacts he had made in the military.

Well aware of Gadsden's usefulness, DuVal put him in charge of orchestrating the most important event in the U.S. subjugation of Florida so far. It consisted of getting Florida's nonwhite inhabitants to agree to what Americans later called the Treaty of Moultrie Creek. The objective of imposing a "treaty" on the Seminoles, rather than simply seizing their land, was to turn the dispossessed into collaborators in their own dispossession. Once Enemathla and the others had been cajoled into approving a Florida-wide "treaty," the piecemeal theft of their lands could be replaced by wholesale confiscation. Foisting on these people a document none of them could read was also morally convenient. Later, when "Indian-givers" claimed they had been tricked, the new owners could lecture them on the importance of respecting solemn agreements, and then have them "punished," in Governor DuVal's words, for not "keeping their promise." This form of land grabbing also had the advantage of making the federal government and U.S. Army responsible for evicting the Seminoles, sparing the new owners the expense and danger of doing it themselves.

Governor DuVal wanted a big turnout at Moultrie Creek: Gadsden made it happen. During the summer of 1823 he traversed the wilds of northwest Florida; in September he reappeared at St. Augustine leading hundreds of Seminole notables. He had persuaded them to travel all that way by promising that, once they did parlay with the governor, their problems could be solved on the basis of honesty and mutual respect. Gadsden did not inform them that he himself already had written the treaty they supposedly were going to negotiate and that it took away from them just about everything.

More than 350 of Florida's nonwhite leaders converged on Moultrie Creek; it was the greatest such conclave ever to occur. The day Governor DuVal opened the talks, entrepreneurs at St. Augustine sold tickets for boat rides down to Moultrie Creek so people could observe the festivities. Joshua Nichols Glenn, a visiting Methodist preacher, got there, as he put it, "in a very comfortable Boat—accompanyed by many other gentelmen and ladies in other boats." The delegation had chosen Enemathla to be its spokesman. Reverend Glenn renders the name as Nehlematha and, like other

Americans, assumes he had powers he did not. "King Nehlematha," he continued, "came forward and Shook hands and after him all the chiefs in rotation." Following these civilities Enemathla made an important declaration. "The King," Glenn writes, "then observed that he considered us gentlemen as Fathers and Brethren and the ladies as Mothers and Sisters." DuVal and Gadsden "then conducted the chiefs in the bark House they had bilt to hold their talk in and after they had all Smoked together they held their first talk."

At Moultrie Creek, Enemathla and the others for the first time were presented with the American ultimatum. It provided that they would be stripped of all human as well as property rights. "The undersigned chiefs and warriors, for themselves and their tribes . . . do cede and relinquish all claim or title which they may have to the whole territory of Florida," was the way Article I of Gadsden's text put it. At a stroke the rights guaranteed to these inhabitants of Florida by the treaty with Spain were abrogated, ostensibly at the request of the victims themselves. Gadsden's document went on to specify that the Seminoles, once removed from their lands, were to be "concentrated and confined" in a barren, landlocked wasteland in central Florida; Governor DuVal himself described it as "by far the poorest and most miserable region I ever beheld."

The Seminoles arrived at Moultrie Creek with flags flying and drums beating. By the time they left, they were pleading with their new masters to be so liberal as to allow their children to learn to read and write. Even more than the request for a school, their plea for a blacksmith is a most telling reference. The day was gone when these "savages" were capable of survival in the Florida wilderness. Just like white Americans, they needed plows to till what scraps of land they could. They needed guns to hunt what game they could find. They also needed imported iron and other metals, since Florida had none, but the treaty also forbade them to trade, as they had traditionally, with the Spanish in Cuba and the British in the Bahamas. DuVal and Gadsden had taken a self-sufficient people and stripped them of their means of sustenance as well as their dignity.

When it came to orchestrating this pageant of dispossession Gadsden's most important enabler was Colonel Gad Humphreys, the U.S. Agent of Indian Affairs. Ostensibly such agents worked on behalf of the Indians; in Florida as elsewhere their actual function was to get them to give the Americans whatever they wanted while putting up as little resistance as possible. The "dishonor to the American character," as Jefferson phrased it, did not stop at that. The U.S. Agent of Indian Affairs also used the "negotiations" to enrich himself. The last section of the Treaty of Moultrie Creek read as follows: "The undersigned chiefs and warriors, for themselves and tribes, have expressed to the commissioners their unlimited confidence in their agent, Col. Gad Humphreys . . . and, as an evidence of their gratitude for their services and humane treatment, and brotherly attentions to their wants, request that one mile square, embracing the improvements of Enehe Mathla, at Tallahassee (said improvements to be considered as the centre) be conveyed, in fee simple, as a present to Col. Gad Humphreys." Enemathla's abundant fields and blossoming orchards were now to be given to the U.S. official who had engineered the details of his dispossession. In an addendum it was stipulated that "five hundred dollars shall be awarded to Neo Mathla, as a compensation for the improvements abandoned by him, as well as to meet the expenses he will unavoidably be exposed to, by his own removal, and that of his connections."

Enemathla never would get what he was promised. Dispossessed and destitute, he and "his connections" were still waiting for his new land and five hundred dollars at the end of 1824 as politicians, speculators and provisioners crowded into the raw new town. Arriving to preside over the first legislative council to be held in Tallahassee's log capitol, Governor DuVal learned that Enemathla, meeting in council with other Seminole leaders, had announced he would not remove his people until Governor DuVal personally came to see him. In *A History of Florida*, the textbook that was required reading for generations of Florida school children, the influential Florida author Caroline Mays Brevard gives the subsequently made-up version of what happened when DuVal and Enemathla did meet. "The governor cried out that Enemathla was a traitor, sprang upon him as he was speaking, seized him by the throat and put him out of the council. Then," she adds, "the governor stood on the platform and spoke to the Indians. He told them Enemathla should no longer be chief, for he tried to keep the Indians from keeping their promise." Following his humiliation, Brevard assures her young readers, Enemathla "never recovered from his mortification at the treatment he had received." "So," this account concludes cheerily, "the Tallahassees passed away from their old fields, leaving only the musical names of their dwelling places to tell of their long possession of the land." "DuVal's Courageous Visit" is the title given to this account of his assault on the Seminole leader.

Governor DuVal was a gifted self-publicist. His tales were too good not to be plagiarized, so as if on cue Washington Irving reappears on the Florida literary scene, once again to misrepresent the tragic events unfolding there. In his latest Florida fiction Irving took Governor DuVal's conspiracy to dispossess Enemathla and the others and turned it into a parable of American virtue and generosity. In "The Conspiracy of Neamathla" the first thing Irving does to trivialize Enemathla and his people is to rob them of their connection to the United States, and so rob the reader of any understanding of who they were and why they reacted as they did to the imposition of U.S. rule. In this telling these people aren't refugees from the United States. They are the degenerate descendants of the aboriginal Floridians—in reality, extinct for generations. "From the time of the chimerical cruisings of Old Ponce de León in search of the Fountain of Youth" right up to the present day, Washington Irving declares, these "Seminoles" had been roaming around Florida, causing nothing but trouble.

He goes on to transform Enemathla the man of peace into a deceitful man of violence; simultaneously DuVal is changed from trickster into a philanthropic idealist, eager to establish schools so that the Seminoles' children "should be instructed like the children of white men." Instead of welcoming DuVal's kindly efforts, Irving has the Seminoles—who had begged for a school teacher at Moultrie Creek—spurning DuVal's kindly offer. "To know how to read and write is very good for the white man but very bad for red men," he has one of his fictional Seminoles warn the governor. "It makes white men better, but red men worse."

Irving then has his fictional Seminole give DuVal a lesson in the inherent superiority of the white race. "I know you white men say we all come from the same mother and father, but you are mistaken. We have a tradition handed down from our forefathers, and we believe it," he continues, "that the Great Spirit, when he undertook to make men, made the black man; it was his first attempt, and . . . he soon saw he had bungled, so he decided to try again . . . and made the red man. [That] was not exactly what he wanted. So he tried once more, and made the white man; and then he was satisfied." Irving's Seminole chief goes on to warn that attempts to create racial equality violate the will of God. To prove it, Irving puts another supposed Seminole tradition into the mouth of his fictional interlocutor.

According to this "tradition," the Great Spirit, having created white, red, and black men, offers them three different boxes containing three different kinds of implements. "The first," Irving explains, "was filled with books, and maps, and papers; the second with bows and arrows, knives and tomahawks; the third with spades, axes, hoes and hammers." "The white man, being the favorite, had the first choice," and chooses the books, maps, and papers. Next, the Indian chooses his bow and arrow. "As to the black man," Irving relates, "he had no choice left, but to put up with the box of tools." In "The Conspiracy of Neamathla," Washington Irving provides supposedly independent validation of what the white man wants to believe, that white men alone are entitled to the rights lauded in America's founding documents. He invents a moral universe in which to do good is the sin. The victim, not the one who victimizes, is the cheat. The great convenience of this role reversal is that the white man's victims now provide the justification for his crimes. "We must go according to the wishes of the Great Spirit," Irving's "chief" cautions the do-gooder DuVal, "or we shall get into trouble."

As Irving had every reason to know, Enemathla and the others were recent migrants from the United States. In their own memoirs and speeches DuVal, Gadsden, Clinch and the others, including Andrew Jackson, never suggest any primordial Seminole attachment to the land in Florida. They present the Seminoles as a motley combination of "runaway slaves" and "renegade Creeks." The text of the

Treaty of Moultrie Creek, among multitudinous other sources, proves that the Seminoles placed a high value on education. In this supposed factual account the Great Spirit would appear to have informed the Seminoles of the existence of white and black men before Europeans and Africans arrived in the New World, indeed before the Seminoles, who begin to emerge as a group only in the 1700s, themselves existed. In a trademark falsification Irving also unilaterally introduces the idea that Enemathla was an old man, the same way he had thirty years earlier with Ponce de León. In the authentic documentation of the time Enemathla is described as "honest and bold, of strong mind and character," also as "tall and of fine bearing." By transforming him into a sullen old man, Irving completes his fictionalization of Enemathla as the degenerate protagonist of a vanishing epoch.

To explore Florida's past is to make many discoveries. The first is how systematically "history" diverges from fact. The second is how deeply ingrained the role of violence is. The third, and certainly the least expected, is how extraordinarily decisive the tales of Washington Irving have been in sustaining false beliefs about Florida's past. Until the 1850s most writings on Florida reflect the controversy which U.S. activities there provoked. Then in 1855 Washington Irving, who never stepped foot in Florida during the times he purports to describe, and makes up his story only after all the supposed participants including DuVal are dead, publishes his strange and unfounded tale. Thereafter scholarly histories of Florida along with educational text books increasingly exclude documented facts which disagree with Irving's lies. These lies, in turn, go on to become the accepted truth of the twenty-first century. Washington Irving left traces of his narrative genius on many landscapes, but it was Florida's destiny to carry the triumph of illusion to a new extreme. When it comes to New York, no one considers fictional characters like Rip Van Winkle or Ichabod Crane to be actual men who lived and breathed. In Florida Irving's fictionalized Ponce and fictionalized Enemathla become figures of "history," driving out the memory of those who actually subdued Florida.

Unlike Washington Irving, Ralph Waldo Emerson took the trouble to go to Florida and see what was happening there with his own eyes. A young clergyman at the time, the philosopher-essayist traveled by sailing ship to St. Augustine, then made his way overland to Tallahassee. "In the journey thither," Emerson reported, he slept "three nights under the pine trees." "The trees, the bushes talk to me," he noted in blank verse that foreshadowed Walt Whitman, "And the small fly that whispers in my ear." Like many future visitors Emerson was impressed most by the mosquitoes, describing how

> *Dulcimer mosquitoes in the woods*
> *Hum their sly secrets in unwilling ears*
> *Which like all gossip leave a smart behind.*

After observing firsthand the workings of the U.S. system of government being implanted there, Emerson formed his own judgment of the Florida Governor DuVal was creating. A gang of "public officers, land speculators and desperados" had taken control of everything, he concluded.

Emerson was right to put "public officers" at the top of his list. The rhetoric was of freedom-loving heroes fighting off bloodthirsty savages in order to tame the frontier with the sweat of their brow. In reality fortune and misfortune alike depended on whether the U.S. government meddled for you or against you. While those they dispossessed starved in their "confinement and concentration" zone, Florida's public officers served up a feast of free land and favors to the "speculators and desperados," reserving the most lavish of these giveaways for themselves. When the government gave out land, DuVal and his friends got the land. When it handed out money, they funneled the money into their own pockets. When Florida's new nabobs speculated in slaves and real estate, the government bailed them out when the bubble burst. When they provoked violence, the U.S. Army rescued them from the consequences of their brutality and avarice.

DuVal was the linchpin of this antidemocratic as well as race-based system of patronage, privilege, corruption and repression. As Emerson put it, in an apt and homey phrase, "Governor DuVal is the button on which all things are hung." Others, when it came to metaphors, preferred nipples. "We have all been here like a litter of hungry suckling pigs," observed one of Tallahassee's new nabobs, "squalling and rooting each other from the teats." Thanks to stolen land and stolen labor, but thanks most of all to the U.S. government, people like DuVal himself, James Gadsden and Colonel Clinch for a time grew rich. Once rich, they imagined themselves to be blue-blooded as well.

Clinch got one of the more dramatic makeovers. The gentrification began with the formal portrait Clinch himself commissioned as soon as he got a hold of enough money to hire an artist. Like Schlesinger's biography of Jackson, the Clinch portrait excludes any Florida reference of any kind. Unbesmirched by mud or blood, or even the presence of a palmetto, Colonel Clinch poses wearing a gilded uniform General Washington might have found a tad too resplendent. Even though Clinch's birthplace was a Nash County, North Carolina, farmhouse and his parents were hardscrabble migrants from Virginia, his biography, when finally published, was entitled *Aristocrat in Uniform*. As a result of his "campaign against the Negro Fort," it states inter alia, "Lieutenant Colonel Duncan Lamont Clinch had won a deserved rest." As with many other books on Florida, the most startling revelation is the date. This whitewash of the man who conducted the Negro Fort Massacre in 1816 was published in 1963. Like the massacre, the biography was government funded, published at Florida taxpayers' expense, copyrighted by the Board of Commissioners of State Institutions of Florida.

When Florida passed into U.S. hands, Clinch was named commander of all U.S. Army forces there. Before basing himself permanently in Florida, Clinch took another step toward turning himself into the aristocrat depicted in the painting. He bought five slaves, two of them children taken from their mothers. Clinch's accounting of his human property illustrates that, by then, many slaves had white fathers. According to his sworn affidavit Daniel, twenty-eight years old; Wallace, nineteen; and Alfred, a seven-year-old boy, were all of "yellow complexion." A pioneer as well as a paradigm of the Florida method of taxpayer-subsidized self-enrichment, Clinch went on to acquire thousands of acres of land, but Americans were not the only beneficiaries of government handouts. In 1824, even as DuVal was tricking Enemathla out of his one square mile, Congress gave as an outright gift thirty-six square miles of land there to a foreigner who would never set eyes on Florida. His name was Marie-Joseph-Paul-Yves-Roch-Gilbert du Motier; Americans knew him better as Lafayette. In honor of his services during the War of Independence, Congress authorized Lafayette to take possession of an entire "township," as a tract of that magnitude was called, anywhere in the United States. Florida's future governor Richard Keith Call, then Florida's territorial delegate in Washington, persuaded the eminent French friend of America to take his township at Tallahassee, where a Gallic version of the usual Florida failure unfolded.

"A number of Frenchmen were sent to colonize the site and to introduce the culture of grapes, olives, figs and silk," notes Dovell in his history, "but for various reasons the project failed." "Hopes that the illustrious Frenchman might come to Florida never materialized," Professor Tebeau likewise acknowledges, "and he eventually sold it to speculators." No history mentions why Lafayette, who could have taken his township in areas where land was more valuable, chose Florida. Lafayette loathed slavery. He aimed to demonstrate that agriculture could prosper without it, and Lafayette failed. By the time he died in 1834, America had embittered Lafayette. "I would never have drawn my sword in the cause of America if I could have conceived thereby that I was founding a land of slavery," he wrote.

The Lafayette land grant at Tallahassee provides an early study in the hidden costs of racism in Florida. It also epitomized the economic irrationality on which U.S. rule was founded. While nonwhites like Enemathla who knew how to make the land flourish were deprived of all they had, fair-skinned foreigners with no idea how to make it productive got land for free. Among the Europeans seeking their fortunes in "Lafayetteville," as it was sometimes called, was Achille Charles Louis Napoleon Murat. Tallahassee's "ladies of the place" who, noted Emerson, numbered exactly eight, preferred to call him Prince Murat. Unlike some later Florida "princes," Murat was no impostor, though his dynasty was freshly minted. Murat's mother was the Emperor Napoleon's sister Caroline. His father was General

Joachim Murat, son of a French innkeeper whom Napoleon named king of the Two Sicilies. Swept from his Naples throne when Napoleon was defeated, the elder Murat was endeavoring to reconquer his lost realm when he was shot dead by his former subjects. "Save my face! Aim for the chest! Fire!" Murat ordered, issuing his last command.

His son and heir fled to America, where once again the vicissitudes of European dynastic politics produced a Florida side effect. Murat married a grandniece of George Washington. He called their twenty-eight-hundred-acre plantation near Tallahassee "Lipona," an anagram of "Napoli," capital city of the kingdom he would never rule. In Florida Emerson and the exiled prince became pals. "I would pay a hundred dollars to live a little while with Murat," he wrote to his brother. Though Murat never wore a crown, he would have the distinction of becoming Tallahassee's longest-serving postmaster. For twelve years Napoleon Bonaparte's nephew sorted letters in Florida's capital city; he also served briefly on the city council, even more briefly as mayor. Tallahassee's Prince Murat Motel, a popular spot for coed trysts, preserves his name. "Cheap, but suitable," noted one satisfied online review.

The fortunes of Florida's new oligarchs rested on a tripod of injustice. Dispossessing Seminoles and enslaving blacks were primal, but restricting the power of poor whites was also central to the process of government-sponsored oligarchic enrichment. When reformers moved to make membership in the legislative assembly in Tallahassee elective rather than appointive, Clinch exploited the fact that, socially as well as financially, Negro Fort had opened doors for him. Less than three years following the massacre, in snooty Charleston, South Carolina, the boy from Nash County, North Carolina, joined President James Monroe for an evening of gala entertainments. Following a fireworks display, they and their ladies watched a performance of Shakespeare's *Julius Caesar*. Then, in lighthearted counterpoint, they enjoyed a farce called *The Sleeping Draught*. Eager to prevent other poor whites from advancing now that he had acquired wealth and position, Clinch later bypassed the chain of command and sent a secret letter of a highly political nature directly to President Monroe. In it he informed the president that he was going to prevent his own soldiers from voting in the upcoming legislative elections—unless the president specifically ordered otherwise. For a second time the "Aristocrat in Uniform" had taken his stand on a matter vital to the future of Florida. As at Negro Fort it was for limiting, not expanding human freedom, though this time it was the rights of white men he curtailed.

In Tallahassee the judiciary was not to be outdone by the legislature or by the executive branch when it came to serving as a font of free Florida riches. By court order actual pioneers, mostly poor whites from Georgia, were evicted from lands they had cleared and cultivated so they could be handed over to powerful, often absentee speculators. The judicial pretext in many cases was the same treaty with Spain that, vainly, had guaranteed the human rights of Florida's inhabitants. Under that treaty the United States also pledged to respect Spain's royal land grants. U.S. officials, picking and choosing, disregarded the treaty's human rights provisions. They then selectively used the treaty's property rights provisions to legitimate the transfer of vast tracts of land to privileged individuals and influential companies.

Gad Humphreys, fresh from tricking Enemathla out of his land at Tallahassee, was one of the first to turn the Spanish land grant provision into a self-enrichment scheme. This time the real estate he coveted was a twenty-thousand-acre demesne located near present-day Ocala. Humphreys did not buy his acreage. Instead he contrived to get himself named co-legatee of one of the king of Spain's land grants. The treaty with Spain specified that all grants made after January 1818 were to be "null and void." That did not stop Gad Humphreys and others like him. With the help of shrewd lawyers and compliant judges, they used Spanish land grants or, more often, alleged copies and unauthenticated translations of them, to acquire millions of acres of Florida land. Thanks to this early form of judicial activism, billions of dollars in Florida real estate today still belong to wealthy individuals and powerful corporations that the Spanish crown originally granted to entirely different persons, for entirely different purposes, before Florida became a U.S. possession.

For nearly forty years Gad Humphreys' attempts to get rich intersected with all the great events of Florida. Then, like many another crucially important Florida protagonists, Gad Humphreys was turned into a nonperson. Most extant histories of Florida fail so much as to acknowledge his existence, even though Humphreys' position as Indian agent put him at the center of the festering Seminole conflict, one of the key events of Florida history. George R. Fairbanks' 1872 *History of Florida* does contain a one-sentence reference. "The agent, Colonel Humphreys, was accused of being too partial to the Indians," Fairbanks recounts, "and influences were brought to bear at Washington, by which his removal was effected in 1830." It bespoke the speed with which a terrible fate was overtaking red, black, and white people in Florida that Humphreys' removal, when it came, should be lamented by the Seminoles and welcomed by whites. Humphreys had not grown less venal. He continued to inhabit a universe in which it was his destiny to become rich, the black man's destiny to be enslaved—and the Seminoles' destiny, once confined to their "concentration area," to get, as promised, their school teacher, their blacksmith, and their periodic cash payments. Though those were the terms the United States itself had imposed, it soon was considered traitorous for any U.S. official to persist in such a view, as Humphreys himself was to discover.

In 1828, the year Jackson won the presidency, Humphreys got into a full-scale administrative row with both Governor DuVal and the secretary of war in Washington. It erupted after Mrs. Margaret Cook requested that her "negro Jack or John" be restored to her forthwith. Mrs. Cook provided no evidence that her errant slave had found refuge in the concentration zone. It did not matter. Mrs. Cook's request was passed to Governor DuVal in Tallahassee, who forwarded it to Colonel Humphreys. The concentration zone, like the rest of Florida, was not bereft of black men named Jack or John, but after making inquiries the Seminole leaders informed Humphreys that the supposed runaway was not to be found, whereupon the wrath of the territorial and federal governments befell him.

Accused of shirking his duties, Humphreys called the War Department's bluff as well DuVal's. "You say the negro Jack or John must be delivered up," he wrote. "Under these circumstances, I have to ask [if] I am authorized to put in requisition the military force stationed near the agency?" As the politicians and paper pushers well knew, the Seminoles had guns; the U.S. supplied them, for hunting and self-defense. To launch a U.S. Army invasion of the concentration zone in search of a runaway who, quite possibly, was not there, risked provoking serious bloodshed. "The military cannot be employed arresting Indian negroes," Governor DuVal replied. "The military will not be employed," the Department of War added emphatically.

Instead of using force, Governor DuVal had what he thought a better idea. He would withhold the financial payments to the Seminoles promised in the Treaty of Moultrie Creek until they delivered up "Jack or John." Once again Humphreys scented trouble. The Seminoles were hungry, he informed DuVal. Denying them funds and food would be reckless and, Colonel Humphreys found himself informing the governor of Florida, also be inhumane. "The last year's crop," he explained, "which was scanty, is entirely exhausted, and they are beginning to feel the pressures of want, from which they receive only such precious relief as is to be found in the woods." Then Humphreys did something truly extraordinary. He begged Governor DuVal to help the Seminoles because they were human beings. He did not want to make "any new calls on the munificence of the government; but if there is any portion of its former bounty that has not reached them, it would be exceedingly acceptable, and an act of humanity to impart it to them, in this their time of need," he wrote.

Denounced by DuVal, Gadsden, Clinch, and many others, Humphreys tried to explain himself to the new administration in Washington. "That I have questioned the policy, and even doubted the justice, of some of the property controversies between the whites and Indians I am free to admit," he conceded. As Jumper, one of the Seminole leaders with whom Humphreys held periodic philosophical discussions, had tried to make him understand, U.S. legal proceedings were not about justice, at least when nonwhites were involved. "The laws of the whites," the Seminole leader reminded him at one point, were "made solely for their own benefit."

Forced from office, Humphreys was scorned as a traitor to his country and his race. Then, in the 1840s, what happened with Negro

Fort happened with him. Someone finally dug up the facts. A U.S. Army officer named John Titcomb Sprague conducted a thorough investigation of the military documents that had accumulated during the Seminole War. The results made him a little uncomfortable. "The voluminous correspondence illustrative of the origins of the war appears at first sight to be a defense of the Seminole agent, Gad Humphreys," Sprague later wrote. More than that, the "voluminous correspondence" revealed Humphreys to have been an essential American figure when it comes to understanding what went wrong between 1821, when the U.S. annexed Florida, and 1835, when the years of misrule exploded into full-scale war.

Humphreys' transformation begins with his appointment as Indian Agent. It seems he has been handed the keys to a kingdom, but Humphreys has the capacity for human empathy and that proves to be his undoing. Where once Florida seemed the blank canvas of his avarice, he comes to see human beings who are hungry, who have been cheated, who deserve better because they are human beings, just like him. The decor may be Washington Irving; the denouement is Joseph Conrad. Only a few years after he uses his government position to take from the Seminoles everything he can, Colonel Humphreys finds himself pleading fruitlessly for "an act of humanity" on their behalf. In official correspondence concerning Indians and blacks, Gad Humphreys actually calls for "justice."

Like de Soto, Gad Humphreys never fully comprehends how lost he is. The official surveyors, as the law requires, survey his royal grant. Rather than accept possession of the twenty-thousand acres the government says is his, Humphreys decides to settle for nothing less than the twenty-thousand acres of his dreams. He sues the government of Florida. When his case finally is heard, he learns firsthand what Jumper told him. Now that Humphreys is no longer a powerful public official, the judge rebuffs him. Undeterred, he pursues his claim all the way to the U.S. Supreme Court; it again gets him nothing except new enemies.

Humphreys' judicial ruination takes decades; his financial ruin unfolds much more quickly. Desperate for money, he rents out his slaves. The sweat of their brows does not suffice to satisfy his creditors; the court orders "certain" of his slaves "to be sold in front of the court house . . . to the highest bidder for cash at Public Auction." Sampson, twenty-four; Katy, eighteen; and "Bob aged about ten years with the future issue and increase of the said female Slave," are put up on the auction block to pay Humphreys' debts. Next time, in order to stave off his creditors, Humphreys sells for $500 "in hand paid, two certain negro slaves (females), ELSY & FLORA, the first about Eleven & the other about nine years of age."

Adrift in Florida, Gad Humphreys fights against injustice; he sells children to the highest bidder. He steals land, and has land stolen from him; he grows more morally aware while remaining deeply venal. The material is there for an emotional and intellectual breakthrough of colossal proportions, but instead of confronting the contradictions, he keeps on wading deeper into them. Having failed to get rich in Tallahassee, then failed again in Ocala, Humphreys fails definitively in St. Augustine. Like Murat in Tallahassee, in St. Augustine Humphreys does get elected alderman, and therefore on two occasions serves for a month as mayor of the sand-blown outpost that only later will be turned into America's Oldest City. Then, in 1859—just after the Seminole War finally ends, just before the Civil War begins—Colonel Gad Humphreys disappears into the Protestant cemetery at St. Augustine, where so long ago Menéndez futilely killed every Protestant he could find.

Gad Humphreys pioneered the paradigm of American failure in Florida. Sooner or later almost all of them wound up like him: Murat, DuVal, Gaines, and scores of others like them, or who wanted to be like them. Florida ruined them all, turning even the mightiest and best connected into wandering exiles, seeking to recoup their losses someplace else. Governor DuVal, after losing everything in Florida, wound up a lawyer of middling esteem in Texas. After going broke, Prince Murat tried to recoup his fortunes by joining the Belgian Foreign Legion; he failed again. His widow—George Washington's grandniece—was saved from financial embarrassment only by a subvention from her dead husband's first cousin, the future emperor Napoleon III.

Why did they fail? Racism was the original sin of these Americans, but it was the fusion of racism with the conquistadors' mortal sin—greed—that doomed their Florida ambitions. By the time Humphreys was dismissed from his post, the most striking feature of life in Florida was how easily the imposition of the new white-supremacist, oligarchic system of U.S. rule had gone. It wasn't a pretty picture, but the situation might conceivably have remained stable were it not for a destabilizing monomania that went beyond avarice and racism.

The problem was that the Americans could not be satisfied with most of everything, or the best of everything. They wanted everything, even when taking everything destroyed whole peoples, along with (as we would note today) ecosystems and other species. This monomania made them seem both crazy and evil to the Seminoles. It blinded most Americans to the meaning and consequences of their actions, but it did not blind Humphreys. He had come to understand that the greatest danger in Florida was not unruly Seminoles or runaway blacks, but the danger Americans posed to themselves. He understood that Jumper got it right, in the course of one of their discussions, when he told him: "It seems that the white people will not rest, nor suffer us to do so, till they have got all the property belonging to us."

10

DEFINED BY MASSACRE

First Negro Fort, then Moultrie Creek: now at a north Florida river crossing called Payne's Landing, James Gadsden again set to work fulfilling in Florida what Andrew Jackson ordained. In 1823 Gadsden had tricked them out of almost everything. Now, in 1832, he deprived them of everything, including who they were. "The Seminole Indians relinquish to the United States all claim to the lands they at present occupy in the Territory of Florida," this latest "treaty" announced, "and agree to emigrate to the country assigned to the Creeks, west of the Mississippi river." Once there the Seminoles, "as such," would cease to exist, or as Gadsden phrased it, the people expelled from Florida "will be received as a constituent part of the Creek nation." All money due the Seminoles, this new piece of paper announced, would be taken away from them and "added to the Creek annuities."

The objective was genocide as the U.S. government later defined it: "Deliberately inflicting on the group conditions of life calculated to bring about its physical destruction in whole or in part." For white-skinned Floridians it was the best of both worlds. Once deprived of their identity, dark-skinned Seminoles could be enslaved while those with Indian features were driven west beyond the Mississippi. Florida would be rid of its "Indians," while getting a new source of slave labor. Practically speaking, the most important result was that this time most Seminoles ignored Gadsden's summons. In their hundreds they had thronged to Moultrie Creek. Ten years later Gadsden managed to prod only seven chiefs to sign. Though the press was barred, Florida newspapers discovered that the translators had been bribed to give the Seminoles a false idea of the proposals he was inflicting on them.

Even so, at their insistence a proviso was added to this latest "treaty" stipulating that, before it could go into effect, the seven "confidential chiefs . . . should be sent at the expense of the United States as early as convenient to examine the country assigned to the Creeks west of the Mississippi River." Only when and if they were "satisfied with the character of that country, and of the favorable disposition of the Creeks" would the "agreement, herein stipulated . . . be binding on the respective parties." As Captain Sprague later observed, "The fulfillment of the treaty was clearly conditional."

On paper the Seminoles had won an important concession. In practice it would be Enemathla's square mile all over again. Though Humphreys was gone, Gadsden had an enthusiastic new accomplice. This was Major John Phagan, whom President Jackson had named the new Indian agent. As Captain Sprague later described him, Phagan personified Jackson's spoils system at its worst: "Without the requisite qualifications for the office, he brought with him the patronage of the executive, as well as the partialities of the people." The new Indian agent, he added, was "totally unqualified, both by education and morals." On their journey to what today is Oklahoma, Phagan and the "confidential chiefs" first traveled by ship across the Gulf of Mexico to New Orleans. Boarding riverboats, they then made their way up the Mississippi and Arkansas Rivers to Little Rock. From there they traveled by horseback to Oklahoma. The Seminoles were horrified by what they found; "we saw Indians bring in scalps to the garrison," one of them later testified. The same Creeks who executed the massacre at Negro Fort and also helped ravage Seminole settlements during General, now President, Jackson's invasion of Florida, were now masters of the land where the Seminoles were supposed to be moved. Nonetheless, in early April 1833, Major Phagan announced that the chiefs had found themselves "satisfied with the character of that country, and of the favorable disposition of the Creeks." More than that, Phagan purported, they were now so eager to get to Oklahoma they wanted to make the move "as soon as the Government will make arrangements for their emigration."

The new Indian Agent had manufactured an "additional treaty" in support of these fabrications. He called it the Treaty of Fort Gibson, after the outpost in the Arkansas Territory where the Seminole group stopped before resuming the journey home to Florida. The delay supposedly gave them more time to "examine the country." In reality they were detained there because Fort Gibson had become the nexus of a conspiracy stretching from the Oklahoma wilderness to Washington. Both President Jackson and Major Phagan were among the coconspirators; their tactics, according to modern research, included "coercion, bribery, alteration of the treaty after the fact." At Phagan's secret request, President Jackson ordered three U.S. commissioners to rush to Fort Gibson in order to intercept the chiefs before they could return to Florida. They carried with them authorization to sign the "additional treaty" that Phagan had generated. Seminole claims that they were victims of a conspiracy were vindicated by James Gadsden himself. Had the chiefs, in Gadsden's words, "been permitted to return and make their report in council," a negotiated settlement still might have been reached. "Unfortunately," Gadsden pointed out, "the fatal mistake was made of meeting the deputation in the West" and imposing the Fort Gibson paper on them before the chiefs could report to "the nation at home. This, as ought to have been expected, created distrust among the warriors."

Like Humphreys, Phagan intended to profit from the Seminoles' misfortune. "The said Seminoles," claimed an article he inserted into the Fort Gibson document, "have expressed high confidence in the friendship and ability of their present agent, Major Phagan, and desire that he may be permitted to remove them to their new homes." Removing the Seminoles would be a major logistics operation involving many lucrative contracts, but Phagan's self-enrichment scheme came to an end when investigators discovered he had been overcharging his own government and then, after involving the subcontractors in his fraudulent schemes, not paying them at all. The Indian Agent also had extorted money from the Seminoles; even more shocking to the sensibilities of the time, he had been soliciting money from Negroes. "I found also that he was in debt," the official investigator reported, "to Abraham, the Seminole interpreter." One later myth was that criminals like Phagan were only doing what was normal back then. That was not the case. The Treaty of Payne's Landing, like the

Negro Fort Massacre, aroused a storm of condemnation, shame and foreboding that only later was excised from accounts of what happened. "A foul blot upon the escutcheon of the nation!" thundered Thomas L. McKenney, a former Superintendent of Indian Affairs. The "evidences of fraud and improper conduct on the part of Major Phagan" added to the disgrace.

Humphreys had come to understand that U.S. abuse of the Seminoles was on the way to provoking an explosion. So now, too, did the person who, along with Gadsden, had done the most to make violence in Florida inevitable. In late 1833 William Pope DuVal resigned as governor of Florida. During his twelve years in office he had turned a territory at peace into a swamp of injustice, ethnic hatred, and smoldering violence. He did not intend to be the one in charge when the chickens came home to roost.

His successor was a very lucky Tennessee politician named John H. Eaton. By then Eaton already had held a number of distinguished positions. His chief qualification for them all was that Andrew Jackson liked him. Appointed to the U.S. Senate in violation of the Constitution at age twenty-eight, Eaton had been promoted to secretary of war once Jackson became president. Soon Jackson's wonder boy was embroiled in one of Washington's first sex scandals, the Petticoat Affair. Slipping out of harm's way, Eaton got Jackson to name him governor of Florida. Callow as he may have been when it came to his personal affairs, Governor Eaton had a sharp nose for political danger. He knew it was a lie when Phagan (and President Jackson himself) claimed the Seminoles agreed to be deported. "I pray you," he asked, "does not this circumstance raise a doubt whether the treaty can be considered valid and binding?" No one listened, so this time he got himself appointed minister plenipotentiary to Spain. "The Indian question of removal is one that should be managed with great caution and care. Tread then cautiously!" Eaton warned as he deftly fled the scene of the expanding disaster, once again to assume an exalted appointive post in an exotic location.

Eaton, like Gadsden, Humphreys and DuVal, knew full well that the Seminoles never agreed to leave Florida. That did not keep most other U.S. officials from pretending they had. "You solemnly bound yourselves to remove," Florida's latest Indian Agent, General Wiley S. Thompson, told the Seminoles when they pointed out that the Treaty of Moultrie Creek authorized them to remain in Florida for twenty years. "You know you were not forced to do it," he added when they stated they had been coerced. Thompson's earnest obliviousness, as much as the lies themselves, provoked sneering contempt. "General Thompson, when communicating to the chiefs," one American remembered, "was repeatedly interrupted by groans, violent grimaces, and language of the most abusive kind, expressed in an under tone." American oppression had created a new, and radicalized generation of militants whom neither the U.S. military nor the traditional elders could control.

In less than twenty-five months General Wiley S. Thompson reenacted in his dealings with the Seminoles the path from Jeffersonian temporizing to Jacksonian brutality it had taken U.S. policy nearly thirty years to traverse. From first to last he worked on the assumption that opposition to anything Americans wanted had to emanate either from his victims' innate childishness or from their savage nature. Hoping for the best, General Thompson first tried treating them like children. Instead of candy and toys, Thompson decided, the way to induce them to be good Indians and go away to Oklahoma was to give them firearms.

Nothing so well epitomized the compartmentalization of American racism as the contrasting attitudes toward blacks having guns, and Indians having them. Blacks with guns were the key element in the nightmare of a slave revolt. Provided they were "friendly," Indians were another matter. As Thompson saw it, by making the Seminoles leave Florida he was helping them set off on a manly adventure. On that adventure they would need weapons and ammunition, so when one young man seemed particularly hostile to Thompson's attempts at persuasion, the Indian Agent sought to win his friendship by giving him a rifle. In some versions, the weapon is a silver-encrusted masterpiece of the gunsmith's art, imported all the way from Savannah. Whatever the details, and from here onward the mythic embellishments get thicker and thicker, we know that Thompson did give such a present. We also know the name of the recipient, which was William Powell Jr., who only later would become known as Osceola—along with Tecumseh, Cochise, and Geronimo one of America's most famous "Indian" leaders.

No one better personified the outraged sense of injustice which American aggression provoked than young Powell. American self-serving moralistic piety, in turn, found precise representation in the personage of Wiley Thompson. What is striking about their encounter is the intimacy. They elicited in each other, by turns, curiosity, amity, forthrightness, disagreement, scorn, disappointment, anger, vengeful-ness, and rage. At Fort King near present-day Ocala, on the fringe of the concentration zone, the lives of these two men intertwined. In the dynamics of their intensely personal interrelationship a centuries-long history of interracial relations, beginning in wary friendship and ending in undying enmity, acted itself out in a matter of months.

Abundant firsthand accounts document that the Seminoles, even after losing almost everything at Moultrie Creek, still wanted to live in peace. "All their 'talks,' petitions, remonstrances, letters, breathe only the wish for peace and fair dealing," Andrew Jackson's own biographer conceded. Had the Americans been willing to leave the Seminoles in possession of the wastes of central Florida which they themselves had allotted to them, great misfortune might have been averted on both sides. Instead, in Parton's words, "The Semi-noles were drawn at last into a collision with the United States by a chain of circumstances with which they had little to do, and the responsibility of which belongs not to them."

Thompson himself provided a vivid example of how U.S. of-ficials radicalized the Seminoles. When, instead of docilely accepting his homilies on the "duty to remove," Powell argued back, the Indian Agent grew increasingly offended. Relations reached the breaking point, Thompson later complained, when the young man "came to my office, and insulted me by some insolent remarks. This was not the first time he had acted disrespectfully but on those occasions," Thompson wrote, "He apologized & I forgave." Now it had happened again, so "on this occasion," Thompson explained, "I confined him in irons." The next day Thompson added emotional duress to physi-cal humiliation. When Powell "begged that I would release him,"

Thompson recounted, "I informed him that without satisfactory security that he would behave better and prove faithful in future he must remain in confinement." The best way to prove he had repented, Thompson informed him, was first to provide "acknowledgment of the validity of the Treaty" and then persuade all his friends and neighbors to accept deportation.

An honest confrontation had been transformed into a psychodrama propelled by humiliation and deceit. In order to obtain his release, Osceola had been forced to proclaim his acceptance "of the validity of the Treaty," but could he now be trusted to "assist in bringing over the refractory portion of the nation," as one witness to their confrontation put it? Soon General Thompson was presented with what he considered conclusive proof that Osceola was a sincere turncoat. "True to his word," the Indian agent wrote, "he this day appeared with seventy-nine of his people Men Women & Children . . . and redeemed his promise." "I now have no doubt as to his sincerity," he added. Giving his erstwhile prisoner an extra supply of gunpowder, Thompson wished Osceola Godspeed as he headed out, once again, into the Florida wilderness. His confidence was still unshaken on the afternoon of December 28, 1835, when Billy Powell killed General Wiley Thompson, his former mentor and tormentor, as in the course of a post-luncheon stroll outside the walls of Fort King. As the U.S. Indian Agent smoked a cigar, Osceola and more than a dozen others opened fire: twenty-four bullets riddled his body, killing him instantly. Thompson's scalp was sliced into many small pieces, so that each member of the attack party might have proof of his role in ridding their people of the person who had come to personify all the evils and injustices inflicted on them. Their resentments had been festering for a long time. As Captain Sprague later acknowledged, "all that was wanting was a heart bold enough to strike the first blow." Thanks to Osceola, that blow now had been struck.

The attack on Thompson was part of a coordinated offensive. Between Christmas and New Year's Eve 1835 a broad-based alliance of Seminoles and blacks—including people of white as well as other racial origins—inflicted "one of the most terrible defeats ever suffered by the U.S. Army at the hands of the native peoples," a U.S.

Senate report later stated. It wasn't just "native peoples." The uprising showed that the two biggest "problems" of American expansion—dispossessing Indians and enslaving blacks—were intertwined conditions produced by the advance of American nationalism. Duncan Clinch, by now promoted to general, recognized the multiethnic nature of the resistance when he referred to the attackers as "a combination of the Indians, Indian Negroes and the Negroes on the plantations." Once again there had been a failure of U.S. intelligence. At the very moment General Thompson imagined Powell was persuading the Seminoles to accept deportation, they had been organizing a war of resistance. The most striking feature of these attacks was the coordination. The Seminoles had what, in today's counterinsurgency parlance, is called an integrated command structure.

"We had been preparing this for more than a year," Alligator later recounted, yet detailed information on where and how the Florida resistance was planned only emerged in 1991. In his pioneering work, *Florida's Peace River Frontier*, professor Canter Brown demonstrated how the proximity of Osceola's central Florida headquarters at Talakchopko on the Peace River (present-day Fort Meade), a black settlement named Minatti fifteen miles to the north on Lake Hancock, and, three miles to the southeast of Talakchopko, a Seminole cattle-grazing center on what still is called Bowlegs Creek, permitted close cooperation between peoples of both African and American origin. Intermingling in the Peace River valley, as they had earlier in the Apalachicola valley, such people were able to share their grievances and, when the time came, combine their forces and orchestrate their attacks. As Brown's research shows, the interracial alliance in the Apalachicola valley had not been destroyed by the Negro Fort massacre. It had been deepened and strengthened by twenty years of U.S. violence, but until he took up the task of verifying what actually happened historians for the most part simply ignored the vital question of how such attacks could have occurred.

White Florida was panic-stricken but the headline writers were unfazed. "The Miserable Creatures Will Be Speedily Swept from the Face of the Earth," the *Niles' Weekly Register* promised; "ten years intercourse with the whites," it explained, "has so far corrupted and demoralized the Seminoles as to make them incapable of protracted resistance." "Intercourse with the whites" in truth had produced a remarkable group of people, none more so than Billy Powell Jr. As news of the military catastrophe in Florida spread, people everywhere wanted to know: Who was this exotic "Indian chief"?

Billy Powell—the now-infamous Osceola—was born on U.S. territory, near present-day Tuskegee, Alabama, in 1804. His father was a white man named William Powell; his mother, Polly Coppinger, was also of European descent. Her mother was named Ann McQueen. Osceola's great-grandfather was a Scotsman named James McQueen who founded a frontier dynasty. If all that mattered was descent from original settlers, Billy Powell would have qualified as an American aristocrat, but James McQueen not only traded with the Indians; he intermarried with them. Around the time the future Osceola was born, the U.S. Indian Agent in the area described the clan in a letter sent to President Jefferson. "Peter McQueen, a half breed," he wrote, referring to Osceola's uncle, "is a snug trader, has a valuable property in negroes and stock and begins to know their value."

There was no place for such "half-breeds" in the new Alabama Jackson and his followers were creating through wholesale dispossession of "Indian savages," followed by the mass importation of black slaves. There was no place for him in traditional Indian society either, which is another way of saying the future Osceola, even before he got there, was a natural Floridian. In Florida the mixed-race boy named Billy Powell would reinvent himself as Osceola. He would transform himself from a marginalized figure into one of Florida's great protagonists.

Thomas Simpson Woodward, a founder of Tuskegee, was an eyewitness to the McQueens' prosperity, and its destruction. Fifty years later he remembered transplanting cedar trees and playing ball with Peter McQueen. He called Osceola's father "the little Englishman," though he was actually born in Georgia. When Peter McQueen and his extended family fled to Florida, Woodward recalled, "Billy Powell was then a little boy, and was with this party." Once in Florida the family dispersed. The senior Powell "moved with his two daughters to the West." Ann McQueen headed east with their son, in the direction of the Suwanee River. The wisdom of dispersing the family was proven in 1818. As Jackson drove his troops toward the Suwanee in search of the Seminole force he imagined he could destroy there, Ann McQueen and her son fell into the hands of a U.S. patrol. Once Jackson abandoned his offensive, the "lad" and his mother continued their flight into peninsular Florida. Osceola's youth and the fact that he was traveling with a group composed of women and children had saved him. He never saw his father or his sisters again.

The preconception was that white supremacy would provide the "basis" of U.S. rule. The reality, by the time the U.S. flag was hoisted there, was that Florida had long served a contrary purpose, evocative of the role Florida plays again today. Back then, Florida was not the refuge for retirees, drifters, sports fishing and NASCAR fanatics, Christian fundamentalists, homosexual rights activists, drug dealers, spare-change waitresses, bootleggers, swampland salesmen, and crazy-scheme millionaires it later became. Instead it had become a refuge for earlier, other kinds of Americans, a place where a spectrum of racial and cultural conditions existed side by side, without any one group considering it necessary to eradicate or subjugate all the others.

Then as later, the human stratifications prevailing farther north blurred. Just as they do today, people acquired new identities once they got to Florida. Ridding themselves of their old tribal names, many though by no means all of Florida's Indians called themselves Seminoles. To the astonishment of Florida's new white rulers, many black people called themselves Seminoles too. Who were the Seminoles? As Americans attempted to impose their tripartite system of white supremacy, black slavery, and Indian removal on Florida, practically anyone who resisted being segregated into those arbitrary categories was turned into a "Seminole." The word itself had first come into use during the War of Independence to describe detribalized Indians migrating into Florida. The ethnogenesis of the Seminole identity—like the emergence of the American identity —demonstrated how human identities, however immutable they seem, are artificial constructs. To this day people insist on calling the Seminoles an "Indian tribe" and Osceola an "Indian chief," but these people were never who white Americans wanted them to be.

By the time the United States took charge, Florida had black cowboys and black farmers, along with black bakers, fishermen, and military commanders. Some of these black people were free. Some, technically speaking, were the property of Indians, Spaniards, or other blacks. Before long, many of these "blacks" weren't black. As Professor Kathleen Deagan points out, "The African refugees from South Carolina married one another, as well as both free and slave black natives of St. Augustine. Some married Indians, and others married whites." Governor DuVal conceded that identity was a social construct when he referred to the "Indian negroes."

Most perplexing of all was the existence of the "Black Seminoles." Even today the term seems self-contradictory simply because race runs too deep in the American psyche to be understood as a social construct—even though today, as they did back then, many American "blacks" have more European than African blood. Like Indian and mixed-race Seminoles, Black Seminoles, beneath the complexities of their interrelationships with each other, and with white Americans, were simply Americans who refused to accept the identities slaveholder America sought to impose on them. Gad Humphreys, who as Indian Agent got to know the Seminoles very well, discovered the prevailing categorizations were inapplicable. "Slaves but in name," he observed, "they work only when it suits their inclination." General Edmund Gaines, who shared Jackson's racial convictions, regarded them as "black vassals and allies" of the Indians.

It was the spectacle of blacks, Indians, and even some white people amicably coexisting that had made Florida such a "post of annoyance." Because Florida continued to annoy them, white Americans would continue devastating Florida for decades. By the time they were finished, virtually every one of these nonwhite persons in Florida had been killed, enslaved, physically removed from Florida, or driven into the Everglades.

Instead of destroying it, Jackson's 1818 rampage had produced an expansion of Seminole settlement in Florida. Driven deeper into Florida by the terror, black, Indian, and mixed-race refugees became true pioneers, establishing more than thirty peaceful multiracial settlements. They succeeded where the Spanish and British had failed because their objective was productive, not extractive—family subsistence, not export riches. An 1821 U.S. intelligence report identified one of those pioneer settlements as "Peter McQueen's village." In seven years McQueen and his connections, including the future Osceola, had migrated some five hundred miles south from Tuskegee to the Peace River valley. Distance did not provide refuge. Starting in 1824, Governor DuVal set out to deprive the inhabitants of McQueen's village of their fishing grounds and gardens, and force them inland, into the "confinement and concentration" area. Unwilling to live under white oppression, Osceola's uncle was hoping to escape to the Bahamas when, Woodward reported, Peter McQueen died "on a little barren island on the Atlantic side of Cape Florida." It may have been the future Miami Beach, or Key Biscayne or Key Largo. Whatever the location, McQueen stands alone on that desolate shore. Like Ribault at Matanzas Inlet and Garcon at Negro Fort, he is a hero whose story deserved to be sung by a Floridian Homer. Instead his odyssey vanished into the sand as the water flowed past him, the water that in Florida outlasts everything.

The circumstances just described display the itinerary, though not the exact geographic and psychological route, that—between 1804 and 1835—took Billy Powell from Alabama, where he enters the world as part of a prosperous, part-white family, important enough to be mentioned in a letter to the president of the United States, to Fort King, Florida, where he strides onto the stage as Osceola—an "Indian," a "savage." Americans were fascinated by this exotic apparition. How, people wondered, had such a person come into being? Had race prejudice not blinded them, they would have recognized that Osceola, as much as any white American hero, was propelled by love of freedom and hatred of injustice. They would have recognized that, historically speaking, Osceola was Andrew Jackson's son.

"In the Revolution, an English officer had slashed him with a saber for refusing to clean a pair of boots," Schlesinger much later wrote, by way of explaining why, forever after, Andrew Jackson had no truck with anyone who got in his way. That the same injustices should provoke the same outrage in nonwhites was something most Americans found it difficult to fathom back then. Osceola's behavior was proclaimed a mystery; the explanation was that he was a "half-breed." The events in Florida actually demonstrated that injustice is color-blind. As a result of American brutality, full-blooded Indians like the Seminole leader Micanopy and blacks like Abraham, the most respected of the Seminole statesmen, as well as mixed-race people like Billy Powell, all became militants and fought together.

Americans still believe no major slave revolt ever occurred within the United States, but in Florida, starting in late 1835, a great slave revolt did erupt. Americans believe their Indian wars were fought out west, but in Florida, beginning in late 1835, the longest Indian war in U.S. history entered its bloodiest stage. Like the Seminoles themselves, the conflict was a product of all the tumultuous forces unleashed by the creation of the United States. Like the whites they fought, the Seminoles were a new people, created by the special circumstances pertaining at the time they arose. That was why this was a new kind of American war.

The same day Osceola was stalking Thompson, a Seminole force, striking forty miles away, wiped out an entire U.S. Army detachment; 107 U.S. officers and men were killed, about a fifth of all American troops in Florida. "The aim of the Indians was well-nigh perfect," one military man later wrote, "and the attack had been carefully planned and discussed by the Chiefs." Not since the British burned Washington had U.S. forces been so humiliated—and this time "savages" were the culprits. "For the first time in the history of our Army," one military analyst observed, "almost an entire Command of trained soldiers had been exterminated in a daylight attack by the Indians."

The die was cast in mid-December 1835 when Duncan Clinch ordered that troops be rushed from Fort Brooke, near Tampa Bay, to Fort King. Richard Keith Call, commander of the territorial militia, warned Clinch it would be suicidal to send the U.S. troops led by Major Dade on such an expedition; "disturbed as the country is through which he must pass, he can never reach you." Reinforcements were needed because, two days before the uprising began, Clinch had abandoned Fort King. Unlike Thompson, "General Clinch had foreseen that hostilities were unavoidable," Captain Sprague later recounted. Deciding that protecting his own plantation was more important than defending Fort King, the highest-ranking U.S. Army officer in Florida had moved his troops more than twenty miles north, leaving only a "little handful of men" at the headquarters of the Indian Agency the day Thompson was killed.

The Seminoles ambushed the doomed relief column as marching two abreast, while lugging a useless cannon along with them, the men in Dade's detachment traversed a patch of palmetto scrub adjacent to the Great Wahoo Swamp. In terms of today's coordinates, the place where they died was located some sixty miles north of Tampa and forty miles south of Ocala. It was also 252 miles east by southeast from Negro Fort. In just under twenty years the ragged knife edge of Americanization, slicing away at Florida, had moved from the Apalachicola valley over and down into the north center of the Florida peninsula. During that same period, as the death of Dade and his men demonstrated, everything Andrew Jackson and most other Americans had said about Florida had been proven false. The Seminoles had not been routed. Florida had not been stabilized. As the sudden loss of U.S. control now demonstrated, Florida was not an American possession except in the same derelict sense it had belonged to Spain.

There were other parallels with the much-scorned Spaniards. Back in 1528 Álvar Núñez Cabeza de Vaca, one of only four survivors of Pánfilo de Narváez' invasion force, walked some two thousand miles from Florida to Mexico. Only then did the Spanish learn of the annihilation of the expedition that had started out to conquer Florida with a force of fifteen hundred. The Americans, 307 years later, had no inkling of what had befallen Dade's detachment until "a private soldier named Daniel F. Clarke, bearing seven wounds, weak from loss of blood and hunger," reached Fort Brooke; "barely alive," he had "crawled almost the entire distance from the scene of one of the most bloody massacres in the history of the American Army." There was also the recurring role the cold played. Later it was claimed that the U.S. troops did not have time to respond because they had to keep their rifles and ammunition under their greatcoats, in order to protect their weaponry from the cold. The Seminoles' rifles and powder seemed not to have required such insulation.

The Indian and black experience in Florida had been defined by massacre since 1816. Now, for white Americans, Florida was defined by massacre too, though the symmetry was lost on Florida's politicians, speculators, military men and historians. While the Negro Fort Massacre remained a nonevent, the Dade Massacre, as it immediately became known, provided proof that only a Florida cleansed of "savages" was safe for white civilization. In the aftermath of the successful Seminole attacks another theme resurfaced: Americans were blameless when bad things happened. The valor of their adversaries could not explain why Americans got themselves killed so easily and in such large numbers, so deceit and betrayal must explain why decades of violence finally had blown up in America's face.

Back in 1818 General Jackson had blamed those two hapless Brits, Arbuthnot and Ambrister, for his failure. In this case the culprit supposedly was a slave named Lewis or Louis or Luis. However they spelled it, Florida's whites agreed that the Dade Massacre wasn't their fault. Holding this one slave guilty was a way to evade responsibility for a self-inflicted defeat. It was also a way to avoid understanding the larger catastrophe white Americans had inflicted on themselves. Because "the expedition was betrayed" by Lewis, the Seminoles knew where Dade was going. Because of Lewis' treachery, "the dreadful work was soon done." Clinch's venality, Dade's gullibility—to say nothing of the viciousness of U.S. policy—played no role.

Like the parable of the three boxes, the tale of Lewis' perfidy was a fiction invented after the fact. Private Clarke, who provided the only American eyewitness account, never mentioned Lewis, nor did eyewitnesses on the Seminole side. Captain Sprague, who fought in Florida before writing his history of the Seminole War, had access to the Army's archives. He interviewed people directly involved in the Dade Massacre. He does not mention Lewis. All these accounts do make it clear that many black people, not just one "traitor," did all they could to help defeat the Americans. Right around Christmas, a Seminole commander named Alligator recalled, the decision was made to attack "the soldiers coming from Fort Brooke, as the negroes there had reported that two companies were preparing to march." Everywhere U.S. forces went invisible spies, black and Indian, monitored their movements. Within the U.S. Army installations, slaves observed what the Americans were planning, just as in the wilderness Seminole observers saw, and reported, all.

This is where Lewis—to use the normal American spelling—entered the picture. A Tampa slaveholder, hearing Dade needed a guide, offered him the services of "a colored man named Louis." Convinced Lewis was just the guide he needed, "Major Dade entered into an agreement with the master for his services in conducting the troops through the forest for twenty-five dollars per month." Until the day he died Lewis vociferously denied having betrayed anyone.

If any single individual was to blame, General Duncan Clinch was. But for Clinch's decision to use the U.S. Army to protect his private property, the killings at Fort King as well as the Dade Massacre might have been averted. Instead Clinch had first ordered the Fort Brooke detachment to march inland. Then, without waiting for Dade's relief column to get there, Clinch and his troops abandoned Fort King, and withdrew to his Auld Lang Syne plantation. There Clinch sat, doing nothing, though he did send some of the troops to guard a relative's property. "Clinch was behind the plan that led to the Dade Massacre," as one military man later put it. As for the underlying causes of the uprising, Thomas Jefferson had identified those decades earlier. "If we do this, we shall have general and perpetual war," he had warned in 1808, cautioning that "nothing ought more to be avoided than the embarking ourselves in a system of military coercion on the Indians."

America had created the Seminoles; America would destroy them. Demography assured it. The certainty the Seminoles would be crushed was there to behold, counterintuitively, in the successful attack on Dade and his forces. Nearly one-half of the U.S. soldiers killed that day were immigrants from Europe. Most of the rest came from the North. Of those victims whose place of birth was recorded, by far the greatest number of those killed, twenty-three, came from Ireland. Among the dead, soldiers born in Germany outnumbered those from North Carolina; immigrants from Scotland outnumbered those from Virginia. Only three came from slave states that would later secede from the Union. Not a single white Southerner from Florida died in the Dade Massacre. Whoever did the dying, sheer numbers would determine who won the Florida War. In 1836 Seminoles numbered at most six thousand people, including women and children. The population of the United States already exceeded fifteen million. The Seminoles could have wiped out dozens of Dade detachments and not affected the capacity of the United States, ultimately and inevitably, to crush them.

On December 29, 1835, General Duncan Clinch finally set out from his plantation to experience war, as opposed to massacre, for the first time. His purpose was not to rescue the survivors at Fort King, nor to rendezvous with Dade's detachment, which he did not yet know had been destroyed. Rather, he undertook a military promenade. He and his men managed to cover twelve miles their first day. That night their bivouac covered half a square mile. The smoke, fires, commotion and noise announced their presence in every direction. In Tallahassee Richard Keith Call had replaced former Governor DuVal as the dominant American figure. As head of the territorial militia he enjoyed the title of brigadier general. In response to the Seminole uprising, he called up his troops and headed out to try to find Clinch. Instead of embarking on a fast, decisive campaign, Call discovered, General Clinch "had set out with every cart and wagon, mule and horse, he could raise on his plantation." Call's own volunteer force did not move silently either. Every soldier, it seemed, had a dog that had decided to come along. Their yelping and their masters' oaths, and the dust kicked up by the supply wagons when they were not mired in mud, filled the Florida air.

Once again the Seminoles saw all, knew all. "Information was brought by the scouts that the troops were approaching the Withlacoochee River," Alligator later recounted. The Seminoles immediately moved to take advantage of the situation. According to Sprague, "Two hundred and fifty warriors, thirty of whom were blacks, started, under Osceola and Halpatter Tustenuggee (Alligator), to intercept them when crossing the river." There they waited while, for a second night, Clinch's force shivered in the near frost of a late December night in interior Florida. The section of the river they reached their third day out was not the "good ford" he had been expecting but, as Clinch himself later described it, "a deep and rapid stream" 150 feet wide. After nineteen and a half years' military experience in Florida, it had not occurred to General Clinch to bring boats. Though Clinch owned five sugar lighters, broad-beamed craft ideal for use on Florida's inland streams and lakes, he had reserved them for commercial use on his plantation.

False intelligence reports had led him into this trap, Clinch explained in a letter of self-exoneration to President Jackson. More than seventeen years earlier Jackson, too, had let supposedly trustworthy guides lead him on a fool's errand. Now, once again, hopes of "surprising the main body of Indians" proved hallucinatory, and Clinch "faced the most important military decision of his career." When one of his soldiers found a sunken canoe, Clinch decided it would suffice to move his entire force to the opposite bank. Having failed to coordinate his advance with Call, Clinch now left one throng of soldiers exposed on one bank of the river, another exposed on the opposite bank, while slowly ferrying his troops, their ammunition, and their weapons across the river a little at a time. Andrew Jackson had known better. When his equally untrustworthy guides led him to the Suwanee, Jackson's survival instincts had taken command. He had abandoned his search for "the main body of Indians," chosen Arbuthnot and Ambrister as his scapegoats, proclaimed victory, and resumed his march toward the White House. General Duncan Clinch, faced with a nearly identical dilemma, plunged into the trap that had been baited with the canoe.

The Seminoles, invisible, watched while Clinch moved his men across the river into their line of fire. This never would be a war fought, Hollywood-style, with bows and arrows. Real bullets tore into real flesh as the Seminoles opened fire and Clinch's "troops broke ranks and ran." Abandoning his troops, Clinch also fled. Brigadier General Richard Keith Call could hardly wait to inform President Jackson of Clinch's cowardice. Appreciating that the most damning account would be an apparently dispassionate one, he adopted a neutral tone as he described his rival's behavior. Clinch "was greatly exhausted from the fatigue of the fight" at the time he fled, "leaving the fate of the army in my hands," Call informed the president.

Had Call not arrived at the last minute, Clinch's "entire force might have suffered a fate similar to that of Major Dade's luckless troops," but with the arrival of Call's reinforcements the balance of battle shifted. American forces now amounted to about 700 armed men. The Seminole force was about 250. Even so Call likewise fled the scene. "In the haste of retreat," according to Clinch's biographer, "many guns were left behind and fell to the Indians as spoils of war."

Clinch's blunders were obvious, but in the official report on what happened it became clear that Call also had disgraced himself. Of "the four hundred or five hundred volunteers" under Call's command, the report noted, "only twenty-seven men and three officers," one of them a rising frontier politician named Leigh Read, actually did any fighting that day. Why so few "took part in the action," he added, "is not explained." The explanation was that the men of Florida refused to fight. Throughout the Seminole War the white men of Florida would mostly fight when and only for so long as the spirit moved them. In this case, the deserters explained, they needed to get home for their New Year's celebrations. In spite of the rout, "one and all, the American newspapers spread the story of the great victory of the Withlacoochee." Clinch, having fled the battlefield, was lauded as "the 'Hero of Withlacoochee' and 'Old Withlacoochee,' who had won a glorious victory for America."

Bitter rivals though they were, Clinch and Call both had opposed Governor Eaton's efforts to avoid violence and had argued loudly for the use of force. Then both of them had run away when their attempt to use force faltered. Now, following the fiasco on the Withlacoochee, Clinch and Call once again agreed on something. The federal government should save them. "We require," Call informed President Jackson, "an army of 2,500 to 3,000 men." The entire standing army of the United States at that time was less than eight thousand, including support troops. President Jackson bore the greatest responsibility for the disaster. He had pressed relentlessly for forced removal; he had promoted reckless, dishonest, and incompetent officials, including Clinch, Phagan, and Thompson. Now Jackson made another series of blunders. Instead of making Call commander of U.S. forces there, and instructing local forces to clean up the mess they had made, he appointed Call to the civilian post of governor. Instead of firing Clinch, he demoted him and ordered General Winfield Scott, a staff officer with no experience of Florida, to take command. Call was outraged; Clinch was vengeful. Scott would turn out to be as incompetent as they were.

Also deeply offended was General Edmund Pendleton Gaines, Jackson's subordinate in the region for more than twenty years. Now Jackson had bypassed Gaines and put a rival general in charge in Florida. In response Gaines, without any orders, invaded Florida himself. Setting out from New Orleans, where the news of Scott's promotion had alarmed him far more than the Seminole attacks, Gaines proclaimed that he was the one who would rid Florida of the Seminole menace. "I shall proceed," he announced, "upon the principle that, to find the enemy, we must search for him; and when we find him, we must take or destroy him." Gaines' main discovery consisted of the decomposing remains of Dade and his soldiers. By then the cadavers had been exposed to the elements for forty-five days. The bodies, Gaines' men noticed, had not been desecrated. "The officers were not robbed of articles of jewelry or personal adornment," a report commemorating Dade's defeat noted with surprise. Why had the "savages" not taken the personal property of those they killed in battle? One popular explanation was that the Seminoles were so shocked that they had been able to kill so many white men that they fled the scene in distraught confusion before having the chance to commit their customary outrages. The Seminoles nonetheless had spent enough time there to dump Dade's heavy cannon in a nearby pond. Nor had the Seminoles been too thunderstruck by the sight of all those white dead bodies to make off with the expedition's weapons and ammunition.

Two days later General Gaines—who had yet to receive a single communication of any kind from his subordinate, General Clinch—reached Fort King. Though he had come all the way from New Orleans, a journey by land and sea of more than six hundred miles, his were the first U.S. reinforcements to reach the fort since Clinch abandoned it. Following the fiasco at the Withlacoochee,

"General Clinch, with his force," once again had retreated to his plantation. The few Americans remaining at Fort King were nearing starvation. There was no way, Gaines realized, to feed his fifteen hundred men, so then and there he decided to abandon his Florida search-and-destroy mission. But how to get from Fort King back to Tampa Bay, where U.S. Navy ships could transport General Gaines comfortably away from Florida?

Seeking to evade the Seminoles, Gaines took his troops on a fifty-mile detour to another spot on the Withlacoochee that supposedly friendly scouts said would provide easy fording. Yet again a U.S. commander found himself facing wide, deep water and yet again the Seminoles "opened a galling fire from the opposite bank." "I have reason to believe that I have now near me the principal force of the Seminole Indians," Gaines had announced. That was true, though not in the sense he intended. Unable to advance, unable to retreat, Gaines gradually came to understand it was the Seminoles who had been doing the searching, and who were now doing the destroying. Sprague, the forgotten Florida Thucydides, lets the scene speak for itself: "The arrival of reinforcements was looked for with anxiety. Hunger began to be felt, though submitted to by officers and men without a murmur. The Indians still fired upon the camp daily, generally at guard-mounting, after creeping within rifle range, in the midst of the bushes and grass, shouting and yelling continually in the distance." Soon Gaines and his men were eating their dogs. "The hindquarter of a stolen dog fetched $5.00 for barbecue; horse entrails went for $6 a piece," soldiers later recounted. One soldier described the survivors among Gaines's force in his diary: "These poor creatures, such was their state of famine, that they represented living skeletons."

Deliverance came in the form of some shouting one night from the Seminole lines. It emanated from "an old negro by the name of Caesar, who at the top of his voice said that the Indians were tired of fighting, and wished to come in and shake hands." Willing to do anything to escape, Gaines falsely promised the Seminoles that, if they stopped firing at him, he would arrange for U.S. commissioners to resume negotiations with them. In the meantime, he pledged, the Seminoles "should not for the present be disturbed." Osceola and the others immediately agreed to the truce, at which point "General Clinch," who had finally appeared on the scene, "wheeled his troops into line, and commenced a vigorous assault" on the peacemakers. In the ensuing melee General Gaines abandoned his troops and handed command over to Clinch, just as Clinch earlier had passed his losing hand on the battlefield to Call. Next, as was standard operating procedure by then, Gaines announced he had won a tremendous victory, and left Florida as suddenly as he had arrived. The Seminoles had been "beaten, and forced to sue for peace," he declared. The promised negotiations never took place.

Even before setting eyes on Florida, General Winfield Scott had concocted a grand three-pronged theory; his idea was to win the Florida War by treating it as a giant turkey hunt. Scott launched his offensive on March 26, 1836. The left wing swept down the Atlantic coast, while the middle wing plunged into the center of the Florida peninsula. The right wing marauded down the Gulf coast. Then all three wings converged at Fort Brooke. The idea was that the Seminoles would be caught up in this great encircling advance like game fleeing beaters on a gentlemen's hunting party. Then, sweeping their quarry before them, the three wings would drive those Seminoles they did not kill to Tampa Bay, where they could be placed on ships and deported to Oklahoma. By early April Scott's combined forces had been able to kill no more than sixty Seminoles, and not even Scott pretended the dead were "warriors." President Jackson was apoplectic. "Why it is that their deposit for women have not been found," the president exclaimed, "I cannot conjecture." He continued to proclaim, from faraway Washington, that if only U.S. forces were ruthless enough, the Seminoles could be defeated in thirty days. By April 1836, four thousand U.S. troops were concentrated at Fort Brooke. This was approximately three times the force Jackson had mustered against the British at New Orleans, but who were they to fight?

After less than a month and a half Winfield Scott, later famous as commander of the 1846 U.S. attack on Mexico, deserted his troops and abandoned Florida. Scott was burned in effigy in Tallahassee; Floridians demanded a congressional investigation into why General Scott had gone off, "leaving the country without defense."

Scott riposted, declaring that the Floridians were "possessed with the general and degrading disease of cowardice." On April 26, 1836, General Clinch, back at his plantation, did Gaines and Scott one better. He resigned from the U.S. Army, then fled Florida forever. One of Clinch's complaints was that President Jackson had expected him to conduct warfare in Florida during the summer time. The United States had shown itself to be as derelict as John Quincy Adams had accused the Spaniards of being when it came "to the protection of her territory," but it was not their fault. U.S. officials were quite explicit about that. The Seminoles' "low cunning and unchivalrous system of warfare" were to blame, Scott testified when asked to explain the disaster. The board of inquiry found every one of them—Scott, Gaines, Call, Clinch, and the martyred Dade—blameless.

A quarter-century earlier "General" Mathews, having disgraced himself politically in Georgia, had sought military redemption in Florida. General Clinch did the opposite. Having disgraced himself militarily in Florida, he sought political redemption in Georgia. Clinch's audiences loved it when he blamed the politicians in Washington for his failures, but the facts showed he was lying. Far from withholding support, Jackson had sent half the armed forces of the United States to Florida. Earlier Clinch had sought to enrich himself at Seminole expense when Dick and Prince, two slaves on Clinch's Auld Lang Syne plantation, had died. No evidence was ever presented as to who killed them, but as at Negro Fort earlier, "a roving band of Seminoles" was declared the guilty party. Therefore, Clinch alleged, the Seminoles should compensate him with cash money. Even as the Seminoles faced starvation, Clinch sued them in federal court, demanding that they reimburse him for the deaths of Dick and Prince.

That claim failed because of a technicality, but after resettling in Georgia Clinch continued his attempts to use his Florida connection to extract money from the U.S. Treasury. In 1842 a federal court ordered the U.S. Treasury to pay Clinch almost $70,000, a stupendous sum at the time. It supposedly was compensation for damages Clinch's late father-in-law had suffered thirty years earlier as a result of the "Patriot" invasion of Florida. It came out of the $5 million with which, twenty years earlier, the United States supposedly had purchased Florida from Spain. Though he had abandoned his Florida plantation without a fight, Clinch also petitioned Congress to take $25,000 out of the funds appropriated for the Seminoles to "compensate" him for his losses there. Instead Congress paid Clinch $25,756.25 for having allowed the U.S. Army's horses and mules to forage on his property for a two-month period. That made Clinch even richer, but it got him into political trouble when he ran for governor of Georgia. "Old Withlacoochee" claimed he had fed Florida's starving volunteers from his own larders as they heroically repulsed the Seminole hordes. When it turned out that the U.S. government had paid him a veritable fortune for letting horses eat his grass, he was denounced as a "dodger." His avarice, not his contempt for human life, caused Clinch to lose his bid to become governor of Georgia.

In November 1849, at age sixty-two, Duncan Clinch, perpetrator of the forgotten Negro Fort Massacre and also the person principally responsible for the much-remembered Dade Massacre, died a millionaire. In addition to a legacy of violence, injustice and corruption, he bequeathed to modern Florida a contempt for productive labor—as opposed to get-rich schemes—that would warp its economy for generations to come. In other parts of America white yeoman ownership of self-sufficient small agricultural holdings was considered the great societal good. In Florida homesteading not only was scorned, it was illegal. To become an "aristocrat" like Duncan Clinch, not some dirt farmer, was the goal which government policy fostered and government money subsidized. Like many another poor boy made good, Clinch once rich became a strong proponent of poor white disenfranchisement. Restrictions on poor white political power would go hand in hand with limitations on poor white property rights into the twentieth century.

Both of his adopted states bestowed honors on this exemplary "hero" of an all too exemplary Florida "victory" that endure to this day. Clinch County, Georgia, perpetuates his name. So does Fort Clinch, Florida, which looks out across the St. Marys River to the place where Mathews had proclaimed that Florida could be subdued in days, that Fernandina and St. Augustine were only stepping-stones on the way to Venezuela.

11

JESUP'S CAPITULATION

The show horses having fled the field, it was left to a war horse, General Thomas Sidney Jesup, to salvage what he could of the Florida disaster. In Jesup's first offensive, yet again on the banks of the Withlacoochee, he failed to dislodge an interracial force composed of some six hundred Seminoles; it included more than two hundred armed blacks. Courageous enough to recognize there was no possibility of a quick, easy victory, Jesup was also astute enough to perceive that only honest negotiations stood any chance of extricating the United States from this quagmire of its own making. Major Dade had been instantaneously transformed into a Florida place-name. Following negotiations at Camp Dade on the Withlacoochee River, the Seminoles agreed to a permanent cease-fire; they pledged to remove themselves from Florida "immediately." Meanwhile, they would withdraw south of the Hillsborough River.

This separation of forces agreement returned to U.S. control the whole swath of central, peninsular Florida—centering on what today is the Interstate 4 corridor—stretching from Tampa Bay to the Atlantic Ocean. Jesup had won back through diplomacy what Gaines, Call, Scott and Clinch had lost on the battlefield. Even more remarkably, he had persuaded the Seminoles to accept Removal.

He called it a Seminole "capitulation," but Jesup had done some capitulating himself. In order to persuade the Seminoles to leave Florida he had pledged, "in behalf of the United States," that the human rights of black Seminoles would be protected. Instead of being sold into slavery, the Seminoles' black "allies, who come in and emigrate to the west, shall be secure in their lives and property." The agreement also explicitly stated "that their negroes, their bona fide property, shall accompany them." This formal U.S. acknowledgment of the interracial nature of the Seminole identity was the breakthrough that made agreement possible. First as individuals, then in family groups, finally whole communities of Seminoles converged on the Tampa Bay transit camp Jesup established. Once registered, each person was issued "provisions and clothing. Twenty-six vessels lay in the harbor to transport them to New-Orleans," Captain Sprague recounted. More than seven hundred Seminoles registered. Even so, less than 12 percent of the total population had come forward. Behind everything lay the question: What would Osceola do? The answer arrived when a U.S. Army "express" rider—Florida's early version of the pony express—galloped into Jesup's headquarters at Fort Brooke. "Osceola or Powell, with his family, [had] expressed his desire for peace, and his approbation of the terms agreed upon in the capitulation."

There remained an unresolved threat to peace. "Any attempt to interfere with the Indian negroes," Jesup warned Governor Richard Keith Call, "would cause an immediate resort to arms." When Call failed to prevent "the interference of unprincipled white men," Jesup attempted to bypass the territorial government. "Responsible as he is for the peace and security of the country," Jesup's headquarters announced, "he therefore orders that no white man, not in the service of the United States, be allowed to enter any part of the Territory between the St. Johns River and the Gulf of Mexico, south of Fort Drane." Whites disregarded the order; Jesup's own troops, who were not about to open fire on other whites, disregarded it too. His attempt to make peace had turned Jesup into the white man white men in Florida hated most.

Unable to modify their behavior, Jesup next tried to win whites over to his plan by betraying the promise that had led the Seminoles to accept his agreement in the first place. He decreed that "escaped slaves" belonging to white residents of Florida, contrary to his original pledge, would not be allowed to go West. They would be returned to their supposed owners. Whites, instead of being mollified, were scandalized. Why should only some blacks be re-enslaved? Why should slaveholders outside Florida not also get their "property" returned to them? At their Tampa Bay camp, the Seminoles recognized that the only significant concession Jesup had offered—equal treatment for black Seminoles—was being taken away from them before their emigration began. In the predawn darkness of June 3, 1837, the entire population of Jesup's internment camp disappeared without their American guards so much as noticing. As General Jesup put it in his report to Washington, "the Indians who had surrendered for emigration . . . and were in readiness to embark, had precipitately fled."

The U.S. Army Surgeon in Florida, Dr. Samuel Forry, explained why any sane human being would have left even before Jesup went back on his word. As soon as Jesup's capitulation was signed, Forry noted, white trading companies were "formed to speculate in the Negro property of the Indians. The negroes became aware of this, grew alarmed, and fled." Meanwhile Seminole women became "the prey of those infernal vampyres . . . who, in violation of all that is honorable in men and all that is sacred in female character have taken advantage of their unprotected condition." Meanwhile, Dr. Forry added, "measles appeared, and as Indians draw no distinction between this disease and small pox, many fled terrified." By then many were convinced that, no matter how cooperative they were, they never would reach Oklahoma alive. If they did not die in Jesup's custody, they feared, once "at sea they would become food for fishes."

Whites had destroyed his peace plan. Seminoles, Jesup now decided, would pay the price. The alternative to a negotiated settlement being a war of attrition, Jesup set out to kill and capture Seminoles any way he could. At his request U.S. Indian agents interrupted the expulsion to Oklahoma of tribes hostile to the Seminoles and diverted them south, down the Mississippi. From New Orleans, the U.S. Navy transported hundreds of warriors by sea to Tampa Bay, where they were set upon the population. Jesup promised these mercenaries "fifty dollars for every negro." When the politicians in Washington refused to pay, Jesup privatized the killing. Mathews had summoned his Georgia "rag-a-muffins." Jackson had unleashed his Tennessee Volunteers. Reversing his previous policy, Jesup invited looters and slave catchers from all over America to kill Seminoles for profit. He could offer his miscreants stolen booty. He could not promise them land. While the orators and editorialists proclaimed it a war to open up Florida to white settlement, homesteading remained illegal. While the killing continued, Governor Call and his allies divvied up the acreage in the safety of their Tallahassee offices.

Following the Seminoles' escape, the familiar reversal of fact and fiction overtook the official American mind. General Jesup's own pledge to protect black people vanished, its place taken by an imaginary obligation on the part of the Seminoles to help re-enslave them. In August 1837 Jesup made it known he wanted to talk with Osceola, and sent him his white truce cloth. When word came that Osceola, as always, was willing to "shake hands," Jesup composed what he called a "Memoranda of Specific Questions to Be Addressed to Osceola." "Ascertain the object of the Indians in coming in at this time," he ordered. "Are they prepared to deliver up the negroes?" Two months later, when Osceola came forward to discuss those very questions, he was seized on the grounds he had "betrayed" his nonexistent pledge to help re-enslave black Seminoles. By capturing Osceola in this manner U.S. troops dishonored their own commander's flag of truce.

This behavior contrasted with Osceola's own much-admired chivalry on the battlefield. In December 1835, as the Seminoles prepared their uprising, Osceola had given an American friend of his, Lieutenant John Graham, what a Florida newspaper described as "a handsome plume of white crane feathers to be worn as a badge of protection in the battle field." Osceola's egret plume was the equivalent of Jesup's white cloth, the difference being that in Osceola's case the dispensation this emblem provided was respected. During the Battle of the Withlacoochee, one of the medics reported, other soldiers crowded around Lieutenant Graham "because Osceola had given his warriors not to fire upon Graham."

By the time he was captured, the story of Osceola's egret feathers had spread throughout the American ranks. "We were all outraged by the cowardly way he was betrayed," one soldier remembered. "Are you prepared at once to deliver up the negroes taken from the citizens?" demanded the commander of the U.S. contingent that surrounded Osceola. He was given no chance to reply: "A signal, preconcerted, was at this moment given and armed soldiers rushed in and made prisoners of the chiefs." When John S. Masters, one of the soldiers who witnessed the capture, pointed out that Osceola had been carrying Jesup's white flag, he was asked: "Did you honor that truce?" "No sir," Masters replied, "no sooner was he safe within our lines than we received the order to seize him, kill if necessary . . . and one of the soldiers knocked him down with the butt of his musket."

The American form of racism relentlessly transformed humans, depending on their skin and facial features, into "negroes" or "savages," but as this incident demonstrated, the knife could cut the other way. The officer who gave the preconcerted signal to beat Osceola to the ground was a St. Augustine–born Spaniard named José Hernández. So far as some Americans were concerned, Floridians like Hernández—Catholic and of Mediterranean origin—were hardly white men at all, but while Billy Powell—born free, on U.S. soil—was being transformed into a "savage," José Hernández had transformed himself into Joe Hernández, a white American figure of consequence.

In 1821, even as Governor DuVal was expelling Enemathla, Hernández arrived in Tallahassee and befriended Florida's new rulers. An Hispanic in an Anglo outpost, a Spaniard in a territory now "appertaining" to the United States, Hernández quickly switched allegiances and ran for territorial delegate to the U.S. Congress. In Florida's first-ever elections, 396 landowning males, almost all of them in St. Augustine, voted for him, more than double the total for his nearest rival. Though Hernández had no vote in the House of Representatives, and held office for less than six months, that arguably made him the first Hispanic elected to the U.S. Congress.

José—the future Joe—Hernández was one of the first in Florida to understand that U.S. annexation presented great opportunities if you were quick enough to grab them. Like Clinch, he used his military-political connections to get rich, notably through federal road-building contracts. To build his roads he needed to "clear" Seminoles from the territory through which they passed. In the resulting conflict the roads Hernández built speeded the arrival of U.S. military forces, necessitating the construction of more forts, which in turn generated more federal contracts. Photographs of Hernández, who was swarthy and hirsute with aquiline features, still exist. At first glance he is no more obviously "white" than Powell is "Indian." That did not stop him from becoming Brigadier General Joseph M. Hernández, head of the territorial militia in eastern Florida, the highest-ranking Florida-born commander to fight on the U.S. side in the Seminole War. The capriciousness, in retrospect, is as striking as the brutality. Had Powell been a few shades lighter, and Hernández a few shades darker, their fates might have been reversed.

Like the war as a whole, Osceola's capture continued the centuries-long tradition of brutality and deceit that characterized the subjugation of America's original population. It was also another step along white America's road to the great bloodletting of the Civil War. The Americans destroyed his life because, in their eyes, Osceola was an "Indian," but it was his refusal to betray black Seminoles that led to his capture. Starting when he was still Billy Powell, Osceola drew his wives and friends from all racial groups. People of Indian, black—and white—descent fought under his command in every battle. They kept fighting even when betraying the blacks among them would have saved them much suffering and, in many cases, saved their lives. Osceola's brutal mistreatment, as Congressman Giddings put it, demonstrated "the intimate relation which this war bore to slavery." General Jesup was even more blunt about it. It was, he pointed out, a war to protect and expand slavery, "a Negro and not an Indian war." Years later, Congressman Jay would come to the same conclusion as he delved into the tragic consequences of the Florida killing. "Slavery, then, is the key which unlocks the enigma of the Florida War," he concluded.

For Osceola, as for Clausewitz, war was a continuation of politics by other means, but a political solution was never possible because the Seminoles found themselves up against a primitive version of total war, in which the objective was not victory but eradication of the enemy, followed by the imposition of a millennial new order. Each time the Seminoles sought a political solution, Americans opted for a continuation of ideological warfare, or what sometimes is called a crusade, a pogrom, or a race war. The mistreatment inflicted on an isolated group called the "Spanish Indians" illustrated the doctrinal and psychological aspects of the Florida War. The Americans were unaware the Spanish Indians existed when the Florida War began; that did not alter their fate. "A small band, composed of Spanish negroes and Indians, among whom were said to be some maroons from Cuba," as Giddings described them, they "resided far down in the Peninsula of Florida." Numbering less than five hundred people, Captain Sprague reported, they lived peacefully, harming no one, subsisting mostly as fishermen, until, "finding themselves attacked and pursued [by U.S. forces], they took arms and resisted." Those Spanish Indians who were not killed were shipped off to Oklahoma with the Seminoles. The arid western plains had become, in the American imagination, the rightful abode of all "Indians," including these subtropical fisher folk.

Scouring a "wilderness of which," as General Jesup put it, "we were as ignorant as of the interior of China," U.S. patrols hunted down their victims one hideaway at a time. Wherever they found them, as one U.S. account later put it, "the soldiers of the United States shot down women and children, destroyed all dwellings, crops and fruit trees they could reach." Two out of every three Seminoles killed, Jesup informed the War Department, were women, children, and old people.

Gradually Jesup captured dozens of Seminole leaders, mostly through trickery. Little by little they were being reduced as an effective military force. In early 1838, a military engagement fought inland from the present-day resort town of Jupiter showed how the lay of the land was changing. The Seminoles were not decisively defeated, but the fighting did reflect the Americans' expanding military superiority. General Jesup called it the Battle of Loxahatchee and proclaimed victory—a victory he set out to turn to his political advantage in Washington.

Jesup by then seemed as malign as Phagan, as mendacious as DuVal, as unscrupulous as Gadsden, your typical Florida villain. Underneath, Florida had been working on him the same metamorphosis it had on Gad Humphreys. The Battle of Loxahatchee was fought on January 24, 1838. Two days later General Jesup made a formal proposal to the War Department, as Sprague later put it, "to put an end to the conflict." "In regard to the Seminoles," he pointed out, "we have committed the error of attempting to remove them when their lands were not required for agricultural purposes; when they were not in the way of the white inhabitants; and when the greater portion of their country was an unexplored wilderness." Jesup also ridiculed the rhetoric of liberty used to justify the war. This was no war for freedom, he had come to recognize; the same omnivorous greed Alligator had discussed with Gad Humphreys propelled the violence.

Jesup had contempt for himself by then; most of all he had contempt for the one American who, more than any other, had engendered America's Florida catastrophe, Andrew Jackson. "If our operations have fallen short of public expectations," he informed the War Department, "it should be remembered that we are attempting that which no other armies of our country had ever been required to do." That was not merely "to fight, beat and drive the enemy before us, but to go into an unexplored wilderness and catch them." Not even "Jackson," he wrote, "was required to do this; and unless the objects to be accomplished be the same, there can be no just comparison as to the results." That last sentence measured the fullness of Jesup's contempt. "Jackson," he called him in a report the president was sure to see, not "General Jackson," not "President Jackson." Like Humphreys before him, Jesup had wound up knowing—in his case that when it came to Florida, Andrew Jackson was a liar and a fraud, a braggart who claimed to have conquered Florida when he had not even crossed the Suwanee. And now, from the comfort of the White House, Jackson blamed others for failing to achieve in Florida what he had not even tried to accomplish.

What, then, should be done with the Seminoles? "I would allow them to remain," Jesup wrote. He went on to propose granting the Seminoles a stretch of inland central Florida, extending roughly from the present site of Disney World "south, to the extreme of Florida. That would satisfy them, and they might hold it on the express condition that they should forfeit their right to it, if they should either commit depredations upon the white inhabitants, or pass the boundaries assigned to them." He went on to warn "that unless immediate emigration be abandoned, the war will continue for years to come, and at constantly accumulating expense."

Jesup frankly admitted that his military duty was "not to comment upon the policy of the government, but to carry it out in accordance with my instructions." The problem, he went on to explain, was that his faithful endeavors had shown him that the entire U.S. policy was wrong. As a loyal citizen, he had decided he no longer could stay silent. The War Department's reply was withering and facile. The fraudulent Treaty of Payne's Landing, he was sternly reminded, "has been ratified, and is the law of the land; and the constitutional duty of the president requires that he should cause it to be executed. I cannot, therefore," the secretary of war continued, "authorize any arrangement with the Seminoles, by which they will be permitted to remain." The disdain was next directed at Jesup himself. "The department indulged the hope," he was informed, "that, with the extensive means placed at your disposal, the war, by a vigorous effort, might be brought to a close." The secretary of war went on to remind him "that every exertion should be made to chastise the marauding Indians." To that end he instructed General Jesup to "address yourself to Colonel James Gadsden for information on this subject." While Jesup had been slogging through the Florida wilderness Gadsden, ever the ingratiator, had been nurturing his contacts in Washington.

The battle-hardened General Jesup also was ordered to transfer frontline prosecution of the war to the latest show horse to arrive on the scene. That was Colonel (and future President) Zachary Taylor, a soldier-politician whose adeptness at turning war to his own advantage would be amply demonstrated in the decades to come. General Jesup tried to use his victory near Jupiter, real if not decisive, to save his country from further dishonor and bloodshed. A week earlier Colonel Taylor, having lost a major battle, turned it into a public relations triumph for himself. In the Battle of Lake Okeechobee, more than eight hundred troops under Taylor's command suffered some of the worst casualties since the Dade Massacre. He did capture some ponies and cattle. News of Jesup's victory and Taylor's defeat reached Washington simultaneously, where the habitual inversion of fact and fiction took place. Taylor became an overnight hero. He was promoted to brigadier general for telling his superiors what they wanted to hear. Rebuked and humiliated for telling the truth, Jesup returned to his old desk job in Washington, as quartermaster general of the U.S. Army. In that capacity he became another of those rare Florida protagonists who manage to live honorably ever after. He remained quartermaster general until 1860 when, still hard at work, he died at age seventy-two, having served longer in that post than anyone else ever has, before or since. Long revered as "Father of the Modern Quartermaster Corps," General Jesup in 1986 was named the first member of the Quartermaster Hall of Fame.

After being humiliated, deceived, and thrown into a dungeon, Osceola—one of Florida's truly prophetic figures—was next turned into a celebrity, then finally into a souvenir. Fearful he might escape his St. Augustine dungeon, his captors transferred him to Fort Moultrie, an island outpost off Charleston, South Carolina. By then his own exploits and the sensationalist tactics of America's emerging newspaper industry had turned Osceola into the first of the country's celebrity Indian chiefs—admired as a heroic embodiment of primitive virtue even as he and his people were being brutalized and dispossessed. Impressed by the heroism of his struggle and the stoicism with which Osceola endured his fate, the famous portrait painter George Catlin traveled south in order to paint his portrait. As artist and subject will, they spent hours discussing life's vicissitudes. "This gallant fellow is grieving with a broken spirit, and ready to die," the artist wrote.

Medical malpractice, not grief, killed Osceola. Respiratory diseases thrive in the cold and damp, and in January it gets chilly in South Carolina. The cold can be especially chilling for a Floridian, especially in an unheated stone cell on a windswept island. The physician in charge, Dr. Frederick Weedon, had accompanied Osceola from Florida, at every turn making sure he was subjected to the conditions that killed him. In his diary the doctor complained that his captive had "for 6 or 7 Days been secured in a warm Room"—not for the sake of his health, but in order to pose for Catlin and other artists. Once the visitors left Dr. Weedon made sure his prisoner was returned to his unheated cell.

Afterward, Weedon acknowledged that Osceola all along had been suffering from quinsy. Better known today as peritonsillar abscess, or PTA, quinsy is a form of aggravated throat infection. Competently treated, it need not be deadly. Lack of proper medical care, combined with unhealthful living conditions, can cause the condition to turn fatal. Dr. Weedon appreciated the effect such conditions were bound to have on his patient. "Probably he will not live through the winter," he reported. His prediction came true on January 30, 1838. That same night Dr. Weedon, using his medical saw and scalpel, set to work severing Osceola's head from its recently dead body.

Fifteen years earlier, the Treaty of Moultrie Creek had initiated the catastrophe that befell the Seminoles. Now Osceola's headless corpse was thrown into a grave at Fort Moultrie. Look across Charleston Harbor from Osceola's grave site, and another symmetry appears. From Fort Moultrie you can see Fort Sumter. Just twenty-three years later, Confederates would open fire on Fort Sumter from Fort Moultrie as the dispute over slavery, whose vast extension was made possible by dispossessing the Indians, unleashed America's greatest bloodletting. As a result of Osceola's decapitation America's two great tragic crimes—near genocide of indigenous Americans; enslavement of Africans—are interconnected across Charleston Harbor.

Later Dr. Weedon's sons recounted how he hung Osceola's head on their bedpost when they were naughty. Eventually he gave his souvenir to his son-in-law, Daniel Whitehurst, who resided in New York City. The gift of a marble bust or suit of armor could not have delighted him more. Osceola's head, Whitehurst boasted, was worthy of being displayed alongside the artifacts "that the classic lands of Greece and Rome, the isles of the sea, and many a well-fought field in Europe, alike have given up." That seems to explain why Whitehurst in turn presented Osceola's head to the Surgical and Pathological Museum in New York, where it vanished in 1866 when the museum, along with its assembled deformities and curiosities, was consumed by fire.

What happened to Osceola's head also happened to the memory of the man. It started while he was still alive. From a human being—the boy with the "English" father who played ball with his white neighbors—Osceola was transmuted into an enemy, a threat to freedom, a "savage." Then he was turned into a celebrity. By the time he died he was America's most famous "Indian," but death was only the beginning. Osceola used a rifle in warfare and was known for his insistent, reasonable voice, yet "Chief Osceola," a Wild West show travesty, complete with flaming arrows and war whoops, was long a feature of halftime shows at Florida State football games. Osceola's head haunted a 2000 science fiction TV show, supposedly bringing doom on whomever possessed it. According to *Osceola's Head and Other American Ghost Stories*, night visitors to the Castillo de San Marcos sometimes "stop and stare. Many have claimed that they see a head," it relates, falsely of course, though this fictional tale does tell a truth that the official iconography does not. Osceola's head floats there to remind us that his capture and subsequent treatment "was one of the most shameful acts of the U.S. Government against the Indians of Florida."

The abstract notion that Florida, to be American, must be Indian-free was the only consistent reason why, under the U.S. flag, it became a crucible of dishonor. One white Floridian was stating the obvious when he wrote that the Seminoles "would have remained peaceable to this day had not an order been issued ordering them all to remove." The needlessness gave the repression its gratuitous flavor, yet even during the worst moments the shared humanity burst out. At Fort King, in 1835, while Thompson and Clinch were haranguing the Seminoles, the makeshift wooden bleachers on which they all were sitting collapsed. Everyone treated it as a marvelous joke: Americans and Seminoles rolled together in the dirt laughing, then helped each other get right up, dust themselves off, and start the same tragic dialogue of the deaf all over again.

Hernández was responsible for an equally memorable outburst of goodwill. It happened on the occasion of his daughter's wedding. By then nearly three hundred captives were jammed into the St. Augustine dungeon. Among them were the Seminole leaders

Coacoochee, also known as Wild Cat, and John Horse. Coacoochee came from a long line of Indian notables. John Horse, as one
U.S. Army officer described him, was racially African but culturally
Seminole: "a long-legged, ill-looking negro boy" who grew up to
become "a fine-looking fellow of six feet, as straight as an Indian, with
just a smile of red blood mantling to his forehead." Close friends,
Coacoochee and John Horse would lead extraordinary lives—first
in Florida, then in the West, finally in Mexico.

Though Coacoochee, like Osceola, had been "betrayed into
being captured," that did not stop Hernández from inviting him to
his daughter's wedding. "Waltzes and Spanish dances were the order
of the day," Forry remembered. "Coacoochee," he added, "was the
lion of the night, attracting special attention of the ladies . . . a perfect
Apollo in his figure." Forry then paid the Seminole leader the highest
compliment he knew: "Coacoochee has the countenance of a white
man." After the party, Wild Cat and the others were returned to their
dungeon. "The Indians are perfectly secure, and do not dream of
escape," Forry wrote. A short time later, Coacoochee and eighteen
other Seminoles did just that. They had starved themselves so as to
be able to wriggle free through prison bars. General—as he now
was—Zachary Taylor chased Coacoochee and his forces across half
of Florida but could never catch him.

Osceola inspired painters; Coacoochee inspired poets. In
Twasinta's Seminoles; or, Rape of Florida, an epic in three cantos, the
hero struggles valiantly, only in the end to be deported by ship the
same way Coacoochee eventually was. More accurate than many
supposedly factual accounts, *Rape of Florida* treated the Seminole
War as the tragedy it was. The poem, an accomplished example
of a genre now out of fashion, was one of the very few works of
imaginative literature of its period dealing with Florida, yet even in
the days when students were made to memorize poetry by the yard,
no teachers taught this poem. Albery Whitman was black. His even
greater disqualification was that he told the truth. In her anthology
of African-American poetry, Joan R. Sherman explains why his poem
suffered the same fate that Jesup's report to the War Department did.
In it the "treacherous rape of Florida is a parable of the American

experience: a land once paradisiacal is corrupted by greed, hatred, and hypocrisy, and its native peoples, red and black, are doomed by race prejudice." Or as the poet himself put it, more pithily: "Freedom is an empty name / And war-worn glory is a glaring shame."

As Jesup warned, the war continued "for years to come." At the end of 1838 General Taylor abandoned southern Florida just as Jesup had proposed. Not even northern Florida was successfully "cleared." That did not stop him from being praised and promoted. Each successive U.S. commander arrived intending to achieve victory in three months. After a year or two they would come to Jesup's conclusion; 1842 marked the ostensible end of what Americans called the Second Seminole War. That year the U.S. military unilaterally ceased operations in Florida. Thousands of Seminoles had died; thousands more had agreed to go West in return for cash payments. These small sums could not begin to compensate them for their losses; nonetheless modern accounts continue to describe them as bribes. As Seminole numbers dwindled, Coacoochee negotiated his own peace settlement. His friend John Horse acted as intermediary. The agreement promised that Coacoochee, plus his family and followers, including black people, could settle freely on land of their own west of the Mississippi. Right from the start the promises were betrayed. As soon as he arrived at the port Coacoochee was chained, then hauled aboard a U.S. Navy transport ship. There he was kept handcuffed, to assure that if he did manage to jump ship, he would drown.

It was the Fourth of July. In celebration a U.S. Navy ship began firing a cannonade. When Coacoochee's captor, Colonel William J. Worth, told him that on this "day many years ago the white people gained their rights as free men," he clutched his handcuffs and said, "Yes! the white man is free." As the ship prepared to weigh anchor Worth and Coacoochee discussed the meaning of life. As a boy, Coacoochee remembered, he had seen his first white man through his rifle sight, while out hunting. "I could not shoot him as I would a wolf or a bear," Coacoochee told Colonel Worth, "yet like these he came upon me." He went on to describe how the white man had treated him and his people: "Horses, cattle and fields he took from me. He said he was my friend. He abused our women and children,

and told us to go from the land. Still he gave me his hand in friendship. He lied and stung us. I asked for but a small piece of these lands,
enough to plant and live upon, far south—a spot where I could lay the
ashes of my kindred. This was not granted me. I was put in prison. I
escaped. I have again been taken. I feel the irons in my heart."

Another of those remarkable Seminole leaders, Halleck Tustenuggee, made shorter work of explaining what happened. "I have
been hunted like a wolf," he uttered with scorn as he, too, was shackled
and shipped West, "and now I am to be sent away like a dog." "A
very Iliad of tragedy" was how another chronicler of the Seminoles,
a white woman named Minnie Moore-Willson, summed up what
had befallen them. As survivors like Coacoochee and John Horse
trekked West, their *Iliad* turned into an *Odyssey*. Facing dangers as
baffling and far-flung as any mythic heroes had, they never stopped
hoping that, if only Americans could be made to appreciate the truth,
justice would be done. In 1844 Coacoochee and John Horse rode
and walked all the way to Washington, D.C. They had to enter the
capital separately. While an Indian could march down the Mall and
be considered quaint, free blacks were banned from so much as stepping foot in the city. Only slaves or servants, in the custody of their
masters, were permitted to see with their own eyes the great temples
of American democracy. John Horse, who had commanded troops
in battle more often than most U.S. generals, had to take a job as a
valet in order to get there.

Their Great Father in Washington would not hear them so they
contacted their old enemy, General Jesup. Jesup welcomed a whole
delegation of the Seminoles into his house on F Street. His wife
cooked for them; his daughters sang for them. By turns in the documentation of the times Jesup seems villainous and noble; gradually
the consistency of his character emerges. He was a man of duty—or
rather duties. His dilemma was that his moral and military duties
diverged, and there was no way to reconcile them. That did not
stop him from trying. Before the Seminoles came to Washington,
he had traveled all the way to Oklahoma to try to help them. There
as quartermaster general, he informed U.S. Army commanders that
those Black Seminoles who had gone West were entitled to their

freedom under the capitulation he himself had imposed. Whether his agreement remained "in full force and effect," as Jesup contended, was an open question, but no commander of a remote outpost likes to offend his source of supplies. The U.S. Army became, fitfully, the Black Seminoles' protector, thanks to Jesup's intervention.

General Jesup also pleaded for their rights in Washington. "I earnestly hope that the Executive will not permit the national faith then earnestly pledged . . . to be violated," Jesup argued, referring to his own pledges, "but that all of the negroes who surrendered to me and have been sent to the West, be protected from capture by, or sale to, either Citizens, foreigners, or Indians." The U.S. government sided with the kidnappers, the bounty hunters, the killers. It was, Jesup was informed, entirely legal to kidnap and enslave Seminoles, so long as they were black.

Nowhere in the United States was there a place, however remote or small, where these people might be safe and free, so Coacoochee and John Horse headed for Mexico. There slavery had been abolished in 1829, and a man of mixed African, Indian, and European descent named Vicente Guerrero had become president more than 180 years before Barack Obama sought the same office in the United States. By then Captain John Titcomb Sprague had finished his history of the Florida War, and been stationed in Texas. There, one day in July 1850, before his very eyes, figures from his book reemerged in the flesh like mirages shimmering on the plains of Texas. Sprague fed the Seminoles and drank whiskey with Coacoochee. Then he gave the group a laisser-passer through U.S. territory. When they reached the Rio Grande, the Seminoles built rafts and crossed into Mexico. There the government granted them what the United States, out of all its land and wealth, had always begrudged them: a place of their own.

Coacoochee died of smallpox at the Seminole land grant in El Nacimiento, Coahuila, in 1857. Though the epic of his life might have spanned generations, he was only forty-five. John Horse, or Juan Caballo as he was called in Spanish, died in 1882 as he lived, trying to speak truth to power, seeking an audience in Mexico City with the president to get renewed protection for the Seminole grant.

Coacoochee, born into the Indian elite in 1812, and John Horse, the son of "runaway slaves" born the same year in north Florida, reincarnated the friendship of Garcon and his nameless Indian companion but with a difference. Unlike them, they survived, and then finally found a place where it was not a crime to be who they were. It was America's tragedy, not theirs, that they could only find freedom outside the United States.

Back in Florida the Seminole War still had not ended, in spite of the official proclamations to the contrary. The "greatest obstacle" to peace, the Indian Agent reported in 1856, remained the adamant opposition of the "citizens of Florida, who, I am sorry to say would dislike this war to be ended." Even after the politicians in Washington realized enough was enough, Florida's white civilians never "lost their appetite for a 'war' that placed numbers of troops in the field, and a market for their produce and gave employment and food to the militia." "Hunting and killing the Indians was more than sport for these people," it was later observed. "Prices on captured Indians were handsome for that day: $500 for warriors, $250 for squaws and $100 for children."

So far as the Seminoles were concerned the war against them never ceased. It only took on additional forms. In 1855 what Americans called the Third Seminole War began after Seminole warriors attacked a U.S. Army detachment that had been devastating their settlements. At most three hundred Seminoles remained in southern Florida. Even so the Florida militia botched operations so badly the U.S. Army had to come to the rescue once again. The Florida militiamen, writes James W. Covington in his study of the conflict, "were given to idleness, drunkenness, and thievery. Most importantly, the militia had failed to prevent attacks against settlers." Though "victory" was again proclaimed in 1858, forced expulsions of the Seminoles continued into 1859. The following year the same white militiamen who disgraced themselves fighting Seminoles rushed to take up arms against federal "tyranny." In the end it would take two wars—the Civil War as well as the Seminole War—to make of Florida a U.S. possession.

Some argue that, except for the Civil War, the Florida War was the bloodiest conflict the United States fought during the nineteenth century. That is certainly true if we stop to consider that the Seminoles were Americans, too. Even counting only U.S. troops, and that phase known as the Second Seminole War, the conflict, with its 1,500 deaths, ranks as one of the major American conflicts. In comparison, U.S. fatalities for the War of 1812 were 2,260 killed; for the Mexican War, 1,773; for the Spanish-American War, 385; for the entire War of Independence, 4,435. The Florida campaign of ethnic cleansing was America's first great counterinsurgency war. It was also America's costliest "Indian" conflict. According to U.S. military statistics, nearly twice as many U.S. soldiers died in Florida as were killed subjugating the entire vast area west of the Mississippi.

The Florida War's most striking feature is the one it shares with so many of Florida's most important and revealing events. It remains the most forgotten major armed conflict in U.S. history. Even Floridians live unaware of the slaughter that occurred in their future backyards. On Wednesday, August 22, 2001, readers of the *Palm Beach Post* were surprised to see the following headline: "Riverbend Park the Site of Historical Battle." Who would have guessed that "just south of Indiantown Road, and west of Florida's Turnpike, sits a plot of land" where "Red and Black Seminoles fought U.S. soldiers?" remarked a local resident, referring to the site of the General Jesup's Battle of Loxahatchee. "Heck, if you drive by and blink you'll miss it."

Jesup's critique of U.S. policy would also disappear, even though its importance was recognized at the time. "General Jesup's letter to the secretary of war and his answer are important records in the history of the general government," Captain Sprague observed in a commentary that, like Jesup's proposal itself, would be suppressed by future historians. Writing in 1848, Sprague went on to describe the situation—as familiar today on C-SPAN as it was back then—that occurs when a competent military professional attempts to acquaint civilian leaders with the realities of a war they have recklessly determined to pursue: "The general, with a candid spirit of wisdom and philanthropy, pleads the cause of his foe, and urges upon the government with cogent reasons, the adoption of measures, the result of experience, which, had they been listened to, would have saved the nation millions of dollars, as well as the lives of valuable citizens and officers," Sprague noted. And then? "[The] secretary of war persists, in answer, to the same mistaken policy which commenced the contest."

Like those whose triumphs, depravities, venality and nobility he documented, Sprague and his definitive account of *The Origin, Progress, and Conclusion of the Florida War* would be expunged from Florida history. The Negro Fort Massacre became a non-massacre; Gad Humphreys became a nonperson; the most comprehensive, accurate account of the Florida War became a nonbook. Thanks to Sprague's thoroughness, everything anyone did not want to know was assembled in one convenient volume. The text of the Treaty of Moultrie Creek, so unaccountably absent elsewhere, is there. So are DuVal's letters, Humphreys's letters, along with the correspondence of dozens of other key figures. Yet Sprague's book is seldom so much as mentioned in Florida "history."

The decision to ignore Captain Sprague's investigation, like the parallel decision to ignore Congressman Giddings' investigation of the massacre at Negro Fort, has to be understood as a choice. Generation after generation, those who do not quote Sprague and Giddings are the same ones who, rather than confront the realities of Florida's past, opt for recycling the tales of Washington Irving. As the Florida War showed, white supremacy was a dynamic, expansive, aggressive system, not one built on passive defense of a society that, as both slaveholders and segregationists later pretended, only wanted to be left alone. "Clearing" Indians was an arduous process. Enslaving black people was a complicated, globe-spanning endeavor. Transforming those twin atrocities into triumphs of freedom was hard work, too. It would keep Florida's—and America's—historians busy for generations.

12

ALTERNATIVE FLORIDIANS

What happened in Florida happened afterward across North America. The seemingly absurd episode of the West Florida Lone Star Republic in 1810 served as a model for the Texas Republic's subversion of Mexican sovereignty in 1845. Florida's race war, masquerading as an Indian war, presaged a continental explosion of violence which would turn back on itself, with America's white men killing incomparably more of America's white men than the Spanish, British, "savages," and slaves ever did.

For famous men of the future like Zachary Taylor and Winfield Scott, Florida was the proving ground first for the conquest of Mexico, then for major political careers. For others Florida was the prelude to achieving immortality on America's road maps. Inside Florida the names of places like Fort Lauderdale, Fort Myers, Fort Pierce, Fort George, Fort White, Fort Braden, Fort Drum, Fort Meade and Fort Walton Beach bear silent witness to the fact that, before becoming resorts or suburbs, they were outposts of America's long campaign to subdue Florida. The name of Dade County, though few in multiracial Miami realize it, perpetuates the name of the commander who led his immigrant troops to their deaths in northern Florida. Farther afield Fort Smith, Arkansas, along with Fort Worth, Texas, are among the places named for U.S. soldiers who first fought in Florida, then went on to conquer more land Out West, before bringing their killing skills back home, for the Civil War.

James Gadsden in particular turned himself into a one-man example of how Florida's history foreshadowed the broader sweep of American expansion. Having begun his career by building Jackson's illegal fortification atop the ruins of Negro Fort, Gadsden went on to leave his name on several other far-flung pieces of territory, including a county in Florida and a city in Alabama. The most extensive territory to bear his name was the Gadsden Purchase, a strip of land, bulging in the middle, stretching from Texas to California. Just as the changing names at Negro Fort bespeak Florida's metamorphoses, the progress of Gadsden's name across the map of North America traces the expansion of the United States prior to the Civil War. Wherever he went Gadsden accumulated wealth—in land, money, and human property. Following his death Shingler Brothers Auctioneers in Charleston sold "A Very Prime Gang of 235 Negroes, belonging to the estate of the late General James Gadsden" to the highest bidders.

A native of South Carolina, Gadsden initially gained Andrew Jackson's favor while serving as a staff officer during the War of 1812. For decades to come, he prospered by making himself useful to powerful men; in the process he become one himself. Gadsden never got rich in Florida; he did learn a valuable lesson there. The future, he understood, was made of steel, not swampland, and it lay to the West, not south of the American heartland of slavery. After leaving Florida Gadsden turned himself into one of the first of the new railroad barons. Railroads like his literally obliterated the homesteads of the people he helped dispossess. One of the new railroads, Thomas Simpson Woodward pointed out, ran "within five feet, it not over the place, where the cabin stood in which Billy Powell was born."

Defeating Mexico opened up boundless opportunities, but for slaveholders like Gadsden the vast territories initially seized were not enough. More land had to be taken for his particular dream to come true. The ensuing Gadsden Purchase of 1854 added thirty thousand square miles to the lands, nearly one million square miles, that the United States seized from Mexico between 1845 and 1848. As a result Tucson and Yuma became part of the United States, but the real importance of the Gadsden Purchase lay in the lands it connected. Starting at El Paso, you could run a railroad through the Gadsden Purchase all the way from Texas to southern California. That explained its oddly elongated shape, but why would anyone want to build a railroad there? California's Gold Rush was far to the north; San Francisco, not Los Angeles, was California's golden boomtown. That was precisely why James Gadsden was so determined to build a railroad to the Pacific following the southern route. If only Yankees had a coast-to-coast railroad, Gadsden warned his fellow slaveholders, slavery's expansion westward would be stymied. But how, exactly, was slavery to be extended from sea to shining sea? As Gadsden planned it, the new railroad—its cattle cars packed with slaves, its parlor cars occupied by their owners—would traverse the desert all the way to Los Angeles, carrying the slaveholders' aggressively expansionist socioeconomic system with it.

Two great problems stood in his way, the same ones encountered earlier in Florida. The land Gadsden wanted belonged to a foreign country. Also, no prudent investor would risk his own money on such a scheme. Connections with powerful U.S. officials had been Gadsden's ticket to success from the beginning; his skills of ingratiation paid off this time too. In 1853 James Gadsden got his good friend Jefferson Davis to intervene on his behalf with President Franklin Pierce. Pierce was one of those many Yankee politicians who believed appeasement the best way to keep the South in the Union; Davis, the future Confederate president, was Pierce's secretary of war. Named by Pierce U.S. plenipotentiary to Mexico at Davis' behest, Gadsden used the techniques he'd perfected in Florida to cajole the Mexicans into relinquishing the land he wanted. Then, in an early example of corporate welfare, American taxpayers were made to foot the bill. The U.S. government paid $10 million in the hard currency of the time for the land Gadsden wanted, and this, unlike the $5 million supposedly paid for Florida, was a real expenditure. The federal government's support for the expansion of slavery, begun in Florida, had assumed continental proportions.

Today the notion of slave auctions in Beverly Hills seems bizarre, but within Gadsden's own lifetime slavery had surged out of Virginia and the Carolinas across Tennessee and Arkansas to Texas. Florida, as the Southern plutocrats saw it, was living proof slavery could be implanted anywhere. Looking back, what's astonishing is how close their scheme came to reality. Had the Civil War not intervened, there might have been a North Arizona and a South Arizona, with South Arizona becoming a slave state. When the Civil War started, secession conventions were held as far west as Tucson. The Confederate Territory of Arizona was established; Confederate troops briefly seized Santa Fe. Hoping to turn southern California into a bastion of slavery, the Los Angeles Mounted Rifles and the California Grays fought for the Confederacy.

As his rivals were defeated, were ruined, or ran away, Governor Richard Keith Call emerged as the dominant American personality in Florida. At age twenty-nine he had become founder and master of Florida's first full-blown political-money machine. Dedicated to concentrating power, hence wealth, in the hands of a small minority centered in Tallahassee, it was called the Nucleus. Speculating in public land, Call made profits of up to 600 percent every year. When favoritism failed, he padlocked the doors of the Land Office, preventing members of the public from bidding on public properties he and his friends wanted. As Florida grew, its counties subdivided. Decisions as to where county seats were to be located could be as lucrative as the initial choice of Tallahassee as the capital had been. The Nucleus also had a monopoly on government transactions, including land transfers. Heavy fines were imposed on those who conducted official business in places other than those they owned or controlled.

Call's personal advancement demonstrated how unfairly the system worked. When, as result of his failures on the battlefield, Jackson was "compelled to relieve his old friend of military command," Call was not demoted; he was promoted to governor. The value of the relationship also was evident in the wealth Call accumulated. "In 1821 he came to the territory possessing little beyond the patronage of Andrew Jackson," notes one account. "By 1840, tax and census records listed him as the owner of 66 slaves, 6,000 prime acres in Leon [County] (and much more elsewhere in Florida), $20,000 in Tallahassee lots." When Jackson's hand-picked successor, Martin Van Buren, named a new governor, Call chose the path of the political turncoat, supporting William Henry Harrison instead. Before dying after only one month in office, President Harrison named Richard

Keith Call governor for a second time. He would remain Florida's unelected territorial governor until 1844.

Between them, William Pope DuVal and Richard Keith Call monopolized the appointive governorship of Florida for more than nineteen of the twenty-three years ending in March 1845, when Florida entered the Union as a slave state. DuVal's leadership had produced the Florida War. Call's legacy was a system based on economic and social, as well as moral and political, irresponsibility, under which Florida lurched first to fiscal ruin, then on to devastation in the Civil War.

Greed had blinded Florida's elite to the need for peace with the Seminoles. Greed also made an honest banking system seem like an avoidable nuisance. While governor, DuVal vetoed the creation of an orderly banking system. A slush fund known as the Union Bank was more to his liking. According to the authors of a 1965 account, it worked as follows: "A planter might subscribe for $3,000 worth of stock, with a mortgage on his land and slaves. He could then mortgage the stock to the same bank and receive $2,000 on a twenty-year loan, leaving the $1,000 in the bank for its routine operation." This seemingly legitimate arrangement amounted to state-sponsored fraud, the government being the victim of its own chicanery. The $2,000 a landowner took out of the bank was a gift, the $1,000 he supposedly left on deposit an illusion.

Slaves provided a convenient way to leverage nonexistent capital. Marching their slaves from one tract of land to another, borrowers "pledged the same Negroes several times by exhibiting them on different pieces of land." The same contempt for equity infested the emerging Florida judicial system. Blacks were cruelly punished for the slightest infraction; the legal gap between rich whites and poor whites also became immense. Misdemeanors like public brawling incurred a 50-cent fine if the miscreant were a rich man's son, $100 if a countryman was involved in the disorder.

Much later, a genteel past of refined manners and aristocratic breeding was invented for Tallahassee. The town actually was "the scene of duels, brawls, knife fights and all the violence" later associated with the Wild West. The political murder of General Leigh

Read was like a Hollywood gunfight, though with a Florida twist. An advocate of reform who incurred the enmity of The Nucleus by promoting Florida statehood and exposing the shady dealings of the Union Bank, Leigh was also one of only three officers who actually stood and fought at the Withlacoochee. Unlike Clinch and Call, he had not fled the Seminole attack, even after being wounded.

Read was Speaker of the Territorial Council when his enemies set out to kill him. The first time Read refused to be provoked into a duel. The second time he accepted the challenge and, forced to defend himself, wound up killing the man sent to kill him. Outraged, the sisters of the failed assassin, Augustus "Bulldog" Alston, extracted the fatal bullet from his corpse, recast it, and urged their brother, who lived in Texas, to use it to avenge their brother's death. "Bulldog" preferred to use a Bowie knife. Having botched that, he then blasted Read in the back, then in the face with a double-barreled shotgun. Florida's triple standard of justice ensured that Willis Alston was never tried, let alone convicted, of murdering one of Florida's most eminent citizens. Allowed to depart to Texas, Willis Alston shot dead a doctor who was so ill-bred as to criticize his actions in Tallahassee, whereupon he was torn apart by a mob. People used words like *honor* to explain such vendettas, but General Read had wound up on a Florida hit list for the same reason welshing drug mules later would. He'd gotten in the way of the money.

Violence upheld the prevailing order, which in turn rested on substrata consisting of "layers and layers of debt." During Call's second term, all three of Florida's principal banks collapsed. Like the Seminole War, the politically motivated creation, scandalous operation and inevitable collapse of Florida's dishonest, unstable financial system was a self-inflicted catastrophe. Millions of dollars and thousands of lives had been expended to make Florida "free," but rather than stay and struggle, many simply headed for the next place where wealth was supposedly there for the grabbing. GTT was the notice bill collectors often found on abandoned property: "Gone to Texas." As their Florida schemes spawned violence and bankruptcy, hundreds of erstwhile "aristocrats" followed former Governor DuVal's lead and "slunk off westward," as one critic put it.

Even without the political institutionalization of economic dis-
incentives that worked against developing a productive civil society,
Florida faced two problems that would have doomed it to backwardness. As the letters, memoirs, diaries, sermons, and speeches of the
time frequently emphasized, Florida was not suitable for "the white
man." At least 90 percent of Florida was unsuitable for anyone when
it came to producing profitable commodities, but even in the Cotton
Belt of Middle Florida, those wanting to make big money fast faced
Florida's other great problem, which was a severe labor shortage.
The person who eventually defined that problem best was Harriet
Beecher Stowe. Following the Civil War, the author of *Uncle Tom's
Cabin* established her winter headquarters in Florida. Once she did,
Mrs. Stowe faced the same problem her pro-slavery neighbors did.

"Who will do the work for us?" she asked. Certainly not white
Americans; on that both abolitionist and slaveholder agreed. They
could not be expected to undertake the physical labor necessary for
"the marshes to be drained, forests to be cut down, palmetto-plains to
be grubbed up, and all under the torrid heats of a tropical sun." "No
white man we know of dares stay in the fields past ten o'clock," she
observed. "Yet the black laborers whom we leave in the field pursue
their toil, if anything, more actively, more cheerfully than during
the cooler months." To prove her point, the creator of Uncle Tom
introduced her readers to Old Simon, whose greatest pleasure, she
happily related, was to drive "his wheelbarrow, heavy with blocks of
muck, up a steep bank" hour after hour in the broiling sun. Intrigued
by this black Floridian incarnation of Sisyphus, Mrs. Stowe inquires:
"Why Simon, how can you work so [in] this hot weather?" To which
Simon replies: "Yah, hah, ho, ho, ho, missee! It be hot; dat so: ho, ho,
ho." "The sun awakes all their vigor and all their boundless jollity,"
added Mrs. Stowe.

Who would do the work for them? In 1820 there were at most
10,000 human beings in the whole of Florida. By 1860 the population
stood at 140,424. Of those, nearly half were black slaves. In the new
plantation areas blacks outnumbered whites five to one. Two-thirds
of Florida's slaves were concentrated in the five counties around
Tallahassee, which produced 80 percent of Florida's cotton. In turn

80 percent of Florida's total wealth was tied up in slaves. Slavery produced enormous inequalities among whites, for "the overwhelming majority of the white portion of Florida's population in 1860 did not own a single slave; of 77,747 whites, but 3,152 were slaveowners." Of them only 1,175 persons were counted as "planters," that is, owners of any significant number of slaves. Nonetheless virtually all of Florida's governors and members of Congress were "planters." Slavery warped the culture as well as politics and the economy. Honest labor was derided, and pioneering, as it would have been called elsewhere, was regarded as uncouth. This Florida never bothered to feed itself. Though Florida later became a major cattle state, meat and draft animals were imported from as far away as Ohio, as were flour and other foodstuffs.

The plutocratic throttlehold on wealth was reinforced by oligarchic limitations on the right to vote. Even a restricted electoral roll threatened the power of the Nucleus and its allies, so in the maneuvering leading up to statehood elitists in the Clinch mold attempted to limit voting rights to affluent property owners. In spite of a terror campaign and attempts—still familiar today—to discourage voting, homespun managed to triumph over broadcloth. Florida's statehood constitution explicitly provided that there should never be a property qualification for voting. Though both bolts of political cloth were exclusively white, Florida had taken a step toward inclusiveness. In 1845 Jefferson's pretense that the Louisiana Purchase extended to the Perdido River was graven permanently on the American political map as Florida, paired with Iowa in order to maintain the balance between slave and free states, was admitted to the Union with the inadvertent borders it had been given more than forty years earlier.

Since the governorship was now elective, Richard Keith Call for the first time faced the wrath of the countrymen. Denounced as the "Bank Nominee," he was defeated. The "aristocratic" elite, which in the most venerable cases dated back a whole twenty-four years, was appalled. One editorialist lamented that in "an awful struggle between virtue and corruption," corruption had won. He was right, though not in the sense intended. With statehood, a somewhat expanded circle of white Floridians got a license to steal. Florida's class politics came into the Union with it, but because race always trumped all other issues, electoral upheaval produced more tumult on the surface than change underneath. Whoever was elected governor, most whites, as well as all blacks, remained victims of a system in which a small number of people monopolized status, education, land and money. Because it had no land grant tradition and its rulers feared an educated populace, Florida would never become a center of excellence in state-funded education. This absence of intellectual excellence, like the absence of the entrepreneurial yeoman, runs like a frayed thread through the whole Florida experience. It links the squatter's shack to the tarpaper shack, the projects to the trailer parks. In 1860 Florida was ranked last in spending on education in the Union; in 2010 it still ranked last in the proportion of its income devoted to education.

The introduction of mass slavery between 1825 and 1865 still marks Florida more deeply than any other single event, but no system can be understood solely in terms of the catastrophes it produces. In the long term, slavery was suicidal. In the short term a society structured on race division fostered the emergence of an inclusive, although exclusively white, American identity. The whiteness of people helped them feel a kinship in America they would not have felt in Europe where, since everyone was white, skin color was useless for purposes of social and political differentiation. In America Irishmen, Jews, Russians, Italians, even Turks and Arabs could be Americanized. Even as they were devastating native Americans and enslaving black people, Americans were announcing to the world that the "wretched refuse of your teeming shore" was welcome, but it had to be white.

The fates of José-Joe Hernández and Billy Powell–Osceola already had shown that Americanization was a double-edged sword. Then, just as it became a state, Florida produced its most spectacular case study in white racist cross-cultural hyphenation. This exotic hybrid was David Levy, a Jew from the Caribbean island of St. Thomas who, once in Florida, transformed himself into David Yulee, a Christian and the state's first member of the U.S. Senate. Levy-Yulee, a master political manipulator, achieved both his political and his personal metamorphoses by causing the Florida legislature to take a vote. Until 1913, when Amendment XVII of the U.S. Constitution came into effect, Americans were prevented from electing their senators. The Founding Fathers reserved that privilege for the state legislatures and the interests dominating them. In one of Florida's more bizarre early exercises in special-interest legislation, Levy first had the legislature name him senator. Then, pursuant to his instructions, it enacted a state law changing his name to Yulee. Down in Tallahassee David Levy was elected senator. Up in Washington David Yulee would be seated in the U.S. Senate. Extremist white racism and his radical pro-slavery stance—plus the liberal application of monies usurped from the public purse—allowed Levy-Yulee to dominate Florida's politics and, through politics, its cash reserves in the crucial years leading up to the Civil War.

His father, Moses Elias Levy, though born in Morocco, had made his money in the Caribbean. Then, like many another rich man, he elected to dissipate in Florida the fortune he had made elsewhere. His particular Florida dream was to create, on sixty thousand acres west of St. Augustine, a proto-Zionist utopia, but Jews were no more adept at raising silkworms in the Florida swamps than Minorcans were. Moses Levy's New Jerusalem went the way of New Smyrna, after which his son—the future Senator Yulee—became Florida' preeminent public personality by betraying his father's moral principles as well as his religious heritage. The elder Levy wrote pamphlets denouncing slavery. Converting to Episcopalianism and marrying the daughter of a Kentucky governor, his son became slavery's ardent proponent while embracing the Florida tradition of using the public purse to build a personal fortune. Just as some claim José-Joe Hernández was the first Hispanic member of the U.S. House of Representatives, others claim Levy-Yulee was the first Jew to serve in the U.S. Congress. It is an honor he himself would have disputed. Not only was he not Jewish, Florida's first senator proclaimed, the royal blood of Morocco flowed in his veins. Yulee, he explained, was the name of his dynasty. Bizarre in its Florida details, this masquerade confirmed an American pattern. In the United States there never has been a moment when Jews have not been passing as gentiles,

blacks passing as whites, people whose parents got off the boat from
Minsk or Palermo palming themselves off as old Back Bay or Pasa-
dena society—blondes having more fun, even though they are really
brunettes. Being an American has always been about forsaking as well
as becoming. What makes this case so Floridian is its brazenness.
Where else would someone get the state legislature to pass a law
proclaiming he was what he wasn't?

In March 1861, Florida celebrated its unusual senator's most
dramatic use of government money for private profit yet, as the
railroad consortium Yulee controlled inaugurated Florida's first trans-
peninsular line. It ran from Fernandina on the Atlantic to Cedar Key
on the Gulf. At Senator Yulee's behest, the state legislature picked up
the tab. This Jewish-Moroccan-Episcopalian-Antillean conquistador
was as rich and powerful as anyone can get in Florida—until he, like
General Clinch and Governor DuVal, wound up ruined. They had
brought on their ruin by provoking the Seminole War. In Yulee's
case the Civil War, which he as much as any Floridian helped to
provoke, proved his undoing. His reversal of fortune, when it came,
would take him from the gilt chambers of the U.S. Senate to a cell in
Fort Pulaski, Georgia, where he was imprisoned for treason against
the United States of America. Once released, the turncoat senator-
speculator built himself another financial house of cards. The names
chosen for his schemes still reek of snake oil: the Peninsular Railroad
Company, the Tropical Florida Railway Company, the Fernandina
and Jacksonville Railroad Company. Serious railroading would not
come to Florida until the Gilded Age. Like Governor DuVal, Senator
Yulee in the end fled Florida, leaving a unique legacy on Florida's
road maps. Both the town of Yulee, Florida, and Levy County are
named for one and the same person.

Richard Keith Call never left Florida. Having first come there
in 1814, he died there in 1862. In 1861 this most eminent of Florida's
Founding Fathers described the human being, in its African variant,
as "an animal [lacking] faculty of mind or feeling of heart, without
spirit or pride of character." The legal system developed while he was
governor reflected that belief. "Any negro" found guilty of stealing,
the Florida penal code specified, "shall suffer death or have his or

her ears nailed to posts and there stand for one hour and receive 30 lashes on his or her bare back at the discretion of the court." Death or a nail through the ear? The capriciousness, like the barbarity, was essential to the slavery system of violence and terror. Individuals were responsible for individual acts of barbarism; Florida's barbaric legal system was the creation of the Florida racist political system. As the Florida state legislature itself later acknowledged, "Florida's first Territorial Legislature . . . and its successors did, over four decades, construct a legal framework that perpetuated African slavery in one of its most brutal and dehumanizing forms."

Between 1820 and 1860, the southeast of the United States was the scene of a double forced migration. While tens of thousands of Indians were uprooted, hundreds of thousands of black slaves were forced into the territories that had been "cleared." The magnitude of these movements was immense, the suffering they produced immeasurable. Not only was slavery, as President Jefferson put it, "a principal source of dishonor to the American character," it was socially and economically so disruptive that, before long, it would drive Americans to kill each other by the hundreds of thousands. There had to be some alternative to this process of national degeneration bred of ethnic cleansing and racism and, amazingly enough, there was someone in Florida who right from the beginning recognized what that alternative was. Even before the Seminoles took up arms, Florida's great forgotten philosopher, Zephaniah Kingsley, unleashed his own rebellion. It took the form of a highly original moral and socioeconomic treatise on conditions in Florida. Kingsley's solution to Florida's problems was that racial hatred be replaced with sexual love. Whites and blacks enjoying sexual relations with each other, he argued, was the way to excise from the American character the poisons generated by "clearing" and slavery. In *A Treatise on the Patriarchal, or Co-operative, System of Society as It Exists in Some Governments, and Colonies in America, and in the United States, Under the Name of Slavery, with Its Necessity and Advantages*, first published in 1829, Zephaniah Kingsley proclaimed interracial sex to be Florida's moral salvation as well as the source of its future prosperity. Its greatest merit, in his judgment, was that which other white men tried hardest to conceal.

Interracial sex produced mixed-race people; that, Zephaniah Kingsley proclaimed, was a great step forward for humankind.

"The intermediate grade of color are not only healthy, but when condition is favorable, they are improved in shape, strength and beauty," he declared, referring to the offspring of masters and their slaves. Sexual intimacy across the color bar, he added, was morally "meritorious and laudable," the ideal way to extirpate a great evil. That evil was race hatred—"a prejudice," he pointed out, which "completely neutralizes the physical strength of the country, by placing one portion of the inhabitants in hostile array against the other." As Kingsley propounded it, eliminating racial prejudice, not establishing white supremacy, was the great challenge Florida faced under American rule. One of slavery's benefits, in his view, was that it made the procreation of a mixed-race population so convenient. Far from being punished or condemned, anyone who participated in that noble as well as pleasurable enterprise, he argued, deserved to be honored as a "philanthropist . . . to whose energy and moral courage mankind were indebted." At the time he wrote about racism neutralizing "the physical strength of the country, by placing one portion of the inhabitants in hostile array against the other," the devastation of the Civil War was still in the future. That early Kingsley foresaw the danger and proposed to avoid the bloodshed by replacing race hatred with sexual love. Like the Seminoles' interracial alliance, Kingsley's philosophy of interracial intimacy was prophetic. It also would have saved many lives, and a great deal of trouble, had people been willing to embrace it.

The first step to transcending racism, Kingsley believed, was to transform slavery from a rigid, static institution into a flexible, evolving condition in which skin color was increasingly irrelevant. Following a generation or two of tutelage, he foresaw most slaves freed. He had no doubt where this process of enslavement followed by manumission would lead. Zephaniah Kingsley may have been the first American thinker not merely to call for the legalization of interracial sex, but to propound interracial sex as a social, cultural, and hygienic desirability. Kingsley's *Treatise* drew on Locke and Rousseau. It also foreshadowed Marx. Kingsley understood that a static economic system based on race, rather than on a fluid division of labor according to class, was bound to be surpassed by competing systems and, in the case of conflict, to be defeated—as the South's slave-based economy would be less than forty years later, by the industrial might of the free-labor North.

An empiricist as well as a theorist, Kingsley was an experimentalist in social psychology who practiced what he preached. At their Florida plantations Kingsley and his wife, Anna, led the familiar life of Southern aristocrats. Astute in business as well as the domestic refinements, Anna Kingsley was a remarkable woman in an age of remarkable American women. What set Mrs. Kingsley apart was that she was pure African. Her American adventure began in 1806, when she was kidnapped on the west coast of Africa, then transported to Cuba in a Danish slave ship. Zephaniah Kingsley, a British-born Floridian of Quaker parentage who had grown up in South Carolina, was on a shopping expedition to the Havana slave market when he saw her, loved her, and bought her. She was about thirteen; he was forty-one; their life together would touch five decades. Anna Kingsley's birth name was Madgigine Jai. She was already pregnant with their first child when Kingsley brought her to Florida.

Today the idea of a middle-aged white man buying a teenage girl at a slave market seems scandalous. What raised eyebrows back then was the deep respect Kingsley showed his African bride. "She has always been respected as my wife and as such I acknowledge her," Kingsley later wrote, "nor do I think that her truth, honor, integrity, moral conduct or good sense will lose in comparison with anyone." Instead of going straight to Fernandina when they left Cuba, he made sure they landed at St. Augustine so she could be registered as his property with the Spanish authorities. The paperwork was important because, by officially enslaving his wife, Kingsley made sure that five years later, when she reached the age of eighteen, he could legally free her. By then the couple had three children, two daughters and a son, all of whom he also freed.

The slave trade was the foundation of their wealth. Madgigine-Anna, herself the prime example of Kingsley's belief in upward mobility through slavery, owned and traded slaves. Managing his own slaves, Kingsley put into practice the policies he advocated in his *Treatise*. He assigned his slaves specific tasks, in the manner of a modern employer. In their spare time they were free to produce crops and handicrafts they could sell for a profit. Kingsley encouraged his slaves to learn useful trades, like carpentry and bricklaying. Any slave who saved enough money could buy his freedom at half the prevailing price. Kingsley also freed a number of slave families without receiving any compensation. In practice he transformed hereditary slavery into a term of indentured servitude that prepared the ex-slave and his children to face the future as self-reliant free men and women.

One of Kingsley's most astute insights concerned the relationship between poor white farmers and rich white plantation owners in the slaveholding South. In places like Georgia and South Carolina, Kingsley noted, the plantations, with their slave populations, were concentrated in the coastal areas. Poor whites tended to settle in the interior. Those poor whites, Kingsley noted, in the kind of statement that was so obvious that only he dared make it, did not benefit from slave labor, but they were there to come to rescue of rich whites if there were a slave revolt. The situation in Florida was different, Kingsley emphasized, because in Florida at that time there were no legions of poor whites to support rich whites in case of an uprising. Kingsley turned that circumstance into another argument for encouraging the growth of a free black and mixed-race population in Florida. "He argued," writes Daniel L. Schafer in his study of contrasting Spanish and U.S. racial policies in Florida, "that whites should unite with free persons of color as a means of controlling the slaves in the territory."

By "adopting the present system of terror," Kingsley pointed out, Florida's racist oligarch were endangering their own "personal safety." This made it all the more necessary for "the free colored population to be attached to good order and have a friendly feeling towards the white population." The alternative was turning non-whites into "our decided enemies by degrading them to the rank of our slaves." That was exactly what Florida's American elite proceeded to do. The repression of the Seminoles was military; the campaign to crush Florida's free blacks was legislative. In 1827 free blacks were prohibited from entering Florida. In 1828 those already there were forbidden to assemble in public. Freeing slaves was made so expensive and so difficult as to be virtually outlawed. Denied the protection of their government, forbidden to vote, hold office, or testify against whites in court cases, free blacks were subjected to taxes far more onerous than those whites paid. Blacks who committed the same crimes were as a matter of legal principle more severely punished. "There is an obvious propriety in visiting their offenses with more degrading punishment," the Florida Supreme Court later ruled, since "the superiority of the white race over the African negro should be ever demonstrated and preserved." As life there was fatally polarized along racial lines, the entire free black population of Florida was legally subjected to a new form of slavery; such persons were allowed to remain in Florida only if they were under the custody of a "guardian." Half the free blacks of Pensacola departed, en masse, for Mexico. The free black population of St. Augustine was also cut in half as government power was used to reduce to poverty and bondage those who did not flee. Less than six years after Kingsley issued his warning about "prejudice . . . placing one portion of the inhabitants in hostile array against the other," black people rushed to fight on the Seminole side. Just as Kingsley had foreseen, the campaign to degrade free blacks had dire consequences for the "personal safety" of Florida's whites.

As a self-described "inhabitant of Florida," Kingsley never lost sight of the universal reality that all the people caught up in the global consequence of the slave economy—kidnapped Africans, European slave traders, English factory workers, American slaveholders—were human beings. How were people to overcome the divisions these new technologies and trade patterns imposed on them? Love! proclaimed Zephaniah Kingsley. Sex will bring us together! Kingsley also understood what, later, even many abolitionists failed to grasp. More than slavery, the problem America faced was racism. Slavery could be abolished. Racism would be another matter.

Kingsley's *Treatise* was the first truly original work of political philosophy to be composed in Florida. It—and he—attracted considerable attention at the time, until his life and *Treatise* were

expunged from the history-production process. On those rare occasions when his wife is mentioned, she is described as an exotic
souvenir. A 1972 account falsely describes her as a "princess whom
he had married in Madagascar." Here, once again, the internalized
race prejudices of the oppressor masquerade as truth. If a white
man like Kingsley did marry an African woman, she had to be not
really black, and therefore be from "Madagascar." And, as in all
fairy tales, she must be a "princess." The idea that a rootless black
girl kidnapped from West Africa could have played the role Mrs
Kingsley did is, to this day, not quite acceptable.

Madgigine Jai–Anna Kingsley was no princess; she was quite
a woman. When George Mathews' Patriots looted her husband's
plantation, she did not wait for the invaders to reach her own property, which was called Mandarin Plantation. She ordered her twelve
slaves to carry away all they could, then burn the place. At the age
of eighteen cold calculation guided her actions; she knew that if the
invading "rag-a-muffins" won, she would lose everything anyway.
She also knew that if the Americans lost, as they initially did, the
Spanish authorities would give her even more land, which they did.
Eventually she and her husband owned a considerable fraction of
modern-day metropolitan Jacksonville.

The Kingsleys continued accumulating property even as the
legislators in Tallahassee enacted ever more vindictive race laws.
Kingsley could have stayed in Florida—had he gone along with the
new mores, and demoted his wife to concubine. His moral stature
would not permit it. Disgusted by the "illiberal and inequitable laws
of this Territory" that denied his "children that protection and justice
which is due in a civilized society to every human being," Kingsley
focused his hopes on the revolutionary island republic of Haiti, where
the world's first successful slave revolt, like the American War of
Independence earlier, seemed to open up new possibilities. In 1837
Kingsley sailed away, leaving behind Florida's "spirit of intolerant
prejudice" forever. Accompanied by more than fifty freed slaves, the
Kingsleys established a plantation in what today is the Dominican
Republic, but changes in latitude did not change human nature.
Haiti's black revolutionaries, like Florida's white speculators, would

leave a legacy of violence and devastation. Zephaniah Kingsley died in New York in 1843, aged seventy-eight. His long search for a human paradise had come to an end within walking distance of the museum where Osceola's head was on display.

In the realm of technology men were also thinking the unthinkable —that is, foreseeing the future—as the slave empire in Florida strode toward its eventual self-destruction. In 1837, the same year Osceola was shipped off to South Carolina and Zephaniah Kingsley set sail for Haiti, a doctor in Apalachicola named John Gorrie decided he was going to rid Florida of yellow fever, as well as malaria, typhus, and typhoid. Apalachicola is far enough north to get cold every winter. That caused Gorrie to notice something interesting. The fever generally struck when it was hot, then disappeared when the weather turned cold. From this correlation Dr. Gorrie drew the logical, though completely erroneous, conclusion that hot weather caused fever. Microbes and mosquitoes, not its sultry climate, caused the epidemics that ravaged Florida, but having propounded his false axiom, Dr. Gorrie went on to derive a corollary that, though erroneous, would change the world. If heat caused the diseases that made Florida so unattractive, Gorrie decided, cold, ergo, could cure them.

After years of tinkering with various contraptions, Dr. Gorrie was granted the first-ever patent for mechanical refrigeration. The date was May 6, 1851, the U.S. Patent number 8080. Gorrie's quest to find a cure for yellow fever through refrigeration was the equivalent of Menéndez' Northwest Passage to China and de Soto's gold mines. In keeping with that pattern, Dr. Gorrie's life ended as many another Florida protagonist's had, and would. Determined to prove that his scheme could revolutionize public health, he abandoned his medical practice, banking interests and civic positions. Ridiculed by locals, he abandoned Apalachicola too. In the last years of his life, in experiments conducted mostly in his laboratory in Ohio, Gorrie produced tons of mushy ice, but no miracle cure.

"Humiliated by criticism, financially ruined, and his health broken, Gorrie died in seclusion on June 28, 1855," notes the biography provided by the National Sculpture Gallery at the Capitol in Washington. In addition to an almost unnoticed sculpture honoring him in the nation's capital, a monument to Dr. Gorrie graces a public park in Apalachicola—a variant on the usual civic monuments glorifying Confederate chivalry. A nearby museum exhibits a replica of Gorrie's ice-producing contraption. With its pipes and valves, it looks like an old moonshine still, and for good reason. Gorrie's momentous breakthrough was to understand, as he explained in his patent application, that by first condensing air in metal tubes and then rapidly expanding it, "very low temperatures could be obtained, even low enough to freeze water." If you want to get an idea of what kind of ice Gorrie's invention produced, go to one of Apalachicola's convenience stores. The "Father of Refrigeration," as local boosters call him, and the grandfather of air-conditioning, Dr. Gorrie was also the great-grandfather of the Slurpee.

Columbus died without understanding he had discovered America. Dr. Gorrie never understood that his discovery, though unable to cure diseases, had the capacity to revolutionize life in other ways. First the Apalachicola oyster industry, then Florida's orange juice manufacturers would prosper because refrigeration made it possible for their products to reach faraway markets in edible condition. Tens of millions of people ultimately would move to Florida once air-conditioning made life there tolerable on a year-round basis. His contraption did not eliminate typhus or yellow fever; it did eventually produce a proliferation of presidential electoral votes.

Kingsley's *Treatise* was one of the most extraordinary works dealing with race, sex, and politics ever composed by a Floridian, or anyone else. Gorrie's work on refrigeration may be the most original independent scientific work ever conducted in Florida. The Americanized African, Madgigine Jai–Anna Kingsley, may be the most fascinating woman the Florida melodrama has produced; the Indianized, mixed-race American Billy Powell–Osceola, may be the most compelling male protagonist. A society that marginalizes people of such originality and valor is a society headed for self-destruction. Their exclusion from Florida, like their exclusion from history, was both a cause and a consequence of Florida's self-inflicted catastrophes. To this day, the magnitude of the loss is scarcely noted, yet the Florida of the future would be their Florida.

By the standards of their own lifetimes, to be sure, these remarkable people were failures, but so was practically everybody else. In consequence of the U.S. annexation of Florida, Zephaniah Kingsley was ruined, but so was "Joe" Hernández. In 1838, the year after Kingsley left for Haiti, Sprague reports, "General Hernández, induced by the situation of his private affairs (his property having been ruined and devastated by the inroads of the enemy)," resigned his military commission. Hernández dreamed of political glory, but he never won another election. Just as Clinch was defeated for governor in Georgia, Hernández was defeated in his bid to become one of Florida's first senators. Bankrupt as well as defeated, he left for Cuba. There he found work managing a sugar plantation. DuVal had wound up in Texas, Kingsley in Haiti, Eaton in Spain, Gadsden wherever money was to be made. Hernández died in Cuba in 1857, the same year Coacoochee died in Mexico. Kingsley had epitomized elite white resistance to the U.S. system being imposed in Florida. Hernández personified cooperation. It didn't matter. Florida stymied them all, so they followed their illusions elsewhere, in the process storing up future disasters so immense that it would be as though the Florida War never happened.

In the end even that master architect of the Florida slave system, Richard Keith Call, found himself marginalized, scorned, turned into another Gad Humphreys, as slavery—its appetite for new land, greater injustice, more money never sated—devoured its friends as well as its foes. Only with the coming and going of the generations would it become apparent that there were alternatives in Florida to genocide, to nailing ears to wooden posts. Yet long before an alternative Florida emerged there were alternative Floridians. These were the people of all colors and both sexes who sooner or later came to understand that, even in Florida, life and governance did not need to be so violent, so unjust, so cruel, so fundamentally selfish, brutish, and vile.

PART FOUR
WHISTLING DIXIE

Slavery is the element of all value.

—John C. McGhee, president of Florida's
secessionist state convention, 1861

13

METROPOLIS OF
THE BRANDED HAND

In Pensacola, in 1845, a brazier with burning coals in it was installed in the courtroom. "When about to be branded," the prisoner later stated, "[a court officer] proceeded to tie my hand to a part of the railing in front. He . . . then took from the fire the branding-iron . . . and applied it to the ball of my hand, and pressed it on firmly, for fifteen or twenty seconds. It made a spattering noise," he added, "like a handful of salt in the fire, as the skin seared and gave way to the hot iron." The American being subjected to this cruel and unusual punishment was a free white man. Jonathan Walker, a forty-six-year-old shipwright, was also exposed in a pillory prior to his branding so citizens of Pensacola could jeer him and pelt him with refuse. When the moment arrived two letters—ss—were seared into his hand. According to Florida law ss stood for "slave stealer." To millions of Americans in the period leading up to the Civil War, though, it stood for "slave savior." Were slaves property that could be stolen, or souls to be saved? On that question the country would be torn asunder.

Like Garcia, Ambrister, and Osceola, Jonathan Walker inadvertently found himself personifying opposition to the misuse of American power, in this case U.S. government support for slavery. A rustic from Cape Cod, he was working as a boat builder in Mobile when he sailed over to Pensacola. Walker was ill, apparently suffering from malaria, but when seven destitute and frightened escaped slaves begged for his help, he decided to transport them to the Bahamas, where slavery had been abolished ten years earlier.

They almost made it to freedom. Walker set to sea on June 20, 1844. First he skirted the north coast of the Gulf of Mexico, then sailed down the western length of the Florida peninsula. Then, avoiding Key West, he and his passengers rounded Cape Florida. At times Walker was delirious with fever; "whenever we landed," he recalled, "we were harassed with swarms of mosquitoes, each anxious to have his bill entered without examination or delay." Thirst caused the greatest torment. "We continued . . . in search of water," Walker later recounted, "without being able to get any." By July 8 they had traversed nearly a thousand miles of gulf, strait, and ocean; freedom sparkled like freshwater on the horizon. Nassau, the Bahamas' capital and chief port, was a half-day's sail away, but that day, in international waters, a Florida maritime scavenger named Richard Roberts seized Walker's ship and imprisoned all eight men on board. They were shipped in chains back to Pensacola. All but one of the slaves were restored to their masters; he escaped re-enslavement by gouging open his stomach, then bleeding to death on the prison floor.

In Bahamian waters Captain Roberts would have been guilty of piracy. Even after they branded his flesh, Walker did not seem to understand that in Florida a different kind of "justice" held sway. "But who delegated to him the right to take charge of me and my boat by force on the high seas?" he wondered. "I do not wish to cast any undue reflections upon Captain Roberts; but I do lament the lack of moral courage, the deep depravity of such professors of Christianity; for surely he hath no pity on those of his fellow creatures. . . . Captain Roberts," he continued, "manifested great seriousness and devotion to the cause of religion. Yet profanity passed freely in the cabin and about his vessel's decks unrebuked." Walker's account is still a good read because on every page its hero-narrator so totally confounds piety with morality and shows himself touchingly devoted to both. Here was a man whose indiscriminate sense of goodness causes him to abhor profanity and slavery alike as affronts to the Creator's Design.

By publicly branding a U.S. citizen in a U.S. courtroom, Florida had meant to show outside agitators that they meddled at their peril. Instead, Up North, following his release, women swooned wherever Walker spoke. Men were moved to tears, and both sexes to moral resolve, as Jonathan Walker held up his hand and his audience saw with their own eyes that not even a free white man was safe from slavery's evil imprint. Daguerreotypes of Walker's mutilated hand were displayed in schoolrooms and at church socials. John Greenleaf Whittier wrote a poem, "The Branded Hand," in Walker's honor:

> *Then lift that manly right-hand, bold ploughman of the wave!*
> *Its branded palm shall prophesy, "Salvation to the Slave!"*
> *Hold up its fire-wrought language, that whoso reads may feel*
> *His heart swell strong within him, his sinews change to steel.*

More and more sinews changed to steel as people realized the mutilation in Florida was part of a systemic crisis of American governance bred of federal favoritism for slavery at every level. A vigilante had captured him but the state of Florida, backed by the federal government, declared Walker a criminal and applied the branding iron. As Richard Keith Call himself unapologetically put it, slavery was "an institution interwoven and inseparably connected with our social and political system, as a domestic institution of the States, and a national institution, created by the American people and protected by the Constitution of the United States." Slaveholders proclaimed that proudly; abolitionists considered it a disgrace. No one denied it was true.

White Americans, not just blacks, were the victims of this systemic commitment to slavery. Because of slavery's privileged place in their governmental system, Americans were (and still are) prevented from choosing their president directly, in a free vote. To give slave owners and slave states greater power, the Constitution ordained that the president be chosen by an electoral college. Thanks to the pro-slavery bias built into the U.S. electoral system, slaveholders got votes for themselves. Then they got extra votes because they had slaves. The "three-fifths provision" of the U.S. Constitution made it official. The slave bonus penalized a midwestern farmer for clearing the land with his own hands; it rewarded Southern planters for making slaves do the work. Inside Florida, the electoral distortion was even more extreme. Since the three-fifths slavery bonus also applied to apportionment within Florida, the slaveholding counties around Tallahassee had far greater representation in the state legislature than counties with fewer slaves.

Slaveholders wanted a powerful federal government, but only so long as that power was used to promote, defend and expand slavery. Whittier's poem summed up the moral outrage the U.S. government's pandering to slavery provoked. In one of his newspaper editorials the worldly Horace Greeley, famous for advising young men to go West, summed up another source of irritation. It consisted of the South's endless, tiresome, ungrateful complaining. "'Why can't you let Slavery alone?' was imperiously or querulously demanded at the North," Greeley observed, "by men who should have seen, but would not, that Slavery never left the North alone." He went on to list a few of the slaveholders' demands and recounted how servilely the rest of the country hastened to satisfy them. "'Buy Louisiana for us,' said the slaveholders. 'With pleasure.' 'Now Florida!' 'Certainly.' Next: 'Violate your treaties with the Creeks and Cherokees; expel those tribes from the lands they have held from time immemorial, so as to let us expand our plantations.' 'So said, so done.' 'Now for Texas!' 'You have it.'" "Slavery," Greeley pointed out, "was using the Union as her cat's-paw—dragging the Republic into iniquitous wars and enormous expenditures, and grasping empire after empire thereby."

The slaveholder reaction to the presidential election of 1860 demonstrated Greeley was right. Abraham Lincoln was chosen president through an electoral process that gave the slaveholding states far greater influence than a strictly democratic system would have. His party's platform explicitly proclaimed "the right of each State to order and control its own domestic institutions according to its own judgment exclusively," but as the votes were cast, the electors chosen, and the outcome tabulated, slavery would not let the American constitutional process alone.

Later, looking back on the Civil War, many claimed slavery was incidental to a profounder clash of philosophies. Those who steamrollered Florida into secession would have scorned such a notion. "Why all this?" John C. McGhee, president of Florida's secessionist state convention, asked in his opening address. "At the South and with our people, of course, slavery is the element of all value." In January 1861, sixty-nine white men met in a room in Tallahassee; sixty-two of them voted to declare Florida "a Sovereign and Independent Nation." Nearly forty-nine years earlier, on March 13, 1812, Mathews' nine "rag-a-muffins" had done the same thing. This latest roomful actually constituted a smaller proportion of Florida's total population in 1861 than Mathews' stage-managed gathering had.

In other states the secession debate consumed months and involved thousands of particpants as well as the state legislatures. The Florida secessionsts opened their meeting in the morning and by dinnertime they were done. In other states a referendum on secession was held. A step so grave as separation from the Union, it was understood, must be approved by the voters. The secessionist clique in Tallahassee made sure Floridians never got the chance to express their views on the single most important issue the state would ever face. Just before proclaiming secession on January 10, they defeated "a resolution . . . that the ordinance be submitted to the people for ratification." Florida's secessionist governor John Milton explained why: "A very large minority were opposed to secession and in many parts of the State combinations existed to adhere to and maintain the United States Government." Even inside the room seven members voted against secession. After only fifteen years of statehood, enemies of democracy had seized power again. Less than forty-seven years had elapsed since Jackson first shot his way into Florida—humiliating the Spanish, massacring Seminoles, killing white men when they got in the way. Now, orating about freedom, Americans would be killing each other.

The debt Floridians owed to the federal government made the rush to secession unseemly as well impulsively ill-advised. Less than three years earlier, the U.S. Army had put down the last Seminole uprising. Florida was more dependent on federal money and protection than any other slaveholder state. In South Carolina and Virginia people could pretend to an identity that antedated the creation of the United States. Florida was a creature of the federal government. Everything they had Florida's secessionists owed to the intervention of the federal government, yet when faced with the choice, they chose slavery over loyalty. More than the "element of all value," slavery had become the value that destroyed all other values.

The presidential election was held on November 6, 1860. South Carolina, ever intemperate, declared secession before Christmas, but no stampede followed. Virginia, Kentucky, North Carolina and Tennessee all held back. It seemed possible that the election crisis of 1860, like the nullification crisis of 1832, might be limited to South Carolina. Then the three slave states so recently gouged out of the southeast frontier—Alabama, Florida, Mississippi—rushed in where the more established slave states hesitated to tread. Alabama beat out Florida by one day to become the first state after South Carolina to secede. Mississippi followed Florida the next day. Florida's secession, nearly three months before Lincoln could take office, marked the first though not the last time that politicians in Florida helped inflict a constitutional crisis on the United States.

In seventy-two hours Andrew Jackson's ambition to expand the Union by expanding slavery had been undone by the three slave states he almost single-handedly had wrung into existence—"clearing" of Indians, Englishmen, and Spaniards and, at U.S. government expense, handed them over to a hand-picked, slaveholding elite which, having initially turned on him, now turned on America itself. Jackson, like Menéndez, had inflicted on Florida yet another self-destructive system that, as events now showed, would lead to the destruction of all his dreams.

All three states, Florida especially, were military liabilities, but thanks to them secession now could claim a hinterland. With secession no longer limited to South Carolina, Montgomery, Alabama, could be proclaimed a capital, and Jefferson Davis of Mississippi be proclaimed president of the Confederacy even before Abraham Lincoln took office as President of the United States. Still, wariness continued to guide the more established slave states. It took another great South Carolina provocation, the attack on Fort Sumter, to unleash the Civil War. Confederate forces attacked the U.S. garrison at Fort Sumter on April 12, 1861, more than five months after the presidential election. Originally the tiny U.S. force there, numbering only 123 officers and men, including thirteen members of a military marching band, was encamped at Fort Moultrie, where Osceola had died. Moultrie was exposed to potshots from nearby settlements. Eager to avoid confrontation Major Robert Anderson, a Kentucky loyalist, and his second in command, Captain Abner Doubleday, moved across the water to Sumter. It was winter. On their little speck of an island these loyal U.S. troops, bereft of candles and heat, huddled under blankets, experiencing the same damp chill Osceola had twenty-three years earlier.

Major Anderson took great care to ensure U.S. troops were not the first to fire on fellow Americans. Only after the Confederates unleashed their artillery barrage did U.S. troops try to defend themselves. Abner Doubleday directed the fire. In his *Reminiscences of Forts Sumter and Moultrie in 1860–61*, published in 1876, Doubleday referred to the widespread belief that he had fired the first Union shot of the Civil War. "In aiming the first gun fired against the rebellion I felt no feeling of self-reproach," he recalled, "for I fully believed that the contest was inevitable, and was not of our seeking." Some are remembered for what they did; Abner Doubleday would be remembered—twice over—for what he did not. Contrary to legend, Abner Doubleday did not invent baseball. He also did not fire the first shot "against the rebellion." Those first shots had been fired in Florida, at Pensacola, more than three months earlier, in January 1861.

There were a multitude of similarities, and one enormous difference, between the forgotten, successful U.S. defense at Pensacola Bay in January 1861 and the celebrated Confederate attack in Charleston Harbor three months later. Pensacola by then was Florida's biggest city, just as Charleston was South Carolina's. In Pensacola the population was as aggressively pro-slavery as it was in Charleston. The besieged Union force at Pensacola was even smaller than the one in South Carolina, consisting of only eighty-one officers and men. At Pensacola, as at Charleston later, defense of the property and honor of the United States fell to two hitherto unknown U.S. Army officers. First Lieutenant Adam Jacoby Slemmer, the acting commander at Pensacola, like Major Anderson at Fort Sumter, was a West Pointer and veteran of the Seminole War. His deputy, Second Lieutenant Jeremiah H. Gilmore, would eventually rise to the rank of general. Also like Doubleday, Gilmore would provide a vivid written account of what happened.

The great difference is that in Florida the besieged U.S. forces never surrendered. With a combination of courage, skill, quick thinking, and pluck—what their pro-slavery adversaries loved to call "valor"—they defeated Confederate attempts to subdue them, and counterattacked. These brave American patriots won the first Union victory of the war even before the war, as people later saw it, had begun. There was, as always, another Florida difference. These Florida heroes—though white and wearing their country's uniform—would be expunged from history as thoroughly as the defenders of Negro Fort were. All over Pensacola and the rest of Florida you still find monuments and plaques praising the Confederates' supposed heroism. Nowhere will you find a memorial honoring the loyal patriots who stood up for America at Pensacola.

Even before Florida formally seceded, looters had started desecrating American flags and stealing government guns and ammunition. This constituted insurrection, as surely as the seizure of Jonathan Walker and his boat had constituted piracy, but in Florida as throughout the South, many military officers vacillated between support for those attacking U.S. installations, and a degree of passive indecision that amounted to dereliction of duty, if not treason. The behavior of the ranking U.S. Navy officer at Pensacola, Commodore James Armstrong, was especially scandalous. As intruders pulled down the U.S. flag and looted U.S. property, Armstrong watched, doing nothing.

Abandoned by their senior commanders the two young lieutenants, Slemmer and Gilmore, decided to make a stand for their country all by themselves, but how and where? In Pensacola Bay the choice was between Fort Barrancas and Fort Pickens. Fort Barrancas, on the grounds of what today is the Pensacola Naval Air Station, was located on the mainland. Fort Pickens, by far the more defensible of the two positions, was located on the opposite side of the channel connecting Pensacola Bay with the Gulf of Mexico, at the extremity of Santa Rosa Island, a long, narrow barrier island separating Pensacola Bay from the Gulf. Having decided to make their stand at Fort Pickens, Slemmer and his men first shifted what supplies, weapons, and ammunition they could from their barracks to the momentary safety of Fort Barrancas. "It was none too soon," Gilmore reported, "for about midnight a party of twenty men came to the fort, evidently with the intention of taking possession, expecting to find it unoccupied as usual. Being challenged and not answering nor halting when ordered, the party was fired upon by the guard."

Slemmer and Gilmore had won their first victory and, small at it was, they understood its significance. "This, I believe," Gilmore added, "was the first gun in the war fired on our side." Thanks to this timely action, they had saved their supplies and weapons, but "the sole force of the United States army in the harbor to guard and hold, as best it might, the property of the United States," as Gilmore described his unit, would have to move quickly to Fort Pickens, on Santa Rosa Island, if it were to defend itself and the U.S. flag against further attack. On the morning of January 9, 1861, Lieutenant Adam Jacoby Slemmer looked across the channel separating Fort Barrancas from Fort Pickens and faced the same question the Frenchman Jean Ribault had at Matanzas Inlet, on the other side of Florida, 295 years earlier. How to cross that water? Two U.S. Navy ships were at anchor in Pensacola Bay. Captain O. H. Berryman of the *Wyandotte*, one of the navy's new steamships, and Captain Henry Walker of the sailing ship *Supply* wanted to help, but pro-Confederate members of Armstrong's staff, as Gilmore later put it, repeatedly "thwarted . . . what they called the mad scheme of resisting the State authorities."

Finally, on the early morning of January 10, 1861, the U.S. Navy steamer *Wyandotte* appeared at Fort Barrancas. Its captain had decided, on his own initiative, to help them. Gilmore relates what happened next: "In a large flat-boat or scow, and several small boats loaded with our men, provisions, brass field-pieces, ammunition, tools, and whatever public property was most needed and could be carried, including, I remember, an old mule and cart (which afterward proved of great service to us), we were towed over to Pickens and landed there about 10 a.m. January 10th, 1861, the day that Florida seceded from the Union." Two days after relocating their force to Fort Pickens, Gilmore reported, "we saw the flag at the Navy Yard lowered, and then knew that it had been quietly and tamely surrendered." As the loyal U.S. troops at Fort Pickens, looking across the water, saw their country's flag pulled down, the silence on the other side distressed them most. Not even a token shot of resistance was fired. "Seeing our flag thus lowered to an enemy caused intense excitement and emotion, a mingled feeling of shame, anger," Gilmore recalled, "and defiance." One flag was pulled down; many others rose in its place. "Not yet having a flag-staff up, we hung our flag over the north-west bastion of the fort," Gilmore later wrote, "that all might see 'that our flag was still there.'" The U.S. Navy ships in the harbor did see. The *Supply* hoisted still more U.S. flags, as did the *Wyandotte*.

While a pro-Confederate crowd applauded the spectacle of America's flag being dishonored, the two U.S. warships slipped out into Pensacola Bay, beyond Confederate reach. As it had been in 1565 with the Spanish and French, so it was in 1861 with the Confederates and the United States. Whoever prevailed on land, control of Florida's waterways determined the ultimate victor. With U.S. forces holding Fort Pickens, no Confederate warship could enter or leave Pensacola. The Pensacola Navy Yard, which might have been the cradle of a powerful Confederate navy, now was strategically useless thanks to what Slemmer and Gilmore had accomplished. The two young officers had something else in common besides military resourcefulness. Both were newlyweds, and "in this hasty and tumultuous 'moving,'" one of Slemmer's Pennsylvania neighbors later marveled, "the patriotic wives of Slemmer and Gilmore did yeomen's service." The work continued once they reached Fort Pickens, as Mrs. Slemmer and Mrs. Gilmore helped make the sand-swept outpost livable as well as defensible. "The heroic wives of Lieutenants Slemmer and Gilmore—refined and cultivated women— . . . form a part of the history of Fort Pickens," another chronicler observed, but he was wrong about that. Like the heroics of their husbands, the bravery of these loyal American women would have no place in the genteel history of pro-slavery female heroics concocted for Florida.

Having first provoked, then botched a confrontation with the U.S. Army and Navy, Pensacola's pro-slavery notables resorted to speechifying about honor in the attempt to have their way. The

Slemmers, the Gilmores and the others were busy shoring up the fort's defenses when the first attempt to talk them into surrendering occurred. Four men appeared at the fort's entrance, demanding admittance, one of them a civilian employee at the navy yard. He, like others, had pretended to be loyal to his military employers; now he showed his true colors. "We have been sent by the governors of Florida and Alabama to demand a peaceable surrender of this fort," he announced. "I am here by authority of the President of the United States," Lieutenant Slemmer replied.

In addition to firing the first shots, Slemmer and Gilmore had won the first strategically significant engagement of the Civil War without losing a single soldier. The casualties had yet to be counted. Relief supplies did not reach Fort Pickens until mid-April. Only in mid-May, as Gilmore put it, was "our company, on the recommendation of the surgeon, the men being much broken down by the severe labor, incessant watching, exposure, and want of proper food of the past four months . . . ordered to Fort Hamilton, New York Harbor." The cost of their valor had begun to emerge before they set sail; "scurvy had already appeared among the men," Gilmore wrote. "On the way North," he added, "one of them died and few of them ever entirely recovered from the effects of the severe physical and mental strain they had endured." Slemmer was among the casualties. A hero on his thirty-third birthday, he was dead at age forty. "He died," as one account later put it, "while in command of Fort Laramie from lingering effects of typhoid fever that he had contracted during the Civil War." He had started his career hounding the Seminoles; he ended it harassing the Indians of the western plains. In between, Brevet General (as he had become) Adam Jacoby Slemmer had done something of which he, and his country, could be proud forever.

Meanwhile, from his office in Washington, Senator David Yulee, Florida's senior public official, incited insurrection against the United States. "The immediately important thing to be done is the occupation of the forts and arsenals in Florida," Yulee wrote to Governor Madison Starke Perry's chief military adviser, Joseph Finegan. Finegan, who was soon to become a Confederate general and eventually author of the worst Florida massacre since the one at

Negro Fort, had no military experience. His qualifications for leading Florida into war were political and financial. His construction
business had become a fountain of wealth thanks to the government-
financed contracts that his close associate, Senator Yulee, got for him.
As a result of a sweetheart deal with Florida officials, Finegan also
acquired five miles of shoreline along Lake Monroe, the section of
the St. Johns water system stretching from Sanford to Deltona, for
$40—not $40 an acre, but $40 for the whole five miles. It was a coup
on the order of Humphrey's acquisition of Enemathla's square mile
in Tallahassee, and for the same reason. Once the U.S. Army drove
out the Seminoles, Finegan found himself sole owner of a veritable
empire from which rival whites, as well as Seminoles, were excluded.
By 1861 Finegan, who had arrived penniless as a child from Ireland,
had a forty-room mansion in Fernandina.

Perry and his successor as Civil War governor, John Milton,
were representative of the psychology, a combination of unjustified
resentment and unmerited self-confidence, that prevailed among
Florida's secessionist leaders. For forty years Florida's eminent men
had depended on the federal government to enrich them and protect them. Now Florida's senators and governors plotted against the
same government to which, directly and indirectly, they owed all
they had. Their plans to overthrow the government of the United
States antedated Abraham Lincoln's election. "This was not an unexpected trouble," one pro-slavery account later conceded, "but had
been long foreseen." For wealthy Floridians like Yulee, Perry, Finegan, and Milton, secession was an opportunity to be grasped, not a
catastrophe to be averted. As they plunged Florida into war, they
were guided by their irrational belief that, if need be, they could
defeat the armed forces of the United States. As the Seminole War
already had shown, and the Civil War would show again, they could
not even defend Florida.

Once secession was proclaimed, the same officials and militia
that had botched operations against the Seminoles faced the U.S.
Army and Navy, and Floridian military incompetence entered a new
phase. If any attempt at secession were to succeed, the essential first
task, as Senator Yulee pointed out, was to gain control of the key

strategic points of the state. Another of the secessionist ultras, John Jackson Dickison, listed the coastal installations that had to be secured if Florida's secessionists were to defy the federal authority with any prospect of success. These were: "Fort Barrancas, with 44 cannon and ammunition; Barrancas barracks, where there was a field battery; Fort Pickens, equipped with 201 cannon with ammunition; Fort McRee, 125 seacoast and garrison cannon; Fort Taylor, Key West, with 60 cannon; Key West barracks, 4 cannon; Fort Marion, 6 field batteries and some small arms; and Fort Jefferson on the Tortugas." No attempt whatsoever was made to secure the island installations at Key West and Fort Jefferson. They stayed in Union hands throughout the war. Florida's pro-slavery militants were equally complaisant when it came to Fort Marion, as the Castillo de San Marcos at St. Augustine was now called. In an effort to avoid confrontation, federal troops evacuated St. Augustine, leaving only a caretaker in charge. When Governor Perry's militiamen finally got there, the caretaker demanded and got a receipt before turning U.S. property over to them. Florida's most fabled fortification had fallen to the secessionists without a fight, but when the need to fight did arise, the Confederates would abandon it without firing a shot.

That left the fortifications around Pensacola. Senator Yulee emphasized that "the naval station and forts at Pensacola were first in consequence," yet Florida officials did nothing as Slemmer's men stripped their barracks, then spiked the guns at Fort Barrancas itself. The ever-kinetic Lieutenant Slemmer also had disabled the artillery at Fort McRee, which commanded the mainland side of the entrance to Pensacola Bay. Even following the Confederate attack on Fort Sumter in April 1861, Florida's secessionist slaveholder regime made no attempt to drive U.S. forces from Fort Pickens. Instead U.S., not Confederate, forces went on the attack. In a night raid on the Pensacola Navy Yard, a landing party from Fort Pickens won the first U.S. victory on Florida soil.

A commercial sailing sloop, the *Judah*, had been allowed to sail unmolested into Pensacola Bay. As Union troops, peering through their binoculars, watched the ongoing work at the navy yard, they discovered that the *Judah*, though it entered the harbor peacefully, intended to leave it a Confederate warship. In his report to the War Department Captain William Mervine, commander of the U.S. Navy Gulf Blockading Squadron, showed he might have prospered as a writer of adventure yarns. "The movements of the schooner had been assiduously watched," he reported, "and I deemed it so morally certain that she was intended for a privateer that I determined the attempt should be made to destroy her, even in the face of the fearful odds which would have to be encountered." The Confederates at the navy yard were routed in fifteen minutes, partly because they were all asleep.

Up in Washington Gideon Welles, secretary of the navy, recognized a public relations triumph when it came sliding across his desk. "An expedition executed in the face of an enemy so much superior in numbers, with such brilliancy and gallantry and success, cannot pass without the special recognition of the department. Its recital," he went on to predict, "hereafter will thrill the heart with admiration." Secretary Welles made sure hearts thrilled by sending Captain Mervine's account straight to the newspapers. "The Destruction of the Judah," an October 20, 1861, headline in the *New York Times* announced over the report of "The Recent Naval Exploit at Pensacola." It was one of the few times Civil War events in Florida made headlines.

The destruction of the *Judah* in October 1861 confirmed what had been evident since January, when Slemmer took possession of Fort Pickens. So long as the United States blocked the entrance to Pensacola Bay, the installations under Confederate control were useless. Still, the Confederates remained unwilling to undertake the expense, human as well as military, of securing Florida's most vitally important strategic objective because, as both Jefferson Davis and Robert E. Lee saw it, Florida was not worth defending. Florida lives, the Confederate administration and the Confederate high command agreed, were better expended fighting for slavery outside Florida, in places they considered more important, such as Virginia.

Only a short time earlier Florida's highest officeholders had denounced every federal action as intolerable tyranny. Now they meekly submitted themselves to the dictates of out-of-state Confederate overlords who, quite soon, would inflict on Florida incomparably greater damage than Yankees ever would. In Pensacola the Confederate overlord was a former U.S. Army lieutenant colonel named Braxton Bragg. Bragg's North Carolina origins were even humbler than Clinch's; people whispered that his mother served time in prison. It was said that during the Mexican war his own troops engaged in what, much later, would be call fragging. Appalled by Bragg's brutality, they tried to kill him by igniting an artillery shell under his cot.

First the war against the Seminoles, then the attack on Mexico had enabled Americans like Bragg to raise themselves from poverty into the officer class. Like Duncan Clinch, Bragg might have wound up a day laborer or tenant farmer had the U.S. government not given him a free education at West Point. American taxpayers then went on paying Bragg's salary, providing his housing allowance, and paying for his children's education until, seeking further enrichment, he left the U.S. Army in 1856 and established himself in Louisiana. There—as Perry, Milton, and so many others did in Florida—Lieutenant Colonel Bragg reinvented himself as a Southern aristocrat. Even before Louisiana seceded, Bragg rushed to take up arms against the U.S. Army.

Arriving in Pensacola Bragg, bearing the Confederate rank of brigadier general, disempowered the civilian authority and proclaimed martial law. When it came to actual fighting, though, he continued the Confederate policy of indolence as U.S. ships landed more than one thousand troops at Fort Pickens. Mostly from the Sixth Regiment of New York Volunteers, these reinforcements brought along an ornery, much-admired billy goat as their mascot. While they transformed the tiny federal presence Slemmer had established into an impregnable redoubt, the Confederates continued to do nothing —until the successful U.S. attack on the *Judah* at last bestirred General Bragg into acting. On the night of October 8, 1861, just shy of nine months after Slemmer seized it, Confederate forces finally made their one and only attempt to attack Fort Pickens.

As the official Confederate report later related, the disaster began even before Bragg's inept and undisciplined troops left the

Pensacola Navy Yard, when the engine broke on the *Ewing*, the steamboat that was supposed to tow them over to Santa Rosa Island. It had not occurred to Bragg's command to verify the ship's seaworthiness. When the Confederates finally did manage to cross the channel, they found that the landing site Bragg's staff had chosen was nowhere near the actual fort. "After a march of 3 or 4 miles" which, the official report complained, was "rendered toilsome and fatiguing by the nature of the ground," U.S. sentries intercepted the Confederates. "The alarm having been thus given, and it becoming impossible to conceal our advance further from the enemy," as the report put it, any possibility of reaching Fort Pickens, let alone seizing it, was gone. In response the Confederates started thrashing around in the dark. One of Bragg's officers, thinking he had cornered the enemy, tried to press home his imaginary advantage: "Without a moment's delay he charged it with the bayonet," the Confederate report noted, "but met with no resistance. The camp was almost entirely deserted, and our troops speedily applied the torch to the tents, storehouses and sheds."

No one was there because U.S. troops had begun to encircle Bragg's force and cut it off from its landing site. The Confederates were in full retreat when "two companies of United States regulars, which had passed us under the cover of the darkness and posted themselves behind a dense thicket to intercept our retiring column," began firing on them. Just getting back to their boats now seemed like victory, but not for long. Hardly had "the order [been] given to the steamers to steer for Pensacola," the Confederate report explained, "when it was discovered that a hawser had become entangled in the propeller of the 'Ewing' and that she could not move." Even after the propeller was finally disentangled, the *Ewing* could not tow the troop barges because its steering mechanism did not work. "The enemy, taking advantage of these circumstances," the report continued, "appeared among the sand hills along the beach and opened a fire upon the masses of our troops densely crowded upon our transports." The Confederates were unable to fire back: "The necessity of using the 'Neaffie' as a tug, and the accident which for some time disabled her, prevented her guns from being brought into play," the report explained.

During their disastrous foray, Bragg's troops had spent much of their time looting. Lauding this undisciplined misbehavior as "worthy of the gallant men who executed it," Bragg granted the troops special permission to keep what they had taken, including personal possessions and money. Florida's political leaders were now bystanders to events. "You will have heard of the affair on Santa Rosa island," Florida's newly installed governor, John Milton, was informed. "The object of the expedition was fully and completely accomplished," it was added, without specifying what that object was.

Bragg's sole achievement was to provoke another U.S. attack. What one pro-slavery account later described as "the most imposing military demonstration in the history of Florida" began on the morning of November 22, 1861, as the Confederate outpost at Fort McRee, just opposite Fort Pickens, came under sustained U.S. artillery fire. Once again it had not occurred to General Bragg that the United States might retaliate for something he had done. He was so surprised by the incoming artillery shells that he made a note of the exact time, 9:30 a.m. Artillery fire came from newly installed guns at Fort Pickens, but the most destructive fire came from two U.S. warships, the *Niagara* and the *Richmond*. They stood offshore, unleashing volley after murderous volley. By late afternoon the Confederates were no longer able to return fire. Two U.S. warships, capable of striking anywhere at any time, had demonstrated that the Confederate coastal defenses in Florida were worthless.

What was true at Pensacola was also true at Mobile, along the Louisiana and Texas coasts, in the sea islands of Georgia, and in Virginia. Pensacola was a prophetic victory for the Union, Charleston a fool's-gold victory for the doomed Confederate cause. Not even South Carolina was safe as U.S. amphibious forces knocked out the Confederate coastal defenses and turned Port Royal Sound into a permanent Union deepwater port and naval base. The fireworks at Fort Sumter fostered the illusion that warfare was still, in spite of the Industrial Revolution, a chivalrous affair in which men died but honor flourished. There was much talk of blood being "spilt," no mention of the pusses and fluids a dying body actually disgorges. While the U.S. Navy's new steamships strangled the South, the new railroads would deliver hundreds of thousands of young men into ever more murderous fields of fire.

This first industrial war was also one of the last to be fought under premodern medical conditions. That compounded the murderousness. U.S. Army surgeons later estimated that 995 out of every 1,000 infantrymen became victims of the "bloody flux," as dysentery was called. Some 5,000 Floridians in uniform died during the war. Only about 1,000 were killed in or as a result of battle. Microbes and sepsis were the great killers. The trail of blood was actually a trail of vomit and feces as Confederate forces surged north, and then after reaching the high-water mark at Gettysburg in Pennsylvania, drained south, until the last Confederate partisans, like the Seminoles before them, had no place left to hide but the Everglades.

The U.S. "military demonstration" at Pensacola heralded a new era in warfare—the age of seaborne firepower, epitomized by the destroyer and the battleship and (when it came to intimidating non-Europeans, and empire building) the gunboat. During the War of 1812 the rockets' red glare provided a dramatic backdrop for "The Star-Spangled Banner"; the British bombardment had not threatened the structural integrity of Fort McHenry in Baltimore Harbor. Less than fifty years later, in 1861, the destruction was so total at Pensacola that Fort McRee never again was used for military purposes. The Clausewitz of the new age was U.S. Navy Captain Albert Thayer Mahan. Like Captain Sprague, Captain Mahan is one of those authorities Florida's valedictorians would never mention, yet he defined to perfection what happened at Pensacola. "Blockade, such as that enforced by the United States Navy during the Civil War," he wrote, "is evidently only a special phase of commerce-destroying; yet how immense—nay, decisive—its results!"

Mahan's acute analysis caught the import of another powerful force the secessionists fatally underestimated. The power of American nationalist sentiment, Mahan observed, "was evidenced by the sudden and rapid rising of the North at the outbreak of our civil war, when the flag was fired upon at Fort Sumter. Then was shown how deeply had sunk into the popular heart the devotion to the Union and the flag, fostered by long dwelling upon the ideas, by innumerable Fourth of July orations, often doubtless vainglorious, sometimes perhaps grotesque, but whose living force and overwhelming results were vividly apparent, as the fire leaped from hearthstone to hearthstone throughout the Northern states." To the "commerce-destroying" naval blockade and the derring-do patriotism of Americans like Lieutenant Slemmer now had been added the stupendous destructive power of nineteenth-century industrial technology, in the form of seaborne high-explosive projectiles.

While General Bragg could not protect Florida's secessionists from American fervor and U.S. firepower, he and the rest of the Confederate leadership could, and did, bring down upon Florida the nightmare they had accused the government in Washington of planning. Just as Yulee, Perry, and Milton predicted, beginning in 1861 the rights of Florida's white people were destroyed, their freedoms usurped by the Confederate administration. One account sympathetic to Florida's slaveholders describes the Confederate emasculation of states' rights in the following way: "In the fall of 1861 the Confederate government stopped the policy of requisitioning the several governors and created military districts in the seceded states under the command of military officers. Requisitions from the central government were passed to the district commands who sought aid from the governor in meeting the quota." In plain English, the governors no longer governed; the states themselves, by Confederate decree, were now only subdistricts of the military commands. The supposed rebellion on behalf of states' rights had turned the states and their elected officials into lower-echelon functionaries in a dictatorial, malfunctioning command economy.

St. Augustine provided an example of how the Confederacy not only failed to defend Florida but made it indefensible. Back in January 1861, following the U.S. withdrawal, a pro-Confederate group calling itself the Marion Artillery of St. Augustine had installed a number of 32-pounder cannon and 8-inch howitzers in the Castillo de San Marcos. Now, just over one year later, on Confederate orders, those same weapons were dismounted and carted off by Confederate troops and, like Florida's soldiers, sent north to Tennessee and Virginia. Then, in an act of gratuitous destructiveness that epitomized their "Florida Last" approach, Confederates stripped the lenses from the lighthouse at St. Augustine. Just as they had in the time of Ribault and Menéndez, ships once again had to pick their way along the Florida coast without benefit of onshore navigational aids.

Much worse was to come. In February 1862 the Confederate high command issued "a sweeping order to the Florida department to withdraw all men and supplies northward." Floridians were expressly forbidden to defend Fernandina, Pensacola, and Florida's other coastal cities and ports. Florida was abandoned, one account sympathetic to the Confederate cause matter-of-factly put it, because "more troops were needed in Tennessee and Kentucky." As the Confederate government, in Governor Milton's own words, abandoned "Florida to the mercy and abuse of the Lincoln Government," the Confederate forces stripped Florida's people as well as the state administration of the material possibility of self-defense. When federal forces landed in Apalachicola, U.S. sailors found people there in an "almost starving condition." The Confederates, after disabling the town's defenses, had burned crops and destroyed food stocks. In Jacksonville Confederate troops, acting under orders, burned down the town's best hotel as well its iron foundry and sawmills. Freelance devastation was encouraged too. "Local 'bushwhackers' roamed as predators" unchecked, destroying what the Confederate armed forces missed.

General Bragg was particularly ruthless; "burn all from Fort McRee to the junction with the Mobile road," he ordered. "Destroy all machinery, etc., public and private," he specified; "disable the saw mills in and around the bay, and burn the lumber. Break up the railroad from Pensacola to the junction, carrying the iron up to a safe point." "The work of destruction . . . began on March 11 and continued through May 10," one friendly summary relates. "Saw mills, lumber stores, warehouses, naval stores, boats and gunboats, forage, food supplies, and clothing . . . were all burned or sabotaged." "Public buildings, camp tents, and whatever was combustible, from the navy yard to Fort McRee, were quickly in flames," another report noted. The U.S. fleet waited offshore, watching as Bragg's Confederate forces defeated Florida for them.

On May 8, 1862, the devastation of Pensacola entered its final phase. On Bragg's orders the civilian population was forced at gunpoint to abandon the city. Written from the Confederate viewpoint, the following passage is particularly revealing because it offers no criticism of this orgy of self-destruction. To the contrary, it finds the visual effect of what the Confederates did picturesque: "Frightened children, bewildered by their strange surroundings, clung weeping to mothers or nurses almost as bewildered as themselves. Notice had been short, and little was clear to any except that by the inexorable decree of war all that stood for security and comfort was left behind. At the last moment, the navy yard, the steamers and the public buildings were set on fire, and the beautiful bay was aglow with the flames." Because the Confederate War Department had ordained it, the ports and towns of coastal Florida, now including the once-formidable fortifications at Pensacola, "were returned to the 'Stars and Stripes' of the United States after but little more than one year under the 'Stars and Bars' of the Confederate States."

After the Confederate abandonment, Florida might not have existed so far as both sides were concerned. Northerners considered Florida an irrelevancy; "the smallest tadpole in the dirty pool of secession," the *Philadelphia Inquirer* called it. Confederates called Florida "the forgotten state of the Confederacy." For generations to come hobbyists and historians would go on peddling the claim that nothing much happened in Florida during the Civil War. Everything happened. A deluded, self-important local elite gratuitously provoked the retaliation of a much more powerful central government. Thanks to racism, the remainder of the white population, not without misgivings, mostly supported this suicidal course of action as well. As a result the preexisting economy and social order were ravaged. The future costs would also be immense. Having lost the slaves they had provoked a war to retain, the political and cultural elite was left, after the war, to cope with a vast uneducated black lumpenproletariat and a poor white population that was also incompetent to deal with the oncoming challenges of the twentieth century. Faced with the destructive consequences of its ignorance, its selfishness, and its folly, the same elite would opt for a policy of black repression and white

inequality that, until federal forces once again intervened, perpetuated poverty, ignorance, and race hatred.

That happened, with variations, in all of the seceded slave states.
It happened first in Florida. Florida was the precursor of all, the meta-
phor as well. What better epitomized what the Confederacy did to
itself than Bragg destroying everything he touched, as Florida's supposed leaders watched passively while talking of valor? As Pensacola
showed, the Confederacy's destruction was, on the most fundamental
level, an act of self-destruction.

One later myth was that no one could possibly have seen what
was coming, but Richard Keith Call foresaw what the secession
would produce: "the most stupendous ruin." For him secession was
the opening scene of a tragedy in which all he built and cherished
would be "madly and rashly destroyed, without reflection." Florida's
"high treason against our constitutional government," he told some
jubilant secessionists on January 10, 1861, the same day Slemmer
fired the first shots on behalf of the Union, had flung open "the
gates of Hell, from which shall flow the curses of the damned which
shall sink you to perdition." Ignoring the distraught old man, they
continued their revelry.

14

DISAMBIGUATION

In Florida two Civil Wars unfolded. First came the war that actually happened. Finite in time, it began in 1861, lasted four years, and ended in 1865. Then there is the imaginary Civil War. An unending pageant, it began after the military conflict was finished, as defeated Confederates and their apologists transformed the brutality and ruin they unleashed into a selfless struggle to defend a noble cause. In this war of gallant charges and no diarrhea, General Bragg, like all Confederate officers, is a gentleman. Genuine heroes like Lieutenant Slemmer figure, to the extent they figure at all, as Yankee ruffians.

It would be nice to limit an account of the Civil War in Florida to what happened during the Civil War, but the subsequent misrepresentations of what actually happened and the ensuing redefinitions of what it meant have come to disfigure America's understanding of itself even more than the original violence did. Until Americans liberate themselves from the fictional Civil War, they may never transcend their national legacy of slavery, racism, hypocrisy, denial, and dishonesty. Even now the Civil War—the real one—remains the biggest bad thing that ever happened to America. The continuing, ex post facto invention of a false Civil War is also a crucially important event in America's life as a nation. There is a lot to be learned from these two separate events, the real and the fake Civil Wars, but only if we are willing to recognize that they are separate events and find some way to disambiguate them.

Today no Fort Slemmer exists to honor the junior officer who kept the U.S. flag flying at Pensacola. Everyone has heard of Fort Bragg. Thousands of U.S. soldiers ship out of Bragg every year.

As America's men and women in uniform set out in the service of their country, few if any realize the name of their home base honors a person who would today be called a terrorist. A U.S. Army history of Fort Bragg, published in 2003, is an exercise in Confederate apologetics. Bragg's "able leadership and superb strategy," it claims, are the reason why this base is named "in honor" of a Confederate general. Bragg's tactics, it adds, "exemplified his military genius." This tribute rolls on until finally it is mentioned that Bragg's "defeat at Bennett's Place, near Durham, North Carolina . . . marked the cessation of Confederate action in this section." Having begun the war by losing Florida, Bragg ended it by losing North Carolina. Pensacola foreshadowed his, and the Confederacy's, trajectory to ruin, yet all these generations later he is treated as a hero. His performance in Florida is nowhere mentioned.

One might expect that, instead of honoring the Confederate loser, the name of a great U.S. Army base would honor the general who defeated him, but even Yankees know why Fort Bragg is not called Fort Sherman. William Tecumseh Sherman is that mean man who burned Atlanta; so the installation honors the general who burned Pensacola. To comprehend the triumph of the mythical Civil War over the real one, all that's necessary is to juxtapose those two events. The burning of Pensacola figures not at all in America's understanding of the Civil War, or of itself. Then there is the burning of Atlanta, as vivid in people's minds as *Gone with the Wind*.

Of all aspects of life in Florida during the Civil War, Confederate abuse of white people is the one the falsifiers most successfully expunged. The widely resented Impressment Act abolished property rights as well as human rights; it empowered Confederate officials to seize the private property of white people, even when it belonged to notables like Senator Yulee. By 1862 Yulee, having lost his Fernandina estate thanks to the Confederate policy of abandonment, was suing the Confederate government in an unsuccessful attempt to stop them from ripping up his Cedar Key railroad. He went to court again when Confederate officials confiscated his sugar crop. He had planned to make half a million dollars off his sugar. Now all he had were lawyers' bills. While the Confederacy was carting away the property of the rich, it was marching poor whites off to the slaughter. Bounty hunters got a bonus for every white boy they delivered. Others preyed on Florida's poor whites by impersonating impressment agents. When authorized agents of the Confederate Conscript Bureau arrived, the families who had paid bribes to the imposters wound up losing their sons as well as their money.

The "Confederate cause," the saying went, "was a rich man's war, but a poor man's fight." The first Confederate conscription act obliged all males between eighteen and thirty-five to fight. Next all males between fifteen and fifty were called up. Then, as sepsis and the Gatling gun devoured conscripts in ever greater numbers, boys of fourteen and men of sixty were drafted. By the end of 1863 four-fifths of its able-bodied white males were outside Florida. The economic, social and emotional stresses on a society stripped of men were multiplied by the fact that the central white male function was controlling the black population.

Throughout the war and long afterward, slaveholders and their sympathizers were sustained by the notion that, by enslaving them, white people did black people a favor. Here is how Governor Richard Keith Call attempted to justify slavery in an 1860 polemic: "Wild barbarians, naked, savage idolaters, black from the burning sun of their native clime, with knotted and combined locks, more like the wool of the beast than the hair of the human head, savage in taste, manner, and disposition," experienced, by virtue of having been enslaved, an "improvement in personal appearance, in feeling and sympathies, in civilization and religion," he argued. Here is what Florida's students were being taught in 1952: "American Negro slavery had become the greatest school for civilizing a race of barbaric savages that the world has ever known."

This sense of slavery as a beneficent institution goes hand in hand with the notion that nothing is ever the slaveholders' fault. They have no choice but to commit savage acts of violence in order to forestall predicted but so far unrealized acts of Yankee barbarism. Tyrannies unknown under U.S. rule must be inflicted on whites as well as blacks since the struggle against potential Yankee tyranny requires it. As the world of slavery self-destructs, the white Southern male is responsible neither for provoking the war nor for losing it. The Yankees are to blame, just as the Seminoles, British, Spaniards and Indians earlier were. Anyway, there was no choice. Honor required it as Yankees were fixing to do the same thing anyhow. Following the Confederate defeat, all sense of responsibility for the catastrophe was expunged as a result of what one scholar, writing in the 1940s, described as the "enshrining, as 'history' [of] that which once was but expedient Conservative political propaganda."

A pervasive mechanism for this "enshrining, as 'history'" of pro-slavery propaganda was what another scholarly paper defines as "The Confederate Monument Ritual." These "fund-raising drives for statues and monuments," it relates, all "involved the same essential ingredients: a parade through the city streets to the site, several brief welcoming addresses by local dignitaries, some musical selections 'appropriate to the occasion,' a poem or two by the local town laureate, and an oration. The draperies were then lifted from around the monument, which would then stand as an enduring symbol of the Lost Cause."

The Ur-granddaddy of Florida's Confederate monuments still occupies a place of honor on the ground of the state capitol at Tallahassee. Its inscription, which inspired the construction of many similar memorials, reads as follows:

> *To rescue from Oblivion*
> *And perpetuate in the Memory of succeeding Generations*
> *The heroic Patriotism of the Men . . .*
> *Who perished in the Civil War from 1861 to 1865*

It is a sentiment anyone could share except, as the Tallahassee inscription makes clear, only those who fought for slavery count as heroes and patriots in this version of Florida's participation in the Civil War. The principal battles in which Floridians died fighting for slavery, twenty-nine in all, are listed on the monument. The most famous are the "Virginia Battles: Williamsburg, Seven Pines, Richmond, Cold Harbor, Manassas, Sharpsburg, Fredericksburg . . . Chancellorsville, Wilderness, Yorktown," and—misspelled as well as misplaced to this day—"Gettisburgh."

The most numerous are the "Western Battles: Richmond, Ky., Farmington, Shiloh, Corinth, Green River, Perryville, Chickamauga, Missionary Ridge, Resaca, Gilgal Church, Cassville, Kennesaw Mountain, Decatur, Jonesboro, Franklin, etc." In addition to those two lengthy lists, there is a third, much shorter list. Taking up by far the least amount of space are the "Florida battles," which number exactly three: Pensacola, Olustee, Natural Bridge.

As its inscriptions demonstrate, this monument tells two stories, one false, the other inadvertently true. The first tale it tells is of how, by putting up monuments like this one, neo-Confederates made it seem the Floridians who died in the Civil War were acting selflessly because war was thrust upon them. The ensuing list of Virginia battles and Western battles shows how, to the contrary, the lives of Florida's conscripts were thrown away in an outward explosion of pro-slavery violence that splattered vast tracts of America with blood, while the list of Florida battles on the monument provides the key to disambiguating the factual from fictional when it comes to understanding what actually happened in and to Florida during the Civil War.

The most salient fact concerning the first of the three Florida battles is that there never was any Battle of Pensacola. The disastrous Confederate raid on Santa Rosa Island in October 1861 was no battle. The Confederates themselves did sack and burn Pensacola in May 1862, but that was no battle either. Nor can the "imposing military demonstration" of November 1861, which saw U.S. artillery destroy Fort McRee, be counted as a battle unless Confederates cowering on the sidelines while great guns blow their defenses to smithereens be counted as combat. That reduces the total number of supposed Florida battles to two, Olustee and Natural Bridge. The initial revelation here is how late in the war both those engagements happened. The Battle of Olustee in northeast Florida was fought in February 1864, after the tide had turned decisively against the Confederacy. The engagement at Natural Bridge in Middle Florida—actually a series of skirmishes—occurred in March 1865, just weeks before the Confederate surrender. Is it really true that nothing worth mentioning on a Civil War memorial happened in Florida between the end of 1861 and the beginning of 1864?

During all that time Key West was serving as the command head-quarters of the Gulf Blockading Squadron. U.S. Navy ships operating out of Pensacola, Fernandina, and other ports were helping to suffocate Confederate commerce. While the Confederates continued to shirk fighting in Florida, Slemmer's once lonely and isolated position became part of a collar of U.S. installations stretching all around the state. Under the protection of U.S. forces, Florida loyalists established outposts in Mayport, at the mouth of the St. Johns River near Jacksonville, and along the Gulf coast from Charlotte Harbor and Cedar Key up to the Pandhandle. U.S. forces also controlled Fort Myers, then deep in the Everglades, as well as St. Augustine. Strategically important to the war effort, these outposts also served as sanctuaries and training bases for loyal Floridians, both white and black, who volunteered to fight for the United States. As more and more people sought refuge in the areas free of Confederate control, two Floridas emerged. A multiracial Florida, where the U.S. flag flew and freed blacks and loyalist whites lived side by side, fringed the coasts. A racist, inland Florida nestled in the center and northern tier of the state. Significant differences developed between life in the U.S.-controlled areas and the Confederate interior as the war progressed. The lifting of Florida's confiscatory race laws allowed Madgigine Jai–Anna Kingsley and other enterprising nonwhites to reclaim their property in U.S.-controlled areas. In Fernandina and St. Augustine blacks, previously liable to be tortured and mutilated for the crime of learning to read and write, now could go to school. The Emancipation Proclamation turned these coastal enclaves into a promised land for all black people in Florida. They knew that if they could make it to the U.S.-held areas, their women and children would be liberated from slaveholder oppression; their young men could join the U.S. Army and fight against slavery.

These two Floridas, U.S. and Confederate, scraped up against each other at Jacksonville. Unique in Florida, it changed hands four times, though not because either side cared much about it. The Confederates, in keeping with their "Florida Last" strat-egy, never bothered to put up a fight there. U.S. forces occupied Jacksonville in March 1862, in March 1863, then again in February 1864. Each time U.S. forces approached, the Confederates abandoned their positions, which is why there is no "Battle of Jacksonville" on any Confederate memorial.

That late in the war the moral and emotional isolation of Florida's secessionist leaders was striking; in their hilly backland preserve in Tallahassee they were militarily as well as geologically detached from the rest of the state. To them this latest loss of Jacksonville, 170 miles to the east, initially seemed of no more consequence than the burning of Pensacola, 200 miles to the west. Then U.S. troops started moving inland. Could it be that President Lincoln's army was finally coming after them? Alarmed at the possibility of actual fighting coming his way, Governor Milton pleaded for protection from the Confederate high command in Charleston, South Carolina. There General P. G T. Beauregard was still in command, nearly three years after his attack on Fort Sumter had commenced the war the Confederacy was now clearly losing. Following Governor Milton's appeal, Beauregard for the first and last time ordered a significant Confederate force into Florida. There it joined the small Florida contingent led by Senator Yulee's partner in business as well as rebellion, Joseph Finegan.

Tallahassee was never the objective of the Union incursion; any such action would have been a violation of U.S. policy. In instructions to Major General Quincy A. Gillmore, who was in overall command of the Florida advance, the General in Chief of the U.S. Army, General H. W. Halleck, reminded him why actions like attempting to take Tallahassee were "in opposition to sound strategy." "If successful they merely absorb our troops in garrisons to occupy the places, but have little or no influence upon the progress of the war." In response Gillmore explicitly disavowed any advance on Tallahassee. "I have no intention to occupy that part of the state," he wrote. He went on to state that his objectives were logistical and economic, not territorial. "First: To procure an outlet for cotton, lumber, timber, turpentine, and the other products of the State. Second: To cut off one of the enemy's sources of commissary supplies. He now draws largely upon the herds of Florida for his beef. . . . Third: To obtain recruits for my colored regiments." Black Floridians by the thousands were eager to fight; Gillmore wanted to arm as many of them as possible.

There was an additional, political consideration at play. In Washington President Lincoln had decided to encourage efforts in Florida to establish a reconstructed state government there. He had sent his secretary, John Hay, to Fernandina and St. Augustine to assess and encourage that possibility. Nothing became of the plan. Taking Tallahassee was never part of it. To the contrary, Hay's instructions limited his activities to Key West and other areas under U.S. Navy control. In his own hand, President Lincoln informed General Halleck that military, not political, considerations should predominate; "you are the master," he assured him. Even so, to the myth that the fighting at Olustee saved Tallahassee would be added the fiction that the battle also foiled Abe Lincoln's plot to turn Florida over to Yankees and their sympathizers even before the fighting stopped.

General Truman Seymour, the operational commander, was explicitly instructed "not to risk a ripost or make an attack when there was a prospect of incurring much loss" yet, as General Beauregard fully understood, that was precisely the prospect which the Union advance created. The force whose presence so agitated Governor Milton was too small, less than six thousand men, and the distance, more than 150 miles, too great for a successful advance on Tallahassee. For that same reasons it offered an enticing target of opportunity, which was why Beauregard did send troops into Florida. Instead of a threat, he perceived "the apparent opportunity of striking the enemy an effective blow."

Easy to find on a Florida road map, the Olustee battle site is located twenty-two miles east of the center of the giant, Confederate-style X that Interstates 75 and 10 form as they intersect near Lake City, Florida. Beauregard's calculation that he could strike "the enemy an effective blow" proved correct. Olustee was the costliest battle ever fought in Florida, yet as the following table shows, the most striking aspect of the casualty lists was the asymmetry in the missing. Confederate and U.S. sources agree that the U.S. missing outnumbered Confederate missing by more than eighty-four to one.

Battlefield Casualties, Olustee, Florida February 20, 1864

	Dead	*Wounded*	*Missing and Captured*
U.S.	203	1,152	506
Confederate	93	842	6

More than a thousand black soldiers fought on the U.S. side at Olustee. They saved the lives of many white troops following the Confederate attack. "The colored troops behaved creditably," General Seymour reported. "It was not in their conduct that can be found the chief cause of failure, but in the unanticipated yielding of a white regiment." These African-American volunteers had joined the U.S. Army to fight for their freedom. At Olustee they did fight. As one white eye-witness put it, "The colored troops went in grandly, and they fought like devils." This was the real Civil War, a struggle to the death over slavery as whites killed black people—and, this time, black people killed back. As always the muck and insects held sway; the foe was unseen until it was too late. It was like the Battle of the Withlacoochee, though this time U.S. troops found themselves being killed by white Floridians, not Seminoles. Also as in the past, the killing achieved nothing. Florida's Confederates, like the Seminoles before them, were doomed to be defeated by an overwhelming power emanating from the north. Nothing happening in the Florida swamplands could change that.

Olustee was the scene of the most consequential massacre in Florida since Negro Fort. That was why the Union missing outnumbered Confederate missing by such an enormous margin. The massacre occurred when, rather than continuing their offensive, Confederate troops halted their advance in order to specially target black soldiers. Once the killing stopped, the Confederates' first step was to segregate their prisoners. "I have forwarded 150 prisoners (not wounded) to Major-General Gilmer," Joseph Finegan reported. It is clear that virtually all of those prisoners were white because Finegan added, "Among them are 3 negroes." He went on to ask: "What shall I do with the large number of the enemy's wounded in my hands? Many of these are negroes." Virtually none of the black soldiers Finegan mentioned were seen alive again.

General John P. Hatch, later commander of U.S. forces in Florida, was able to shed light on what happened. "Soon after the battle of Olustee," he wrote, "a list of wounded and prisoners in the hands of the enemy was forwarded to our lines." He added: "The very small number of colored prisoners attracted immediate attention, as it was well known that the number left wounded on the field was large." "It is now known," General Hatch reported, "that most of the wounded colored men were murdered on the field." In their eagerness to murder wounded blacks, the Florida forces had thrown away the one chance that arose in Florida during the Civil War to inflict a significant defeat on the U.S. Army. When asked why they were letting the U.S. forces escape, one field officer responded, "Shooting niggers, sir." More than two years later U.S. officers came upon a reminder de Soto had passed this way. "The bodies of the Union soldiers killed in the Battle of Olustee," a U.S. lieutenant named Frederick E. Grossman wrote, "were disinterred by the hogs within a few weeks after the battle, in consequence of which the bones and skulls were scattered broadcast over the battlefield."

Olustee, the greatest of the Florida battles celebrated on the Tallahassee memorial as a triumph of "heroic Patriotism," it turns out, tops another list. Consisting of "Olustee, Fort Pillow, Poison Spring, and the Crater," it is a list of "the war's most notorious massacres" compiled by Gregory J. W. Urwin, editor of *Black Flag over Dixie*, which examines atrocities inflicted on nonwhite U.S. troops by Confederates during the Civil War. Racism, which had and would cost the state so much, cost the Confederates what might have been their only meaningful military success in Florida; "the fruits of the victory were insignificant," Beauregard sourly informed Jefferson Davis, "mainly because . . . no serious attempt [was] made to pursue" the federal forces as they withdrew.

Decades later, the Olustee massacre was transformed into a triumphalist tale of valor, culminating in glorious victory, of which every white man, woman, and child in Florida could be right proud. "In this battle," declares one widely read account, "the Confederates

won a complete victory over a much larger force than their own."
Beauregard's comment puts paid any notion of "a complete victory."
As for the pretense the Confederates defeated "a much larger force
than their own," Confederate military documents state that their
forces at Olustee numbered fifty-two hundred. The U.S. force numbered fifty-five hundred. Because of their knowledge of the terrain
and because they had the element of surprise, the Confederates had
the clear advantage when the battle began. Like many such accounts,
"Victory at Olustee" goes on to create the impression that heroic
Confederates ran the spineless Yankees clear out of Florida: "After
the hasty retreat from Olustee to Jacksonville," it states, "most of the
invading party sailed away to South Carolina." Confederates, not the
Yankees, were the ones who abandoned Florida. Recognizing the futil-
ity of further operations there, General Beauregard ordered his troops
out of Florida. Then, pushing its "Florida Last" strategy to its ultimate, the Confederate command ordered the Florida troops out of
Florida too. Finegan and his Florida Brigade arrived in Virginia on
May 25, 1864, only three months after the Battle of Olustee. Over
the next ten months U.S. forces ground the Floridians to pieces. In
April 1865 the last remnants of the Florida expedition were disarmed
by U.S. cavalry commanded by General George Armstrong Custer,
rounded up in stockades as the Seminoles had been, and herded south.

The "Victory at Olustee" was the invention of Caroline Mays Brevard, one of the most influential Floridians who ever lived. Just as
Washington Irving's fables, in defiance of the factual documentation,
were metamorphosed into Florida "history'" during Territorial times,
Brevard's fictionalizations became the "history" that prevailed over
what really happened during the Civil War. Born in 1860 into two of
Florida's best-connected families, the Calls and the Brevards, Brevard
rewrote family history as she fictionalized Florida events. Her father,
who rose to the rank of brigadier general in the Confederate army,
was directly involved in the Battle of Olustee. Her grandfather on
her mother's side was Governor Richard Keith Call, Florida's most
trenchant critic of secession.

The military records of the war—especially the Confederate
war archives—tell what happened at places like Olustee. Brevard's

accounts tell us what didn't. Fabricating some incidents, excising others, she created a fantasy Florida where rich, powerful whites, most especially her own forebears, incarnate virtue and progress. Their manly treatment of insubordinate Seminoles provides a prologue, in her telling, to the magnificent victories of Florida's better class of white folks during the Civil War. A child of five when the Confederacy surrendered, she never experienced slavery or war first hand. That allowed her, like Washington Irving, to write elegiacally, falsely and with complete authority of times and places she never knew. Even Confederate heroes are allowed to say only what she lets them say. She censors General Beauregard's comments on the Battle of Olustee.

She also censors her own grandfather. Richard Keith Call's jeremiad on the folly of secession is one of the clairvoyant moments of Florida history. It is what redeems him before the bar of history, yet his granddaughter suppressed all that because her grandfather's astute insights did not fit in with her white lace version of events. "There was the wildest excitement," she writes of the festivities accompanying secession. "Amid shouts and cheers men embraced each other and cried that the day of liberty had come." Brevard then adds, referring to her grandfather but declining to identify him, quote him, or explain why he felt that way: "There were some, however, who felt no gladness; some still loved the Union and honored the old flag, and their hearts were sad, and tears filled their eyes." Later, in a monograph entitled *Richard Keith Call by His Granddaughter*, she transformed her eminent forebear into the kind of critter Washington Irving might have invented; in her telling, his loyalty to the United States becomes an eccentric peccadillo. Brevard never mentions that secession divided her family as deeply as it divided America, let alone that Ellen Call Long—his daughter, her aunt—also remained unashamedly and publicly loyal to the United States. Instead, thanks to her niece and the lies she propagated, this remarkable woman was turned into another of the nonpersons Florida's histories of gentility triumphant would never mention.

During the last decades of the nineteenth and first decades of the twentieth centuries Brevard was Florida's most powerful racist apologist and neo-Confederate propagandist. Two institutions proved especially effective when it came to imposing her bias on Florida's public idea of itself. The first was the Florida division of the United Daughters of the Confederacy. The second institution Brevard turned to her purposes was the government of the state of Florida. Before the Civil War her ancestors had used the state power to grab land and money. She used Florida's public funds to finance and the state government to enforce her fabricated vision of Florida past. Her magnum opus was *Government and History of Florida*. Black as well as white children were forced to study its pro-slavery account of Florida's past. Thanks to legislation Brevard and her supporters got enacted, Florida law required that her text be taught in every school. A popular lecturer, she was famed for "telling in the most charming manner of slavery times, colonial balls, duels, and all those romantic things which we associate with the early social life of the South," but Brevard, who lived until 1920, did not limit her propagandizing to words. All over Florida her racist propaganda was enshrined as "history" in stone, as she and her acolytes transformed Florida's public spaces into a kind of statewide slavery nostalgia theme park. "The monument dedicated to the Confederate veterans for keeping Tallahassee free from invasion by Union troops was made possible through her writings and influence," wrote one admirer following her death.

Brevard's campaign to cover Florida with monuments honoring nonexistent, militarily meaningless, or disgraceful Confederate "victories" reached its climax in the years just before World War I as she and the United Daughters of the Confederacy turned the massacre site at Olustee into their biggest celebration of pro-slavery valor yet. Her first step in transforming the meaning of the massacre was enshrining Olustee as one of the Florida battles on the Tallahassee monument, while simultaneously transforming it in her history book. Next Brevard and her allies reshaped the Olustee battlefield itself. As always, they used other people's money; at their behest the Florida state legislature paid for the land and provided money for the monument. When the Olustee monument was dedicated in 1912, some four thousand Floridians, the most to gather there at one time since the battle itself, converged on the site. The object of their veneration was a stone tower that, in keeping with the dawning age of Florida tourism, more resembled a Spanish Revival–style resort hotel than a war memorial; "this granite tower," one orator declared, "stands sentinel over the field where the Confederate soldier won admission to the temple of fame." No mention was made of the U.S. dead as the tower honoring those who killed them was dedicated.

Like Ponce de León's fictional exploits in St. Augustine, the nonexistent Confederate triumph at Olustee long ago superseded what really happened there and become the attraction that anchors the local tourist industry. Every February celebrants, souvenir salesmen, and people who like to dress up in Civil War uniforms and shoot off heavy artillery converge on the site of the 1864 massacre. Scale models are not permitted: "full scale artillery only," the regulations emphasize. The most spectacular event occurs the night before the supposed reenactment of the battle, as hobbyists fire their cannon into the adjacent Osceola National Forest. Every year the Confederates advance gloriously. Everyone whoops and hollers as the United States gets defeated. Neither the organizers' promotional literature nor their websites mention the words *massacre, colored, black*, or *Negro*. None of the participants reenacts white Confederates murdering wounded black U.S. soldiers.

The dramatizations of the imaginary Battle of Olustee illustrates how the falsification of Florida's past is an ongoing process. The first "reenactment" did not occur until 1977, 113 years after the real battle was fought. At first, one participant relates, impersonators had to thrash their way through the thick undergrowth covering the actual battle site, so the reinvented battle was moved away from the actual battle site to a place "where visibility was far better." The reenactment field was subsequently "clear-cut" in order to remove all vegetation. In addition to the battle "reenactment" and the amateur artillery firings, the Annual Olustee Battle Festival & Olustee Battle Re-Enactment includes Little Miss, Petite Miss, Preteen Miss, Junior Miss Tiny Tot, and Miniature Miss Battle of Olustee Festival pageants. The Florida state Department of Environmental Protection helps subsidize the festivities. The merchants, weapons hobbyists,

JUAN PONCE DE LEON AT THE FOUNTAIN OF YOUTH.

Ponce de León's fictional discovery of the Fountain of Youth.

Florida's Founding Fabricator, Washington Irving (1783–1859): best-selling inventor of the Ponce myth and many another historical falsehood.

This Fountain of Youth, circa 1930, served up tap water with free paper cups.

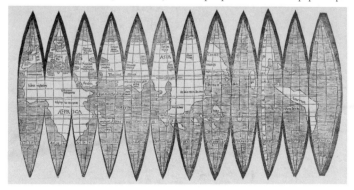

The 1507 Waldseemuller map. Well before Florida was "discovered," it started appearing on maps.

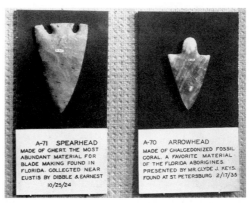

Mankind's genius for killing: Florida had no stone;
even so it had a Stone Age, complete with murderous
spear points.

de Soto's lasting legacy: Florida's feral hogs.

Thomas Moran's 1878 study of de Soto's mad wanderings, renamed *Ponce de León in Florida*
in hopes of cashing in on the Irving myth.

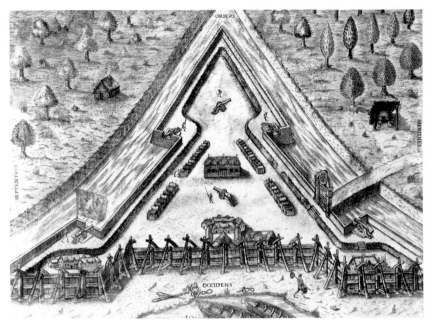

French Fort Caroline, not Spanish St. Augustine, was Florida's first European settlement until Spain, transposing Europe's blood feuds to America, massacred its settlers, unleashing the violent rivalries that would drive Florida history for the next 350 years.

Florida's factual founding father, Pedro Menendez de Aviles (1519–1574). The first of its major protagonists to be expunged from history, he—not Ponce de León—founded St. Augustine after massacring the French.

Ruins of British New Smyrna, Florida's Heart of Darkness. Within two years 627 of the 1,255 colonists were dead; the survivors' "Minorcan" descendants included Hollywood's singing cowgirl, Judy Canova, and the poet Stephen Vincent Benét.

Lieutenant, later General Duncan Clinch (1787–1849) orchestrated Florida's definitive massacre at Negro Fort; later fled to Georgia.

Governor William DuVal (1784–1854) sowed the seeds of catastrophe by establishing Florida's first "concentration zone;" later fled to Texas.

Also cited in official reports for battlefield cowardice, Governor Richard Keith Call (1792–1862) turned Florida into his money machine; He loved the Union as much as he revered slavery and foresaw the ruin pro-slavery rebellion would bring.

David Levy; Senator Yulee (1810–1886). Two names, one scoundrel. At his behest, the Tallahassee legislature transformed him from the son of a Jewish merchant into an Episcopalian-Moroccan prince.

William Powell, Jr., later known as Osceola (1804–1838). He carried a rifle, never a bow and arrow, but this representation of a white man striking a pose out of Greco-Roman classical antiquity, Apollo-like, captures Osceola's cultural and genetic complexity and conveys the truth of his valor. Note the similarities with Osceola's death mask.

Jose, later Joseph, Hernandez (1793–1857) originally Spanish, tricked and brutalized the American-born Osceola; got rich on U.S. government contracts; fled to Cuba when Florida ruined him too.

Osceola death mask

Massacre of the Whites by the Indians and Blacks in Florida.

The above is intended to represent the horrid Massacre of the Whites in Florida, in December 1835, and January, February, March and April 1836, when near Four Hundred (including women and children) fell victims to the barbarity of the Negroes and Indians.

The crucial role played by black Americans would be expunged from accounts of both the Seminole War and the Civil War in Florida.

Captain, later General John Titcomb Sprague (1810–1878), also expunged from history, fought and befriended the Seminoles, wrote the Florida war's definitive history, and was the key U.S. military figure in Florida under Reconstruction.

More than three months before Fort Sumter, Lieutenant Adam J. Slemmer (1828–1868) won the first and signal U.S. victory of the Civil War at Pensacola. No monument honors him.

United States Marshal branding the author

Florida's court-ordered branding of white U.S. citizens for helping escaped slaves scandalized America, then was excised from history too.

Confederate General Braxton Bragg (1817–1876) burned Pensacola long before Sherman burned Atlanta; Fort Bragg honors him.

The 1912 dedication of the Olustee monument at the site of one of the Civil War's worst massacres. Remains of the U.S. troops massacred there have never been retrieved.

Caroline Mays Brevard (1860–1920), white supremacist. Her ideas are still being propagated on the Internet and in academia.

The greatest Floridian since Osceola, perhaps ever, Governor Ossian Hart (1821–1874) integrated Florida's schools, righted its chaotic finances and proclaimed his loyalty to America and its values.

Marcellus Stearns (1839-1891). Following its notorious 1876 vote-counting crisis, Florida's one-armed governor peacefully left office rather than risk further bloodshed as racist violence and judicial election rigging undid democracy in America.

Robert Meacham (1835–1902) helped write Florida's enlightened 1868 Constitution.

Representative Josiah Walls (1842–1905) proposed social security and equal rights legislation that was only adopted generations later. Historians later turned him and other accomplished black men into "mulattos." First hand descriptions emphasized their dark skin and African features.

Incapable of saving itself from the clutches of yellow fever, Florida is saved by the same America that came to its rescue during the Seminole War, and would have to rescue it again and again, most often from itself.

Judge James Dean (1858–1914). Born a slave in central Florida, he was elected judge by white as well as black voters. Purged from office by Governor Francis Fleming for "moral turpitude."

Governor Fleming's black niece, Louise (1862–1899). Sent to the Congo as a medical missionary she contracted sleeping sickness while yellow fever in Florida was killing her white and Latin relatives. Fleming's final campaign was to make the pro-slavery Confederate "saltire"—diagonal cross—the dominant feature of the Florida state flag. His flag still flies.

Governor Francis Fleming (1841–1908).

Florida's gulag, circa 1940. Turpentine workers were slaves in all but name. The state's notorious turpentine camps were not outlawed until 1949.

A Florida panoply: The old capitol, with Brevard's monument celebrating Florida's fake victories; the Florida flag, with Fleming's racist saltire; the state flower, imported from China; the state anthem, written by a Yankee who never saw the Suwanee, adopted at the behest of a Miami state senator from Versailles, France; the mockingbird, so called because of its habit of purporting to be what it is not.

Henry Plant's Tampa Bay Hotel, opened in 1891.

HOTEL PONCE DE LEON, ST. AUGUSTINE. FLA. *Built 1885* A-13522

Flagler's Ponce de Leon Hotel, its name inspired by Washington Irving's fictional figure, opened in 1888. Like his railroad, the hotel lost money and had to be taken over by the state.

Gasparilla parade in honor of Tampa's non-existent pirate hero, Jose Gaspar, invented in 1904.

Flagler's Folly, inaugurated in 1912.

Negro Fort eternal. The 1923 Rosewood massacre was also expunged from history, as well as from newspaper archives.

Governor Charley Johns (1905–1990) updated Florida hate-and-fear politics with his crusade against the "Negro-Communist-homosexual conspiracy." He introduced the roving electric chair.

Florida's playboy segregationist Senator George Smathers with John F. Kennedy in 1963. Smathers also introduced Richard Nixon to banker Charles "Bebe" Rebozo.

Anita Bryant: homophobe activist and smiling face of Florida orange juice, she updated Charley Johns' sexual conformity crusade.

Sea World, opened in 1973, fifty miles inland, replaced Marineland as Florida's most visited salt water attraction.

The hurricane as permanent feature of Florida life. For more than five hundred years storms like Betsy (1965), David (1979, pictured here), Andrew (1992) and Katrina (2005) have laid low conquerors and stymied get-rich schemes while inspiring novels and movies as well as bad PR and fear.

The Space Shuttle *Challenger* moments before the disaster, January 28, 1986.

Systemic dysfunction following the 2000 presidential election

Continuing a long tradition, Governor Rick Scott, Florida's latest newcomer oligarch opportunist, extols traditional values at The Villages in 2012. Due to age restrictions, the youths staged behind him would not be allowed to live there.

and "reenactors" fire off their weapons, then party while treading over and around the scattered, unnoticed remains of the U.S. soldiers killed at Olustee. "Park personnel told me that there was a mass grave containing the remains of about 400 Union soldiers that died there that day," one visitor blogged in 2007, "but no one knows the names or the exact location of the grave."

Brevard's male counterpart in the fabrication of Florida's imaginary Civil War triumphs was John Jackson Dickison. Among the most extreme of the ultra-secessionists, he helped raise two cavalry regiments, but when the Confederate quartermaster general refused to furnish feed, Dickison refused to fight. While Florida's conscripts slogged north, on foot, he stayed at home with his horses. Like many of its most extreme chauvinists, Dickison was a self-invented Floridian; he had been living there only four years when Florida seceded. In his *Confederate Military History of Florida*, still popular with pro-slavery nostalgists, Dickison himself plays the starring role even though, as his own account makes clear, he avoided serious fighting. One of the incidents he describes occurred in March 1865, only a month before the Confederacy surrendered. He at first makes it seem he was pursuing a U.S. Army unit but, as he eventually concedes, "the enemy" consisted only of some black families trying to reach freedom. "I marched all night at times at half speed and reached Fort Peaton, 7 miles from St. Augustine, where," Dickison announces, "I overtook four negroes." This is followed by what he presents as an even more consequential military achievement: the capture, less than a mile from Union lines, of twenty more escaping slaves, "also a wagon and six ponies." In this self-selected vignette of Confederate valor Dickison's vigilantes fire not a shot at the nearby U.S. troops, just as General Finegan and his troops did not pursue the U.S. troops at Olustee. On both occasions, they target the blacks. For Dickison too, the war in Florida ends as it began: a war for slavery, fought by kidnapping and killing black people.

In another incident Dickison did exchange fire with U.S. troops, though they weren't Yankees. In early 1865, a force of 386 U.S. troops headed inland from Cedar Key on one of their periodic forays. Then, as planned, they turned back to the coast. The U.S. withdrawal was so far advanced that by the time he heard about it, Dickison had to race after the U.S. troops in a vain attempt to catch up with them. By the time he got there, Dickison and his troops were too tired—"almost broken down by fatigue," as he puts it—to actually engage the U.S. troops in battle, so they all went to sleep. The next morning he did get some U.S. troops to fire back, though, as always in these accounts of Confederate valor, there was a hitch. At St. Augustine Dickison blamed the fact "that the wind blew very strong" for his failure to catch the "escaping negroes" sooner. This time he had not brought along enough ammunition. "Had our ammunition come in time," Dickison complained, "the entire force would have been captured." There was another reason Dickison failed to land his catch. When he did attempt to take prisoners, U.S. soldiers would "rally again and again and renew the attack." Repulsing Dickison's fruitless raid on their rear, U.S. forces continued the withdrawal they had begun before Dickison interrupted them.

Generations of Florida schoolboys would grow up learning how Dickison whipped the Yankees, but what made Cedar Key such a great victory? Dickison claimed he, too, had foiled a plot to take Tallahassee, more than 130 miles away. How the U.S. command expected to do that with 386 men Dickison does not explain. Why he had to chase after them in the opposite direction, toward the coast, in order to get them to exchange gunfire with him, he does not elucidate either. Thanks to his Cedar Key triumph, Dickison would have us believe, Florida's white womanhood was saved. At the approach of the invaders, he later wrote, "the bravest hearts among our fair women trembled and sweet lips grew pale. . . . Had it not been for the timely arrival of our heroic little band," he adds, referring to himself, "fearful indeed would the result have been."

As at Olustee, the biggest lie here is of omission. Dickison does not mention that he was fighting black soldiers. The majority of those U.S. troops who would "rally again and again and renew the attack" were ex-slaves, many of them from Florida. The whites Dickison attacked weren't Yankees either. Of the 386 U.S. troops involved in the Cedar Key raid, 186 were white men from the Second Florida Regiment of the U.S. Army; 200 were black men from the U.S. Colored

Infantry. Something historic did happen at Cedar Key, but it wasn't that, as usual, the Confederates ran out of ammunition, or lacked reinforcements, or got tired, or that the wind started to blow just as the great victory was about to materialize. White men and black men fought side by side out of loyalty to the United States of America, just as they had at Olustee. One of the greatest lies told about the Civil War in Florida is that it was a struggle between Florida's valiant sons and "Yankee invaders." The greatest lie of all is that black Americans were too shiftless, or contented, or inherently stupid, to fight for their freedom. By early 1865 the main U.S. force in Florida consisted of Southerners, not Northerners. Black men with guns were now able to fight back; white Floridians were marching with them. That was why Confederate lips trembled, and not just female lips.

While U.S. forces regularly advanced into Confederate Florida, Confederate forces almost never went on the offensive. A rare attempt to take a federal position did occur at Fort Myers in the wilderness of southwestern Florida in early 1865. Confederate irregulars on horseback demanded that the U.S. forces inside the fort surrender. The officer in command refused. A few days later the Confederate posse returned, carting an artillery piece. The Confederates opened fire. The U.S. troops inside Fort Myers returned fire. The Confederates went away. U.S. forces had won "the southernmost land battle of the Civil War," but the incident was significant for a reason that goes beyond latitude. Black as well as white U.S. troops manned Fort Myers. At the time Fort Myers sheltered more than three hundred people, white and black, about the same number who had sought refuge at Negro Fort fifty years earlier. This time, because the fort's multiracial defenders had received proper training, no massacre occurred.

Natural Bridge, the third of the Florida battles inscribed on the Tallahassee monument, followed the Olustee–Cedar Key pattern. U.S. troops advanced inland for a time. Then, after meeting much, some, or no resistance, they returned to the coast. Though this incursion, too, was later portrayed as a "Yankee invasion," U.S. Colored Infantrymen bore the brunt of the fighting, along with the Second Cavalry composed of white soldiers recruited in Florida. The ages of those who allegedly fought on the pro-slavery side at Natural Bridge also would become an important detail in neo-Confederate fictionalizations. Here is how Caroline Mays Brevard reinvents the incident in an account published in 1904: "The cadets of the West Florida Seminary with their teacher in command shouldered their rifles, and with brave hearts marched proudly away to their first battle. The little boys of the school . . . were bitterly disappointed at being left, and some cried, thinking it hard they should have no part in the dangers and glory of the day." She adds: "By this battle the interior of the State was again saved from invasion and its capital from seizure."

As at Olustee, official Confederate documentation rebuts the neo-Confederate version. Eyewitness reports show the Battle of Natural Bridge was not a "significant Southern victory." They also show that the Confederates, not the Union troops, on this occasion were the ones possessing "overwhelming force." The Confederate archives also make it clear that on their side hardly anyone did any fighting at all, which explains the near nonexistence of Confederate casualties. Though by then the Confederates were conscripting young boys, none of the Confederate accounts mention any fighting by any cadets. Official Confederate documents explicitly state that "our artillery," not underage cadets, decided the outcome.

The series of skirmishes and maneuvers later called the Battle of Natural Bridge unfolded at two different places along the St. Marks River. Hearing that U.S. soldiers were heading up the river, Confederate forces rushed first to a place called Newport, where the last remaining bridge across the St. Marks River was located. Here is how General Sam Jones, the highest-ranking Confederate officer left in Florida, described developments after he got to Newport on the evening of March 5: "I found Brigadier-General Miller, who had promptly gone there with a company of cadets and a small body of militia." That is the only mention of the cadets in the official Confederate report. Had the cadets seen any military action, General Jones would have mentioned it. Instead Jones reports the opposite, that Confederate regulars, not schoolboys, were doing the fighting. U.S. troops, he writes, were being "retarded in their march by part of Fifth battalion Florida cavalry." Jones makes no mention of U.S.

forces attempting to take the bridge or cross the river in the direction of Tallahassee for an understandable reason. Since the U.S. forces were coming up the river in boats, they had no need to cross the bridge. Even so, the Confederates destroyed their last remaining bridge across the St. Marks River.

The actual fighting occurred the next day, March 6, eight miles farther upstream at a place where the river flows underground for a few hundred yards. Hence the name: "Natural Bridge." The Confederate "reserves, militia and two sections of artillery . . . arrived at the Natural Bridge about 4 o'clock in the morning," General Jones reported. Though he had caught the U.S. troops by surprise, Jones encountered stiff resistance. "The enemy," he wrote, "kept up an obstinate fight at intervals for ten or twelve hours." In his official report Jones makes no mention of cadets being under fire. Nor would Dickison mention them in his account, even though that kind of detail was a hallmark of his depictions of Confederate valor. Instead, mentioning the cadets not at all, he writes: "Our troops made a most gallant and determined charge, repulsing the Federals at every point until they were forced to fall back to their gunboats, sustaining a very heavy loss." It is a rare infantry charge, however "gallant and determined," that results in only three people getting killed. That was the total dead the Confederates listed for the entire two-day action, not just the fighting at Natural Bridge.

As with Olustee and Cedar Key, the firsthand U.S. and Confederate accounts agree as to what really happened. Captain Thomas Chatfield, a U.S. Navy officer who helped ferry troops up the St. Marks River, left an eyewitness view of the encounter. By the time they got to Natural Bridge, Chatfield relates, the U.S. forces believed they had left the Confederates behind. The next morning, as they came under fire from General Jones' reinforcements, they discovered they were wrong about that. "Evidently the Rebel force was nearly or quite equal with our own," Captain Chatfield wrote, "for at the end of two hours' fighting, while our fellows had captured one field piece, they had failed to clear the woods of the enemy, and they had been losing men fast. It was then that they heard car whistles in the rear of the enemy, and in a short time the Rebel fire increased to

such an extent that General Newton knew they had received reinforcements, and that he must retreat at once, or lose the whole of
his little army." Here, as elsewhere, the U.S. tactic was to withdraw
whenever the Confederates did manage to concentrate sufficient
forces to provide effective resistance.

In his report the Confederate commander says exactly the same
thing: "our artillery opened a brisk fire," whereupon the Union forces
were ordered to withdraw. The Confederate infantry charge that
later became so celebrated occurred only after the U.S. withdrawl
had begun, at which point the "Confederates . . . pressed forward
like a flock of sheep," Chatfield reported. When the crowd got close
enough, a U.S. officer ordered his troops to pivot and fire at the approaching throng. They "fired three rounds," Chatfield relates, "then
ceased: and when the smoke lifted, not a single man was on his feet."
It was clear that hardly anyone on the Confederate side had been hurt.
"Probably a goodly number were not hit at all," Chatfield observed,
"but simply dropped with their stricken comrades unable to understand such a hailstorm of death-dealing lead." It is a scene anyone
who has ever seen a large crowd come under fire would recognize.

That was the end as well as the beginning of what later would
become the famous Confederate infantry charge at Natural Bridge.
As General Jones' own report makes clear, he made no more effort to
pursue the withdrawing U.S. forces than Finegan had at Olustee or
Dickison had at Cedar Key. "But our victory at Natural Bridge was
a signal one," Dickison later insisted, "and again were the invaders
foiled in their long cherished design to get possession of Tallahassee."
The greatest rebuke to the Florida Confederates' unfounded sense
of self-importance is that the U.S. Army's "long cherished design
to get possession of Tallahassee" is another myth. U.S. documentation makes it clear that, in this case, too, the aim never was "to get
possession of Tallahassee." It does, intriguingly, suggest that one
objective may have been to bypass Tallahassee and go on to Georgia
instead. According to Captain Chatfield, the objective of such a raid
would have been a place that, in the last weeks of the Civil War, figured far more acutely in U.S. calculations, and hearts, than Florida's
backwater state capital. That was the Confederate prisoner-of-war

camp in Thomasville, Georgia, located only fifteen miles beyond the Florida state line. According to the Chatfield account, the purpose of the expedition up the St. Marks River was to bypass Tallahassee and make "a dash for Thomasville, relieve the Union prisoners, and return by the way they came." He adds that this daring operation was entrusted entirely to the "colored troops."

Things did not turn out that way. "Instead of carrying out the plan," Chatfield added, "they were attacked as soon as they were clear of the swamp by a Rebel force . . . hidden in the woods." Here again his account dovetails with General Jones' account. The only difference lies in what the Florida Confederates thought the purpose of the U.S. incursion was. Believing they were halting a "Yankee invasion" of Tallahassee, it may be, instead, that Florida's Confederates thwarted an attempt by black Southern U.S. soldiers to liberate white prisoners from a prison camp in Georgia. There were worse ironies than that. At the end of 1864 thousands of U.S. prisoners had been crammed into a five-acre stockade at Thomasville. Lack of shelter and sanitation killed many of them. Then, when smallpox broke out, the Confederates abandoned their holding pen just north of the Florida border. They marched their prisoners to the even more notorious Confederate prison at Andersonville, Georgia. Had the Confederate attack not stymied the U.S. advance, the strike force would have found nothing when they got to Thomasville. The Confederates had removed their prisoners nearly four months earlier, in December 1864.

Future accounts would laud the West Florida Seminary cadets, not mentioning General Jones' artillery pieces. They would make it seem that the U.S. forces struggled to cross the bridge when they came in boats. They would leave out another detail. The U.S. soldiers who, according to General Jones, "kept up an obstinate fight at intervals for ten or twelve hours" were black men. The fog of war obscures why men do things, not just what they do, but after the war ended two categories of protagonists were unjustly erased from Florida history even though their exploits entitled them to conspicuous and honorable mention in any truthful account of what happened there during the Civil War. One consisted of the white Floridians who fought for the United States. In his memoir Captain Chatfield recalled a white Floridian named Strickland, who led a U.S. patrol. "Strickland never returned," he wrote. "He, with his small party, was captured by some irregulars at the head of the big swamp, and he was shot as a deserter a day or two after, the alternative to the execution being that he should join the Confederate Army, which he refused to do. He had never been with the Rebel colors, had escaped conscription, that was all: but they called it desertion and shot him. He was just a common cracker of the better sort, and refused to fight against the United States."

In another epitaph worthy of Thucydides, Chatfield commemorates a black soldier "lost in that battle. He was a sergeant of the 9th regiment, of the color of an ordinary negro, with kinky hair, but with a Caucasian face, something over six feet in height, spare of flesh, rather inclined to slenderness. In language and deportment a gentleman, evidently well educated, with nothing servile about him, fit to command a regiment. I had had him with his squad on board my little vessel for forty-eight hours, while getting troops up the Caloosahatchee to Fort Myers, some months before: and when we had reached the front, instead of hustling ashore as enlisted men invariably do, he stopped aft, lifted his cap, and thanked me for the courteous treatment he had received while on board."

Today there are no monuments to them either, but American patriots like Strickland and the nameless black sergeant whom Captain Chatfield describes, like Garcia and his nameless Choctaw friend at Negro Fort, prefigured the America where we live today. They are the same bivouac buddies we see in *Platoon*. They star in countless adventure movies. Because their country, or only the president, asks it, they fight together in places like Iraq and Afghanistan. They play professional football together; they man our country's fire stations and emergency rooms. Americans like them were the first responders on 9/11, but there is still no place for them in conventional Florida history. Instead Dickison's meaningless histrionics at St. Augustine and Cedar Key remain the official version, along with Caroline Mays Brevard's edifying tales of how genteel whites saved Florida "from invasion and its capital from seizure"—when, in reality, Confederate Florida would collapse, and the flag of the United States of America once again fly over the capitol at Tallahassee, within months of her "decisive" victories. The Confederate "victory" at Natural Bridge was decisive, though not in the way later pretended. Until then Tallahassee had been like a twig on the outer edge of a giant whirlpool. Florida's officials were so remote from the vortex, the motion of events on Florida's far edge of the whirlpool so slow, it was possible to pretend the steadily accelerating movement of events was not downward into darkness. After Natural Bridge that pretense no longer was sustainable. It had shown that Tallahassee, in spite of General Jones' successfully improvised attack, would soon fall under U.S. administration.

One test of leadership is impending defeat. In the four weeks and five days separating the Confederate "victory" at Natural Bridge from the Confederate surrender at Appomattox, an honorable leadership would have prepared Florida's people to face the inevitable with courage and stoicism. Instead, Governor John Milton abandoned his duties at the moment Florida needed leadership most. Earlier he had watched, doing nothing, as the Confederates burned Pensacola and stripped the state of its food supplies and ability to defend itself. Now, again doing nothing, Governor Milton fled to his plantation, Sylvania, near Marianna. At secession time Governor Milton had personified the ingratitude and folly of the Florida slaveholding elite. Throughout the war he epitomized its passive acceptance of every Confederate dictate. Florida's secession had been an act of suicide. Now he personified that, too. On April Fool's Day 1865 the governor of Florida, not having bothered to resign his office, shot himself through the head and was thereupon transformed from a colorless Florida politician into a beloved Confederate martyr. Milton himself, by then, was no fan of the Confederacy. "She has never received a musket from the Confederate States," he complained, referring to Florida's lack of armaments, before doing away with himself.

Milton's life had followed the Florida trajectory. A native of Georgia, he speculated in land and slaves before his failures in Alabama and Louisiana propelled him, in his fortieth year, to try his luck in Florida. By then he already had taken two wives, sired fourteen children, and gotten himself mixed up in a duel. Thanks to the usual mixture of personal connections and public money, he acquired thousands of acres in his latest home state. At Marianna "Milton's holdings consisted of 2,600 acres, a manor house, a school and family chapel, barns, blacksmith shop, and quarters for 50 slaves," according to the state of Florida plaque currently marking the site of his plantation. For Milton, as for the other secessionist leaders, all the benefits Florida heaped upon him had not sufficed so now, four and a half years later, in the form of Governor Milton's blood-spattered corpse, the prophecy of another Florida governor, Richard Keith Call, had come true. The "gates of Hell" had opened wide inside the mind of Florida's Civil War governor as the state he led sank "to perdition." Governor Milton's bullet-shattered skull, like Osceola's head earlier, epitomized Florida's moral as well as its material condition.

In the aftermath of Governor Milton's suicide Florida's chroniclers disinfected history the way family members scrub down the room where a relative has killed himself. The dreadful prospect of Yankee rule, they made it seem, had given him no other choice. A 1966 description of the circumstances surrounding the governor's death noted that, as a consequence of the war, Milton's family had been obliged to prepare its own meals. "There were no servants to greet him this time," it recounted. "And so, as one of his daughters busily prepared his 'homecoming dinner,' Milton quietly went to his room, took a pistol, and shot himself in the head." "Governor Milton was dedicated to a lost cause," is how a 1974 Florida text book explained it, as though that excused the abandonment of his duties. Most accounts simply excise the unpleasant fact that Florida was the only Confederate state whose governor lacked the guts to see the conflict through to the end.

Fear of white Floridians apparently drove Governor Milton to kill himself. Earlier he had complained about "Confederate army deserters" roaming Florida. By March 1865 undisciplined bands of white Floridians—not "Yankee invaders" or liberated blacks—were the ones posing the great threat to law, order, and life in the heartland of Florida slavery stretching from the governor's mansion in Tallahassee to Milton's house at Marianna. Though the threat of the vengeful, lustful black almost always lurks in the underbrush of their narratives, Brevard, Dickison, and most others leave out another factor that, by the end of the Civil War, had become a source of pervasive alarm. Thousands of homeless, landless defeated white men roamed Florida. Florida's rich white men had gotten Florida's poor white men into a fight they were bound to lose, and now they had lost it. Bloodied, dispirited, despairing, and angry, they were coming home. The slaveholder elite that brought catastrophe down on these men also had made sure most of them had no property, hence no way of surviving honestly, once the war was lost. Now these defeated men, possessing guns, knives, and little else, roamed Florida alone, in small groups, or in organized bands. By early 1865 Florida's governor had become convinced that Confederate "deserters" were plotting to kidnap him and sell him to the Yankees.

It was inside U.S.-controlled Florida that the most famous single Florida incident of the Civil War era occurred—and it didn't involve Confederate troops, valorous or otherwise. Fort Jefferson in the Dry Tortugas, which Ponce de León had named after the turtles he found there 350 years earlier, was a base for the U.S. Navy blockade. The island fortress also served as a prison for Union deserters and malefactors. Contrary to popular belief, no Confederate prisoners of war were held there. Fort Jefferson became the most famous federal outpost in Florida when Samuel A. Mudd, the doctor who treated President Lincoln's killer, John Wilkes Booth, was transported by sea to Florida and placed in the custody of the Eighty-second United States Colored Infantry.

The belief that Dr. Mudd, scion of a Catholic slave-owning family in Maryland, was shackled permanently and not allowed access to sunlight is legendary. So, it would appear, is the belief he was an innocent man. Dr. Mudd had met with the assassin before Lincoln was killed. He sheltered Booth and treated him after he killed the president; Mudd then lied about his contacts with Booth and withheld other evidence. The military commission that tried him acknowledged the ambiguity of Dr. Mudd's situation by sparing him the death penalty. People who have never heard of Fort Pickens, Olustee, or Cedar Key know the story of the doctor who was imprisoned in that dreadful fort, though even today the tale continues to be tinged with neo-Confederate misrepresentations. In most accounts, including depictions in the movies and on TV, no black soldiers are shown; Mudd is assumed to have been wrongly convicted. Entirely absent is any sense of what the imprisonment in Florida, in a fortress manned by a black U.S. Army unit, of someone involved in the assassination of President Lincoln, tells us about Florida's real as opposed to imaginary role in the Civil War, which is that Florida throughout the war was a federal asset and a Confederate liability.

15

EMPOWERING
THE BETWEENITY

"Death would be preferable to reunion," Governor Milton had informed the Tallahassee legislators, a preference for suicide over living as a loyal American in his judgment being "the sentiment of all true Southern men." Ex-senator David Levy Yulee was not one to share that sentiment. Even before U.S. troops could reach Tallahassee, he was rushing back to Washington. Yulee's mission, as he saw it, was to achieve "the restoration of normal relations between Florida and the Washington government," while turning himself into a major player again.

When it came to historical detritus the Florida tide continued to wash both ways. While Yulee headed north, dozens of Confederate notables het off for Florida. The most eminent and also the most colorful of these pro-slavery fugitives was former Senator Judah Benjamin. Born in the West Indies of Jewish parentage, Benjamin, like Yulee, was a secessionist notable with an exotic pedigree. In 1860 Senator Benjamin of Louisiana, like Senator Yulee of Florida, repudiated his allegiance to the United States. He became—first as secretary of war, then as secretary of state—the Confederacy's highest-ranking Jewish officeholder. Then, as the slaveholder cause collapsed, Benjamin helped himself to the Confederate Treasury. Donning goggles and a floppy hat, he disguised himself as a wandering Frenchman and slipped into Florida. Using the Confederate gold he'd sewn inside his costume, Benjamin paid a local wrecker $1,500 and set sail for Nassau on a sponge boat, which sank.

Free Bahamian sailors saved him from drowning. Adrift "with three negroes for my companions in disaster, only five inches of the boat out of water," Benjamin was contemplating "the certainly that we could not survive five minutes if the sea became the least rough" when a British naval vessel rescued him a second time. Safe in London, the former Confederate secretary of war wrote a classic legal treatise (*Benjamin's Sale of Goods*, still in print) and, having become a British subject, was named Queen's Privy Council. The final act unfolded in Paris, in 1884. At age seventy-two, the man whose face had appeared on the Confederate two-dollar bill fell on his head whilst alighting from a carriage, died, and was buried in the same Père Lachaise Cemetery where, eighty-seven years later, another figure with a Florida past, Jim Morrison of the Doors (born in Melbourne, Florida, on December 8, 1943) was also interred.

In basic ways defeat in the Civil War changed nothing in Florida. Even after U.S. troops took control, racist rule continued to prevail in the formerly Confederate-controlled parts of the state. To the dismay and astonishment of loyal whites and blacks, racist rule was also expanded into those parts of Florida that, by then, had been free of the racist regime for several years. As a result black Floridians who had enjoyed a variety of civil and human rights in the Union-controlled parts of Florida now were stripped of those rights. For white people as well, the U.S. victory produced paradoxical results: an actual extension of the powers of those who had supported the Confederacy, as well as the disfranchisement of loyal white Floridians.

"This is a country for white men, and by God, as long as I am President, it shall be a government for white men," explained President Andrew Johnson, when members of Congress questioned his favoritism for ex-Confederates. Under Presidential Reconstruction, as it was called, only those permitted to vote in Florida in the 1860 presidential election were allowed to seek election to the all-powerful 1865 constitutional convention, where the key questions about postwar political control would be decided. Since only white men, the great majority of them secessionists, had voted in the 1860 election, restricting membership to them guaranteed that Florida's postwar political system would be "reconstructed" by people whose aim was to restore, not replace, the three-tiered system of elite white supremacy that, as events now showed, had only been disrupted by the Civil War. Black Floridians who had fought in the U.S. Army were forbidden to vote. So were white Americans who had established residence in Florida after 1860. This meant that many white men who had fought for the Union were denied the vote, too.

The administration of justice also retained its three-tier structure. Poor whites went on being heavily fined for misdemeanor offenses. Unspeakable cruelties continued to be inflicted on blacks for the most trivial infractions while justice for big-time miscreants remained problematical. Having helped provoke the deaths of thousands of Floridians, the turncoat Senator Yulee, instead of being tried for treason, once again becomes the kingpin of Florida's convoluted financial shenanigans. Nothing better epitomized the defeated Confederates' postwar revival of fortunes than the fate of Dr. Mudd, Florida's most famous prisoner. President Andrew Johnson pardoned him after less than four years in prison. The man mixed up in President Lincoln's assassination left Florida in triumph, a neo-Confederate hero. Just as Yulee planned, there was a "restoration of normal relations between Florida and the Washington government"—if by "normal" is meant the federally supported restoration of the power and privileges of the very people the United States had a fought a four-year war to defeat.

"The prominent pro-slavery men, the active rebels during the rebellion," one Florida loyalist noted sadly, were being rewarded for their disloyalty, while those who had stood fast for their country were stripped of their rights. Florida's population by then included at least thirty-five thousand adult white males. Fewer than four thousand voted in Florida's first post–Civil War election. Severely restricting the electorate produced the intended results. Confederate sympathizers, having dominated the constitutional convention, also dominated the supposedly reconstructed legislature; they gained control of the state administration as well. Instead of entering a new age, Florida had regressed to pre-statehood Territorial days. A few privileged magnates, controlling a few hundred (or now, a few thousand) votes, decided who got the power, the land, the money.

The newly elected governor, a proponent of absolute white supremacy named David S. Walker, personified neo-Confederate expectations. Though an advocate of slavery, he had briefly opposed secession, then supported the Confederacy once Florida's Secession Ordinance was enacted. The assumption was that, as a result of embracing Walker's combination of pro forma loyalty to the Union and militant white supremacy, an oligarchic white elite would continue to control the state's government and the allocation of its land and money. As in the past, white countrymen with limited political rights would enforce those privileges, when and as necessary, by keeping nearly half the state's population "in its place." In this somewhat altered system of state-enforced inequalities the juridical situation of black people would be modified; their political and socioeconomic condition would not change. No longer slaves, black people would remain chattels, with the difference that controlling them now became the principal responsibility of the state of Florida, not individual owners. Florida's ex-slaveholders still would have access to black labor; the advantage now was that they no longer would have any legal responsibility to clothe, feed, and house them.

The band played "Dixie" as Florida's neo-Confederate legislators, with far less opposition than might have been expected, revoked the 1860 Secession Ordinance and adopted Article XIII to the U.S. Constitution, which abolished slavery. Florida's new rulers then turned to their main business: establishing a harsh new system of racist repression to replace the old one. While white loyalists and black people watched, disenfranchised and powerless, the new rulers codified as law a comprehensive system of state-sponsored racist violence. Under Florida's new "Black Codes," flogging and the pillory were authorized for blacks, though not whites. "Vagrancy"—being someplace where whites did not want you to be—could be punished by forced, unpaid labor, that is, what used to be called slavery. Among other restrictions, no black person could testify against a white person in a court of law. The ban on black people voting was extended, permanently, to all elections, at all levels.

Denied political rights, Florida's black people were also denied the chance to liberate themselves economically. Even to aspire to self-sufficiency was declared insubordinate. At public meetings Florida's re-empowered racist politicians "cautioned the Negroes against appearances of insolence and laziness and against the myth of a presidential gift of forty acres of land and a mule." For generations to come, white indignation at the indolence and disrespectfulness of the Negroes would go hand in hand with astonishment at the idea they should be allowed to acquire sufficient property and tools to support themselves.

By the end of the Civil War many Southerners had come to agree with General Robert E. Lee that it was time, as he put it, for slavery to be "extinguished." The pivotal question was under whose control and to whose benefit the termination of slavery would occur. As the Florida legislature's speedy adoption of the Thirteenth Amendment demonstrated, white supremacists did not consider abolition an intolerable price to pay in order to end U.S. military occupation, so long as slavery was replaced by a new, state-run system of black subjugation.

Voting rights were another matter. In the 1860s, as in the 1960s, the right to vote was the key that unlocked every possibility. If black people could vote, the weight of their votes would lead to the establishment of a system of greater equality. As we have seen in our own time, it would also lead to black people being elected to high public office. That was why Florida's neo-Confederates reacted so differently when the Fourteenth and Fifteenth Amendments to the U.S. Constitution were enacted. Article XIV for the first time specifically established the most basic right of someone born in America, the right to be an American. "All persons born or naturalized in the United States, and subject to the jurisdiction thereof, are citizens of the United States and of the State wherein they reside," it specified. It went on to ban "Black Code" laws of the kind enacted in Florida, and also make it unconstitutional for "any State [to] deny to any person within its jurisdiction the equal protection of the laws." Thanks to the "equal protection" clause, there no longer could be one set of laws for white people, another for black people. Article XV was even more specific. "The right of citizens of the United States to vote," it provided, "shall not be denied or abridged by the United States or by any State on account of race, color, or previous condition of servitude."

Florida's neo-Confederate governor and legislature reacted with horror and defiance. Abolishing slavery was one thing. White rights for black people was an entirely different matter. It was a question of honor, they proclaimed, "honor" as usual being a code word for abusing black people. "We have lost much, many of us our all—all but our honor. Let us preserve that," Governor Walker urged. The Florida legislature, which had adopted Article XIII, almost unanimously rejected equal rights for black people unanimously.

In 1867 Congress won its greatest battle in the struggle it ultimately would lose to impose the principles of human equality on the defeated Confederacy. Overriding President Johnson's vetoes, it annulled the neo-Confederate state constitutions tolerated under Presidential Reconstruction. Under Congressional Reconstruction, Congress would have to approve all new state constitutions; U.S. military occupation would not end until it did. In order to regain its representation in Congress, each state would also have to ratify the Fourteenth Amendment and extend full voting rights to all men, whatever their race or color. (Women would not gain the same right for another fifty years.)

With this expansion of the right to vote in Florida, the shift away from oligarchic, whites-only politics was dramatic. In the elections the neo-Confederates had organized, only 7,042 people, all of them white, had been registered to vote. By the end of 1867, just two years later, a total of 26,582 voters had been registered in Florida. More than half—15,434—were black, but 11,148 white voters, more white people than ever before, also were enrolled. In Florida's 1868 elections the Republicans, the party of equal rights, won a substantial majority, but Southern-born white men continued to hold the most seats. Black ex-slaves were proportionately the least represented, holding only nineteen of the seventy-six seats in the Florida House and Senate.

"Negroes Franchised; Whites Disfranchised." Once again Caroline Mays Brevard provided the fictional version of events that, generations later, would still be filling history books. "In the first Legislature that met after this constitution was formed, there were many negroes who could neither read nor write," Brevard also claimed. In truth the relatively few black members of the legislature included some of the best-educated Floridians of any race. Presenting racist paranoia as fact, Mays (like generations of similar writers) went on to provide a classic expression of white fears about what supposedly happens when black people are not kept in their place. "The negroes were so excited by politics," she laments, "that few were willing to make a living by regular work. They were not satisfied to work in the fields when they thought they might go to the Legislature or perhaps to Congress." With blacks overrunning the legislature, she adds, "Florida suffered greatly from high taxation." "The white people grew poorer and poorer," she continues. In reality Florida levied almost no taxes, and whites there did not get "poorer and poorer." Incomes slowly rose following the Civil War, though Florida, along with Andrew Jackson's two other orphan states, Mississippi and Alabama, would remain poor for generations as a result of the diseconomies inherent in the system of rigid racial repression they imposed.

Florida's white people still had all their rights, including the right to vote, but something had been given to others. That was why all Floridians, not just some, were represented in the Tallahassee legislature, why the debates there reflected the convictions and dreams of all Floridians now. Thousands of books on the subject were to be written, tens of thousands of speeches given, but the essential difference between Presidential Reconstruction and Congressional Reconstruction could and still can be summed up in five words: Now blacks could vote too.

The Confederate defeat was like all the disasters that previously had overtaken Florida. Florida's whites were definitionally blameless. The chaos and destruction of the Seminole War had not been their fault; now it was the ruin and defeat of the Civil War for which they were blameless. Since nothing was ever their fault, the real villain responsible for Florida's backwardness, violence, and poverty therefore had to be the Outside Agitator, a miscreant whose costume changes periodically, but whose function never does. In the racist demonology of the 1860s the font of all mischief is the Carpetbagger. Like the nonexistent "British agents" General Gaines denounced in 1818, the Carpetbagger is "one of those self-styled Philanthropists" whose "pretended care and kindness" stir up needless trouble by "fomenting a spirit of discord." What makes things worse is that the "pretended care and kindness" are only a mask for the avarice of the Carpetbaggers. They are really there to grab hold of Florida's unspecified riches.

The Carpetbagger fiction purports that Congressional Reconstruction pitted long-established Floridians against alien intruders. In reality some of the most obdurate neo-Confederate racist extremists were opportunistic newcomers from the North. While many of those denounced as "Carpetbaggers" had considerable experience there and a great love of the place. Notable among them was Florida's most powerful official under Congressional Reconstruction, a man who had an unparalleled knowledge of Florida going all the way back to 1839. This was Colonel John Titcomb Sprague. The same never-mentioned Sprague who had written the definitive account of the Seminole War and drunk whisky with Coacoochee as he and his fellow former Floridians headed toward sanctuary in Mexico now became the pivotal figure in another crucial phase of Florida history.

By the time Sprague assumed his duties as Commanding Officer in Florida, his life had expanded into another of those widescreen epics Hollywood would never make. Out West Sprague and his cavalry had escorted giant wagon trains across the desert, fighting and, when he could, conciliating Comanches, Navajos, and Apaches. The New Mexico legislature passed a vote of thanks, but in March 1861 this U.S. Army officer was insulted and abused by secessionists in New Orleans. Worse awaited him in Texas. Attempting to rejoin his regiment, Sprague was kidnapped by a pro-Confederate mob. Finally released, he composed a monograph which he later read to a special meeting of the New York Historical Society. It chronicled the secessionist seizure of power even as the legendary Sam Houston warned that disaster would be the consequence.

As the U.S. Army's Commanding Officer in Florida, Colonel Sprague's mission was to oversee its transition from the racist rule to full respect for the human rights that now were the law of the land. No one understood Florida's need for justice better than Sprague did. No one had a deeper grasp of Florida's tragic past and of its human inequities. Throughout his far-flung exploits as warrior, scholar, author, and conciliator, Sprague had developed an abiding empathy for his enemies. He also brought to his duties a muck-level grasp of war, diplomacy, politics, and human nature that was matchless. Most important, Sprague was morally unassailable. As Florida plunged headfirst into multiracial democracy, Sprague needed all those qualities as he sought to channel the passions and empower the aspirations of thousands of newly franchised black and white people.

The difference was on display at Florida's 1868 constitutional convention, called to provide a replacement for the racist 1865 constitution. For the first time in Florida people of every hue and persuasion were free to chart Florida's future together. As one press report memorably phrased it, the delegates comprised the "black and white as [well as] the betweenity." Florida's previously whites-only factionalism already had recast itself in multiracial form by the time the 1868 constitutional convention convened. Future governors Harrison Reed and Ossian Hart, founding members of the powerful Jacksonville Republican Club, were two of the most prominent factional leaders. Each used his federal connections to build a biracial power base. Hart had served as chief registrar during the Florida-wide voter enrollment campaign, sending his registrars into the woods to enroll "squatters" and into former slave quarters to register black voters, in the process turning himself into a leader with a fervent statewide following. Hart's rival, Harrison Reed, used his position as chief U.S. postal agent in Florida to build his own political organization as he gave dozens of poor white and black people their first taste of political patronage by making them local postmasters.

The unforgettably named Liberty Billings was one of those "Carpetbaggers" who would never get rich, never give up the struggle for human rights, and never leave Florida, even after white supremacists reestablished control. A Unitarian minister, Billings was wounded while leading colored troops in battle during the Civil War. Mustered out of the army in 1863, he purchased property in

Fernandina; his house there still stands. Billings' federal source of
support was the Republican Party. It sent him money. It also sent
him a remarkable black political organizer named William U. Saunders, who would become a major force in Florida politics. Billings,
Saunders and another voting rights organizer sent to Florida by
the Republican Party, Daniel Richards, founded the Florida branch
of the Loyal League of America. Liberty Billings' commitment to
Florida was also permanent. He died in Fernandina in 1877. Colonel
Thomas W. Osborn was another leader of the 1868 constitutional
convention. Born in New Jersey and raised in New York, Osborn
had been promoted on the battlefield for bravery in combat. Sent to
Florida, he headed the most important federal agency of all. Usually
called the Freedman's Bureau, its full name, the Bureau of Refugees,
Freedmen and Abandoned Lands, gives an idea of the opportunities
it provided before it, too, had its powers revoked. Osborn's grassroots
organization was called the Lincoln Brotherhood. Both the Loyal
League and the Lincoln Brotherhood provided a means for recently
liberated slaves to meet, discuss their problems, debate policy, or-
ganize for political action, and, as we would put it today, network.

These ever-wrangling factional alliances acquired some colorful
names. Billings and others got together to form the "Mule Team."
The "Fishing Party" included Reed and his allies. Whatever the labels, the different factions all supported equal rights out of principle,
but also because their leaders understood what mainstream Florida
reformers would not fully appreciate for another hundred years. Only
black voting on a massive scale could lead to fundamental change. "I
foresaw at the beginning of the rebellion," future Florida governor
Ossian Hart later remembered, "that the ordinance of secession was
the death knell of slavery, and that with four millions of freedmen the
subject of equal rights could not be kept out of sight . . . and I told our
people so." Reconstruction politics adumbrated twenty-first-century
politics in another way. Even when black people could vote, even
when Florida's Loyalists and recent migrants were counted, Florida
teetered on the edge. "We need a few thousand more Yankees to
outvote them," wrote Reverend John Sanford Swaim, referring to the
neo-Confederates who, in the previous constitutional convention,

had denied newcomers like him the right to vote. That, he believed, was the way to establish state government "founded on the eternal principles of freedom and equal rights."

Eternal principles were not enough to ensure unity at the January 1868 constitutional convention. Even before deliberations could begin the Mule Team named its own president and took possession of the chamber in the state capitol where the convention was to be held. The Fishing Party regrouped in Monticello, twenty-five miles away. Then, one night, the Monticello faction returned and dislodged the Mule Team from the hall. Two rival conventions now purported to be in charge, at which point Colonel Sprague, like a proctor breaking up a school-yard fist fight, restored order. Under Sprague's guidance Florida's multiracial factions produced a most remarkable new constitution. The neo-Confederate constitution of 1865 had sought "to reinstitute the slave system in fact if not in law." The 1868 constitution guaranteed ex-slaves the right to vote and hold office. In a measure reflecting the deep empathy for their plight Colonel Sprague had developed during his military service in Florida, it also allocated to the Seminoles one seat in the Florida Senate and one in the House. It further specified that the Seminoles had to be represented by a Seminole, "and in no case by a white man." Had Osceola lived to see the day he would have been sixty-four years old.

No lie was baser than the subsequent claim that the "colored people" involved in Florida politics were a disruptive, ignorant rabble. Among the notable black leaders who helped frame the 1868 constitution was a native of Gadsden County named Robert Meacham. Meacham's mother was a black woman. His father, a white doctor, homeschooled him after parents of the white students had him expelled. The boy then taught other children to read and write. After playing a key role writing the 1868 constitution, Meacham served in the Florida Senate. Under different circumstances he today might be remembered as one of modern Florida's Founding Fathers. Instead, after white supremacists purged blacks from office, they also purged them from the history books.

Josiah Walls was another remarkable leader who would never become a role model because the story of his life was suppressed.

Born a slave in Virginia, he joined the advancing U.S. Army. After fighting in the major Florida engagements, he decided to stay in Florida. Walls taught himself the law, formed one of the state's first black law firms, and served as mayor of Gainesville. In an effort to promote crop diversification, he also transformed an abandoned slave plantation into a vegetable farm. The name of the newspaper he started, the *New Era*, summed up his dream. Josiah Walls went on to be elected three times to the U.S. House of Representatives from Florida. Because of racially motivated political maneuvering he ultimately was denied his seat in the House two of those three times. The first time his opponent challenged the validity of his election. He ran again and was vindicated. After serving his second term unmolested, Walls ran again. Again he got the most votes but, shades of Florida elections to come, the candidate who came in second took office. So great was racial political repression in subsequent decades that another black person would not be elected to Congress from Florida until 110 years later.

While in Congress Josiah Walls had the authority to name cadets to the U.S. Military Academy at West Point. How he used that privilege puts into perspective subsequent claims that "radical" Reconstructionists denied white Floridians their rights while heaping unearned privileges on undeserving blacks. One of the West Point cadets Walls appointed was a young black man, the son of Jonathan Clarkson Gibbs, Florida's first black cabinet member. The other cadet he nominated was the son of former governor David S. Walker. This was the same Governor Walker who had signed into law the Black Codes and equated "assent to Negro suffrage" with dishonor. A century before such measures finally were enacted, Representative Walls also introduced legislation to establish a national education fund and proposed a Social Security–type program for retired persons.

In response whites tried to kill him. On one occasion the bullet missed his head "by inches." Driven from public service by the same white supremacists he had conciliated while in office, Walls fought successfully to have public land set aside near Tallahassee for the establishment of a training school for black students. Initially known as the State Normal College for Colored Students, it later became the Agricultural and Mechanical School, later still, the legendary Florida A&M. Marginalized and ignored, Walls passed the final years of his life working on the school's farm. He died, another of Florida's valiant nonpersons, in 1905.

"The most cultured member of the [1868] convention, probably, was Jonathan Gibbs, a negro," William Watson Davis remarked in his 1913 study, *The Civil War and Reconstruction in Florida*. Born into a free black family in Philadelphia, Gibbs graduated first in his class at Dartmouth, then studied theology at Princeton. Returning to Philadelphia, he battled segregation in public transport more than a hundred years before Rosa Parks refused to go to the back of the bus. Gibbs flicked aside suggestions that black people weren't ready for equality. The question, he pointed out, was whether white people were ready to put "away their stupid prejudices." Gibbs did not deny that many ex-slaves were unschooled. Even so, he added, "we do ask that if the ignorant white man is allowed to vote, that the ignorant colored man shall be allowed to vote also."

In 1865, with the Confederacy in its death throes, Jonathan Gibbs headed South. "The destitution and suffering of this people extended my wildest dream," he wrote. Sexual melodrama as well as moral principle caused Gibbs to reinvent himself in Florida. A bitter divorce from his first wife scandalized his Philadelphia congregation; his trip south distanced Gibbs from the scolders. He intended to spend only a few months traveling. Instead, he found new love as well as a new life waiting for him. In Jacksonville Gibbs and his new wife started a school open to children of all races. Gibbs was a major force at the 1868 constitutional convention, which turned out to be one of the most impressive assemblages of human talent in Florida history.

How to explain the remarkable aptitude black people showed for the arts of democracy, all the more impressive coming so soon after the abolition of slavery? Attempting to demonstrate that Florida's black leaders were not really black, its neo-Confederate chroniclers reconfigured the DNA as well as the facts. At the time there was no question as to the racial identity of the civil rights leader William U. Saunders. The authentic documents of the time refer to him as

"William U. Saunders, black," or "WM Saunders (negro)" or "the negro Saunders." In the hands of Florida's white race revisionists, this outstanding protagonist in the struggle for racial justice in Florida was transformed into "the Maryland mulatto, William Saunders," as a 1952 account puts it—"a mulatto ex-barber from Baltimore," according to a 1971 account.

A similar mutation was inflicted on Florida's black representative, Josiah Walls; he was transformed into a "mulatto from Pennsylvania." Walls actually was from Virginia, the state from which so many white Floridians proudly claimed antecedence. Documents of the time emphasize his dark complexion, but demonizing Walls as both a Northerner and a product of miscegenation served a double purpose. It robbed Florida's black people of a hero. It sustained whites in their illusion that half-breeds and Yankees caused all that trouble. Delegitimizing the struggle for racial justice served a deeper purpose than that. By turning blacks into "mulattos," black achievement was transformed into another demonstration of white supremacy. The alleged presence of white blood, which supposedly explained such achievements, also rendered black achievement in and of itself dishonorable since it necessarily carried with it the odor of sexual misadventure.

In the political free-for-all that followed adoption of the 1868 constitution, a rainbow coalition took office. Harrison Reed was elected governor. Osborn was sent to represent Florida in the U.S. Senate. Spreading around the spoils, Governor Reed named Ossian Hart to the state supreme court, making him the first Florida-born member of that body. Upon Jonathan Gibbs, the new governor bestowed an unprecedented distinction; he named Gibbs an officer of the Florida state militia. Sixty years after the massacre at Negro Fort, etiquette dictated that white men call a black man "Colonel" in Florida. Though Gibbs had supported the rival Mule Team, Reed also named him to a far more consequential post, Florida secretary of state.

The 1868 constitution, as prophetic in matters of education as it was in other fields, stipulated that Florida have a uniform system of racially integrated public schools, in which both black children and white children were prepared for the future. To ensure that happened, it established a statewide board of education, with the secretary of state one of its three members. In addition to education, Gibbs made the integrity of Florida's electoral process a priority. In his efforts to curb political violence, Gibbs conducted some of the nation's first investigations into the terrorist activities of the Ku Klux Klan. After his term as secretary of state expired, he became superintendent of public instruction. Gibbs was another of those Carpetbaggers who never got rich and never went home. He would live in Florida for the rest of his life.

To this day Governor Harrison Reed, in office from 1869 to 1873, figures in the stereotypes as the paradigmatical Carpetbagger. In reality the trajectory of Reed's life was the normal one for someone who winds up making history in Florida. Like Mathews and DuVal, Billy Powell and John Milton, Harrison Reed arrived there only after misfortune elsewhere led him to reinvent himself in a Florida setting. Massachusetts-born and raised in Vermont, Reed was an influential Wisconsin newspaper publisher, famed for his editorials promoting Abolition; his two newspapers, the *Milwaukee Sentinel* and the *Wisconsin State Journal* in Madison are still in business today. Then, in October 1862, his wife of more than twenty years died just as a federal appointment became available in the U.S.-controlled area of Florida. When Reed arrived there to start his new life, he found romance waiting in the form of Chloe Merrick, a volunteer school teacher from Syracuse, New York. They met on Fernandina Island.

She was there because, in February 1862, when Senator Yulee, future Confederate general Joseph Finegan, and other secessionists abandoned Fernandina, more than one thousand black people as well as a smaller number of white people welcomed the Union forces as liberators. Recognizing their desperate need for education, employment, and medical care, the federal authorities appealed for "philanthropic people" to come to the aid of those newly freed of slaveholder control. Once in Florida, Chloe Merrick found that her work only began in the classroom. Nearly all of Fernandina's able-bodied black men, more than two hundred of them, had volunteered to fight in the U.S. Army. That left some 250 women and more than four hundred children without income or protection. Worst off were the children with no mothers. Merrick found herself running an orphanage as well as a school. It was located in the mansion Joseph Finegan had abandoned when he took up arms against the United States. It was there, in May 1863, that the future governor Reed first met his future wife. Chloe Merrick had invited him to her students' graduation ceremony.

It was a memorable moment. In Florida children who once would have been punished for learning now were receiving diplomas. Neither of them ever forgot that day, though not solely because of its educational significance. Florida had smitten Harrison Reed; so had Miss Chloe Merrick. "I want to live in Florida to assist in bringing it in as a free state," he declared. He also wanted to work alongside the woman he loved. By then, her earnestness had acquired a spinsterish edge. Nearly twenty years her senior and with an editorialist's proclivity for punctiliousness, Reed reminded one acquaintance of "an old granny." In short, these Florida romantics were made for each other. As usual in Florida whenever love and fine feelings seem ascendant, a villain appeared on the scene. It was Joseph Finegan. Having commanded Florida troops during the Olustee massacre and then killed more U.S. soldiers in Virginia, he wanted his Fernandina mansion back—and, thanks to the federal government, he got it. As Florida's loyalists, whose comrades had died for the Union at Olustee, looked on with disbelief, Chloe Merrick's orphans were evicted so that the ex-Confederate general could resume his lavish way of life.

A conciliator and temporizer, Governor Reed sought to unite the rival factions within the Republican Party, mostly without success. Like Representative Walls, he also attempted to conciliate the state's most notorious Confederates, entirely without success. When it came to maintaining law and order, Governor Reed was also a failure, as ineffective at suppressing Florida's chronic violence as slaveholder governors like DuVal, Call, and Perry had been. The difference was that while the U.S. Army had come to their rescue during the Seminole uprisings, Reed the "Carpetbagger" got no military help from the government in Washington when white terrorists went on the rampage. Determined to keep the peace, Governor Reed got a loan of $21,000; he ordered two thousand rifles for the state militia. Shipped by sea from New York, the rifles were off-loaded at Jacksonville for the 165-mile transshipment to Tallahassee, but long before the train got there the weapons had vanished. Vigilantes led by that ertswhile paladin of Confederate chivalry, John J. Dickison, had seized the rifles and ammunition. Governor Reed found himself in the same situation the Spanish authorities had in the years before U.S. annexation. Titular sovereignty rested in the hands of the governor, but lawless, unaccountable men of violence acted with impunity in Florida.

The hijacking of Governor Reed's rifles foreshadowed the permanent failure of Florida state governments to control white violence. Reconstruction governments lacked the means. Segregationist state governments would lack the will to do it. What ensured the triumph of violence, however, was dereliction of duty on the part of the federal government. In 1868, as in 1835 and 1858, only the U.S. Army could quell the Florida violence, yet Governor Reed's pleas for help were rejected.

By the time Reed's term ended, Florida's factions had wound up replicating the political schisms in Washington. Like President Johnson, Governor Reed was impeached—twice. Also like him, Reed was acquitted. The second vote to acquit, 10–7 in the Florida Senate, was a typical triumph of Florida factionalism: "Six Democrats and four Republicans sided with the governor; three Democrats and four Republicans opposed him." Ex-Confederates had saved an Abolitionist governor, showing paradoxically enough that political expediency could bridge the chasm dividing the ex-enemies of the Civil War. A stereotypical Carpetbagger would have quit Florida after his term expired, as ex-Governor DuVal and so many other "true Southern men" had when their dreams of power and money came unstuck. Unlike them ex-Governor Reed stayed in Florida; he would remain there until he died. Having demonstrated that editorialists seldom make effective chief executives, he returned to publishing.

Periodically Florida politics poses an intriguing question. What would happen if the "Cracker of the better sort," as Captain Chatfield put it, made common cause with Florida's ex-slaves? At the Florida Republicans' 1872 nominating convention, opponents of the popular front-runner, Ossian Hart, tried to pull a fast one. Agents of a rival grouping, the Ring, brazenly announced that their candidate, Marcellus Stearns, had already won the nomination for governor. Hart's supporters quickly made it clear they would not let victory be snatched away from them. "Many of the Hart men, mostly colored . . . mounted chairs, tables, desks and everything else that would elevate them," a white observer later recalled, "and yelled, and bawled, and shouted, and swore they would not submit to such a nomination." Ossian Hart, a Florida-born white man, won the nomination thanks to the fervor of his black supporters. With their continuing support, he won the election to succeed Harrison Reed as Florida's governor.

The results of Florida's 1872 election, like the proceedings of the 1868 constitutional convention, refute claims that during Reconstruction white people were denied their rights. In the race for governor Ossian Hart's opponent got some thirty-five hundred more votes than the white supremacist candidate had the last time, but Hart did even better, getting five thousand more votes than his party's candidate previously had. Hart had won by getting more people to vote for him, not by preventing other people from voting for someone else. A total of thirty-three thousand citizens voted in 1872. That exceeded the total number of citizens, voters and nonvoters, white as well as black registered only three years earlier. The 1872 results also showed that the best cure for democracy's ills was more democracy. The 1868 elections had produced an unsuccessful governor. In the form of Ossian Hart the 1872 elections produced an inspiring one. Eager to consolidate Florida's biracial democracy, Governor Hart's first priority was to ensure that equal rights were protected by Florida, not just federal law. To that end he persuaded the legislature, after four years of delay, to approve an "Act to Protect All Citizens of the State of Florida in their Civil Rights and to Furnish the Means for their Vindication." The Republicans remained too factionalized to pass it by themselves, so Governor Hart got this landmark equal rights bill voted into law with support from Democrats representing south and central Florida.

These Democrats, like their north Florida counterparts, had in the great majority supported slavery and the Confederacy. Economic self-interest and a differing conception of Florida's future explained why these particular white supremacists now supported civil rights legislation. Florida south of Gainesville was now cattle country. New harbors and roads, not pro-slavery plantation nostalgia, were needed to get their cattle to market and to bring in new settlers and money. I'll help you develop south Florida, Governor Hart promised, if you help me get my civil rights legislation. Such expediency marked a potential breakthrough to a politics in which racism was no longer "the element of all value." Hart's alliance with the cattlemen also prefigured the emergence of peninsular Florida as the dominant region of the state.

Until Ossian Hart took office all Florida governors—racist or not, both Confederate and Unionist—were "Carpetbaggers" in the sense that all had migrated there from some other place. Now a Florida-born white finally got to be governor—and no one was more authentically Floridian than Governor Ossian Bingley Hart. His grandfather had infiltrated Spanish Florida in the years before annexation. His father, Isaiah Hart, spent his youth killing Seminoles and kidnapping blacks in what he and "General" Mathews liked to call the "Patriot War." By 1821, when his son Ossian came into the world, Isaiah Hart had acquired a plantation and a river transport company. He also had some book learning. That was why he named his son after Ossian, a Gaelic bard whose poems, though later proved to be anachronistic forgeries, were at the time considered the epitome of romantic literary refinement. The Harts' neighbors along the St. Johns included Zephaniah and Anna Kingsley. The place where Isaiah Hart's most valuable properties were located was called Cowford; he perceived possibilities there that went beyond a cattle crossing. Buying up land adjacent to his ferry slip, Isaiah Hart started planning what would eventually become the city of Jacksonville.

Ossian Hart was not merely the first Florida-born governor. He was the first whose life experience reflected Florida's chaotic realities.

All previous governors had arrived there as adults, bringing with them attitudes and agendas forged elsewhere. Hart's life experience was a product of what happened in Florida. He was born into the cosmopolitan little world of relatively flexible racial attitudes that characterized plantation life under the Spanish. As a boy he saw that world purged of freethinkers as the race laws enacted in Tallahassee restricted the freedoms of both white and black people. Hart was a teenager when the war to extirpate the Seminoles was at its height, in his twenties as tens of thousands of African-Americans were herded into Florida as slaves. In those days young men normally pursued their ambitions in Tallahassee and in the nearby Cotton Counties. Ossian Hart's path to the governorship was far more circuitous. At age twenty-two he migrated more than two hundred miles down the Florida coast. The Armed Occupation Act of 1842 had briefly made honest pioneering possible in Florida, and he seized the chance. Arriving in the south Florida wilderness, Ossian Hart pursued the dream that would ruin many others besides him. The day was coming, he had convinced himself, "when vessel after vessel shall leave our ports and harbours, laden with the Sweet Orange, the well-flavored Lemon as fine as ever grew in Sicily—the Guava, the Citron and the Lime—Bananas, Pine Apples and Plantains."

The normal catastrophe ensued. Trying to turn the viscosity of the Everglades into arable land, Hart and his neighbors almost drowned when their drainage canal, instead of creating dry land, unleashed a mighty surge of floodwater. The Great Hurricane of 1846 completed the process of ruination. Man-made catastrophes—one ending, another yet to be—were also personified at Fort Pierce at that time. The U.S. Army, thinking the Seminoles defeated, had abandoned the military camp there, allowing Dr. Frederick Weedon—the same Dr. Weedon who cut off Osceola's head—to take over the fort and its stockade. There he rented space to incoming settlers. His crops failed but at Fort Pierce Ossian Hart's political career took root. The area was entitled to send one delegate to the Tallahassee legislature. When all ten votes were counted, Hart squeaked into office with five of them, his two opponents having split the other five. After the hurricane terminated his legislative as well as his horticultural career, Hart moved to Key West. There, again, he got himself elected to something. In this case the post was solicitor of the state's Southern Judicial Circuit. During his two-year term, Hart acted as an itinerant prosecutor, riding circuit in parts of the Everglades that are still wilderness today.

Opportunity next seemed to beckon in Tampa; by 1859 Ossian Hart was one of Tampa's up-and-coming attorneys. Then one of those events that define a man's character, and with it his destiny, overtook him. A white man was found murdered. In keeping with local custom, a slave was selected to be killed in retribution. Ossian Hart, recognizing the injustice of it, defended the innocent black man, whose name was Adam. In such cases the distinction between legal process and lynching was procedural. The jury convicted Adam. The judge sentenced him to death, but in a remarkable legal maneuver Ossian Hart succeeded in getting the Florida Supreme Court to declare a mistrial. It made no difference. A mob seized Adam from his cell and hanged him.

Even before the Civil War began, Ossian Hart held convictions most Americans admire today. He preferred to work his own land instead of watching while slaves did it. At a time when women were chattels, he supported the Married Women's Property Act while serving in the legislature. Adam's lynching, followed by the harshness of Confederate rule, confirmed Ossian Hart in his opposition to injustice, whomever it victimized. Loyalists like Hart assumed that once the Confederates were vanquished, the U.S. government would reward their patriotism. "To their dismay," as Hart himself put it, they instead found themselves victims of "a policy which tended directly to their ruin." Aiming to provide a countervailing voice, Hart sought election to Florida's first postwar, whites-only constitutional convention. He had, after all, been eligible to vote in Florida in 1860. He was defeated the same way many another enlightened Floridian would be. "Hart wants to put the nigger on a level with the white man, and I don't," his opponent, James Gettis, declared. Hart, the native-born Floridian, was defeated by James Gettis, who was from Pennsylvania. It is a stratagem that still wins elections in Florida, where contests pitting Yankee racists against Floridians committed to civil rights have been a recurring feature of politics for more than one hundred years.

"This is not a white man's government nor a black man's government, but a government of the people," Hart declared, during torch-lit Fourth of July celebrations held at the state capitol in 1868. Hart had no time for states' rights, especially when they were states whose governments enforced a system of racial oppression and economic injustice. "Some say 'the State is Sovereign,'" he added in his 1868 oration. "That is not true, the people only are sovereign."

"There is no one to buy the Legislature," one editorialist lamented after Hart became governor. Under his leadership, sixteen constitutional amendments were proposed and adopted. They provided for reform in fields ranging from public finance to reorganization of the state judicial system. Progress in education was Governor Hart's greatest source of satisfaction. "Florida has cause to rejoice greatly," he declared as his second year in office began, "that we now have numerous public free schools (500 schools, attended by 18,000 pupils), increasing in number and efficiency open to all the children of the state alike. To a large majority of the people who never saw such a thing before reconstruction," the governor added, "this great blessed fact is ever new and delightful." Maintaining equality before the law, as Hart saw it, was the way to keep Florida "staunch, safe and free." Sound finances and universal education would make sure Florida was "well equipped and manned." Essential above all else to Florida's future prosperity, this Southern loyalist believed, was loyalty to the United States of America. Only under "the old flag, with all its glories ever radiating from it," he declared, could Florida achieve its potential.

At the end of 1873, as another Tallahassee winter began, Florida's prospects were more hopeful than at any other time since U.S. annexation. Then, once again, meteorology acted like a deus ex machina in the Sunshine State. Previously neither fever nor hurricanes had stopped him, but during the 1872 campaign Hart caught pneumonia. Once he took office Tallahassee's "winter weather compounded the situation as it ranged from poor to worse, with storms, rain, drizzle, and cold alternating and combining." By the end of March 1874 he was dead. Together Ossian Hart, Florida's most notable "Cracker of the better sort," and Jonathan Gibbs, the most accomplished of the black men who dedicated their lives to Florida's betterment, had shown what could happen when politics transcended racism, but there was something about the Tallahassee climate, when it came to officeholders there, that seemed either to induce longevity or inflict an early death. Hart died on March 18, 1874, aged fifty-three. Gibbs died the following August 14, aged forty-seven. In less than five months Reconstruction Florida lost its two most forceful leaders.

Ossian Hart was Florida's most inspiring political leader since Osceola, its most courageous public thinker since Zephaniah Kingsley. So what happened to him was only to be expected. Oblivion: it was the fate Florida inflicted on its very best. Today Ossian Hart's father is honored as Jacksonville's founder. The official name of the city's giant cantilever bridge, a local landmark, is the Isaiah D. Hart Bridge. No edifice, institution, or historical marker honors his son, even though, as his biographer Canter Brown has noted, "Hart when alive had numbered among the region's leading men, contributing to it as frontier settler, legislator, prosecutor, civic leader, entrepreneur, jurist and politician." The state of Florida's official Great Floridians Program, overseen by what is described as "a group of seven distinguished historians from across the state," excludes Florida's first Florida-born governor, even though, in addition to Senator Yulee, it honors Governor William Pope DuVal, dispossessor of the Seminoles. White, black, mixed-raced, Florida-born or not: there was room for them all in Florida's forgetfulness. Colonel Sprague was one of the most significant, principled, and insightful figures to traverse Florida during the mid-nineteenth century. Not a single history of Florida so much as takes note of the continuous role he played during two of Florida's most crucial events: the Seminole War and Reconstruction. He was a "Carpetbagger" after all.

The Carpetbaggers were vile enough, but in the neo-Confederate schema Ossian Hart appertained to an even more depraved subset of humanity, the Scalawags. One of those distinctively American terms "scalawag," according to one editorialist, originally was "applied to all of the mean, lean, mangy, hidebound skinny, worthless cattle in every particular drove." Following the Confederate defeat, "scalawag" acquired a new meaning. It was applied to white men deemed not sufficiently racist and not sufficiently disloyal to the United States to count as honorable.

"There are few men whose lives have been more thoroughly interwoven with the history of the State," one eulogist remarked when Hart died in 1874, "and whose death leaves so rich a legacy to the living." To rip him out of Florida's history was to destroy that legacy, and that was what happened, even more entirely in Hart's case than in most others. In the ongoing process of falsification that constitutes Florida's past, Clinch is kept but his Negro Fort Massacre is not. Governor Milton is kept, but his suicide disappears. Then there are those, like Ossian Bingley Hart, whose triumphs and defeats are so revelatory that they have been expunged in their entirety from Florida's understanding of itself.

What endures, like contempt for "Indian givers," is the myth of the Scalawag—the enduring belief that Floridians like Ossian Hart were "traitorous opportunists who had deserted their countrymen and ingratiated themselves with the hated Radical Republicans for their own material gain," as one recent account puts it. Ossian Hart was Florida's white Osceola with the difference that after Osceola was killed, dismembered, and trivialized, some little hint of Osceola's valor lingered in the FSU halftime show. In Florida's ever-duplicitous memory of itself, Ossian Hart wound up less than Osceola: "a damn Scalawag [with] no honesty about him . . . a traitor to his country and to his race," as one white Floridian described him and his ilk. Nowhere else, one newspaper complained, were "the white Radicals of a lower type of humanity than they are in Florida."

To this day it is a commonplace that state government during the period when black as well as white people were allowed to vote was horribly more depraved than when only white folks had the chance to squabble and pilfer. That's not true. Scrape away the "history," and it is clear that governance in Reconstruction Florida was both unremarkable and remarkable. It was unremarkable for the reasons its detractors professed to find it so shocking. The period following the Civil War was one of turbulent venality throughout the United States; Florida, no exception, exemplified a national condition. What is remarkable is how principled Florida's Reconstruction leaders were in their approach to the well-being of Florida's people—all its people. They, unlike those who replaced them, understood that education, justice, and access to economic opportunity were the preconditions of a better future for everyone. A final point needs to be made about Reconstruction in Florida. Governance then, whatever its failings, was much, much less corrupt than it had been under whites-only rule prior to the Civil War.

Writing in 1951, a Florida historian who, that late, still praised slavery as a beneficent institution, could not gainsay the accomplishments of the Reconstruction era. "Regardless of the charges and the countercharges," wrote J. E. Dovell in his two-volume compendium of white male exploits, "improvement from 1868 to 1876 was made in public education, in a penal system, an intermediate court system of circuits, labor lien statues, revision of the civil and criminal codes, homestead legislation, and the establishment of an agricultural college." The growth in public education was particularly impressive, as was the progress made in reforming Florida's notorious finances. "By 1875 there were 678 public schools with some 28,000 students" and Florida's "financial reform program stood as model for other southern states."

The crimes and corruptions for which Florida's Reconstructionists were blamed had thrived, and would thrive again even more luxuriantly under white racist rule. It was the good these Carpetbaggers, Scalawags, and mulattos tried to do that caused them to be condemned so harshly. A photograph taken in April 1874 in Tallahassee is a snapshot of what Florida briefly was and, in time, would become again. It shows a crowd of civic leaders gathered there to honor a distinguished guest, Harriet Beecher Stowe. The author of *Uncle Tom's Cabin*, who had a knack for showing up at crucial moments in Florida history, was surprised at the friendly welcome she received.

White Floridians showed her their gardens and held a gala reception in her honor at city hall. The next morning she came to the capitol to be photographed with a throng of people who wished to commemorate her visit. Though the beards and hats on the gentlemen and the bonnets and long skirts on the ladies lend an archaic air to the scene, it was a photograph of Florida's future. In it successful black and white people mingle comfortably on the capitol steps, including on the top step. Replace their funny clothes with modern wear; then mix in a goodly portion of Hispanics. You have a scene that occurs often these days when the Tallahassee legislature is in session. A celebrity shows up, and people of all factions and colors gather to get their pictures taken with, in this case, her.

"What earthly interest have we now to separate us?" Mrs. Stowe wondered as she reflected on her visit. "Why should we not be friends?" The "earthly interest" was racism, above all else the racist fear of interracial sex. Beneath the many other rationalizations, the reason whites and blacks could not be friends was that Zephaniah Kingsley was right. Human nature being what it is, friends become lovers, and wed.

Shakespeare, along with everything else, understood the slaveholder's horror at such a prospect:

> *You have among you many a purchased slave*
> *Which, like your asses and your dogs and mules,*
> *You use in abject and in slavish parts*
> *Because you bought them. Shall I say to you*
> *"Let them be free, marry them to your heirs.*
> *Why sweat they under burdens?"*

asks Shylock in *The Merchant of Venice*. Marry them to your heirs! Long after slavery was gone, even after segregation had been declared unconstitutional, the ban on white people and black people loving each other would remain on the books.

To keep them from loving each other, it would be necessary in the years ahead to lynch people, to massacre free communities, to keep people ignorant and poor and, most vital, keep them hate-filled and frightened. For one hundred years blaming the Carpetbagger, the Scalawag, and the "mulatto" would serve as a substitute for acknowledging that Floridians themselves were responsible for their backwardness. For those seeking to maintain, and expand, their powers and privileges in Florida its utility would not end there.

16

TRIUMPH OF VIOLENCE

Sixty years earlier, back in 1816, the Negro Fort Massacre had initiated the process of Florida's "Americanization" leading to genocide, slavery, and civil war. Now once again terrorism determined what Florida's future would be. Had half-breeds, outlanders, and traitors dishonored Florida with their "assent to Negro suffrage"? Violence was the tried-and-true means of restoring "honor." They couldn't win free elections, but as one account published following World War II put it, "Ruthlessly suppressing the negroes with halter, shot-gun and whip conspired to gather strength unto [their] cause." Florida's white terrorists were called "Regulators," as though by killing people they were adjusting a faulty functioning of the body politic.

Regulators targeted white as well as black voters. "I got up one morning and found a piece of paper . . . informing me that if I remained three days longer I was in danger," a native-born white Floridian stated in 1871 testimony to the Joint Select Committee of Congress investigating the political murders there. "There was a . . . big notice on the store," another white man testified, "that they would give me 24 hours to leave." Testifying in his capacity as Florida secretary of state, Jonathan Gibbs produced documents indicating that, in two years, hundreds of Floridians had been murdered for political reasons. He may have understated the toll. Gibbs estimated twenty people had been killed in Madison County; the "white sheriff of Madison put the number in his county at 37, not 20." Another white official estimated the toll at about 75 murders in Jackson County, but one Regulator bragged "that probably 175 murders were perpetrated in Jackson County."

In Marianna, the late governor Milton's hometown, "Samuel Fleishman, a Jewish merchant, was called before a committee of citizens and told that he must leave the county because he had expressed opinions derogatory to 'white supremacy.' Fleishman had been for twenty years a citizen of Jackson County. 'They gave me two hours to arrange my affairs and get out of the town,' he said. 'I told them . . . that I would rather die than leave.'" That was what happened. "A week later his body was found in the public road." As usual the victim was to blame. "He had disregarded the warning of those who had expelled him," a person familiar with the proceedings remarked.

In sworn congressional testimony Florida state senator William James Purman, also a resident of Marianna, provided graphic evidence of white terrorism. It consisted of "an ugly scar" on his own neck. At the time of the attempt to assassinate him, Senator Purman was walking home from a concert with Dr. John L. Finlayson, a Marianna-born white Floridian. The sniper, hiding in the dark, opened fire as they crossed the town square. The cowardliness harked back to the political vendettas of Territorial days. It also continued the Florida tradition of botched political violence. The bullet intended to kill Senator Purman smashed through Dr. Finlayson's skull instead. The next day Jackson County's black citizens gathered to show their support. Terrified that any show of resolve would result in the demonstrators being massacred, Senator Purman forced the protesters, as he himself described it, to "hold up their right hands and swear to me to go and call off their friends and return home."

His reaction to the neo-Confederate terror campaign provided a cameo of the larger calamity overtaking Florida. Even when they themselves were victims of Regulator terrorism, white leaders never ceased to counsel nonviolence. In response these conciliators were scorned, as well as tortured and killed. In the spring of 1868, Senator Purman testified, "unfriendly notices" in west Florida started bearing a curious signature: "Ku Klux Klan." Dickison's supposedly gallant freedom fighters were transforming themselves into an organization whose ideology was terror.

Although they were denounced as unscrupulous interlopers, in real life people like William James Purman, originally from

Washington, D.C., personified the idealism that brought many honorable Americans to Florida. In Jackson County Purman helped negotiate labor contracts between planters and freedmen laborers. He struggled to establish schools for African-American children and also organized democracy seminars, which educated former slaves in their duties as citizens. Working under Ossian Hart's supervision, Purman led the voter registration drive in Jackson County. In the 1868 constitutional convention he emerged as a moderate, counseling conciliation and compromise.

Avoidance of individual responsibility was a key feature of racist violence directed against such people. "Samuel Sullivan was killed by a mob at Newmansville; Moses Smith, at Gordon; and Henry Franklin, at Gainesville." The killers sometimes chose their victims at public meetings, thus absolving the killers in advance. "After the meeting Matt Nickels, his wife and son," according to one account, "were all three taken a short distance out of town, shot to death, and their bodies thrown into an old lime-sink." These, as one observer put it, were merely "specimens of assassination, not a list of casualties." Beyond the towns and off the dirt roads were the unidentified, unclaimed "bodies of dead men found putrefying in 'sinks' and ponds." "They whipped me from the crown of my head to the soles of my feet," one woman testified. "The blood oozed out through my frock, all around my waist, clean through." Black women were considered fair game, but when a white woman was in any way affected the indignation was unbounded. One spate of terror killings erupted after two white women desecrated the graves of Union soldiers, and a local official then had the temerity to tell the two, "girls of refinement and elevated social position," that they had done wrong. The next day white gunmen ambushed picnickers riding in an oxcart. Women were targeted; a little boy was killed.

Though the Regulators saw threats to white womanhood lurking everywhere, there is only one known claim of a white woman being killed in Reconstruction-related violence in Florida. The gunman, it was alleged, had been trying to kill "the generalissimo" of the local white terrorist squads. How he could have mistaken a male gang leader for a young woman was never explained. When John

Quincy Dickinson, the justice of the peace who earlier had testified on the violence, ordered the town constable to investigate, the very people who claimed the attack had "been planned by Radical whites and negroes" killed the constable, a black man named Calvin Rogers. They then killed Justice of the Peace Dickinson, too. Whoever killed Miss Maggie McClellan was never brought to justice.

Typical of the political changes terrorism produced was the outcome of the 1874 legislative election in Pensacola. There a white supremacist candidate named Charles W. Jones defeated his opponent by only five votes. Two years earlier Jones had been soundly defeated in his first try at winning election to public office. This time enough voters, white as well as black, were sufficiently intimidated to squeak him into the Florida House of Representatives. Like many white supremacists, Charles W. Jones was as much a Carpetbagger as any of the Reconstructionists were. This adroit practitioner of racist politics was born and spent his early childhood in Ireland. He grew up in New York, attending public schools there and in St. Louis, but no one ever described him as "a damn Yankee who came here to rule us." What differentiated an acceptably "Southern" politician like Jones from a Carpetbagger like Harrison Reed was not his origins, ethnic or geographic. The willingness to condone political violence, and to benefit from it in the name of white supremacy, was what made candidates like him "authentic" Floridians.

The same 1874 election that brought Charles W. Jones into the Tallahassee legislature left the state senate deadlocked, 12–12. White supremacists resolved that impasse by murdering Republican senator Elisha G. Johnson with a shotgun blast to the face. "The assassination . . . broke the tie," a 1996 account notes, "but reminded everyone of the fragility of relations between native white Conservatives and their Republican opponents." That late the reference to "native white Conservatives" perpetuated the fiction that the struggle was between Yankee outsiders and "native white" Southerners. While Jones, the paladin of the neo-Confederate cause, was a New York Irishman, the assassinated Republican senator, Elisha Johnson, born and bred in North Carolina, had fought for the Confederacy before settling with his family in Florida. If stereotypes prevailed, he would have been warmly welcomed by the state's neo-Confederate elite. Instead, because Johnson, accepting the full outcome of the struggle, had embraced Abolition and supported the human rights amendments to the Constitution, he was first killed, then expunged from memory.

While Elisha G. Johnson, a Confederate war hero, was removed from the Florida legislature through assassination, Charles W. Jones, who avoided military service during the Civil War, had conferred on him by that same legislature its most consequential honor. In 1875 it named him to be one of Florida's U.S. senators. Johnson's murder had allowed neo-Confederates and their allies to gain the upper hand in the Tallahassee legislature; that in turn allowed Jones to assume one of America's higher offices without having to face the voters. Up in Washington Senator Jones helped forge the paradigm of a successful Florida member of Congress that would prevail through the Cold War era. While simultaneously lamenting and denouncing the horrors of federal tyranny, "Senator Jones," notes Judy Nicholas Etemadi in her study of his senatorial career, "was highly regarded in Florida for having obtained appropriations for the Pensacola naval base, additional postal routes, and public buildings." An unashamed proponent of the racist mores of the ex-Confederacy, Jones also personified the growing power of America's Irish-American electorate, and so combined two of the most colorful and corrupt strands of the Democratic partisan politics of last half of the nineteenth and first half of the twentieth centuries—Deep South racist and Big City machine politics. Statesmen up to and including President Grover Cleveland considered Jones of Florida one of the soundest men in Congress to have in your corner until, politicians in Tallahassee and Washington noticed, they had not actually seen the senator for quite some time.

The long and short of his mysterious disappearance was that the Florida senator from Balbriggan, Ireland, had been undone by a heroine out of a Henry James novel. The millionairess in question lived in Michigan. For her Jones had abandoned the brass spittoons of the U.S. Senate as well as the ice-free shores of his adopted state in order to become a street person in Detroit. "He has been living a vagabond life about the city for the past year or two," the *New York*

Times later reported in a story headlined "An Insane Senator." Though her name—Clothilde Palms—had a Florida resonance, the *Florida Times-Union* described her as "a plain looking woman of 35 years." Hoping to escape Senator Jones' attentions, Miss Palms, a spinster, first married a local physician, then fled to Europe. Senator Jones never went back, either to Congress or Florida. Years later he died in a Dearborn insane asylum.

Ex-senator Yulee was another solon whose life ended far away from the scene of his Florida triumphs. His financial maneuverings there finally having bankrupted him as well as his victims, Yulee forsook Florida for Washington, D.C. He aimed to live out his life in the capital of the country he had tried to destroy; fate had another twist in store. Having been born on a Danish island in the Caribbean, he died on the formerly Dutch island of Manhattan, on what proved to be his last money-hunting expedition. It was Yulee who had first proved that racism, not region, was what counted in Florida politics. You could be an ex-Jew from the Virgin Islands or a Catholic from Ireland—and no one would call you a Carpetbagger so long as you were racist enough. At the time of his death the obituaries recounted the devastation which Yulee's manipulations, in both war and peace, had inflicted on Florida. "From beginning to end Mr. Yulee has shown himself a trickster," a Tampa editorialist remarked. Since then, the usual transmogrification has occurred. In 1999 Yulee was officially determined by the state of Florida to have been a "Great Floridian."

Ossian Hart's successor, Marcellus Lovejoy Stearns, was Florida's only one-armed governor; he had lost a limb fighting in the U.S. Army. Under Governor Stearns Florida's finances, administration, and schools continued to improve. In 1876 Stearns was seeking election in his own right, but by then murder and terror no longer were political sidelines. As one account later put it, unjudgmentally, "Outlawry and lynch law became part of the political campaign." While the Democrats pursued their "shot-gun policy," the Republicans continued to urge nonviolence. "In view of the excited condition of the public mind, and the in some degree well-founded apprehension of coming trouble growing out of the bitter political canvass now in progress in this State," the governor appealed for peaceful behavior.

Another Republican statement summed up what was at stake. "The coming election is the crisis of free government in Florida," it stated.

In the excitement over the 1876 race for governor, the outcome of the presidential contest, pitting the Republican Rutherford B. Hayes against the Democratic candidate, Samuel J. Tilden, at first was scarcely noticed. Returns telegraphed from around the nation showed Tilden had won a clear majority of the popular vote. Then news spread that, in spite of his success at the ballot box, the Democratic candidate had fallen one vote shy of victory in the electoral college. Suddenly, people all over America realized, Florida had the capacity to undo the will of the nation. Electoral votes also were in dispute in Louisiana, South Carolina, and Oregon, but Florida was at the vortex of the struggle. "If the Republicans have carried that State, as they claim," the *New York Times* reported in November 1876, "they will have 185 votes, a majority of one." That in turn would mean that the candidate who finished second would become president of the United States.

With control of the national government depending on how the votes were counted in Florida, private railroad cars—the executive jets of the Gilded Age—converged on Tallahassee. So did legions of lawyers. Once installed in their Tallahassee hotel suites these "visiting statesmen," as they were called, dispensed cigars from their humidors, bourbon from their decanters, and cash from their valises as, under their watchful eyes, the members of the Florida Board of State Canvassers picked their way through the disputed returns, county by county. The best-remembered of these itinerant politicos on the Republican side was General Lew Wallace, later celebrated as the author of *Ben Hur*. Among the Democratic Party notables was General George Washington Biddle, of the Philadelphia Biddles; he represented the United States in the Bering Sea fisheries dispute with Great Britain. Now something more than seal rookeries was at stake.

Though neo-Confederates and segregationists later made it seem that Yankee Carpetbaggers had stolen Florida's electoral votes, the three-member Florida Board of State Canvassers had not a single Yankee on it. Heading the board was Samuel B. McLin, a native of Tennessee. Because McLin, like thousands of other Tennesseans, had stayed loyal to the Union during the Civil War, he would be denounced as a "deserter from the Confederate army." The other Republican on the board, Dr. Clayton A. Cowgill, would be denounced as a Carpetbagger from Delaware even though Delaware, like Tennessee, was both a slave state and located south of the Mason-Dixon Line. The third member, and its sole Democrat, William Archer Cocke, also had immigrated to Florida from a slave state. Since Cocke supported white supremacy, he got the conventional laudation: "a native Virginian, an old resident of Florida, a lawyer of some repute, an historian, and a Democrat" is how one account enshrines him.

According to the initial tally Rutherford B. Hayes had indeed carried the state for the Republicans by 43 of the some 45,000 votes cast. There was a hitch, though. Tiny Baker County submitted three rival sets of returns—two by Democrats, one by Republicans. It was the Republican return, validated by a judge named Elisha W. Driggers and the local sheriff, a black man named Bill Green, which gave Florida's electoral votes to Hayes. If either of the Democratic returns from Baker County were accepted, the presidency would go to Tilden. None of the returns from Baker County complied with state regulations, so the canvassing board conducted its own investigation. In spite of their political differences, the two Republicans and one Democrat unanimously concurred that Tilden, not Hayes, had prevailed in Baker County, by a vote of 238 to 143. That transformed Hayes's paper-thin victory into a slender statewide victory for Tilden. If the new total stood, Tilden would be the next president of the United States, but the new total did not stand for long as the members of the board went on to adjudicate the disputed results from other counties. When the statewide tally was complete, Hayes' narrow victory had increased from 43 to 924 votes.

Though the notion prevails that the Republicans stole Florida, if anyone stole the election it was the Democrats. To win, all the Republicans needed was a fair, peaceful election that allowed the state's black as well as its white citizens to vote freely and safely. Only through violent intimidation and fake electoral returns could the Democrats be sure of carrying Florida. While irregularities did occur on both sides, the election results revealed a clear pattern of white supremacist interference on the whole beneficial to Tilden and the Democrats—not Hayes and the Republicans—extending from one extremity of Florida to the other. In Key West one precinct gave Tilden 401 votes, Hayes 59. Local officials produced this lopsided result by carrying off the ballot boxes to a secret location. They only announced their spurious result in favor of Tilden the next day. At another precinct at the far north end of the state, winter weather was the excuse. "The evening being chilly and the polling room being without fireplaces or proper lights," it was explained, the "inspectors had gone to count the votes in a nearby house." "Nearby" turned out to be two miles away. In some counties the location of the polling places was kept secret in order to prevent Republicans, especially black people, from voting.

In other places electoral politics was literally the continuation of the Civil War, and not by other means. "Former Confederate cavalry commander J. J. Dickison led . . . mounted men in cavalry charges through crowds of potential voters," notes one account. "On the morning of the election, before daylight," Governor Stearns later testified, "several persons came to my house, and said that the Democrats were coming into town armed. I . . . went downtown, and found that quite a large number had come there with arms, and had deposited them . . . at different points around the court-house square." Those prevented from voting, Stearns reported, "were universally Republicans."

After nearly two months of sifting through the disputed voting totals, the Board of State Canvassers announced that the Republican presidential candidate had won Florida's four electoral votes even though the two Republican members of the Florida Canvassing Board had allowed many dubious votes for Tilden to stand. "The board did not throw out votes . . . on the score of intimidation; yet no one familiar with the evidence . . . will for a moment doubt that there was sufficient intimidation to change the whole result," noted Paul Leland Haworth in his masterful but forgotten 1903 account, *The Hayes-Tilden Disputed Presidential Election of 1876*. "While a fair count of the votes cast in the state of Florida might have resulted in a small majority for Tilden," he concluded, "a free election would with far greater certainty have resulted in a substantial majority for Hayes." That comment raised the great question that the state of Florida, as well as the Congress and Supreme Court of the United States would never address. How could there be a fair count when there had not been a free election?

Because of the electoral chaos in Florida, the candidate a majority of America's voters had chosen would not become president; another man would. It was not a trivial undoing of the popular will. Tilden, nationwide, had won 51 percent of the vote. Slim as that margin might seem, it was more than Presidents John Quincy Adams, Martin Van Buren, Zachary Taylor, James Knox Polk, Franklin Pierce, James Buchanan, and Abraham Lincoln had gotten. Tilden also had a bigger share of the vote than Presidents James Garfield, Grover Cleveland, Benjamin Harrison, Woodrow Wilson, Harry S Truman, John F. Kennedy, Richard Nixon, Jimmy Carter, Bill Clinton, and George W. Bush would get when they won the White House.

The problem was not simply that politicians are venal or that the Florida electoral system malfunctioned. Democracy was defeated because the U.S. electoral system was skewed against the people. Attempting to assure that the Civil War had not been fought in vain, America's human rights activists had amended the Constitution three times, but they left intact its single most antidemocratic electoral provision. While keeping the electoral college, Article XIV ordained that all human beings, including black people, now must be counted as whole human beings, not three-fifths of one. This produced one of the most bizarre unintended consequences of the Union victory in the Civil War because it meant that the defeated ex-Confederate states automatically increased their representation in Congress, and so were given an even stronger voice in the electoral college after the Civil War than they had before they seceded.

If the ex-slave states could continue to prevent black people from voting, white supremacists in the defeated ex-Confederate states would enjoy a political advantage even greater than the one they had enjoyed under slavery. Article XIV foresaw that danger and attempted to deal with it. "But when the right to vote at any election . . . is denied to any of the male inhabitants of such State," it provided, "the basis of representation therein shall be reduced in the proportion which the number of such male citizens shall bear to the whole number of male citizens twenty-one years of age in such State." The more people they prevented from voting, this provision of Article XIV specified, the greater the reduction would be—except that never once would any state ever be penalized in that way, no matter how many people were prevented from voting.

By 1876, the states of the former Confederacy comprised a significantly smaller proportion of the total population of the United States than they had before the Civil War began, yet their total strength both in Congress and in the electoral college was substantially greater than it had been before the Civil War. The secessionist states, which had eighty-eight electoral votes in 1860, had ninety-five electoral votes in 1876. Florida was the prime example of how this perverse triumph of the law of unintended consequences corrupted democracy nationally as well in the states. Thanks to Article XIV, Florida got an extra seat in Congress, and therefore an extra vote in the electoral college. That one electoral vote sufficed to undo the majority vote for Tilden across the nation, at the very same time the black people of Florida were being prevented from exercising their right to vote. It was the worst of both worlds. The rights of tens of thousands of people in Florida and the other ex-Confederate states who had wanted to vote for Hayes were violated with impunity. Simultaneously the rights of the majority of Americans who had voted for Tilden were also violated.

In the furor over the 1876 presidential results, it was little noticed that the electoral chaos in Florida had produced an additional undoing of democracy, when the Republican candidate was denied the governorship by an alliance of Yankee jurists and gun-toting Southern terrorists. "The object [of] the murder of the leaders of the Republican party in the state, and the intimidation of the other Republicans," as Senator Purman explained, all along had been "in this way to obtain possession and control of the state government." In the 1876 state elections the conspiracy of "halter, shot-gun and whip" had almost, but not quite, prevailed. In spite of the electoral terror campaign, the canvassing board found that the Republican candidate for governor, Marcellus Stearns, had managed to defeat his Democratic opponent, George F. Drew, by 458 votes but then, in a stunning act of judicial interventionism, the Florida Supreme Court "commanded" the board to restore the fraudulent votes it had disallowed. That reversed the election result, making the white supremacist candidate governor by a margin of 195 votes. Next the Court ordered reversals in all the other election results. In this manner every statewide electoral office was taken away from those whom the canvassing board determined had actually gotten the most votes. Thanks to this early instance of "conservative" judicial activism, Florida's white supremacists gained control of the entire state government and every office in it—secretary of state, comptroller, treasurer, commissioner of immigration, attorney general, adjutant general, superintendent of public instruction, and surveyor general.

Even as it rewarded political violence and legitimized electoral fraud, the Florida Supreme Court refuted regional stereotypes. Chief Justice Randall, the judge who had "given the governorship" and, with it, control of Florida's future to neo-Confederate racists, was a Yankee. A native of upstate New York, Chief Justice Randall first attained political influence in Wisconsin. Then he had been appointed to federal office in Florida. Reed himself had named Randall chief justice. Chief Justice Randall did not deny there had been gross irregularities. He merely ruled it didn't matter when votes were stolen in Florida. No matter how outrageous the "irregularities or fraud in an election," he claimed, the board had no right to go "behind the face of the election returns."

The chief justice was the one who had exceeded his authority. Florida law explicitly compelled the canvassing board "to determine the true vote." In every case where the "returns shall be shown or shall appear to be so irregular, false or fraudulent that the Board shall be unable to determine the true vote," the law explicitly ordered, they "shall not include such return in their determination." That did not stop Chief Justice Randall from ordering the state canvassers to violate the law and include stolen and fabricated votes in their final totals. In his 1913 volume, *The Civil War and Reconstruction in Florida,*

William Watson Davis summed up what had happened: "Since the murder of Senator Johnson in 1875 the Conservatives had controlled the Senate." Now, "through this pronouncement the executive branch of the government passed into their hands."

The beneficiary of this "Conservative" judicial activism was also a Yankee. A farm boy from New Hampshire, Governor Drew, like Governor DuVal before him, had fled the family homestead following a dispute with his father over domestic chores. Arriving friendless and unskilled in the factory town of Lowell, Massachusetts, by age nineteen he had advanced from mill hand to professional machinist. Fate took another turn when he was sent south to oversee the installation of an engine works in Georgia. There George Drew discovered that black slaves did the farm work that he had found so disagreeable. He stayed, eventually becoming one of the richest slaveholders in Lee County, Georgia, but with the outbreak of the Civil War, Drew ran away again, this time to the safety of the federally controlled region of Florida. There, as one account puts it, he safely "remained with the fleet until the end of the war." Only after the Union crushed the Confederacy did Drew decide to settle permanently in Florida. As with DuVal, Call, and other Florida governors before him, a brush with war had introduced him to the idea that, in Florida, a man could get rich if he had the right connections.

As Florida politicians still do, Drew cloaked both his non-Florida origins and his oligarchic ambitions in the gaudy cloak of Southern-sounding chauvinism, but in reality he was pioneering a new, more complete form of outside exploitation. "Buying entire mill outputs he would wholesale it to buyers in the northern states," writes Don Hensley in "The Rise of the Drew Family and Their Sawmills." By 1869 George Drew, in partnership with Louis Bucki, a New York moneyman, had gained control of vast tracts of unfelled Florida timber. This grab-it-all, grab-it-now form of Florida capitalism was strip mining with trees. As soon as one sector was devastated, Drew would get the legislature to cede him another sector of public land.

The same racist vigilantes whom Dickison used to hijack Governor Reed's rifles and to terrorize Drew's black laborers now became the henchmen behind the neo-Confederate seizure of state power. On inauguration day Drew and his supporters "had stationed in an old cotton storehouse close by the capitol, between three and five hundred men, armed with repeating rifles, with the intention of slaughtering the men who might attempt to inaugurate the defeated candidate." Governor Stearns had seen it all coming. "Our Democratic opponents realize already that their defeat is inevitable," he told his supporters on the eve of the vote, "unless they can stifle the voice of the people by fraud and violence and deter the masses of our party from casting their ballots." He had foreseen, too, that "evil, designing men" were intent on "wresting from our people the rights guaranteed by the constitution." What neither he nor anyone else had foreseen was the capricious intervention of the judicial branch on behalf of the neo-Confederates.

Tallahassee was spared a blood bath, once again, because of Governor Stearns' commitment to nonviolence. Early that morning the outgoing governor, who had been grievously wounded fighting in the Civil War, paid a courtesy call on the incoming governor, who had sat out the war protected by the U.S. Navy. After informing his rival that he would not stand in his way, Stearns boarded a horse-drawn carriage, rode out of town and out of history too.

Once installed in office, Governor Drew took up the task of reimposing white supremacy with as much ruthlessness as any Southern-born zealot might have. Nonracist whites as well as blacks were purged from the state administration. Notable among the radical reactionaries taking their place was John J. Dickison. In return for Dickison's help repressing his laborers as well as his political opponents, Drew named Dickison his adjutant general. In this way the state's most famous terrorist was transformed into its chief military administrator.

Florida had made fiscal progress in the later years of Reconstruction, but until it found a way to fund its expenditures through broad-based taxation, the state government would remain destitute. Foreshadowing present-day politics in Florida, Governor Drew's "solution" was to give the rich more while taxing them less and regulating them not at all, while eliminating, to the greatest extent possible, the useful functions of government. In his judgment those needless fripperies included prisons. "Convict leasing," an early form of outsourcing, turned Florida's penal system into a profit center while providing Florida's land barons, including Governor Drew himself, with a government-subsidized supply of slave labor. Also dating from Governor Drew's administration were Florida's turpentine camps. Under slavery the slave knew it was in his master's interest to keep him nourished and healthy. The convicts on the chain gang could hope for the day when they became free men again. The turpentine camps, state-authorized, were Florida's gulag. Innocent men disappeared into them and never came out. The camps were not abolished until 1949.

Up in New Hampshire Drew's father had whipped him for reading a book. As governor he did the same thing, figuratively, to the children of Florida. At a time when states like California and Iowa were creating the great land-grant universities, Florida's governor "advocated the elimination of public high schools." In many places in Florida, especially those with large black populations, public education was closed down completely. Like the politics of environmental destruction, epitomized by Drew's own logging operations, his devastation of Florida's educational system had consequences that endure to this day, yet after four years of "cost-cutting," Florida remained as bankrupt as ever. No matter how many convicts were leased, or children turned out of school, Florida's finances would remain a wreck so long as the tax base there was composed by and large of a wealthy minority who would not pay taxes and a poor majority who could not pay them. As Zephaniah Kingsley had pointed out half a century earlier, the remedy was the creation of a freeholder class, but "Conservative" Floridians considered it "incendiary," not admirable, that "radicals" like Liberty Billings had called for "homesteads and equality." Outrage was added to incredulity when it was hinted that black as well as white folks might benefit from some sort of homesteading scheme that would allow people to feed their families, educate their children, and work themselves out of debt.

Ossian Hart had foreseen what the costs would be if racists once again were allowed a free hand. The prospect of a racist restoration filled him with dread because he knew that, once in power, they would make sure no more free elections were held. And then? "There is no telling how far back they would drag Florida before the solid countermarch could be arrested," he correctly predicted.

17

KING IGNORANCE

While allotting poor Floridians forty acres and a mule was denounced as mischievous and immoral, letting a Yankee millionaire grab millions of acres of Florida real estate was lauded as an example of the "wise plans" put into practice by Drew's successor, Governor William Bloxham. The Disston land scandal of 1881 was one of the biggest such scams to unfold since George Mathews presided over the Yazoo affair, up in Georgia, in 1795. Under this latest scheme to "develop" Florida, a Philadelphia plutocrat named Hamilton Disston acquired four million acres of Florida land in a deal that mimicked the "purchase" of Florida from Spain sixty years earlier. Though Governor Bloxham claimed the deal would rescue the state financially, Florida never got a penny. The money went to out-of-state creditors who had acquired claims to the debts that Senator Yulee had failed to pay on his railroad schemes.

Under Bloxham's successor, Edward Aylesworth Perry, there was no land for the landless; homesteading remained illegal. There was unlimited acreage for the speculators whose bankruptcies, like the hurricanes, frosts and epidemics, now became a recurrent feature of Florida's boom-and-bust melodrama. Governor Perry's solution was ever more lavish giveaways. "In 1885, when Perry became governor," according to one account, "the state controlled 5,367,265 acres of land. On January 1, 1889, just prior to the end of Perry's term, the state controlled 2,104,898 acres." Governors Bloxham and Perry had given away enough land—more than three million acres of it—to turn every Florida family, white and black, into the possessor of a substantial domain.

Governor Perry was one of the most extreme racists ever to hold that office. In light of his future Florida activities, the name of his birthplace—Richmond, a hamlet in western Massachusetts—had a prophetic edge to it. Perry attended Yale; he did not move south until he was a grown man. Once there he, like Governor Drew, recognized that the key to acquiring wealth and power was to side with the forces of violence and racism. He had the love life of the up-and-coming Florida politico, too. His Southern belle was an Alabama woman, Wathen Virginia Taylor. When not politicking, the Perrys were At Home at their Pensacola mansion. A Greek-columned, twin-balustraded paragon of slaveholder elegance, the residence was later converted into a Masonic lodge.

Governors Reed and Stearns were castigated as "damn Yankee[s] who came here to rule us." Perry, as much a New Englander as they were, would get a Confederate war memorial erected in his honor. The monument, a thirty-foot-tall obelisk, was one of Florida's most grandiose, but its location posed a problem. "Pensacola was one of the communities whose citizens felt the need to remember the sacrifices made in behalf of the Confederacy," but considering the inglorious Confederate record there, what and who was there to memorialize? "If a local area could not boast of an authentic hero," W. Stuart Towns explains, "they dedicated their monument to the 'Confederacy,' or the 'Boys in Gray.'" In Pensacola's case the monument was topped by an eight-feet-tall generic Confederate soldier. Through stone eyes, he still stares out over the city where Jonathan Walker was branded and which the Confederates burned, toward Santa Rosa Island where, defied by Lieutenant Slemmer and his loyal U.S. troops, the Confederates suffered their first, defining defeat.

Further down on the monument, the Massachusetts-born Perry is lauded as one of the "Uncrowned Heroes of the Southern Confederacy." It was a case of getting what you paid for when it came to self-glorification in public spaces. Mrs. Perry led the Confederate Ladies' Monument Association's fund-raising campaign for the memorial intended to immortalize her spouse. Collecting pennies from orphans and nickels from widows of the Confederate war dead, the

Confederate Ladies raised $5,000 for their obelisk, which, Florida limestone being considered an insufficiently noble substance, was made from imported granite.

For the design of their monument the Confederate Ladies looked to the Washington, D.C., headquarters of the government that had crushed the rebellion their monument celebrated, and the J. F. Manning Company. Among the firm's clients were Ohio and New York infantry units that had helped crush the Florida Brigade during its post-Olustee foray into the Virginia fighting, but the company took money from ex-Rebels, too. Their "matchless heroism shall continue to be the wonder and inspiration of the ages," read the all-purpose inscription its Yankee designers engraved on the Pensacola monument. Though the Pensacola monument was ostensibly a private edifice, the cost of maintaining the monument there, as at Olustee, long ago was shifted to the public, in this instance to the taxpayers of Pensacola, approximately one-third of whom are the descendants of slaves. Like other racist figures, Perry continues to be honored at state expense. "His Great Floridian plaque is located at the Scottish Rite Temple, 2 East Wright Street, Pensacola," the Florida Division of Historical Resources advises, Perry having been confirmed in that honor in 1998.

The most enduring legacy of this Massachusetts racist's governorship was Florida's notorious 1885 "poll tax" constitution. By 1884, the year Perry was elected, the rampant abuses of the Drew and Bloxham administrations were sufficient to engender great popular revulsion. Perry managed to win, but only after an alliance of disaffected Democrats and black and white Republicans, campaigning for "a free ballot, a full vote and a fair count," got 46 percent of the vote. The 1876 election had shown that not even a monopoly on violence could ensure a racist victory; the courts had to intervene. The 1884 election showed that, even when great numbers of black citizens were prevented from voting, a reduced black electorate nonetheless still had the potential to shift the balance of power to whites who favored greater equity in fields such as education and the criminal justice system. The lesson Florida's racist elite drew from all of this was that a governmental system deliberately engineered to guarantee one-party racist rule on a permanent basis was required. First the much-admired constitution of 1868, along with its human rights protections, was revoked. Then a new system of white race supremacy was imposed.

In the name of cost-cutting, Governor Drew had inflicted on Florida one of the features that still define governance there. That was the refusal to raise and spend adequate sums of money for the public good. The result is that, no matter how much money flows into the state or how immense its population becomes, Florida chronically lags the nation in fields like education, environmental protection, safety in the workplace, and health. In the form of the Disston deal, Governor Bloxham initiated a second defining feature of Florida governance. That was the use of "development" projects to benefit wealthy, mostly out-of-state magnates, as opposed to Florida's finances or its people. Adoption of the 1885 constitution added a third defining feature of governance that would endure for generations. This was Florida's de facto transformation into a one-party state. That was achieved, most famously, by authorizing the state legislature to impose a poll tax. As America's first chief justice, John Marshall, had pointed out back in 1819, "the power to tax involves the power to destroy." Destroyed in this instance was the power of the citizens of Florida to govern their state by means of voting in free elections.

Even if you did have enough money to pay the Florida poll tax, you couldn't just show up at the polling place. In order to vote, people had to have "paid on or before the second Saturday in the month preceding the day of election, their poll taxes for two years preceding the year in which the election is held." Voters also had to prove that they had "resided in the State for one year and in the county six months at the time of any election." Visiting relatives in Alabama or Georgia could cost you your right to vote, though only if you were black. Easier yet, your boss could send you on an errand to another county, then inform on you. Polling officials disqualified thousands of black voters without challenging the qualifications of a single white person, but what if a black citizen somehow did thread his way past all those snares? In the manner of some mythical protagonist, he next faced the Ordeal of the Boxes, as Washington Irving's parable assumed electoral form. A 1928 article in the *Florida Historical Quarterly* described how it worked. "The law provided separate ballots and separate ballot-boxes for each of the chief elective offices," it explained. "All ballots for a certain officer were to be placed in the box specified. No ballots in a wrong box were to be counted." "Since most of the negroes were illiterate and since the white Democratic election commissioners refused to tell them in which boxes to place the ballots, the black vote, which was almost entirely Republican, was practically eliminated."

In spite of all the restrictions, it was still possible in some localities for black voters to swing the result to less racist candidates. To prevent that from happening, the Tallahassee legislature "passed laws seizing control of the municipal governments" wherever coalitions of white and black voters held office. First in Pensacola, then in Jacksonville and Key West, democratically elected mayors, councilmen, and commissioners were purged from office as the state government legislated multiracial, two-party politics out of existence. Such violations of due process and equal protection of the laws never faced effective legal challenge because the new constitution also destroyed the independence of the Florida judiciary. Once again in the name of "democracy," the state's judges, including its supreme court justices, were made elective. As a result, the "unwritten laws" of a restricted, whites-only electorate—not what was written in the law books—would be the supreme law of the land.

Another widely abused pretext for disfranchising black people was the provision disqualifying convicted criminals from voting. Anyone convicted "of any infamous crime in any court of the State or any other State" could be denied the right to vote. There was no factual standard or legal appeal. A mere rumor of supposed misconduct somewhere, at some time, sufficed to prevent a citizen from voting for the rest of his life.

The felony voting ban, still in force, is one of the most enduring legacies of the triumph of racism in Florida. With 6 percent of the country's population, Florida currently accounts for more than 20 percent of all Americans who are disfranchised. Since the American legal system punishes the kinds of crimes that poor whites as well as black people tend to commit much more harshly than it does the kinds of crimes that affluent Americans commit, the felony voter ban injects a class as well as a racial bias into Florida's electoral process. Approximately 10 percent of Florida's white citizens as well as nearly 20 percent of its black citizens are prohibited from voting.

Denying black people the vote could not eliminate the possibility that someday some Florida governor might appoint some eminent black person to a position of authority. To prevent another Jonathan Gibbs from ever serving Florida, the 1885 constitution stripped the governor of the power to appoint his own cabinet. Florida's cabinet positions became statewide elective. Like the election of Florida's Supreme Court justices, it sounded democratic, but this provision meant that blacks were effectively excluded from statewide office, even by appointment. As racists rewrote Florida's history as well as it constitution, it was forgotten how well black people in Florida had taken to electoral politics. According to Canter Brown's study, *Florida's Black Public Officials, 1867–1924*, nearly one thousand black people, the great majority of them Florida-born ex-slaves, held office following the Civil War. By profession they ranged from farmers and laborers to craftsmen and preachers.

Though white racists had state power as well as political violence at their disposal, thousands of black and white citizens voted against the abolition of the 1868 constitution. Tens of thousands of Floridians also voted against the "poll tax" constitution. The final official tally was 31,803 to 21,243. The difference the new constitution made was to be seen in the elections for governor. In 1880 the Republican candidate for governor got 26,485 votes. The Republican candidate for president, James Garfield, got 23,654 votes, 45.83 percent of the total. In 1896 the Republican candidate for governor got 8,200 votes, the presidential candidate only 11,298, even though by then the state's population had nearly doubled.

Because it restricted the electorate so effectively, the 1885 constitution guaranteed that into the 1950s Florida would be controlled, with some exceptions, by racially bigoted neo-Confederates, many of them as implacably hostile to improved conditions for white people as they were opposed to justice for black people. Nowhere was the corruption of public service on more exquisite display than in the state legislature, which was expressly forbidden to meet more than once every two years. Following a flurry of special-interest legislation, it was legally obliged to disband for another two years. Because Florida's legislators met so seldom and their sessions were so fleeting, there was no check on executive abuses of power. As in Territorial days, the rich and well-connected got the cake; the crumbs fell to neo-Confederate "countrymen." White supremacist terrorists—and eventually their sons and grandsons—filled the halls of the legislature, while also taking up residence in local sheriffs' offices and, as the automobile age dawned, preying on both blacks and Yankees at Florida's notorious speed traps.

In segregationist mythology as well as the history books, Florida's "solid countermarch" would be celebrated as a triumph of patriotic Southerners over venal Northern interlopers. In this instance, too, the birth certificates tell a different story.

Florida Governors 1868–1889

Governor (in office)	Birth State	Party	Political Tendencies
Harrison Reed (1868–1873)	Massachusetts	Republican	Abolitionist, civil rights activist
Ossian B. Hart (1873–1874)	Florida	Republican	Loyal U.S. citizen, black liberationist
Marcellus Stearns (1874–1877)	Maine	Republican	Abolitionist, U.S. combat veteran
George F. Drew (1877–1881)	New Hampshire	Democrat	Radical racist, avoided military service
William D. Bloxham (1881–1885)	Florida	Democrat	White supremacist
Edward A. Perry (1885–1889)	Massachusetts	Democrat	Confederate racist

Whites-only politics was only the beginning; state-enforced segregation, now constitutionally mandated in Florida's schools, was expanded to travel on railroads and buses and access to hotels and restaurants. By the time the segregationists were finished, private sexual acts would become a matter for state regulation. Who could drink from a public water fountain was also subject to a racial test. The poll tax remained the defining example of a constitutional depravity of governance. Ostensibly imposed for the purpose of funding education, it did nothing to elevate educational standards because, as with almost everything Florida did, the stated purpose was never the real purpose, in this case to deny black citizens their rights, whatever the consequences. Those consequences would be dire because, thanks to this latest of its constitutions, Florida had a government that by its nature tended to be morally and intellectually, as well as financially, bankrupt—and because racist rule was written into the state constitution, there was now no way for Florida's voters to change it.

There was nothing new in that. By themselves the people of Florida—white and black—never could have rid their state of slavery. They never could have thrown off oligarchic Confederate tyranny. It was the same with the backwardness that gripped Florida into and across the first half of the twentieth century. Only the government of the United States could make sure that the civil and human rights of U.S. citizens were respected. That the federal government was never fully willing to do, not even under Congressional Reconstruction, and by 1876 the government in Washington would not so much as a lift in a finger in that regard. Why should it, when on the whole the people of the United States, who had fought a terrible war to preserve the Union, no longer cared what went on in the ex-Confederate states? As the white supremacists tightened their vise in the ex-Confederacy, California beckoned. The great factories of the North belched out money! Rockets would carry men into outer space from Florida before the constitutional perversion of democracy there ceased being abetted by dereliction of constitutional duty in Washington.

Florida's racist 1885 constitution would remain in force, with modifications, until 1968. One result was that Florida's people remained mired in ignorance. The perennial disregard for scientific as well as human advancement was on full display in 1888 as Florida endured its latest spate of pestilence. As yellow fever consumed Jacksonville, people sprayed their homes with a poisonous mercury solution in the false hope that could save them. Floridians also fired off artillery shells in the belief that "concussion would kill the microbes." The spread of the disease touched off Florida's biggest spate of self-inflicted devastation since the Confederates burned Pensacola in 1862. In Jacksonville they started by burning down the hotels, in keeping with the idea that outsiders invariably were to blame.

The refusal to foresee consequences also continued to prevail. Fifteen years earlier a Florida doctor, John P. Wall, had discovered that "the Aedes aegypti mosquito carried the disease." Cuban researchers confirmed his findings; still no one bothered to drain the stagnant pools of untreated water where the mosquitoes thrived. When the fever first appeared, "Dr. Wall came down from Tampa on an inspection tour." Warned in advance that an epidemic was imminent, the Jacksonville medical authorities refused to diagnose the disease, one diarist noted. Even as the telltale black vomit spewed out of people's mouths, "the attending physician [was] denying its being Yellow Fever all the time." The next entry reads, inevitably: "In a few days more were sick." As always an outside agitator was to blame; fifty-three years before the attack on Pearl Harbor, Yellow Jack—the squinty-eyed personification of the disease—leered out at his victims from billboards and newspapers.

As during the Civil War, officials in Tallahassee did nothing until the fear arose that Yellow Jack might use his Jacksonville beachhead to advance on the state capital. To avert that, Governor Perry ordered that people fleeing the epidemic be rounded up at gunpoint and, like the Seminoles earlier, "concentrated." One of the biggest holding pens for the sick and dying was named Camp Perry, and justly so. During more than three years as governor Perry had done nothing to protect Floridians from the killer diseases endemic there. Lack of funding was the habitual excuse, but there was more than enough to increase the money the Tallahassee treasury paid every Floridian who had fought for slavery from $5 to $8 a month. There was no land for the veterans, though. Since homesteading of state land remained illegal, the main effect of this state-financed Confederate "pension" program was to stifle self-sufficiency while enhancing the white racist sense of entitlement.

Governor Perry demonstrated that it didn't matter where you were born, so long as you were racist enough. His successor, Governor Francis Philip Fleming, in office from 1889 to 1893, demonstrated that having a black sister was also no bar to becoming a successful white racist politician in Florida. Fleming's grandfather, a migrant from the British Isles, had acquired a Spanish land grant abutting the St. Johns River. His Florida-born father, Lewis Fleming, like his neighbor Zephaniah Kingsley, found romance during a youthful foray to Cuba, though not in the Havana slave market. The eventual Florida governor was the son of Lewis Fleming's second wife, Margaret Seton, a Florida-born woman of Scots extraction whom he wed after his Cuban wife died. As a result of his father's first marriage, Governor Fleming had two Cuban half brothers and a Cuban half sister. Then there was Governor Fleming's black half sister, Chloe, his father's child by a slave at the family's Hibernia plantation.

While Francis Fleming made speeches about the patriotic necessity of preserving the purity of the white race, he and his multi-hued siblings lived together at Hibernia. Skin color determined each one's place in the hierarchy of domestic cohabitation. The Cuban children, being more or less fair skinned, became "Anglo" in spite of their Hispanic origin. Chloe, being half-African, was accorded the status of "personal maid of the lady of the house," the lady in question being her own stepmother, Margaret Seton. Through his half sister Chloe, Governor Fleming had a truly exceptional black niece. Like Anna Madgigine Jai Kingsley, Louise Cecilia Fleming, better known as Lulu. was one of the remarkable female Floridians of her time.

A slave at the time of her birth, Lulu Fleming received an excellent education. As a result of medical studies at Shaw University in North Carolina and at the Women's Medical College in Philadelphia, she became one of the most qualified Floridians of any race in the field of public health. Though her skills were desperately needed in Florida, this half-white, half-black Floridian was sent to the Congo Free State, that tortured part of Africa then being ravished by Leopold II, king of the Belgians, and other rapacious investors, including Florida's own Henry Sanford. Aspiring to work as a medical missionary, Lulu Fleming sailed up the Congo River in 1887, two years before Joseph Conrad got there. Meanwhile Lulu's uncle, the future governor Francis Fleming, was rising higher and higher inside the neo-Confederate racist power elite.

"The climate seems quite like that of my own beloved birth State," she wrote from Africa, a statement that proved sadly true. In the Congo Lulu Fleming contracted sleeping sickness. Lapsing into coma, she was brought back to America to die. Following Fleming's election as governor in 1888, two of his Cuban siblings died of yellow fever. Not even those deaths produced any substantive change in Florida's public priorities or those of its governor. John F. Kennedy would be elected president before the state of Florida got around to graduating its first doctor.

Even after the 1885 constitution was adopted, people in Florida kept up the struggle for civil and human rights. Nor, as the 1888 elections results showed, did white supremacists win every battle. That November Francis Fleming's statewide victory in the contest for governor was a foregone conclusion, but the voting down in Monroe County—the Florida Keys and adjacent mainland—produced a result that shocked Florida's white politicians. In spite of all the racially rigged electoral machinery, a black man was elected judge of Monroe County. The candidate who won this victory, Judge James Dean, was a native Floridian ex-slave. Born in Ocala in 1858, he was only ten when Florida's 1868 human rights constitution was adopted. He was nineteen in 1877, when white racists began dismantling Florida's equal-opportunity educational system. This meant the future judge was of school age during that brief period when Florida was committed to educating all its children. The boy first got a basic education at the Cookman Institute in Jacksonville, which Ossian Hart helped found. Then, in 1883 Dean earned a bachelor of arts degree at Howard University in Washington, D.C. A year after that he was awarded his master's by the Howard Law School. Both times he was first in his class.

At age twenty-three Dean was a delegate to the Republican national convention. He could have stayed in Washington, becoming a pillar of its black elite. He returned to Florida because he had a dream. It went back, he explained, to his graduation from the Cookman Institute when, "with a deep sympathy aroused for my people and my youthful heart heaving with great purpose, I departed from that Institute and stepped out on this land of flowers to grapple with King Ignorance, who reigns in high places." The young lawyer established himself in Key West.

By then Key West, with nineteen thousand people, had become Florida's first American boomtown. When Commodore Matthew Perry, later celebrated for his expedition to Japan, arrived there in 1822 to take possession of the island for the United States, it was uninhabited. The island was too exposed to hurricanes and pirates, also too small and too close to Havana to have any strategic or economic value for the Spanish. Its most numerous inhabitants, once the U.S. flag was raised, were neither Americans nor Cubans, but migrants from the Bahamas. Most were free black Bahamian seafarers. Others were white loyalists who had fled the United States during the War of Independence. While peninsular Florida was still trackless wilderness, Key West's position athwart the sea route from New York to New Orleans gave it a vital connection to the rest of the United States. Key West's main source of early prosperity, though, was wrecking, more politely known as the "salvage" business. Starting in the 1500s Floridians—first Indians, then Europeans—preyed on the shipwrecks the sea periodically delivered to their shores. Under U.S. rule, wrecking became a form of legalized plunder. These licensed looters, as Jonathan Walker and his escaped slaves discovered, did not wait for ships to be wrecked before seizing "contraband," both material and human. When the sea failed to provide sufficient booty, the wreckers generated shipwrecks themselves—using fake lights and buoys to lure seafarers to their doom.

Wreckers and the loot they brought ashore gave life in Key West a devil-may-care aspect that still persists there. During the Civil War Key

West's location insulated it psychologically as well as geographically from Confederate repression. Then, starting in 1868, thousands of refugees migrated to Key West in order to escape the bloodletting in nearby Cuba. Long after Spain lost Florida (and all its other possessions on the continental mainland of the Americas), it clung to Cuba. As its vicious repression of the independence movement there demonstrated, Bourbon Spain had learned nothing from its previous colonial tragedies.

By the time Dean arrived there, Key West was Florida's most populous as well as least intolerant community. Only twenty-nine when he launched his campaign for judge of Monroe County, Dean was so successful he carried into office on his coattails a black candidate for sheriff as well. "It was conceded alike by Democrats and Republicans," one newspaper reported, "that Mr. Dean was the best qualified of all the three candidates, he being the only lawyer among them." Only racist sex paranoia could generate the political poison capable of destroying the career of an elected official like Judge James Dean, so sex, inevitably and almost immediately, came to the fore. Among the new judge's responsibilities was the issuance of marriage licenses. Soon the scandalous, shocking and false information reached Tallahassee that Judge Dean had authorized a white man to marry a black woman. It wasn't so. Dean upheld the matrimonial segregation of the races as vigilantly as any white judge. The bride was black. Under oath the bridegroom swore he was of mixed-race parentage, that is a "mulatto."

The controversy was cultural as well as racial. DNA testing would not be available for another one hundred years, but even had it been possible to put Mr. González' genome in the witness box, his "race" would have remained a sociological construct. In the Cuban context González probably would have been considered "white" because of his fair complexion. In Florida, where one drop of African blood sufficed to make a man "colored," González was nonwhite by law as well as social custom. To have denied González and his fiancée a marriage license, Judge Dean would have had to rule that a person who swore he was not white actually was of the white race. Such a court-ordered change in racial status would have constituted a far more egregious meddling by a black judge in the white race's reproductive affairs than that of which Judge Dean was accused.

Since no legal grounds existed to fault Judge Dean's decision, Governor Fleming removed him from office on moral grounds; "his official misconduct," it was asserted, provided "palpable evidence of his moral unfitness to hold an office of trust and responsibility." "Our city has been in a state of excitement for the past two weeks over the suspension of Judge Dean from office by Governor Fleming," one citizen wrote from Key West at the end of July 1889. "The act," he added, "is considered by all classes irrespective of race, nationality or politics as an outrage perpetrated on him from mere race prejudices and not for malfeasance in office." The Florida Supreme Court refused so much as to consider Dean's challenge to the legality of his dismissal. In this manner one of Florida's most qualified jurists was removed from the judiciary, and a person with no legal training installed in his place. The *Florida Sentinel* explained why: "it [was] simply because he's colored."

As of 2012 the state of Florida was still portraying Judge Dean as the guilty party and Governor Fleming as the hero who had meted out the appropriate retribution, personal as well as political. "Governor Francis P. Fleming removed him from office in 1889 for marrying a black woman and a white man (although the groom said he was mulatto)," according to the Florida Memory Project of the State Archives and Library of Florida. "He left Key West penniless and disgraced, for Jacksonville where he died a pauper," but that's fiction too. Driven from the judicial pulpit Judge Dean, like many ambitious black Americans, turned to religion, in his case to the African Methodist Episcopal Church, of which he became a national leader. By then the railroad had replaced water transport as the nexus of Florida moneymaking; Jacksonville had replaced Key West as Florida's biggest city. Former governor Fleming and ex-judge Dean would cohabit the same city for decades.

Winter in Florida finished off them both. When Fleming expired, in "December, 1908, at his home in Jacksonville, after a long and painful illness," he got a neo-Confederate send-off too lengthy to fit on an obelisk. "A . . . brave soldier, a loyal and patriotic citizen, a faithful public officer, a wise counselor, an ardent and zealous church-man, and a conscientious, charitable and consistent Christian gentle-man," he was declared to have been. Reverent, lengthy obituaries marveled that while serving as "president of the Old Confederate Soldiers' and Sailors' Home Association," Francis Fleming had yet found time to assume the duties of "commodore and trustee of the Florida Yacht Club." As "president and an active member of the Florida Historical Society; and editor and frequent contributor to that Society's Quarterly Publication," he also had helped transform the military, economic, social and moral disasters which, thanks in part to his own activities, had overtaken Florida into triumphs of honor and courage.

Dean's death, in December 1914, made news as far away as New York where, one paper reported, his funeral attracted "a large concourse of people. Hundreds filed by and took their last look on the face of him who so many knew in life." White supremacist re-pression had prevented Dean from holding public office; it had not stopped him for battling King Ignorance on his home ground. Dean bequeathed a spirit of struggle that, in Florida, would continue to be viciously repressed, yet never be extinguished.

Francis Fleming's most enduring achievement was visual. Flor-ida's state flag acquired its distinctive red diagonal cross, or saltire, at the ex-governor's persistent behest. Then as now the state seal occupied the center of the flag. Ever since 1868 Florida statute has ordained that the seal display "the sun's rays, a cocoa tree, a steam-boat, and a female Indian scattering flowers." In 1895, in deference to Florida's flatness, the mountain on the seal was removed. The "female Indian" eventually lost her Wild West feathers; today she wears a Seminole blouse and skirt. Otherwise the great seal is the same as it was back in Governor Fleming's day.

What Fleming found wanting was not the great seal, but the field upon which it was displayed. Back then the Florida flag, except for the seal, was entirely white. Some considered this feature an ap-propriate assertion of white supremacy. To Fleming, white signaled surrender to Yankees. After leaving office he devoted his energies to eliminating what he considered the Florida flag's defeatist aspects. In a whites-only referendum Fleming's campaign to superimpose the red-crossed Confederate war flag on the white Florida flag was crowned with success. Alabama, Mississippi and Georgia also made versions of the Confederate battle flag their state flags. In those states the pro-slavery symbolism eventually engendered controversy; Georgia removed the Confederate saltire from its flag in 2000. In Florida Governor Fleming's pro-slavery version of the Florida flag to this day continues to fly, unprotested, over highway patrol outposts, toll booths and post offices, as well as over the state capitol and other public buildings, including Florida's schools. No one seems to notice that Florida's most conspicuous state symbol still celebrates armed insurrection against the United States.

PART FIVE

PROJECT FUTURE

I would have been a rich man,
if it hadn't been for Florida.

—Henry Flagler, on his Florida expenditures

18

PIONEERS IN PARADISE

Starting in around 1500, belief that gold and a shortcut to China were to be found in Florida or thereabouts propelled events. Later the idea that using slave labor was a good way to get rich fostered dreams and produced disaster. As the twentieth century approached, a new Florida myth took hold. This was the pretense that Florida was Paradise. Like the earlier beliefs, this one flourished independent of reality. Yellow fever epidemics could not kill it, nor could hurricanes blow it away. If human epochs were organized around their dominant miscomprehension, it could be said that we are still living in Florida's Third Great Epoch of Illusion.

We can trace the myth of El Dorado in the Spanish archives. We can see how the ideology of Confederate valor and victory was propagated by studying inscriptions on public monuments. The Paradise myth also has its paper trail. Like belief in the Fountain of Youth, it was an import—in this case imposed from the North following the Civil War. Before then, anyone suggesting Florida was Paradise would have been told to have his head examined. Better a year in hell, one soldier opined during the Seminole War, than a month in Florida. That was before influential outsiders started talking, and acting, as though Florida were Paradise. One of the first recorded instances of Florida being marketed as Paradise dates to 1868. That year the Englishman H. H. Williams named his St. Augustine attraction the Paradise Grove and Rose Gardens. The year after that James Fenimore Cooper's niece, Constance Fenimore Woolson, started spreading the new notion of Florida's wonderfulness.

Woolson was the one who warned her readers not to trip over the human bones during their romantic moonlit strolls, but in her telling what formerly had been lamented as dangerous and dreadful was presented now as inviting and attractive. That included swamps and alligators.

> *The sluggish stream from the everglade*
> *Shows the alligator's track.*
> *Ah, Destiny! Why must we ever go*
> *Away from the Florida beach?*

elegized Ms. Woolson. Referring to the derelict little town as "The Ancient City," Woolson also helped spread the notion that St. Augustine was a kind of North American Troy or Carthage.

Among the converts to Florida-boosting was ex-governor Harrison Reed. After white supremacists seized power Reed, a publisher before he became a politician, resumed his old profession. His new monthly magazine, *Semi-Tropical*, was the precursor of all the fun-in-the-sun Florida lifestyle publications of the future. Even as racist vigilantes as well as Yellow Jack terrorized the place, Reed and those who wrote for him proclaimed Florida's salubriousness; they prophesied a glorious future lay just around the corner. The switch was especially notable in the case of the Reverend Charles Beecher. An important antislavery agitator in his own right, Harriet Beecher Stowe's younger brother came to Florida following the Civil War for the familiar reasons. Accused of heresy by his fellow Congregationalists Up North, he opted for a new beginning. Uplifting the ex-slaves was initially Charles Beecher's great project, but with the reimposition of racist rule Beecher's mission underwent a metamorphosis. Previously, in works such as *The God of the Bible Against Slavery*, Florida had figured as a spiritual wilderness; now increasingly, he portrayed it as consisting of real estate.

In the rapidly approaching twentieth century, Beecher promised, high-speed bullet trains would encircle the state, allowing land transport to compete with Florida's as yet uninvented airships. Thirty years before it happened, Beecher predicted the eradication of malaria and yellow fever. With epidemics banished, he informed the readers of *Semi-Tropical*, Florida would be transformed into an ultramodern paradise where millionaires as well as "the magnates of the general government had semi-tropical winter residences." "Southern Florida," Beecher predicted, "would be the home of a large population of Yankees and Canadians." One interesting feature of this future Florida was the absence of Floridians. Neither black people nor white "countrymen" were mentioned in his article. That was not the only transformation he foresaw. "As a result of the state's growth," one account explains, "Beecher thought that the Everglades would no longer exist."

Florida worked an even more remarkable transformation on Charles Beecher's famous sister, Harriet Beecher Stowe. Prior to taking up Florida as her enthusiasm, Mrs. Stowe had deployed her literary tirelessness on behalf of human freedom. Once installed on a plantation near Jacksonville, the gated-community view took hold. What Mrs. Stowe did not see did not bother her. What she did see gratified her. Florida's transition from abominability to acceptability is summarized in a comment she made after relocating there. "For ourselves," she wrote, "we are getting reconciled to a sort of tumble-down, wild, picnicky kind of life—this general happy-go-luckiness which Florida inculcates." Florida was still "tumble-down" and "wild," but those qualities were now portrayed as alluring rather than repulsive.

Harriet Beecher Stowe was to Florida following the Civil War what Washington Irving was before it, the outsider literary celebrity who replaces reality with myth. Even slavery days glimmered pleasantly in Mrs. Stowe's description of the plantation she and some friends rented near Jacksonville. In those happy bygone times, Mrs. Stowe claimed in an article in *The Atlantic Monthly*, her Florida plantation "had raised quantities of the long-staple cotton, and . . . was said to have had a fine productive orange grove, of which by the bye, not a trace remained." No trace remained because all of the orange trees had been killed, Stowe herself conceded, by "the great frost of 1835." Stowe's plantation had made money once, through smuggling slaves, not from agricultural production. We know this because Stowe had settled on Zephaniah Kingsley's and Madgigine Jai's former plantation, Laurel Grove. Without mentioning their names, Mrs. Stowe evoked "the splendor of the former occupants of the house; how they kept a French cook and an elegant table, and gave superb dinners." She did not inform her readers that the hostess presiding over that "elegant table" was an African ex-slave. Instead, Stowe spun a tale of fabricated gentility where Florida's sweaty human dramas, like its humid geography, dissolved "dreamily into purple mists."

Stowe and her fellow investors had convinced themselves that, by planting some cotton there, they would wind up, like "our predecessors, living in abundance and comfort in a beautiful and highly cultivated place on the St. Johns River." Every cotton "blossom spoke of a golden future" until boll weevils devoured their crop and Stowe and her friends were forced to abandon Laurel Grove. "One [of us] went to editing a paper," she recounted, "another set up a land agency. As for us, we and ours bought an orange grove on the other side of the St. Johns." It was what people did after the initial get-rich-in-Florida scheme failed. They went into PR, or became real estate salesmen, or, like Mrs. Stowe, moved their dreams to another parcel of land where, the promoters claimed, everyone was sure to get rich this time. At Stowe's new location the novelistic improbabilities ramified. The "orange grove on the other side of the St. Johns" was Anna Kingsley's old Mandarin Plantation. It was too far north for citrus not to fail, but Mrs. Stowe did produce a bumper crop of words. In 1873 she published a book called *Palmetto Leaves*. In chapters with titles like "A Flowery January in Florida," it portrayed Florida as Paradise Waiting. The key chapter was entitled "Buying Land in Florida."

It was as though something truly was in the water. White supremacists and Abolitionists; Northerners and Southerners; poets and travel hacks: they drank of Florida and the panegyrics started flowing. There was an underlying reason why so many different kinds of people wound up doing what was PR, even when you called it literature or history. Aside from timber and phosphate Florida had little to sell for money, but what if its millions of acres of empty, unproductive and waterlogged land could be turned into a commodity? The urge to turn worthless acreage into real estate united them all in the great enterprise of making people believe Florida was what it wasn't.

Did it freeze in Florida? Sell it as a place to escape the cold! Was Florida (except for Louisiana) America's rainiest state? Call it the Sunshine State! The most bizarre of the fictions was that Florida was good for your health. Into the twentieth century the greatest factor limiting population growth there wasn't hurricanes or the heat. It was that Florida would kill you. Medically it was the worst of both worlds. Exotic fevers and infections throve there. So did the diseases—ranging from influenza to polio—that afflicted people Up North. This doubly dangerous situation was exacerbated by the refusal of Florida's public officials to spend money on public health. The public paid with their lives. So did the politicians who wouldn't spend the money. As early as 1841 Governor Robert Reid died of yellow fever; as late as 1908 Senator William James Bryan died of typhoid.

Like the idea it never froze there, the proposition that "the conditions necessary to insure life to the consumptive are admirably provided in the climactic resources of the peninsula" became a permanent part of the Florida publicity repertoire. The poet-publicist Sidney Lanier, who fought for slavery during the Civil War, was linked closely with claims that Florida could save you from TB. In 1875 the impoverished, sickly, and romantic Georgia poet, in return for free travel and lodging, produced a book called *Florida: Its Scenery, Climate, and History*. In the pivotal chapter, "For Consumptives," Lanier counseled heavy doses of moonshine as well as sunshine. Once they relocated to Florida's panacean clime, he promised health-seeking migrants, "regular doses of whiskey administration at intervals of from an hour to an hour and a half through each entire day from sleep to sleep [would] effect marvels." Only a year after completing his ode to Florida's salubriousness, Lanier died of the disease he claimed Florida could cure, aged forty-one.

In *Palmetto Leaves*, Mrs. Stowe slapped down one visitor who had been so ill-bred as to describe Florida accurately. "Many," he wrote, "are deceived by the milder climate here; and down they come—to die." In rebuttal Mrs. Stowe blamed the victims. "Some invalids do come here," she conceded, "expose themselves imprudently, and die." Should Florida be blamed because invalids were imprudent? Typhus and polio were among the diseases that hit children hard in Florida. Those who survived were likely to grow up unschooled. "Truly it is a child's Eden," Mrs. Stowe enthused. "All day long we hear their running and racing,—down to the boat-wharves . . . catching crabs, or off after flowers in the woods, with no trouble of hail, sleet, or wet feet." Pity the little ones up north "kept close prisoners" in school-rooms. She next resorted to the perennially favorite tactic of the Florida publicist: evoking the horror of life in the temperate zone. "We cannot better illustrate this," Stowe concluded, "than by two experiences this year. Easter morning we were waked by bird-singing; and it was a most heavenly morning." "Now," she added briskly, "for the North. A friend in Hartford writes, 'I was awaked by the patter of snow and sleet on the window-pane. Not a creature could go out to church, the storm was so severe. . . .'" Who, confronted with the horrors of Connecticut, where the climate impiously conspired to frustrate even the worship of God, would not prefer Florida?

Among those lured to Florida by such publicity was the stu-pendously wealthy Henry Flagler, cofounder of Standard Oil and personification of the triumph of industrial finance in the United States. Flagler first came to Florida in 1877, believing residence there would restore the health of his first wife, Mary Harkness. It didn't; she died, but when his daughter also became seriously ill Flagler ordered her transported to Florida—first by rail to Norfolk, Virginia, then aboard Flagler's yacht, the *Oneida*, for the 850-mile voyage to St. Augustine. There is no way to know how she might have fared had she not been subjected to the ordeal, but when Flagler's yacht anchored in Florida it disembarked a corpse.

Thanks to Flagler Ponce de León finally showed up in St. Augustine —376 years after the historical markers claim he did, in 1889. He arrived by railroad. Henry Flagler, who along with Andrew Jackson and Walt Disney was one of the great Americanizers of Florida, had decided to take his Standard Oil millions and use them to run a railroad down the Atlantic coast to a place where it didn't get cold in winter. Four centuries earlier the seagoing caravel, capable of sailing against the wind, had revolutionized Florida's relations with Europe. Now Flagler's railroad revolutionized its relations with the rest of the United States. Once they got there in their private railroad cars, the superrich would need a stage upon which to flaunt themselves and, coincidentally, eat and sleep, so at St. Augustine Flagler had built to his specifications the most grandiose hotel Florida had ever seen. With its two ornate towers, each 165 feet high, this magnificent edifice looked as though it were transposed stone by stone from haughty Seville. Like the railroad, like the millionaires who arrived on the railroad, it actually was a by-product of the Industrial Revolution. Flagler disguised its steel girders with Spanish-seeming architectural details in order to create an attraction of European-style voluptuousness that the superrich of the belle epoque could not resist.

He named his stupendous caravansary the Ponce de Leon Hotel. The choice made no sense from a Florida perspective. In all the hundreds of years they owned the place the Spaniards had never named anything after Ponce de León, but Flagler did not have a Florida perspective. He was a Yankee multimillionaire; he had in mind a place like the Mediterranean resorts he and his fellow tycoons visited on their yachts—and by then a mythical character bearing Ponce's name, but having very little to do with the actual Ponce de León, had been a fixture of the American boyhood imagination for several generations, thanks to Washington Irving's schoolboy tales. In addition, a craze for fantasy Spanish architecture arrived in Florida with the railroad and Flagler's grand hotel. So why not call it the Ponce de Leon Hotel?

After the Ponce de Leon Hotel opened, people in St. Augustine started celebrating Ponce de León Day each April. For a time vestiges of historical accuracy endured. The Indians fled when they espied Ponce de León's approach, as they had during his first landings back in 1513. Then, starting in 1909, the Indians—as acted out by locals wearing Wild West costumes—came whooping and hollering at the Spaniards like actors in a Tom Mix movie. They were preparing to sacrifice the captured Spaniards to the sun god, just like in the movies, until Ponce's diplomatic overtures turned them into friends. As late as 1926 you still found no Fountain of Youth in St. Augustine, but gradually the idea took hold that the historical Ponce de León and the tourist attraction "Old St. Augustine" were somehow linked. Soon streets, schools, and real estate schemes all over Florida bore his name; the history books followed suit. Ponce de León had become a major figure not because of what he had done during his lifetime, but because, more than 360 years after his death, an American millionaire decided to name a hotel after him.

As Florida's population grew, fiction masqueraded as fact all over the state. Unaware of Florida's actual history, newcomers confected a mythical Florida that melded the plots of Hollywood westerns with the decor of hotel lobbies. Celebrations of nonexistent historical events helped transform strangers into neighbors. They also gave Florida's newcomers a sense, entirely false, of historical context that made irrationality seem logical and destructive behavior seem, as many a public relations press release would put it, "visionary." They did this by deceiving themselves as to the nature of the land they settled and their place in it. Tampa became the Gulf coast's front-runner in historical fakery. Many people attending Tampa's great civic fete, Gasparilla, imagine it mirrors an actual event—an early raid by the pirate José Gaspar. Gaspar never existed. He, along with Gasparilla, was dreamed up by a society editor of the *Tampa Tribune*, Mary Louise Dodge, and some friends in 1904. Inventing Gaspar gave Tampa a "history" overnight. It also gave local movers and shakers the chance to ape the social distinctions of older cities. Now that Tampa had its own version of New Orleans's pirate Jean Lafitte, it could hold an annual fiesta modeled on New Orleans's Mardi Gras.

The fact that Gaspar never existed did not stop a subsidiary myth from gaining currency, that Gaspar buried a treasure somewhere in the vicinity of Tampa Bay. Searching for the nonexistent pirate's nonexistent treasure, fortune hunters have "bulldozed Indian mounds, damaged valuable wetlands and destroyed mangroves in their determination to find silver and gold," writes Kevin McCarthy in his book on Florida buccaneers. As late as 1992 fortune hunters were arrested for desecrating legitimate historical sites in the hunt for José Gaspar's "treasure." It was a paradigmatic Florida event: destroying the state's actual history in the attempt to profit from its illusory past.

By the time his hotel opened Flagler had dispensed a fortune. What he had to show for it was personal tragedy and a hotel that never would turn a profit. That was only the beginning of it. Flagler's second wife would go mad in Florida. His only son, appalled by his father's extravagance and unwillingness to listen, would flee Florida; they would never speak again. Someone with a less grandiose idea of Florida's, and his own, possibilities might have been deterred, not Henry Flagler. "I have found a veritable paradise," he announced upon launching his next great spate of Florida expenditures. Fever and cold had quickly defeated Flagler's hope that St. Augustine was safe enough and south enough to be America's Paradise. But then, following a shipwreck, a cargo of coconuts from Cuba washed ashore south of the Jupiter lighthouse, where they sprouted. Palms, in contradistinction to scrubby palmettos, are not native to Florida; like the feral pigs, they are descendants of imports. The then-unusual sight of those palms flourishing on that seashore aroused in Henry Flagler a vision of Palm Beach as a frost-free winter playground for the world's richest people, a combination Monte Carlo and Tahiti. No such Florida existed, so Flagler set out to create one.

First he uprooted the mangroves; stately palms, he decreed, must be everywhere. Until then, even the rich in southern Florida lived in wooden houses built on stilts to raise them above the damp. He and his Palm Beach neighbors, Flagler decided, would live in marble palaces. Palm Beach was exclusively for the rich. To contain the workers and servants necessary to operate his Paradise Flagler constructed the town of West Palm Beach, which served as his new railhead and freight depot. Until then Henry Flagler, though enormously rich, had been outshone by his partner in conquest, John D. Rockefeller. In Florida Flagler no longer played de Soto to Rockefeller's Pizarro; he transformed himself into numero uno. In order to do that, he had stopped producing wealth and started consuming it on a gargantuan scale. All by itself Whitehall, Flagler's Palm Beach palace, would cost more than $4 million.

By the winter of 1895 Flagler, using his own money, had pushed his Florida East Coast Railroad more than three hundred miles down Florida's Atlantic coast. It was tremendous fun, playing railroads with Florida, but then, as it inevitably does, Arctic air surged south, once again undoing his dream of a frost-free Paradise. His third and latest wife was shivering in her furs when a bouquet of fresh orange blossoms arrived. Unlike the ones in Palm Beach, these orange blossoms weren't dead from the frost. A wealthy widow named Julia Tuttle had sent them from some property she owned seventy miles farther down the coast. The orange blossoms were only one part of the presentation Tuttle had prepared; it also included photographs, newspaper clippings, and weather records.

Like Flagler, Julia Tuttle had come to Florida to transcend death and reinvent herself, after her father and husband, both multi-millionaires, died. Flagler's dream was to build a railroad to a place where the thermometer never, ever, dipped below thirty-two degrees Fahrenheit. Tuttle dreamed of creating a Florida metropolis to rival their mutual home town, Cleveland. No roads or railroads reached her lands, so she arrived by barge, carrying tons of possessions, including two milk cows. Tuttle's dream of turning her scrubland into a city depended on finding a way to connect it to the outside world, hence her courtship of Flagler. Her ploy worked. Within a year his railroad would start turning Tuttle's land into the instant metropolis of Miami. At least that's the story. According to the historian of the Florida Department of Environmental Protection, "Flagler already had plans to extend his railroad to Miami. He and Mrs. Flagler set up the orange blossom incident as a PR gimmick."

The cold that helped make Tuttle's dream come true killed off the dreams of countless others. Former U.S. representative Josiah Walls had survived assassination attempts. He prospered even after white racists drove eminent blacks like him from public life, but the Great Freeze of 1895 defeated the pioneer of black enterprise in Florida; he lost everything. That same winter another Florida farmer, a white man named Elias Disney, also had his crops ruined. He fled north, eventually settling in Missouri. There his son Walt

Disney grew up hearing stories of the family's adventures in Florida. In 1963, having decided to build his gargantuan leisure park, Disney narrowed his choice to two sites. He chose Florida over Missouri. Today it's hard to envision America, let alone Florida, without Miami and Disney World. Neither might exist in their present form but for the Great Freeze of 1895.

In 1500 you could have known all it was possible to know about Florida, but that knowledge would not have prepared you for what was about to overtake the place and its people because those changes did not originate in Florida and could not be explained by anything previously happening there. The changes in full flood in Florida by 1900 also might as well have come from outer space. Thanks to the Industrial Revolution, Americans took things that did not exist in Florida—notably iron ore, coal, petroleum, and quality education—and transformed them into the machines, implements and ideas that propel the modern world. As a by-product of this all-encompassing transformation, boys like Flagler who'd grown up reading Washington Irving by candle light became multimillionaires in a world ablaze with electric light. Now that the dollar was mightier than the sword, these titans of industry each summer reversed the voyages of the conquistadors, sailing off to explore, and loot, Europe in their oceangoing yachts. Then, each winter, these plutocrats quested after warmth and luxury in their private railroad cars.

To chart the expansion of the railroads these men built and used is like charting the advance of slavery earlier. It is to map the conquests of a new form of human organization. In this instance too, Florida was at the tail end of events. The transcontinental railroad to California was completed in 1869. The railroad would not span Florida end to end until 1912. Building railroads to California helped America get rich on a continental scale. Copper, silver, lead, and, later, uranium, were all to be found Out West, along with iron ore, oil and coal. In comparison to the Golden West, Florida had nothing to offer but weeds, disease, hurricanes and heat, but once money is made, money cries out to be spent. That was why Florida belatedly started to play its new role in American life and manners. Thanks to Henry Flagler, his rivals in railroad- and resort-building, and their many imitators, Florida became part of the pageant of conspicuous consumption which the economist Thorstein Veblen analyzed (and satirized) in *The Theory of the Leisure Class*.

"Conspicuous consumption of valuable goods," explained Veblen, whose famous treatise was published at the height of the Florida railroad-building craze, "is a means of reputability to the gentleman of leisure." Veblen was to money what Mahan was to sea power; his great insight into what he called the age of "pecuniary emulation" was that a rich man, having consumed a pound of caviar, does not elevate his status further by eating five pounds of it. "As wealth accumulates on his hands, his own unaided effort will not avail to sufficiently put his opulence in evidence," Veblen explained. "The aid of friends and competitors is therefore brought in, by resorting to the giving of valuable presents and expensive feasts and entertainments." Central to Veblen's analysis was the concept of "conspicuous leisure." Since the rich man now has enough wealth to nourish, clothe, and shelter himself for many lifetimes work, in its authentic sense, no longer is necessary. The status associated with successful endeavor nonetheless remains vital, hence the mania among members of the "leisure class" for disturbing their leisure with all sorts of strenuous pursuits. Sailing, hunting, art collecting, travel, golf, sponsoring ever more elaborate costume balls on behalf of ever more bizarre maladies: J. P. Morgan defined the essence of conspicuous leisure when he observed that anyone who needed to know how much it cost to keep a yacht could not afford one.

Flagler's empire cost him more than a thousand yachts, and he was only the most conspicuous of Florida's new consumers. Now that Florida, like oceangoing yachts, had become fashionable, hundreds of rich people took on Florida as their hobby. Towering above all others was a trio of multimillionaires, all named Henry. Henry Bradley Plant (1819–1899) and Henry Shelton Sanford (1823–1891) could have been brothers of Henry Morrison Flagler (1830–1913). Henry Flagler's involvement in oil typified the Industrial Revolution. More than a century before Federal Express started operations, Henry Plant founded his fortune on an express parcel service that guaranteed speedy delivery of what you needed, if you could pay the premium. Plant, like Flagler later, first visited Florida in hopes it would improve his wife's health. In her case, too, the supposed "Soothing and Strengthening Effect of Florida Climate" failed to produce the anticipated result. His wife also died. As in Henry Plant's case, the loss prompted both new romance—he, too, quickly took a second wife—and an opulent self-reinvention.

While Flagler would concentrate his energies on the Atlantic coast, the Gulf coast of Florida became, as his biographers later put it, "Mr. Plant's Hobby." The gaudiest ornament of his empire was the Tampa Bay Hotel. A quarter-mile long and often described as "Moorish," beneath its exotic domes and cupolas the Tampa Bay Hotel was, like the Ponce de Leon Hotel, an industrial product, built of reinforced concrete, with private baths and telephones in every room. Like Flagler, and unlike earlier Yulee-style wannabe Florida tycoons, Plant did not need to trick investors out of their money. He had, for the time being, an unlimited personal supply of the stuff. He used it to buy up bankrupt Confederate railroads, and then spent as much constructing the Port of Tampa, $3 million, as he did on the Tampa Bay Hotel. No sooner were these embellishments in place than the Spanish-American War broke out. As the might and wrath of the United States, which earlier smote Seminoles and Confeder- ates, was unleashed on the remnants of Spain's once-mighty empire, a new epoch—the American Century—was launched: Florida was the launch pad. Tampa's new prominence was signed, sealed, and de- livered when Theodore Roosevelt himself strode into the grandiose lobby of Plant's hotel, on his way to histrionics on the battlefield and the presidency of the United States.

Flagler and Plant personified the new era's fusion of technology and excess. Florida's third Henry—Henry Shelton Sanford—epito- mized its ruthlessness and amorality. All three millionaires had used their wealth and influence to avoid military service during the Civil War; Sanford got himself commissioned a general in the U.S. Army while doing it. Putting an ocean between himself and the bloodshed, "General" Sanford next got himself named U.S. envoy to Belgium. There, as the *New York Times* later observed, he "became well and favorably known to the Belgian King." Exploiting the financial opportunities his U.S. government position provided, Sanford become the financial partner of King Leopold II, whose avaricious mistreatment of his African colonial subjects made him one of Europe's richest and most despised heads of state. It was Sanford who, on the king's behalf, recruited Henry Morton Stanley—the Welsh-born Confederate battle veteran and American journalist—to head off in search of "Dr. Livingston, I presume?"

Leopold's headquarters in the Congo was called Leopoldville. Sanford named the headquarters of his central Florida domain Sanford. They weren't called slaves anymore in either place, but now that the state of Florida leased out its convicts, thousands labored without pay to make it possible for some of America's most privileged people to create the pleasant, comfortable Florida they now required as part of their seasonal migrations across the map of fashion and luxury. Plant would get Teddy Roosevelt, but in 1883 President Chester Alan Arthur checked into Sanford House, his lakeside version of the Tampa Bay Hotel.

The nucleus of Sanford's empire was the territory in central Florida that Joseph Finegan had first grabbed from the Seminoles, then gotten the federal government to restore to him following the Civil War. The former Confederate commander at Olustee had vanquished Chloe Merrick and her orphans, but he was no match for the Yankee "general" who'd spent the Civil War years making money in Belgium. Henry Sanford forced Finegan to sell out for less than $20,000.

Until then, the scrublands of central Florida were considered good for nothing except grazing cattle. Florida's limestone structure made both temperate and tropical commercial agriculture unprofitable, but here as in the Congo Sanford quickly devised new ways of extracting wealth. One of limestone's many avatars is phosphate: immense quantities of it underlie central Florida. Phosphate has two remarkable, indeed paradoxical, qualities. Nothing can grow in it, and nothing can grow without it. In its natural state it is so inert that Florida's phosphate deposits contain perfectly preserved remnants of many of the creatures that millennia ago roamed there—and, before that, swam there while Florida was still ocean bottom. These include the fossilized remains of giant tigers and mastodons—and of enormous sharks whose individual teeth are larger than many fish are today.

Phosphate makes agricultural production impossible in the places where it is found, yet the phosphorous it yields is essential to food production around the world. Until Sanford and other Northern magnates arrived, there was no easy way to extract the phosphorous, and no way at all to get this immensely bulky material out of Florida. Sanford's railroads and Plant's Port of Tampa changed that. In 1880 Florida produced no phosphate, in 1888 just 3,000 tons. By 1898, thanks to the development of diesel and electric-driven extraction devices, nearly 600,000 tons were extracted. The figure was 860,000 tons in 1903, more than a million tons just one year later. Back then it took a year for the phosphate companies to strip fifteen acres. Today it takes a month, and the production figures show it. By 2003, more than 20 million tons of phosphate rock were being ripped out of Florida every year, devastating vast stretches of central Florida. Once the rock is extracted, immense quantities of sulfuric acid are used to refine it. One by-product of Florida phosphate production is a radio-active substance called phosphogypsum. More than a billion tons of it litter the state. Another by-product is a multimillion-dollar public relations campaign portraying the phosphate processors as friends of the environment. Because of its abundance, its accessibility and Florida's traditional absence of corporate regulation, Florida accounts for three-quarters of the phosphorous used for agricultural purposes inside the United States and about one-quarter of the entire world's production. The product, essential for root formation in crops that feed billions of people, is also used by terrorists to make explosives.

The Industrial Revolution also transformed John Gorrie's invention into an economic force reshaping both the land and people's lives. The age of domestic air-conditioning would have to wait until after World War II, but with the development of refrigerated railroad cars it became possible to get Florida oranges to market in edible condition. Yellow fever was spread by mosquitoes. "Orange fever" was spread by newsprint. Starting with "a log cabin and 160 acres of scrub wilderness" in Florida, *Lippincott's Magazine* assured potential investors, everyman could wind up just like Sanford, Plant and Flagler, with "the income of a nabob."

Although Christopher Columbus brought some of Seville's famous sour oranges with him on his second voyage to the New World in 1493, production of the fruit used to make the orange juice we drink today only became significant in Florida toward the end of the nineteenth century, when sweet oranges from China were introduced on a massive scale. There was a reason for the long delay. Citrus does thrive in limestone-rich soil, but as both the Kingsleys and Harriet Beecher Stowe discovered, Florida's freezing temperatures inevitably destroyed citrus groves and the hopes of the growers. The new belief that oranges, when squeezed, produced liquid gold disregarded that reality. In 1894, in a frenzy of production, speculators shipped nearly six million crates of citrus. Then the Great Freeze of 1895 struck, and only 150,000 were shipped. The cold had done to Florida's citrus industry what the U.S. naval blockade thirty years earlier had done to the South's cotton exports.

Orange Fever showed what Yellow Jack had demonstrated in 1889. In Florida the moments of seeming linearity were the aberrations. All three Henrys aimed "to build for all time," as Flagler put it, but even as they and their imitators reshaped Florida, Florida oozed back. One of the first to be undone was Henry Sanford. "With his fortune inextricably mired in Florida," notes one of his biographers, "Sanford had no choice but to continue" pouring good money after bad into the place. He, too, might have remained a rich man, were it not for Florida. Also undone was Julia Tuttle, whose ambitions had ignited south Florida's first great battle between preservationists and developers. The redoubt of the preservationists, led by Commodore Ralph Munroe of the Biscayne Bay Yacht Club, was Coconut Grove. More than a century later, it remains a refuge of foliage and greenery. The developers' lair, as it still is, was the area north of the Miami River. Today that is skyscraper Miami; back then it was Julia Tuttle's landholding. Her successful courtship of Henry Flagler tipped the balance, irrevocably, in favor of the developers. It also led to Julia Tuttle's ruin. In return for extending his railroad to her lands, Tuttle deeded over to Flagler half her holdings, though not in a single block. In what seemed a clever move, Tuttle intermingled their lots, like white and black spaces on a checkerboard. She had not reckoned with Flagler's mania for building, or with bubble economics. The shoddiness of Tuttle's own get-rich-quick construction led to the first disaster when fire swept through the new town. While Tuttle's burnt-out lots lay empty, waiting for demand to catch up with supply, Flagler made sure that never happened. Commodore Munroe could not disguise his gratification. "Flagler continued to build ahead of demand," he wrote. "The result was bitter disappointment for Mrs. Tuttle, whose land remained vacant, weed-grown and little in demand until her death."

As a result of building "ahead of demand," Miami since its inception has been a city of unsold real estate and unfinished "developments." Flagler helped establish another Florida tradition, skimping on public necessities. No embellishment was too lavish for Palm Beach. Shoddiness was the rule "in the service town of West Palm Beach," writes Les Standiford of the permanent inequalities Flagler helped create. In Miami, Flagler's "waste disposal planning, with short-fall pipes pouring tons of raw sewerage into the beautiful Miami river, would create serious health problems within the decade," recounts Gene M. Burnett. Measles and typhoid fever started killing people immediately. Then one day in September 1898 Julia Tuttle complained of a headache. Hours later she was dead at age fifty. A mosquito-borne infection had developed into brain fever, as they called meningitis then. Seven years earlier Julia Tuttle, rich and healthy, had barged her way into pristine wilderness. Now her children had to sell off what remained of her land to pay her debts.

What making cars was for Detroit and drilling for oil was for Texas, throwing your money away turned out to be for Florida—the economic activity that determined its identity and defined its soul. To this day it's what links the Hobe Sound yachtsman and the Ocala retiree in his mobile home. One is squandering, the other eking out money both made somewhere else. Henry Flagler was to the new age of "pecuniary emulation" what Andrew Jackson had been to the wilderness. He personified the latest great tide of events to slop

over into Florida and dissipate itself, but there comes a moment
for all Florida's protagonists when they stand by the water, looking
out, trying to figure out what to do next. Will reason prevail, the
moment asks, or illusion? The winter of 1905 was Henry Flagler's
fateful moment. Extending his railroad south, Flagler had paid no
more attention to Florida's underlying geological structure than the
Spaniards had while searching for gold, yet by accident his railroad
ran straight down that low-lying but vital coastal ridge that protects
most of the peninsula's Atlantic coast from being entirely inundated
by hurricane surge tides. South of Miami the ridge disappears into
the muck of the Everglades. That did not deter Flagler. In 1905 he
announced his most astounding project yet. He would, his public
relations department informed the world, extend his railroad to the
offshore island city of Key West.

Previously railroads had crossed plains, bridged rivers, tun-
neled under mountains. Now what Henry Flagler called his Overseas
Railroad would traverse one of the more storm-tossed corners of
the Atlantic Ocean. By then comparisons to the conquistadors had
become obligatory. "Ponce de León's first visit there in 1513 was
hardly more significant than Flagler's first trip" was the conventional view. That was correct, though not for the reasons usually
given. In both instances that first foray set the stage, years later,
for a final, transcendent act of folly. Ponce's discovery in 1513 was
that Florida wasn't worth colonizing, but then Cortez' conquest of
Mexico, and his own vanity, provoked Ponce to return. The great
project of building the Panama Canal provides the context that, by
1905, made constructing a railroad across 125 miles of open sea seem
so imperative to Henry Flagler. Flagler, by then seventy-five years
old, regarded President Theodore Roosevelt, who at that time was
forty-seven and at the height of his powers, as a vainglorious upstart.
His Overseas Railroad, Flagler convinced himself, would show the
world who was the true visionary.

Concrete capable of hardening in salt water had to come from
as far away as Germany in order to construct Flagler's railroad across
the ocean. Northern oak, harder than Florida pine, was necessary to

support the trestles. Immense quantities of coal also were imported, to run Flagler's giant dredges. Since Florida's educational system did not produce skilled workers, engineers and craftsmen had to be imported as well. Once there they discovered what Jonathan Walker had sixty years earlier. It was the mosquitoes, not the alligators, that drove men mad with desperation and fear. Thousands fled Flagler's work camps. Hundreds died, including the project's chief engineer, before the project was completed. Flagler's publicists, like future historians, emphasized the obstacles he had to overcome while constructing his "Eighth Wonder of the World." They did not mention that the state of Florida gave Flagler eight thousand acres of free land for every mile of railroad he built, even though the mileage, in many cases, served no public purpose and never would. In total Flagler got more than one million acres as a gift from the state. The Florida militia as well as its sheriffs were there to intimidate Flagler's workers on those occasions when they were tempted to strike. Florida had no safety regulations, no workmen's compensation, so Flagler was spared the expenses other employers faced when their decisions cost the lives of hundreds of their workers, as his did. He also paid no taxes. The state of Florida never collected a penny from Flagler; to this day it collects no income tax, not even from the richest of the rich.

The state of Florida also enabled Henry Flagler to change wives as he wished. Following his first wife's death, he had married her nurse, a woman named Ida Alice Shourds. Flagler was quite a catch, but the second Mrs. Flagler soon came to believe a more brilliant matrimonial destiny awaited her. After consulting with spirits summoned via her Ouija board, she announced the tsar of Russia soon would make her his empress. Not since Senator Charles W. Jones ran off to Detroit had a prominent Floridian been so afflicted by romantic delusion. Flagler had the latest Mrs. Flagler confined to an asylum for life, but back then even robber barons married "for better and for worse." Henry Flagler had no way to dispose of his insane spouse legally—until the Florida legislature enacted a special law allowing him to divorce her, and then repealed it so average folk could not avail themselves of its provisions.

His third wife, Mary Lily Kenan, was with him on January 22, 1912, when Henry Flagler culminated his Florida expenditures by traversing the ocean in his private railway car. By now, in the columns of the local press, he had surpassed the conquistadors, become biblical; "the railroad magnate has extended his rod, the sea has been divided," one paper exulted. The telling event had occurred more than two years earlier. In late 1909 Henry Flagler, for the first time ever, went into debt to cover his Florida operations, securing $10 million in financing through bonds issued by J. P. Morgan and Company. The income from his hotels and railroads never covered his costs, nor had sales of the free land the state of Florida gave him provided anything like a rational return on the money he expended. Then, in October 1909, a great hurricane struck the Keys. More than forty miles of track, half of all that had been completed, was swept away. A previous storm in 1906 had killed more than 150 of Flagler's workers. Later hurricanes would inflict much worse damage. The crucial revelation of the 1909 hurricane was that such devastation was periodic, normal, and inevitable, but Henry Flagler did not let the certainty of hurricanes dissuade him. He encumbered his fortune in order to finance the final rush to finish the great project before he died.

His critics called the Key West Extension "Flagler's Folly." That, precisely, was what it turned out to be, a railroad version of those carefully faked Greek temples and exquisitely ruined Gothic chapels the rich loved to erect on their estates. At the heart of Flagler's Folly was the delusion that connecting Key West to peninsular Florida by rail could confer some sort of commercial advantage, but what was there to connect? A railroad running up the Keys and along the Florida coast, after more than five hundred miles of jostling them over bridges, across swamps and through palmetto barrens would carry its cargoes and passengers all the way—to Jacksonville and its ample port and rail depots. Great ports like New York, San Francisco, and New Orleans linked the high seas with inland empires. Plant's Port of Tampa already connected Florida's rail lines with shipping to Latin America. As Flagler refused to see, running his railroad to Key West was pointless.

Flagler had taken his money and, as so many others in Florida did, he had used it to create an attraction. Thanks to Flagler you could attach your private railway car to a train at New York's Pennsylvania Station. At Key West the railroad cars rolled onto an ocean-going ferry, which transported them to Cuba. Artists depicted the Overseas Railroad as a futuresque projectile, rushing its occupants above the waves to the Latin tropics. Its practical benefits proved to be imaginary, too. The transit to Key West was so complicated and dangerous that, even when hurricanes weren't blowing, the train in some places had to crawl along at fifteen miles an hour. Cuba, being an island, provided no route onward to South America. The most numerous passengers arriving in Havana were swine, bound for Cuba's slaughterhouses.

Key West went into decline following the arrival of Flagler's railroad. In less than twenty years, it lost fourteen thousand jobs; both city and county went bankrupt. The hurricane-force irony was that, before dispensing a penny on his Key West Extension, Flagler already had established the future "metropolis of the Southern Seas." Miami, "the city Flagler built," would become everything he incorrectly predicted Key West would be.

As Miami quickly demonstrated, it had a gift for survival. In September 1926 one of the most powerful hurricanes ever recorded lashed Miami. As the immense dome of water advanced over the land, misinformation was the greatest killer. The local newspapers, ever averse to saying anything negative, had avoided using the word "hurricane" in their weather forecasts. The 1926 hurricane was one of those catastrophes that periodically generate pronouncements that Miami is doomed, yet between 1920 and 1930 its population more than tripled. Geology was the underlying reason it survived. Located near the southern extremity of that hard limestone ridge running down Florida's Atlantic coast, Miami in spots was a whole twenty feet above sea level. That was high enough to spare it from total catastrophe when, inevitably, the hurricanes struck. The underlying limestone was capable of supporting the tallest skyscrapers; the Miami River provided the nucleus for what eventually became a major port. Miami, not Key West, was the southernmost point in the United States where it was practical to ship, and transship, large quantities of building materials and consumer goods. It was also the southernmost place where millions of people could conveniently converge not just in winter, but all year round.

It was a different story nine years later, when it was the turn of the railroad Flagler built to be hit. Everything except the exact timing of the Great Labor Day Hurricane of 1935 was predictable yet, as Marjory Stoneman Douglas later recalled, "There was no organized relief" as the storm destroyed Flagler's railroad while killing more than 400 of the 1,000 people on the islands between Key West and Key Largo. Many more would have been killed but for two reasons. Flagler's railroad had led to depopulation, not development, as locals seized the chance to find work elsewhere, and it was a holiday. More than 350 people who would have been in the hurricane's path had gone up to Miami that weekend. Most of those killed were outsiders —not tourists, but "broken-down army veterans, forlorn stragglers from the bonus army that had marched on Washington" who had been sent to work camps in the Keys. Many were swept out to sea; even so, cadavers littered the islands. About 250 veterans were killed; for the locals, too, the impact was devastating. "There were, after all, only about four hundred Key people, closely related and clannish, like Captain John Russell, postmaster at Islamorada, and his seventy-nine kinfolks." Of those seventy-nine Russells, sixty-eight were killed by the storm.

Flagler's railroad, supposedly a lifeline, contributed to the death toll and was also one of the causes of its own destruction. Before it was built storm tides had sloshed freely through the Keys from the Atlantic into the Gulf of Mexico, and back again. That no longer was possible because "the rock embankment of the railroad . . . had dammed up the natural channels into Florida Bay." When the pent-up storm tide finally did burst through these man-made constraints, "the undertows created by the irresistible force of its going out . . . sucked everything away with it: men, wreckage, and the very sand under toppling concrete walls and foundations."

The population statistics rebuke the notion that humans can foresee, let alone determine, what the consequences of their actions will be. They also document a triumph of geographical determinism. Miami had what Key West lacked, the physical attributes to become a metropolis, and the population numbers showed it.

Growth versus Stagnation in South Florida, 1900–2010

	Key West	Miami	Miami Metro
1900	17,114	1,681	—
1930	12,831	110,637	214,830
1960	33,956	291,688	1,497,099
2010	21,500	505,000	5,250,000

Henry Flagler never saw the disasters his hubris engendered. In early 1913 he tripped and fell descending a staircase at Whitehall. A pneumatic door—one of the many mechanical amenities he installed there—propelled the multimillionaire headfirst down the steps. According to the obituary writers, Flagler had done Florida a stupendous favor by dissipating his capital there. "But that any man could have the genius to see of what this wilderness of waterless sand and underbrush was capable and then have the nerve to build a railroad here," a spokesman for J. P. Morgan and Company declared, "is more marvelous than similar development anywhere else in the world." One commentator did get to the nub of the matter. Up North Flagler had been "determined on making money," it was observed, "whereas after he began his developments in Florida he was satisfied to be a money spender." Flagler was Florida's biggest "money spender" to date and so he, better than anyone else, had wound up personifying its fundamental conundrum. While Florida soaked up wealth like a sponge, it remained impossible to squeeze long-term profits out of the place.

In 1994 the *Palm Beach Post*, in keeping with its role as civic promoter, published a book that reflected the continuing insistence on transforming Florida's past into a comfort zone free of moral complications. The title of the book—*Pioneers in Paradise*—fused the Florida myth of paradise with the American myth of the pioneer. Subtitled *West Palm Beach, the First 110 Years*, it fostered the misapprehension that the city had come into existence as a result of independent yeomen hewing out free lives for themselves. Instead of a work camp for convict gangs, the book's cover showed vintage photographs of two adorable little children. One was white, the other black, adding a third falsehood. This was the pretense that, in spite of its long refusal to invest in education, whatever your race, Florida was and always had been a wonderful place to raise your kids.

The Paradise myth also misshapes what people consider culture. The first time I saw that painting in Jacksonville of "Ponce de Leon" lost in the forest clearing, it was at an exhibition called *Florida as Paradise: Five Centuries of Art*. That was the name; the nature the paintings portrayed was something else. Within their gilt frames, they depicted a Florida of bugs, swamps, shipwrecks, and desolation. That did not stop either the curators or the gallerygoers from needing to believe that Florida was a place that, for half a millennium, everyone had agreed was a paradise. At this art exhibit, as in the history books, the duty of the past was to pre-justify the present, in this instance the belief that Florida was just the right location for your next condo, your next vacation, the next chapter of your life. That night a great storm lashed Jacksonville. When I turned on the Eleven O'clock News, the Nice Guy Next Door weatherman was gesturing to a radar image. Where the city should have been was an all-consuming black gyre. He grinned and said: "Well that's the price we pay for living in Paradise."

In Florida no activity is safe from the paradise moniker. *War in Paradise*, its cover copy explains, deals with "the impact of World War II on the Sunshine State." Though the invocations of Paradise began in earnest only during the final third of the nineteenth century, *The Florida Reader* is subtitled *Visions of Paradise, from 1530 to the Present*. The theme of *Paradise Lost* also constantly reworks itself in Florida titles (and subtitles). So we have *Some Kind of Paradise: a Chronicle of Man and the Land in Florida* and *Fifty Feet in Paradise: The Booming of*

Florida. Last Train to Paradise tells the story of Flagler's Key West Extension. *Slow Train to Paradise* recounts "how Dutch investment helped build American railroads." *Cutting Through Paradise* is "a Political History of the Cross-Florida Barge Canal," though the waterway, never finished, actually cut through barrens and swamps. Efforts to protect the environment are equated with *Saving Paradise*, the title of a study of "the Florida Environmental Land and Water Management Act of 1972." Public Television calls its version of *The Florida Story: Struggle for Paradise. Borders of Paradise* is a study of antique maps; *Picketing in Paradise* portrays unionizing efforts in the laundry industry.

As late as 1949 black people continued to be barred from nearby Silver Springs, where generations of (whites-only) tourists had ridden its famous glass-bottom boats. A truly authentic Florida shrine, Silver Springs' wild life consisted of rhesus monkeys, imported to give the place the jungle-safari look its promoters wanted. Six of the original Tarzan movies were filmed at Silver Springs. What made this evocation of an African jungle truly Floridian was that no people of African descent were allowed inside, but as one publicity poster put it, they could "See Silver Springs from . . . PARADISE PARK for Colored People." The irrelevant, bizarrely tasteless and fraudulent use of the term inevitably engenders disdain, disillusion and disenchantment, so we have "Polluted Paradise" and "Evil in Paradise," also "Fool's Paradise: Players, Poseurs, and the Culture of Excess in South Beach." *Paradise Screwed* is a collection of writings by the genially shameless south Florida columnist Carl Hiaasen. Over the decades he has made more money sneering at Florida than most promoters have by claiming Florida is wonderful. Nonetheless Hiaasen has wound up another classic Florida loser. A King Canute of a columnist, he has had no more success turning back the human tide flooding into Florida than Harriet Beecher Stowe had discouraging boll weevils.

The most fitting Paradise-Florida fusion occurred in the title of a movie: *Stranger than Paradise*. Made in 1984 by cult cineast Jim Jarmusch, his grainy, low-budget film recapitulated Florida's modern history in the form of a zonked-out hegira. First the heroine, like many eventual Floridians an immigrant from Eastern Europe, links up with a New York adventurer. In section two of the film they wind up in Cleveland, Ohio, city of Henry Flagler and Julia Tuttle. The climactic section of the film is titled "PARADISE." "Bikinis! Beaches!" the guy enthuses. "They got alligators, too," she remarks. In one memorable shot, Jarmusch immortalizes on film the way the bottoms of doors in cheap Florida motels get all icky from slovenly housekeeping and humidity. How bedraggled the roadside sand looks does not escape his camera as it plays across the stunted, scrubby palmettos, interspersed with the stubs of crushed-out filter-tip cigarettes. By showing the Florida that was there, Jarmusch helped spawn a cinematic genre that would link John Sayles and Wayne Wang with the Coen brothers and Quentin Tarantino.

What the auteur of *Stranger than Paradise* took care to notice had not been lost on The Master. In 1904 Henry James, America's most persnickety as well as its greatest living author, honored Florida by visiting it. James's observation that the St. Johns River was "Byronically foolish," geologically speaking, was right on target, though it came enveloped in so many references to the prolificacy of the foliage and zephyrousness of the air that Mrs. Stowe might have felt flattered. His comments on the "florid local monument" Jacksonville's neo-Confederates had erected were also phrased so as to allow the unwary to imagine he was saying something nice. He let the full venom flow in his private correspondence. "Florida is a fearful fraud," he wrote to a friend once he was safely away "—a ton of dreary jungle and swamp and misery of flat forest monotony to an ounce or two of little coast perching place—a few feet wide between the jungle and the sea."

It didn't matter. Neither Jarmusch's counterculture irony nor James' High Anglican sensibility could dislodge the myth that, in Florida, hype plus swampland equaled wealth and happiness. Even after Boom turned to Bust in their erstwhile paradise, people seldom if ever asked themselves: How did such a notion arise in the first place?

19

SWANEE

While Tuttle, Flagler, and their ilk promoted Paradise, Florida's "solid countermarch" continued full speed. In 1907 Governor Napoleon Bonaparte Broward proposed that every black person be physically evicted from the state. What made his proposal characteristically Floridian was the role he wanted the federal government to play. As with the Seminoles, the American taxpayer was expected to put up the money "to purchase territory, either domestic or foreign . . . and to transport them" there, the U.S. Army to round up, expel, and then "prevent Negroes from migrating back to the United States."

An arms smuggler as well as a racist, Broward personified Florida's piratical insouciance when it came to the rule of law. An indicted felon when elected sheriff of Duval County, Broward made "law and order" his top priority. In the move that got him the biggest headlines, he slapped handcuffs on Gentleman Jim Corbett, but what grounds could there be for his arrest? After Corbett knocked out his opponent in the third round, Broward charged the champ with assault and battery. The future governor initially aimed to get rich as a "wrecker," but now that steam had replaced sail, ships could outrun the wreckers' boats; wireless transmissions allowed ships to call for help. Broward's business was foundering when the Cuban struggle for independence, which the Spanish imagined they had crushed for good after ten years of bitter fighting in 1878, re-erupted in 1895. More than seventy years after John Quincy Adams predicted that, once the U.S. got Florida, the "laws of political as well as of physical gravitation" would cause the island to fall into American hands, the Spanish still clung to Cuba. Spain's generalissimo on the island, Valeriano "Butcher" Weyler, was infamous for his cruelty, but the Spanish soldier with the biggest long-term impact was a recruit named Ángel María Bautista Castro y Argiz who, later returning to Cuba, would father a son named Fidel.

By the time Broward got himself embroiled in Florida politics two wings of the Democratic Party, which had monopolized power since 1877, were vying for control. The "Antis" were against everything, including daylight saving time. The "Straightouts" wanted a better deal for common white folks. On one occasion when the Antis tried to pull a fast one on Broward's Straightouts, white delegates "stood on chairs and roared their approval or condemnation" just as blacks had, back in the day when they had been permitted to participate in Florida politics. In addition to cleansing Florida of Negroes, Governor Broward proposed "punishing any newspaper editor or writer or publisher who deliberately or intentionally writes or publishes an article that is untrue." He also proposed road construction, state-sponsored grade school education, and the creation of a railroad commission (to replace the one Flagler had gotten abolished). The prospect of a Florida rid of Negroes, in which the state dealt sternly with smart-aleck reporters and hoity-toity tycoons, and which had paved roads and public schools, was one to delight its poor white "countrymen." Unfortunately for them Broward's achievements were exclusively rhetorical.

Racism was the reason Broward achieved next to nothing. Proposals to use public money for such things as educating children divided the white vote. Since "dividing the white vote raised the specter of Negro domination," no program of serious reform ever got anywhere. Broward's proposal for a publicly sponsored life insurance program was typical. Praised by outside observers but rejected by the legislature, it was never anything more than an oratorical flourish. Broward's other trademark proposal, in addition to Negro Removal, was to make the Everglades "fit for civilization." In 1906, he fought for an amendment to the 1885 constitution that would have mandated the destruction of Florida's wetlands. The measure was soundly defeated, not out of concern for the environment but out of fear Floridians might have to pay for it. "The treasury will be drained before the Everglades," one editorialist warned. In the meantime fortunes were made and lost speculating on swampland that supposedly was going to be turned into real estate by the proposed drainage programs.

In some ways Napoleon Bonaparte Broward (1857–1910) had so much in common with Ossian Bingley Hart (1821–1874) they might have been father and son. Both were Florida-born governors of Florida, which was still unusual. Both came from families that early settled in the St. Johns basin—and delighted in giving their sons peculiar names. Like Ossian Hart, Napoleon Bonaparte Broward died at age fifty-three following an arduous political campaign, in part because of Florida's lack of public sanitation and medical facilities.

Both Hart and Broward empathized with the downtrodden, but Broward differed from Hart in one all-important way. Hart had proclaimed aloud what generations of white "progressives" never admitted. Progress could come only—and then not surely, and only with difficulty—once Florida reempowered the black voter. So long as Florida's electorate remained exclusively white, Florida would remain corrupt, backward, ignorant, and poor. Broward's failure to transcend—or even appreciate the need for transcending—racism has not stopped him from being accorded a most exalted place in the pantheon of Great Floridians. "Broward's example will never cease to be a challenge and an inspiration," claims one panegyric. Initially, in such laudations, Broward's proposal for racist cleansing was dismissed as an amusing eccentricity. These days his plan for an all-white Florida is completely excluded from accounts of his putative achievements.

Though Broward's priorities were different, his objective was the same as Flagler's, to turn Florida into something it wasn't. Get rid of black folks! Then Florida will be what we want it to be. Since it was no more possible to rid Florida of black people than it was to rid it of swamps, the trajectory of racist expectations was also one of boom and bust. Lynchings, massacres, Ku Klux Klan death squads: whether the violence was community-based or state-sponsored, it failed to make the Negro disappear. White racists coped with the failure of reality to conform to their expectations the same way real estate speculators coped with sinkholes and termite infestations, by taking refuge in an imaginary Florida. In geographical reality, the actual Suwannee River is little more than a blackwater trench flowing out of the Okefenokee Swamp across the narrow neck of north Florida into the Gulf of Mexico. No great plantations have ever been worked there. No porticoed mansions line its banks. The real-life Suwannee is a mere rivulet compared to the Swanee, which in racist mythology became a combination mighty Mississippi, holy Jordan, and blue Danube.

In this case too, it was a Yankee who fabricated a fake version of Florida which posterity found preferable to the truth. The composer was Stephen Collins Foster, a Pennsylvanian who would support the Union during the Civil War. The composer's brother, Morison Foster, later recounted how it happened: "One day in 1851, Stephen came into my office, on the bank of the Monongahela, Pittsburgh, and said to me, 'What is a good name of two syllables for a Southern river?'" When Morison suggested the Pee Dee, a South Carolina stream, his brother said: "Oh, pshaw . . . I won't have that." So, Morison related, "I took down an atlas from the top of my desk and . . . my finger stopped at the 'Swanee,' a little river in Florida emptying into the Gulf of Mexico. 'That's it, that's it exactly,' exclaimed he delighted, as he wrote the name down; and the song was finished, commencing, 'Way Down Upon de Swanee Ribber.'"

Foster never set eyes on the Florida river, but what truly made this hymn of homesick yearning as much a nonsense song as his first great hit, "Oh! Susanna," is that the singer apparently is a freed or escaped slave. Since the song was performed by whites in blackface, the emotion expressed is doubly false. A fake black man expresses his longing to return to the place of his enslavement, which, thanks to a stroke of Foster's pen, is now located in a place where there never were any such plantations. In Florida Foster's fictionalization—like Henry James's condescension—was welcomed as a celebrity endorsement.

The Suwannee's lack of qualifications when it came to serving as a mythic waterway did not stop lightning from striking twice. In 1919 George Gershwin, a young Brooklyn-born Jew, was riding a bus up

Broadway when the melody popped into his head. The lyricist who put the "Swanee" in Gershwin's tune was Irving Caesar (who later wrote "Tea for Two" and lived to be 101). It originally was performed by scantily clad chorus girls, the stage dark except for electric lights flashing from their tap-dancing toes for one of those revues that back then opened and closed faster than hibiscus blossoms.

Gershwin, like Foster, had never set eyes on the Suwannee. Nor had his lyricist. "We had never been south of Fourteenth Street when we wrote 'Swanee,'" Caesar jested decades later. Nearly seventy years earlier Foster's song had soared in popularity as printed sheet music and a piano in the front parlor became American amenities. The success of Gershwin's "Swanee" came hand in hand with mass production of the phonograph and, a little later, the development of commercial radio and talking movies. Al Jolson was the one who made "Swanee" a hit by turning it into one of the first songs ever to sell more than a million records. Gershwin's "Swanee," like Foster's song earlier, was a technological landmark in the commercialization of American popular culture.

While the bons vivants of Palm Beach were tapping their toes to "Swanee," Florida suffered through its worst spate of political terrorism since 1876. As the 1920 presidential election approached, the question—as always—was who would be allowed to vote in Florida and, once they did, whose votes would be counted. World War I had just ended; service overseas had shown black soldiers a world where to be black was considered interesting, not repulsive. Then, in May 1919, Amendment XIX to the U.S. Constitution finally passed Congress giving women the vote. It was possible to believe that Congressman Josiah Walls's "new era" at last was at hand as "African Americans throughout Florida . . . created the first statewide civil rights movement in U.S. history." Racist rule had not destroyed it, only driven "the vibrant interior life of the Florida movement" for human rights underground. Now that the struggle was out into the open again James Weldon Johnson, one of the Florida founders of the NAACP, posed the question the 1920 election would answer: "Have not our weary feet come to the place for which our fathers sighed?"

The answer was No. On this Election Day, as on so many others, black citizens who attempted to vote were terrorized, whipped, castrated, murdered. This latest triumph of political terrorism showed that World War I, like the Civil War, had not changed the violence-based racist nature of Florida's civic culture. It also showed, once again, that only the American government could protect the rights of Americans in Florida and that, once again, it would not be bothered to do that. Instead congressmen exchanged blackface jokes as witnesses attempted to describe what had happened. "The willingness of the U.S. Congress to set aside the Fourteenth and Fifteenth Amendments to the Constitution spelled the final doom of the Florida movement," notes Paul Ortiz in his definitive exhumation of this forgotten tragedy. The electoral repression of 1920 became another of those events that would be expunged from history, and not just in Florida. "American history has completely erased the martyrs of 1920," Ortiz discovered as he researched *Emancipation Betrayed*, his account of *The Hidden History of Black Organizing and White Violence in Florida from Reconstruction to the Bloody Election of 1920.*

Sidney Johnston Catts, governor of Florida at the time these outrages occurred, blamed the victims. Instead of making a fuss when whites murdered African-Americans for trying to vote, the "Cracker Messiah" as he was called, informed the NAACP it should teach black "people not to kill our white officers and disgrace our white women." The problem for Catts was that picking fights with the NAACP wasn't of much use politically. All the candidates for governor were loudly and reliably racist. A different variety of fear- and hate-mongering was required, so Catts introduced anti-Catholicism into Florida politics. Catholics constituted only 3 percent of the population. Many of them were Minorcans, more Floridian than most anyone else, and for generations Florida had elected both Catholics and Jews to public office so long as they supported slavery or white supremacy fervently enough. That didn't stop Catts from first inventing, then pledging to protect Florida from the Negro-Papist conspiracy.

A teetotaler as well as a racist and bigot, Catts—campaigning against Rome and rum, though not rebellion—became the only candidate running on the Prohibitionist ticket ever to get himself elected governor of an American state. The victory of the Panhandle Bible-thumpers was likewise a triumph for the Tampa mafiosi. Prohibition and the rum-running it engendered provided Florida's smugglers their greatest windfall since the Cuban gunrunning of Broward's time. Like smuggling slaves earlier and drug smuggling later, it enriched the pious and impious alike, making Florida's Sunday School pontificators and crime bosses allies in fact, though, to be sure, not in name. Mainstream Florida racists denounced Catts as an extremist. In reality his self-serving coalition of hate and fear—and opportunism—presaged a modern kind of politics in which exploitation of a carefully crafted set of wedge issues can, and frequently does, make the difference between victory and defeat in Florida's free-for-all factional politics.

As the 1920 election showed, the struggle for freedom in Florida never stopped. As the New Year's Day 1923 Rosewood massacre showed, Andrew Jackson's reign of terror also remained an unchanging feature of life. In 1816 white Americans massacred the people at Negro Fort because they were trying to live normal lives. In 1923 whites destroyed the Negro settlement of Rosewood, ten miles inland from Cedar Key, for the same reason. As at Negro Fort, leaders who tried to defend their community were tortured to death. In addition to the violence Florida's latest massacre exemplified the continuing role the cold played in Florida's misfortunes. In his book on the Rosewood massacre, *Like Judgment Day*, Michael D'Orso provides a classic description of how Florida cringes when a hard freeze hits: "A half century later they would remember . . . how frost glistened on the palms and palmettos, how sheets of ice sparkled in the swamp and crystals of rime coated the moss sagging from the branches of the oaks."

At least "the ones who were still alive" did. During that cold snap white Floridians shot, bludgeoned, murdered, lynched and terrorized Rosewood out of existence. Then, also in keeping with the habitual pattern, white folks banished the Rosewood massacre from mind and memory. Decades later, when descendants of the victims tried to piece together what happened, they discovered that, so far as Florida's newspaper, morgues and academic archives were concerned, nothing had happened. Arnett Doctor, whose family was among the victims, at first found the tales of arson, mutilation, and murder hard to believe. "Who," he wondered, "could believe any of this could have happened in the first place without it becoming a matter of record, something that could be looked up at the local library?" But, as Michael D'Orso recounts in his investigation of the Rosewood massacre, "Arnett . . . had gone and searched through every text he could find on Florida history. Nowhere was there a mention of Rosewood. Not a single sentence."

Occasionally someone like Ortiz or D'Orso drew attention to some particular outrage. Otherwise the repression of the truth went hand in hand with the human repression. That made it all the more striking when the fate of Rubin Stacy, a black sharecropper who had lost his farmland, made the front pages. It was 1935, in the depths of the Great Depression. Stacy had gone door to door begging for relief. Annoyed, the white people he solicited called the police. The police handed Stacy over to a Fort Lauderdale lynch mob, who invited reporters to cover the public killing. The killers posed proudly for the photos, which immediately ran on the front pages of Florida's newspapers. It was an open-and-shut case of premeditated murder, but as they grinned at the cameras Stacy's killers knew in advance the state of Florida would never prosecute. They never did, which was why Florida consistently led the nation in lynching.

Impunity for the killers was the keystone of Florida's "system of terror," as Zephaniah Kingsley had called it, but Up North what Governor Catts described as "a concourse of white people taking revenge" was known as a lynch mob—and, as the solons of Florida's tourist and real estate interests pointed out, Florida's tradition of extrajudicial murder was bad for business. Instead of a crime, killing Stacy was regarded as the latest instance of a recurring public relations problem. A member of the Florida state senate, Simon Pierre Robineau, had an idea on how to counter the bad publicity. At his behest the Tallahassee legislature discarded the state's longtime anthem, "Florida, My Florida," and replaced it with Stephen Collins Foster's panegyric to the delights of slavery along the Suwanee.

Written by a clergyman who was also a professor of languages at Florida Agricultural College in Lake City, the lyrics of "Florida, My Florida," the discarded anthem had noted correctly that its shores were washed "by the Gulf and Ocean grand," while also praising "thy phosphate mines." In order to make "Swanee" Florida's state song, its legislators threw out an anthem composed by an actual Floridian that described Florida as it actually was. They did it at the behest of someone, Marjory Stoneman Douglas remembered, who was "as French as anyone you'd meet in Paris." A native of Versailles and graduate of Harvard Law School, Simon Pierre Robineau had practiced law in Lake Forest, Illinois, before moving to Florida and basing his political career on appeals to Confederate nostalgia.

Today the Suwannee Valley does boast one slave owner–style plantation so picture-perfect it could be a transplant from a Hollywood movie. Like many of Florida's other neo-Confederate shrines, this porticoed mansion is maintained at taxpayers' expense. Its official name is the Stephen Foster Folk Culture Center State Park; it more appropriately could be called the Florida Slavery Celebration Center. One of its eye-riveting displays shows rag-clad pickaninnies thrashing about in rhythmic ecstasy, pleased as punch to be slaves in Florida, as they gaze in envyless bug-eyed delight at the white folks' fancy-dress goings-on. As with the adoption of Foster's song as the Florida anthem, the significant detail here is the date. This apparently venerable plantation was constructed in 1954, the same year the U.S. Supreme Court handed down the first of its decisions banning racial segregation. As they habitually did, Florida's politicians had responded to the challenge of changing times by barricading themselves inside a fake past. Attended by Florida's governor, senators, and other civic leaders, the Center's inauguration was the most notable public event to unfold in the area since the Confederate victory memorial at nearby Olustee was dedicated.

20

THE TOTAL TRIUMPH
OF WALTER P. FRASER

The Great Florida Real Estate Bubble of the 1920s was America's version of the Netherlands' Tulip Craze of the 1630s. At the height of the mania, prices for Florida swampland rose by the day. When the bubble burst in 1926 they fell by the hour. This time, too, Florida provided a portent no one noticed. The hysterical rise and panic-stricken collapse of Florida real estate values foreshadowed America's hell-bent rush toward the 1929 Wall Street Crash.

As the Great Depression gripped America, Florida found itself littered with unfinished and unsold Boom-time projects with grandiose and exotic names. Behind many of them stood a "visionary" who, until his wealth evaporated, imagined he could turn Florida into his idea of Paradise. One of most notable was an anti-Semite ex–bicycle repairman named Carl Fisher. Like Julia Tuttle, he was a millionaire from the Midwest, in his case Indiana. Like Henry Flagler, Fisher was on the cusp of a great transformation, in his case America's switch to automobiles. Transforming his bicycle business into America's first automobile dealership, Fisher and his partner Barney Oldfield, creator of the Oldsmobile, founded the Fisher Automobile Company. Then he started the Indianapolis 500.

You could build cars, sell cars, and race them, but until Americans had someplace to drive their cars long-distance, travel would be dominated by the railroads. In 1913, the same year Flagler, Florida's apostle of the railroad, died, Fisher and his fellow promoters inaugurated the Lincoln Highway. America's first coast-to-coast highway, it ran from New York to San Francisco. Once again a revolution in how, and where, Americans traveled followed the pattern: California first, Florida later, but this time there was only a three-year lag. In 1916 Fisher opened the Dixie Highway, leading a caravan of goggled, horn-tooting motorists out of the Midwest all the way down to Miami.

Carl Fisher had launched the Automobile Age and set the stage for the Sunbelt Shift. The moment had come for the immensity of his achievement to be swallowed up in Florida. Fisher's Folly was a vermin-infested swamp on the ocean side of Biscayne Bay. This boggy wilderness, he decided, was going to be to people with automobiles what Palm Beach was to those with private railroad cars. In places Fisher's land was so boggy and Biscayne Bay so shallow it was hard to tell which was which. Turning this to his advantage, he dredged up millions of tons of sand and muck, filling in his land, then creating more new real estate in the form of artificial islands between Miami and what he now proclaimed was Miami Beach. By 1925 Florida real estate prices had become so inflated that Fisher's holdings were valued at $100 million, more than twice what Flagler had spent in all his decades there. Then, after the 1926 hurricane struck, the real estate bubble burst; Fisher's seaside empire collapsed. The 1929 stock market crash finished him off once and for all. Penniless and power-less, he died in 1939 of ailments brought on by alcoholism. By then Florida had laid him low in another way. Miami Beach, intended to be a Gentiles-only Paradise, had become America's premier Jewish resort.

The inventor-entrepreneur Glenn Curtiss was to airplanes what Fisher was to cars. Curtiss developed seaplanes and also planes that could land on aircraft carriers. He pioneered long-distance flying, broke speed records, and trained women pilots. Then, in 1920, Glenn Curtiss decided to go into Florida real estate. It was the age of flappers doing the Charleston on airplane wings, when the "aviatrix" symbol-ized glamour. His first project was the Florida airfield from which Amelia Earhart started her fatal flight around the world. This was also the time when the women of America swooned over Rudolph Valentino, so Curtiss complemented the glamour of aviation with an Arabian Nights–themed real estate development called Opa-locka. After Curtiss in his turn went bankrupt, the U.S. military took over the airfield. Eventually the CIA launched its Bay of Pigs operations against Cuba from there. His slapdash bungalows with minarets turned into one of Miami's first slums.

Florida's weather systems seemed to bear a double grudge against George Merrick. This visionary's vision, forty years before the Cubans arrived, was movie palace Hispanic. The lots he was attempting to sell, inland from Miami, were not even on the water, so he built a boulevard bedecked with banyan trees to lure buyers back toward the Everglades. Merrick called his thoroughfare Coral Way. He named his development Coral Gables though there was no coral there. Ruined by the 1926 hurricane, he relocated to the Keys. There the Labor Day Hurricane of 1935 ruined him for a second time. He was working for the post office when he died in 1942, aged fifty-five.

At the height of the Florida land speculation two Jacksonville journalists, Frank Parker Stockbridge and John Holliday Perry, made a fortune with their book, *Florida in the Making*, a sky's-the-limit cyclopedia of Florida's supposed opportunities. The Great Depression turned their original volume, published in 1926, into the relic of a vanished age, so in 1938 they brought out a new book with a new title. *So This Is Florida* explored the changes that had overtaken Florida since the boom went bust.

Nowhere, they found, was the change more extraordinary than in St. Augustine. In spite of the bad times, they wrote, it had become the scene of "a revolutionary venture in the field of history and science." "Quite the most interesting and quite possibly the most important development of recent years in Florida," Stockbridge and Perry announced, "if not of all time, is the program of historical restoration of St. Augustine." Of all time? It was as though these two hard-nosed newspaper men had been mesmerized by some snake oil salesman. In a way they had been. "The inspiration for this huge project came in the first instance from Mr. Walter B. Fraser, mayor of St. Augustine. Mr. Fraser is manager of the Fountain of Youth Gardens, St. Augustine's most popular tourist resort," they explained.

Walter B. Fraser, not Pedro Menéndez de Avilés, was the founder of the St. Augustine that the millions of tourists still visit every year. Like Mary Louise Dodge, inventor of José Gaspar, Tampa's nonexistent pirate, and Henry R. Schoolcraft, discoverer of the non-existent de Soto trail, Walter B. Fraser is one of those forgotten go-getters who have made Florida what it is. Like his Fountain of Youth, Fraser himself was newly invented, in his case self-invented. In 1926 the future mayor cum "manager of the Fountain of Youth" was still living in rural Georgia. There he held down a job with the local school board in the town of Sylvester. One of nine children of a Methodist preacher, he might have gone on working in the Worth County, Georgia, school system almost into the days of court-ordered desegregation except that, in 1927, Walter Fraser took a vacation.

Only one year earlier, the Georgia preacher's boy might have felt out of place among all those high rollers populating the Ponce de Leon Hotel. What a difference a year made! Real estate agents were so desperate that even someone living on a Georgia school board salary was welcomed like a king. During his visit Fraser made a cash down payment on some land belonging to the estate of a lady named Dr. Luella McConnell, thereby acquiring one of the most storied bits of land in the whole of Florida. Back in 1565 Pedro Menéndez de Avilés and his men had camped on what now became Fraser's property. Later the same ground served as a graveyard for dying Indians who had converted to Christianity. In 1869 James Fenimore Cooper's niece had stumbled on human bones in the course of her moonlit perambulations there. This same parcel of land was also the site of H. H. Williams's failed and abandoned Paradise Grove.

Thanks to Flagler, Ponce de León had finally reached St. Augustine in 1889. Now, thanks to Fraser, the Fountain of Youth would gush there, too. Fraser's inspiration was to transform his moldering graveyard into an attraction celebrating eternal youth, but the property had a serious defect. It abutted a malodorous mud flat that rendered swimming and boating impossible, to say nothing of such activities as discovering Florida. People nonetheless would pay by the millions to visit his fetid property, Fraser foresaw, if he could convince them that this was the very spot where Ponce de León had first discovered Florida, then drunk from the Fountain of Youth. He in turn realized that, in order to do that, all he needed was to foist on the American public a new and entirely fraudulent understanding of

St. Augustine's place in the history of the United States—as well as an equally ersatz versions of the discovery and subsequent settlement of the whole of Florida, North America, and the Western Hemisphere.

A tall tale, but this was Florida: Fraser's first step was to transform the nature of the mud flat in people's minds. Changing its name, he referred to it as a "salt marsh" in his publicity campaign. Whatever you called it, any conquistador stepping ashore there would have sunk up to his breast plate in sodden muck. No problem, Fraser declared. "A study of the early maps and charts and check of land-changes caused by tides and currents," Fraser announced, "indicate that . . . a very different condition prevailed then from what we know today. Sandbars, now vanished," he declared, "blocked the north and south channels" leading from the Atlantic Ocean into what now is St. Augustine, thereby making his place the place where Ponce had landed.

The many authentic maps going back to the Spanish era conclusively demonstrate the opposite: St. Augustine's shoreline had changed hardly at all from what it was hundreds of years ago. To solve that problem, Fraser installed a pyramidal monument inspired by the Washington Monument, only made of limestone, with a plaque on it saying Ponce had landed there. Understanding that the appearance of scholarship was vital to such a hoax, Fraser also paid an "expert" with no known scholarly qualifications the then very large sum of $20,000 to "prove" his tales were true. Though, as one contemporary scholar puts it, this "shallow, poorly researched and error-filled document should have no interest to the serious student of history." Lawson, Edward, *The Discovery of Florida and Its Discoverer Juan Ponce de Leon* keeps showing up in bibliographies—notably in 2012 as various books, pamphlets, and press releases started celebrating the quincentennial of Ponce's supposed discovery.

A generation before the marketing concept of "hidden persuaders" entered the pitchman's vocabulary, Fraser also understood the importance of sex. The cover illustration on one of his (supposedly) well-researched monographs depicted a beautiful white girl—her arms raised invitingly above her head, her nipples shaded a delicate pink. By the standards of the time the image was pornographic— except the young woman was shown cloaked in what seemed to be an enticing though diaphanous veil. Though the girl's seductive image dominated the cover, her image was not actually on the cover. Instead, one perceived her inviting contours through an ovum-shaped aperture on the cover. Upon probing deeper, the purchaser of Fraser's pamphlet found that the diaphanous veil enveloping the pale beauty was actually the spray created by the magic waters of the Fountain of Youth cascading about her delectable silhouette. Also visible, though only after opening the cover, was the image of an elderly white-bearded caballero. This portly gentleman—who in his Ponce de León costume might be some modern-day retiree attending a St. Augustine masquerade ball—bowed from the hips to the nubile female in the Fountain, age paying homage to perpetual youth.

On April 13, 1934, an event occurred that might have brought down a less resourceful charlatan's house of cards. "On that day," Fraser himself later remembered, "a laborer . . . uncovered a skeleton. Further diggings discovered others." Before he was finished "over one hundred skeletons were uncovered." Instead of reburying these human remains speedily, and with respect, Fraser ordered the skeletons stripped of their jewelry and other effects. "These ancient remains were then covered with a preservative," he wrote, and turned into a new exhibit at the Fountain of Youth attraction where "skeletons of infants can be seen lying on adult female skeletons, and were evidently buried with their mother." Also on display were "two skeletons of infants, one [who died] shortly after birth, and the other a babe of a few months," Fraser added, in one of his advertisements.

Nearly a century earlier Dr. Frederick Weedon of St. Augustine, after cutting off Osceola's head, attempted to keep secret what he had done. Fraser, sensing a new public relations opportunity, described what he did next: "Realizing the historical importance of the discovery, Mr. Walter B. Fraser, Manager of the Fountain of Youth Park, notified the Smithsonian Institute in Washington, D.C." His mass exhumation, Fraser claimed, proved "that these people were among the most advanced in culture of North American Indians. Their beautiful ceremonials," he added, on the basis of no evidence other than his own vivid imagination, "suggest those of the great Indian civilizations of Mexico," but these were not the ancient remnants of a pre-Columbian civilization. They dated from the period of Spanish rule. The presence of infant skeletons indicated many had perished in epidemics. As the crucifixes and rosaries Fraser stripped from these human remains proved conclusively, he had been profaning the graves of Catholic, not sun-worshipping Indians.

In 1939 Fraser added American gadgetry to the faked Indian archaeological site he had confected atop a desecrated Spanish cemetery. The Fountain of Youth "radio station is built of 'Tabby,' a construction typical of Spanish Florida," he announced. Fraser told his customers that, for the price of admission, they could see how Florida's history unfolded. That was what they did get to see. His bizarre collage faithfully replicated the process of despoliation which had made Florida what, by then, it had become. A complimentary paper cupful of the immortal elixir was included with the ticket price.

The Fountain of Youth was entirely fake. What many people still do not understand is that Fraser's claims concerning St. Augustine were false too. The Spanish-style tower on what was proclaimed "the oldest house in the United States" dated only to 1888. Second only to the Fountain, St. Augustine's "oldest wooden school house" was Fraser's most enduring invention. Though the little building was claimed to have been used briefly as a schoolhouse in the 1860s, it actually was the home of the Gianopoulos family, survivors of New Smyrna. Built in 1788—twelve years after America declared its independence—it was newer than thousands of more important structures up and down the east coast of the United States. This building, which millions would pay to see, was so unimportant it was not even built of coquina, the stucco-like substance used for serious building in St. Augustine. That very defect, once Fraser passed his magic wand over it, was precisely what made it worth the price of admission. This wasn't just any oldest schoolhouse, he announced. It was the "oldest wooden school house."

It was never history or archaeology—nor concern for St. Augustine's few remaining colonial artifacts—that inspired him. Nor was it any interest in either the historical or mythical personage of Ponce de León. Rather, as Fraser explained to Stockbridge and Perry, it was the grandeur and luxury of Flagler's 1889 resort that inspired him to invent a St. Augustine that never existed. It was, likewise, "the great Ponce de Leon Hotel," Fraser proclaimed, that would inspire and tie "together all the elements constituting the restored and reconstructed historical monument into which archaeologists, engineers and builders began to convert St. Augustine in the Spring of 1937."

It was with the objective of creating a new St. Augustine modeled on an American resort hotel built less than fifty years earlier, they went on to explain, that "archaeologist, architect, engineer, geologist, astronomer, botanist, the student of cartography, physical and human geography, languages, medicine, agriculture, plant ecology, anthropology and paleontology" all would labor together in order to make of "St. Augustine a great laboratory of history, as well as in the fine arts and social democracy." What made his project so epochal, Fraser had convinced them, was that "the pan-scientific method will be used." This was another way of saying that St. Augustine's actual past would be destroyed. "The plan [was] to telescope the centuries," they explained.

One of Historic St. Augustine's most revealing edifices is the "original Ripley's museum opened in 1950." It is housed in "Castle Warden, an 1887 historic landmark," the Believe It or Not website explains. Its Prince Valiant–style gewgaws are made of reinforced concrete. Never a castle, it started out as the vacation home of Standard Oil plutocrat William Grey Warden. It was like living inside a Tiffany lamp shade. A gigantic stained-glass skylight dominated the interior balconies and staircases, the white marble floors and black marble fireplaces. Today its adornments include the shrunken head of what, in a publicity photo, appears to have been an American Indian. This fleshy cranial remain, about the size and shape of a pulpy supermarket lemon, is shown cupped in the palm of the hand of a woman with long, white tapering fingers. Her fingers are tipped with bloodred nail polish. The tiny dour eyes of this former human being stare out into ours from between her fingers, as if playing peek-a-boo.

After the Warden family abandoned it, "'Castle Warden' was owned by Pulitzer Prize Winner Marjorie Kinnan Rawlings," the museum's official history reveals. Rawlings was the author of *The Yearling*, a 1938 novel set in Florida which was made into a Hollywood movie starring Gregory Peck. Rawlings' evocations of poor white folks were what made her writing seem so important for a time. Her tale of a Florida country boy who must kill his pet deer because it eats the family crops, appearing in the depths of the Great Depression, seemed to combine the cosmic exotic themes of Pearl Buck with the gritty Americanisms of John Steinbeck.

Rawlings' initial purpose in relocating to Florida from Washington, D.C., was to make money growing citrus; when her trees died she turned to writing. It was a Florida tradition by then. The composer Frederick Delius was also among those who had gone bust growing oranges and so made art instead. It was while observing the laborers she hired to work her seventy-four-acre plantation that Rawlings got the idea of writing *The Yearling*, which proved to be her only literary triumph. Today Rawlings is to American literature what the objects on display at the Believe It or Not "castle" are to Florida history: an oddity, a curiosity, an irrelevancy that nonetheless reveals a lot if you take the trouble to look.

What went wrong with Florida's momentarily great novelist? In spite of its ostensible realism, Rawlings' novel portrayed a Florida as fake as the Fountain of Youth. There were no "colored people," as they would have been called at the time, in her book, even though black people at the time constituted nearly 40 percent of Florida's population. Her take on whites was deficient too. In real life, Florida's poor white folks didn't subsist on the edge of hunger because they were noble countrymen. They were denied land, opportunity and education because Florida's political and financial oligarchs grabbed everything for themselves. Rawlings' writings seemed to promise that her backwoods yeomen would endure in their rustic Eden as long as Florida's pine barrens and swamps did. In a way, that was how long they did last. For as relentlessly as those barrens and swamps were turned into resort communities and tourist attractions, Rawlings' protagonists were relegated to the trailer parks and "projects" of a new Florida.

Though Rawlings' novel, as Richard Feynman's father would have put it, tells us "absolutely nothing" about the nature of events in Florida, her real-life travails would provide illumination. Rawlings' citrus grove having failed, and with her literary endeavors failing as well, she took in boarders at Castle Warden. Florida's most renowned novelist was making sure the sheets were clean when the latest misfortune struck. Two guests were burned to death as fire swept through Rawlings' hotel. Having served as plutocratic hideaway and tourist firetrap, Castle Warden was ready for its next reinvention—as the Original Ripley's Believe It or Not! Museum. It opened only after millions already had visited Ripley's earlier exhibits in Chicago and New York.

If some deconstructionist doctoral candidate ever wrote a thesis on St. Augustine's Believe It or Not Museum, Rawlings herself would be a prime exhibit. Unlike her fictional characters she was a true Florida protagonist; her literary reputation underwent the same riches-to-rags-to-plastic metamorphosis that Ponce's place in the conquest of the Americas did. Another chapter could be written on that shrunken Indian head cupped in the white woman's beautifully manicured fingers, and its Florida resonances. Though today Osceola's name is vaguely known to many people in Florida, only the tiniest proportion know that he was imprisoned in St. Augustine. No historical marker indicates the house where Dr. Weedon kept his grotesque trophy.

The city of St. Augustine now concedes that not a single building there antedates the "destruction of the city by invading British forces in 1702." War and hurricanes played their role, but an American-style cycle of neglect, abandonment, "development" and "restoration" did the greatest damage. One municipal publication contains the interesting information that, of all the structures still standing when the town passed into the custody of the United States, there remain today only thirty-six buildings able to claim any kind of colonial origin—that is, any remnant dating any further back than 1821. That is fewer such buildings than can be found in dozens of towns in Virginia and the Carolinas that motorists pass without stopping on their way to visit America's "oldest city."

The result of these ceaseless deceptions, as an Ohio college student discovered in 2002, is "A City with Schizophrenia." That year Shauna Henley, then an undergraduate at Miami University in

Oxford, Ohio, spent her summer vacation in St. Augustine. In a few months she discovered all by herself what the tenured notables of the Florida history establishment seemed never to notice: "The entire area and its narrative has been reformulated for the sole purpose of creating a more appealing travel destination." She continued: "Therefore, what visitors find when they come to St. Augustine is a twentieth-century invention of a blended past." On the surface, she observed, "The city has evolved in a way that it seems content to live in unreality."

The problems, she noted, arose when reality intruded. Blacks, for example, started playing a key role in St. Augustine long before the Spanish left, yet there was no place for black people in St. Augustine's fictitious version of itself. As a result it came as a shock, in the 1960s, when Dr. Martin Luther King Jr. arrived in St. Augustine to lead a struggle against racial segregation. White people in St. Augustine were deeply offended that blacks, of all people, should disrupt the genteel Anglo-Hispanic tranquillity of America's "oldest city." The ensuing struggle was especially bitter because, as the Ohio college student pointed out, "the civil rights movement not only disrupted the status quo, but it affected a highly constructed outward image." Black residents had a more vivid way of putting it. "In St. Augustine," the saying went, "the horses could drink water from the fountains; we could not." When black people were finally allowed to integrate St. Augustine's hotels, the owners of one hotel poured acid into the swimming pool.

Fraser, one of the most inventive—and nuttiest—Florida pre-varicators of all time, did more than falsify the past. His "oldest city" was the precursor of the theme parks—and theme communities —of twenty-first-century Florida. It prefigured an age when—in fields ranging from politics to science, in war as well as peace— entertainment value is decisive. Fraser's dream of festively mixing history and real life, complete with "folk-lore, traditions, religious observances, historical plays, pantomimes, pageants, festivals, fiestas and pilgrimages," as he put it, also foreshadowed more responsible efforts, a generation later, to revive historic areas like Quincy Market in Boston and to give new relevance to old public spaces like Union

Station in Washington, D.C. Today Fraser could win backers by pointing out that, in truth, St. Augustine's relics were more atmospheric than historic. Yet that, above all else, was what Fraser felt he needed to conceal, so he kept foisting history-shattering "discoveries" on the public.

The result is a situation rich in conceptual and emotional irony. Visitors are told they are getting a view of America's origins; they actually are observing what developed into a harbinger of its future. It's not that the truth cannot be seen. In 1976 and 1985 excavations by the noted Florida archaeologist Dr. Kathleen Deagan established that: Ponce de León never landed there; no fountain ever flowed there. Several large signs, erected at Dr. Deagan's request, draw the visitors' attention to these realities. For an hour I watched as people walked past the signs without reading them. When I asked one of the guides if every visitor believed Ponce de León had discovered the Fountain of Youth, he answered: "Ninety-five out of a hundred do. The other five tell us Christopher Columbus discovered St. Augustine."

What gets obscured most successfully is Walter P. Fraser's own great importance. Chronologically as well as ethically, Fraser was one of Florida's great transitional figures. He is what links the Confederate war memorials and the mechanical presidents at Disney World. Fraser's "attraction" has endured longer than anything Ponce de León built in Florida. With the passage of time his Fountain of Youth— the one that flows from the city of St. Augustine water mains—has become the single most important artifact in the history of Florida tourism. Better than anyone else, he epitomizes the truth that had molded Florida's past and continues to determine its future, which is that reality there is never a deterrent. Authentic exhibits at those places would show Fraser digging up dead babies, ripping jewelry off skeletons, faking parchments, laying the pipes connecting his Fountain to the municipal water works. Instead Fraser himself has become a victim of the relentless denaturing of Florida's past.

As the Fountain of Youth itself demonstrates, the truth is never unfindable. People like Dr. Deagan are always digging it up, which seldom if ever stops protagonists like Fraser from defeating the truth. They triumph, often, for no more complicated a reason than that people do not like to be reminded of unpleasant things. The Fountain's greatest revelation to be found there is that Fraser's triumph over the truth was not his alone. With the complicity of the paying public, the migrant from Georgia's peanut capital stole the meaning of Florida's history. He was so adept, and they were so complaisant, that St. Augustine—and Florida—have never regained possession of their stolen goods.

During the decades when Walter P. Fraser was turning the debris of Florida's past into a mock-up of its future, Florida did produce one public figure who, like Ossian Hart in the previous century, transcended his situation. A Southerner by birth, breeding, and heritage, Senator and later Representative Claude Pepper (1900–1989) was born in a sharecropper's shack outside Dudleyville, Alabama. He worked in a steel mill near Birmingham before making it all the way to Harvard Law School. Alabama didn't have much to offer a big-dreaming young law graduate back then, so in 1925 Pepper set up shop in Florida and within four years got himself elected to the Tallahassee legislature. Then in 1936 Florida in the form of Claude Pepper chose the most independent-minded U.S. senator it would ever have. No one personified the New Deal's hopes and opportunities better than Florida's Senator Pepper did. Other politicians supported particular policies. He was living proof of the difference a new deal could make in a person's life.

Pepper strongly supported the federal programs—ranging from the Civilian Conservation Corps to the WPA—that directly helped poor and struggling Floridians survive the Great Depression. He warned of the dangers of isolationism long before the attack on Pearl Harbor, but by 1950, when he sought a third Senate term, the Cold War had erupted and during a wartime mission to Moscow Pepper had publicly praised the Communist dictator, Joseph Stalin. Pepper's nemesis was a New Jersey–born sophisticate named George Armistead Smathers. Born in Atlantic City, Smathers was the son of a federal judge. His uncle represented New Jersey in the U.S. Senate. As Florida's beaches supplanted the Jersey Shore, Smathers' family relocated to Miami; there he developed into a lifelong Big Man on Campus. President of the student body and of his fraternity at the

University of Florida, he captained the varsity basketball team before joining the Marines during World War II.

In the 1946 congressional elections Smathers—like John F. Kennedy and Richard M. Nixon—became one of the first young veterans of World War II to be elected to the U.S. House of Representatives. Nicknamed "Gorgeous George," Smathers the congressman from fast-living Miami became close friends with John F. Kennedy, the fast-living congressman from Boston. The two never let such issues as voting rights and racial segregation disrupt their shared passion for sexual adventure. "Together or singly, they were wolves on the prowl," the TV anchorman Roger Mudd recalled, "always able to find or attract gorgeous prey." Many of their conquests took place on yachts while Kennedy was vacationing at the family estate in Florida. Mudd remembered "squinting through binoculars to find out who was coming and going but always having our view blocked by a Secret Service boat just as another long-legged Palm Beach beauty climbed aboard."

In 1950 Smathers sought election to the U.S. Senate. The ensuing confrontation with Pepper was a classic Florida slugfest, down to the fact that its most celebrated incident was entirely fictional. Crisscrossing backwoods Florida, the story goes, the Yankee Smathers warned rural white folks to beware of the un-Floridian depravities personified by elitist Claude Pepper (who truly was a son of the South). In its April 17, 1950, edition, *Time* magazine, playing the Washington Irving role, provided the standard version of what never happened. "Smathers," *Time* related, "had a little speech for cracker voters [which] went like this: 'Are you aware that Claude Pepper is known all over Washington as a shameless extrovert? Not only that, but this man is reliably reported to practice nepotism with his sister-in-law, and he has a sister who was once a thespian in wicked New York.'"

This "yarn," as *Time* described it, was to twentieth-century Florida politics what the Parable of the Boxes had been a hundred years earlier—the lie that revealed many truths. Though Smathers never gave any such speech, his campaign was based on contempt for the electorate and exploitation of its ignorance. The magazine also got it right when it observed that "Smathers was capable of going to any length in campaigning." "I don't travel under the Crimson banner of Harvard," *Time* quoted Smathers as declaiming. "I was never a classmate of Alger Hiss." Smathers made the Confederacy as well as anticommunism his cause. At the opening rally of his campaign, the *Miami Herald* reported, "Rebel yells resonated through the Orlando Coliseum and spectators draped themselves in Confederate battle flags." Resorting to techniques that both prefigured the disruption of the presidential recount in 2000 and harked back to the terror tactics of 1876, the "Smathers Sergeants" were sent to polling places "to keep order on election day and make up a permanent anti-Communist force." The real purpose, Pepper alleged, was "to keep newly qualified Negroes from voting."

In the Senate Pepper had fought for programs that benefited the people of Florida even more than they did those in most other states. With the support of congressional leaders like Pepper, the United States and its Allies had vanquished the Nazis in Europe; then, almost single-handedly, the United States had defeated the Japanese in the Pacific. To repudiate Claude Pepper was to repudiate the politics that had enabled the United States to go from despair to affluence, from isolationism to world power. In 1950 that is what Florida's voters did. The revelation of the times was how the rest of the country reacted. Smathers' hate- and fear-based campaign was considered amusing. "Fast-talking George Smathers," *Time* chuckled, "had learned how to pour salt in Pepper's old wounds." What was true in Florida turned out to be true across America in the general election the following November. From Pennsylvania and Maryland to Utah and Idaho, Smathers-like challengers defeated Pepper-like incumbents. Nowhere was the triumph of smear tactics more consequential than in California. There Richard Nixon, like Smathers, denounced his opponent as a crypto-Communist un-American, and coasted to victory.

Debonair while partying in Palm Beach, in Congress Smathers was as stubborn as a Gadsden County mule in his support for white supremacy. In 1964 he voted against the first civil rights act to be passed by Congress since 1868. He did offer to post bail for the Reverend Martin Luther King Jr., though only on condition that the future Nobel Prize laureate leave Florida and never return. Then, starting in 1968, George Smathers reinvented himself. Quitting the Senate, he became a multimillionaire entrepreneur whose lobbying firm sold contacts for money. Smathers had fixed up Kennedy with complaisant ladies; he also introduced Richard Nixon to Charles "Bebe" Rebozo. Smathers' friendship with the disgraced president became financially as well as politically profitable when he sold his Key Biscayne mansion to his great friend Nixon. Not since David Levy Yulee had political amorality taken finer Florida form.

Politicians like Pepper and Smathers got more attention, but Charley Johns, governor from to 1953 to 1955, demonstrated how power continued to be won and wielded in Florida, whoever was in office. For one thing, Johns was a governor no one elected. When they wrote the 1885 state constitution, Florida's neo-Confederates did away with the office of lieutenant governor. Upon the incapacity of a sitting governor, it was provided, the president of the state Senate, almost certain to be a white supremacist from rural north Florida, would become governor. That is what happened in 1953 when the elected governor was incapacitated after less than two months in office, and state Senator Charley Johns, the political boss of tiny Bradford County, which even today has less than seven thousand people, became Florida's chief magistrate. Governor Johns' signature innovation was the portable electric chair. It moved around Florida, along with its own electric generator, in a special truck. Though the device tended to cook rather than kill those strapped into it, Johns proclaimed it a vital weapon in his war against crime and immorality.

Before, during, and after his spell as governor, Johns was deeply preoccupied by what he denounced as the Homosexual-Communist-Negro threat to Florida. Johns struck his most notorious blow against the forces of ideological-sexual nonconformity after returning to his old power base in the state legislature. The Johns Commission Report "Homosexuality and Citizenship in Florida," was the product of eight years of taxpayer-funded probing into Floridians' private lives. When finally published in 1964, the "Purple Pamphlet," as everyone called it, became a collector's item in the dirty book stores

362 Finding Florida

of New York City's Times Square thanks to its explicit photographic depictions of the Homosexual Threat. To those summoned to room 202 in Gainesville's Thomas Hotel, places such as the commission's "interrogation suite," Johns' inquisition was no joke. With the help of those they blackmailed, Johns' investigators infiltrated such haunts as Burger House in Gainesville. A "Confidential Report" revealed the results of these field trips, which was that there were places in Florida where homosexuals congregated.

More than 130 years earlier the Nucleus had turned the government of Florida into its money machine and political bludgeon. Johns and his clique, the latest of the corrupt cabals to dominate Tallahassee, were known as the Pork Chop Gang. While the labels occasionally changed, the source of power and lucre never did. Into the 1960s Florida's antidemocratic political system remained rooted in its 1885 constitution, under which the members of the legislature represented alligators, sink holes—and vested interests—not people. The consequence was fiscal as well as political injustice. Every year people in places like Miami and Tampa sent millions in tax revenues to Tallahassee. In return the legislature thwarted efforts to finance education and rejected pleas for hurricane relief. As always equality was invoked to enforce inequality. The Pork Chop Gang ordained that every one of Florida's sixty-nine counties receive an equal share of the state's budget. "As a result," the legal historian Stephen H. Wainscott notes, "Dade (Miami) got twenty cents per person, while tiny Liberty County got sixty-one dollars per person."

Because population growth was so much greater in peninsular Florida the magnitude of the injustice was constantly expanding. By 1960 Pinellas County (county seat: Clearwater) had 374,665 people. Hillsborough (Tampa) had 397,788 people. Broward (Fort Lauderdale) had a population of 333,946. The 1,106,399 people in those three counties had fewer representatives in the state legislature than a handful of north Florida counties with a combined population of less than 30,000 people. According to the 1960 U.S. census, Liberty County, site of the Negro Fort Massacre, had 2,868 inhabitants. Dade County (Miami) had 935,047 inhabitants, 326 times as many people. In Tallahassee that counted for nothing; "12.3% of the population could elect a majority in the state senate and 14.7% could do the same in the lower house," notes Seth A. Weitz, in his unpublished study, *Political Immorality in Florida*. The Pork Choppers "implemented institutional barriers which virtually left Florida's political system disconnected from the profound changes engulfing the state," America, and the world. So disconnected were Johns and his allies that they were still blocking attempts to reapportion the legislature on March 2, 1966. That day the federal district court ruled Florida's electoral districts were so unjustly skewed that they could not be used in the upcoming primary election, scheduled to be held less than two months later.

No one called it Reconstruction, but starting in 1962 the U.S. Supreme Court finally did what it had failed to do back in 1877 when the neo-Confederates seized power. It ruled that travesties of democracy like the one in Florida were unconstitutional. "Legislators represent people, not trees or acres," decreed Chief Justice Earl Warren. As at ease in their Tallahassee lair as their Confederate precursors had been during the final days of the Civil War, the Pork Chop Gang might have gone on stymying reform indefinitely, but now, under federal court order, officials in Tallahassee finally were compelled to redraw the political map of Florida so that its election districts somewhat corresponded to the state's actual distribution of population. Though the courts soon ordered still further changes, the results were momentous.

Until then Charley Johns personified a Florida system that, except for a brief period following the Civil War, had thwarted democracy for 140 years. Now he became an example of what could happen when the federal government protected the rights of U.S. citizens. The reapportioned legislative district Johns now sought to represent had twenty-three counties in it and some three hundred thousand people. Most of those voting in the May 1966 primary were Southern-born whites, but in spite of "the fact that Johns carried 15 of the 23 counties in his district," he was denied renomination by the paper-thin margin of 50.1 percent to 49.9 percent. People with an eye for poetic justice noted the votes to oust Johns had come from "Alachua County, where the Johns

Committee's witch hunts had terrorized the University of Florida community a decade earlier."

Florida finally was rid of ex-governor Johns for the same reason that, back in 1865, it was rid of Governor Milton. At long last the government of the United States had exercised its sovereignty, and taken steps to remedy Florida's fetid situation.

21

LOCATION, LOCATION, LOCATION

In October 1957 the Soviets launched *Sputnik*, the first man-made earth satellite. The Soviet success was a critical turning point for Florida as well as the American psyche, but that was only the latest far-flung event to have an enormous impact. In July 1955, on the other side of North America, fireworks filled the sky in Anaheim, California, as Disneyland was inaugurated. Florida would be the launchpad for America's come-from-beyond lunar triumph over communism, but the exurban population explosion Disney helped unleash would have effects outlasting the Cold War. Disney World, his even bigger theme park in Florida, would attract hundreds of millions of visitors. Tens of millions would settle in Florida, transforming it from a demographic backwater into the crucible of the changes reshaping America.

Florida's north-south geography continued to determine its destiny, though with a difference. Previously change had come predominantly from one direction at a time, either north or south. Now it came simultaneously from both north and south as technological innovation introduced by outsiders once again revolutionized Florida's place in the world. One result was that Florida, so long a backwater, once again found itself at the center of world events. The 1962 Cuban Missile Crisis replicated the clash of superpower ambitions that had occurred in Florida in 1565, but the main protagonists of the new era were individual human beings, surging into Florida by a multitude of paths, propelled by an infinity of motives. Over the coming decades, events would show, people had more power to change the world than nations and ideologies. One reason people made such a big difference was that there were so many more of them. A population explosion in Latin America was one of the events propelling change in Florida, but however exotic Florida seemed to become, the most numerous newcomers remained North American: Midwesterners fleeing the Snowbelt, refugees from the Northeast whose idea of Paradise previously had been the Jersey Shore. Millions of Canadians would come too, just as Reverend Charles Beecher had predicted. By 2010 more than three million Canadians—nearly 10 percent of that country's entire population—were visiting Florida each winter.

The nature of the times had changed. As for the names, it was like the parable of the blind men and the elephant. Terms like "post-industrial," "postmodern," and "globalization"—along with "suburbanization" and "Sunbelt Shift"—proliferated. Whatever you called it, people were too mobile now to be contained within one nation, their movements limited to one direction. When it came to empowering people, most important were the automobile and the airplane. Americans whose parents had been tied to farms or factory jobs now could jump into their cars and drive to Florida. Latin Americans whose parents had never seen airplanes now could fly to Florida. Even when they had to get there on inner tubes, Florida was just ninety miles off Cuba's shores, the rest of the Caribbean not much farther away. As technology transformed lives everywhere, India, Eastern Europe, West Africa and the Mideast also would draw closer to Florida—closer than they had been since the Age of Discovery.

New Year's Day 1959 is a good date to mark the moment when Florida's future became bidirectional. The night before, on New Year's Eve, Batista fled Cuba while revelers enjoyed the fabled excesses of the Havana nightlife for the last time. Fidel Castro would be the latest conquistador to bring about major change in Florida—Florida, not Cuba. Miami was the place where Castro touched off a real revolution, as the failures of his regime sent wave after wave of Cubans fleeing in Florida's direction. Nothing so epitomized the failure of violent revolution in Latin America as Miami's emergence as *Mistress of the Hemisphere*, as one study of its growing importance felicitously put it. America's own shortcomings also would be on full display. The United States, events in Florida would show, could send a man to the moon, but not cope rationally with a regime it disliked on an adjacent island. It could make an amusement park the center-piece of a civilization. It could not make its voting machines work.

Centuries earlier Floridians had pursued their lives obliviously, cracking open oysters atop their middens as the first white-winged bird-ships from Europe dropped their iron anchors. Now, equally oblivious, they puttered around on their powerboats and did dishes in their trailer parks as American rockets soared into outer space and Soviet ships carrying rocket launchers sailed down the coast. The Pork Chop Gang, Timicuan chieftains to this new time, had not real-ized their system was now archaic, but even if you did understand that something transformational was happening, how to make sense of it? Exactly one hundred years earlier the Frenchman Jules Verne had shown why the eyes (and TV cameras) of the world were destined to focus on Florida. In 1865 Verne predicted Americans would go *From the Earth to the Moon* and when they did go, he foresaw, it would be in a "projectile-vehicle" launched from Florida.

Jules Verne was one of those Florida visionaries who never set eyes on the place. Unlike those who brought their fantasies with them, and tried to make Florida conform to them once they got there, he observed Florida from a distance, with detachment. Writing at the exact moment Americans were killing each other at Olustee, he recognized Florida possessed two crucial advantages so far as future space travel was concerned. First, it was located inside the United States. Like his fellow Frenchman, Alexis de Tocqueville, who had written *Democracy in America* thirty years earlier, Verne foresaw that the United States was going to be one of the most powerful nations ever. He took it for granted that, having crushed the Confederacy, the United States then would go on to become rich, inventive, and powerful enough to undertake the risks and costs of lunar explora-tion. He also understood the importance of human nature, including that variant of it called American nationalism. Verne's Americans don't send an expedition *From the Earth to the Moon* because they love science or lust for adventure. They shoot a big bullet into outer space because, now that the Civil War has ended, they can't shoot at each other anymore.

Florida was the part of the continental United States closest to the equator—and when launching a rocket latitude is crucial because escape velocity from earth's gravitational pull diminishes the closer the launch site is to the equator. Readers to this day marvel at Verne's gift for the fantastic; his respect for the laws of physics was what made his prognostications so prescient. As future events demonstrated, the uses to which Florida's equatorial tilt could be put were not limited to space travel. In activities ranging from organizing Caribbean cruises in the age of jumbo jets to laundering drug money in a globalized economy, Florida's combination of tropical access and U.S. location made it a place of many different possibilities, where many different people and activities converged, for many different reasons.

The other renowned fantasist who realistically assessed Florida's possibilities was Walt Disney. He spent Friday, November 22, 1963, the day President Kennedy was killed, taking a detached view of Florida. Ordinarily Disney just being there might have unleashed a spate of real estate speculation. On this traumatic day no one noticed as he overflew a wasteland southwest of Orlando where alligators outnumbered people and the main amusement was shooting wild turkeys. Far from Florida's beaches, this sludgy realm was hot and muggy most of the year, yet periodically got so cold that frost killed what did grow there. This was the wasteland where the Seminoles, normally so self-sufficient, had been reduced to begging for federal handouts.

"That's it," Disney proclaimed, pointing down to the future site of the fantasy land he had decided to create in the midst of this Florida desolation. Who would pay to visit such a place? Disney, foreseeing the future as clearly as Verne had, knew generations of Americans would, once he had worked his marketing magic. By then suburbs were replacing traditional neighborhoods. In this new America of split-levels, deep freezers and TV dinners, Disney understood, the real neighbors were the ones in the sitcoms. Even when it was snowing outside, the real neighborhood was the one that, seen through the TV screen, was located in that safe, seasonless paradise eventually known as the Sunbelt. He also understood that for millions of Americans the problem, increasingly, was not that what people saw on television was unrealistic, false, a fantasy. The problem was that the realities of their lives did not correspond to what they saw on television. Disney understood something else. Thanks to an immense new federal government spending program, Florida was becoming a human catchment zone.

The Dwight D. Eisenhower National System of Interstate and Defense Highways, to use its full official name, had a push as well as a pull effect. As the new expressways cut through big cities and bypassed small towns, they destabilized established urban and industrial areas, destroying their business districts, isolating the people who lived there, creating an incentive for people to relocate elsewhere. The highways themselves transformed getting to Florida from a time-consuming, sometimes dangerous ordeal into a stress-free, high-speed journey. Thanks to the interstates, the speed traps of the Deep South became as obsolete as whites-only water fountains because, in this matter, too, the federal government finally took a hand.

The expanding interstate highway system funneled people into Florida along converging multilane thoroughfares: I-95 ran down the Atlantic coast, channeling traffic from the most densely populated parts of North America straight into Florida. Interstate 75 funneled people out of the Midwest and Upper South, while I-10 carried them from the Mississippi valley across the Panhandle into peninsular Florida. Near the Olustee battlefield I-75 and I-10 converged in the shape of the giant X on the Confederate battle flag. North of Cape Canaveral I-4, splitting off from I-95, also channeled people into central Florida. In a few decades, Disney foresaw, these new pathways would channel millions more people into Florida than previously had arrived there during the whole of human existence, but with a difference. These new migration paths flowed into Florida's empty middle, not just down the coasts. Right in the middle of that middle was the territory Disney selected.

As usual the changes transforming America had overtaken California first. While Miami briefly captured America's imagination,

Hollywood during the 1920s permanently enthroned itself as the manufacturing capital of America's dreams. During the Dust Bowl 1930s and again during World War II, when many war industries relocated there, California kept on booming because it offered what Florida didn't, the chance to make money, not just spend it. Like countless Midwesterners Walt Disney as a young man went west. There, in southern California, he turned himself into one of the controlling spirits of the American Century. He did this by monetizing America's most cherished conceptions of itself, while also divorcing the idea of what it meant to be American from nature and making it postliterate. Thanks to Disney America's imagination of itself no longer was confined to schoolbooks and classrooms. It pranced, it danced, it sang to you in movie theaters and on your TV set. Disney recycled the tales of Washington Irving (and many others, including Jules Verne) in ways that continued to make the American past seem a perpetual and pleasant triumph of valor and virtue over everything that got in its way, while at the same time making the actual experience of being an American more and more passive. Disney marketed adventure; what the customers got for their money was freedom from freedom for a while, as Disney preprogrammed your life, and also your understanding of life.

Only after becoming a legend twice over in California, first for his cartoons, then for his theme park, did Disney unleash his organizing genius on Florida. He focused on Florida for the same reason Flagler and de Soto had. His previous triumphs had left him deeply dissatisfied. Because it covered only about three hundred acres, the original Disneyland had been quickly ringed, Disney lamented with "the jungle of signs, lights and fly-by-night operations that have 'fed' on Disneyland's audience." In Florida's boggy, buggy midsection he intended to rectify all that by creating an Adventureland where nothing was left to chance. He would do it by turning *The Hidden Persuaders* Vance Packard analyzed in his 1957 best seller into invisible determinants. First step was to exclude free market forces. On the Magic Kingdom's Main Street every shop would be Disney-owned or -licensed. In every window and on every shelf would be displayed only products Disney authorized. Next came human choice. As Disney and his imagineers organized it, visitors surrendered their freedom before they got out of their cars. Smiling factotums told them where to park; people were not allowed to choose their own parking spaces.

In Disney's world the color of water was controlled. Disney lakes could not be tannin brown, as bodies of water in central Florida naturally were. They must be sparkling blue, so the sinkholes were drained, the sludge removed, liners installed, filtered water pumped into the resulting lagoons. Visitors entering the theme park imagined they were traversing a tropical Paradise. They actually were walking on the landscaped roof of the underground control center from which Disney's operatives, thanks to the crowd-control techniques the Disney organization pioneered, determined where they went, what they did, and how much they spent. Ticket sales revealed what Fraser's Fountain of Youth, in its smaller, tackier way, already had. Vast numbers of the paying public preferred the passive experience these denatured "attractions" provided to the inconvenience of interacting with reality. Today more people visit Disney's Magic Kingdom (some eighteen million annually) than Venice (seventeen million). More pay to see Disney World's Cinderella Castle than take the trouble to visit Versailles and the Parthenon combined.

The expanded horizon of control was reflected in the names. In Florida Disneyland became Disney World, nearly 150 times the size of the original in California. This new world, Disney proclaimed, was founded on "the ideals, the dreams and the hard facts that created America." It certainly was founded on the hard facts that created Florida. Disney's acquisitions continued the tradition of state-sponsored, for-profit land grabs going back through the plutocrats of the Gilded Age to Spanish times. Like Menéndez and Jackson, Disney cleansed the land of all that, and all who, did not conform to his requirements. He then went on, like Flagler, to superimpose his fantasy on the place.

Determined to get his land at below-market prices, Disney and his operatives engaged in a far-ranging conspiracy to make sure sellers had no idea who was buying their property. The Latin-American Development and Management Corporation fostered the false impression that foreign investors were behind the acquisitions. Though he wasn't in the cattle business, Reedy Creek Ranch, Inc. was another Disney front. Once these dummy corporations served their purpose, they and the land they now owned were merged into another wholly owned Disney entity known as the Compass East Corporation. By resorting to such tactics Disney acquired more than forty square miles of land for just over $5 million, or less than $200 an acre. When news broke that Disney was the buyer, some adjacent land changed hands for as much as $75,000 per acre.

"The theme of 'control' would serve as one of the leading factors in most decision-making related to the project," notes one Disney-friendly account, but how to maintain control once Disney's empire had been acquired? As developers going back to Joseph Finegan and Gad Humphreys had discovered, even the most expansive land grants were worthless if government officials had the power to regulate them or if litigants could challenge their validity in court. The solution turned out to be both cartoon-simple and in keeping with Florida tradition: maintain control by barring democracy and turning the courts into your accomplices. Get rid of the rule of law as you celebrate America's hometown values. In Disney's case help also came from the Central Intelligence Agency. Disney's closest contact within the "intelligence community" was the consummate cloak-and-dagger operator, William "Wild Bill" Donovan. As much a legend in the realm of covert operations as Disney was in family entertainment, Donovan was the founder of the CIA's predecessor organization, the Office of Strategic Services. Sometimes called the "Father of the CIA," he was also the founding partner of Donovan, Leisure, Newton & Irvine, a New York law firm whose attorneys included future CIA director William Casey.

Donovan's attorneys provided fake identities for Disney agents; they also set up a secret communications center and orchestrated a disinformation campaign. When word leaked out that someone was buying up all that land, Disney agents spread false reports that the Ford Motor Company was behind the move. Psyops played their role, but in the grander sense every Disney enterprise was an integral part of a self-reinforcing campaign. Disney's movies, cartoons and television shows, long before the term came into use, were infomercials for his theme parks. Those operations in turn reinforced demand for other Disney-themed products and services ranging from lunch boxes to time-shares. Each individual profit center helped produce a cybernetic impact greater than the sum of its parts, namely the belief that what was good for Disney was good for America. When the *Orlando Sentinel* caught wind of Disney's clandestine activities, the newspaper forbade its reporters to investigate for the same reason the *New York Times* had refused to report the CIA's planned invasion of Cuba. To oppose Walt Disney was like revealing government secrets, something no loyal citizen would do.

Disney's principal legal strategist in Florida was a senior CIA operative named Paul Helliwell. Having helped launch the CIA secret war in Indochina, Helliwell relocated to Miami in 1960 in order "to provide business cover for the CIA's Cuban operations." Helliwell had links to organized crime; he also took on Disney as one of his clients. At a secret "seminar" Disney convoked in May 1965, Helliwell came up with the approach that to this day allows the Disney organization to avoid taxation and environmental regulation as well as maintain "control" over its immense Florida holdings. It was the same strategy the CIA pursued in the foreign countries where Helliwell had operated. Set up a puppet government; then use that regime to control what goes on there.

Though no one lived there, Helliwell advised Disney to establish at least two phantom "cities," then use these fake governments to control land use and make sure the public monies the theme park generated stayed in Disney's private hands. Though nothing was grown there, the rest of the land would be classified as "agricultural" so as to avoid commercial taxes on what already was the biggest commercial enterprise ever undertaken in central Florida.

On paper Disney World's "cities" would be regular American home towns—except that their only official residents would be the handful of hand-picked Disney loyalists who periodically "elected" the officials who, in turn, ceded complete control to Disney executives. Meanwhile the hundreds of thousands of people actually living and working in the area would be denied any say in what happened, including the right to vote. It was traditional Florida politics, the same type of gerrymandering that had kept the Pork Chop Gang in control. That was why Disney found himself facing the same problem Florida's white supremacist politicians did. The U.S. Supreme Court's new insistence that elected officials must represent people, not alligators or special interests, applied to out-of-state entertainment moguls and their theme parks as well as Dixiecrats and Florida counties. In order to maintain "control over the overall development," Disney and his advisers quickly realized, "the company would have to find a way to limit the voting power of the private residents" even though, they acknowledged, their efforts "violated the Equal Protection Clause" of the U.S. Constitution.

In Florida, as in most states, laws are enacted under various "titles." In the Florida Statutes, Title XII deals with "Municipalities," Title XIII with "Planning and Development." Title XXXIII is concerned with "Regulation of Trade, Commerce, Investments, and Solicitations." Title XXXVI deals with "Business Organizations." Title XXXIX laws regulate "Commercial Relations." Disney's ambitions encompassed all those titles, but none of them would be used to establish either his theme park or the phantom municipalities it contained. Instead Disney World was established under what the statues of Florida define as "Title XXI, Drainage." As always in Florida drainage was necessary to prepare the ground for construction, but that wasn't why Disney's legal experts chose that tactic. Treating construction of the world's most grandiose amusement park as a drainage project allowed Disney's lawyers to turn Disney World into a "drainage district." Under Florida law such districts, though privately owned, had quasi-governmental powers exempting them from many forms of regulation. No legislation was needed to establish a drainage district; no referendum or public hearings were required. All you had to do was have a friendly Florida judge decree that your land was now a drainage district. Presto!—you truly did possess a Magic Kingdom, independent of both governmental and citizen control.

On March 11, 1966, Disney's dummy corporations, concealing their common ownership and representing themselves as individual landowners, petitioned Florida's Ninth Judicial Circuit, located in

Orlando, to transform their properties into a drainage district. Establishing the district sealed off the land Disney already owned from governmental interference. It also empowered him to seize other people's homes and property or, as the law put it, "to condemn and acquire property outside its boundaries" when uncooperative owners refused to sell. Control of the drainage district also gave Disney the power to disrupt Florida's ecosystem with impunity. If a creek flowing down to the Everglades happened to traverse the theme park, Disney's landscapers now could block its flow, no matter how severe or far-flung the consequences. Damming up these natural waterways allowed Disney to create the artificial lakes that dominate Disney World's landscaping. Since state and county agencies could only regulate streams that having first flowed into, then flowed out of a drainage district, destroying natural waterways also insulated Disney World from environmental accountability. This hydraulic impunity was a template for the jurisdictional immunity Disney also sought, and won, in matters ranging from property taxes to consumer safety.

The drainage district's prior existence, brief and self-serving though it was, also allowed Disney lawyers to purport nothing exceptional was happening when, one year minus one day later, they got the Tallahassee legislature to transform the drainage district into an "improvement" district with quasi-sovereign powers. According to its preamble, this special-interest legislation was merely "AN ACT relating to the establishment, powers and functions of the Reedy Creek Improvement District; changing the name of the Reedy Creek Drainage District . . . to the Reedy Creek Improvement District; setting forth new territorial boundaries of the District." There followed, according to a computer word count, 11,226 words of fine-print legalese, not including indexes and appendices, which effectively placed Disney World above the laws of Florida and, as events would show, beyond the writ of the U.S. Constitution.

Though enacted by the Florida legislature, this crucial piece of legislation, which would reshape central Florida socially and economically and affect the lives of tens of millions of people, was written by teams of Disney lawyers working in New York at the Donovan firm, and in Miami at Helliwell's offices. Disney lawyers in California signed off on the text before it was flown to Tallahassee where, without changing a word, Florida's compliant legislators enacted it into law. "No one thought of reading it," one ex-lawmaker later remarked.

Had Florida's state senators and representatives taken the trouble to read the text they were approving they would have discovered that Disney's lawyers had engineered one of the most notable Florida land grabs of the past two hundred years. They also had obligated Florida's taxpayers to reward them for having done it. As they drew up Reedy Creek's "new territorial boundaries," Disney's lawyers added thousands of acres not originally in the district; they then exempted those additions from future taxation. Not satisfied with that, they also obligated local and state authorities to provide "for re-fund of taxes heretofore levied on lands excluded from the District." This meant that home owners, small businessmen and retirees were now required by law to subsidize Disney World's profits twice over. Local people would have to pay increased taxes to finance the roads, rescue services and other public improvements now that Disney's holdings were exempt from property taxes. Disney also profited directly as tax monies collected on family homes and local businesses were paid directly into Disney's accounts into order to "re-fund . . . taxes heretofore levied on lands excluded from the District" as the Disney-written law required.

The same day it created the improvement district, the state of Florida, enacting additional Disney-written legislation, also created Helliwell's two "cities," both named for the artificial reservoirs Disney engineers created by obstructing the area's natural water flow. When you visit Disney's Magic Kingdom, you are visiting the City of Bay Lake, Florida. The other was the City of Reedy Creek, later renamed the City of Lake Buena Vista. It contains such attractions as Downtown Disney and Disney's Old Key West Resort. The same laws that created them stripped each "city" of its independence by mandating that "the exercise of the powers and duties vested in the city . . . conform to plans, programs, resolutions and other actions adopted or undertaken by the board of supervisors for the District." It then made provision for the cities' actual operations to be controlled "without limitation" by "a central agency," in turn controlled by "the board of supervisors for the District," who were themselves ciphers for Disney corporate control.

Disney's legal experts next did away with representative government altogether, imposing restrictions on civil liberties not seen in Florida since pre-statehood days. The law they wrote required that each candidate for office there "must be the owner, either directly or as a trustee, of real property situated in the City" in order "to be eligible to hold the office of councilman." The same held true for the ex-drainage district's all-powerful board of supervisors. "At all elections of supervisors, each landowner shall be entitled to one (1) vote . . . for every acre of land and for every major fraction of an acre owned by him in the District," the Disney voting law required. This meant that if you owned a thousand acres, you were a thousand times more "equal" than someone who owned only one acre. Even back when most white men, as well as all blacks and women, were denied the vote, those white males who could vote got only one vote each, no matter how much or how little land they owned.

Imposing a property qualification for public office violated the U.S. Constitution. It also reversed nearly a century and a half of fitful progress toward equal rights in Florida. Article One, section 4, of Florida's statehood constitution had proclaimed that "no property qualification for eligibility to office, or for the right of suffrage, shall ever be required in this State." Disney undid that. For the first time since 1845, a person had to own property in order to vote in a Florida municipal election. You did not have to live there, however. As Disney's lawyers arranged it, the governing supervisors could reside in California (if they were Disney executives) or New York (if they were Disney lawyers), or in a foreign country (if they were stationed at one of Disney's overseas theme parks). They did not even have to be U.S. citizens.

As Florida's own Attorney General later put it, the legalistic mumbo-jumbo about drainage was a "mere subterfuge" used to by-pass both democratic process and constitutional rights in order to create a "multi-county, multi-purpose special improvement district with numerous and diverse powers." Among those powers was the unilateral right to generate public revenue for Disney's private use through "the issuance of general obligation and revenue bonds." This power, in effect, to print public money for private profit harkened back to the days when Florida's magnates, using banks instead of drainage districts, also had used the government to generate unearned cash for their private benefit.

In an appeal to the Florida Supreme Court, the state Attorney General pointed out that state-backed drainage bonds were meant to finance water projects beneficial to the public, not subsidize out-of-state corporate profits on magic castles and monorail rides. Adhering to its long-established traditions, the Florida Supreme Court sided with the special interests. Disney's "issuance of public funds for a private purpose" was permissible because, in the court's opinion, once Disney World was up and running "the contemplated benefits of the District will inure to numerous inhabitants of the District." Whatever gave the Florida Supreme Court the idea that Disney World someday would have "numerous inhabitants" who somehow would derive "benefits" from this special-privilege legislation? For more than two years Disney and his surrogates had been orchestrating a disinformation campaign designed to make people believe they were going to create a new city, not just open a theme park.

Walt Disney reiterated his pledge to create a living city with "numerous inhabitants" many times, never more persuasively than in a speech given in Florida on February 2, 1967. The governor and his cabinet came down from Tallahassee. TV crews were in attendance, along with Florida's most eminent civic leaders. Right on schedule, the curtains parted. Walt Disney gave his much beloved, self-deprecating smile, then announced that in Florida he was going to create a new kind of America, not just a theme park. Of course, he reassured his audience, there would be space rides and magic mountains, but "by far the most important part of our Florida project," he pledged, "will be our Experimental Prototype Community of Tomorrow. We'll call it Epcot," Disney informed them.

If Florida, among all the many melodramas of the last five hundred years, could be said to have had only one defining moment, this was it because in this place, at this particular time, the distinction between reality and fantasy—nature and names—vanished entirely. Walt Disney was dead when he made this presentation. A chronic smoker, he had died of lung cancer seven weeks earlier, on December 15, 1966. What defined the moment was that it didn't matter. As the lips of the dead Disney moved, people in the audience murmured their agreement. As his hands gestured, they nodded their approval. It was a Tinker Bell moment. The same Tinker Bell who all these years later you still see in the commercials that day sprinkled on one and all the sparkling dust of credulity as Disney assured them Epcot would be a real live city, not just another make-believe attraction.

A month before he died Disney confirmed it was all a trick. There would "be no landowners, and therefore no voter control," Disney responded, when asked how he planned to maintain control. That wasn't what he told them in Florida. "Everything in Epcot will be dedicated to the happiness of the people who will live, work and play here," he declared. When he finished speaking "from the other side," as Mrs. Flagler might have put it, the applause was at first reverential. Then it grew to a crescendo of belief, trust, and approval. The posthumous Walt Disney, like the mechanical Andrew Jackson in the Hall of the Presidents, had joined Mickey, Donald, and the Sorcerer's Apprentice in that special world where it doesn't matter whether you're real or not; it doesn't matter whether you tell the truth or not. People believe in you anyway.

Epcot never became a city. According to the 2010 Census, the total population of the City of Bay Lake is forty-seven; the population of the City of Lake Buena Vista is ten. "For legal reasons" it had been necessary to project an image of democracy because "only a popularly elected government could exercise planning and zoning authority and gain exemption from land-use laws." That was why "the Disney Co. needed to say that they were building a city." Once those special privileges were safely in hand, Epcot was demoted to a second-tier attraction.

By turning the state of Florida and its statutes into their enablers, Disney and his successors pioneered a business model based on public subsidy of private profit coupled with corporate immunity from the laws, regulations, and taxes imposed on people that now increasingly characterizes the economy of the United States. In the decades since the Reedy Creek District was empowered, "Privatizing Traditional Public Areas of Governance," as Professor Chad E. Emerson calls it, has become a national trend. At the time Disney World was established, the United States had approximately 38,000 traditional "governmental units"—cities, counties, boroughs, townships, and other "general purpose forms of local government," some dating back to colonial times. There were also about 15,000 "special districts," mostly school districts. By 2007, according to the U.S. Bureau of the Census, the balance of governance had shifted. According to the latest enumeration, more than 37,381 "special districts" were spread across the country, many operated for a profit and wielding powers unimaginable in the past. This extra-constitutional "alternative approach to governance" insulates for-profit private entities from regulation and helps them make more money. It also allows private corporations to position themselves outside the realm of democratic accountability, empowering them to misuse their employees and their customers, as well as the environment and their investors' capital, with impunity. The advantages don't necessarily stop there. In a lot of cases, malefactors then get bailed out by the same government whose taxes they never paid and whose regulations they never obeyed.

Over the decades Disney World has showed that, once tasted, partial impunity is never enough. As Disney World's powers increased, its lobbyists made sure the state of Florida lost even the authority to protect the public from injury and death there. The first Disney World monorail crash occurred in February 1974, four months after it began operating. In July 2009 seven persons were injured and an operator of the monorail was killed. In response Disney spokesmen announced that three employees had been temporarily suspended. In June 2005 Rob Jacobs, at the time chief of Florida's Bureau of Fair Rides Inspection, summed up the human meaning of such impunity. "We don't have the authority to close the park down or close the ride down," he explained when a four-year-old boy died after taking Disney World's simulated ride into outer space, and the state of Florida did nothing.

Disney World opened for business in 1971. A decade later Frances Novak-Branch, a student at Rollins College in Orlando, conducted an investigation, published as *The Disney World Effect*. Examining official statistics, she made some more of those Florida discoveries they never teach in history class. "From 1970 to 1980, the wage level for the three-county area decreased by 6%," official statistics showed. Novak-Branch, who in the end had to have her scholarship published privately at her own expense, also discovered that per capita expenditures on public services, including education and health, declined after Disney World opened. As early as 1972 other statistical indicators emerged. Crime rose; orange production went down—to the extent that orange production in Orange County, Florida, has virtually ceased. The most remarkable change Disney World engendered was demographic. "Whereas many once traveled to Florida for its beaches, by the 1980s, Disney World accounted for roughly 40% of Florida vacationers," an official report noted.

One effect of this change in migration patterns was the decision by SeaWorld Parks & Entertainment to locate its Florida SeaWorld Adventure Park more than fifty miles from the nearest sea. For its grand opening in 1973, sharks and whales were plucked from the ocean and, in tank trucks, transported inland. Florida already had a marine-life attraction. Marineland, on the Atlantic Ocean three miles south of Matanzas Inlet, was one of Florida's oldest theme parks. It had been founded in the 1930s by a relation of Cornelius Vanderbilt Whitney and one of Count Leo Tolstoy's sons. Marineland proclaimed itself the world's first "oceanarium," but its seaside location could not compete with SeaWorld's proximity to Disney World. The landlocked theme park quickly became America's most-visited saltwater attraction.

Today SeaWorld attracts some six million visitors a year, so it was a major news event when a twelve-thousand-pound killer whale called Tilikum killed his keeper during a show there in February 2010. Aged thirty, Tilikum, a male, had been captured in subarctic waters off Iceland while still a calf. First in Canada, then in Florida he had spent most of his life confined to the whale equivalent of a saltwater bath tub. Every day Tilikum consumed some 250 pounds of seafood. Elaborate filtration systems were required to remove the animal's feces. Chemical additives were used to approximate ocean water. The artificial seawater also had to be chilled to a temperature of about fifty degrees Fahrenheit. Nothing could compensate for the confinement. Killer whales normally migrate tens of thousands of miles in the course of their lives; this immense powerful beast would never course the oceans.

Tilikum previously had killed a human at a Vancouver theme park that later failed, allowing SeaWorld to acquire him for a bargain price. This time Dawn Brancheau, the SeaWorld employee, was first dragged into the pool, then drowned while the audience watched. Afterward members of the audience expressed concern. Would any harm come to Tilikum? What about people who'd paid in advance for the "animal interaction" option? Just as the Fountain of Youth now calls itself an archaeological park, SeaWorld markets itself as a marine-life zoological park, so the death also was lamented as a setback for science. The fact that a six-ton, twenty-two-foot-long captive mammal had killed a human being, SeaWorld spokesmen in safari gear emphasized, would not deter SeaWorld from its "mission." "We're not in the business of punishing our animals," added James Atkinson, the theme park's manager. Within two days Tilikum was back on public display.

While the goings-on at SeaWorld were treated as a kind of reality show, another species of melodrama was unfolding behind closed doors a thousand miles away, at the New York City headquarters of The Blackstone Group, the venture capital hedge fund that owned Tilikum along with most of the world's other captive orcas. As part of its strategy to diversify profits following the financial meltdowns at the world's stock exchanges, Blackstone had set out to corner the market in performing killer whales. Thanks to a September 2009 $2.7 billion leveraged buyout of SeaWorld and other attractions, including the Busch Gardens African safari theme park near Tampa, Blackstone had wound up "more heavily invested in orcas than anyone else," the *Wall Street Journal* reported, owning "more than half the 42 held in captivity around the world." For accounting purposes, a valuation of approximately $10 million was placed on each whale. Tilikum, twice the size of the company's other performing whales, would have been worth many millions more because, in addition to his stage presence, he had stud value, having since his capture "sired 13 calves, more than half the number of killer whales born at its parks."

Until his involvement in a second human death this testosterone-propelled leviathan had been to the marine-mammal entertainment industry what Mickey Mouse was to the universe, "the identifiable icon . . . responsible for generating hundreds of millions of dollars," as one industry consultant explained. Seeking to counter the perceived threat to the financial viability of its icon, Blackstone went on the offensive. Instead of making excuses for what had happened, it asserted that "its orcas receive excellent care and thrive through interaction with their trainers." The public was reminded that over the previous thirty-one years SeaWorld "and partner parks" had contributed some $20 million to wildlife conservation, which worked out to about $1/_{135}$, or about 0.75 percent, of Blackstone's purchase price.

Fears of financial meltdown proved unfounded. Following the "unfortunate tragedy," as the entertainment news networks described it, SeaWorld ticket sales increased. The death of Dawn Brancheau was like those signs at the Fountain of Youth pointing out that Ponce de León never stepped foot in St. Augustine. A great truth had been revealed, that is to say a great falsehood exposed, and now? People, instead of stopping at the Atlantic Ocean, still preferred to turn inland.

Today more than fifty thousand people are employed within the boundaries of the Reedy Creek Improvement District. Not one of them is allowed to live or vote there. In addition to the traditional Disney attractions, there now are, according to Reedy Creek's Supervisors, "over 25,800 hotel rooms in 26 resorts, renowned golf and athletic attractions and an abundance of retail and entertainment areas," but you can't buy a house or an apartment there. You can purchase a time-share although, this being Disney World, it is called a "Disney Vacation Club Membership." However much you pay, you will not actually own property. No matter how much time you spend there, you never will be allowed to establish residence or vote. Legally speaking, Disney World is the godson of the Disston deal that scandalized Florida in 1881, but with a difference. Cloaked in the wholesome Disney imagery, the Reedy Creek Improvement District has proved to be immune from the scrutiny as well as the outrage previous schemes provoked. One reason no federal court has ever ruled on the unconstitutionality of Disney World's violation of voting rights is that no one so far has challenged it. It is as though a crucial sector of the New York metropolitan area—Wall Street, for instance—were exempted from democracy as well as taxation, government regulation, and the rule of law, and no one so much as protested.

PART SIX
FLORIDA MILLENNIUM

"Reality must take precedence over public relations, for Nature cannot be fooled."

—Richard Feynman, 1986

22

THEME PARK UNIVERSE

A different Disney creation did turn into America's experimental prototype. Celebration, a preplanned "community" where the control techniques prevailing inside the theme park were applied to how people lived, not just how they vacationed, started out as an integral part of the Reedy Creek District. Once the houses there were sold Disney executives got the district's boundaries redrawn again, this time to exclude the new town they had built and, just as Disney promised, deprive Celebration's residents of the right to participate in local governance. Its combination of democratic disenfranchisement and home town decor made Celebration America's experimental prototype community of tomorrow—a prototype for theme communities all over Florida that today offer the decor of freedom while sealing off their residents from democratic responsibility and, to an extent not apparent on the surface, control over their own lives.

Especially at Christmastime, when immense white snowmen—some Styrofoam, others inflatable plastic—stand guard in the front yards, Celebration seems like Currier-and-Ives America perfected with palm trees. All that's missing is the town meeting–style freedoms that once upon a time supposedly were what made America America. Celebration's design team, headed by a key Disney executive named Peter Rummell, made sure their plans included an imposing city hall. They also made sure Celebration had no municipal government. Today nearly ten thousand people live in Celebration, but nobody elects anybody there. Unlike nearby Bay Lake and Lake Buena Vista, Celebration is not a "City." It is only what, in Census jargon, is known as "an unincorporated census-designated place."

No one remembers Menéndez de Avilés or Duncan Clinch; it's the same with Peter Rummell, Florida's paradigmatical conquistador of the theme park age. Rummell, like James Gadsden, grew rich and powerful making himself useful to the rich and powerful. Also like Gadsden, he saw his conquests, starting in Florida, span continents. Euro Disney Resort, today known as Disneyland Paris, was one of Rummell's creations. Critics said it rained too much there but Rummell, whose corporate title was chairman of imagineering, understood about chilly, rainy Marne-la-Vallée what Disney had about muggy, buggy Orlando. The place didn't matter. Accessibility was all. Europe's autoroutes converged on the site Rummell chose. Euro Disney's customers, Rummell foresaw, would drive right past the real Europe in order to pay to get inside Disney's version of it.

For decades Rummell prospered in his powerful but secondary position. Then in the 1990s Rummell—like de Soto and Flagler—decided to become numero uno in his own private empire. The realm he chose was located in the same piney reaches of northern Florida where, nearly two hundred years earlier, Duncan Clinch had attacked Negro Fort and Andrew Jackson rampaged.

By deciding to colonize north Florida with a series of Celebration-style residential theme parks, Rummell brought history full circle. Back in 1803 Thomas Jefferson had proposed a market-driven approach to ethnic cleansing. His idea was to set up U.S. government trading posts providing the Indians with such consumer items as potbellied stoves and calico dresses, all on credit. Once enticed into debt, President Jefferson assured Congress, the Indians would be forced to sell their land in order to pay their bills. President Jackson ultimately preferred violence to evict them, but in Spanish Florida a variant of Jefferson's scheme set in motion the process that ultimately made Peter Rummell master of what had been one of the Spanish Crown's most munificent giveaways.

Whether of African, Native American, or mixed-race origin, Spanish Florida's "runaways" needed tools and weapons. When its Florida customers couldn't pay, the trading establishment of Panton, Leslie and Company demanded compensation, and they got it, in the form of hundreds of thousands of acres of free land. Alexander

Arbuthnot was trading with Panton, Leslie when Andrew Jackson seized his ship and killed him. Following the Negro Fort Massacre, Colonel Clinch handed over the Spanish-speaking blacks he kidnapped to Panton, Leslie; they had been farming land granted the company by Spain. That was only the first installment of the giveaway. Because some "Indians" failed to pay, in full and on time, for the rifles and plows that an enterprise operated by America's British rivals had enticed them into buying, Panton, Leslie and its successors were granted some 1.4 million acres by the Spanish crown. Because U.S. courts later upheld those claims, a territory nearly half the size of Connecticut became private property in America, all without its owners having to pay a penny for it. Finally, in an iconic triumph of privilege, the whole 2,188 square miles of it passed into the realm of the Du Pont family's vast and intricate holdings.

The name of the family's Florida holding company, run by a legendary Du Pont in-law named Ed Ball, was the St. Joe Company; its New York Stock Exchange ticker symbol is JOE. "If you don't know JOE, you don't know Florida," a 2007 press release, since removed from the company's websites, correctly asserted. Most people truly have no idea of how the symbiosis of land and privilege in Florida affects their lives because they have no idea of how interests like the St. Joe Company have wielded enormous power and accumulated enormous wealth, mostly for the benefit of a tiny group of people, few of whom live in Florida except, perhaps, in the winter.

For generations JOE's profits, based on timber extraction, financed the trust funds of dozens of that fortunate family's heirs. Then, as the twenty-first century approached, its owners began to understand that real estate lay beneath all that timber. That was where Peter Rummell entered the picture. In 1997 he laid out his master plan for transforming the old turpentine-and-creosote St. Joe Company into a lifestyle manufacturing enterprise. Deeply impressed, the company's directors gave Rummell full power to orchestrate the theming of a private empire fifty times the size of Disney World.

As the Age of the Theme Park superimposed itself atop the conquests of Florida's original conquistadors, image control became central to JOE's operations. "With a focus on the big picture," one press release announced, "we take great care in creating authentic, organic and original 'true places' for people to live, work and escape." Typical of these "true places" was a development called WaterColor. Like Celebration, it was an example of the corporate appropriation of an aesthetic principle for the purpose of profit diversification. Built on land that once formed the core of the Seminole "confinement and concentration area," Celebration merged theme park crowd-control techniques with the suburban illusion of freedom. WaterColor did the same with the environmental aesthetic, mimicking, surrounding, and co-opting the values of a much smaller development called Seaside. Started in 1980 by an Alabama department-store heir named Robert Davis, Seaside stood on land his grandfather had purchased in 1946 as a summer camp for his employees. The original idea was that, along this pristine stretch of coastline, low-wage workers would get the same chance to enjoy Florida's sand, sea and sunshine as rich people did. It was another of those utopian schemes that never came true. Blue-collar white folks did throng to northwest Florida's beaches, though not in the bucolic manner originally intended. Instead, chaotic speculation turned the Florida Panhandle into the raucous Redneck Riviera. By 1980 the Redneck Riviera was being turned into a wall of high-rise cement. In many places the area between the widened highway and the receding shoreline became so narrow, and the condos so closely packed along the water's edge, that each new building needed its own concrete overpass connecting it with an entrance ramp on the opposite side of the road. When the killer hurricanes of the early 2000s struck, many of these monstrosities became high-rise death traps.

Alarmed by the ugliness and devastation, Davis decided to create an alternative model for real estate development. The result was an idiosyncratic masterpiece of what was starting to be called postmodernism. Seaside's most revolutionary feature was the way it turned its back on the sea. Most houses were located along byways that encouraged the people living in them to relate to each other. The beach itself was easily accessible along sandy lanes on foot or by bicycle. Removing the residences from the seaside in Seaside meant the beach remained pristine. The risk of hurricane damage was reduced. "I believe that the lessons they've worked out at Seaside have very serious applications both in rural areas and in our cities," enthused the Prince of Wales, one of many famous people who made the pilgrimage to Seaside.

Executives at JOE were impressed. Any real estate venture that could get a free endorsement from a future king of England was worth co-opting. WaterColor made the decor of Seaside the centerpiece of its marketing strategy as, once again, a valid human experience was turned into a theme. In spite of its marketing image of intimacy, WaterColor was a sprawling, energy-intensive suburb—though, unlike in America's traditional suburbs, you couldn't give birth there and, should you happen to die there, you couldn't be buried there either. Rummell and his imagineers had created one of those "family-oriented" Florida "communities" with no schools, as well as no hospitals, no cemeteries, also no public transportation.

"WaterColor offers endless opportunities!" its sales brochures claimed. The right to vote was not among them. As at Celebration, democracy was written out of the prospectus. The neighbors were left to foot the bill for the costly public improvements the creation of these new housing estates made necessary. In one instance, taxpayer money was used "to reroute a major highway . . . when 3.5 miles of US-98 were moved inland to enhance the value at WindMark Beach," another of Rummell's newly invented "real places." This, too, continued a Florida tradition: public money being used to generate private wealth. In this case it also deprived the taxpayers of access to their beaches.

JOE's stock price, around $30 a share when Rummell took power, nearly tripled, but the real test of a "real place" is what happens when the bubble bursts. JOE's stock was trading for $85 a share in 2005. "Then," as one friendly account put it, "came the national market downturn, and St. Joe's sales dried up." By 2012 JOE was trading for $15 a share, about half of what it was before Rummell's extravaganza of theming was unleashed. Peter Rummell's essay at empire building had wound up demonstrating what Hernando de Soto's foray into the same territory had 450 years earlier. Florida was a great place to launch visionary schemes, so long as your source of money kept flowing. And when the money stops? Florida, pushed and pummeled, once again had oozed back. So much land had been frittered away in these lifestyle sales pitches that once-mighty JOE no longer was Florida's biggest private landowner.

While Celebration and WaterColor are paradigms of upscale theming, the little town of Christmas demonstrates how, in its down-scale versions as well, transforming what is into something that isn't continues to be Florida's grand unifying principle. Christmas was not established by some god-fearing congregation in order to reverence the birth of the Savior. Originally called Fort Christmas, it was set up, at federal government expense, to facilitate killing Seminoles on December 25, 1837. Once the Seminoles were gone, Fort Christmas faced the familiar problem. What to do now that the outside money no longer was flowing? This time the Post Office was the agency of the federal government that rode to the rescue, by dropping the "Fort" from Fort Christmas. Thanks to that alteration in its name, an abandoned relic of a forgotten war was transformed into an "attraction," the attraction being its new, festive postmark.

"Cracker Christmas," on the first weekend in December, is the biggest draw. For $5 you can park your RV and partake of such holiday treats as BBQ gator while watching broom-making demonstrations. Like Gasparilla in Tampa, Cracker Christmas has become the centerpiece of a year-round tourist attraction festival cycle. "Militia Encampments" is a twice-annual event. As at Olustee "cannon firing demonstrations" highlight the festivities. The Cracker Christmas theme carries over into the demography. According to the U.S. Bureau of the Census, Christmas is more than 95 percent white and only 0.43 percent African-American; per capita income was less than $15,000 a year, little over a third the national average.

Just twenty-one miles east of Christmas, right beside the Atlantic Ocean, you run into Florida's most powerful example of the transformational force of theming. Though its official name is the John F. Kennedy Space Center, most folks know it better by its Spanish colonial name, Cape Canaveral. They called it Canaveral because of the reeds growing in the marshes there, *cañaveral* being cognate to the English word cane, as in sugar cane and walking cane.

The space center is one of Florida's most heavily promoted attractions. The multimedia campaign, funded at U.S. taxpayer expense, centers on marketing NASA's launch headquarters as a Disney sideshow. "A Day of Fun. A Lifetime of Inspiration," proclaims one ad. Though it's a 130-mile round-trip, NASA describes the space center as "just east of the most popular Orlando attractions and theme parks." "Experience more on your Orlando, Florida vacation," exhorts another NASA ad, "with a daytrip to Kennedy Space Center Visitor Complex." It'll cost you if you do. As of 2010 general admission for Mom, Dad, and three kids to the U.S. government facility cost $160, plus tax. Take the "Then & Now" and "Today & Tomorrow" tours: you're up to $334. At Disney World the kids get to hug Mickey. At Cape Canaveral you can buy tickets for "Lunch with an Astronaut,'" bringing the cost of NASA's "Day of Fun" to $427.95, plus tax, not including souvenirs purchased at "The Space Shop," where astronaut costumes, including imitation moon boots, space gloves, and utility pack, cost out at $181.75 each.

What makes the Kennedy Space Center such a powerful example of the transformational force of theming is that the usual theming process in this case has been reversed. Most attractions take nothing and pretend it's something. At the Kennedy Space Center, a site of great historical and cultural as well as scientific importance has been turned into another ride. The only living creatures to reach the moon departed from Cape Canaveral, but its significance goes beyond rocketry. Some of the most consequential events of modern world history also unfolded there. One was NASA's failure to launch, on December 6, 1957, what was supposed to have been America's first earth satellite. While millions watched on their black-and-white TV sets, NASA's Vanguard rocket exploded on the launch pad. Like the bungled Bay of Pigs invasion five years later, this bungled attempt to put a satellite into orbit made it seem like America was under threat in outer space as well as right here on earth. Suddenly winning the "space race" seemed as essential to the free world's survival as fighting counterinsurgency wars in the tropics. In those overheated ideological times the moon was to superpower politics what Florida had been 450 years earlier—remote, barren and irrelevant, until it appeared that the other guy might get there first.

In spite of all the alarums, Americans eventually would see both the Soviet Union and communism collapse; America also came from behind to win the space race, becoming the first and so far only nation to send human beings more than a quarter-million miles out beyond the earth, then bring them home safe and sound. That feat was proclaimed a decisive victory, but of what, and over whom? Between 1969 and 1971, eight lunar expeditions blasted off from Florida. No one since then has returned to the moon because the only real reason for going there in the first place—defeating communism in outer space—vaporized long ago.

While failing to fulfill any scientific purpose, the manned space program has served as a geopolitical barometer. The original moon shots reflected how cold war priorities dominated everything. Then, years before the Berlin Wall fell, the abandonment of the program foreshadowed a new age in which ideological competition was increasingly irrelevant. The man-in-space barometer registered its biggest shift yet in 2011, when the United States terminated its space shuttle missions entirely. By then the notion that private enterprise could succeed wherever "big government" failed had become, like the communist threat in outer space earlier, a key element in America's public theology. In due course, it was promised, private enterprise would propel Americans back into space—all the way to Mars, NASA promised this time. In the meantime Americans would go into orbit as paying guests on Russian rockets. Once this would have provoked outrage, shame, and fear. Now people hardly noticed.

For fifty years the manned space program also has held up a mirror to America's changing vision of itself. Those first forays were all about All-American white guys proving they had *The Right Stuff*, as the title of Tom Wolfe's book on the astronauts put it. In all, thirty-two America-born white males either landed on the moon or orbited it. Only one of them, a geologist who flew on the final mission, was an actual scientist. Following abandonment of the lunar program, America entered its greatest epoch of immigration since Ellis Island days; the birth certificates of the astronauts reflected that too. In 1986 Franklin Chang-Diaz became America's first Hispanic in space; through his father, Chang-Diaz was also America's second Chinese-American astronaut. Since his family had emigrated to the United States from Central America, he was also the first Costa Rican–American astronaut.

America, Florida, and human nature being what they are, it was only a matter of time until sex cast off its earthly tethers. Nine married couples have flown in space. Four of them have since divorced, another reflection of how America lives. Human inevitability took another step out into the cosmos in 2007 when the first astronaut tabloid sex scandal erupted. Cocaine busts episodically occur at Cape Canaveral, though if, how, and when an astronaut first got high in outer space has yet to be determined.

Even after it stopped launching them into orbit, the theme NASA offered remained the same—that the astronauts are America's celebrity pioneers, conquering the extraterrestrial frontier just as past heroes subdued the earthly one. In this invention of a blended future, outer space is an Adventureland where the laws of physics and finance are suspended, and every episode ends with PR values triumphing over the spirit of scientific inquiry. It is all on display at the United States Astronaut Hall of Fame, Cape Canaveral's trademarked version of Disney World's Hall of the Presidents, where the Heroic Astronaut takes pride of place the same way the Valiant Conquistador, the Confederate Gentleman and the Millionaire Visionary do in their respective shrines.

At Cape Canaveral as at SeaWorld the shared community of unreality makes it all the more shocking when reality intrudes, as happened on January 28, 1986. That morning one of the rockets propelling the space shuttle *Challenger* broke off from the rest of the launch assemblage. There was no explosion and the space capsule carrying the astronaut crew of seven was not damaged. "However, the shuttle had no escape system and the astronauts did not survive the impact of the crew compartment with the ocean surface," as one summary bureaucratically put it. This lapse derived from the systemic peculiarities of what investigators described as NASA's "organizational culture and decision-making processes."

Across America schoolkids were watching as the astronauts died; this was supposed to have been the grand inaugural of the Teacher in Space Project, part of NASA's permanent publicity campaign. Christa McAuliffe, one of ten finalists in NASA's spelling bee–type competition to be the first teacher in space, had no aeronautical experience. She taught civics, not science, but as one judge of the contest later explained, "She had an infectious enthusiasm." Just prior to launch NASA handlers booked McAuliffe on both the *Today Show* and *Good Morning America;* she was a hit on the *Johnny Carson Show* as well.

NASA had been equally painstaking when it came to selecting McAuliffe's supporting cast. As part of another competition, this one a precursor to *American Idol,* NASA challenged TV and movie stars to talent-scout for astronauts. Judith Resnik, the second women chosen for the *Challenger* launch, had been recruited by Nichelle Nichols, the actress who played Lieutenant Uhura on the space ship *Enterprise* in the cult series *Star Trek.* Resnik's hair, it was later explained, had led to her choice for the mission. During her one previous ride into space, NASA surveys revealed, the viewing public had found it fascinating to watch Resnik's long wavy hair undulating in weightlessness. Her selection also complemented NASA's diversity policy. Following the disaster, NASA officials pointed out that Judith Resnik had been the first Jewish woman in space. The mission's black astronaut, Ronald McNair, had brought along his saxophone. His space project was to play jazz of his own composition. Hawaii-born Ellison Shoji Onizuka was scheduled to become the first Japanese-American in space.

Three more or less stereotypical white men rounded out the *Challenger* crew. U.S. Air Force Lieutenant Colonel Francis Richard Scobee was mission commander; Gregory Jarvis, the payload specialist, was an employee of the Hughes aerospace corporation. *Challenger's* pilot was Michael John Smith, a graduate of the U.S. Naval Academy who had bombed Hanoi during the Vietnam War. Following a careful study of Cape Canaveral weather conditions, Smith had decided it was not safe to launch that day. When higher-ups overruled him, he said something that in the aftermath was seen as prescient. "You know," this experienced pilot observed, "you've got people down here making decisions who've never even flown an airplane." It later emerged that NASA's managers frequently violated their own safety regulations in order to synchronize their space spectaculars with network television's prime viewing hours as well as with celebrity visits to the Cape.

When disaster struck they did their best. The *Challenger*'s pilot, Michael Smith, pulled the levers necessary to unlock the switches on his control panel. It was not because of him that those controls connected to nothing. Four of the astronauts' personal egress air packs were found to have been activated. It was not because of them that the shuttle, though it had egress packs, had no egress. *Challenger*'s commander, Colonel Scobee, "fought for any and every edge to survive. He flew that ship without wings all the way down," one investigator later concluded, adding, "They were alive."

The specially convened Presidential Commission on the Space Shuttle Challenger Accident, headed by former secretary of state William P. Rogers, was with one exception composed of people committed to reassuring the American public that all was well with NASA. That exception was Richard Feynman. The Nobel Prize–winning physicist had been chosen to be the token scientist on a panel composed almost entirely of well-connected Washington lawyers and photogenic ex-astronauts. In a way it was surprising that Feynman, whose career intersected with so many revelatory events and situations, had never intersected with Florida before. In another way it wasn't. No serious science took place in Florida for reasons going back beyond the Civil War. NASA itself—so adept at courting celebrities and politicians—had no outreach program to scientists of Feynman's caliber.

Ever since his boyhood bird-watching days, Feynman had devoted his life to differentiating between natures and names. Now, in the form of NASA, he found himself investigating an organization which had spent decades, and billions of dollars, denying that such a distinction existed. It wasn't merely that those running America's space program had little scientific or technical expertise. As Feynman questioned them, he discovered they had no understanding of the basic mathematics of risk calculation. That, in turn, had led "official management" to claim that "the probability of failure [was] a thousand times less" than NASA's own scientists had determined. As he delved into the specifics of what had gone wrong, Feynman came upon what might well have been the most glaring discrepancy between nature and name of all. A device that NASA called a safety feature had caused the astronauts' deaths.

The items in question were the O-rings on *Challenger*'s booster rockets. Imagine a garden hose with a nozzle that lets you regulate the flow of water. Inside that nozzle is a little rubber ring. If that rubber gasket doesn't work properly, the nozzle can't control the water; instead of going where you want it to go, water spurts all over the place. The same thing happened as *Challenger* lifted off its launchpad. Only it was the hot, high-pressure gases produced by the burning solid propellant inside the booster rocket, not water, that spurted uncontrollably out of the nozzle.

The O-rings caused the space shuttle launch to fail, but what caused the O-rings to fail? The O-rings on America's space shuttles, Feynman discovered, were not built to the same temperature specifications as your garden hose. Your garden hose will work until temperatures drop to freezing; Morton Thiokol, a Utah firm that was one of NASA's preferred contractors, only warranted its O-rings to work safely at temperatures higher than fifty-three degrees Fahrenheit. Later, looking back on that memorable day, people in Florida said about the *Challenger* disaster what others had said about the Dade Massacre 150 years earlier, what they said again at Rosewood in 1923. It was so "unnaturally cold" that morning they died, but the cold was not unnatural. At Cape Canaveral, 226 miles north of Miami, it gets cold every winter. That's why Henry Flagler pushed south.

That night at the Kennedy Space Center ice formed on the launch service platform. NASA did postpone the launch for a few hours to let the ice melt. It then ordered *Challenger* to blast off at 11:34 a.m. The scientific fact which the launch managers disregarded was that a rising thermometer could not undo the damage the cold already had done. The O-rings lost their elasticity at low temperatures. They did not regain it simply because a frosty Florida night was followed by a sunny day.

NASA had equipped space vehicles costing hundreds of millions of dollars with gadgets which malfunctioned whenever the weather got nippy and, as the Rogers Commission began its televised hearings, only Richard Feynman seemed to find that of much interest. The tried-and-true bureaucratic response was to smother Feynman's truth telling in a suffocating balm of obfuscation. Unfortunately for the obfuscators Feynman, a superstar academic performer as well as one of the twentieth century's most respected scientists, had been stealing the show at boring conferences and stodgy colloquia since the days of vaudeville. All he needed this time was a piece of rubber and a glass of ice water. As the TV cameras swiveled toward him, Feynman held up his little piece of rubber, then plunged it into the glass of ice water, then removed it. As could be seen clearly on TV screens across America (and still can be seen on YouTube), the rubber had been deformed as a result of its brief exposure to the cold. Millions of viewers also could see that, even after being removed from the cold, the rubber did not regain its original flexibility.

NASA's disregard for science and safety did produce one of the Rogers Commission's more memorable circumlocutions. This was the bland observation that the *Challenger* disaster was "an accident rooted in history." History repeated itself in 2003 when seven more people were killed when the space shuttle *Columbia* disintegrated. Once again the bureaucratic obfuscators inserted words like "probably," "rather likely," and "to some degree," even as the facts forced them to concede that the *Columbia* "accident was probably not an anomalous, random event but rather likely rooted to some degree in NASA's history and the human space flight program's culture." That is to say, it was not an accident, but the result of "a broken safety culture" at NASA, as one investigator put it. It was an old story by then. Back in 1986 NASA's computers already were so antiquated that, like the O-rings, they constituted a safety risk. "There is not enough room in the memory of the main line computers for all the programs of ascent, descent, and payload programs in flight," Feynman had pointed out. "It is becoming more difficult to find manufacturers to supply such old-fashioned computers," he warned.

By 2002, the year before the *Columbia* astronauts were inciner-
ated, *The New York Times* reported that in order "to keep the shuttles
flying, the space agency has begun trolling the Internet—including
Yahoo and eBay—to find replacement parts." "Aging NASA Labs
Need $2 Billion Makeover," read one headline. The calls for more
money ignored the fact that NASA—whether or not it sent men
to the moon, whether it launched space shuttles or abandoned that
program too—has been costing America's taxpayers, in real dollars,
approximately $15 billion every year, for fifty years. All that money
had not prevented a "steady and significant decrease in NASA's laboratory capabilities, including equipment, maintenance, and facility
upgrades."

Back in the 1960s, as they gave it a futuresque new name, politicians and promoters imagined that theming the area around Cape
Canaveral was only a first step toward a Florida-based theming of the
universe, but Silicon Valley in California, not Florida's "Space Coast,"
was the place where the future was invented. Florida was left behind
by the revolutionary developments in fields ranging from microbiol-
ogy to nanotechnology occurring in states that, unlike Florida, had a
tradition of financing education and encouraging scientific research.
The astronaut icon also had proved to be a franchise of limited appeal
for the real estate market. Exploring the tidal flatness of the Space
Coast, you find no astronaut-themed communities. Instead, where
Ribault's French colonists were castaways so long ago, the theme
communities have names like Tuscan Hills and Painter Hills. Here,
where the pelican is king, you find Quail Run.

Though his attempt to get NASA to operate in the "world
of reality" was fruitless, the *Challenger* disaster did cause Richard
Feynman to make a comment so insightful that it may have been
the most important thing ever said by anyone at any time about
something happening in Florida; "reality," he argued vainly, "must
take precedence over public relations, for nature cannot be fooled."

Neither the manufacturer nor anyone at NASA was ever held
accountable, either civilly or criminally, not even after it was verified
that for nine years both NASA administrators and Thiokol executives
had known about the design flaw in the O-rings and its potential

to cause human death, yet took no corrective action. It wasn't just NASA officials and Thiokol executives who got off the hook. No one ever implicated Harriet Beecher Stowe. Juliet Tuttle and Carl Fisher were never indicted either. Even Feynman stopped short of resolving the great mystery. What could have led all those supposed experts to spend all that money on some rubber seals that got all bent out of shape whenever it got cold enough to wear a sweater? You can search all the reports, study all the testimony, follow the research and development process of the O-rings from its inception out in Utah to its conclusion in the skies above Florida. You still won't find the answer, though like "The Purloined Letter" in Edgar Allan Poe's tale, the reason the O-rings failed was always out there, right in front of everybody, implicating not only NASA and the manufacturers, but all those others who for generations had striven to make people believe Florida was something it was not, and so wound up fooling themselves.

The myth that it never gets cold in Florida killed the astronauts just as once upon a time the myth of gold lured conquistadors to their doom.

23

CITIES OF THE FUTURE

Study Disney; you find out what people have wanted and hoped, and pretend and market Florida to be. To understand what has become of Florida in Feynman's "world of reality" you must delve into the activities of another authentic American genius. Jack Kerouac—guru, bad boy and literary superstar of the Beat Generation—showed up in Florida even before Disney, the astronauts and the Cubans did. In 1957, in a two-week frenzy, he wrote *The Dharma Bums* in a rented Orlando apartment with a tangerine tree out back. In the interval Kerouac shocked America and thrilled nonconformists everywhere with the publication of his counterculture classic, *On the Road*. Like Kerouac himself, it will be remembered as long as Walt and Mickey are—that is, as long as American civilization exists.

Disney chartered a private plane. Kerouac arrived by bus. Disney used celluloid and plastic attempting to make America conform to what he put on TV. Kerouac put his howling rant against the plastic shackles he perceived imprisoning the American spirit down on paper, yet even to Kerouac, Florida initially seemed a kind of Paradise. "Why not come to Orlando and dig the crazy Florida scene of spotlessly clean highways and fantastic supermarkets?" he wrote Lawrence Ferlinghetti, the Beat poet, in 1961. Ferlinghetti never showed. Florida for Kerouac became a series of shabby sublets as he wandered from Orlando to Tampa and finally to St. Petersburg where, in 1969, a few months after the United States landed men on the moon, death caught up with the Beat apostle who personified youthful rebellion. He was forty-seven; the protean artist who better than anyone else since Walt Whitman replicated America in the bursting energy of his prose never got to be a crazy old man with a long white beard. *Kerouac in Florida: Where the Road Ends* was how the title of one book put it. As Ponce and de Soto could have told you, it was Florida's oldest theme. In another surrealist denouement, the world's most comprehensive collection of Salvador Dalí's art also found its final resting place in St. Petersburg. Like Tuttle, Flagler and LeBron James, all those Dalís (and their donors) reached Florida via Cleveland, Ohio.

Never were two creative geniuses so totally American and so different, yet Orlando (like Florida, like America) transcended them both. It today is a place where you can go for years without entering a theme park or reading a book.

Today more people than ever wait in line for their theme park adventures. More than ever Kerouac's lonely defiant spirit prowls the RV parks and hangs out at the discount shopping malls. As new multitudes thronged into Florida, Orlando turned into what they were trying to escape—America's newest expanse of exurban sprawl, a place so gigantic and diverse that there was a dream home or a crawl space there for everyone. Disney himself was the Sorcerer's Apprentice who ignited the transformation. By coming to Florida, he imagined he could escape "the jungle of signs, lights and fly-by-night operations," but Disney World today is but one nodule of an immense glob-like conurbation of theme parks and trailer parks, gated communities and broken-window slums where vast cookie-cutter suburbs are interspersed with corporate-logo skyscrapers. Sprawling across Florida's midsection, Greater Orlando has become what sociologists sometimes call an "Edge City," a place where millions pursue Disney dreams while leading Kerouac lives.

Head out Epcot Center Road; minutes later you're traversing Kissimmee, one of America's true cities of the future. A redneck rodeo town when Disney arrived, Kissimmee today is where many of the people who operate the rides and pick up the litter at Disney World live—and are allowed to vote. Just beyond the intersection of U.S. 192 and 7 Dwarfs Lane you'll find Capone's Dinner and Show. Farther on you'll pass Pirates Island–Kissimmee, which is not on an island. There's also a place offering cut-rate helicopter rides. The whirring machine sits, rotors spinning, right next to the moving traffic. It's scarier than any theme park ride.

The dollar stores and fast-food franchises cling to the edges of Disney World like junkyard scrap drawn to a gigantic magnet, yet the wackiness, the wildness, and the gratuitous inventiveness that makes America America also are on display. So is the thirst for something more. It goes without saying there's no coral at the Coral Cay Resort, but right across the street is Wat Florida Dhammaram. There real monks chant real vedas at Florida's first authentic Theravada Buddhist temple. The Vietnamese were the first Asians to colonize Orlando. Since Disney World opened it also has become the Indian capital of Florida: not as in Seminoles, but as in Tamil and Punjabi, iddly and naan roti. Should you wish to study Sanskrit, head for the Hindu University of America, located on Econlockhatchee Trail.

At Meadow Woods Middle School, out on the cutting edge of Orlando, concrete walls abut untouched swamp. Kids from nearly one hundred countries study there. Every time a pupil from a new country enrolls, they put up a new flag. Flags you normally see nowhere except at the UN decorate the trailers that serve in place of the classrooms the state of Florida does not provide. Here, where the soggy scrubland that once served as the Seminole concentration zone is visible just outside the window, you also can see the future. Both whites and blacks are in the minority in this school where the flags of the whole world fly. According to the U.S. Bureau of the Census, soon that will be true of America as a whole.

"No one warned us this was going to happen," complained Pulitzer Prize winner Jane Healy, on finding out one morning that the Orlando easy-listening station on her car radio had turned into Rumba 100.3 FM. She was wrong about that. There had been plenty of warning. For decades, if you wanted to know what would happen next in Orlando, all you had to do was look at that other instant American metropolis, Miami. Healy herself was an example of how Miami forecast the future. When she arrived in Orlando the *Miami Herald* was already winning Pulitzers. The *Orlando Sentinel* still expected her to be a ladylike civic booster. Instead she blew the lid off corruption in the real estate market. Disney and the moon shots got the prime time coverage, but of all of the transformations overtaking Florida, none was more consequential than Miami's metamorphosis into America's city of the future—unless it was the refusal to recognize what was happening. "Will the last American to leave Miami please bring the flag?" the saying went—as though invading immigrants, bootleg drugs, and shoot-outs were not as all-American as Ellis Island, Prohibition, and Al Capone.

Orlando was supposed to be the blue-eyed Dick-and-Jane refuge from everything Miami epitomized, but today nearly twice as many Hispanics—536,922 of them, according to the U.S. census—live in the Orlando area as there were people of all kinds living there when Disney arrived. In this case, too, the die was cast by an invisible corporate hand. Sales were slow at a development called Buenaventura Lakes until its marketing strategists started advertising in Spanish in Puerto Rico. Suddenly Puerto Ricans started flowing into the Orlando area, creating an Hispanic alternative to predominately Cuban Miami. Invisible corporate manipulators were also behind the change on Healy's car radio. Profit analysts at Clear Channel Communications, the giant radio conglomerate, had decided that her middle-aged, middle-American demographic, heretofore synonymous with Orlando, no longer had enough revenue-growth potential.

Like Chicago a century earlier, Miami was a harbinger of Americas, not just Floridas, to come. Chicago was created by the Industrial Revolution's unquenchable appetite for markets and raw materials. Miami was the first major American city to be transformed by the globalization of population movements as well as goods and services. Its traumas, considered so "un-American" at the time, exemplified trends that since then have become pervasive. One of them was the emergence of new kinds of inequality. Poor black people always had been ghettoized in Miami; with the arrival of the Cubans Florida's old three-tiered hierarchy of inequality, dating back to slavery days, took new form. As they themselves often emphasized, black people in Miami weren't second-class citizens anymore; they were third-class citizens now.

History was rhyming again. In the nineteenth century colonialism had lingered on in Cuba long after Spain was driven from the rest of its New World empire. Now, once again, Cuba was the last redoubt of an old-fashioned faith—Marxist-Leninism rather than the divine right of kings. Other deeply entrenched patterns were repeating themselves in Florida, too. Upon arrival in Miami, Cubans (and only Cubans) became beneficiaries of one of the most all-encompassing affirmative-action programs ever undertaken in the United States. In keeping with the Florida tradition of using the legal system to enforce inequality, the United States also rewarded Cubans for acts it punished other people for committing. A Haitian who made it ashore, if caught, would be detained at a holding camp in the Everglades. All Cubans who set foot on U.S. soil automatically got benefits that would have been denounced as "welfare" had they been Florida-born white and black folks in need. They also were put on a fast track to U.S. citizenship, hence the right to vote. As it had in DuVal's and Yulee's time, and in Charley Johns' time, reserving special privileges for one group at the expense of others would deeply mark Florida politics, while warping its cultural development, including its culture of civic responsibility.

Florida's racist legacy was like the pro-slavery saltire on the state flag—so omnipresent as to be virtually invisible until some particular event revealed what it meant. One night in February 1962 Dewey McLaughlin, a merchant seaman, was sitting alone in the apartment at 732 Second Street in Miami Beach he shared with his girlfriend, Connie Hoffman, when two policemen barged into the apartment without warrant or warning and arrested him. It wasn't drugs. They hadn't been playing their radio too loud, but Hoffman was a white woman; McLaughlin, in the detectives' opinion, was black. They therefore were charged with violating section 798.05 of the Florida Statutes, which read as follows: "Any negro man and white woman, or any white man and negro woman, who are not married to each other, who shall habitually live in and occupy in the nighttime the same room shall each be punished by imprisonment not exceeding twelve months, or by fine not exceeding five hundred dollars."

No one disputed Connie Hoffman was white, just as seventy-three years earlier no one disputed Annie Maloney was black. In

Miami Beach in 1962 as in Key West in 1889, the controversy de-
volved upon the racial identity of the male partner. Their landlady
had been spying on the couple. She told the policemen she had
observed McLaughlin taking a shower. After checking for themselves, the arresting officers agreed that "certain features that are
predominant in colored males" warranted the conclusion that Mr.
McLaughlin was nonwhite. McLaughlin himself proclaimed he was
not "colored" for the same reason that Antonio González in 1889
had sworn that he was—namely, he was Latino. In spite of his Irish
surname, McLaughlin's native language was Spanish. Official documents proved he was from La Ceiba, Honduras. McLaughlin did not
consider himself a "colored male" because in the Spanish-speaking
Caribbean, categorization along purely racial lines is far less common than in the United States. Besides, this was Miami Beach; it was
1962. This was not the Florida of chain gangs and turpentine camps.
It was the Florida of Jackie Gleason, of kosher Chinese restaurants,
where people danced the Twist.

Connie Hoffman protested she had "never heard of any law
that said a Negro and a White woman couldn't live together and
she didn't believe it." She was wrong. It had been the law in Florida
since Governor Fleming's time. On June 28, 1962, a Dade County
jury—not some Crackers up in the Panhandle—found Hoffman
and McLaughlin guilty as charged. They were sentenced to thirty
days' hard labor. In 1845 the branding of a shipwright in Pensacola
had revealed with exactitude the state of civilization in the state of
Florida. In 1962 sentencing a waitress and her boyfriend to hard labor
had the same effect. The greatest revelation was the extent to which
white racist attitudes permeated the behavior of people who were
not stereotypical white Southerners. The landlady who called the
police, Dora Goodnick, was no Daughter of the Confederacy. Had
they applied for membership in the Ku Klux Klan the two detectives
who arrested them, whose names were Stanley Marcus and Nicolas
Valeriana, might have been rejected.

Hoffman, remonstrating with her accusers, vowed to "go to
the Supreme Court." In the end the case did go all the way to the
Supreme Court for the simple reason that so many people in Florida

considered it appropriate that a white woman who slept with a black man should be declared a criminal. First the arresting officers, then their superiors, then the prosecutor, then the judge, then the jury, then the appellate court, then the Florida Supreme Court could have ended the ordeal to which Hoffman and McLaughlin were being subjected, but they did not. In October 1964, a team of Florida's top lawyers put on their best suits, packed their briefcases, and flew up to Washington, D.C. There with straight faces they defended white supremacist notions of legality that had prevailed since the neo-Confederate takeover in 1877. Their argument was a paradigm of legal logic. Criminalizing cohabitation by unmarried mixed-race couples, these taxpayer-paid attorneys alleged, was justified by the need to buttress Florida's ban on interracial marriage. In their words, sending an unmarried couple to prison was "ancillary to and serve[d] the same purpose as the miscegenation law itself."

The argument of the Florida lawyers prevailed. The Supreme Court ruled that the legislators in Tallahassee could make it a crime for white people to have sex with black people, and vice versa, but in that case the state would have to pass a "necessity test." That is, Florida would have to prove there was some specific justification for treating interracial sex in a different manner than it treated intra-racial sex. Florida, the justices ruled, had failed to meet this "heavier burden of justification." On that technicality the state law under which Connie Hoffman and Dewey McLaughlin had been sentenced to hard labor was judged invalid. Only two of the nine justices—Justices Potter Stewart and William Douglas—"refused to accept that there could be any such 'overriding statutory purpose,' which would require such discrimination based on skin color."

Like Floridians going back to Garcia and the Choctaw, the waitress and the merchant seaman had not been looking for a fight. Even so, they had taken their stand against the dominant force propelling injustice in Florida, which in 1962 as in 1816 was white American racism. Like Negro Fort, the place where they lived, 732 Second Street, is one of those historical sites which make Florida understandable. Though no "Great Floridian" plaque marks the spot, it's easy to find. All you have to remember is that in Miami Beach street numbers run from south to north. The iconic Fontainebleau Hotel, which defined fashionability at the time Hoffman and McLaughlin were arrested, is located forty-two blocks to the north of the place where they lived. The famous South Beach Deco District starts three blocks north, at Fifth Street. For decades the area south of Fifth Street was a low-rent annex of "God's Waiting Room," where thousands of retirees waited to die. Then, starting in 1980, the area was overrun by "Marielitos," newly arrived boat people from Cuba. Then everything changed again. Today 732 Second Street is at the center of a snazzy neighborhood that its promoters call SoFi, for South of Fifth. A modern condo complex now stands where Dora Goodnick's tatty efficiency apartments once were. Though new, the Deco-reminiscent building has been designed to evoke a glamour and style that, at this particular site, never existed.

The beaches, clubs and roving sports cars are all essential to SoFi's ambience, but what gives their old neighborhood its new edge is its sexiness. Straight, gay, bi; white, black, brown, tan: SoFi's racial and sexual permutations give new meaning to the concept of "betweenity." Wandering through SoFi, you see that Dewey McLaughlin and Connie Hoffman were true Florida pioneers. The interracial nature of their relationship made them pioneers. So did its cross-cultural aspect, for it is not just the different races that now mingle freely in their old neighborhood. Different cultures mix and match there as well. The mating long ago transcended the English-Spanish divide. These days you'll also hear people flirting in Portuguese, Russian, German, French, Chinese, and, depending on the season and time of day, many other languages.

The legal drama involving Dewey McLaughlin and Connie Hoffman was part of an advance from the North into the South of constitutional human rights protections which, culminating in the civil rights revolution of the 1960s, resumed the work of national integration that had been abandoned nearly one hundred years earlier. The United States' regional racism, it is less often noticed, was also steadily pushed back by another great movement—this one emanating from the Caribbean and Latin America. People like Antonio Gonzales and Dewey McLaughlin did not arrive in Florida with strong notions of constitutionally guaranteed rights. They were unashamed protagonists of a culture where the idea that you could be sent to prison for having sex with a woman of a different color was considered an insult to a man's virility. In the matter of interracial sexual rights, as in so many others, Florida as a result turned out to be a place of convergence. In this instance the Latin macho ethos and the U.S. Constitution converged as two different advances from two different directions—one legal and philosophical, from the North; the other demographic and cultural, from the South—reshaped the sexual as well as the legal landscape. In Key West in 1889, a black judge was not powerful enough to protect from racist persecution a couple who wanted to marry. He could not protect himself. In Miami Beach in 1962, an unmarried couple was able to prevail at the federal, though still not at the state level. That late rights considered self-evident today had to be litigated all the way to the highest court in the land.

What's revealing are all the many varieties of interracial sex Florida Statute did not outlaw. The furtive embrace, coerced sex, sex on the side, short-time sex, sex with the house maid, sex with the field hand: Florida law was silent on everything except what happened when an interracial couple's coupling went beyond the sex act—when people chose to "habitually live in and occupy in the nighttime the same room." Only then did Florida law decree that they "shall each be punished." What the statutes criminalized was treating interracial sex as though it were not something shameful, which had to be hidden. Hiding something does not remove its existence. As America's highest court pondered whether or not a sailor and a waitress could share an apartment in Miami Beach, social scientists pointed out that the "white" lawyers from Florida had at least a 20 percent likelihood of having a black ancestor. The "black" attorneys from the NAACP were nearly 80 percent likely to have some white blood.

Miami also was a harbinger when it came to sports and the business of franchising sports for money. As early as 1888 the Washington Capitals held a training camp in Jacksonville. The Philadelphia Phillies arrived the following year. By the beginning of World War I Spring Training had become, like the horse races at Hialeah, an integral part of the Florida calendar of attractions. Following World

War II more than fifteen major-league teams established training bases in Florida. Then, starting in 1966, something new started to happen in Miami. For the first time a Florida city established its own professional sports team instead of playing host to outsiders. An even bigger change: Miami's Dolphins didn't play baseball. They played football, and they played it so well that by 1972 they were the national champions—playing a perfect season, winning seventeen games, losing none. In 1976 the Tampa Bay Buccaneers became Florida's second major-league football team. Florida now played in big leagues, with the Miami Heat and Orlando Magic teams emerging as star performers in the basketball industry. Miami eventually would also have its own ice hockey team, the Florida Panthers. So long as it wasn't suited to Florida's climate, Florida fans seemed to love the sport, whatever it was.

The greatest continuity when it came to Miami's emergence as America's newest metropolis was the intrusion of the unanticipated catastrophe. New Year's Eve of 1980 in Miami proved to be like New Year's Eve of 1959 in Havana. Those who lived through Miami's fateful year of 1980 still lament how badly "things went wrong" that year. Nothing went wrong. It was simply that once again reality had the temerity to intrude. The Great Freezes of the 1890s had been followed by the killer hurricanes of 1926 and 1935 and the Cuban crises of 1961 and 1962. Then, in just one year, the latest double whammy struck as smoke rose in angry columns from Miami's ghetto neighborhoods and more than one hundred thousand Cuban boat people converged on south Florida.

How and why had racial violence at its worst, and migration into the United States at its most chaotic, converged on Miami at the same time? As always, most folks opted for the weather-report approach. One day the weather report tells you to tape up your windows: a hurricane's coming. Another day it tells you not to wash your car: there's a drought. You will never learn from the TV weather reports that the earth tilts on its axis, causing seasons, or that the second law of thermodynamics explains why we have hurricanes; life, like history, consists of unrelated disruptions. Then there is the contextual approach to understanding why people do things. Could

it be that those Seminoles massacred Dade and his men for reasons
other than that they were "bad Indians"?

To understand the Miami riots of May 1980, you had to go back
no further than December 17, 1979. That morning, after handcuff-
ing a motorcyclist named Arthur McDuffie and removing his safety
helmet, police "beat him to death with their batons, put his helmet
back on, and called an ambulance, claiming there had been a mo-
torcycle accident," as one account austerely put it. It goes without
saying McDuffie was black. Had the police questioned McDuffie
before brutalizing him, they would have learned that he, like them,
had served as a law-enforcement officer. An insurance agent with
two young daughters, McDuffie had been an MP while in the U.S.
Marines. In 1980 the Florida legal system worked as it would have
in 1920 or 1880, or 1860 or 1835. As an all-white, all-male, six-man
jury made clear, it remained okay to kill black men in Florida. They
found every one of the policemen not guilty. There was another
parallel with the past. Miami's black people, not its police officers,
would be the ones blamed for giving Miami a bad name.

Liberty City and Miami's other black neighborhoods had reacted calmly to the original news of the McDuffie attack. They
stayed calm when official investigations documented the brutality
of McDuffie's murder and the ensuing cover-up, calm throughout
the trial as well. Then, on May 17, 1980, five months to the day after
the attack, came the policemen's acquittal. That evening thousands
marched peacefully to the Dade County Justice Department. "The
marchers were made up of all elements of the Black community—
businessmen in suits, young children in shorts, and old ladies in
aprons," Patrice Gaines-Carter wrote afterward. "Their numbers
grew as they marched." It took only a spark to ignite the blaze.
When a speaker called for prayer, someone shouted: "We are tired
of praying."

One spark also touched off the invasion from Cuba. On April
Fool's Day 1980 five Cubans, desperate to escape the island, forced
their way onto the grounds of the embassy of Peru in Havana. Within
a few days some ten thousand people had crowded onto the embassy
grounds. In response Fidel Castro indulged in one of his theatrical

gestures. If people wanted to abandon the Revolution, he announced, let them. On April 15, 1980, the port of Mariel, twenty-five miles east of Havana, was declared open to anyone wanting to leave Cuba. By the following October 124,779 Cubans, according to official statistics, had fled. They took off for Florida on rafts; they paddled themselves onto the open sea clinging to plastic containers. Most of the Marielitos, as they were called, were rescued by Cubans from Miami. They came to Mariel in every watercraft imaginable: speedboats, yachts, fishing boats, cigarette boats, putt-putts with outboard motors.

It was the Miami Cubans' finest hour, but their Dunkirk moment soon gave way to new images of mayhem. In addition to his dissidents Castro sent Miami his misfits, his "undesirables" and, in some cases, his hardened criminals. Once in Miami many converged in Felliniesque abandon on the by-then-unfashionable South Beach area. Decades earlier people had danced to "Moon Over Miami" there, but by then the mostly Jewish white- and blue-collar workers who retired there were dying off. No one was replacing them. That changed once the Marielitos arrived, unleashing a crime wave that also resembled a transvestite carnival. Suddenly South Beach was the scariest place in America. To put it another way, history was repeating itself. Decade after decade Florida undid people's dreams as well as their schemes, yet the adherents of the Paradise myth kept multiplying, until the failure of reality to correspond to illusion was what made the news.

"Paradise Lost!" screamed the headlines, as though Florida ever had been a place where calamities, human and natural, were not the norm. It was not lost for long. Just as one group—English-speaking Americans in general, retirees in particular—discovered they had not been living in Paradise, another group—Latinos in general, Cubans in particular—decided: Yes, it was Paradise! The Marielitos filled the TV screens while, less noticed, hundreds of thousands and, ultimately, millions of hardworking Latinos converged on Florida.

Resiliency remained Miami's great continuity. Typhoid and hurricanes hadn't stopped it earlier; these new traumas didn't either. Miami's latest Julia Tuttle was an ex–Atlantic City newshen by way of Chicago and New York named Barbara Baer Capitman. Combine in

your mind's eye the Mad Woman of Chaillot and Betty Friedan. Give
her a screechy voice and a hairdo that would do Medusa proud. Add
PR smarts equal to those of Walter P. Fraser. You will have an inkling
of her impact. Many were convinced Barbara Capitman was crazy,
and why not? She stated as a certainty that South Beach—the Deco
District, she called it—would soon become "a great world resort, like
Monte Carlo or Rio, where people from all over the world meet to
enjoy themselves." The "developers" sneered. Their idea of saving
South Beach was to destroy it. One blue-ribbon panel proposed pul-
verizing all those art deco masterpieces, crisscrossing South Beach
with canals, floating fake gondolas in them, then rebranding South
Beach as New Venice. The idea that Miami Beach, with its Jews,
retirees, and (now) Hispanics, could become more fashionable than
WASPy resorts like Palm Beach struck most in Miami as ludicrous,
but not Capitman. She was that rarity, a "visionary" who actually
foresees something.

Capitman's greatest insight was into the changing nature of
power in America. Instead of pandering to Miami's traditional movers
and shakers, she built a nationwide, grassroots activist support base
for art deco preservation. Then, in March 1980, just before Liberty
City exploded and the Marielito tsunami hit, Capitman took Andy
Warhol on a tour of South Beach. As she of the blurry lipstick and he
of the dead-white hair surveyed the fading Deco treasures, a passerby
could have mistaken them for just two more south Florida freaks.
That would have been another of those Feynmanesque confusions,
for this may have been Florida's most fateful encounter between a
man and a woman who were not sexually interested in each other
since Flagler met Tuttle. Few figures since Rubens had a keener eye
for spotting those nodal points where money meets art than Warhol, and following his tour with Capitman he pronounced the Deco
District delightful! Where Warhol trod, Capitman understood, the
trendsetters were sure to follow.

Of Florida's previous inventors Capitman most resembled Harriet Beecher Stowe. A tireless propagandizer as well as a moralizer,
she never let reality stand in her way. Though there were many art
deco buildings in South Beach, the Deco District was a jumble of

different styles. Along Ocean Drive, the Via Veneto of South Beach, the most conspicuous building was the Betsy Ross Hotel, a rip-off of George Washington's Mount Vernon. A number of Mediterranean-style extravaganzas also overshadowed the art deco creations. One of them, an imposing Spanish Revival edifice, was to Ocean Drive what the Dakota was to New York's Central Park West—and not just because of the architectural idiosyncrasy. John Lennon would be assassinated outside the Dakota in 1980; Gianni Versace would be murdered outside this South Beach palazzo in 1997. Long after Capitman's prophecy had been fulfilled, and South Beach became the hottest style-destination in the entire United States, danger like drugs remained inherent to Miami's sizzling mix.

As usual the federal government was there to subsidize this latest fantasy of what Florida should be, in this case by putting the "beach" back in Miami Beach. By the 1980s it was so eroded that the most infirm retiree could make it into the water in a few steps. That all changed as the U.S. Army, using funding from our national defense budget, created an artificial offshore reef (composed partly of used automobiles) and imported millions of tons of sand to re-create the picture-postcard version of Miami Beach. As for Capitman, the familiar fate of the Florida visionary awaited her. She first went broke, then was turned into a road sign. Today, as the people with designer bodies flit from beach to bar to boutique, few notice that they are on Barbara Capitman Way, yet they are acting out their dreams in a world she created. What she invented is for them reality.

Two other trendsetters who became enamored of Miami's possibilities at the moment Miami supposedly was doomed were Jeanne-Claude Denat de Guillebon and her husband, Christo Vladimirov Javacheff. Born on the same date (June 13, 1935)—he in Bulgaria, she in Casablanca—they fell in love (where else?) in Paris before moving to New York. There, known jointly as "Christo," the couple became a powerful force in the world of the avant-garde; their installations redefined people's understanding of their surroundings, and themselves, from Berlin to Australia. As the smoke cleared over Miami, they came up with an idea that at first seemed even nuttier than Capitman's. Why not wrap those scruffy, garbage-strewn landfills in Biscayne Bay in 6.5 million square feet of pink-colored cloth?

Surrounded Islands transformed the world's vision of Miami when it was inaugurated in May 1983. Whether viewed from land, air, or the promenade deck of your yacht, the Christo installation conjured up a vision of a true Paradise of sky and water that, like Miami itself, was both out of this world and the absolute center of Right Now. What made this soul-gripping delight truly, authentically, completely Miami was that it all was fake. The islands were fake, landfills left over from dredging Biscayne Bay to create real-estate. The fabric was fake, made of synthetic polypropylene, yet what a vision of harmony plus excitement all this fakery produced!

Fifty years later and three hundred miles south of St. Augustine, right there in Biscayne Bay, Walter P. Fraser's "pan-scientific method" had produced a living work of art that combined the expertise of engineers, architects, and construction crews, marine biologists, ornithologists, specialists in mammalian behavior (human as well as dolphin), along with world-class couturiers and draftsmen. Especially honored were the garbage collectors; they removed tons of trash from the islands, including a well-publicized kitchen sink. Most astonishing, lawyers and politicians played a nondestructive role, arranging and approving the many permits necessary for the project. A truly memorable work of art that deeply touched all who participated in its construction, *Surrounded Islands* was also prophetic in the questions it raised about responsibility. Would we revere our surroundings or despoil them? Nearly thirty years later sludgy black oil, not buoyant pink fabric, surrounded other islands on the other side of Florida. People called it the Gulf Oil Spill; it could have been named *Surrounded Islands* (2). Miami's *Surrounded Islands* and BP's surrounded islands formed a diptych. Two "installations," one truth: together they showed how our choices reflect what kind of people we are, not just what we do to the earth.

Only seventeen months after *Surrounded Islands* delighted the world, on September 16, 1984, *Miami Vice* created a sensation when it premiered on network TV. Those guys! Those women! Plus all those cars and boats, and the music, those colors! Beyond its riveting sense of pace, place, and style, *Miami Vice* reflected truths about America that the press, politicians, and academics, along with Miami's publicists, had spent decades denying. One of those truths was that the frontier-suburban-theme park version of America was mostly bunk, and always had been. America was created in cities (Independence Hall in Philadelphia, Bunker Hill in Boston, the Charleston and New Orleans slave markets, the counting houses of New York, the stock yards of Chicago, the dream factories of Los Angeles). Now, as *Miami Vice* showed in living color, it was being reinvented in cities once again.

During the 1950s and '60s the de-Americanization of cities had played as central a role in U.S. domestic affairs as belief in the domino theory did in the conduct of U.S. foreign relations. Cities were alien, scary, where America's trash got dumped; suburbs were where "real" Americans lived happily ever after. Then, in the late 1970s, Hollywood started showing Americans something the official custodians of the national self-image had forgotten. Cities could be exciting as well as dangerous, fun as well as violent. On *Miami Vice* the colors were more vivid; the music danced in your ears. Barbara Capitman's Deco pastels and Christo's pink had gone national, with car chases, on prime time TV.

Like *Saturday Night Fever* (1977), *Escape from New York* (1981), and *Blade Runner* (1982), *Miami Vice* was part of an American cultural transformation. Skin color no longer decided your place, nor did ethnicity. Crockett (blond, blue-eyed, and cool), Tubbs (black, stubbly cheeked, and cool), and, coolest of all, their brooding, utterly cool (and Latino) boss, Lieutenant Castillo, belonged to a new American elite. These guys weren't rich. In the conventional sense they were not successful, yet they were indivisibly and unalienably what Kerouac, up in Orlando, had called "hip." The sociology was fascinating but what made *Miami Vice* essential viewing were those bodies—not just the breasts and biceps on the guest stars, but all those sexy extras crowding those beaches and bars.

Who were all those gorgeous people? According to the news reports Miami was a war zone. A peek into people's bedrooms revealed that Miamians all along had preferred to make love, and not just with the girl (or boy) next door, and this change, too, presaged an American transformation. As recently as 1962 Dewey McLaughlin and Connie Hoffman had been jailed for living together, but by the time *Miami Vice* premiered in 1984, cross-cultural, artistic, political, and financial—as well as romantic—cohabitation had turned Miami into America's hottest, and coolest, place to pursue your dream. Whether it was Miami's signature design firm, Arquitectonica, or Miami Sound Machine, or Miami-Dade politics, behind many if not most Miami success stories there was an interethnic coupling—sexual, not just professional. It had taken a very long time, but what Florida's forgotten philosopher of sex and love had written nearly 160 years earlier was finally demonstrated to be correct. "The intermediate grade of color are not only healthy, but when condition is favorable, they are improved in shape, strength and beauty," Zephaniah Kingsley had declared in 1829. No one, watching *Miami Vice*, could deny that now.

Miami Vice offered a glimpse of an America of the future (that is today) that was eclectic, synthetic, polyglot, and multiracial. Also like America today, *Miami Vice* was full of drugs, violence, designer labels, and technological toys, but also imbued with a capacity for empathy and tolerance unimaginable in the past. In 1980 Miami had laid bare America's racial and ethnic divisions. Now, only four years later, *Miami Vice* reveled in another truth about America. For all that divides them, when Americans fuse their talents they thrill the world. Long after its last episode was shown in the United States, the show's uniquely American hybrid dynamism made it a big hit in both Estonia and the United Arab Emirates, among other places.

What the show nailed most accurately was the multiplier effect of excess cash. By the 1980s more than two-thirds of America's cocaine imports were reaching their consumers via Florida. The U.S. Treasury calculated some $5 billion in excess currency was circulating in the Miami area. The *Miami Herald* discovered that it was impossible find a $100 bill in Miami without traces of cocaine on it. People used all that money for purposes other than snorting coke. They bought cars, condos, houses, boats—also clothes, accessories, food, wine, sex, and people and, sometimes, after the sex and people paled, they hired hit men. Much as they complained about drugs and crime, few of Miami's movers and shakers complained about all that cash flowing into their businesses and bank accounts, even when the white powder did stick to their money.

In this realm of multiple convergences, good and bad commingled as inseparably as heat and humidity as Jules Verne's great insight into Florida's importance took sociological and macroeconomic form. Because of Miami's geography and U.S. and Cuban politics, Miami had become what the French scholar Fernand Braudel called a world city existing in world time. This was in contradistinction to the Florida "attraction," which exists out of time (or in false time) and also (whether theme park or gated community) occupies an artificial space deliberately contrived to exclude reality. It all had happened before in Florida. More than 150 years earlier the sailing ships that carried the ideals of the Enlightenment across the Atlantic also made possible the globalization of the African slave trade. Fernandina had domiciled both Zephaniah Kingsley's idealistic speculations and the slaves he traded. It was the same now, only with a billion times more intensity.

As it was with Miami, so also it would be with Orlando, then Florida—and not just Florida. With each passing year life in America grows more Miami-like. To see that, all you need do is take the masks off the costumed "characters" at Disney World. Beneath the plastic you find people from all over the world—humanity in all its forms. Orlando today is as all-American as Ellis Island. It is a denouement full of irony and revelation, the convergence of the American situation in these two Florida cities, each the product of a different variant of the American Dream.

People could flee Miami, or sneer at it, but if other cities wanted to cash in on how the world was changing they had to change too. Before airplanes and superhighways reduced travel times, Jacksonville was Florida's dominant city. Its location at the northeast extremity of the state gave it access up the East Coast to the sources of political money in Washington and private capital in New York. It was one of the few places in Florida where rich people could bear to live year-round prior to the invention of air-conditioning. The newfangled hatred of winter, followed by the invention of the motorcar and the advent of air travel, struck heavy blows to Jacksonville's hegemony, but when it came to exploiting new possibilities Jacksonville was always its own worst enemy. Penny-pinching in public health had turned Jacksonville into yellow fever's Florida stronghold in 1889. Unregulated working conditions and shoddy construction produced the Great Fire of 1901, as a blaze starting in a mattress factory took less than ten hours to consume more than two thousand buildings. The Jacksonville fire, as much as the railroad, moved the locus of Florida development southward. Though the old pine and tar-paper town was rebuilt in brick and concrete, Jacksonville's foundations remained sectional and racist.

Jacksonville's destruction of its film industry—twice over—epitomized the city's intolerance of alternatives to its pretentions to lily-white gentility. Jacksonville's first movie was made in 1908; within a decade it was rivaling New York as the movie-making capital of the United States. *The Gulf Between*, shot entirely in Florida in 1917, was the first Technicolor film, but even before Hollywood had a chance to overtake it, Jacksonville drove the film production studios out of town. The city's upper crust—the civic heirs of Francis Fleming and his ilk—complained that movies were filmed on Sundays, also that movie folk lowered the social tone. And the immorality one could see flickering there, with Jacksonville in the background! Though it was filmed in St. Augustine, the lesbian theme portrayed in *A Florida Enchantment*, released in 1914, disenchanted the guardians of propriety all over the state.

Rid of riffraff like Mary Pickford and Oliver Hardy, Jacksonville next destroyed its colored film industry. To the alarm and disgust of the local elite films like *The Bull-Dogger* and *The Crimson Skull*, dating from 1921 and 1922, made Jacksonville the capital of the African-American film industry. The preachers and politicians found it particularly unseemly that these films portrayed black folk in a positive light—as war heroes, airplane pilots, and handsome cowboys, not as the bug-eyed buffoons usually seen on the screen. The subsequent destruction of Jacksonville's colored film industry—through vigilante violence as well as government restriction—showed that the idea of white supremacy, like white supremacy itself, aggressively sought out and destroyed even implicit alternatives to itself.

What limited Jacksonville's possibilities most was the old extractive ethos of self-enrichment, going back to racist Carpetbaggers like George Drew (as well as bona fide homegrown racists like Broward). Into the civil rights era Jacksonville clung to the notion that you got rich ripping things out of Florida (notably timber products and phosphate) and stayed rich by keeping your white as well as your black workforce poor, unskilled, cheap, and powerless. That zero-sum approach meant Jacksonville lost its comparative advantage when other places found other ways to attract people and money.

Tampa had an immense natural harbor, a central location and a climate better suited to tourism than Jacksonville's. For a long time it also had Florida's biggest Cuban community. Certainly the mafia found Tampa an agreeable headquarters for its Florida operations. In one of the more exotic examples of Florida hybridization, the Ku Klux Klan made common cause with the mafiosi, dominated by the notorious Trafficante crime family. Tampa's Anglo elite used them both to break unions, terrorize blacks, keep the cigar workers in Ybor City in line—and limit Tampa's possibilities.

Instead of Jacksonville or Tampa, Florida's two made-up cities—Miami and Orlando—became the pacesetters. Their artificiality was key to their success. People could make of Miami and Orlando whatever they wanted. Jacksonville and Tampa carried the burden of having a there there, though that wasn't the end of the story. Today JAXPORT (the Jacksonville Port Authority) is to America's trade deficit what Miami once was to its drug problem. Every year more than half a million imported automobiles, and their internal combustion engines, enter the United States through the ancient lagoon system people call the St. Johns River. Maybe someday some statistician or philosopher will determine which has harmed Americans more: cars or drugs? The globalized economy doesn't care whether our addiction is to cocaine or gasoline, or both, any more than once upon a time it cared whether you trafficked in slaves or printing presses.

With its globalized import-export sector, its theme parks, and its major-league sports franchises, Tampa also plays in the big leagues now. Its much-appreciated airport is to the age of mass migration through the air what Henry Plant's Port of Tampa was to the age of steamships. Though the ways plutocrats get their money change with time, both Henry Plant, paradigmatic plutocrat of the belle epoque, and George Steinbrenner, prototype postindustrial billionaire, wound up reinventing themselves in Tampa. Never changing here as elsewhere is the importance of government spending, especially military spending. At the end of the nineteenth century America's wars in the Caribbean were launched from Tampa. At the beginning of the twenty-first century the wars in Iraq and Afghanistan were run from Tampa, headquarters of the U.S. military's Central Command.

Whether it's a large and growing immigrant population, a dynamically expanding involvement in foreign trade, or the continuing marginalization of several sectors of society, Florida's urban centers now share the characteristics that once supposedly made Miami aberrant. That doesn't mean they are identical. Look at a big sports crowd in Miami. You will see much the same blend of people as you might at the Meadowlands in New Jersey, only with suntans and wearing shorts. In Tampa you will see much the same crowd as you would at one of the big midwestern sports arenas. Florida, like America, has become bicoastal, as Midwesterners flow down its west coast while people from the Northeast populate its east coast. In the course of this region-by-region colonization, whole congressional districts in places like Illinois and New York did not so much disappear as transport themselves to Florida.

A similar pattern prevails in migration from Latin America. Traditionally people from the Caribbean and South America head toward Miami. Migrants from Mexico and Central America reach north and central Florida first, though the days are gone when any simple diagram could represent the jumbled peopling of Florida. Brazilians are now big players in Miami; the 2010 Census gave the Orlando megapolis Florida's first "Puerto Rican" congressional district.

Successful cities know how to specialize. They also must be generalists, forever ready to reinvent themselves by acquiring new specialties if they are to prosper in the face of social as well as economic upheaval. Miami Beach reinvented itself, spectacularly, when it transformed itself from "God's Waiting Room" into a fashionista playpen. So did Fort Lauderdale when it deliberately, and successfully, transformed itself from the Spring Break Capital of the United States into the Yachting Capital of the World. Smaller Florida cities like Lakeland have also figured out how to reinvent themselves—as places where a genuine as opposed to a manufactured small-town approach to life prevails.

One of America's most telling examples of urban specialization is to be found on the expanding fringe of the Central Florida Megapolis. Located some sixty miles north of Orlando, it is known as The Villages. In keeping with the first law of Florida nomenclature, The Villages is the antithesis of everything a real village is. Villages produce crops, tools, handicrafts, art, and, by means of the human family, the future. The Villages produces nothing, though it does have nearly five hundred holes of golf, because the normal chain of human existence is aborted there. At other times and places various groups have oriented themselves around hostility to Seminoles, to black people, to abolitionists, to Carpetbaggers, to "outside agitators." The Villages is founded on the exclusion of children. Any resident who actually brought forth new life there, whether biologically or through adoption, and then tried to rear the child there would be driven from its gates—and gates and security fences proliferate in The Villages.

The Villages exemplifies one of contemporary America's most conspicuous trends. The more "American" people proclaim themselves to be, the more detached in many cases they have become from the values that make America America. Inside The Villages' security perimeter the principal form of transport is the golf cart. During the Iraq invasion of 2003, war fever swept through The Villages. Golf carts remodeled to look like Humvees were festooned with military emblems. Flags flew everywhere, yet The Villages' system of segregation meant that many of the young soldiers risking their lives in battle would be physically evicted if, having been wounded in Iraq or Afghanistan, they attempted to convalesce in their parents' homes. Should the widow and young children of a fallen soldier attempt to move in with his parents, she and her infants would be evicted too.

There are exceptions. For thirty days each year, not at a stretch but in total, children are permitted to stay with their parents in The Villages. Thereafter they must leave.

In The Villages rights normally considered universal are restricted to one group. Once upon a time that privileged group would have consisted of people who were white, or who owned property, or were males. In The Villages the privileged caste consists of people over the age of fifty-five. The younger you are, the more severe the denial of your civil liberties. People in their thirties and forties may live in The Villages, though only if cohabitating with at least one person fifty-five or older. If under nineteen, you are forbidden to live there under any circumstances, not even in your own parents' house—not even if you are handicapped, and certainly not if, like more and more young people these days, you can't afford a place of your own.

The American family has been eradicated in The Villages; so has American democracy. The Villages has no mayor, no city council, no municipal elections. Entities known as Community Development Districts dictate how people live. The most powerful of them is the Village Center Community Development District, locally known as the VCCDD. As one account puts it, the "VCCDD provides water and sewer utility services, recreation, security services, fire protection and paramedic services to the residents." It also taxes without representation, unilaterally determining how much in "amenity and utility fees" residents must pay for access to services ranging from emergency medical care to use of The Villages' adults-only swimming pools. Disney World's two "cities" do have a few residents. In The Villages the boundaries of the VCCDD have been configured so that it has no people, hence no voters at all. Its all-powerful Board of Supervisors is chosen by The Villages' developer-owner, his family, and their agents.

Not very long ago The Villages did not exist. Neither did its developer-owner, Gary Morse. It was desolate scrubland and he was Harold Schwartz Jr. His father, Harold Schwartz Sr., originally came to Florida to run trailer parks. He called his encampment Orange Blossom Gardens, another classic misnomer. In this northerly stretch of central Florida the blossoms froze many winters; most months it was stiflingly hot and humid. In territorial times Governor DuVal had included these forlorn wastes in the Seminole concentration zone. Nothing much changed until 1983. That year, in a move equivalent to Flagler's decision to relocate to Florida, Schwartz's son, who had been living up in Michigan, decided to join the family business. Before he was finished, he would transform his family's mobile home park into a real estate empire with holdings larger than the island of Manhattan. Harold Schwartz Jr. already had transformed himself—into a public relations "counselor" named H. Gary Morse.

Opportunities bred of traumatic change propelled the growth of this latest Florida empire. Alarmed by drug violence and a spate of drowning boat people, many Americans were now scared of the places on the Florida coast where they once dreamed of retiring. They could head inland to Orlando, but where to go once Orlando also failed to provide a refuge from reality? By then millions of Baby Boomers were starting to approach retirement age. As the boomers cashed in their life savings, Gary Morse foresaw, immense profits were to be made attracting buyers for whom a sense of security was more important than sunsets over open sea. Working outward from the family trailer park, he began amassing not acres, or even thousands of acres, but square miles of land. Eventually he got a hold of more than thirty-three square miles of land. This unknown son of a trailer park manager had created for himself one of the great Florida land grants, virtually the same size as the realm that Congress conferred on Lafayette back in 1823.

The name change wasn't the only thing Schwartz-Morse had in common with David Levy Yulee. Like most Florida empire-builders he was a firm believer in the role of big government so long as the public purse subsidized his private fortune. Having set up his Community Development Districts, Morse then used them to issue the equivalent of municipal bonds while simultaneously ensuring that no municipal governments, which might have served as a check on his powers, were established. He also unilaterally exempted himself from Florida sales taxes. He had no authority to do that, but also like Yulee—and other Florida visionaries going back through Disney and

Flagler to Call and Menéndez—Morse understood nothing is illegal in Florida, not even the usurpation of sovereignty, unless and until some prosecutor claims it is, some judge agrees, and then, finally, someone actually enforces "the law."

Drawing up the plans governing life inside The Villages, Morse didn't hire urban planners. He had theme park designers from Universal Studios gouge out a shallow depression, fill it with water, and call it Lake Sumter. Thanks to the bulldozers and a marketing label, The Villages now had waterfront property plus a subliminal link to Florida's triumphant Confederate heritage. Morse's land remained about as far from salt water as you can get in Florida, some fifty miles distant from the Gulf of Mexico, nearly eighty miles from the Atlantic Ocean. Morse's imagineers nonetheless also created Florida's first landlocked lighthouse; they named the nearby shopping center Lake Sumter Landing. Though the Spaniards had left no trace there, Spanish Springs was the name chosen for the development's other commercial center.

"Not democracy, but freedom from democracy" was the source of Disney World's enormous appeal to vacationers, as Richard Foglesong had understood nearly a generation earlier. Now Morse grasped that, for many Americans, the need to escape freedom had become an entire life need, so he filled every aspect of life there with theme-park controls. Halloween trick-or-treating was forbidden. So were clothes lines and mail boxes. Morse headed off the danger freedom of the press might pose by buying the independent local newspaper and turning it into his publicity organ. Then the developer-owner and his family established control over The Villages' radio stations as well as the local Fox News TV affiliate, which for many residents is their sole source of information about what goes on beyond the fences, in the "world of reality." Morse's understanding that people would pay you to take away their freedom made him the paradigmatical Florida conquistador of the late twentieth century. It also made him rich. In its best years The Villages did nearly half a billion dollars in sales. This being Florida, Morse and his family paid no state income tax, in addition to no sales tax.

Like New Smyrna in the eighteenth century, The Villages was an experiment in for-profit oligarchy. As in Clinch's and Call's time, a tripartite hierarchy of social relations both enforce and perpetuate the misdistribution of power. At the bottom—as in pre–Civil War days—were those with no rights whatsoever: service workers; those who tend the golf greens but will never play golf there; people still in their reproductive years; the young. Above them, those fifty-five and older occupied the position "countrymen" once did. Except when their user "amenity fees" are arbitrarily raised, or they are reprimanded for some violation of The Villages' infinity of rules, they seldom considered that, like Florida in slaveholder times, The Villages exists to enrich a tiny elite, not them.

In times past that top tier consisted of those who owned slaves, and later, of those who controlled the railroads and the legislature. In The Villages it consists of the Schwartz-Morse clan. The regulations governing others do not apply to them. Members of the governing clan can and do have as many children as they wish. By century's end Morse's grandchildren had begun to inherit some of his powers. In a sealed society where letting your dog off its leash can incur a penalty when other people do it, they also were free to ignore The Villages' lifestyle restrictions. An oft-cited example of their immunity was the Schwartz-Morse private herd of water buffalos, long one of the local sights.

Holding together this structure of systemic inequality was a myth as powerful as the myth of white supremacy once was. Nothing could be more radically subversive of American values than forbidding children to live with their parents, yet almost everyone you meet in The Villages will tell you they are "conservative" and proud of it! You may never have heard of Gary Morse, but "family values" politicians snap to attention when he offers them rides in his private jet to one of his stage-managed rallies. In a typical political event thousands cheer as the candidates denounce the threat big government poses to our freedoms and call for a resolute defense of our traditional American way of life. The politicians then fly off in Gary Morse's airplane while those in the audience return to homes where sheltering a child, let alone a water buffalo, would expose them to retribution.

As has been the case in Florida from the beginning, the rhetoric of freedom obscures a reality of dependence. "Big government" provides residents of The Villages with Medicare health insurance and Social Security payments. Florida taxpayers pay for The Villages' roads, which then are gated in order to discourage their use by the "outsiders" whose taxes paid for them. Big government's biggest beneficiary in The Villages is Gary Morse, yet this rich and powerful man laments the threat government poses to America in general and The Villages in particular. "Excessive and inefficient regulation is an expensive, continuing challenge. For a country built by free enterprise, we sure make it tough on ourselves," he complained in one of his rare interviews.

So taken are its residents with the nomenclature of The Villages that they imagine they have escaped the tumultuous changes reshaping America—not recognizing that they are that change. They descry the erosion of "traditional values"—unaware that they themselves personify the breakdown of traditional values. Those enclosed behind its fences don't think of The Villages as a radical repudiation of traditional values. They also don't think of The Villages as a city, yet precisely because of them moving there that is what it has become. In 1980 only a few thousand people lived in the area. By 2006 it was America's fastest-growing Micropolitan Statistical Area. By 2010 the population was 51,442, an increase of 517.3 percent in ten years.

Today about the same number of people live in The Villages as live in Fairbanks, Alaska or Charleston, West Virginia. Inside Florida, it has about the same population as the cities of Ocala and Pensacola. The difference is that in those places the rule of law and democratic process prevent one person or one family from creating a system of self-perpetuating hereditary rule. There's another difference, one that makes the situation in The Villages truly un-American. Unlike people fleeing to Florida from places like Cuba, the people in The Villages have come there to have their freedoms taken away from them. They willingly divest themselves of their rights, "and they're happy with that," notes Andrew Blechman, who wrote a book, *Lei-sureville*, about The Villages. "You know, they've traded in the ballot box for the corporate suggestion box."

Another trend The Villages epitomizes, in addition to the shrinking writ of responsible government, is America's dissipation of productive wealth—the erosion of savings; the growth of debt. De Soto and Ponce dispensed their fortunes in a quixotic attempt to reenact in the Florida swamps a golden age of conquest that already had passed. People inside places like The Villages are dispensing the capital they accumulated elsewhere in the attempt to re-create an America that no longer exists. The difference is the scale. More people live in The Villages than ever lived in the whole of Spanish Florida. Sooner or later all utopian communities must answer a question not even Henry Flagler was able to evade. How do we pay our way? In places like The Villages the future is demographically, hence fiscally clear. Over the next few decades the same system of age segregation that created The Villages will destroy it. All those now over fifty-five will die. If current projections hold, there will not be a "replacement population" sufficient to maintain the demographic status quo. As Social Security payments become increasingly inadequate, and people find themselves obliged to work longer and longer, the whole premise of founding cities on the idea of "retirement"—that is, consuming, not producing, wealth—will become, like the idea of covering Florida with Spanish missions, ridding it of Negroes, or eliminating the Everglades, archaic.

As a result Florida's age segregationists face choices similar to those Florida's race segregationists once did. Whether they choose to embrace change or fight it, the law of unintended consequences will continue governing Florida's mutations with a hand both imperious and capricious, though one thing already is evident. The more people keep coming to Florida, the more they will go on creating cities—cities that turn into bigger cities. Tampa and the Tampa Bay area, Jacksonville and Duval County, like Miami and Dade County, long ago became coterminous. Currently the whole midsection of Florida is turning into a sprawling supercity stretching from Tampa

Bay across the peninsula to Daytona on the Atlantic Ocean, and from Ocala south toward Sebring. Like Kissimmee, The Villages has become another nodal point in the central Florida megalopolis.

You can see it happening from Outer Space. When America's first satellite was launched from Cape Canaveral in 1958, Florida from earth orbit looked like two dimly lit lowercase letter *l*'s standing side by side. One long string of lights ran down the Atlantic side of the peninsula. Another line of light ran along the Gulf of Mexico. In between was the dark emptiness of interior Florida. Today those former swamps and barrens shine so brightly it's as though Florida has switched from low to high beam. The shape as well as the intensity has been transformed. So many formerly dark spaces shine so brightly now that, instead of two parallel *l*'s, Florida resembles a lopsided capital H. The extent and intensity of the glow give an idea of the consumption of resources, the upheaval of human population, and the alteration of the natural landscape involved in a sudden transformation this immense. Florida, once so empty, glows as though gigantesque phosphorescent alien creatures are replicating even though it's not aliens down there. It's us.

24

A FATEFUL CONVERGENCE

As the portentous zeros of the year 2000 clanked into place some claimed the new millennium would witness the end of history. After all, the contest with communism had wound up like the race to the moon, with America in first place. Now that the age of obscure wars fought in obscure places for obscure reasons was ending, surely we would spend all that money doing nondestructive things? Others, perceiving menace in those millennial zeros, predicted that they would cause a digital domino theory to kick into operation. As our computers crashed, currencies collapsed, and planes and earth satellites fell from the sky, our ICBMs would self-launch, obliterating us as well as those they targeted. It was one of those gigantic nonnews nonevents that go on forever, no news driving out any news, until another buzz erupts.

More and more it was Florida that kept buzzing like a broken bedside alarm. Night after night on the network news, which people still watched back then: Florida. Morning after morning in the newspapers, which people still read back then: Florida. One night on Fox, as the latest feed from Florida wormed its way across the bottom of the screen, the bleach-blonde opinionator looked unscripted for a moment. Then she said: "Why does Florida keep doing this to us?" No one showed any interest in what the answer might be. Content was so last century! Climate change? Stem cell research? Natural selection? The irrelevance of fact, which had always prevailed in Florida, was turning out to be a hallmark of the new epoch.

The new millennium's precursor took the form of an angelic little boy floating up to Florida on a waterborne manger. Imagine

Botticelli's *Venus* as the sweetest, friendliest, most lovable little kid you ever saw. Change the sea shell into an inner tube: there you have Elián González as the tempest-tossed tides of history bore him onward toward the free shores of the United States of America and its 24/7 news cycle. Elián wound up on an inner tube because generation after generation, Americans placed hegemony ahead of hemispheric equity, because, starting in 1492, the Spanish placed greed ahead of goodness. From beginning to end, under Castro as under the conquistadors, the sword trumped the cross and violence crushed freedom. Those were among what history books used to call the underlying reasons why Elián was found floating in the Atlantic Ocean in November 1999. The immediate cause was that his mom and her boyfriend fled without informing Elián's dad, let alone asking his permission to abscond with the child. Their boat, unseaworthy, sank. Only the boy survived.

Had an American endangered her child in such a manner she would have been denounced, possibly imprisoned, but this was Florida. Elián's mother was lauded as a noble martyr who had given her life that her only son might live in Miami-Dade County. When Elián's father asked that his son be restored to him, the Hispanophone south Florida polemicists denounced him as an ogre. Up in Washington agitated legislators proposed a special Act of Congress conferring immediate U.S. citizenship on Elián. José Martí, Cuba's national hero, had never been so honored. In Miami the mayor, supposedly a nonpartisan figure, took the same position Florida's Confederates had in 1860. The law and loyalty to America counted for nothing when it conflicted with local passions. In the ensuing disgrace for Florida's leadership, Anglo as well as Hispanic, no one had the guts to say: The Boy Belongs with His Father. Besides It's The Law, so the six-year-old was held hostage (though none dared call it that) for more than four months in Little Havana.

Pending inquiries, U.S. authorities had entrusted Elián to relations he'd never met, whereupon the boy's supposed guardians turned their household into a proto-reality show, themselves into instant celebrities. "You think we just have cameras in the house?" one of his keepers threatened. "If people try to come in, they could be hurt." Along with the journalists besieging the house in Little Havana, symbolism was out in full force. Elián's boat had sunk on November the 22nd—Kennedy Assassination Day, Disney Decision Day. He was brought ashore on Thanksgiving Day; certainly Elián gave photo editors reason to give thanks. There was not a Cuban grandmother in south Florida who did not see both the Christ Child and her own dear little ones in his bashful media-compelling grin.

The prospect of Elián being returned to Cuba profoundly offended the Miami Cuban sense of entitlement. The notion that America owed them whatever they wanted whenever they wanted it, in return for not having rid them of Castro, had been transgressed. At Save Elián rallies Cuban-Americans who owned two houses and four cars recalled the trauma of having to sleep in a garage on a mattress for a few weeks back the 1960s. People who had multimillion-dollar art collections proclaimed they, too, were but orphans of the storm. Soon it wasn't only Cubans who were demonstrating. Their Anglo neighbors started asking, out loud, questions that had been nagging them privately for years. Did these Cubans have no appreciation for what America had done for them? Were they nothing but takers? Florida's other Latin Americans were also sick and tired of the preferential treatment Cubans got.

As counterdemonstrations erupted the "Anglos," it could be seen, included black people as well as people of Irish and many other non-English, indeed traditionally anti-English origins. Once again special privilege for some had brought on a general crisis for all that would not be resolved until the federal authority of the United States, as it had been doing since Seminole times, saved Florida from itself. Onlookers threw empty beer bottles and fist-fights broke out among swarming photographers as Justice Department community relations officers, Border Patrol SWAT teams, and agents of the U.S. Immigration and Naturalization Service rescued Elián.

The usual Miami-is-doomed obituaries followed but post-Elián Miami did not die. It turned itself into America's newest great metropolis: sexy as Rio; stylish as Milan, with a semitropical edge all its own. The Latin American Cafeteria on Coral Way was a good place to observe how Miami put Hurricane Elián behind it. At the height of the crisis you could feel the tension dividing Anglos and Cubans when you sat down at the counter. That didn't stop both ethnicities from packing in there to get those wonderful Cuban sandwiches. What made Latin American Cafeteria's sandwiches so perfect? Was it the way the sandwichmen toasted them in what looked like laundry irons? Maybe it was the horseshoe shape of the cafeteria's counter, the way it let you take in the conversations of the customers plus the acrobatics of the sandwichmen. Most of all, the contents of the sandwiches made them taste so good. In what other cuisine was it possible to combine ham plus pork, then cheese plus mayo plus mustard, all compressed gently within a length of warm crusted bread, and the result be refined, not coarse? All Cuban food is comfort food, but in that symphony of carbs and calories, there was something exalted as well.

While passions were running highest, someone turned the wall behind the Latin American Cafeteria's parking lot into a large-as-life mural of Elián rising out of the sea. After Elián disappeared back into Cuba the mural disappeared too. A real estate ad replaced it. Then the Latin American Cafeteria itself disappeared, ostensibly to make way for some superprofitable real estate–selling venture. This being Miami, by the time the Latin American Cafeteria's sandwichmen were evicted the latest bubble had burst. The shell sat empty, evidence of how in Miami greed in an average year destroys more property than hurricanes and civil disturbances do.

Five months after Elián went home, starting in November 2000, Florida became the pivot of another defining controversy. This time America's electoral values were betrayed as, for a second time, democracy in America was undone as the result of electoral dysfunction in Florida. Nationwide the Democratic candidate, Al Gore, had defeated his Republican opponent, George W. Bush, by more than half a million votes. In total he had gotten more votes—50,999,897 of them—than any other candidate for president up to that time with the exception of Ronald Reagan's reelection total. Even so, the U.S. Supreme Court, in a radical act of "conservative" judicial activism, made the candidate who came in second president of the United States.

In 2000, as in 1876, Floridians were denied their right to vote because of acts of repression directed against citizens who were nonwhite and poor. The pretext in many cases was the ban, dating back to the days of chain gangs and turpentine camps, on convicted felons voting even after they "paid their debt to society." Its proponents claimed denying citizens the right to vote for the rest of their lives was an anticrime measure. As the 2000 election made clear, the felony voting ban was no more an anticrime measure than the poll tax had been a revenue measure in the days of whites-only primary elections. Nowhere was the racial bias built into the electoral system on more blatant display than in Gadsden County, the only one in the state that still had a majority black population. As the *New York Times* eventually noted, Gadsden County "had the highest rate of disqualified ballots in Florida in 2000: 12 percent of those cast in the race between George W. Bush and Al Gore," but it wasn't just there. All over Florida nurses, school teachers and decorated war heroes were prevented from voting because they had names similar to supposed felons.

In 2000, unlike 1876, the repression was state-sponsored. Acting in her capacity as Florida secretary of state, the Republicans' campaign chairman purged nearly sixty thousand citizens from the voting rolls even before the voting began. The governor of Florida was the brother of one of the presidential candidates; as the votes were cast, counted, and recounted, his appointees and allies manipulated the system to favor one candidate over the other candidate. As in the days of The Nucleus and the Pork Chop Gang, special privilege, not the popular will, prevailed.

The voting process had been corrupted, but the more fundamental problem was the electoral system itself. The presidential electoral results of 2000 bore witness to the fact that for more than 120 years America had an electoral time bomb ticking in its constitutional suitcase, and not bothered to defuse it. Decade after decade the question was not whether, but when, the electoral college again would thwart the majority. The problem was not simply that so many votes went uncounted in such a prejudicial way. It was that so many citizens were prevented from voting in the first place. In 2000 Florida remained, as it had long been, the state where, proportionately, more citizens—white and black—were denied the right to vote than anywhere else, yet in the constitutional crisis that followed, neither the state of Florida nor the Supreme Court of the United States addressed the essential question—the same one that also had gone unanswered back in 1876. How could there be a fair count when there had not been a free election?

Because of the electoral chaos in Florida, the candidate a majority of America's voters had chosen would not become president. As events from Langley, Virginia, to Baghdad, Iraq, would show, this was not a trivial undoing of the popular will. The election connected with Florida's past in another way. Back in 1818 the killings of Arbuthnot and Ambrister had provoked outrage because, in their case, Andrew Jackson's victims were white. The massacre of hundreds of nonwhites attracted far less attention, and then mostly long after the fact. In 2000, the disenfranchisement of African-Americans attracted relatively little attention. It was the electoral dysfunction in white areas that riveted attention. Another similarity was that in 2000, as in 1876, white thugs disrupted the vote count, but this latest crisis for democracy in America was also new millennium in one very significant respect. The technology supposedly empowering people had stripped them of their rights. Thanks to those malfunctioning voting machines tens of thousands of white people as well as black people had their voting rights traduced.

Following all the polemics the electoral college did not get abolished, or even reformed. America's crazy quilt of voting regulations stayed in place. Florida's presidential election fiasco was to America's malfunctioning political system what the *Challenger* disaster was to NASA's malfunctioning manned space program. It was the event which revealed fundamental flaws that America would never fix. Then, on May 2, 2001, two Florida newcomers walked into the Department of Motor Vehicles office in Lauderdale Lakes. There they got driver's licenses. In Florida anybody can escape taxes. Many suppose they can escape death, or indefinitely defer it. No one escapes that visit to the DMV. The whole of Florida lines up there—the society lady with the helmet-like Palm Beach hairdo and the woman wearing plastic curlers; men sporting $500 sunglasses, men in greasy coveralls; brain surgeons and those who bag groceries at Publix. Most of all you see nervous parents, as Anglo kids, black kids, Hispanic kids, kids arguing with their parents in Creole, Romanian, and Malayalam all prepare to take that first big turn out onto the American freeway of life.

Had you gone to the Lauderdale Lakes DMV on May 2, 2001, you might have stood in line with two Florida residents who, like Andrew Jackson and Walt Disney, were going to change America forever. Their names were Marwan Yousef Mohamed Rashid Lekrab al-Shehhi and Mohamed el-Amir Awad el-Sayed Atta. Four months and nine days later, on the brilliant blue morning of September 11, 2001, they flew two hijacked passenger jets into the twin towers of the World Trade Center in New York City. In addition to getting driver's licenses in Florida, the hijackers also learned to fly—but not land—the planes they hijacked there because in Florida government, after all these generations, still existed to enable moneymaking schemes, not protect the public from them. Atta and al-Shehhi had chosen Florida because in Florida it was as easy to set up shop teaching people to fly big passenger jets, no questions asked, into skyscrapers as it was to sell submachine guns as the local strip mall. Of course they didn't hijack the planes in Florida. On the morning of September 11 the Booton airport security checks were like the Florida driver tests, that is to say like the O-rings made in Utah and the voting machines manufactured in Ohio. It wasn't one thing or five things that didn't work. There was systemic dysfunction in America. Months after Atta and al-Shehhi and more than three thousand other people were dead, the U.S. Immigration and Naturalization Service renewed the hijackers' visas.

In 2003 the United States invaded Iraq because weapons of mass destruction supposedly were there, only they were not there. Then, in October 2005, Hurricane Katrina joined the expanding gallery of dysfunction. At first it seemed just one more Florida breaking-news event—until Katrina, like Andrew Jackson 191 years earlier, charged out of Florida, hell-bent for Louisiana. As the ensuing mayhem demonstrated, hurricanes don't turn American cities into death traps.

Slack maintenance by the U.S. Army Corps of Engineers of the dikes protecting them does. Hurricanes don't abandon people in downtown sports arenas, or gun them down when they try to reach safety. Our government officials and those supposedly there to protect us do. In this instance, too, Florida provided perspective. While neglecting flood control for New Orleans, public officials, using public dollars, had been making sure everything was in tip-top shape for the yachts coursing down to Florida on the Intracoastal Waterway.

Today most Americans believe the main effect of the upheavals of the 1960s was that black citizens got to vote, but in Florida the expansion of voting rights meant that an immense cross-section of the white population also was empowered as never before. Now that Florida's legislators represented people, and migration was turning northern, central, and Gulf coast Florida into densely populated outposts of the Upper South and plains states, two things happened simultaneously. Progress in civil rights meant that more previously disenfranchised Americans, in spite of continuing restrictions and impediments, were voting. That increase was vastly outstripped by the increase in white voters produced by migration into Florida from other states.

As Florida's perfomance in the 2012 presidential election showed, today, most Americans believe the main effect of the upheavals of the 1960s was that black citizens got to vote, but in Florida the expansion of voting rights meant that an immense cross-section of the white population also was empowered as never before. As migration turned northern, central, and Gulf coast Florida into densely-populated outposts of the Upper South and Plains states, two things happened simultaneously. Great numbers of previously disenfranchised Americans were voting. That increase was outstripped by the increase in white voters produced by migration into Florida from other states. Meanwhile more and more Latinos acquired U.S. citizenship.

As a result two electoral narratives emerged, the same ones that now dominate politics across America. One was the upbeat linear narrative of the American Dream come true. In this narrative America overcomes the legacy of slavery and its other inequities, vindicating the idea that America can be made perfect. What better proof of that could anyone want than Barack Obama's 2008 election as President of the United States, who as he triumphs gets the Florida electoral votes that, only eight years earlier, were snatched away from Al Gore? That is not a false narrative. As the election of 2012 showed, it is incomplete because simultaneously a second narrative unfolds. It is the narrative of (predominantly) white fear and anger. Its protagonists are (predominantly) politicians who exploit the negative energy unleashed by change in America.

Nowhere else was the election harder fought or more closely contested, but once all the votes were counted, the 2012 results proved once again that Florida was the paradigm of America. Not even Florida's blatantly racist voting restrictions, its governor's attempts to intimidate non-white voters—not even Florida's inevitable snafus at the polling place—could undo the profound human changes reshaping America, as Florida demonstrated that here, as all across the country, demography was destiny.

The new political contours began to emerge in 1963 when former Senator Pepper returned to Washington as Congressman Pepper, representing one of the new districts Florida gained following the 1960 census. Florida now had new kinds of voters to go with its new congressional districts; Pepper's political metamorphosis demonstrated that. The better to please these new kinds of constituents, the senator who once praised Stalin now became the representative who condemned Fidel Castro. As Florida's population of exiled Central Americans grew, Pepper also supported Ronald Reagan's war against the Sandinistas in Nicaragua, including the CIA's secret (and illegal) support for the "contras." In Pepper's later years a typical oration, having commenced with a fervent denunciation of communist subversion, would be followed by a heartfelt reminder of every American's duty to stand steadfast in the defense of Israel. Then the grand old man would segue into a discussion of what was on his mind that day. In many though far from all cases, it was securing some benefit or protection for Florida's, America's—and his congressional district's—senior citizens. Having served three terms in the U.S. Senate, Pepper would stay in the House of Representatives for twenty-six years.

Eighty years earlier Judge James Dean, after being purged from office, had resettled in Jacksonville where his persecutor, former governor Francis Fleming, also lived. Now that Miami was the place where friend and foe converged, Pepper's constituents included his former nemesis, George Smathers. Florida's "Venereal Soil," as the poet Wallace Stevens called it, also transformed Smathers, gradually shifting his focus from the earthly nexus of money and influence to a concern for his status in the hereafter. As the judgment of history closed in on him, he arranged for a donation totaling $24 million to be made to his old alma mater, the University of Florida. In return, Florida's publicly financed university library system renamed itself the George A. Smathers Libraries in honor of the politician whose disregard for fact had made him nationally famous. Rich, remarried, and renowned, Smathers lived until age ninety-three. In its January 2007 obituary the *Washington Post*, along with many other publications, recycled the amusing story of how Smathers had accused Pepper's sister of being a thespian.

Pepper adapted himself to change. Smathers let the changes overtaking Florida flow around him. Governor Claude Roy Kirk Jr., in office from 1967 to 1971, was that change. A promoter of the death penalty like Charley Johns, and an opponent of racial integration like Smathers, Kirk was also a longtime Democrat until, in 1960, he rebranded himself as a Republican. Until Kirk gave it its new, strident face, the Republican Party, so far as most Florida-born white folks were concerned, was the party of that folkloric oppressor, the Carpetbagger. Claude Kirk changed all, in the process helping to usher in the age of code words in Florida politics. Kirk didn't praise lynching; he turned militant support for the death penalty into a litmus test of Florida politics. He and the growing crowd of newly converted Republican politicians did not orate about colored water fountains and white womanhood, as their Dixiecrat forebears had. They railed against "court-ordered" busing, while denouncing civil rights legislation on the grounds it, too, extended federal tyranny.

When he wasn't confronting convicted murderers, Kirk was treating Florida's school teachers as though they were criminals, turning contempt for learning into his political tool. Kirk's opponent for governor was Robert King High. The Tennessee-born son of a carpenter, he had been elected mayor of Miami on a reform ticket. "Good Government" was his pledge, his only pledge; his constituents agreed he had delivered. Kirk (who lived in Jacksonville) denounced High as the candidate of big-city depravity. Kirk also pioneered the use of scare-and-smear tactics on television. Decades before Willie Horton showed up in attack ads for George H. W. Bush, one of Kirk's commercials showed a darkened room. Though viewers could not see what was happening, they could hear a white woman screaming. Kirk denounced his opponent as "a rubber stamp for Washington, backed by the ultra-liberals." In a very early example of what later would be called swiftboating, an outfit called the Committee for Integrity in Government distributed a cartoon caricature of Mayor High. "Black power is with you 100 percent," the caption read. "Bob, let's march."

The very embodiment of Richard Nixon's "Southern strategy," Kirk channeled Barry Goldwater's extremism-in-defense-of-liberty approach. He also foreshadowed the Bush brothers with his rhetorical opposition to nonmilitary federal spending on everything except programs benefiting his own friends and supporters. Until Kirk won the governorship, Florida was turning into an anti–death penalty state. Governor LeRoy Collins had opposed capital punishment, and won. So had his more traditionally minded successor, Haydon Burns. Kirk's me-first Republicanism repudiated the party's traditional values, yet it was the Republican label that made Kirk's tactics acceptable to hundreds of thousands of voters who never would have voted for Dixiecrats, along with the hundreds of thousands who had voted for overtly racist candidates, and now switched to the Republicans. In 1966 Kirk—a multimillionaire native of California—was elected governor of Florida at the same time Illinois-born Ronald Reagan, another Sunbelt transplant and Democrat-turned-Republican, was elected governor of California. Like Reagan, Kirk was a divorced politician who, campaigning against his monogamous opponent, proclaimed himself the champion of family values.

Upright Floridians dismissed Claude Kirk as a ruffian, his triumph a fluke. As Florida's next watershed election demonstrated, they were wrong about that. The 1968 Senate race pitted former governor LeRoy Collins (born in Tallahassee) against Edward Gurney (born in Portland, Maine). Collins was a fourth-generation Floridian; Gurney, Collins' opponent, had studied law at Harvard just like Claude Pepper. It didn't matter. Like Governors Drew and Perry before him, and Governors Jeb Bush and Rick Scott later, Gurney the Yankee managed to "out-Southern" his Florida-born opponent. While serving as governor Collins had headed off the kind of racist confrontations that disgraced Alabama and Arkansas. Later he assumed the role of national peacekeeper, becoming the first director of the Community Relations Service under the 1964 Civil Rights Act. When violence broke out in Alabama, Collins was there to calm the situation. As a result his opponent was able to circulate photographs of Governor Collins walking alongside Reverend Martin Luther King Jr. in Selma. Gurney, the migrant from Maine, trounced Collins, the native-born Floridian whose forebears had fought Seminoles as well as Yankees, and whose wife was a direct descendant of Richard Keith Call, to become the first Republican to represent Florida in the U.S. Senate since Reconstruction.

Over the next thirty years Republicans would replace Democrats as the dominant party in the Tallahassee legislature as well the Florida congressional delegation. Events foreshadowed Florida's future another way when a young, Connecticut-born recent Yale graduate showed up in Florida and volunteered to work on Gurney's campaign staff. The younger George Bush had avoided military service in Vietnam by getting himself assigned to an aviation training program in Alabama; he then took "what amounted to a two-month-plus vacation that enabled him to head to Florida to work for a Republican candidate for the U.S. Senate, Edward J. Gurney," the *Washington Post* later reported. It was the beginning of a relationship with Florida that, for America as well as the Bushes, would be fateful.

Florida's culture wars also became prophetic in those days. In 1977 Anita Bryant—best known until then as the all-American face of Florida's orange juice industry—took up Charley Johns' anti-homosexual crusade. A second runner-up in the Miss America pageant, Bryant provided the All-American (that is to say, all white and nonethnic) public face for an industry where the migrant workers who picked and processed the liquid sunshine were like homosexuals— people who had no place in the highly processed world of Florida's self image.

Bryant's crusade against gays was one of the first of the great Florida lifestyle controversies to obsess the nation. Behind the scenes, though, the impresario orchestrating the citrus industry's marketing strategy was a figure as all-Floridian as David Levy Yulee. The Walter P. Fraser of Florida OJ was a native of Messina, Sicily, named Anthony T. Rossi. His process of self reinvention was set in motion by an earthquake back in Italy which, in his case caused a spiritual upheaval too. As Rossi's quest for God and Wealth unfolded he first abandoned Roman Catholicism; then he set out to discover a place where life was earthquake-proof.

In Florida the earth never, ever quaked, but how to make his other dream come true, of building an empire all his own? In 1947 Rossi made a down payment on a third-tier orange juice outfit in Bradenton, on the southern side of Tampa Bay. The perilous ambiguities of Florida's subtropical climate propelled the never-ending melodrama of its citrus industry, yet Rossi did not call his company Subtropicana. He called it Tropicana, and over the next twenty years he made Tropicana synonymous with sunshine itself.

Bryant could not reverse the gradual acceptance of sexual diversity in America. By the time she abandoned her Florida crusade, gay and lesbian days had become big moneymakers at Disney World: Rita Mae Brown had become the most famous Florida-born author since Zora Neale Hurston, following publication of her lesbian breakthrough novel, *Rubyfruit Jungle*. Bryant's sitcom-perfect Florida never had existed, nor had that zephyrous clime where the sunshine supposedly grew on trees. Though the producers kept denying it, their great problem was that evolution never equipped the orange to survive Florida's freezes, though for a time American know-how seemed able to solve that problem. The rootstock of the sour orange, *Citrus aurantium*, being more resistant to frost than the sweet orange and the grapefruit, growers grafted Florida's sweet citrus trees onto sour orange rootstock. That did not solve the problem for long. Killer freezes—what those in the citrus industry call "impact frosts"—had terminated orange and grapefruit cultivation in northern Florida in 1835. The impact frosts of 1895 and 1896 had traumatized production everywhere in Florida. Heavy freezes in 1899, 1917, 1934, 1946, and 1957 caused wide devastation. Then, in the 1980s, two successive impact frosts would kill off citrus production almost everywhere north of the I-4 corridor. Meanwhile each new orange hybrid seemed more prone to infestation and disease.

Everything was more complex now, but like the saltire on the Florida flag, the question of race was always there, ready to be exploited. No one could accuse Governor Jeb Bush of being racist. So why did so many poor whites prefer to vote for privileged Republicans, in this case the scion of one of America's most privileged political dynasties, over one of their own? In the 2002 election for governor, Bush's opponent was a Tampa lawyer named Bill McBride. Unexotic as Wonderbread at first glance, McBride was one of those Floridians who upon closer inspection demonstrated that everyone there was exotic, or married to someone who was. "Would you like to see my family album?" asked his wife, Alex Sink, when I remarked that there seemed something almost Oriental about her eyes. When she returned, she provided the interesting information that, though North Carolina–born and a longtime resident of Florida, she was a descendant of one of the original, famous "Siamese Twins." "Chang and Eng weren't Siamese," she informed me, as she showed me their pictures. "They were Chinese, though born in Siam."

There were many reasons why McBride lost his bid for the governorship. That day he described one of them. While campaigning he'd run into an old acquaintance. Things weren't going well, the man told him. He and his family had lost their home; they were forced to sleep in their car. After making some phone calls, McBride got back to the homeless family. He'd found a decent place for them at a rent they could afford. Later McBride ran into the same man again. He asked how his family liked their new house. They were living out of their car again, the man told him. Was there something wrong with the house? No, the man replied, but he didn't like his wife and children living in such close proximity to colored people. American-style slavery was only introduced there in the 1820s. It was practiced in Florida for less than forty years, yet the most persistent legacy of slavery—race fear and the politics it engenders—still casts Florida's longest shadow. There hasn't been an election yet in which Florida's poor white men didn't vote to perpetuate the privileges of its rich white men, so long as it helped keep black Americans in their place—and this election was no exception. "I pretty much realized I'd lost at that point," McBride told me. "I'd done my best to help him, but I could tell he was going to vote for my opponent."

Nearly two hundred years of Florida's "hidden history" came into play in 2010 when one of the truest Floridians ever was elected governor. For one thing, Rick Scott had spent his whole life outside Florida before arriving there to dissipate the fortune he'd made elsewhere. Just like Flagler and Tuttle, he'd started out in Ohio. Like Carl Fisher and Glenn Curtiss and Plant and Sanford and de Soto, Florida's new governor had made his fortune off one of the transformative moneymaking schemes of his era. America's deepening financial health care crisis was Rick Scott's El Dorado. Up North he'd made his fortune turning hospitals into profit centers: *Forbes* magazine described him as the entrepreneur who "bought hospitals by the bucketful and promised to squeeze blood from each one." Like most of Florida's conquerors, Scott had gotten even richer thanks to big government. His company eventually had to pay $1.6 billion in fines for ripping off Medicare, but he had moved on by then. Florida had beckoned.

Initially Scott, in keeping with the Yulee tradition, intended to buy himself one of the Florida seats in the U.S. Senate. Political consultants he hired counseled him to run for governor instead. Henry Flagler had spent $50 million on his Florida pet project; though Rick Scott spent $70 million to make himself governor, his greatest asset was the disconnect he offered from reality. Both Scott's rival for the Republican nomination and his Democratic opponent for governor each had the disadvantage of being bogged down in the realities of Florida. His main opponent in the primary was Bill McCollum, a tried-and-true Florida politician of the Charley Johns school. While in the House of Representatives McCollum stage-managed the effort to impeach President Clinton. As Florida attorney general, McCollum paid one witness more than $120,000 in state funds to testify that placing adopted children in homosexual households was as dangerous as placing them in households "with a pedophilic-behaving adult, households with practicing criminals, households with drug dealers and drug abusers, households with unemployed adults, households that advocate the overthrow of the U.S. government [and] households with an active terrorist" in them.

McCollum's polyester used-car salesman–like immersion in the nittier aspects of Florida politics contrasted with the contentlessness of Rick Scott's political past. With the help of his out-of-state fortune and his Washington political consultants, Scott defeated his Florida-born opponent in the primary, then ran for traditional values against big government in the general election. The result was poetic injustice, for this time the hapless Democrat defeated by the wealthy newcomer was Alex Sink, whom Scott dispatched with the same efficiency that Jeb Bush had her husband.

Once in office Governor Scott moved to cut those few taxes that rich people like him paid in Florida. He also vetoed funding for rape crisis centers. His goal was to close down Florida's public hospitals, while his supporters in the Tallahassee legislature fought to turn educating Florida's children into a for-profit operation. During his preinaugural Forging a Path to Prosperity Appreciation Tour, Scott praised Disney for exemplifying the best in American values and Epcot for providing a model for America's future. After taking office in Florida's most expensive inaugural ever, Scott urged Floridians to honor Ponce de León who, he stated, had "named the land La Florida because of its lush plant life." Then, in the latest reinvention of Florida's past, Ponce's Florida failure was portrayed as a triumph of multiculturalism. "WHEREAS, the expedition of Ponce de León included people of diverse culture and ancestry," the new governor urged all Floridians to celebrate "the anniversary of Ponce's landing." In later actions, Scott used his line-item veto to block health care funding for farmers suffering serious illnesses due to pesticide use.

Rick Scott was the George Drew of the new millennium. In his case, too, the effort to restrict voting rights defined his approach that, as his predecessor and fellow Republican Charlie Crist put it, ran "contrary to our democratic ideals." As part of Scott's effort to "make it more difficult for people to register and reduce the availability of early-voting opportunities," organizations like the League of Women Voters were threatened with criminal prosecution. In a state where, more than once, miscounting a few hundred votes had tipped the scales against democracy in America, Scott set out to purge more than one hundred thousand Floridians from the rolls. Among them was a ninety-one-year-old World War II veteran who had won the Bronze Star for bravery fighting in the Battle of the Bulge. His name was Bill Internicola. Civil liberties advocates pointed out that Scott's purge principally targeted nonwhites, Latinos, and people with foreign-sounding names.

It was impossible to call Governor Scott a racist. That was because he had selected a black woman to be his lieutenant governor, that post having been reinstated after the 1885 constitution was finally repealed. Having been born in Trinidad, raised in New York, gone to college in New Mexico, and served in the U.S. Navy, Lieutenant Governor Jennifer Carroll brought to her high office a life experience as detached from Florida's past history of racial tribulations as Scott's was from the hardscrabble travails of its white folks. Her résumé did resonate with Florida's past in another way. For the first time since Yulee had the legislature make him a senator, Florida had a high elected official born in the Caribbean.

In Florida labels always had been detached from meaning. Now that race and ethnicity were too, it was a situation to confound Heidegger as well as Rousseau until some clarifying event occurred. That happened on February 26, 2012, inside a gated community called The Refuge at Twin Lakes, located in the central Florida megalopolis about halfway between The Villages and Disney World. That night

an unarmed seventeen-year-old boy named Trayvon Martin was shot
dead for wearing a hooded sweat shirt and being black. According to
the killer, George Zimmerman, it was the victim's fault. His presence
had made him feel threatened. That was why he had followed the
boy, and ultimately killed him, so the police said what they would
have in 1980, 1935, 1920—or 1876 or 1818. It had been okay to kill
him. They told Zimmerman he could go home.

As this latest Florida melodrama caused Americans to shout at
each other on phone-in talk shows, the evidence once again demonstrated that in some fundamental sense Florida never changed.
Would Zimmerman be punished or not? It was the same question a
"countryman" would have faced back in the 1850s. While "white,"
Zimmerman's social status did not automatically confer on him the
immunity it gave Florida millionaire John Goodman, who killed another man by ramming him with his Bentley, but then went free "on
appeal," even though he had been found guilty of both manslaugh-
ter and failure to provide the aid that might have saved his victim's
life. Meanwhile a Jacksonville black woman, Marissa Alexander, was
sentenced to twenty years in prison for firing a "warning shot" into
a wall in the course of an altercation with her husband, who had
a history of domestic violence. Twenty years for wounding a wall,
when the perpetrator was black. Freedom for a millionaire when
someone actually was killed: Florida's three-tiered system of justice
was still thriving.

The vigilantism, the violence, the notion that the black male by
his very existence constitutes an unacceptable danger: these themes
went straight back to Jackson, Gaines, and Clinch. In other ways
the Trayvon Martin homicide was as up-to-date as the cell phones
killer and killed used as their encounter moved toward its climax.
There also was the multicultural aspect of the homicide. The killer's
last name was Zimmerman; his father was white and from Virginia.
His mother was Peruvian, which explained why so many reports
described him as "Hispanic."

Mentally and emotionally, as well as by his physical appearance, George Zimmerman demonstrated that in twenty-first-century

America there was no need anymore to have blue eyes and blond hair in order to act as stereotypical Florida white males previously had. Trayvon Martin was killed in the same once-barren midsection of Florida where Joseph Hernández, having assimilated white American notions of race and violence, had Billy Powell battered to the ground 175 years earlier. The gated "community" where Zimmerman killed Martin also defied profiling. Rebutting the notion that only affluent white folks inhabited such places, it showed how Florida's culture of violence infected every race and class even when—especially when—those in the grip of such prejudices had no suspicion that they were perpetuating the tragedies of Florida's past.

So there they were: one human stalking another in the heart of the old Seminole concentration zone. This place had been nothing but two sinkholes when Disney first appeared in the sky overhead. Now, like every trailer court and McMansion enclave, it had a fancy name, but what was its nature? What was the nature of what this place had become? Had George Zimmerman looked up that night, he might have seen an earth satellite making its tumbling progress across the sky. As he fired on Trayvon as though he were "a wolf or a bear," its unblinking eye gazed down on all those who believe we can be safe from our fears once we put up the fences, hire the security guards, buy the gun at the mall and, sooner or later, find a reason to use it. It also gazed down on the victims.

EPILOGUE
NO ESCAPE FROM AMERICA

When you take the very, very long view, it becomes evident that occasionally changes occur so immense they make what people do, as well as what they say, irrelevant. Starting in 1500 Spain writhed in dispute over how to treat the conquered populations of the New World. In Florida it didn't matter if missionaries sang psalms to them or conquistadors whipped them. The arrival of the killer microbes determined what would become of Florida's people. The introduction of monoculture slavery decided things again. Not even the Civil War could excise the race stain of slavery, once imprinted. Then, starting in the twentieth century, people happened to Florida, enormous numbers of people. In 1900 just over half a million people lived there; today thirty-five times as many people do.

As late as 1940 Florida, demographically as well psychologically, was still the ex-Confederacy's tadpole. The South's least populous state, it had fewer people than Arkansas. By 2010 Florida had out-stripped Illinois and Michigan to become the fourth most populated state, surpassed (only barely) by New York and those two other Sun-belt behemoths, Texas and California. Texas and California, unlike Florida, had a plentitude of natural resources. They had industry as well as accumulated intellectual property; Florida had the myth of sunshine, the allure of escape. Those immaterial assets had sufficed to unleash a sudden shift of population as consequential as the great migration of the 1820s, which created the conditions that produced the Civil War. That earlier influx had swept away the Indian nations of the southeast frontier; almost overnight it turned Mississippi, Alabama, and Florida into "pens to breed more slaves." Now—just as speedily—people crammed themselves into Florida and, by so doing, re-created every frustration they sought to escape.

The Miami Metropolitan Statistical Area continued to be the most stunning example of what, were a nonhuman species involved, biologists would call the Florida infestation. Also known as the south Florida metropolis, it as accurately could be called the oolite mega-lopolis, in honor of the underlying limestone that makes it possible for so many millions of people to perch there, between the Atlantic Ocean and the Everglades. More than 120 miles long yet seldom more than 20 miles wide, this narrow strip of north-south limestone stretching from Jupiter down to Homestead today is the seventh most populous agglomeration in the United States. Three of America's historic metropolitan centers—New York, Chicago, Philadelphia—still are larger. Los Angeles and the two great Texas conurbations, Houston and Dallas–Fort Worth, also are bigger, but by 2010 Greater Miami had outstripped the Washington, D.C., area in population. It also had surpassed what previously had been the South's dominant metropolitan region, Atlanta. The metropolis Flagler and Tuttle built on a desire to escape freezing temperatures also had overtaken such long-established urban centers as Boston and San Francisco, as well as rust belt cities like Detroit, Sunbelt comers like Phoenix, high-tech centers like Seattle, and regional capitals like Denver and Minneapolis–St. Paul.

It isn't just Miami and Orlando. In less than two lifetimes the state of Florida had become the most densely populated state out-side the northeastern Boston-Washington megalopolis. At previous turning points the Spanish, the Seminoles, and the Confederates discovered there is no escaping change in America once its full force is unleashed. Today that's true again, as all over Florida people find themselves coping with the complications of life in a state that now not only has more people, but is more densely packed with people than Pennsylvania or Ohio.

Vast cultural changes and an infinity of individual choices brought people as various as Rick Scott and George Zimmerman, LeBron James and John Travolta to Florida, but at every turn this de-mographic implosion has been accelerated and subsidized by govern-ment, both big and small. Long after population loss became a crucial problem Up North, states like New York continued to force retirees to head south with taxation policies that punished school teachers and hardware store managers for keeping the homes where they had raised their families. Long after population gain was recognized as a crucial problem in the Sunbelt, states like Florida continued to incite unchecked growth with low (or no) taxes, producing a double dysfunction of governance. States that did have the infrastructure, both physical and institutional, to serve the public found their fiscal foundations, and well as their highways and school houses, disintegrating. States like Florida, which didn't bother much with education and public works, found themselves having to cope with a population explosion that overburdened their already inadequate facilities.

This failure of government to govern intelligently, or at all, has turned out to be of more than polemical import. In 2012 census data established that Miami, America's newest metropolis, was also its least educated. The rest of Florida—and America—was not far behind in its accumulating neglect of the nation's intellectual infrastructure. With its low-skilled work force, Florida still did not produce much of anything. That also made it a national indicator of what, by the beginning of the twenty-first century, America as a whole was becoming. This was a debtor nation, consuming more than it produced, dependent on imported goods as well as borrowed money to sustain its frivolities and, increasingly, its necessities. Dissipating capital was nothing new, but the universality—the democratization—of the capacity to squander was new. Every man was like Ponce and Flagler now, dispensing money that originated someplace else, and not just in Florida.

Florida most obviously provided an environmental prototype, and not just because of its geographical vulnerability. For decades it had done nothing meaningful to slow or soften the impact of its stupendous population growth. Increasingly the do-nothing model applied nationally, as Americans responded to climate change either by lamenting it or denying it existed. Neither verbalization stopped the glaciers melting. Here, too, Florida was in danger of leading the way. Water pressure increases volumetrically, which means a three-inch rise in ocean levels produces a ninefold extra push of salty ocean water inward on Florida's freshwater aquifers.

When it came to Florida's hallmark agricultural activity, the production of orange juice, the chickens already had come home to roost. Successive frosts kept driving the citrus industry farther down the peninsula, but that couldn't save the orange and grapefruit, themselves alien species, from attack by wave after wave of invading killers. In 1995 the brown citrus aphid, or *Toxoptera citricida*, which means "toxic mobile citrus killer," invaded Florida. Having displaced the comparatively inoffensive black citrus aphid, this truly disgusting-looking newcomer began ravaging its way across the state's citrus groves. Then, in 2005, Doomsday seemed truly to be dawning as a murderous bacterium with the friendly-sounding name, citrus greening, took up residence. By 2013 about half of Florida's sixty million or so citrus trees had been infected. Unless some miracle cure came to the rescue, every orange and grapefruit tree in Florida seemed likely to die of the disease sooner or later.

At the peak about a million acres had been under citrus cultivation; now just over half a million acres were. Florida's orange exports were down to 145 million boxes from a peak of 244 million boxes in the late 1990s. Both Brazil and China had overtaken the United States in citrus production. Beneath all that, a deeper drama was unfolding. The Florida orange had originated in China; so had the disease now killing it. Citrus Greening is also known as HLB after its Chinese name, *huang long bing*, which means Yellow Dragon Disease. Just as Europeans had once chased Europeans all the way to Florida in order to kill them, the Yellow Dragon had pursued its prey halfway around the world. Like so many other exotic interlopers, this Chinese bacterium and its Chinese prey now faced their moment of truth in a Florida Garden of Eden.

For nearly two hundred years people had kept on pretending that Florida was, as H. H. Williams called it, a "Paradise Grove." A good place to see with your own eyes the long-term consequences of trying to fool nature is Clermont, Florida, located about twenty-five miles northeast of Disney World. When they incorporated it in 1916, local boosters named their development after Clermont-Ferrand, France, but something more than a fancy-sounding name was needed to turn the place into an attraction. Clermont's "Citrus

Tower," its website proclaims, "stands unrivaled as a majestic and monumental tribute to Central Florida's famed citrus industry and its lush subtropical groves." Today those groves are gone; just about the only orange blossoms left to see there are the ones on the license plates on the cars in the parking lot. Thanks to frost, disease and the advance of another invading species—*Homo sapiens*—the orange trees that gave Orange County its name now belong—like the Seminoles who once were concentrated there—to history, but no matter! "The glass enclosed observation deck," according to the Citrus Tower's promoters, now "serves as a beacon guiding a burgeoning new business and population base to the scenic South Lake County region."

Earlier secessionist slaveholders, instead of addressing the problems that their excesses created, turned against their principal benefactor, the federal government. Now neo-Cons (neo-Confederate as well as neoconservative) also ranted against federal tyranny, even though in this new age, full of unrecognized consonances with the old one, the conquistadors in golf carts, like their predecessors on horseback, were government-subsidized. Medicare and Social Security checks had given people the security and leisure to complain about big government. Federally insured bank deposits and government-guaranteed home mortgages helped inflate Florida's real estate bubbles. Boom or Bust, federal transfer payments sloshed more money into Florida every month than all the robber barons of the Gilded Age ever had.

One reason for the distraught response to what America was becoming was that, like Florida, America now had an economic system skewed to make the few richer while shortchanging the many. Once it had been oligarchs versus countrymen. Now across America it was the expanding privileges of One Percent versus the declining possibilities of what people still called the "middle class." Economically speaking, America's trend lines in the early twenty-first century posed questions similar to those the Disney World approach raised from the start. What is the point of a "boom" in which wages stagnate or decline and personal savings diminish? What's the benefit of a "jobless recovery" in which foreclosures multiply and personal debt (often at usurious credit card rates) soars, and going to college is a one-way ticket to penury too? Why are corporate malefactors exempt from the laws normal folks must obey?

One of the more daunting aspects of America's increasingly Floridaesque situation was its inability to solve its own problems, let alone provide solution-oriented models for the rest of the world. Over the past five hundred years Florida successively has been a by-product of the Age of Discovery, a pawn in Europe's dynastic struggles, an offshoot of the expansion of slavery, a symptom first of the industrialization, then of the deindustrialization of the United States. Now that the whole country was being redefined by forces it neither created nor controlled, maybe that was how the future of America would work itself out too. All those smart Asians and hard-working Latinos, leavened by sophisticates from other continents, and helped out by lots and lots of native-born New Millennium Scalawags: Was that Florida's terrible great lesson? Not to worry! Things will get a better—at least they will get different—once all those billionaires from Fujian and Nizhny Novgorod and entrepreneurs from São Paulo and Oaxaca start playing with America as though it's Play-Doh. Would the history books someday laud them as "visionaries" or would they be condemned as Carpetbaggers? Or would the conquistadors from Seoul and Shenzhen wind up like de Soto in the painting? One thing every one of us shares with Ponce de León and Julia Tuttle and Gary Morse is that whatever we do, we can be certain that the consequences of our actions will be different from what we intend them to be. That, generation upon generation, was Florida's unchanging lesson.

When people are unwilling or unable to come to terms with reality, a politics based on unreality becomes necessary to sustain what the Florida scholar Eugene Lyon describes as the "utopia of mutual hopes." The utopia in question can be a gated community or an indigo plantation—or the insistence that America always is and always will be number one so long as it makes up its past as it goes along. You can call the lies illusion or ideology or doctrine or traditional values, or talking points or wedge issues if you prefer. The key function of such a politics, whatever you call it, is to sustain the prevailing but now endangered disconnect with reality. The problem, which Florida has been demonstrating for half a millennium, is that maintaining the disconnect makes it even more unlikely that practical solutions to real problems will be found. Lyon was referring to the utopia the Spaniards failed to find in Florida five centuries ago. By the beginning of the twenty-first century America had also become such a place. Like the New World the Spaniards discovered, America was still an empire of marvels, but not those marvels which the "utopia of mutual hopes" had promised.

Of Florida's marvels, the most wondrous remained the ineradicability of hope. Even after the boll weevils ate her cotton crop, Harriet Beecher Stowe still believed "the malarial fevers here are of a mild type," just as, today, it never occurs to the millions upon millions who have followed her that Florida's function may not be to make their dreams come true. You see them at the Department of Motor Vehicles; you see them again at Florida's drawbridges, the people trapped in history and not knowing it. It's happened to almost everyone who has spent any time in Florida. To get to your favorite beach you probably have to cross a bridge. Chances are, it's a drawbridge, and just as you get to it, the drawbridge will be raised, forcing you to stop. The drawbridge is raised because some fortunate person who owns a boat too big to fit under the drawbridge has decided to take it out that day.

In Florida those who own boats take precedence over people who don't. So while the yacht goes under the bridge, the people in the cars waiting to go over the bridge sit there in the stalled traffic. The real estate broker in his leased Audi; the black family with the beach balls in the secondhand station wagon; the Latino kids playing their boom box; the fellow with spiked hair in the pickup truck with the Confederate-flag decal; the guys in the Miata wearing yarmulkes and thongs all wait without complaint. Everyone accepts that Yachts First is the Florida order of things. No horns honk. Not one person demands to know: Why is it that the people with boats take precedence over us? No one shouts in a loud angry voice: It's not fair! Most everyone who's ever gone to the beach in Florida has sat there, waiting for that shared moment when the flashing red lights turn green, and all the cars move forward together as if they share a common purpose, and have a common goal.

They wait so patiently because Richard Feynman, so right about everything else, was wrong about Florida. He of course was right in the technical sense. Nature cannot be fooled, but that misses the point. Florida isn't about fooling nature; it's about fooling people. Most of all it's about people fooling themselves. All around them Florida shouts No! No! You are foolish to believe that life can or ever will be easy! Can't you see history is sorrowful, history is painful; history is a process of ripping things off? Your ancestors were not Southern gentlemen! They did not own big haciendas in Cuba! Can't you see that so far as the credit card companies and the wedge issue consultants are concerned, you're all Seminoles! But the people waiting at the drawbridge don't see.

They don't see because they have many complications in their lives. They also do not see because their schools don't teach them to see, and the politicians and the media don't either. Most of all they don't see because they prefer not to see. They wait patiently—innocently, as Henry James might have put it, describing the pattern in the carpet—because, whatever their real-life experience tells them, they prefer to believe that life for them, too, tends toward a yacht. They believe someday it will be their boat, and then the drawbridge, rising in salute, will open wide for them.

THANKS

For more than thirty years Florida, my happenstance birthplace, has been the scene of sporadic comings and goings on my part. Recently it also has become one of the places where I live, but my work as a journalist, not heredity or residence, is the reason why this book now exists. Thanks, first of all, therefore must go to the publications that paid me to go to Florida and to learn about Florida, and so enabled me to develop the perspective which informs this book.

My 1980 article in *Esquire* changed the way the way the world sees Miami and helped alter how Miami sees itself; it changed my life in ways I am still discovering. Thanks to the editors of the Atlantic Monthly Press, I was able to write my first book with a Florida setting, *Miami: City of the Future*, a volume that continues to lead a life of its own. Much later Barbara Paulsen edited my 2007 *National Geographic* article on what Orlando means to America with tact and grace. In between, Tina Brown and *Vanity Fair* sent me to Florida to learn about Mario Antonio Noriega and his colorful Miami lawyers; *Penthouse* sent me to the Gulf coast as I delved into the lives of the church women killed in El Salvador. Looking back on these seemingly separate projects, I realize I was already exploring the diverse worlds whose convergence there makes Florida so fascinating, and so important.

Among all the people who helped me in my earlier work on Florida, I must especially thank Joyce Johnson and Oliver Payne for their decades of support, both as editors and friends. It was because of Chuck Sudetic that I embarked on this enterprise. The form this book would take crystallized in a 2002 transatlantic voyage undertaken for the specific purpose of determining how, why, and which book I would write next. Like Florida, the *Golden Princess* was an ark of diversity. The crew spoke more than forty languages including, to my delight, Nepali. My talks with members of the crew about who they were, and how and why they had arrived where they were, I realize now, constituted rehearsals for the many more such learning experiences I would have in Florida. There is another parallel which I only notice now, as I write this. The crew, not the passengers, were the most interesting people aboard this ship, just as in Florida history the most important characters are the ones the historians usually treat like servants—and, of course, the functioning of the great ship was far more interesting than its clichéd destinations. Wherever future voyages may have taken these interesting people many, no doubt, have wound up in Florida.

Most of this book was written in France, and most of the rest of it in New York. For their tolerance of my writerly ways I want to thank some of my neighbors in Lauzerte: Nicole de Renzy-Martin, Ildiko and Jean Francais, Justin and Momoe Downes, Pierre Dessarts, Francoise Ducasse and Frederic Berthaux, Libby Pratt and Craig Resnick, Nicole Dardelou and Rene Beziat, Jill Morgan and Tim Abadi, Anne Noirot-Nerin and Jean-Pierre Maitre, Frederic Noyer. Surtout je voudrais offrir ma gratitude à mes amis depuis plus que vingt ans, Patricia et Dominique Darniere. Leur aide était indispensable. My thanks also go to Claude and Patrice Brassier, who introduced me to the French idiom of it raining in ropes. Daphne Morgan Barnicoat, I love you!

In Paris I must thank Chantal and Peter Curtis in whose apartment in the Sixteenth one empty September morning I realized I could get this damn thing tamed without breaking its spirit. Deep thanks also go to Anthony, Glenda and Luca Curtis; to my namesake Timothy Curtis; to Nathalie Curtis Lethbridge, and to the incomparable Ouane who kept me well-nourished with veritable vats of piquant Lao sauce and near lorry-loads of gigantic, homegrown squashes. Fond thanks, too, to Nuria Almiron for her Shiatsu massages and views of the moons of Jupiter.

In New York I have first and foremost to thank Jamison Stoltz and Morgan Entrekin. Their fascination with what I wrote, and their enthusiasm for editing it and publishing it provided me with the greatest gift a writer can receive: genuine appreciation of what he has tried to do. Honorable mention must go to my old friend Carl Bromley and my new friend, John Sherer. Thanks also to Vincent Douglas, Nikki Smith and Gloria Martinez. My thanks also go to Leslie Morris, curator of Modern Books and Manuscripts at the Harvard College Library, for providing a home for my Florida and other archives. Transcending time and place is my gratitude to Martha Didinger Franklin.

Some wonderful scholars have done their best to tell the truth about Florida. Among them I must single out for highest praise Canter Brown. He and Barbara Brown were steadfast in their support throughout my long adventure of *Finding Florida*, then transforming what I found into a book. I also owe a special debt to Ben Kiernan and Gloria Gilmore at Yale; they never let me forget that this book needed to be published. Also through Yale I was able to benefit from the very helpful suggestions of Ben Madley. Thanks also to J. B. Bird for his Texas perspective on the Seminoles, and much else.

Among the Floridians to whom I owe so much, the incomparable JoAnn Bass tops the list of those whom I must thank for their support. She will have to keep her balance up there on the pinnacle of my esteem, because she must share it with Maurice Ferre, a truly original Florida intellectual, as well as the elegant and spiritual Mercedes Ferre. For nearly forty-five years Princess Moune Souvannaphoma and Perry Stieglitz have been constant in their friendship. It is both accidental and appropriate that our lives, having first intertwined in Laos, now intertwine again in Florida. Unpremeditated reintertwinings, as Wallace Stevens might have phrased it, define Florida.

The great danger in thanking other people is that by expressing my gratitude to some I omit thanking so many others, but here goes! My thanks to Rose McDaniel, Mark Pinsky, Wilfredo Fernandez, Joe Garcia, Jeanette A. Toohey, Peter Rummell, Elizabeth Krist, Connie Moore, Steve Baker, Rob Johnson, Pamela Iorio, Alex Sink, the late Bill McBride, Robert Shaw, Bob Graham, Arva Moore, Ewald Horwath, Jim Henry, Cecelia Montesinos, Dylan Thomas, Thomas Van Lent, Donna Shalala, Frank Billingsley, David Russin, Bruce Fitell, Robert Davis, Fred Levin, Gary Mormino, Harris Rosen, Kevin Bouffard, Jane Healy, James Moore, Peg Couch, Alexandra Kristoffersen, Linda

Chapin, Stacey May Brady, Woody Graber, Anthony Arneson, Archbishop Tom Wenski, Wendy and Lester Abberger. Undying gratitude must also be extended to the never-to-be-forgotten Minnie Hickman and the utterly indelible Barbara Baer Capitman. A comradely wave, also, to Jim DeFede, Don Wright, Les Standiford, and Carl Hiaasen. I take this opportunity to honor Mitchell Kaplan for his lifelong commitment to books in Florida—and to thank Anders Gyllenhaal for coming to the rescue at a particularly opportune moment.

To all the many others whose help I have not explicitly acknowledged I offer this book. In it I have sincerely tried to the best of my ability to tell the truths which so many people have so generously shared with me.

Billy, Zephaniah, Ossian, William—at last I can call you by your first names! Like the shepherd in *Montaillou*, you prove life is always worth having been lived. I close by saluting all those, from Windover times through Negro Fort onward to this very day, who have sacrificed so much in hopes of making Florida better than it is.

BIBLIOGRAPHY

Significant historical works on Florida fall into two broad categories: those which tell the truth and those which perpetuate Florida's
myths. For most of the past two hundred years the mythmakers
have reigned triumphant, while a number of superb studies of what
actually happened there have moldered in the archives, ignored by
academics and best-selling authors alike. The digital age has given
these truth tellers a new chance to be heard. Many of even the most
obscure titles mentioned here are now available online. Several of
them are literary as well as historical masterpieces. They open up a
world of factual information that, for generations, has been smoth-
ered in historical publicists' apologetics. That does not mean the
works of the panderers and dissemblers should be ignored. They
provide a detailed record of each generation's need to be told the
past is exactly what they imagine it was, while sometimes also telling
truths the authors never intended.

TRUTH TELLERS AND EYEWITNESSES

Presented Chronologically

Jacques Le Moyne de Morgue. *Narrative of Le Moyne: An Artist Who
Accompanied the French Expedition to Florida Under Laudonnière,
1564.* Translated from the Latin by Frederick B. Perkins [1875].

Garcilaso de la Vega (Gómez Suárez de Figueroa). *La Florida del Inca*
[1605]; *The Florida of the Inca.* Translated and edited by John
Grier Varner and Jeannette Johnson Varner [1951]. This earliest and least unreliable of de Soto's chroniclers makes it clear
how psychologically as well as geographically lost he became
in Florida.

Bernard Romans. *A Concise Natural History of East and West Florida* [1775]. Into the 1970s Florida historians dismissed his account of the savagery at New Smyrna as reflecting "animus" against the ruling class, but this book will last forever.

Treaty of Amity, Settlement and Limits Between the United States of America, and His Catholic Majesty. Also known as the "Adams-Onís Treaty" and the "Transcontinental Treaty" [1819]. I will pay one thousand dollars to any reader who finds anything about the United States purchasing Florida in this text.

Treaty with the Florida Tribes of Indians [1823]. Also known as the Treaty of Moultrie Creek, in Charles J. Kappler (editor), *Indian Affairs: Laws and Treaties, Vol. II, Treaties* [1904].

John James Audubon. *The Birds of North America* [1827–1839].

Zephaniah Kingsley. *A Treatise on the Patriarchal, or Co-operative System of Society as It Exists in Some Governments, and Colonies in America, and in the United States, Under the Name of Slavery, with Its Necessity and Advantages* [1829].

John Titcomb Sprague. *The Origin, Progress, and Conclusions of the Florida War* [1848]. The Thucydides of the Seminole War. A good test of scholarly integrity is whether a "history" of Florida cites Sprague. Most do not so much as mention his name.

Jonathan Walker. *The Branded Hand: Trial and Imprisonment of Jonathan Walker, at Pensacola, Florida: For Aiding Slaves to Escape from Bondage with an Appendix Containing a Sketch of His Life* [1848]. The touching tale, told by himself.

John Giddings. *The Exiles of Florida: or, The Crimes Committed by Our Government Against the Maroons, Who Fled from South Carolina and the Other Slave States, Seeking Protection Under Spanish Laws* [1858]. A definitive investigation expunged from history.

James Parton. *The Life of Andrew Jackson* [1860]. Published more than 150 years ago, this three-volume study makes most contemporary works on Jackson seem like cartoon strips.

Richard Keith Call. *Union—Slavery—Secession: Letter from Governor R. K. Call, of Florida, to John S. Littell of Germantown, Pennsylvania* [1861]. An anguished cry from a heart passionately devoted to both slavery and the Union.

Florida State Archives. *Constitution of 1868* [1868]. One of the most enlightened constitutional documents in American history.

Florida State Archives. *Constitution of 1885* [1885]. Florida's charter of racist reaction; in force, with modifications, until 1968.

J. H. Gilman. "With Slemmer in Pensacola Harbor." In The Century Co., *Battles and Leaders of the Civil War* [1887].

Alfred Thayer Mahan. *The Interest of America in Sea Power, Present and Future* [1893].

Minnie More Willson. *The Seminoles of Florida* [1896].

Charles H. Coe. *Red Patriots: The Story of the Seminoles* [1898].

Thorstein Veblen. *The Theory of the Leisure Class: An Economic Study of Institutions* [1899].

Thomas Chatfield. *Reminiscences of Captain Thomas Chatfield: Cotuit, Massachusetts* [1904]. Eyewitness account of events at Natural Bridge, never cited in conventional histories.

Paul Leland Haworth. *The Hayes-Tilden Disputed Presidential Election of 1876* [1906].

Isaac Joslin Cox. *The West Florida Controversy, 1798–1813: A Study in American Diplomacy* [1918].

James Weldon Johnson. *Along This Way: The Autobiography of James Weldon Johnson* [1933].

A. J. Hanna. *Flight into Oblivion* [1938]. How Confederate nabobs followed the Seminoles into Everglades oblivion.

Federal Writers' Project. *Florida: A Guide to the Southernmost State* [1939].

Stetson Kennedy. *Palmetto Country* [1942].

Stefan Lorant. *The New World: The First Pictures of America* [1944].

Marjory Stoneman Douglas. *The Everglades: River of Grass* [1947]. The Rachel Carson of Florida's wetlands.

Philip D. Ackerman. "Florida Reconstruction from Walker Through Reed" [1948].

Rembert W. Patrick. *Florida Fiasco: Rampant Rebels on the Georgia-Florida Border, 1810–1815* [1954].

Florence Fritz. *Unknown Florida* [1963]. Interesting focus on southwest Florida.

Joe M. Richardson. *The Negro in the Reconstruction of Florida, 1865–1877* [1965].

Henrietta Buckmaster. *The Seminole Wars* [1966]. Unusual for being a truthful account aimed at young readers.

Samuel Eliot Morison. *The European Discovery of America: The Southern Voyages* [1974].

J. Leitch Wright Jr. *Britain and the American Frontier, 1783–1815* [1975].

Eugene Lyon. *The Enterprise of Florida: Pedro Menéndez de Avilés and the Spanish Conquest of 1565–1568* [1976]. Who really founded Florida, and why; see also his *Adelantimiento of Florida: 1565–1568* [1973], doctoral thesis, University of Florida, George A. Smathers Libraries.

Peter C. H. Pritchard (series editor). *Rare and Endangered Biota of Florida* [1976–1982]. Seven volumes were required to list them all.

Virginia Parks, Alan Rick, and Norman Simons. *Pensacola in the Civil War* [1978].

W. Stuart Towns. "Honoring the Confederacy in Northwest Florida: The Confederate Monument Ritual," *Florida Historical Quarterly*, vol. 57, no. 2 [1978].

Edward D. Davis. *A Half Century of Struggle for Freedom in Florida* [1981].

Frances Novak-Branch. *The Disney World Effect* [1983].

Joseph Burkholder Smith. *The Plot to Steal Florida: James Madison's Phony War* [1983].

Jean Parker Waterbury. *The Oldest City: St. Augustine Saga of Survival* [1983]. Reliable, in spite of the title; does not mention the Fountain once.

David Nolan. *Fifty Feet in Paradise: The Booming of Florida* [1984].

Richard P. Feynman. "Personal Observations on the Reliability of the Shuttle" [1986]. This definitive explanation for NASA's failures was relegated to an appendix in William P. Rogers et al., *Report of the Presidential Commission on the Space Shuttle Challenger Accident* ("The Rogers Commission Report").

T. D. Allman. *Miami: City of the Future* [1987].

Kathleen Deagan. *Spanish St. Augustine: The Archaeology of a Colonial Creole Community* [1987].

Hap Hatton. *Tropical Splendor: An Architectural History of Florida* [1987].

Frank Oppel and Tony Meisel (editors). *Tales of Old Florida* [1987]. Vivid original accounts of wilderness Florida.

Ronald L. Myers and John J. Ewel. *Ecosystems of Florida* [1990].

Canter Brown, Jr., *Florida's Peace River Frontier* [1991].

Joel Garreau. *Edge City: Life on the New Frontier* [1991].

Patricia C. Griffin. *Mullet on the Beach: The Minorcans of Florida, 1768–1788* [1991].

Douglas T. Peck. *Ponce de León and the Discovery of Florida* [1993]. A valiant attempt to dispel the myths.

Robin Brown. *Florida's First People: 12,000 Years of Human History* [1994].

Jack Lane and Maurice J. O'Sullivan Jr. *The Florida Reader: Visions of Paradise* [1994]. Shows how writers find in Florida what they want to see.

Kevin McCarthy. *Twenty Florida Pirates* [1994]. The most important pirates are the fictional ones.

Kathleen Deagan (with Darcie McMahon). *Ft. Mose: Colonial America's Black Fortress of Freedom* [1995]. She keeps unearthing the past.

Walter T. Howard. *Lynchings and Extralegal Violence in Florida* [1995].

Allen Morris. *Florida Place Names: Alachua to Zoleo Springs* [1995]. Every one of them tells a story.

Michael D'Orzo. *Rosewood: Like Judgment Day: The True Story of the Rosewood Massacre and Its Aftermath* [1996]. Admirable reconstruction of another forgotten Florida massacre. The movie "based" on this book is a travesty.

Arva Moore Parks, Gregory W. Bush, and Laura Pincus. *Miami, the American Crossroad: A Centennial Journey 1896–1996* [1996].

Canter Brown Jr. *Ossian Bingley Hart: Florida's Loyalist Reconstruction Governor* [1997]. The definitive biography of a great American.

Al Burt. *Al Burt's Florida: Snowbirds, Sand Castles, and Self-Rising Crackers* [1997].

David J. Coles. "'They Fought Like Devils': Black Troops in Florida During the Civil War." In Mark I. Greenberg, William Warren Rogers, and Canter Brown Jr. (editors), *Florida's Heritage of Diversity* [1997].

James M. Denham. *A Rogue's Paradise: Crime and Punishment in Antebellum Florida, 1821–1861* [1997].

Daniel Simberloff, Don C. Schmitz, and Tom C. Brown. *Strangers in Paradise: Impact and Management of Nonindigenous Species in Florida* [1997].

Canter Brown Jr. *Florida's Black Public Officials, 1867–1924* [1998]. Disproves the claim that Florida's black people were politically incompetent.

Gene M. Burnett. *Florida's Past: People and Events That Shaped the State* [1998]. Illuminating miscellany.

Mark Derr. *Some Kind of Paradise: A Chronicle of Man and the Land in Florida* [1998]. Its transformation from wilderness into real estate.

Jerald T. Milanich. *Florida Indians and the Invasion from Europe* [1998].

James J. Miller. *An Environmental History of Northeast Florida* [1998].

Susan Orlean. *The Orchid Thief* [1998].

Russ Rymer. *American Beach: A Saga of Race, Wealth, and Memory* [1998]. Segregation at the seashore and its legacy.

Robert W. Torchia. *A Florida Legacy: Ponce de Leon in Florida* [1998]. Thomas Moran's Cinerama-like canvas and what happened to it.

John T. Foster Jr. and Sarah Whitmer Foster. *Beechers, Stowes, and Yankee Strangers: The Transformation of Florida* [1999]. Who these eminent "Carpetbaggers" really were.

Mark S. Foster. *Castles in the Sand: The Life and Times of Carl Graham* [2000].

Jane Landers. *Black Society in Spanish Florida* [2000].

Larry E. Rivers. *Slavery in Florida: Territorial Days to Emancipation* [2000].

Robert W. Saunders Sr. *Bridging the Gap: Continuing the Florida NAACP Legacy of Harry T. Moore* [2000].

Carl Hiaasen. *Paradise Screwed* [2001].

Walter E. Meshaka. *The Cuban Treefrog in Florida: Life History of a Successful Colonizing Species* [2001].

Jeffrey Toobin. *Too Close to Call: The Thirty-Six-Day Battle to Decide the 2000 Election* [2001]. The best account of what it meant.

Edward E. Baptist. *Creating an Old South: Middle Florida's Plantation Frontier Before the Civil War* [2002]. How rich whites used poor whites to repress blacks while inventing a fake past of aristocratic gentility.

Steven Brooke. *Seaside* [2002].

Shauna Henley. "A City with Schizophrenia" [2002]. An undergraduate essay more accurate than most history books.

John M. Williams and Iver W. Duedall. *Florida Hurricanes and Tropical Storms, 1871–2001* [2002]. The hurricane as permanent feature of Florida life.

Richard E. Foglesong. *Married to the Mouse: Walt Disney World and Orlando* [2003]. Remarkable for its insights into Disney's co-option of democratic values.

Les Standiford. *Last Train to Paradise: Henry Flagler and the Spectacular Rise and Fall of the Railroad that Crossed an Ocean* [2003].

Mark I. Pinsky. *The Gospel According to Disney: Faith, Trust, and Pixie Dust* [2004].

Diane Roberts. *Dream State: Eight Generations of Swamp Lawyers, Conquistadors, Confederate Daughters, Banana Republicans, and Other Florida Wildlife* [2004].

J. B. Bird. *Rebellion: John Horse and the Black Seminoles* [2005]. A fascinating and factually rigorous website.

David J. Coles. "Shooting Niggers, Sir." In Gregory J. W. Urwin (editor), *Black Flag over Dixie: Racial Atrocities and Reprisals in the Civil War* [2005].

Gary Ross Mormino. *Land of Sunshine, State of Dreams: A Social History of Modern Florida* [2005].

Paul Ortiz. *Emancipation Betrayed: The Hidden History of Black Organizing and White Violence in Florida from Reconstruction to the Bloody Election of 1920* [2006].

Kathryn Ziewitz and June Wiaz. *Green Empire: The St. Joe Company and the Remaking of Florida's Panhandle* [2006].

Jay Barnes. *Florida's Hurricane History* [2007].

Andres Resendez. *A Land So Strange: The Epic Journey of Cabez de Vaca* [2007].

Seth A. Weitz. *Bourbon, Pork Chops, and Red Peppers: Political Immorality in Florida, 1945–1968* [2007].

Andrew D. Blechman. *Leisureville: Adventures in a World Without Children* [2009]. The strange new world of The Villages.

Chad D. Emerson. "Merging Public and Private Governance: How Disney's Reedy Creek Improvement District 'Re-Imagined' the Traditional Division of Local Regulatory Powers," *Florida State University Law Review* [2009].

Karen Graves. *And They Were Wonderful Teachers: Florida's Purge of Gay and Lesbian Teachers* [2009]. One of the many reasons Florida lags educationally.

Larry Eugene Rivers and Canter Brown Jr. *The Varieties of Women's Experiences: Portraits of Southern Women in the Post–Civil War Century* [2009]. Tells the story of Lulu Fleming and other fascinating, forgotten female protagonists.

Vincent Virga and E. Lynne Wright. *Florida: Mapping the Sunshine State Through History: Rare and Unusual Maps from the Library of Congress* [2010].

William C. Davis. *The Rogue Republic: How Would-Be Patriots Waged the Shortest Revolution in American History* [2011].

Larry Eugene Rivers. *Rebels and Runaways: Slave Resistance in Nineteenth-Century Florida* [2012].

MYTHMAKERS AND THEIR PROPAGATORS

Presented Chronologically

Duncan L. Clinch. Descriptions of the Negro Fort Massacre. *National Intelligencer* [1819]; *Army and Navy Chronicle* [1836]. These two slightly varying accounts provide both a model of the Florida whitewashing, blame-the-victims methodology and, like a number of the most biased accounts, also present indispensable factual information that cannot be ignored.

Washington Irving. *Voyages and Discoveries of the Companions of Christopher Columbus* [1831].

Henry Rowe Schoolcraft. *The American Indians: Their History, Condition and Prospects, from Original Notes and Manuscripts* [1851].

Washington Irving. "The Seminoles" [1855].

Theodore Irving. *The Conquest of Florida by Hernando de Soto* [1857]. Like uncle, like nephew.

George R. Fairbanks. *History of Florida from Its Discovery by Ponce de Leon, in 1512, to the Close of the Florida War, in 1842* [1872]. A prominent lawyer, Fairbanks turned his land-grabbing clients into valiant heroes in this pioneering paean to the white male's seizure of Florida.

Harriet Beecher Stowe. *Palmetto Leaves* [1873].

Sidney Lanier. *Florida: Its Scenery, Climate, and History with an Account of Charleston, Savannah, Augusta, and Aiken; A Chapter for Consumptives; Various Papers on Fruit-Culture; and a Complete Hand-Book and Guide* [1877]. He died of consumption after praising Florida's curative powers.

The Works of Washington Irving. Volume 3: [1882]. "Origin of the White, the Red and the Black Men. A Seminole Tradition," "The Conspiracy of Neamathla: An Authentic Sketch."

John J. Dickison. *Confederate Military History of Florida* [1898].

Caroline Mays Brevard. *A History of Florida* [1904].

Hubert Bruce Fuller. *The Purchase of Florida: Its History and Diplomacy* [1906]. Shows how the conventional wisdom periodically is flipped to suit current needs. Previously none dared call it a purchase. Thereafter everyone did.

William Watson Davis. *The Civil War and Reconstruction in Florida* [1913, reprinted 2009]. Valuable for its documentation of white terrorism during Reconstruction, in spite of its various biases.

Frank Parker Stockbridge and John Holliday Perry. *Florida in the Making* [1926]. Tons of hype, barrelfuls of fascinating detail; this book captures the euphoria of the Florida real estate boom just before it went bust. See their sequel, below.

William Thomas Cash. *History of the Democratic Party in Florida; Including Sketches of Prominent Florida Democrats* [1936]. Racist hagiography.

Frank Parker Stockbridge and John Holliday Perry. *So This Is Florida* [1938]. They still find Florida fabulous, in spite of the Great Depression.

Walter P. Fraser. *The Fountain of Youth Ancient Indian Village and Burial Grounds* [1939]. Archaeological and historical sacrilege, described by its perpetrator.

John R. Swanton. *Final Report of the United States De Soto Expedition Commission* [1939]. This government-financed fiction made Schoolcraft's mythology official U.S. educational doctrine.

Arthur M. Schlesinger Jr. *The Age of Jackson* [1945]. Scholarly crimes of omission.

Edward Lawson. *The Discovery of Florida and Its Discoverer Juan Ponce de Leon* [1946]. This fraud is still being quoted.

Samuel Proctor. *Napoleon Bonaparte Broward: Florida's Fighting Democrat* [1950]. His plan to racially cleanse Florida does not tarnish his status as a "progressive" in this account.

J. E. Dovell. *Florida: Historic, Dramatic, Contemporary* [1952]. An indispensable and massive treasure trove of information and misinformation.

Rembert W. Patrick. *Aristocrat in Uniform: General Duncan L. Clinch* [1963]. An academic whitewash full of fascinating facts about the perpetrator of the Negro Fort Massacre, published at taxpayers' expense.

Charlton W. Tebeau and Ruby Leach Carson. *Florida: From Indian Trail to Space Age* [1965]. Having triumphed over the Spanish, British, Seminoles and Yankees, Florida's white males conquer outer space in three volumes. Many major authorities never so much as mentioned.

Rembert W. Patrick. *Florida Under Five Flags* [1966]. According to this book, massacring Negro troops at Olustee "made the victory all the more satisfying."

Charlton W. Tebeau. *History of Florida* [1971]. The one-volume successor to Brevard's apologetic, updated periodically to conform to the latest conventional wisdoms and stereotypes.

Ormonde De Kay. *Meet Andrew Jackson* [1973]. What our children are still being taught.

Joan E. Gill and Beth R. Read (editors). *Born of the Sun* [1976]. A negation of the past in honor of the America Bicentennial; an archetype of its genre.

Richard R. Beard. *Walt Disney's Epcot Center: Creating the New World of Tomorrow* [1982].

William P. Rogers et al. *Report of the Presidential Commission on the Space Shuttle Challenger Accident* ("The Rogers Commission Report") [1986].

Michael Gannon (editor). *The New History of Florida* [1996]. The usual hodgepodge.

Robert V. Remini. *Andrew Jackson and His Indian Wars* [2001]. According to Professor Remini, the official historian of the U.S. House of Representatives, Jackson did the Indians a favor.

Michael Gannon. *Florida: A Short History* [2003]. Lauds Brevard's racist inventions as a model of the historical arts; dismisses the Seminole eradication in a paragraph.

Sean Wilentz. *Andrew Jackson* [2005]. One of the more recent refictionalizations of what Jackson did in Florida.

Maria Antonio Sainz Sastre. *Florida in the 16th Century: Exploration and Colonization*. Translated from the Spanish by Bella Thomas and Miguel de Avendano [2011]. Intended to provide a Spanish perspective on Florida's origins, this work, financed by wealthy hispanophone donors, is as ethnocentrically arrogant and factually skewed as any screed any American ever wrote. "MISSION ACCOMPLISHED" is how this account sums up Menéndez' massacre of the French.

FINDING FLORIDA

Fiction

Stephen Vincent Benét. *Selected Works Vol. 2* [1954]. Contains many of his Florida-related writings.

Harry Hart Frank. *Alas, Babylon* [1959]. Nuclear war overtakes fictional Fort Repose, Florida.

John D. MacDonald. *The Deep Blue Good-by* [1964]. This first Travis McGee novel marked a Florida literary watershed.

Rita Mae Brown. *Rubyfruit Jungle* [1973].

Douglas Fairbairn. *Street 8* [1977]. An early stab at noir in Little Havana.

Elmore Leonard. *LaBrava* [1983]. The first of his Florida novels.

Russell Banks. *Continental Drift* [1985]. The first of Banks' explorations of Florida's white losers and those who encounter them.

Carl Hiaasen. *Hurricane Season* [1986]. With this first of his Florida novels, Hiaasen launched a genre of his own.

Jimmy Buffett. *Tales from Margaritaville* [1989].

James Michener. *Recessional* [1994]. His last compendious opus dealt with the retirement home where he was living.

Tom Wolfe. *Back to Blood* [2012]. All the silly stereotypes writhe here.

TV Series

Surfside 6 [1960 to 1962]. Like Sonny Crockett a quarter-century later, Detective Troy Donahue inhabits a Miami houseboat.

The Jackie Gleason Show [1963 to 1970]. The comedian accelerated Sunbelt shift when he moved his show to Florida.

Flipper [1964 to 1967]. The underwater Lassic lived in Cape Coral.

¿Qué Pasa, U.S.A.? [1977 to 1980]. This bilingual sitcom caught the Americanization of Miami's Cubans just right.

Miami Vice [1984 to 1989].

The Golden Girls [1985 to 1992]. Showed how lots of retirees lead interesting, happy lives.

Dexter [premiered 2006]. Where else would a series about a serial killer–homicide detective be set, but Miami?

Magic City [premiered 2010]. Best visuals since *Miami Vice*.

Movies

A Florida Enchantment [1914]. Filmed in St. Augustine, this may have been the first lesbian-themed movie.

The Gulf Between [1917]. First Technicolor film, shot entirely in Florida. Lost when no one preserved Florida's film archives.

The Bull-Dogger [1921]. Jacksonville was the capital of the African-American film industry until it was run out of town.

The Crimson Skull [1922]. "An All-Colored Cast," the posters proudly proclaimed.

The Flying Ace [1926]. A World War I hero turned Florida detective goes after the bad guys. The first of countless such on-screen transformations.

The Cocoanuts [1929]. The Marx Brothers, in their first feature-length film, run riot in a Florida hotel.

Prestige [1932]. Real-life chain gangs were working nearby when this film, supposedly set in a penal colony in French Indochina, was filmed in Florida.

Reap the Wild Wind [1940]. Hollywood's version of Florida's wreckers.

Tarzan's Secret Treasure [1941]. Filmed at Wakulla Springs. One of the many jungle and underwater adventures made in Florida between the world wars.

The Palm Beach Story [1942]. A Preston Sturges classic.

Thirty Seconds over Tokyo [1944]. Actually over Eglin Air Force Base, which, like Cape Canaveral later, was the stage set for many films featuring American heroics.

Key Largo [1948]. The power of the hurricane is revealed in the performances, especially by Claire Trevor as the drunken songstress.

On an Island with You [1948]. Jimmy Durante and Xavier Cugat cavort with Esther Williams by, in and under Florida's crystalline waters.

The Barefoot Mailman [1951]. A con man tries to cash in on the Florida railroad boom.

The Greatest Show on Earth [1952]. Cecil B. DeMille does Ringling Brothers in Sarasota. Only film with a Florida locale to win Best Movie Academy Award.

Beneath the 12-Mile Reef [1953]. The 1950s were Creature Time in Florida.

Seminole [1953]. Utter balderdash filmed in Everglades National Park. Anthony Quinn plays Osceola, Rock Hudson his U.S. Army pal.

Creature from the Black Lagoon [1954]. From Silver Springs, actually.

Revenge of the Creature [1955]. It lurked in Marineland.

Yellowneck [1955]. "Five Rebel Confederates Alone Among the Terrors of the Everglades!"

The Creature Walks Among Us [1956]. It did if you were walking in Fort Myers.

Wind Across the Everglades [1958]. An unusual, beautiful, and forgotten film in which Gypsy Rose Lee, Emmett Kelly, and MacKinlay Kantor wind up embroiled in a battle between an honest teacher–turned–game warden (Christopher Plummer) and vicious bird poacher Burl Ives. This "philosophical adventure story set in turn-of-the-century Florida" was derived from the real-life murder of a Florida game warden by plume rustlers.

The Bellboy [1960]. Jerry Lewis causes chaos in Miami Beach's Fontainebleau Hotel.

Midnight Cowboy [1960]. Failed Times Square hustler finds clean clothes in Florida.

Where the Boys Are [1960]. Groovy L.A. starlets play beach blanket bingo in Fort Lauderdale.

Nude on the Moon [1961]. The lunar nudist colony scenes were filmed in Coral Castle, a Miami-Dade attraction where the bizarre Latvian-American megaliths are made entirely of Florida limestone.

Two Thousand Maniacs! [1964]. Low-budget gore plus historical resonance: pro-Confederate locals lure Yankees to a fake reenactment, then mutilate and murder them.

Lady in Cement [1968]. This time Frank Sinatra plays the disillusioned detective who reinvents himself in Florida.

Frogs [1972]. The low-budget horror flick that foresaw Florida's actual frog invasion.

Gates of Heaven [1978]. Death and life in the Bubbling Well Pet Memorial Park.

Smokey and the Bandit II [1980]. Yet more adventures in Florida, Land of Sequels.

Against Wind and Tide: A Cuban Odyssey [1981]. Oscar-nominated.

Honky Tonk Freeway [1981]. The denizens of tiny Ticlaw will do anything to get themselves an exit on the freeway to Miami. Anything.

Scarface [1983]. Oliver Stone's foulmouthed film is unfair to Miami.

Stranger Than Paradise [1984]. Jim Jarmusch's Florida-bound masterpiece.

A Flash of Green [1985]. Lovable preservationists fight off evil developers. One of the locals organizes fake Florida historical festivals as a sideline.

Nightmare Beach [1988]. In this Italian-American coproduction the killer's motorbike doubles as an electric chair.

Revenge of the Nerds II: Nerds in Paradise [1988]. They, too, wind up in Florida.

Apollo 13 [1995]. Ron Howard's big-screen treatment of NASA's safety problems turns an institutional failure into a triumph of American heroism.

The Birdcage [1995]. The Broadway (originally Paris) romp translated to South Beach.

Fair Game [1995]. Rogue KGB agents stalk Cindy Crawford in Metro Miami-Dade.

William Shakespeare's Romeo + Juliet [1996]. The warring clans have relocated to Verona Beach.

From the Earth to the Moon [1998]. HBO's adoring twelve-part salute to the astronauts rips off Jules Verne's title.

Great Expectations [1998]. Miss Haversham retires to Florida.

Palmetto [1998]. Nouvelle Vague cinephilia and Hollywood neo-noir converge as director Volker Schlöndorff immerses Woody Harrelson in Florida's moral viscosity.

Space Cowboys [2000]. Clint Eastwood and his fellow NASA rejects save the world.

Olive Juice [2001]. Pet shop romance in Central Florida Megalopolis.

Adaptation [2002]. Florida's orchid-rustling subculture and its Seminole cowboys, derived from Susan Orlean's *The Orchid Thief.*

Monster [2002]. South African–born Charlize Theron's portrayal of Michigan-born Florida female mass murderer Aileen Carol Wuornos won her an Academy Award in California.

Snow Dogs [2002]. Arctic sled dogs struggle through blizzards of fake Orlando snow.

Sunshine State [2002]. John Sayles' exploration of Florida race relations filmed on real-life Amelia Island.

Sydney White [2007]. Snow White and the Seven Dwarves also relocate to Florida.

Never Back Down [2008]. Survival of the fittest among Orlando's white Iowa-transplanted lumpenproletariat.

Hollywood East: Florida's Silent Film Legacy [2010].

NOTES AND CITATIONS

Works previously listed in the Bibliography are cited here initially by author and date, as well as by title if necessary for clarity, and thereafter by author or short title.

EPIGRAPH

vi *"Why do we flee to lands warmed by a foreign sun?"*: Horace, *Odes*, vol. 2, pp. 16, 18–20, quoted by Michel de Montaigne, *Essays*, "On Solitude." Montaigne was among the first Europeans to recognize, and lament, the effects of the European intrusion on the peoples of the New World. He also was familiar with what happened at Fort Caroline. Socrates made comments to the same effect on travel as Horace did.

PROLOGUE

ix **"Feynman's book"**: Feynman, *The Pleasure of Finding Things Out* [2005]. The comments on his father on are on pp. 4–5.

x **St. Johns not a river**: Miller, [1998].

x **"fateful ambiguity of water and land"**: Myers and Ewel, [1990]; John Edward Hoffmeister, *Land from the Sea: The Geologic Story of South Florida* [1976].

xi **Jefferson on Florida**: Thomas Jefferson Randolph, *Memoirs, Correspondence, and Private Papers of Thomas Jefferson* [1829], vol. 3, p. 513.

xiii **"Florida has no gold"**: In keeping with the tradition of never saying anything negative about Florida, geological surveys across the decades don't say it has no metals. See, for example: Albert C. Hine, *Geology of Florida* [2009]; Anthony F. Randazzo and Douglas S. Jones (editors), *The Geology of Florida* [1997]; Ed Lane (editor), *Florida's Geological History and Geological Resources* [1995], going back to "Sketch of the Geology of Florida," *The Florida Review*, June 1911, pp. 488–90.

xvii   "freezes in Frostproof": *Time* magazine, January 14, 2010.

Michelangelo abandoning fixed perspective: Giorgio Vasari, *Lives of the Most Excellent Painters, Sculptors, and Architects*, first published in 1550, p. 354.

PART ONE

1   "Ships at a distance": Zora Neale Hurston, *Their Eyes Were Watching God* [1937]. This comes from the opening sentence of her book.

CHAPTER 1

3   "Fountain of Youth National Archaeological Park": Visits and interviews there, 2005.

4   Cabot and Florida: William Grimshaw, *History of the United States from Their First Settlement as Colonies to the Cession of Florida* [1830], p. 19.

4   "five hundred people were lured onto Spanish ships": Milanich, [1998].

4   "Waldseemüller Map": Virga and Wright, [2010].

5   "The most famous of them": Peter Martyr d'Anghiera, *De Orbe Novo* [1511].

5   Treaty of Tordesillas: Visits and interviews there, 2005. Translation of text: The Avalon Project, Lillian Goldman Law Library, Yale Law School.

6   Ponce and Fountain myths: Peck, [1993]; Morison, [1974], pp. 502–16; Leonardo Olschki, "Ponce de Leon's Fountain: History of a Geographical Myth," *Florida Historical Quarterly*, August 1941; David O. True (editor), *Memoir* of *Fontaneda* [1944].

CHAPTER 2

13   De Soto "only anxious to finish his existence": Frederick A. Ober, *Ferdinand De Soto and the Invasion of Florida* [1906], p. 236.

13,19   "The younger Irving's fantasy version"; "money to be paid . . . on the first discovery of any gold": Theodore Irving, [1851], pp. ii, 103, 189.

14   "why de Soto 'discovered' nothing"; "The Inca": Garcilaso de la Vega, [1605].

14 **Schoolcraft method:** Henry Rowe, Schoolcraft, *History of the Indian Tribes of the United States* [1857], especially chapters 7 and 8.

15 **De Soto's fantasy route:** Swanton, [1939].

16 **"kids are falsely taught":** U.S. National Parks Service, De Soto National Memorial website. Accessed 15 May 2012.

16 **"De Soto Oak Plaque":** Floyd E. Boone, *Florida Historical Markers & Sites* [1989], p. 149.

16 **"legendary gas-guzzler":** Dave Duricy, *DeSaga: A Brief History of DeSoto* [2005]. Online at desotoland.com. Accessed 10 May 2012.

17 **Moran's painting and its adventures:** Torchia, [1998].

19 **"500,000 Feral Hogs Causing Problems":** Associated Press, 5 August 2005; see also "Hog Wild in Florida!" *IFAS News*, Institute of Food and Agricultural Sciences—University of Florida, 2 June 2005.

19 **"The conquest continues":** *National Feral Swine Mapping System*, April 2012 update. Southeastern Cooperative Wildlife Disease Study, College of Veterinary Medicine, University of Georgia.

19 **Pigs "especially at home in Florida":** ABC News, 8 June 2005.

CHAPTER 3

20 **Failure of the Spanish expeditions:** Recounted by many different authors. John Francis Bannon, *The Spanish Borderlands Frontier, 1513–1821* [1970] provides an overview; Ann L. Henderson and Gary Ross Mormino (editors), *Spanish Pathways in Florida, 1492–1992* [1991] offers a bilingual perspective.

21 **Advance of European diseases:** Henry F. Dobyns, "The Invasion of Florida: Disease and the Indians of Florida," in Henderson and Mormino, *Spanish Pathways*, 58–78; Alfred W. Crosby Jr., *The Columbian Exchange: Biological and Cultural Consequences of 1492* [1976] revolutionized popular understanding of what happened; Samuel M. Wilson, *The Emperor's Giraffe: And Other Stories of Cultures in Contact* [1999] contextualizes the Florida tragedy.

21 **Failure of Florida missions:** Bonnie Gair McEwan (editor), *The Spanish Missions of La Florida* [1993]; Mark Frederick Boyd, Hale G. Smith, and John W. Griffin, *Here They Once Stood: The Tragic End of the Apalachee Missions* [1951, reprinted 1999].

484 Notes and Citations

21, 22 "Charity and kindness were here, 7,000 years ago"; spear points and chert; Windover excavations: Brown, [1994].

23 Extinction of original fauna: Robin C. Brown, *Florida's Fossils* [1988].

25 Cold weather in Florida: Thomas F. Giella, *Florida Historic Cold Weather Archive* [2012].

25 "greatly in need of a coat": Dwight Young and Margaret Johnson (editors), *Dear First Lady: Letters to the White House* [2008], p. 200.

26 "The monstropolous beast"; "mother of malice": Zora Neale Hurston, *Their Eyes Were Watching God* [1937], pp. 156, 202.

28 "Celebrity Frog": *Tampa Tribune*, 26 March 2005.

28 Frog infestation: Jacki Lyden, *Frogs!* National Public Radio report, 18 October 2002.

31 Invasive species: Simberloff et al., [1997].

32 *Schizoporella floridana*: K. Hill, Smithsonian Marine Station report, Fort Pierce, 25 July 2001.

34 Only 3,096 inhabitants: Verne Elmo Chatelain, *The Defenses of Spanish Florida, 1565 to 1763* [1941], pp. 128–32.

34 Discovery of pre-Columbian culture and artifacts in Florida: Frank Hamilton Cushing, *Preliminary Report on the Exploration of Ancient Key-dweller Remains on the Gulf Coast of Florida* [1896]; Jerald T. Milanich, *Florida's Indians from Ancient Times to the Present* [1998].

35 Varying population estimates: Dovell, [1952], pp. 6–8; Tebeau, [1971], p. 16; Dobyns, "Invasion," p. 58.

35 Extinction of original peoples: Jerald T. Milanich, *The Timucua* [1996], xv–xvi; also Milanich, *Florida's Indians*, pp. xiii–xvi.

CHAPTER 4

36 "killer-courtier named Pedro Menéndez de Aviles": Lyon, [1976] is the unparalleled source for an understanding of what, beneath the mythology, happened in and to Florida in the sixteenth century. Lorant [1944] is valuable, as is Charles E. Bennett, *Laudonniere & Fort Caroline: History and Documents* [2001].

36 Menéndez massacres: At least nine of the French survivors left written accounts. The most valuable of them found its way into English centuries later as: *Narrative of Le Moyne: An Artist Who Accompanied the French Expedition to Florida Under Laudonnière, 1564*, translated from the Latin by Frederick B. Perkins [1875]. Jacques Le Moyne de Morgue's engravings of the original Floridians, done from memory many years later, remain the single most valuable document of Florida prior to the imposition of Spanish rule. The French commander left a memoir published in English as Jean Ribault, *The Whole and True Discovery of Terra Florida* [1582], later republished in the *English Historical Review* [1917]. For attempts to excuse the massacres, see Professor Michael Gannon's foreword to Albert Manucy, *Menéndez: Pedro Menéndez de Avilés*, in which he dismisses the massacres as "legend." A more recent whitewash is to be found in Sastre. [2011]. To get the perspective of the Spanish who were actually there, seek out the memoir of Menéndez's brother-in-law, eventually rendered into English as: *Pedro Menéndez de Avilés, Adelantado, Governor and Captain-General of Florida: Memorial by Gonzalo Solís de Merás*, translated by Jeanette Thurber Connor [1923].

45 **"Castillo de San Marcos":** Ian K. Steele, *Warpaths: Invasions of North America* [1994], p. 36.

PART TWO

47 **"a disease, corrupting the moral sense of each succeeding administration":** K. C. Babcock, *Rise of American Nationality* [1906], p. 22.

CHAPTER 5

49 **"future marauded into Florida in 1702":** Fairbanks, [1872], chapters 13–14.

50, 51 **"Diplomacy caught up with reality in 1763"; "British ruled Florida only from 1763 to 1783":** see Matthew C. Cannavale and Robert Olwell, *Florida, 1513–1821* [2006].

52 **New Smyrna catastrophe:** Romans, [1776], pp. 267–73.

53 **"'Blame the Victim' methodology"; "animus toward colony management":** Tebeau and Carson, [1965], pp. 73–74.

53 **"a death-camp like existence":** Griffin, [1991], p. 136.

53 **Descendants of the Minorcans:** Stephen Vincent Benét, *Selected Works, Volume 2* [1954] contains many of his Florida-related writings.

54   Adams and Hancock burned in effigy: Fairbanks, p. 223.

54, 55   Gálvez and Spain's military success; Spain's vital contribution ignored: Thomas E. Chavez, *Spain and the Independence of the United States: An Intrinsic Gift* [2010], chapters 11–12, pp. 213–14.

55   1783 Treaty of Paris; Florida's borders: James W. Raab, *Spain, Britain, and the American Revolution in Florida, 1763–1783* [2008], pp. 162–73.

55   Treaty of Ildefonso: *Preliminary and Secret Treaty Between the French Republic and His Catholic Majesty the King of Spain, Concerning the Aggrandizement of His Royal Highness the Infant Duke of Parma in Italy and the Retrocession of Louisiana* [1801]. Translation of text: The Avalon Project, Yale Law School.

58, 59   Jefferson's disregard of U.S. Constitution, amendment draft, hopes for getting Florida, comments on Baton Rouge: John P. Foley (editor), *The Jefferson Cyclopedia* [1900], p. 510.

58   Henry Adams comment: Widely cited; see Peter P. Hill, *Napoleon's Troublesome Americans: Franco-American Relations, 1804–1815* [2005], p. 1, for a contemporary exploration of this episode.

59   "The Floridas will fall to us peaceably": Paul Leicester Ford (editor), *Writings (of Jefferson)* [1897], vol. 8, pp. 261–63.

60   "an imperial expansion of the United States": Frederick Jackson Turner, *Review of Reviews* [May 1903].

62   President Madison's Florida conspiracy: Smith, [1983]. See also James G. Cusick, *The Other War of 1812: The Patriot War and the American Invasion of East Florida* [2003].

62   Loyalist murdered: St. Tammany Parish Government, *(Online) History of St. Tammany Parish* [2007].

62   "Butterfly Effect": See, inter alia, Robert L. Devaney, *Introduction to Chaotic Dynamical Systems* [2003]; James Gleick, *Chaos: Making a New Science* [2011].

63   "an epitome and a prophecy of expansion": Cox, [1918], p. 6.

63   West Florida Lone Star flag: Ibid., chapters 11–14; David A. Bice, *The Original Lone Star Republic* [2004]; Davis, [2011].

64   "unprovoked seizure of a foreign colony": U.S. Congress, *American State Papers*, Class I, vol. 3, p. 542.

CHAPTER 6

65 **Folch's ploy, "equitable capitulation":** U.S. Congress, *American State Papers*, Class I, vol. 3, p. 398.

66 **"a subversion of the Spanish authorities":** James Madison, Special Message to Congress, 3 January 1811, Gaillard Hunt (editor), *The Writings of James Madison* [1908], vol. 8: 1808–1819, pp. 130–31.

66 **Mathews imbroglio:** Patrick, [1954], cover to cover.

67 **Need for discretion and delicacy:** Smith, [1983], p. 116.

69 **"suspicion of an existing design of any foreign Power":** Weston Arthur Goodspeed, *The Province and the States: A History of the Province of Louisiana Under France and Spain, and of the Territories and States of the United States Formed Therefrom* [1904], vol. 2, pp. 330–31.

67 **Mathews, Washington, and "the Lord Almighty"; Folch foils West Florida intrigue:** Patrick, [1954], pp. 5, 31–39.

69 **"staggering ineptitude":** David Stephen Heidler, *Journal of Military History*, vol. 68, no. 2 [2004].

70 **Race relations in Spanish Florida; "first legally sanctioned free black community":** See Deagan, [1995]; Jane G. Landers, *Black Society in Spanish Florida* [1999].

71 **"Felicia the Fortune Teller" and other denizens of Amelia Island:** Patrick, [1954], pp. 40–55.

73 **"unseen foe"; Laval-Mathews animosity; events at Fernandina:** Ibid., pp. 56–99.

74, 75 **"Jews, rogues, traitors, conspirators"; "rag-a-muffins from the fag-end of Georgia":** Ibid., pp. 81, 89.

76, 78 **"On to Venezuela!" St. Augustine harder to take than Quebec:** Ibid., pp. 107, 142.

78 **"Disgraceful in the extreme":** Smith, p. 229.

78 **"Mathews has been playing a strange comedy":** Hunt (editor), *Writings of James Madison*, vol. 8, p. 190.

78 **Monroe's disavowal of Mathews:** *The Secretary of State to General Matthews*, 4 April 1812, *American State Papers*, Class I, vol. 3, p. 572.

79 **"ravange," "rest in oblivion":** Patrick, [1954], pp. 175, 178.

79 "**blow them all up in Washington**": Dovell, [1952], vol. 1, p. 187.

79 "**Poor old Mathews**": William Junius Pratt, *Expansionists of 1812* [1949], p. 114.

80 "**the figment of imagination, the hallucination of old age**": Patrick, [1954], pp. 125–26.

80 "**a paper maneuver**": Dovell, vol. 1, p. 186.

81 "**Canada or Florida?**": Thomas Jefferson, "To James Madison," 6 June 1812, in Paul Leicester Ford (editor), *The Writings of Thomas Jefferson: Volume IX: 1807–1815* [1897], p. 355.

81 **Seizure of Mobile**: Michael Thomason, *Historic Mobile: An Illustrated History of the Mobile Bay Region* [2010], pp. 20–26.

CHAPTER 7

82 "**Madison's War commenced in folly . . . carried on with madness . . . end in ruin**": Robert Mann, *Wartime Dissent in America: A History and Anthology* [2010], p. 25.

82 "**Treaty of Ghent guaranteed**" restoration of "**all lands taken from Indians**": David Stephen Heidler and Jeanne T. Heidler (editors), *Encyclopedia of the War of 1812* [1997], p. 25.

83 "**hickory**," "**Americanize**": Noah Webster, *A Compendious Dictionary of the English Language* [1806].

84 "**for the benefit of the white man**": Stephen Arnold Douglas, *Life of Stephen A. Douglas: With His Most Important Speeches and Reports* [1860], p. 144.

84 **Description of Negro Fort and surroundings**: Visits and interviews there, 2005.

85 "**scene horrible beyond description**": Duncan L. Clinch, "Negro Fort," *Niles' Weekly Register,* 20 November 1819.

86 "**force of the Negroes**"; "**plantations on the fertile banks**": Daniel Patterson, *Commodore Patterson to the Secretary of the Navy,* 15 August 1816, text in "Message from the President of the United States . . . in Relation to Our Affairs with Spain," 28 December 1818.

86 "**The result appeared miraculous**"; "**Neither vessel boasted of a furnace**"; "**valuable stores that escaped destruction**": Patrick, [1963], pp. 31–34.

87, 91   Victims "almost entirely Spanish-speaking;" Garcon shot: Choctaw scalped: Dovell, [1952] pp. 195–96.

87   "their ancestors had owned the ancestors of the prisoners": Department of the Interior, National Park Service, "British Fort," nps.gov. Accessed 31 May 2012.

87, 88   "gallant daring"; "self-governing Negro communities": Patrick, [1963], pp. 32–33, 35.

89   "Jackson sought pretexts"; "Negro brigands": See Bird, [2005]. Accessed 1 June 2012. See also Bird, [2012]. Larry Eugene Rivers, *Rebels and Runaways: Slave Resistanc in Florida* [2012] offers even more depth than Mr. Bird's excellent work.

89   "unprovoked war against the citizens of the United States": *American State Papers*, Class V, vol. 1, pp. 704–5, Jackson note to War Department, 25 March 1818.

91   "Indian chief and black commander were sentenced to death for the murder of the four Americans": Visits to Fort Gadsden.

93, 95   "possession of the Floridas . . . in sixty days"; "a situation 'to exasperate the mind of General Jackson'": Parton, [1860], vol. 2, pp. 485, 434, 460.

95   Letter from Arbuthnot: "From A. Arbuthnot to his Son, John Arbuthnot, Fort St. Marks, 2 April 1818," in John D. Lawson (editor), *American State Trials*, vol. 2 [1914], p. 868.

95   "Hapless Arbuthnot!" "provisional government" in Pensacola: Parton, vol. 2, pp. 439, 448, 423.

95   "self-styled Philanthropists": "From Edmond Pendleton Gaines (to Jackson)," 2 April 1817, in Harold Moser et al. (editors), *The Papers of Andrew Jackson*, vol. 4: 1816–1820 [1994], p. 107.

96   "East Florida . . . now an American possession": Remini. [2001], pp. 161–62.

96   "Seminole War . . . at a close": U.S. Congress, *American State Papers*, Class V, vol. 1, p. 708, Jackson to Secretary of War Calhoun, 2 June 1818.

96   "one of the most heated controversies in American history": Tebeau, [1971], p. 113.

97   Monroe and Jackson alike exonerated: *Appleton's Cyclopaedia of American Biography*, vol. 3 [1877], pp. 377–78.

98   Marx on tragedy and farce: Karl Marx, *The Eighteenth Brumaire of Louis Bonaparte*, translated by Daniel De Lion [1913], p. 9.

CHAPTER 8

99   "Adams . . . finally got Florida": William Earl Weeks, *John Quincy Adams and American Global Empire* [1992] explores his role as an American expansionist.

99   "post of annoyance" ultimatum: "To Don Luis de Onis," 30 November 1818, in Worthington Chauncey Ford (editor), *Writings of John Quincy Adams*, vol. 6: *1816–1818*, pp. 503–11.

100   Text of Onis-Adams Treaty: *Treaty of Amity, Settlement, and Limits* [1819].

100   U.S. to renounce "forever" any claims to Texas and California: Article III, Paragraph 2.

100   "five millions of dollars" for citizens of the United States: Article XI.

101   America's western "boundary-line" the Sabine River: Article III, Paragraph 1.

101   "fundamental maxims . . . insensibly change from liberty to force": Walter LaFeber, *John Quincy Adams and American Continental Empire* [1965], pp. 43–47.

102   Florida "strategic but useless": Isaac Joselin Cox, "Florida, Frontier Outpost of New Spain," in James Alexander Robertson and Alva Curtis Wilgus (editors), *Hispanic American Essays* [1942, reprinted 1970], pp. 150–66.

102   Jackson disenchantment, no business can be profitable: Dovell, [1952], vol. 1, p. 219.

103   Florida populated by "runaway slaves, renegade whites and Indians, and foreign adventurers and pirates": Tebeau, [1971], p. 115.

103   Florida populated principally by "criminally inclined persons": Patrick, [1963], pp. 24–25.

104   Reports of Florida-based arson false: Ibid., p. 29.

104   Delayed congressional investigation: William Jay, *A View of the Action of the Federal Government, in Behalf of Slavery* [1839].

105 Victims as honorable as "the patriots of 1776": Gidding, [1858], pp. 37–38.

105 "Negro banditti roamed the country": Dovell, vol. 1, pp. 197–98.

105 Massacre "removed any immediate danger to users of the river": Tebeau, p. 110.

106 Massacre "did not end the problem": Gannon, [1996], p. 156.

107 "Spain sold Florida to the United States": De Kay, [1973], pp. 64–65.

107 "Who was General Andrew Jackson"; "For the decade past": Schlesinger, [1946], pp. 5, 35.

108 Jackson's "rude violence . . . a legend": Ibid., p. 37.

108 Jackson's ethnic cleansing "part and parcel" of "victories" over Nazis in World War II: Ibid., p. x.

110 "So much for the 'negro menace'": Remini, [2001], pp. 130–32.

110 "the nation's southern border" threatened; Florida miscreants "raided and harassed American settlements in south Georgia"; "Spanish, goaded by British agents, were encouraging the attacks"; "Spanish command center"; Jackson's rampage led to "America's purchase of Florida": Wilentz, [2005], pp. 35–40.

111 "an episode . . . I could wish might remain unwritten": Patrick, [1954], p. 303.

111 "truth about Florida . . . concealed by . . . three different methods": *Critic*, 15 July 1882.

PART THREE

113 "I would allow them to remain": General Thomas Sidney Jesup, 1838, in Sprague, [1848], p. 200.

CHAPTER 9

115 DuVal's tales: Brevard, [1904], pp. 105–7.

117 Jefferson's changing views on Indian Removal: Albert Ellery Bergh (editor), *The Writings of Thomas Jefferson* [1907], vol. 3, "Confidential Message," 18 January 1803, pp. 489–91; Thomas Jefferson Randolph (editor), *Memoirs, Correspondence and Private Papers of Thomas Jefferson* [1829], vol. 3, "To General Gates," 11 July 1803, p. 518.

118 Desirability of Enemathla's land: 1821 journals of the two commissioners, John Lee Williams and D. H. Simmons; "The Selection of Tallahassee as the Capital," *Florida Historical Quarterly*, April, July 1908.

119 Moultrie festivities: Joshua Nichols Glenn, *Diary*, St. Augustine entry, *Florida Historical Quarterly*, October 1945, pp. 148–49.

120 Treaty provisions: *Treaty of Fort Moultrie Creek*, 2 January 1824. Full text in Sprague, [1848], pp. 20–24.

120 "most miserable region": William Pope DuVal, "Letter to the Secretary of War," 22 February 1826, U.S. House of Representatives, Committee on Indian Affairs; "Letter from the Secretary of War Relating to the Present Location of the Florida Indians," 18 April 1826, pp. 5–7.

121 "dishonor to the American character": John P. Foley (editor), *The Jefferson Cyclopedia* [1900], p. 424.

121 "present to Col. Gad Humphreys" Moultrie Treaty, Article X.

121 "five hundred dollars" for Enemathla: Moultrie Treaty, "Additional Article."

122 "DuVal's Courageous Visit"; "Enemathla Disgraced": Brevard, pp. 121–26.

122 Irving's Florida fables: *The Works of Washington Irving*, vol. 3 [1882], p. 423.

124 In real life Enemathla "of strong mind and character": Brevard, 110, citing Lee's comments.

125 Dulcimer mosquitoes; observations on Florida: *Journals of Ralph Waldo Emerson*, vol. 2, 1824–1832, pp. 152–87.

125 "suckling pigs": Baptist, [2002], p. 99.

126 "dramatic makeovers": Patrick, [1963].

126 Massacre earned Clinch "a deserved rest"; buys child slave: Ibid., pp. 37, 48–49.

127 Lafayette "project failed": Dovell, [1952], vol. 1, p. 235.

127 Lafayette visit "never materialized." Tebeau, [1971; 1981 edition], pp. 136–37.

127 Lafayette never would have drawn his sword: Comment to Thomas Clarkson, quoted by Victor Hugo, *Letter to Louis Kossuth: Concerning Freedom and Slavery in the United States* [1852], p. 39. See also American Friends of

Lafayette, *Lafayette and Slavery: From His Letters to Thomas Clarkson and Granville Sharp* [1950].

128 Murat and Emerson: Ralph L. Rusk (editor), *The Letters of Ralph Waldo Emerson*, vol. 1 [1939], p. 312.

128 Prince Murat Motel: Yahoo! Travel Contributor, 26 December 2006.

129 Clinch's soldiers prevented from voting: Patrick, [1963], p. 52.

130 Humphreys "too partial to the Indians": Fairbanks, [1872], p. 277.

132 "voluminous correspondence" favorable to him: Sprague, pp. 46–48, 5.

133 "ELSY & FLORA": Territory of Florida, Alachua County Public Records, Gad Humphreys Affidavit on sale of his slaves, 3 June 1837. Transcribed by Jim Powell Jr. from records provided by Buddy Irby, Clerk of the Court, Alachua County, Florida 1999.

134 "white people will not rest": Sprague, p. 51.

CHAPTER 10

135 Treaty provisions: *Treaty of Payne's Landing*, 9 May 1832. Full text, Sprague, [1848], pp. 74–76.

135 "genocide as the U.S. Government later defined it": *Convention on the Prevention and Punishment of the Crime of Genocide*, enacted by U.S.-supported Resolution 260 (III) of the U.N. General Assembly, 9 December 1948.

136 "treaty . . . clearly conditional"; Phagan "totally unqualified": Sprague, pp. 76, 72.

136 "scalps to the garrison": *Public Documents* (of the U.S. Senate, relating to Seminole Removal), vol. 3, 7 December 1835, p. 151.

137 Fort Gibson imbroglio: Sprague, pp. 76–79.

137 Phagan and "additional treaty": Sprague, pp. 76–77, 72–73.

137 Gadsden on "fatal mistake": Dovell, [1952], vol. 1, p. 243.

138 "A foul blot": Thomas L. McKenney, *Memoirs, Official and Personal* [1846], pp. 274–75.

138 Eaton on treaty and Florida dangers: Sprague, p. 82.

139 "You know you were not forced to do it": Woodbine Potter, *The War in Florida: Being an Exposition of Its Causes, and an Accurate History of the Campaigns* [1836], p. 63.

139   **Radicalized generation of Seminoles:** Sprague, pp. 79–80.

139   **Silver-mounted rifle:** Patricia Riles Wickman, *Osceola's Legacy* [2006], pp. 13, 88–91.

140   **seminoles "breathe only the wish for peace":** Parton, [1860], vol. 2, p. 393.

141   **Thompson's death:** Sprague, p. 89.

142   **"Indians, Indian Negroes and the Negroes on the plantations":** Patrick, [1963], p. 71.

142   **"Miserable Creatures":** *Niles' National Register*, 4 November 1837.

142   **McQueen and Powell families:** Wickman, *Osceola's Legacy*, chapters 1–2.

143   **"a snug trader":** Ibid., p. 37.

143   **"little Englishman"; boy and mother captured; McQueen-Powell family life:** Thomas Simpson Woodward, *Reminiscences* [1939], pp. 9, 45–50.

145   **Intermarriage among Seminoles:** Deagan, [1995].

145   **"Black Seminoles":** Giddings, [1858]; William Jay, "Miscellaneous Writings on Slavery" [1853]; and Sprague provide the clearest firsthand accounts of who they were. Kenneth Wiggins Porter, Alcione M. Amos, and Thomas P. Senter, *The Black Seminoles: History of a Freedom-Seeking People* [1996] offers a contemporary perspective. Kevin Mulroy, *The Seminole Freedmen: A History* [2007] covers a vast canvas.

145   **"Slaves but in name"; "vassals and allies":** Bird, [2005]; also Mulroy and Porter et al.

145   **"McQueen's village":** Wickman, *Osceola's Legacy*, p. 56.

146   **McQueen died "on a little barren island":** Woodward, *Reminiscences*, p. 44.

146   **"for refusing to clean a pair of boots":** Schlesinger, [1946], p. 36.

147   **"exterminated in a daylight attack":** Fred Cubberly, "The Dade Massacre," U.S. Senate, *Documents*, vol. 9, 1921, pp. 122–32.

149   **Lewis blamed:** Brevard, [1904], p. 132.

149   **"negroes'" and Seminoles' joint action:** Sprague, p. 90. Brown pp. 3–46.

149   **Lewis's hiring and outbreak of fighting:** Giddings, pp. 97–107.

150   **"If we do this, we shall have general and perpetual war":** Albert Ellery Bergh, *The Writings of Thomas Jefferson* [1907], p. 142.

150   Birthplaces of troops killed with Dade: W. S. Steele, "Last Command: The Dade Massacre," *Tequesta* magazine [1986], no. 46, pp. 9–10; Mark F. Boyd and Joseph W. Harris, "The Seminole War: Its Background and Onset," *Florida Historical Quarterly*, July 1951, pp. 3–115; visit to Dade Memorial, West Point, NY, June 2009; Cubberley, "Dade Massacre."

151   "every cart and wagon": *Niles' Weekly Register*, 19 August 1837, "The Florida War."

151   "near frost": Patrick, [1963], p. 102.

152, 153   Clinch reserves boats for his private use; leaves battlefield; weapons abandoned; "Hero of Withlacoochee": Ibid., pp. 125, 109, 111.

152   Withlacoochee fighting: Patrick, [1963], p. 109; Sprague, pp. 91–93.

154   Gaines imbroglio: Sprague, pp. 109–12, 122.

155   "hindquarter of a stolen dog": Patrick, [1963], p. 126.

156   Scott's misadventure: Patrick, [1963], pp. 134, 138–39; Dovell, vol. 1, p. 245.

156   Jackson apoplectic: Bird, [2012], p. 102.

157, 158   Federal payments; Clinch "a dodger"; "a millionaire": Patrick, [1963], pp. 156, 179, 49.

CHAPTER 11

161   Dr. Forry's descriptions: "The Letters of Samuel Forry, Surgeon U.S. Army 1837–38," *Florida History Quarterly*, January, April, and July 1928.

162   Osceola "betrayed" his nonexistent pledge: Giddings, [1858], pp. 166–67.

162   Egret feathers: Patricia Wiles Wickman, *Osceola's Legacy* [2006], pp. 83–86.

162   Osceola's capture and brutalization: Giddings, pp. 166–67; Willson, [1896], pp. 25–39.

164   "intimate relation which this war bore to slavery": Giddings, p. 275.

164, 166   "a Negro and not an Indian war": Thomas Sidney Jesup, Letter to Acting Secretary of War, 9 December 1836, U.S. House of Representatives, 13th Congress, 2nd session, *Public Documents*, p. 52.

164   "Spanish Indians": Giddings, pp. 275–76; Sprague, [1848], pp. 99, 243–44.

165 Troops "shot down women and children": Minnie More Willson, pp. 25–27.

165 Jesup report urging end to ethnic cleansing: Thomas Sidney Jesup, "To the Secretary of War," 11 February 1838; text in Sprague, pp. 199–201.

166 "Slavery . . . unlocks the enigma": William Jay, "Miscellaneous Writings on Slavery" [1853], p. 312.

166 Not even "Jackson": Sprague, p. 250.

167 "withering and facile" reply: Text in Sprague, pp. 201–2.

168, 169 Weedon's treatment of Osceola; "quinsy": Weedon's diary, quoted in Wickman, p. 148.

170 Head haunts Castillo: Walter Harder, *Osceola's Head and Other American Ghost Stories* [1974], pp. 26–29.

170 Seminoles "would have remained peaceable": Dovell, [1952], vol. 1, pp. 252, 261.

171 John Horse description: Bird, [2005], p. 22.

171 "countenance of a white man": "Letters of Samuel Forry."

171 Florida tragedy as epic poem: Albery Allson Whitman, *Twasinta's Seminoles; or, Rape of Florida* [1885].

171 Florida War as parable: Joan R. Sherman (editor), *African-American Poetry: An Anthology, 1773–1927* [1997], p. 258.

172 Coacoochee encounter with Worth: Sprague, pp. 288–91; Bird, [2005], pp. 153–54.

173 "sent away like a dog": Sprague, p. 483. See also Milton Meltzer, *Hunted Like a Wolf: The Story of the Seminole War* [2004].

173 "A very Iliad of tragedy": Willson, p. 1.

174 John Horse encounters Sprague in Texas; Seminoles cross Rio Grande: Bird, [2005], pp. 187–89. The principal work is Kevin Mulroy, *Freedom on the Border: The Seminole Maroons in Florida, Indian Territory, Coahuila, and Texas* [1993].

175 Floridians "greatest obstacle" to peace; "Hunting and killing the Indians" for money: Dovell, [1952], vol. 1, pp. 258, 260, 236

CHAPTER 12

178 Seminole War in place-names: See Allen Morris, *Florida Place Names: Alachua to Zoleo Springs* [1995].

178   **Gadsden "one-man example":** The scope of Gadsden's importance emerges from his apparition and reapparition in many different
episodes of American expansion. No major biography of Gadsden has
ever been assayed.

179   **"A Very Prime Gang of 235 Negroes":** *Charleston Mercury*, 6 December 1859. Cited by Magnolia Plantation Foundation of Charleston,
Lowcountry Africana website. Accessed 18 May 2012.

180   **Gadsden Purchase for $10 milion:** *Gadsden Purchase Treaty: De-
cember 30, 1853.* The Avalon Project, Yale Law School.

181   **Call's ingratitude and wealth:** Baptist, [2002], p. 93.

182   **Territorial banking abuses:** Larry Schweikart, *Banking in the
American South from the Age of Jackson to Reconstruction* [1987], p. 198.

182   **"pledged the same Negroes several times":** Tebeau and Carson,
[1965], p. 142.

182   **Killing of General Leigh Read:** Burnett, [1998], pp. 227–31; Baptist, p. 173.

183   **"G.T.T.";** **DuVal "slunk off westward":** Baptist, p. 186.

184   **"Who will do the work for us?":** Stowe, [1875], pp. 279–81.

184, 185   **Florida population growth; concentration of slavery; only
"3,152 were slaveowners"; Statehood vote:** Dovell, [1952], vol. 1,
pp. 332, 274

184, 185   **Concentration of slaves and wealth:** Dovell, vol. 1, p. 320.

188   **Call life details:** Herbert J. Doherty, *Richard Keith Call, Southern
Unionist* [1961].

188   **Views on slavery and Union:** Call, [1861].

189   **"ears nailed to posts":** U.S. Senate, Committee on Slavery, *Report
by Charles M. Sumner*, 29 February 1864, p. 15.

189   **"a legal framework that perpetuated African slavery in one of its
most brutal and dehumanizing forms":** State of Florida, *A Concurrent Resolution Expressing Profound Regret for the Involuntary Servitude of Africans and Calling
for Reconciliation Among All Floridians*, 26 March 2008.

191   **Kingsley family:** Daniel L. Schafer, *Anna Madgigine Jai Kingsley:
African Princess, Florida Slave, Plantation Slaveowner* [2010]; also *Anna King-
sley* [1994]. Faye L. Glover, *Zephaniah Kingsley: Nonconformist, Slave Trader,
Patriarch* [1970].

191, 194 "always been respected as my wife"; "illiberal and inequitable laws": Kingsley Will, cited in *Kingsley vs. Broward et als.*, Cases Adjudicated by Florida Supreme Court, 1883, pp. 739–40.

192 Kingsley's observations: Kingsley, [1829].

193 "obvious propriety . . . [of] degrading punishment": *Cases Adjudicated by Florida Supreme Court*, 1853, p. 195.

194 falsely described as princess: Tebeau, [1971], p. 96; Schafer, *Anna Madgigine Jai Kingsley.*

000 Phosphate production and impact: George Charlton Matson, *The Phosphate Deposits of Florida* [1915]; U.S. Geological Survey, "Output of Phosphate Rock in Florida, 1888–1907," *Mineral Resources of the United States, Part 2* [1908], p. 653; "Phosphate Rock Production, 1890–2003," *Florida Almanac 2007–2008*; University of South Florida, Florida Industrial and Phosphate Research Institute, *Florida Phosphate Mining History* [2012].

195 Gorrie and refrigeration: Visit and interviews, Apalachacola, 2005.

195 Gorrie "ruined": U.S. Capitol, National Sculpture Hall, "John Gorrie."

197 Hernández "ruined": Sprague, [1848], p. 220.

197 Hernández to Cuba: Sprague, p. 220.

PART FOUR

199 "Slavery . . . element of all value": *Journal of the Proceedings of the Convention of the People of Florida*, 3 January 1861, p. 8.

CHAPTER 13

201 Walker's ordeal: Walker, [1848]. Cover to cover.

203 "The Branded Hand": N. H. Dole (editor), *The Early Poems of John Greenleaf Whittier*, pp. 172–76.

203 slavery "a national institution": Call, [1861], p. 6.

203 "three-fifths provision": U.S. Constitution, Article 1, Section 2, Paragraph 3.

204 "Slavery never left the North alone": Horace Greeley, *The American Conflict: A History of the Great Rebellion* [1865], vol. 2, p. 354.

207 "first gun fired": Abner Doubleday, *Reminiscences of Forts Sumter and Moultrie in 1860–61* [1976], pp. 145–46.

207   Slemmer's stand at Pensacola: J. H. Gilmore, "With Slemmer" in *The Century Co., Battles and Leaders of the Civil War* [1885–1887], vol. 1, pp. 40–49.

210   "patriotic wives": "Brigadier General Adam J. Slemmer," in Moses Auge, *Lives of the Eminent Dead: and Biographical Notices of Prominent Living Citizens of Montgomery County, Pa.* [1879], pp. 224–31.

210   "refined and cultivated": Benson John Lossing, *Harpers' Popular Cyclopaedia of United States History* [1890], vol. 1, p. 516.

211, 220, 221   Civil War details, including Yulee urging seizure of federal "forts and arsenals," Bragg's ruthlessness, ports "returned to the 'Stars and Stripes'": Franklin Lafayette Riley et al. (editors), *The South in the Building of the Nation: History of the States*, vol. 3, pp. 45–63.

213   Dickison enumerates forts: Dickison, [1898, reprinted 2002], p. 12.

000   "not an unexpected trouble": Brevard, [1904] p. 156.

213, 216, 217   The Judah affair; Confederate report on Santa Rosa fiasco; "most imposing military demonstration": Dickison, pp. 14–23.

218   "how immense—nay, decisive—its results!": Mahan. [1897], pp. 133.

222   "madly and rashly destroyed": Call, p. 3.

CHAPTER 14

224   Bragg apologetics: "Fort Bragg History," sandhillsnc.com. Accessed 2 June 2012.

224   Confederate impositions: Dovell, [1952], vol. 1, pp. 480–82.

225   "rich man's war, but a poor man's fight"; absence of white males: Dovell, vol. 1, pp. 511, 504.

225   "American Negro slavery . . . civilizing . . . barbaric savages": Dovell, vol. 1, p. 504.

226   "enshrining, as 'history'": Philip D. Ackerman, "Florida Reconstruction from Walker through Reed," cited in Dovell, vol. 2, p. 570.

226   Confederate Monument Ritual: Towns, [1978].

226, 227   "Gettisburgh"; "Florida Battles": Tallahassee visit, 2005; photos of monument by Wendy Abberger, June 2012.

227   Details on Olustee, including Union objectives, behavior of troops, U.S. strategy, Confederate response: U.S. Senate, Reports of Committees: 30th Congress, 48th Congress, 1st session [1864], "The Florida Expedition," pp. 274–355. Available (and ignored) in libraries for 150 years, this trove is now online. Military policy, 22 January 1864; Gillmore's objectives, 31 January 1864; orders "not to risk a ripost," 7 March 1864; behavior of black troops, 26 March 1864; Beauregard's disenchantment, 3 March 1864.

231   Olustee casualties: *Florida Almanac 2007–2008*, p. 126. All sources provide virtually identical numbers.

231   General Hatch's comments: Stuart B. McIver, *Dreamers, Schemers and Scalawags* [1993], vol. 1, p. 176.

231   "Many of these are negroes": U.S. Senate, "The Florida Expedition," p. 328, Finegan report dated 23 February 1863.

232   "disinterred by the hogs": *Report of Lieutenant Federick E. Grossman, Seventh United States Infantry, on the Reburial of Union Troops at Olustee, Florida*, 25 May 1866. Full text at http://battleofolustee.org/reports/grossman.htm. Accessed 4 June 2012.

232   "war's most notorious massacres": Coles, [2005], pp. 65–89.

232   "fruits of the victory were insignificant": Dickison, [1898], p. 47.

233   "Victory at Olustee": Brevard, [1904] pp. 166–67.

234   "felt no gladness": Ibid., p. 157; Caroline Mays Brevard, "Richard Keith Call by His Granddaughter," *Florida Historical Quarterly*, July, October 1908.

234   Ellen Call Long: Rivers and Brown, [2009], pp. 25–91; Tracy J. Revels, *Grander in Her Daughters: Florida's Women During the Civil War* [2005], p. 77.

235   "telling in the most charming manner": Caroline Mays Brevard, "The Association of History Teachers of Florida" [undated], Call Family Papers, Florida Memory, Division of Libraries and Information.

235   "keeping Tallahassee free from invasion": Lewis Publishing Co., *The History of Florida: Past & Present* [1923], vol. 3, p. 141.

235   "this granite tower": "The Confederate Monument at Olustee," *United Daughters of the Confederacy Magazine*, vol. 69, 2006, p. 24.

236   Miniature Miss Battle of Olustee Festival pageants; artillery firing; history of reenactment: See http://www.olusteefestival.com/. Accessed 12 June 2012.

236 "**Park personnel told me**": Baker County Florida Archives, *Cemeteries: Olustee Battlefield Memorial Cemetery.* Accessed 1 June 2012.

238 "**our heroic little band**"; **artillery halted Union advance:** Dickison, pp. 77–79, 81–82.

240 Cadets saved the "**capital from seizure**": Brevard, p. 177.

241 Chatfield account of Natural Bridge: David Churbuck (editor), *Reminiscences* [1905], published online at http://www.churbuck.com. Accessed 1 June 2012.

242 "**our artillery opened a brisk fire**": Dickison, p. 82

242 "**our victory . . . a signal one**": Ibid., p. 81.

245 Florida "**never received a musket**": John Thomas Scharf, *History of the Confederate States Navy* [1887], p. 49.

246 "**dedicated to a lost cause**": Merlin G. Cox and J. E. Dovell, *Florida from Secession to Space Age* [1974], p. 25.

247 Mudd's imprisonment: Robert Summers, *Dr. Samuel A. Mudd at Fort Jefferson* [2008] relies on actual documents and letters.

CHAPTER 15

249 "**Death . . . preferable to reunion!**": Dovell, [1952], *Florida* [1952], vol. 1, p. 516.

249 Levy-Yulee to Washington: Tebeau and Carson, [1965], p. 217.

249 Judah Benjamin to Florida: Hanna, [1938], pp. 202–6.

250 "**government for white men**": Hans Louis Trefousse, *Andrew Johnson: A Biography* [1989], p. 236.

251, 269 "**prominent pro-slavery men**" **rewarded;** "**policy . . . tended directly to their ruin**": Brown, [1997], pp. 153–54.

252 Blacks repressed economically and politically: Dovell, vol. 1, pp. 537–38.

254 "**Negroes Franchised; Whites Disfranchised**": Brevard, [1904], p. 187.

256 Sprague's adventures; return to Florida: John Titcomb Sprague, *The Treachery in Texas, the Secession of Texas, and the Arrest of the United States Officers and Soldiers Serving in Texas* [1862]; Ben E. Pingenot, "John Titcomb Sprague," *Handbook of Texas Online* (http://www.tshaonline.org/

handbook/online/articles/fsp30). Accessed 4 June 2012. Published by the Texas State Historical Association. Bird, [2012].

257 **1868 convention and constitution:** Dovell, vol. 2, pp. 553–57.

258 **"foresaw ... rebellion ... death knell of slavery":** Brown, [1998], p. 115.

258, 270 **Swaim comment; "blessed fact ... ever new and delightful";** **"the old flag, with all its glories ever radiating from it"; "rain, drizzle, and cold":** Ibid., pp. 231, 292, 271, 282

259 **1868 constitution:** Full text accessible, Florida Memory, Division of Libraries and Information.

259 **"reinstitute the slave system":** Gannon, [1996], p. 48.

259 **Robert Meacham:** Canter Brown, [1998], p. 110.

259 **Josiah Walls:** Burnett, [1998], pp. 46–49.

260 **"assent to negro suffrage":** Dovell, vol. 2, p. 538.

261 **"most cultured ... a negro":** Davis, [1913], p. 494.

261 **"suffering ... extended my wildest dream":** Jonathan C. Gibbs, Letter to *Christian Recorder*, 15 April 1865.

262 **"William U. Saunders, black"; "WM Saunders (negro)"; "the negro Saunders":** Davis, pp. 470, 493, 479.

262 **"the Maryland mulatto, William Saunders":** Dovell, vol. 2, p. 561.

262 **Saunders "a mulatto ex-barber from Baltimore":** Tebeau, [1971], p. 248.

262 **Walls a "mulatto from Pennsylvania":** Dovell, vol. 2, pp. 561, 252.

263 **Reed and Chloe Merrick:** See Foster, [1999].

265 **Reed's hijacked rifles:** Davis, p. 290; John Wallace, *Carpet Bag Rule in Florida* [1888], p. 92.

265, 267 **Impeachments; bipartisanship under Hart:** Brown, [1998], pp. 257, 278.

265 **Reed stayed in Florida:** Ibid., pp. 237, 244.

266 **1872 nominating convention and election; Hart civil rights laws:** Brown, [1998], pp. 254–56, 275–76.

268, 269 **"vessel after vessel shall leave our ports"; Hart elected solicitor; defense of Adam; defeated by Yankee racist:** Ibid., pp. 66, 73, 103–6, 160–61.

271 "Hart . . . among the region's leading men": Ibid., p. xiii.

272 "damn Scalawag": Davis, p. 609.

272 Florida "white Radicals . . . lower type of humanity": Dovell, vol. 2, p. 553.

273 Achievements under Reconstruction: Dovell, vol. 2, pp. 575–76.

273 Florida's "financial reform program . . . as model": Brown, [1998], p. 29.

273 Mrs. Stowe in Tallahassee: Photo in Foster, [1999].

CHAPTER 16

276, 277 "Regulators"; first use of the Klan's name: Daniel R. Weinfeld, *The Jackson County War: Reconstruction and Resistance in Post–Civil War Florida* [2012], p. 65.

276 "halter, shot-gun and whip": Davis, [1913], p. 621.

276, 277, 278 Personal narratives of threats; Fleishman murder; abuse of women; bodies in sinkholes: Davis, p. 558; United States Congress, *Report*, "Joint Select Committee on the Condition of Affairs in the Late Insurrectionary States" [1872], p. 60; Weinfeld, *Jackson County War*, pp. 180, 140.

277 Events in Marianna: Davis, pp. 575–78.

279 Jones affair: Judy Nicholas Etemadi, "A Love-Mad Man: Senator Charles W. Jones of Florida," *Florida Historical Quarterly*, October 1977, pp. 123–37; "An Insane Senator," *New York Times*, 30 May 1890.

279 False stereotyping of "native white Conservatives and their Republican opponents": Jarrell Shofner, "Reconstruction and Renewal, 1865–1877," in Gannon, [1996], pp. 257, 260.

281 Yulee "Great Floridian": Dickie Anderson, "Famous Floridians: David Levy Yulee," *Amelia Islander*, June 2012. Accessed 5 June 2012.

281 Marcellus Stearns' life and background: Claude R. Flory, "Florida's Last Reconstruction Governor," *Florida Historical Quarterly*, vol. 44, no. 3, January 1966, pp. 181–92.

281 "lynch law . . . part of the political campaign": Dovell, [1952], vol. 2, p. 562.

282 "crisis of free government": Davis, p. 701.

283 **"43 of the some 45,000 votes":** Tebeau, [1971], p. 253.

284 **"Dickison . . . cavalry charges through crowds of potential voters":** Shofner, "Reconstruction and Renewal," p. 257.

284 **Testimony on electoral violence:** U.S. Senate, Reports of Committees: 30th Congress, 1st Session–48th Congress, p. 76.

284 **Fair count, free election conundrum:** Haworth, [1906].

287 **Drew "given the governorship" by court:** Gannon, [2003], p. 50.

286 **"basis of representation therein shall be reduced":** U.S. Constitution, Article XIV.

287 **Stolen votes ordered counted:** *Cases Argued and Adjudged in the Supreme Court of Florida, During the Years 1876–7–8, Reported by George P. Raney, Attorney-General*, vol. 26, 33, pp. 36; Davis, p. 608.

288 **Drew business affairs:** Don Hensley, "The Rise of the Drew Family and Their Sawmills," in *The Rise and Fall of the Florida Railway*. Online publication. Accessed 4 June 2012.

289 **"evil, designing men"; "wresting from our people":** Davis, p. 701.

289 **Stearns' peaceful exit:** John Wallace, **Carpet Bag Rule in Florida** [1888], p. 343.

289 **"Drew named Dickison his adjutant-general":** Dovell, vol. 2, p. 578.

290 **Turpentine camps; "elimination of public high schools":** Samuel Proctor, "Prelude to a New Florida," in Gannon, [1996], pp. 266–68.

290 **"homesteads and equality":** Dovell, vol. 2, p. 553.

CHAPTER 17

292 **Bloxham's "wise plans":** Brevard, [1904], p. 190.

292 **Disston scandal:** Dovell, [1952], vol. 2, pp. 644–45; Tebeau and Carson, [1965], pp. 250–56.

292 **three million acres given away:** Dovell, vol. 2, p. 659.

293 **Perrys and Pensacola monument:** Towns, [1978].

294 **1885 "poll tax" constitution:** Full text accessible, Florida Memory, Division of Libraries and Information.

296 **Florida election boxes:** James O. Knaus, "Growth of Florida's Election Laws," *Florida Historical Quarterly*, July 1926, p. 10.

296 Blacks "eliminated" as political factor: Jarrell Shofner, "Reconstruction and Renewal, 1865–1877," in Gannon, [1996], p. 262.

297 one thousand black officeholders: Brown, [1998].

300 Belief "concussion would kill the microbes": Dovell, vol. 2, p. 658.

300 Yellow Jack; warning ignored: E. Lynne Wright, "Disasters and Heroic Rescues of Florida," Periodical, pp. 9–10; E. E. and E. B. Johnson, "Diary of the 1888 Epidemic," Periodical; John W. Cowart, *Yellow Jack in Jacksonville: The 1888 Epidemic* [2005], online history. Accessed 5 June 2012.

301 Lulu Fleming life and meaning: Rivers and Brown, [2009], pp. 122–50.

301, 302 Francis Fleming; siblings dead of yellow fever; political rise: Dovell, vol. 2, pp. 559–60.

303 "King Ignorance," Judge Dean education, travails, legacy: Canter Brown Jr. and Larry E. Rivers, "The Pioneer African American Jurist Who Almost Became a Bishop: Florida's Judge James Dean, 1858-1914," *Florida Historical Quarterly*, vol. 87, no. 1, Summer 2008, pp. 16–49.

305 Judge Dean died "disgraced": Florida Memory, "Judge James Dean—Monroe County, Florida." Accessed 5 June 2012.

306 Fleming panegyric and life details: "In Memorium: Francis Philip Fleming," *Florida Historical Society Quarterly*, vol. 2, no. 1, April 1909, pp. 4–8.

306 Florida flag saltire: Joseph E. Miller, "Governor Francis P. Fleming (1841–1908)," *Jacksonville Observer*, 2 October 2009.

PART FIVE

309 Flagler "rich man, if it hadn't been for Florida": Standiford, [2003], p. 212.

CHAPTER 18

311 Woolson and changed view of Florida: Constance Fenimore Woolson, "The Ancient City, Part I," *Harper's Monthly*, December 1874, pp. 1–25; "The Ancient City, Part II," *Harper's Monthly*, January 1875, pp. 165–85; Sharon Kennedy-Nolle, "'We Are Most of Us Dead Down Here': Constance Fenimore Woolson's Travel Writing and the Reconstruction of

Notes and Citations

Florida," in Victoria Brehm (editor), *Constance Fenimore Woolson's Nineteenth Century: Essays* [2001], pp. 141–60.

313 **"Everglades would no longer exist":** Foster, [1999], pp. 104–6.

313, 314 **"picknicky" life; "Buying Land in Florida":** Stowe, [1873], pp. 39, 279–81.

314 **Stowe crop failures:** Stowe, "Our Florida Plantation," *Atlantic*, vol. 43, 1879, p. 643.

315 **Disease kills high officials:** Tebeau [1971], p. 333.

315 **False health claims; whiskey as curative:** Lanier, [1877], "For Consumptives," pp. 210–17, 213; Anne E. Rowe, *The Idea of Florida in the American Literary Imagination* [   ], pp. 36–37.

316 **Stowe denounces Florida critics:** Stowe, [1873], p. 120.

316 **Flagler's daughter's death:** "Dies on the Yacht; H. M. Flagler's Invalid Daughter Expires While Hurrying South," *New York Times*, 27 March 1889.

318 **Gasparilla invention:** See Nancy Turner, *The History of Ye Mystic Krewe of Gasparilla, 1904–1979* [1979].

319 **Gaspar's "treasure":** McCarthy, [1994], pp. 55–57.

322 **"Conspicuous consumption":** Veblen, [1899, republished 2008], p. 46.

323 **"Mr. Plant's Hobby":** George Hutchinson Smyth and George Sherwood Dickerman, *The Life of Henry Bradley Plant* [1898], pp. 87–116.

324 **Sanford in Congo and Florida:** Joseph A Fry, "Struggling for Survival in Florida," in *Henry S, Sanford: Diplomacy and Business in Nineteenth-Century America* [1982], pp. 112–30; Adam Hochschild, "From Berlin to Florida," in *King Leopold's Ghost* [1998], pp. 76–87; *New York Times*, 23 May 1891.

326 **Freezes and citrus industry:** Dovell, [1952], vol. 2, p. 629.

327 **Tuttle and Flagler:** Burnett, [1998], p. 19; Standiford, [2003], p. 60.

328 **Flagler and Ponce de León:** Dovell, vol. 2, pp. 616–19.

331 **Key West decline:** Garry Boulard, "'State of Emergency': Key West in the Great Depression," *Florida Historical Quarterly*, vol. 67, no. 2, October 1988, pp. 166–83.

331 **Newspapers avoided word "hurricane":** Barnes, [2007], pp. 111–26.

332, 333 **"no organized relief"; Russell family deaths; undertows:** Marjory Stoneman Douglas, *Hurricane* [1958], pp. 158–168.

332   **Overseas Railroad blown away**: Willie Drye, *Storm of the Century* [2002], pp. 42–43.

333   **Population statistics comparison:** All figures from U.S. Census Bureau.

333   **Flagler biggest "money spender"**: Stuart W. Martin, "Florida's Flagler."

334   **Art vs. cultural packaging**: Cummer Museum of Art, *Florida as Paradise: Five Centuries of Art* [2001].

335   **"PARADISE PARK for Colored People":** Tim Hollis, *Glass Bottom Boats & Mermaid Tails: Florida's Tourist Springs* [2006], p. 27.

336   **"helped spawn a cinematic genre"**: Geoff Andrew, *Stranger Than Paradise: Maverick Film-Makers in Recent American Cinema* [1999], pp. 135–65.

336   **"fearful fraud"**: Henry James, *The American Scene* [1907], pp. 433–35; Leon Edel, *Henry James, The Master: 1901–1916* [1971], p. 275.

CHAPTER 19

337   **Negro Removal**: Proctor, [1950], pp. 75–76.

337   **Adams and political "gravitation"**: Louis A. Pérez, *Cuba Between Empires, 1878–1902* [1983], p. 59.

338, 339   **Broward policy proposals; praised as hero**: Proctor, pp. 64–5, 252.

340   **"Swanee"**: Morison Foster, *My Brother Stephen* [1896, full text published 1932], p. 47.

340   **Gershwin's Swanee**: Howard Pollack, *George Gershwin: His Life and Work* [2006], pp. 237–38.

341   **1920 election**: Ortiz, [2006], pp. 227–29.

342   **Sydney Johnson Catts**: David R. Colburn and Richard K. Scher, *Florida's Gubernatorial Politics in the Twentieth Century* [1980], p. 222.

343   **"frost glistened on the palms"; "Nowhere . . . a mention"**: D'Orzo, [1996].

344   **Ruben Stacey lynching photos**: Dora Apel, *Imagery of Lynching: Black Men, White Women, and the Mob* [2004], p. 41.

344   **Robineau**: Marjory Stoneman Douglas, with John Rothchild, *Voice of the River* [1987], p. 110.

345   "thy phosphate mines": C. V. Waugh, "Florida, My Florida," Laws of Florida, Concurrent Resolution no. 24 [1913], p. 517.

345   Steven Foster Folk Culture Center: Visit and interviews, 2005.

CHAPTER 20

346, 347   Fisher; automobiles; Miami Beach: See Foster, [2000].

347, 348   Glenn Curtiss and George Merrick: See T. D. Allman, "Circumspice," in *Miami: City of the Future* [1987].

348   Boom-time "cyclopedia": Stockbridge and Perry, [1926].

348   "revolutionary venture": Stockbridge and Perry, [1938].

348   Walter Fraser in St. Augustine: Interviews with his son, John Fraser, and staff at Fountain of Youth, 2005.

350, 351   "land-changes" and skeletons: Fraser, [1939].

350   False scholarship on Fountan: Lawson, [1946].

350   "error-filled document": Peck, [1993].

352   "oldest wooden school house": Steve Rajtar and Kelly Goodman, *A Guide to Historic St. Augustine, Florida*, [undated], p. 89.

353   "great Ponce de Leon Hotel"; "telescope the centuries": Stockbridge and Perry, [1938].

353, 355   "original Ripley's museum opened in 1950"; "Castle Warden"; Rawlings hotel: Rajtar and Goodman, *Guide*, p. 50.

355   No building older than 1702: City of St. Augustine Official website, "The Nation's Oldest History." Accessed 6 June 2012.

356   "invention of a blended past": Shauna Henley, "A City with Schizophrenia." Online report, 2002. Accessed 10 April 2007.

356   St. Augustine racial strife: David R. Colburn, *Racial Change & Community Crisis: St. Augustine, Florida, 1877–1980* [1991].

357   Proof Ponce never there: Kathleen A. Deagan (editor), *America's Ancient City: Spanish St. Augustine, 1565–1763* [1991]; Deagan placards at the Fountain.

357   "Columbus discovered St. Augustine": Interviews with Fountain personnel, 2005.

358   Claude Pepper's life, including 1950 contest: Claude Pepper and Hays Gorey, *Pepper, Eyewitness to a Century* [1987]; Reginald Thomas, "Claude

Pepper, Fiery Fighter for Elderly Rights, Dies at 88," *New York Times*, 31 May 1989; Tracy E. Danese, *Claude Pepper and Ed Ball: Politics, Purpose, and Power* [2000]; "Florida: Anything Goes," *Time*, 17 April 1950.

358   Smathers' career and life, including 1950 contest: Brian Lewis Crispell, *Testing the Limits: George Armistead Smathers and Cold War America* [1999], especially pp. 54–75.

361   Charley Johns' life and details: Allyson A. Beutke (producer), *The Dark Legacy of the Johns Committee* [2000]. The film's website is informative.

361   Johns investigation: James Anthony Schnur, *Closet Crusaders: The Johns Committee and Homophobia: 1956–1965*; John Howard (editor), *Carryin' On in the Lesbian and Gay South* [1997], pp. 132–63; State of Florida, Legislative Investigation Committee, *Homosexuality and Citizenship in Florida* [1964].

362   Pork Chop Gang: "Florida's Dubious Dynasty," in Burnett, [1998], pp. 106–9.

362   Antidemocratic finance and legislature: Weitz, [2007].

363   "represent people, not trees": Stephen H. Wainscott, "From the 'Political Thicket' to 'One Man, One Vote," in John W. Johnson (editor), *Historic US Court Cases* [2001], pp. 258–66.

363   Johns denied renomination: Weitz, p. 241.

CHAPTER 21

366   Miami and Latin America: Jan Nijman, *Miami: Mistress of the Hemisphere* [2011].

367   Verne on Florida: Jules Verne, *Les Voyages Extraordinaires: Autour de la Lune* [1867]; *From the Earth to the Moon: Direct in Ninety-seven Hours and Twenty Minutes: And a Trip Aroud It* [English translation, 1890].

368   Disney in Florida: Foglesong, [2003].

369   Impact of interstates: Dennis W. Johnson, "Ribbons of Highway: The Interstate Highway Act of 1956," in *The Laws That Shaped America: Fifteen Acts of Congress and Their Lasting Impact* [2009], pp. 261–92.

372   "theme of 'control'": Emerson, [2009].

372   Control mechanisms at Disney World: T. D. Allman, "Beyond Disney," *National Geographic*, March 2007.

373 Helliwell CIA connection: Joseph J. Trento, *Prelude to Terror: The Rogue CIA and the Legacy of America's Private Intelligence Network* [2005], pp. 24–27; Foglesong, p. 42.

374 "a way to limit the voting": Emerson, p. 193.

374 Disney special privilege laws: Statutes of Florida, Title XXI Drainage, Statutes of Florida, chapter 67-764 for the Reedy Creek Improvement District; Chapters 67-1104 and 67-1965 for the two "cities."

378, 379 "numerous inhabitants of the District"; Disney posthumous appearance; "needed to say that they were building a city": Foglesong, pp. 75, 64–68, 103.

380 Special districts "a national trend": Emerson, pp. 179–81; U.S. Bureau of the Census, 2002 "Census of Governments, Individual State Descriptions" [2005], pp. 54–62; Helisse Levine, Eric A. Scorsone, and Jonathan B. Justice, "Growth of Special Municipal Districts, 1992–2007," in *Handbook of Local Government Fiscal Health*, pp. 370–74, 513.

380 Injuries and death at Disney World: Numerous press reports, 1974–2011.

380 "We don't have the authority": Associated Press, 18 June 2005.

381 Adverse ecoomic impact: Frances Novak-Branch, *The Disney World Effect* [1983].

382, 383 Captive whale ownership; Blackstone operations; "identifiable icon": Mike Esterl, "Marine Park Operator Faces a Big Dilemma," *Wall Street Journal*, 9 March 2010.

PART SIX

385 "Reality must take precedence": Feynman, [1986], p. 169.

CHAPTER 22

387 Celebration: Visits 2003, 2005, 2006.

388 "paradigmatical conquistador of the theme park age": Interview with Peter Rummel, Jacksonville, 2005.

389 JOE, Du Ponts, and Spanish land grant: Ziewitz and Wiaz, [2006].

389, 390 "If you don't know JOE"; "original 'true places'"; 2007 company press release: Accessed 17 July 2008; subsequently deleted from Web, but reference remains at http://groups.yahoo.com/group/HopeForCleanWater/message/4014.

390 Seaside alternative: Visit and interviews with Robert Davis, Seaside and San Francisco, 2005; Brooke, [2002].

391 "WaterColor offers endless opportunities!"; expropriation of conservationist aesthetic: Visit and interviews 2005; *water-color vacation rentals* website.

391 Public highway moved: Desiree French, "Proactive Community Builder: Peter S. Rummell," *Urban Land* magazine, June 2006.

391 Rise and fall of JOE's stock price: New York Stock Exchange, ten-year chart. Accessed 6 June 2012.

392 "JOE no longer was Florida's biggest private landowner": *Florida Trend* magazine, 27 May 2009.

392 "Cracker Christmas": "Places to Go and Things to Do: Fort Christmas Historical Park," *North Brevard—Titusville—Community Directory*. Accessed 6 June 2012.

393 NASA as theme park: "A Day of Fun. A Lifetime of Inspiration," Kennedy Space Center, *Performance Group Reservation Form*. Accessed 6 June 2012; visits to Cape Kennedy, 2003, 2005, 2006.

394 White male heroics: Tom Wolfe, *The Right Stuff* [1973, republished 2008].

395 "first astronaut tabloid sex scandal": Pew Research Center, Project for Excellence in Journalism, PEJ News Coverage Index, 4–9 February 2007.

399 "an accident rooted in history": Rogers et al., [1986].

396 Profiles of the astronauts: Staff of the *Washington Post, Challengers: The Inspiring Life Stories of the Seven Brave Astronauts of Shuttle Mission 51-L* [1986].

396, 397 "infectious enthusiasm"; "never even flown an airplane"; "They were alive": Jay Barbree, *The Challenger Saga: An American Space Tragedy* [2012]. Print version of 1997 television series.

398, 399, 400 NASA cultural failure; "reality . . . must take precedence"; "antiquated" computers; O-rings: Feynman, [1986]; Alan J. McDonald, *Truth, Lies, and O-Rings: Inside the Space Shuttle Challenger Disaster* [2009]; Diane Vaughan, *The Challenger Launch Decision: Risky Technology, Culture and Deviance at NASA* [1996].

400   lack of spare parts: Feynman, [1986], ; "For Parts, NASA Boldly Goes . . . on eBay," *New York Times*, 12 May 2002.

CHAPTER 23

402   Kerouac and Ferlinghetti; tangerine tree out back; *Dharma Bums*: Visit to Kerouac house, Orlando, 2005; *New York Times*, 14 March 2004; Bob Kealing, *Kerouac in Florida: Where the Road Ends* [2004].

403   Dalí in St. Petersburg; donors from Cleveland: Cindy Cockburn, "The New Dalí Museum" [press release], 11 January 2012; "Why Is the Dali Museum in St. Petersburg, FL?" Dali Museum website. Accessed 7 June 2012.

403   Kerouac and Disney: T. D. Allman, "Beyond Disney," *National Geographic*, March 2007.

403   "jungle of signs": Emerson, [2009], p. 188.

403   "glob-like conurbation": Garreau, [1991].

403   Kissimmee attractions: Visits there 1987, 2003, 2006.

404   Learn Sanskrit: Hindu University of America, *Catalog 2007*, "Academic Programs in Sanskrit Studies," pp. 63–65.

404   Meadow Woods Middle School: Interview and visit, 2005.

404   "No one warned us"; Orlando transformation: Interviews with Jane Healy and others, 2005, 2006, 2010, 2012.

406   Connie Hoffman and Dewey McLaughlin: Rachel F. Moran, "Love with a Proper Stranger: What Anti-Miscegenation Laws Can Tell Us About the Meaning of Race, Sex, and Marriage," *Hofstra Law Review*, October 2004; Richard Moran and Rachel F. Moran, *Interracial Intimacy: The Regulation of Race and Romance* [2003], pp. 91–93; Marc Stein, *Sexual Injustice: Supreme Court Decisions from Griswold to Roe* [2010], pp. 45, 113.

408, 409   No "overriding statutory purpose"; subsequent rulings on sexual freedom: U.S. Supreme Court, *McLaughlin v. Florida* [1964]; *Loving et Ux. v. Virginia* [1967]; Ariela R. Dubler, "From *McLaughlin v. Florida* to *Lawrence v. Texas*: Sexual Freedom and the Road to Marriage," *Columbia Law Review*, vol. 106, no. 5 [2006].

412   McDuffie killing; disturbances: Patrice Gaines-Carter, "McDuffie: The Case Behind Miami's Riots," *Southern Changes*, vol. 2, no. 7, 1980, pp. 20–23; Bruce D. Porter and Marvin Dunn, *The Miami Riot of 1980: Crossing the Bounds* [1984].

413 Mariel boatlift: Benedict L. Stabile and Robert L. Scheina, *U.S. Coast Guard Operations During the 1980 Cuban Exodus* [2012], USCG website. Accessed 7 June 2012. Alex Larzelere, *The 1980 Cuban Boatlift* [1988]. *El Mariel Boat and Passenger Records*, ongoing *Miami Herald* database. Accessed 7 June 2012.

413, 415 South Beach; Capitman; Christo: Interviews and visits, 1980–2012; Allman, [1987], pp. 38–39; "Barbara Baer Capitman," *New York Times*, 31 March 1990; Barbara Baer Capitman, *Deco Delights: Preserving Miami Beach Architecture* [1988]; Christo et al., *Christo, Surrounded Islands: Biscayne Bay, Greater Miami, Florida, 1980–83* [1985].

416 *Miami Vice:* Visits to set; interviews with Don Johnson, Edward Olmos, other cast members, 1985–1987.

418 "intermediate grade of color . . . improved in shape, strength and beauty": Kingsley, [1829], p. 10.

418 Miami awash in money: "South Florida: Trouble in Paradise," *Time*, 23 November 1981.

420, 421 Jacksonville fire; revival: Visits and interviews, 2005–2008; Jacksonville Port Authority, *Jaxport Master Plan* [1990]; Ennis Davis and Robert Mann, *Reclaiming Jacksonville: Stories Behind the River City's Historic Landmarks* [2012].

420 Florida filmmaking: Norman Studios *Silent Film Museum, Hollywood East: Florida's Silent Film Legacy* [2010]; James Ponti, *Hollywood East: Florida's Fabulous Flicks* [1992].

421 Tampa mafia; Ybor City: Scott M. Deitche, *Cigar City Mafia: A Complete History of the Tampa Underworld* [2005]; Ron Chepesiuk, *The Trafficantes: Godfathers from Tampa, Florida* [2010]; Gary Mormino, *The Immigrant World of Ybor City* [1998]; Ferdie Pacheco, *Ybor City Chronicles* [1994].

421 Tampa evolution: Canter Brown, *Tampa Before the Civil War* [1999]; *Tampa in Civil War & Reconstruction* [2000].

423, 429 The Villages; "happy with that": Visit and interviews, 2006; Andrew D. Blechman. *Leisureville: Adventures in a World Without Children* [2009]; "The Villages: Florida's Disney World for Retirees," *National Public Radio* transcript, 31 March.

CHAPTER 24

431 Elián affair: National Public Radio, "The Elián González Case: An Online NewsHour Focus" [1999–2000]. Accessed 7 June 2012. Terrence Smith, "Dueling Images," NewsHour Media Unit transcript, 24 April 2000. Accessed 7 June 2012.

433 Latin American Cafeteria: Numerous visits, 1987–2004.

434 2000 Florida election crisis: See Toobin, [2001].

436 Florida and 9/11: *The 9/11 Commission Report: Final Report of the National Commission on Terrorist Attacks upon the United States (9/11 Report)* [2004].

437 Flight training; driver's licenses; posthumous visas: *9/11 Report*, pp. 251–52, 224–27; CNN Miami Bureau, "Six Months After Sept. 11, Hijackers' Visa Approval Letters Received," 12 March 2002.

440 Claude Kirk politics: "Claude R. Kirk Jr.," *New York Times*, 29 September 2011; Edmund F. Kallina, *Claude Kirk and the Politics of Confrontation* [1993].

442 George W. Bush and Florida: George Lardner Jr. and Lois Romano, "At Height of Vietnam, Bush Picks Guard," *Washington Post*, 28 July 1999.

444 Family living in car; original "Siamese Twins": Interviews with Bill McBride and Alex Sink, 2005.

443 "impact frosts": Florida Citrus Mutual, Inc., "Timeline of Major Florida Freezes." Mongi Zekri, "University of Florida Citrus Freeze Fact Sheet" [2011].

444, 445, 446 Rick Scott activities; "squeeze blood" from hospitals; "$1.6 billion in fines"; attacks Florida education; vetoes help for pesticide victims: *Forbes*, 15 December 2000; *New York Times*, 18 December 2002; David DiSalvo, "How Governor Rick Scott Is Sabotaging Florida's Universities," *Forbes*, 23 April 2012; *Florida Independent*, 20 April 2012.

446 Ponce expedition "included people of diverse culture and ancestry": Rick Scott, *Proclamation*, "498th Anniversary of the European Discovery of Florida," The Capitol, Tallahassee, 31 March 2011.

446 Approach like Drew's: *Miami Herald*, 16 February 2011.

446 Voter suppression "contrary to our democratic ideals": Charlie Crist, "Florida Laws Erect Barriers to Voter Participation," *Tampa Bay Times*, 10 April 2012.

447 Jennifer Carroll: State of Florida, "Meet Lt. Governor Jennifer Carroll." Online biography accessed 7 June 2012.

451 Historical context of Trayvon affair: Adam Weinstein, "Trayvon Martin's Death Extends Sanford's Sordid Legacy," *Mother Jones*, 28 March 2012; David R. Dow, "George Zimmerman Will Never Be Convicted of Murdering Trayvon Martin," *Daily Beast*, 22 May 2012. Accessed 30 May 2012.

EPILOGUE

451 Florida population statistics and demographic profile: All statistics come from U.S. Bureau of the Census.

454 Citrus "Doomsday": Interviews with Kevin Bouffard, May 2012. Also his reports in the *Lakeland Ledger:* "Citrus Land in Florida Down 2.3 Percent This Year," 22 September 2011; "Threat of Citrus Greening to Industry Worse Than Feared," 15 November 2011.

454–455 "Citrus Tower": See http://citrustower.com/clermont. Accessed 8 June 2012.

457 "utopia of mutual hopes": Eugene Lyon, *Adelantimiento of Florida* [1973], 207.

INDEX